20/9/q

Tolstoy

Tolstoy

Tales of Courage and Conflict

INTRODUCED AND EDITED BY
Charles Neider

Cooper Square Press

First Cooper Square Press edition 1999

This Cooper Square Press paperback edition of *Tolstoy: Tales of Courage and Conflict* is an unabridged republication of the edition published in New York in 1985. It is reprinted by arrangement with the editor.

Published by Cooper Square Press,
An Imprint of Rowman & Littlefield Publishers, Inc.
150 Fifth Avenue, Suite 911
New York, New York 10011

Distributed by National Book Network

Library of Congress Cataloging-in-Publication Data

Tolstoy, Leo, graf, 1828–1910
    [Short stories. English. Selections]
    Tolstoy—tales of courage and conflict ; introduced and edited by
Charles Neider.
       p.   cm.
    Translated from the Russian.
    Originally published : New York : Carroll & Graf, 1985.
    ISBN 0-8154-1010-7 (pbk. : alk. paper)
    1. Tolstoy, Leo, graf, 1828–1910—Translations into English. I. Neider, Charles,
1915- . II. Title. III. Title: Tales of courage and conflict.
PG3366.A15N45   1999
891.73'3—dc21   99-32572
                                                                                              CIP

☉™ The paper used in this publication meets the minimum requirements of American National Standard for Information Sciences—Permanence of Paper for Printed Library Materials, ANSI/NISO Z39.48-1992.
Manufactured in the United States of America.

CONTENTS

TO ARRI SENDZIMIR

ACKNOWLEDGMENTS

All of the stories in this collection with three exceptions were translated by Nathan Haskell Dole. The three Sevastopol stories were translated by Isabel F. Hapgood.

All unascribed footnotes are by the translators.

The editor is indebted to the Library of Congress for courtesies extended to him.

INTRODUCTION

I have been aware of the name Tolstoy since my childhood. My grandfather, who had met Tolstoy, used to utter it with admiration. I can still see his whiskered mouth say it and can still hear the sound as it emerged. "Tol-stóy." It came to me with such a ring of inevitability that it seemed not to be attached to a human being, someone frail and perishable, but to a thing, a color or quality. It was as though my grandfather said "door" or "sky." When on rare occasions he preceded the word with "Lev Nikolayevich" I was always disturbed, in the way I might be if he had suddenly referred to an Andrew Door or a Mary Sky or a Jimmy Purple.

He was a strong old man, my grandfather, with kindly eyes and a long gray beard, and he had some of Tolstoy's later "style." That was in Virginia, for although I was born in Odessa I was brought to Virginia at an early age. My grandfather's saying the name that way, with relish and a piercing glance and with a way of suddenly holding his head imperiously, lent it an authority for me which I never forgot, even when in my early teens I was indifferent to and on the verge of being contemptuous of all writers of fiction. When I was a boy, hiking and camping in the woods around Richmond, the great thing for me was "fact," or so I thought. It seemed to me that there were so many wonderful facts to be learned that it was silly to spend time reading someone's fiction, what someone had "made up" out of his own head.

A fact, I thought, was indisputable. That was what made it fine. The knowledge of certain facts made camping a pleasure. Without them it could be uncomfortable and even dangerous. I was eager to experiment and to check life for myself. A fact could be ascertained, checked. But when it came to novels and to the thousands of assertions each of them contained—regarding emotions, psychology, certain actions and so on—I was repelled, for I didn't know how to check these assertions. It seemed too easy to spin stories out of one's head. Didn't I do the same thing with great ease and involuntarily in my daydreams? And so I avoided good fiction and had a ready answer when some adult urged me to read it. Curiously enough, none of those adults knew how to answer me. (But this undoubtedly is the falsification of memory.) None of them said what was obvious: that serious fiction, besides being a wonderful entertainment (and primarily an entertainment), had much to teach me about the human way. At any rate, I was too close to nursery rhymes and fairy tales to care for books which somehow resembled them. And I was too passionately Americanizing myself to care for anything which wasn't clearly a fact.

Besides, how could I check in my heart the assertions about the human way which the good novels contained? When I was forced to read *Silas Marner* in school I was bored and contemptuous. The prose was as thick as molasses and the portrait of the miser had no correspondence to anything in my experience. I took it as a kind of grown-up child's play, nothing more, and resented having to spend precious time reading such a book when I might be out running with my dog, and even more resented the humiliation of having to respond to questions in class the answers to which were obvious and silly. I and my friends could teach the author a few things, I thought. Or when it came to reading about Ichabod Crane and Sleepy Hollow—it was spooky enough and of course titil-lated me, but who could believe in the existence of Crane, who could check the author's assertions regarding the kind of guy he was? It was all a game and had nothing to do with the serious business of life, which was girls, dogs, spending money, chums, camping, hiking, and above all *facts*.

I would read books on astrophysics, architecture, chemistry, and avoided for a long time the books certain of my friends were reading—the Boy Allies, Tom Swifts, Altshelers, Tarzans. Very early I realized that in my circle of friends there were three classes of book readers: the non-readers, who were the large majority; the readers of light fiction; and the readers of non-fiction, the latter being an almost infinitesimal category. The non-readers were the respected group, those who excelled in baseball, track, swimming and camping. The readers of light fiction were regarded as either effeminate or, if they were muscular, per-verse. And the readers of non-fiction, unless the books were automotive or carpentry handbooks and the like, were thought to be "stuck up" or lacking in some essential moral fiber or under the influence of some decadent authority. Who but someone who was "stuck up" would read books on the temperatures of stars or on the evolution of the skyscraper—when everybody else was content to read Richard Halliburton's travel adventures or the latest scout handbook?

How I came to fall into the latter category I don't know, But it's clear that as a lover of fact I was already a good American, even if my relation to facts was largely in books. Americans have been too busy settling a vast part of a new continent and experimenting with a new way of life to have much time for such luxuries as daydreams and theories. Besides, they have an English heritage, and the English have long been noted for their opposition to overstatement, most theories and daydreams about life being overstatements of one sort or another and lacking the wry humor necessary to a sane handling of facts. Yet even in those days I would dip into the stories of Tolstoy, chiefly under the urging of my grandfather. My mother loved Chekhov and Turgenev. When she said Chekhov she smiled gently and her eyes reflected distant and poetic images, the way they did when she mentioned certain romantic operas. When she said Turgenev she always said he was "fine," and said it as though she were describing the feel of a taffeta. My father, with a wry smile, preferred Gogol. But neither my father nor my mother had for me in this particular realm the authority of my grandfather, and so it was Tolstoy's stories that I read.

By good luck the first things I picked up were the Sevastopol sketches. Their intense realism overwhelmed me and shook my notions about fiction. There could be no question that here were tales which could compete with any actuality; that they were more intense than actuality as I usually knew it. There was nothing vague in them. Everything was specified: the horrors of war, the horrors of operations without anesthetics, the courage, fatalism, patriotism of men who seemed close to me because they too were Russians (I still thought of myself as Russian in some ways), but above all because they were so human as to seem palpable. I dimly realized then what I later came to understand: that Tolstoy is tremendous in capturing the feel of life. Of course I sensed he had written the sketches after close observation of the Sevastopol scenes, that they were highly autobiographical; and my grandfather confirmed this. But there was no hiding the fact that in the last two of the three sketches a great deal of imagination was in play. Tolstoy had never died, yet he closely described the sensations and thoughts of dying men, and the descriptions convinced me to such an extent that my heart beat wildly and I felt slightly sick.

I began to have an inkling of the value of good fiction, but the inkling was vague, my resistance strong, and I began to regard him as a special case. When I read some of his moral fables, written in his later phase, with their intense idealism, I was put off. Being very young, I was very idealistic and didn't see the relevance of such passionate, insistent idealism, not having had much experience of the cynicism at loose in the world. My grandfather fortunately helped me, although at times he disconcerted me by chuckling or giggling at the sound of Tolstoy in English. Under his guidance I read "Lost On the Steppe" (also known as "The Snowstorm") and again was struck by the factual clarity of the fiction. Here was a man who *knew* certain things and could describe them authoritatively. On the other hand, there was a poetic side to him in the intensity of his perception and in the flow of waves which emanated from his story beyond its confines, which I dimly appreciated as being magical.

I was confused, uncertain. The shell of my dogmatism had been punctured. It was fortunate for me that this was so, for that tiny hole let in the fresh air of a new perception, which was soon to become strengthened—the perception that facts in themselves are cheats, dry as dust and fluid as water; that they are an insidious diet without the influence of poetry; and that in good fiction one finds facts and poetry and a knowledge of the human way all brought together in interesting forms and all free for the enjoying.

I no longer recall how I came, step by step, to change my attitude toward fiction, nor what the essential causes for this change were, but I remember, as I have indicated, that Tolstoy had a hand, and a strong one, in that change. He made it easier for me. He was not involved in some philosophy of style or structure of thought. He was not interested in "literature" as such but in "life" and in capturing as much of "life" as he could, in his diaries and in his stories and novels. And I as a young man, like other young men, was intensely interested in "life" and repelled by speculation about it, by moralizing and philosophizing, and above all by fiction which was mannered. When in time I became a passionate admirer of fiction I realized that I had early encountered a great practitioner of it—the greatest, the zenith of achievement in the medium, a man who had done titanic things and who was possessed of titanic energy, a man of whom even Henry James, so different in vision and scope, had written, "The perusal of Tolstoy—a wonderful mass of life—is an immense event. . . . Tolstoy is a reflector as vast as a natural lake; a monster harnessed to his great subject —all human life!—as an elephant might be harnessed, for purposes of traction, not to a carriage, but to a coach-house. His own case is prodigious, but his example for others is dire: disciples not elephantine he can only mislead and betray."

When I think of Tolstoy two other great artists come to mind. The first is Michelangelo. Tolstoy shares with him the same great energy, the same fascination with the physical life, the same tremendous scope, and the same effect of being larger than life. Michelangelo's Sistine Chapel frescoes bring to my mind *War and Peace*; his Moses, brooding in the shadows of the little Roman church, Daddy Eroshka in *The Cossacks*; and his unfinished sculpture of Christ being removed from the cross, so touching in its tenderness, several splendid moments in *Anna Karenina*. The other artist is Mozart, whose spontaneous, singing quality was considered remarkable even in his own time. Tolstoy's effects, like Mozart's, never resemble effects. He can almost be said not to have a "style," and there is no interposition, or very little, of a manner between the reader and Tolstoy's stage. It is as if the reader, the spectator, were on the stage itself. So it is in Mozart, whose music seems stripped of all encumbrances and to be the essence of music. Both artists give the effect of effortlessness. Mozart is said to have composed many things while playing billiards and to have merely written them out later. If this is true, then Tolstoy differs here, for he is known to have been a savage overhauler of his drafts. But the effect is the same: of witnessing a restless, singing life force expressed in the essence of a particular artistic medium. In encountering all three men one experiences intense purity, a devotion for which only the word religious seems adequate, and an incredible fertility. No wonder one is shaken by these encounters.

It seems that there was never a time when Tolstoy was a blundering beginner. (The same can be said of the other two men.) He began his artistic career with several stories and with *Childhood, Boyhood and Youth*, which immediately brought him great praise. *Childhood* is an acclaimed masterpiece and even the earliest stories are worthy of him and contain in a surprisingly developed form the hallmarks of his genius. In "The Invaders," for example, everything is so well realized physically, so simple, and the descriptions of manners so fine. Tolstoy seems to miss nothing, yet he never lingers, being always restless and energetic, always muscular. There are wonderful touches, such as the meeting between the general and the countess, and the nature descriptions are superb. When the battalion marches at night you are *there*. In "The Wood-Cutting Expedition" there is the same brilliant detail, and the delight in being alive, of having vibrant senses, and there is much raw nature, and men concerned with behaving according to their station in society or to their duty or their notions of themselves. Tolstoy writes as though he has been writing a long time. He is already on the way to being a master. And he always writes like a novelist, with breadth and with incomparable reserves. In "Lost on the Steppe" he shows how he can sustain one note without ever being boring. How powerful the details are and how they keep coming! One is bowled over by the fertility and the accuracy and by the sense of the storm. And there are wonderful surprises, such as the startling and beautiful recollection of summer. Nowhere is there any evidence of sentimentality or of literary tricks or of putting on the dog. Suspense, psychology, action, intense characterization, a breadth of experience, a wonderful feeling of story: all these gifts are to be found in his earliest fictions. He is tremendous at the very opening of his career.

I was lucky to have had my Tolstoy experience at a fairly early age and I knew it. I was also in a sense prepared for it. As a former Russian I felt a kinship with Tolstoy. As an American I felt I had a special basis for understanding him: both our countries were immense; both very energetic and experimental, both sensitive to questions of good and evil and both still young in literary tradition. And as a young man delighting in muscular energy, I was ready to admire it in Tolstoy.

Paradoxically, it was that very energy, especially in its sexual manifestations, from which he later so strongly recoiled, trying to expunge it or to rechannelize it in the old way of the saints, through self-abnegation, chastity, poverty, humility and various other forms of asceticism, which became the talk of half the world. After his religious conversion he theorized about many things, including literature and art, and shocked his admirers by denouncing his own great works as products of an idle brain. It was during this later phase that he wrote his moral fables, stories such as "Where Love Is, There God Is Also" and "Walk in the Light While There Is Light," the latter probably the most didactic of all his fictions. I still don't like them as much as his less moralistic stories, and many people share my preference. Yet such a sensitive reader as James Joyce wrote of one of the stories: "In my opinion 'How Much Land Does a Man Need?' is the greatest story that the literature of the world knows." Which indicates how much room there is for differing tastes and opinions regarding Tolstoy.

The conventional conception of Tolstoy's literary career is that it was broken approximately in half, that the first period, of about twenty-five years, ending with the completion of Anna Karenina in 1876, was a free and good and highly productive one, in which Tolstoy's genius was not encumbered by theories and false notions; and that the second period showed a crotchety interest in propaganda, a falling away of creative powers, and an increasing retreat from the real world. This view, however, overlooks the fact that Tolstoy from the beginning was passionately interested in questions of what was just and what unjust, what noble, what evil, what pure, what impure, and was intensely curious about men's motives and behavior, and that as he grew older all the early tendencies were merely intensified and came into full flower.

He was a nobleman, with good prospects in life and with important connections in all avenues of Russian power. As a young man he didn't stray into literature because of a desire for fame or because of family precedents. Nor was he seduced into it by the hope of earning large sums of money in an easy way. What then made him a devotee of it? What caused him to work at it so stubbornly and with inspiration even in such a place as Sevastopol, with the terrible battles raging and with his life constantly in danger, and with the thousand and one preoccupations and chores of such a life? It seems to me that any motive short of a passionate ethical one is insufficient in his case. Tolstoy greatly felt the need to examine and improve himself, and in the process of trying and of sometimes succeeding he decided that he had to examine and improve Russian society. But it wasn't so much a pedagogical seduction as an evangelical one.

Like Hemingway, who paid him great praise, Tolstoy wanted to know and later to describe (but perhaps he could only truly know by describing) what it was to be brave in the trenches, or to be afraid, or cowardly, or to die, or face imminent death. He wanted to know how men behaved in extreme situations and to know if they were noble or mean and why they were so, and what their behavior meant, to themselves and their comrades. He also wanted to know what kind of man he himself was. Such an interest, it seems to me, clearly underlines his earliest writings and is almost monstrously obvious in his early diaries and outweighs any other considerations in an attempt to understand what caused him to write under such unpropitious circumstances. He possessed and was possessed by a moral passion which first manifested itself in the form of curiosity and later in indignation, a passion so strong that at times it seems to amount to a specific emotion, and an emotion on the verge of seizure.

Its effects can be seen in his early stories. How do officers behave on campaign, what is expected of them, what is their relation to the soldiers, how do they differ in type ("The Invaders")? What is it like to be possessed by a gambling demon, to watch one's own degradation, and what is the way out ("Recollections of a Billiard-Marker")? How do men behave in a terrible snowstorm, why is the Russian peasant so beautifully fatalistic, and what is the secret of his great moral strength ("Lost on the Steppe")? What causes a well-born man to disgrace himself, to become declassed, and to end by behaving like a beggar; and how does such a man specifically behave, what are the details of the way he comforts himself ("An Old Acquaintance")? And so on.

Such a passion stimulated and strengthened his work so long as it was subordinated to the legitimate needs of the fictional medium. But when moral indignation got out of hand, as in "Lucerne," it harmed the story, making one feel that the author's condemnation of the tourists was excessive and his admiration of the beggarly singer verging on the sentimental. The author's emotion stands between us and the stage, like a highly colored screen through which we peer, trying to see the action unvarnished. The same may be said of the stories which Tolstoy set himself to write for children, and two of which were his favorites as an old man ("The Long Exile" and "A Prisoner in the Caucasus"). These tales contain a surprising amount of cruelty and suffering and are hardly good fare for children. But even if we ignore such a point, the fact remains that Tolstoy is deliberately hamstringing himself by writing in an artificially abbreviated and oversimplified style, as also in "Desire Stronger Than Necessity."

These three stories immediately preceded the writing of *Anna Karenina*. In the very late tales, as in "The Kreutzer Sonata," some of the views expressed are extremely eccentric, and are fictional counterparts, in their eccentricity, of such published views as that Harriet Beecher Stowe was a more effective writer than Shakespeare and that *War and Peace* and *Anna Karenina* did not merit the term of serious art. In his attacks on doctors in "The Kreutzer Sonata"

Tolstoy is patently unfair, and Chekhov, himself a doctor as well as a sensitive writer, justifiably resented them although he admired the art and power of the tale. And Tolstoy's views of sexual relations are nothing if not shocking. But then he loved to shock, partly in order to cover his shyness, partly to stimulate opposition.

Speaking of the "half-crazy saints" who used to come to the house at Yasnaya Polyana, the Tolstoy estate south of Moscow, when he was a boy, and one of whom he portrayed in *Childhood* as Grisha, Tolstoy wrote in later years: "They accomplished what Marcus Aurelius speaks of when he says: 'There is nothing higher than to endure contempt for one's good life.' So harmful and so unavoidable is the desire for human glory, which always contaminates good deeds, that one cannot but sympathize with the effort not merely to avoid praise, but even to evoke contempt." Tolstoy may well have been recollecting two sides of his own behavior, one when he was part of the literary set centering around the *Contemporary* and goading Turgenev to the point of hysterics, and the other when he took to giving away his copyrights (infuriating his wife), wearing peasant clothes, soling his own shoes and espousing singular views.

It would be a mistake, however, to conclude that because of his oddities, excesses and moral indignation he inevitably harmed his creative work. Despite its flaws, "The Kreutzer Sonata" is a mighty creation and is better balanced than appears at first encounter. Many of its views are indeed Tolstoy's, but the character who utters them is not quite sane, as the author takes pains to show us, and the psychological structure of the work holds water. That it is an almost incredible *tour de force*, as is "The Death of Ivan Ilyitch," is almost universally conceded. Why Tolstoy's moral indignation did not get out of hand sufficiently to spoil these two great tales is a mystery. Tolstoy is a genius and as such is not very predictable. These long tales, and others of his later phase are sufficient evidence that his creative powers didn't fail him.

I have not given up reading Tolstoy since my boyhood. I have been reading him now for many, many years and am witness of the fact that his power over the reader and his intense quality of being alive do not fade.

—Charles Neider
1985

Tolstoy

THE INVADERS

A VOLUNTEER'S NARRATIVE

1

On the 24th of July, Captain Khlopof, in epaulets and cap,—a style of dress in which I had not seen him since my arrival in the Caucasus,—entered the low door of my earth hut.

"I'm just from the colonel's," he said in reply to my questioning look; "to-morrow our battalion is to move."

"Where?" I asked.

"To N——. The troops have been ordered to muster at that place."

"And probably some expedition will be made from there?"

"Of course."

"In what direction, think you?"

"What do I think? I tell you I know. Last night a Tartar from the general came galloping up,—brought orders for the battalion to march, taking two days' rations. But whither, why, how long, isn't for them to ask. Orders are to go—that's enough."

"Still, if they are going to take only two days' rations, it's likely the army will not stay longer."

"That's no argument at all."

"And how is that?" I asked, with astonishment.

"This is the way of it: When they went against Dargi they took a week's rations, but they spent almost a month."

"And may I go with you?" I asked, after a short silence.

"Yes, you *may*; but my advice is—better not go. Why run the risk?". . .

"No, allow me to disregard your advice. I have been spending a whole month here for this very purpose,—of having a chance to see action,—and you want me to let it have the go-by!"

"All right, come with us; only isn't it a fact it would be better for you to stay behind? You might wait for us here; you might go hunting. But as to us,—God knows what will become of us! . . . And it would be glorious," he said in such a convincing tone that it seemed to me at the first moment that it would actually be glorious. Nevertheless, I said resolutely that I wouldn't stay behind for anything.

"And what would you see there?" pursued the captain, still trying to dissuade me. "If you want to learn how battles are fought, read Mikhaïlovsky-Danilevski's 'Description of War,' a charming book; there it's all admirably described,— where every corps stands, and how battles are fought."

"On the contrary, that does not interest me," I replied.

"Well, now, how is this? It simply means that you want to see how men kill one another, doesn't it? . . . Here in 1832 there was a man like yourself, not in the regular service,—a Spaniard, I think he was. He went on two expeditions with us, . . . in a blue mantle or something of the sort, and so the young fellow was killed. Here, batyushka, one is not surprised at anything."

Ashamed as I was that the captain gave such a poor interpretation of my motives, I did not attempt to argue him down.

"Well, he was brave, wasn't he?" I asked.

"God knows as to that. He always used to ride at the front. Wherever there was firing, there he was."

"So he must have been brave, then," said I.

"No, it doesn't signify bravery,—to put one's self where one isn't called."

"What do you call bravery, then?"

"Bravery, bravery?" repeated the captain, with the expression of a man to whom such a question presents itself for the first time. "A *brave man is one who conducts himself as he ought*," said he, after a brief consideration.

I remembered that Plato defined bravery as *the knowledge of what one ought and what one ought not to fear*; and in spite of the triteness and obscurity in the captain's definition, I thought the fundamental conception of both was not so unlike as might at first sight appear; and that the captain's definition was even more correct than the Greek philosopher's, for the reason that, if he could have expressed himself as Plato did, he would in all probability have said that that man is brave who fears only what he ought to fear and not what there is no need of fearing.

I was anxious to explain my thought to the captain.

"Yes," I said, "it seems to me that in every peril there is an alternative, and the alternative adopted under the influence of, say, the sentiment of duty, is bravery, but the alternative adopted under the influence of a lower sentiment is cowardice; therefore it is impossible to call a man brave who risks his life out of vanity or curiosity or greediness, and, *vice versa*, the man who under the influence of the virtuous sentiment of family obligation, or simply from conviction, avoids peril, cannot be called a coward."

The captain looked at me with a queer sort of expression while I was talking.

"Well, now, I don't know how to reason this out with you," said he, filling his pipe; "but we have with us a yunker, and he likes to philosophize. You talk with him. He also writes poetry."

I had only become intimate with the captain in the Caucasus, but I had known him before in Russia. His mother, Marya Ivanova Khlopova, the owner of a small landed estate, lives about two versts[1] from my home. Before I went to the Caucasus I visited her. The old lady was greatly delighted that I was going to see her Pashenka (thus she called the old gray-haired captain) and, like a living letter, could tell him about her circumstances and give him a little message.

[1] One and a third miles.

Having made me eat my fill of a glorious pie and roast chicken, Marya Ivanova went to her sleeping-room and came back with a rather large black relic-bag,[2] to which was attached a silken ribbon.

"Here is this image of our Mother-Intercessor from the September festival," she said, kissing the picture of the divine mother attached to the cross, and putting it into my hand. "Please give it to him, batyushka. You see, when he went to the *Kapkas*, I had a Te Deum sung, and made a vow that if he should be kept alive and safe, I would order this image of the divine mother. And here it is seventeen years that the Virgin and the saints have had him in their keeping; not once has he been wounded, and what battles he has been in, as it seems! . . . When Mikhaïlo, who was with him, told me about it, my hair actually stood on end. You see, all that I know about him I have to hear from others; he never writes me anything about his doings, my dove,—he is afraid of frightening me."

I had already heard in the Caucasus, but not from the captain himself, that he had been severely wounded four times; and, as was to be expected, he had not written his mother about his wounds any more than about his campaigns.

"Now let him wear this holy image," she continued. "I bless him with it. The most holy Intercessor protect him! especially in battle let him always take it with him! And so tell him, my dear friend, that his mother gave him this message."

I promised faithfully to fulfil her commission.

"I know you will be fond of him, of my Pashenka," the old lady continued,— "he is such a splendid fellow! Would you believe me, not a year goes by without his sending me money, and he also helps Annushka, my daughter, and all from his wages alone. Truly I shall always thank God," she concluded, with tears in her eyes, "that He has given me such a child."

"Does he write you often?" I asked.

"Rarely, batyushka,—not more than once a year; and sometimes when he sends money he writes a little word, and sometimes he doesn't. 'If I don't write you, mamenka,' he says, 'it means that I'm alive and well; but if anything should happen,—which God forbid,—then they will write you for me.' "

When I gave the captain his mother's gift (it was in my room), he asked me for some wrapping-paper, carefully tied it up, and put it away. I told him many details of his mother's life; the captain was silent. When I had finished, he went into a corner, and took a very long time in filling his pipe.

"Yes, she's a fine old lady," said he, from the corner, in a rather choked voice; "God grant that we may meet again!"

Great love and grief were expressed in these simple words.

"Why do you serve here?" I asked.

"Have to serve," he replied, with conviction. "And double pay means a good deal for a poor man!"

The captain lived economically; he did not play cards, he rarely drank to excess, and he smoked ordinary tobacco, which from some inexplicable reason he did not call by its usual name, but *sambrotalicheski tabak*. The captain had pleased me even before this. He had one of those simple, calm Russian faces, and looked

[2] *Ladanka*, the bag containing sacred things worn by the pious, together with the baptismal cross.

you straight in the eye agreeably and easily. But after this conversation I felt a genuine respect for him.

2

At four o'clock on the morning of the next day, the captain came riding up for me. He had on an old well-worn coat without epaulets, wide Lesghian trousers, a round white Circassian cap, with drooping *kurpeï*[1] dyed yellow, and an ugly-looking Asiatic saber across his shoulder. The little white *mashtak*[2] on which he rode came with head down, and mincing gait, and kept switching his slender tail. Though the good captain's figure was neither very warlike nor very handsome, yet there was in it such an expression of good-will toward every one around him, that it inspired involuntary respect.

I did not keep him waiting a minute, but immediately mounted, and we rode off together from the gate of the fortress.

The battalion was already a quarter of a mile ahead of us, and had the appearance of a black, solid body moving in waves. It was possible to make out that it was infantry, only from the circumstance that while the bayonets appeared like long, dense needles, occasionally there came to the ear the sounds of a soldier's song, the drum, and a charming tenor, the leader of the sixth company,—a song which I had more than once enjoyed at the fort.

The road ran through the midst of a deep, wide ravine, or *balka*, as it is called in the dialect of the Caucasus, along the banks of a small river, which at this time was *playing*, that is, was having a freshet. Flocks of wild pigeons hovered around it, now settling on the rocky shore, now wheeling about in mid-air in swift circles, and then disappearing from sight.

The sun was not yet visible, but the summit of the balka on the right began to grow luminous. The gray and white crags, the greenish yellow moss, the clumps of different kinds of bushes, wet with dew, stood out extraordinarily distinct and rotund in the pellucid golden light of the dawn.

On the other hand, the ravine, hidden in thick mist which rolled up like smoke in varying volumes, was damp and dark, and presented an evanescent mixture of colors—pale lilac, almost purple, dark green, and white.

Directly in front of us, against the dark blue of the horizon, with startling distinctness appeared the dazzling white, silent masses of the snow-capped mountains with their marvelous shadows and outlines exquisite even in the smallest details. Crickets, grasshoppers, and a thousand other insects were awake in the tall grass, and filled the air with their sharp, incessant clatter; it seemed as if a numberless multitude of tiny bells were jingling in our very ears. The atmosphere was fragrant with waters, with foliage, with mist; in a word, had all the fragrance of a beautiful early summer morning.

The captain struck a light, and began to puff at his pipe; the fragrance of sambrotalicheski tabak and of the punk struck me as extremely pleasant.

We rode along the side of the road so as to overtake the infantry as quickly as possible. The captain seemed more serious than usual; he did not take his Daghestan pipe from his mouth, and at every step he dug his heels into his horse's

---

[1] Lambskin.—Author's Note
[2] A small horse.—Author's Note

legs as the little beast, capering from one side to the other, laid out a scarcely noticeable dark green track through the damp, tall grass. Up from under his very feet, with its shrill cry, and that drumming of the wings that is so sure to startle the huntsman in spite of himself, flew the pheasant, and slowly began to fly up. The captain paid not the slightest attention to it.

We had almost overtaken the battalion, when behind us were heard the hoof-beats of a galloping horse, and in an instant there rode by us a very handsome young fellow in an officer's coat, and a tall white *papakha*, or Circassian cap. As he caught up with us he smiled, bowed to the captain, and waved his whip. . . .

I only had time to notice that he sat in the saddle and held the bridle with peculiar grace, and that he had beautiful dark eyes, a finely cut nose, and a mustache just beginning to grow. I was particularly attracted by the way in which he could not help smiling, as he noticed that we admired him. If by nothing else than his smile, one would have known that he was still very young.

"And now where is he going?" grumbled the captain, with a look of dissatisfaction, not taking his pipe from his mouth.

"Who is that?" I asked.

"Ensign Alanin, a subaltern officer of my company. . . . Only last month he came from the School of Cadets."

"This is the first time that he is going into action, I suppose?" said I.

"And so he is overjoyed," replied the captain, thoughtfully, shaking his head; "it's youth."

"And why shouldn't he be glad? I can see that for a young officer this must be very interesting."

The captain said nothing for two minutes.

"And that's why I say 'it's youth,' " he continued, in his deep bass. "What is there to rejoice in, when there's nothing to see? Here when one goes often, one doesn't find any pleasure in it. Here, let us suppose twenty of us officers are going: some of us will be either killed or wounded; that's likely. To-day my turn, to-morrow his, the next day somebody else's. So what is there to rejoice in?"

3

Scarcely had the bright sun risen above the mountains, and begun to shine into the valley where we were riding, when the phantasmagoric clouds of mist scattered, and it grew warm. The soldiers, with guns and knapsacks on their backs, marched slowly along the dusty road. In the ranks were frequently heard Malo-Russian dialogues and laughter. A few old soldiers in white linen coats—for the most part non-commissioned officers—marched along the roadside with their pipes, engaged in earnest conversation. The heavily laden wagons, drawn each by three horses, advanced step by step, and raised a thick dust, which hung motionless.

The mounted officers rode in advance; a few *jigited*, as they say in the Caucasus;[1] that is, applying the whip to their horses, they would spur them on to make four or five leaps, and then reined them in suddenly, pulling the head back. Others listened to the singers, who, not withstanding the heat and the sultriness, indefatigably tuned up one song after another.

[1] Show off.

A hundred sazhens in advance of the infantry, on a great white horse, surrounded by mounted Tartars, rode a tall, handsome officer in Asiatic costume, known to the regiment as a man of reckless valor, and one who always tells the truth in any one's eyes.

He wore a black Tartar beshmet trimmed with silver braid, similar trousers, closely fitting new leggings, with *chirazui*,[2] a yellow *cherkeska*, or cloak, and tall papakha worn jauntily on the back of his head. On his breast and back were silver lacings, to which were attached his powder-flask and pistol behind; another pistol and a dagger in a silver sheath depended from his belt. On top of all this was buckled on a saber in a red morocco sheath adorned with silver; and over the shoulder hung his musket in a black case.

By his garb, his carriage, his manner, and indeed by every motion, it was manifest that his ambition was to ape the Tartars. He was just saying something, in a language that I did not understand, to the Tartars who rode with him; but from the doubtful, mocking glances which these latter gave one another, I came to the conclusion that they did not understand him either.

This was one of our young officers of the dare-devil, jigit order, who get themselves up in the style of Marlinsky and Lermontof. These men look upon the Caucasus no other wise than through the prism of the "Heroes of our Time," Mulla-Nurof,[3] and others, and in all their activities are directed, not by their own inclinations, but by the example of these models.

This lieutenant, for instance, was very likely fond of the society of well-bred women and men of importance, generals, colonels, adjutants,—indeed I believe that he was very fond of this society, because he was in the highest degree vainglorious,—but he considered it his unfailing duty to show his rough side to all important persons, although he offended them always more or less; and when any lady made her appearance at the fortress, he considered it his duty to ride by her windows with his kunaki,[4] dressed in nothing but a red shirt and with nothing but chuviaki on his bare legs, and shouting and swearing at the top of his voice—but all this not so much with the intention of insulting her, as with the wish to show her what handsome white legs he had, and how easy it would be to fall in love with him if only he himself were willing.

Or he often went by at night with two or three friendly Tartars to the mountain into ambush by the road so as to take by surprise and kill hostile Tartars coming along; and though more than once his heart told him that there was nothing brave in such a deed, yet he felt himself under obligations to inflict suffering on men who he thought had caused him to lose some of his illusions, and whom he affected to hate and despise. He wore two things which he never took off,—an immense holy image suspended around his neck, and a dagger above his shirt; he even went to bed with them. He firmly believed that enemies surrounded him. It was his greatest delight to argue that he ought to wreak vengeance on some one and wash out some insult in blood. He was persuaded

---

[2] Gold braid

[3] The name of a character in one of Marlinsky's novels. The poet Lermontof's most famous novel was entitled *Heroï nasheva vrimeni*, a "Hero of our Time"; Lermontof, of Scotch origin, was killed in 1841 in a duel in the Caucasus at the early age of twenty-seven.

[4] *Kunak*, friend, guest-friend, in the dialect of the Caucasus.

that spite, vengeance, and hatred of the human race were the highest and most poetical of feelings. But his mistress,—a *Cherkeshenka*, or Circassian girl, of course,—whom I afterward chanced to meet, said that he was the mildest and gentlest of men, and that every evening he wrote in his gloomy diary, cast up his accounts on ruled paper, and got on his knees to say his prayers. And how much suffering he endured, to seem only to himself what he desired to be! because his comrades and the soldiers could not comprehend him as he desired!

Once, in one of his nocturnal expeditions with his Tartar kunaks, it happened that he put a bullet into the leg of a hostile Chechenets, and took him prisoner. This Chechenets for seven weeks thereafter lived with the lieutenant; the lieutenant dressed his wound, waited on him as if he were his nearest friend, and when he was cured sent him home with gifts. Afterward, during an expedition when the lieutenant was retreating from the post, having been repulsed by the enemy, he heard some one call him by name, and his wounded kunak strode out from among the hostile Tartars, and by signs asked him to do the same. The lieutenant went to meet his kunak, and shook hands with him. The mountaineers stood at some little distance, and refrained from firing; but, as soon as the lieutenant turned his horse to go back, several shot at him, and one bullet grazed the small of his back.

Another time I myself saw a fire break out by night in the fortress, and two companies of soldiers were detailed to put it out. Amid the crowd, lighted up by the ruddy glare of the conflagration, suddenly appeared the tall form of the man on a coal-black horse. He forced his way through the crowd, and rode straight up to the fire. As soon as he came near, the lieutenant leaped from his horse, and hastened into the house, which was all in flames on one side. At the end of five minutes he emerged with singed hair and burned sleeves, carrying in his arms two doves which he had rescued from the flames.

His name was Rosenkranz; but he often spoke of his ancestry, traced it back to the Varangians, and clearly showed that he and his forefathers were genuine Russians.

4

The sun had traveled half its course, and was pouring down through the glowing atmosphere its fierce rays on parched earth. The dark blue sky was absolutely clear; only the bases of the snow-capped mountains began to clothe themselves in pale lilac clouds. The motionless atmosphere seemed to be full of some impalpable dust; it became intolerably hot.

When the army came to a small brook that had overflowed half the road, the troops made a halt. The soldiers, stacking their arms, rushed to the stream. The battalion commander sat down in the shade, on a drum, and, showing by his broad countenance the degree of his rank, made ready, in company with a few officers, to take luncheon. The captain lay on the grass under the company's transport-wagon; the galliard lieutenant Rosenkranz and some other young officers, spreading out their *burki*, or Caucasian mantles, threw themselves down, and began to carouse, as any one could see by the flasks and bottles scattered around them and by the extraordinary liveliness of their singers, who, standing in a half-circle behind them, whistled an accompaniment to the Caucasian dance-song sung by a Lesghian girl:—

> *Shamyl resolved to make a league*
> *In the years gone by,*
> *Traï-raï, rattat-taï,*
> *In the years gone by.*

Among these officers was also the young ensign who had passed us in the morning. He was very entertaining; his eyes gleamed, his tongue was a trifle entangled. He wanted to exchange kisses with every one, and show his good-will to them all. . . .

Poor lad! he did not know that in acting this way he might be ridiculous, that his frankness and the gentleness which he showed to every one might win for him, not the love which he so much desired, but ridicule; he did not know this either, that when at last, thoroughly heated, he threw himself down on his burka, and leaned his head on his hand, letting his thick black curls fall over, he was extraordinarily handsome.

Two officers had crept under a wagon, and were playing cards on a hamper.

I listened with curiosity to the talk of the soldiers and officers, and attentively watched the expression of their faces; but, to tell the truth, in not one could I discover a shadow of that anxiety which I myself felt; jokes, laughter, anecdotes, expressed the universal carelessness, and indifference to the coming peril. How impossible to suppose that it was not fated for some never again to return along that road!

5

At seven o'clock in the evening, dusty and weary, we entered the wide, fortified gates of Fort N——.

The sun was setting, and shed oblique rosy rays over the picturesque batteries and lofty-walled gardens that surrounded the fortress, over the fields yellow for the harvest, and over the white clouds which, gathering around the snow-capped mountains, simulated their shapes, and formed a chain no less wonderful and beauteous. A young half moon, like a translucent cloud, shone above the horizon. In the *aul*, or native village, situated near the gate, a Tartar on the roof of a hut was calling the faithful to prayer. The singers broke out with new zeal and energy.

After resting and making my toilet, I set out to call upon an adjutant who was an acquaintance of mine, to ask him to make my intention known to the general. On the way from the suburb where I was quartered, I chanced to see a most unexpected spectacle in the fortress of N——. I was overtaken by a handsome two-seated carriage in which I saw a stylish bonnet, and heard French spoken. From the open window of the commandant's house came floating the sounds of some "Lizanka" or "Katenka" polka played on a wretched piano, out of tune. In the tavern which I was passing were sitting a number of clerks over their glasses of wine, with cigarettes in their hands, and I overheard one saying to another:—

"Excuse me, but taking politics into consideration, Marya Grigor'yevna is our first lady."

A humpbacked Jew of sickly countenance, dressed in a dilapidated coat, was creeping along with a shrill, battered hand-organ; and over the whole suburb echoed the sounds of the finale of "Lucia."

Two women in rustling gowns, with silk kerchiefs around their necks and bright-colored parasols in their hands, hastened past me on the plank sidewalk. Two girls, one in a pink, the other in a blue frock, with uncovered heads, were standing on the terrace of a small house, and affectedly laughing with the obvious intention of attracting the notice of some passing officers. Officers in new coats, white gloves, and glistening epaulets were parading up and down the streets and the boulevard.

I found my acquaintance on the lower floor of the general's house. I had scarcely had time to explain to him my desire, and have his assurance that it could most likely be gratified, when the handsome carriage which I had before seen rattled past the window where I was sitting. From the carriage descended a tall, slender man, in uniform of the infantry service and major's epaulets, and came up to the general's rooms.

"Ah! pardon me, I beg of you," said the aide, rising from his place: "it's absolutely necessary that I notify the general."

"Who is it that just came?" I asked.

"The countess," he replied, and, donning his uniform coat, hastened up-stairs.

In the course of a few minutes a short but very handsome man in a coat without epaulets, and a white cross in his buttonhole, appeared on the steps. Behind him came the major, the aide, and two other officers.

In his carriage, in his voice, in all his motions, the general showed that he had a very keen appreciation of his high importance.

"*Bon soir, madame la comtesse,*" he said, extending his hand through the carriage window.

A dainty little hand in dogskin glove pressed his hand, and a pretty, smiling little visage under a yellow bonnet appeared in the window.

Of the conversation, which lasted several minutes, I only heard the general saying in French, with a smile, as I went by:—

"You know that I have vowed to fight the infidels; beware of becoming one!"

A laugh rang from the carriage.

"*Adieu donc, cher général.*"

"*Non, à revoir,*" said the general, returning to the steps of the staircase; "don't forget that I have invited myself for to-morrow evening."

The carriage drove away.

"Here is a man," said I to myself, as I went home, "who has everything that Russians strive after,—rank, wealth, society,—and this man, before a battle the outcome of which God only knows, jests with a pretty little woman, and promises to drink tea with her on the next day, just as if he was meeting her at a ball!"

There also at that adjutant's I became acquainted with a man who still more surprised me; it was the young lieutenant of the K. regiment, who was distinguished for his almost feminine mildness and cowardice. He came to the adjutant to pour out his peevishness and ill humor against those men who, he thought, were intriguing against him to keep him from taking part in the matter in hand.

He declared that it was hateful to be treated so, that it was not doing as comrades ought, that he would remember him, and so forth.

As soon as I saw the expression of his face, as soon as I heard the sound of his voice, I could not escape the conviction that he was not only not putting it on, but was deeply stirred and hurt because he was not allowed to go against the

Cherkess, and expose himself to their fire; he was as much hurt as a child is hurt who is unjustly punished. . . . I could not understand it at all.

6

At ten o'clock in the evening the troops were ordered to march. At half-past nine I mounted my horse and started off to find the general; but on reflecting that he and his aide must be busy, I remained in the street, and, tying my horse to a fence, sat down on the terrace to wait until the general should come.

The heat and glare of the day had already vanished in the fresh night air and in the obscure light of the young moon, which, infolding around itself a pale gleaming halo against the dark blue of the starry sky, was beginning to decline. Lights shone in the windows of the houses and in the chinks of the earth huts. The gracefully proportioned poplars in the gardens, standing out against the horizon from behind the earth huts, the reed-thatched roofs of which gleamed pale in the moonlight, seemed still taller and blacker.

The long shadows of the houses, of the trees, of the fences, lay beautifully across the white dusty road. . . . In the river rang incessantly the voice of the frogs; in the streets were heard hurrying steps, and sounds of voices, and the galloping of horses. From the suburb came floating, now and again, the strains of the hand-organ: now the popular Russian air, "The winds are blowing," now one of the Aurora waltzes.

I will not tell what my thoughts were: in the first place, because I should be ashamed to confess to the melancholy ideas which without cessation arose in my mind, while all around me I perceived only gayety and mirth; and, in the second place, because they have nothing to do with my story.

I was so deeply engrossed in thought, that I did not notice that the bell was ringing for eleven o'clock, and the general was riding past me with his suite.

The rear-guard was just at the fortress gate. I forced my way across the bridge, amid a crush of cannon, caissons, military wagons, and commanding officers shouting at the top of their voices. After reaching the gate, I rode at a brisk trot for almost a verst, past the army stretched out and silently moving through the darkness, and overtook the general. As I made my way past the mounted artillery dragging their ordnance, amid the cannon and officers, a German voice, like a disagreeable dissonance interrupting soft and majestic harmony, struck my ear. It screamed: —

"Agkhtingkhist,[1] bring a linstock."

And a soldier's voice replied, quick as a flash, "Chevchenko! the lieutenant asks for a light!"

The greater part of the sky had become enveloped in long dark gray clouds; here and there gleamed from between them the lusterless stars. The moon was now sinking behind the near horizon of dark mountains which were on the right; and it shed on their summits a feeble, waning half-light, which contrasted sharply with the impenetrable darkness that marked their bases.

The air was mild, and so still, that not a single grass-blade, not a single mist-wreath, moved. It became so dark that it was impossible to distinguish objects, even though very near at hand. On the side of the road, there seemed to me some-

---

[1] German mispronunciation for *Antichrist.*

times to be rocks, sometimes animals, sometimes strange men; and I knew that they were bushes only when I heard them rustle, and felt the coolness of the dew with which they were covered. In front of me I saw a dense, waving black shadow, behind which followed a few moving spots; this was the vanguard of cavalry, and the general with his suite. Between us moved another similar black mass, but this was not as high as the first; this was the infantry.

Such silence reigned in the whole detachment, that there could be plainly distinguished all the harmonious voices of the night, full of mysterious charm. The distant melancholy howls of jackals, sometimes like the wails of despair, sometimes like laughter; the monotonous ringing song of the cricket, the frog, the quail; a gradually approaching murmur, the cause of which I could not make clear to my own mind; and all those nocturnal, almost audible motions of Nature, which it is so impossible either to comprehend or define,—united into one complete, beautiful harmony which we call "the silence of night."

This silence was broken, or rather was unified, by the dull thud of the hoofs, and the rustling of the tall grass through which the division was slowly moving.

Occasionally, however, was heard in the ranks the ring of a heavy cannon, the sound of clashing bayonets, stifled conversation, and the snorting of a horse.

Nature breathed peacefully in beauty and power.

Is it possible that people find no room to live together in this beautiful world, under this boundless starry heaven? Is it possible that, amid this bewitching Nature, the soul of man can harbor the sentiments of hatred and revenge, or the passion for inflicting destruction on his kind? All ugly feelings in the heart of man ought, it would seem, to vanish away in this intercourse with Nature—with this immediate expression of beauty and goodness!

7

We had now been marching more than two hours. I began to feel chilly, and to be overcome with drowsiness. In the darkness the same indistinct objects dimly appeared; at a little distance, the same black shadow, the same moving spots. Beside me was the crupper of a white horse, which switched its tail and moved its hind legs in its vigorous stride. I could see a back in a white Circassian shirt, against which was outlined a carbine in its black case, and the handle of a pistol in an embroidered holster; the glow of a cigarette casting a gleam on a reddish mustache, a fur collar, and a hand in a chamois-skin glove.

I leaned over my horse's neck, closed my eyes, and lost myself for a few minutes; then suddenly the well-known hoof-beat and rustling came into my consciousness again. I looked around, and it seemed to me as if I were standing still in one spot, and that the black shadow in front of me was moving down on me; or else that the shadow stood still, and I was rapidly riding down on it.

At one such moment I was more strongly than ever impressed by that incessantly approaching sound, the cause of which I could not fathom; it was the roar of water. We were passing through a deep gulch, and coming close to a mountain river, which at that season was in full flood. The roaring became louder, the damp grass grew taller and thicker, bushes were encountered in denser clumps, and the horizon narrowed itself down to closer limits. Now and then, in different places in the dark hollows of the mountains, bright fires flashed out and were immediately extinguished.

"Tell me, please, what are those fires," I asked in a whisper of the Tartar riding at my side.

"Don't you really know?" was his reply.

"No," said I.

"That is mountain straw tied to a *tayak*,[1] and the light is waved."

"What for?"

"So that every man may know the Russian is coming. Now in the auls," he added with a laugh, "*aï, aï!* the tomasha[2] are flying about; every sort of khurda-murda[3] will be hurried into the ravines."

"How do they know so soon in the mountains that the expedition is coming?" I asked.

"*Eï!* How can they help knowing? It's known everywhere: that's the kind of people we are."

"And so Shamyl is now getting ready to take the field?" I asked.

"*Yok* (no)," he replied, shaking his head as a sign of negation, "Shamyl will not take the field. Shamyl will send his naïbs,[4] and he himself will look down from up yonder through his glass."

"But does he live a long way off?"

"Not a long way off. Here, at your left, about ten versts he will be."

"How do you know that?" I inquired. "Have you been there?"

"I've been there. All of us in the mountains have."

"And you have seen Shamyl?"

"Pikh! Shamyl is not to be seen by us. A hundred, three hundred, a thousand murids[5] surround him. Shamyl will be in the midst of them," he said, with an expression of fawning servility.

Looking upward, it was possible to make out that the sky, which had become clear again, was lighter in the east, and the Pleiades were sinking down into the horizon. But in the gulch through which we were passing it was damp and dark.

Suddenly, a little in advance of us, from out the darkness flashed a number of lights; at the same instant, with a ping, some bullets whizzed by, and from out the silence that surrounded us from afar musket-shots were heard, and a loud shrill cry. This was the vanguard of the enemy's pickets. The Tartars of which it was composed set up their war-cry, shot at random, and fled in all directions.

Everything became silent again. The general summoned his interpreter. The Tartar in a white cherkeska hastened up to him, and the two held a rather long conversation in a sort of whisper and with many gestures.

"Colonel Khasanof! give orders to scatter the line," said the general, in a low, deliberate, but distinct tone of voice.

The division went down to the river. The black mountains stood back from the pass; it was beginning to grow light. The arch of heaven, in which the pale, luster-less stars were barely visible, seemed to grow higher; the dawn began to glow

---

[1] Pole.—Author's Note.

[2] Slaves—Author's Note.

[3] Goods and chattels—Author's Note.

[4] Officers whom the great Circassian chieftain Shamyl endowed with special authority.

[5] Something between adjutant and body-guard.—Author's Note.

brightly in the east; a cool, penetrating breeze sprang up from the west, and a bright mist like steam arose from the foaming river.

8

The guide pointed out the ford; and the vanguard of cavalry, with the general and his suite immediately in its rear, began to cross the river. The water, which reached the horses' breasts, rushed with extraordinary violence among the white boulders which in some places came to the top, and foaming, gurgling whirlpools were formed around the horses' legs. The horses were surprised by the roar of the water, lifted their heads, pricked up their ears, but slowly and carefully picked their way against the current along the uneven bottom. The riders held up their legs and firearms. The foot-soldiers, literally in their shirts alone, lifting above the water their muskets, to which were fastened their bundles of clothing, struggled against the force of the stream by clinging hand to hand, a score of men together showing noticeable determination on their excited faces. The artillerymen on horseback, with a loud shout, put their horses into the water at full trot. The cannon and green-painted caissons, over which now and then the water came pouring, plunged with a clang over the rocky bottom; but the noble Cossack horses pulled with united effort, made the water foam, and with dripping tails and manes emerged on the farther shore.

As soon as the crossing was effected, the general's face suddenly took on an expression of deliberation and seriousness; he wheeled his horse around, and at full gallop rode across the wide forest-surrounded field which spread before us. The mounted line of Cossacks were scattered along the edge of the forest.

In the forest appears a man in cherkeska and lambskin cap; then a second and a third. . . . One of the officers shouted:—

"Those are Tartars!"

At this instant a puff of smoke comes from behind a tree—a report—another. . . . The quick volleys of our men drown out those of the enemy. Only occasionally a bullet, with long-drawn ping like the hum of a bee, flies by, and shows that not all the shots are ours.

Here the infantry, at double quick, and with fixed bayonets, dashed against the line; one can hear the heavy reports of the guns, the metallic ring of flying grape-shot, the whiz of rockets, the crackling of musketry. The cavalry, the infantry, and the artillery converge from all sides on the wide field. The smoke from the guns, rockets, and firearms unites with the early mist arising from the dew-covered grass.

Colonel Khasanof gallops up to the general, and reins in his horse while at full tilt.

"Your excellency," says he, lifting his hand to his cap, "give orders for the cavalry to advance. The standards are in sight," and he points with his whip to mounted Tartars, at the head of whom ride two men on white horses with red and blue streamers on their lances.

"S Bogom, God speed it, Ivan Mikhaïlovitch," says the general.

The colonel wheels his horse round on the spot, draws his saber, and shouts "Hurrah!"

"Hurrah! hurrah! hurrah!" echoes from the ranks, and the cavalry dash after him.

All look on with excitement: there is a standard; another; a third; a fourth! . . .

The enemy, not waiting the assault, fly into the forest, and open a musket fire from behind the trees. The bullets fly more and more thickly.

"*Quel charmant coup d'œil!*" exclaimed the general, rising easily in English fashion on his coal-black, slender-limbed little steed.

"*Charmant,*" replies the major, who swallows his R's like a Frenchman, and, whipping up his horse, dashes after the general. "It's a genuine pleasure to carry on war in such a fine country," says he.

"And above all in good company," adds the general, still in French, with a pleasant smile.

The major bowed.

At this time a cannon-ball from the enemy comes flying by with a swift, disagreeable whiz, and strikes something; immediately is heard the groan of a wounded man. This groan impresses me so painfully that the martial picture instantly loses for me all its fascination; but no one besides myself seems to be affected in the same way: the major smiles, apparently with great satisfaction; another officer with perfect equanimity repeats the opening words of a speech; the general looks in the opposite direction, and with the most tranquil smile says something in French.

"Will you give orders to reply to their fire?" asks the commander of the artillery, galloping up.

"Yes, scare them a little," says the general, carelessly, lighting a cigar.

The battery is unlimbered, and the cannonade begins. The ground groans under the report; the firing continues without cessation; and the smoke, in which it is scarcely possible to distinguish those serving the guns, blinds the eyes.

The aul is battered down. Again Colonel Khasanof dashes up, and at the general's command darts off to the aul. The war-cry is heard again, and the cavalry disappears in the cloud of its own dust.

The spectacle was truly magnificent. One thing only spoiled the general impression for me as a man who had no part in the affair, and was wholly unwonted to it; and this was that there was too much of it,—the motion and the animation and the shouts. Involuntarily the comparison occurred to me of a man who in his haste would cut the air with a hatchet.

9

The aul was already in possession of our men, and not a soul of the enemy remained in it when the general with his suite, to which I had joined myself, entered it.

The long neat *sakli*, or huts, with their flat earthen roofs and red chimneys, were situated on rough, rocky hills, between which ran a small river. On one side were seen the green gardens, shining in the clear sunlight, with monstrous pear trees, and the plum trees, called *luitcha*. The other side bristled with strange shadows, where stood the high perpendicular stones of a cemetery, and the tall wooden poles adorned at the ends with balls and variegated banners. These were the tombs of jigits.

The army stood drawn up within the gates.

After a moment the dragoons, the Cossacks, the infantry, with evident joy, were let loose through the crooked streets, and the empty aul suddenly teemed with life.

Here a roof is crushed in; the ax rings on a tough tree, and the plank door is broken down; there hayricks, fences, and huts are burning, and the dense smoke arises like a tower in the clear air. Here a Cossack is carrying off sacks of flour, and carpets; a soldier with a gay face lugs from a hut a tin basin and some kind of a rag; another with outstretched arms is trying to catch a couple of hens, which, cackling furiously, fly about the yard; a third is going somewhere with a monstrous kumgan[1] of milk, and drinking as he goes, and when he has had his fill throws it on the ground with a loud laugh.

The battalion which I had accompanied from Fort N—— was also in the aul. The captain was sitting on the roof of a hut, and was puffing from his short little pipe clouds of smoke of sambrotalicheski tabak with such an indifferent expression of countenance that when I saw him I forgot that I was in a hostile aul, and it seemed to me that I was actually at home with him.

"Ah! and here you are?" he said, as he caught sight of me.

The tall form of Lieutenant Rosenkranz flashed here and there through the aul. Without a moment's pause he was engaged in carrying out orders, and he had the appearance of a man who had all he could do. I saw him coming out of a hut, his face full of triumph; behind him two soldiers were dragging an old Tartar with his arms tied. The old man, whose garb consisted merely of a many-colored, tattered beshmet, and ragged drawers, was so feeble that it seemed as if his bony arms, tightly tied behind his misshapen back, were almost falling from his shoulders; and his crooked bare legs moved with difficulty. His face and even a part of his shaven head were covered with deep wrinkles; his distorted, tooth-less mouth, encircled by gray clipped mustache and beard, incessantly mumbled as if he were whispering something; but his handsome eyes, from which the lashes were gone, still gleamed with fire, and clearly expressed an old man's indifference to life.

Rosenkranz through an interpreter asked him why he had not gone with the others.

"Where should I go?" he replied, calmly looking away.

"Where the rest have gone," suggested some one.

"The jigits have gone to fight with the Russians, but I am an old man."

"Aren't you afraid of the Russians?"

"What will the Russians do to me? I am an old man," he repeated, carelessly glancing at the circle surrounding him.

On the way back, I saw this old man, without a hat, with his hands still tied, jolting behind a mounted Cossack, and he was looking about him with the same expression of unconcern. He was necessary in an exchange of prisoners.

I went to the staircase and crept up to where the captain was.

"Not many of the enemy, it seems," I said to him, wishing to obtain his opinion about the affair.

"The enemy?" he repeated with surprise; "there weren't any at all. Do you call these enemies? . . . Here, when evening comes, you will see how we shall

[1] Pitcher.—Author's Note.

retreat; you will see how they will go with us! Won't they show themselves there, though!" he added, pointing with his pipe to the forest which we had passed in the morning.

"What is that?" I asked anxiously, interrupting the captain, and drawing his attention to some Don Cossacks who were grouped around some one not far from us.

Among them was heard something like the weeping of a child, and the words:—

"Eh! don't cut . . . wait . . . you will be seen . . . here's a knife, Yevstigneïtch . . . give him the knife." . . .

"They are up to some mischief, the brutes," said the captain, indifferently.

But at this very instant, suddenly from around the corner came the handsome ensign with burning, horror-stricken face, and, waving his hands, rushed among the Cossacks.

"Don't you move! don't kill him!" he cried, in his boyish treble.

When the Cossacks saw the officer they started back, and allowed a little white goat to escape from their hands. The young ensign was wholly taken aback, began to mutter something, and stood before them full of confusion. When he caught sight of the captain and me on the roof, he grew still redder in the face, and springing up the steps, joined us.

"I thought they were going to kill a child," he said, with a timid smile.

10

The general had gone on ahead with the cavalry. The battalion with which I had come from Fort N—— remained in the rear-guard. The companies under command of Captain Khlopof and Lieutenant Rosenkranz were retreating together.

The captain's prediction was fully justified; as soon as we had reached the narrow forest of which he had spoken, from both sides the mountaineers, mounted and on foot, began to show themselves incessantly, and so near that I could very distinctly see many crouching down, with muskets in their hands, and running from tree to tree.

The captain took off his hat, and piously made the sign of the cross; a few old soldiers did the same. In the forest were heard shouts, the words, "*iaï! Giaur! Urus! iaï!*"

Dry, short musket reports followed in quick succession, and bullets whizzed from both sides. Our men silently replied with a running fire; only occasionally in the ranks were heard exclamations in the guise of directions: "*He*[1] has stopped shooting there;" . . . "*He* has a good chance behind the trees;" . . . "We ought to have cannon," and such expressions.

The cannon were brought to bear on the range, and after a few discharges of grape the enemy apparently gave way; but after a little their fire became more and more violent with each step that the army took, and the shouts and war-cries increased.

We were scarcely half a mile from the aul when the enemy's shot began to

---

[1] The collective expression by which the soldiers in the Caucasus indicate the enemy.—Author's Note.

hail down on us. I saw a ball with a thud strike one soldier dead—but why relate details of this terrible spectacle, when I myself would give much to forget it?

Lieutenant Rosenkranz was firing his musket without a moment's cessation; with animating voice he was shouting to the soldiers, and galloping at full speed from one end of the line to the other. He was slightly pale, and this was decidedly becoming to his martial countenance.

The handsome ensign was in his element; his beautiful eyes gleamed with resolution, his mouth was slightly parted with a smile; he was constantly riding up to the captain, and asking permission to charge.

"We'll drive them back," he said impulsively,—"we'll drive them back surely."

"No need of it," replied the captain, gently; "we must get out of here."

The captain's company occupied the edge of the forest, and was fully exposed to the enemy's fire. The captain, in his well-worn coat and tattered cap, slackening the reins for his white trotter and clinging by his short stirrups, silently stayed in one place.—The soldiers were so well trained, and did their work so accurately, that there was no need of giving commands to them.—Only now and then he raised his voice, and shouted to those who exposed their heads. The captain's face was very far from martial; but such truth and simplicity were manifest in it, that it impressed me profoundly.

"There is some one who is truly brave," I involuntarily said to myself.

He was almost exactly the same as I had always seen him; the same tranquil motions, the same even voice, the same expression of frankness on his homely but honest face; only by his more than ordinarily keen glance it was possible to recognize him as a man who was calmly attending to his business. It is easy to say *the same as always*; but how different were the traits that I noticed in others! one tried to seem calmer, another rougher, a third gayer, than usual; but by the captain's face it was manifest that he did not even understand *how to seem*.

The Frenchman who at Waterloo said, *La garde meurt, mais ne se rend pas*, and other heroes, especially among the French, who have uttered notable sayings, were brave, and really uttered notable sayings; but between their bravery, and the bravery of the captain, is this difference, that if a great saying in regard to any subject came into my hero's mind, I believe he would not have uttered it: in the first place, because he would have feared that in saying something great he might spoil a great deed; and, secondly, because when a man is conscious within himself of the power to do a great deed, there is no need of saying anything at all. This, in my opinion, is the especial and lofty character of Russian bravery; and how, henceforth, can it fail to wound the Russian heart when among our young warriors one hears French platitudes which have their vogue because they were the stock phrases of the old French nobility? . . .

Suddenly, from the direction in which the handsome ensign with his division was stationed, was heard a faint hurrah from the enemy. Turning round at this shouting I saw thirty soldiers who, with muskets in their hands and knapsacks on their shoulders, were going at double-quick across the plowed field. They stumbled, but still pushed ahead and shouted. Leading them galloped the young ensign, waving his saber.

All were lost to sight in the forest. . . .

At the end of a few moments of shouting and clash of arms, a frightened horse came dashing out of the woods, and just at the edge soldiers were seen bearing the killed and wounded. Among the latter was the young ensign. Two soldiers carried him in their arms. He was pale as a sheet, and his graceful head, where could be now detected only the shadow of that martial enthusiasm which inspired him but a moment before, was strangely drawn down between his shoulders and rested on his breast. On his white shirt, under his coat, which was torn open, could be seen a small bloodstain.

"Akh! what a pity!" I said, as I involuntarily turned away from this heart-rending spectacle.

"Indeed, it's too bad," said an old soldier, who with gloomy face stood beside me leaning on his musket. "He wasn't afraid of anything! How is this possible?" he added, looking steadily at the wounded lad. "Always foolish! and now he has to pay for it!"

"And aren't you afraid?" I asked.

"No, indeed!"

11

Four soldiers bore the ensign on a litter; behind them followed a train-soldier, leading a lean, foundered horse laden with two green chests in which were the surgeon's implements. They were expecting the doctor. The officers hurried up to the litter, and tried to encourage and comfort the wounded lad.

"Well, brother Alanin, it'll be some time before you dance and make merry again," said Lieutenant Rosenkranz, coming up with a smile.

He probably intended these words to sustain the handsome ensign's courage; but, as could be easily seen from the coldly mournful expression in the eyes of the latter, these words did not produce the wished-for effect.

The captain also came up. He gazed earnestly at the wounded young fellow, and his ever cold, calm face expressed heartfelt pity.

"How is it, my dear Anatoli Ivanuitch?" said he, in a tone which rang with a deeper sympathy than I had expected from him; "we see it's as God wills."

The wounded lad looked up; his pale face was lighted with a mournful smile.

"Yes, I disobeyed you."

"Say rather, it was God's will," replied the captain.

The doctor, who had now arrived, took from his chest bandages, probes, and other instruments, and, rolling up his sleeves, approached the sufferer with a reassuring smile.

"So it seems they have been making a little hole through you," he said, in a tone of jesting unconcern. "Let us have a look at the place."

The ensign listened, but in the gaze which he fixed on the jolly doctor were expressed surprise and reproachfulness, to which the latter paid no heed. He began to probe the wound and examine it from all sides; but at last the sufferer, losing his patience, pushed away his hand with a heavy groan. . . .

"Let me be," he said, in an almost inaudible voice; "it makes no difference; I am dying."

With these words he fell on his back; and five minutes later, when I joined the group gathered about him, and asked a soldier, "How is the ensign?" I was told, "*He has gone.*"

12

It was already late when the detachment, deploying in a broad column, entered the fortress with songs.

The sun had set behind the snow-covered mountain crest, and was throwing its last rosy rays on a long delicate cloud which stretched across the bright pellucid western sky. The snow-capped mountains began to clothe themselves in purple mist; only their upper outlines were marked with extraordinary distinctness against the violet light of the sunset. The clear moon, which had long been up, began to shed its light through the dark blue sky. The green of the grass and of the trees changed to black, and grew wet with dew. The dark masses of the army, with gradually increasing tumult, advanced across the magnificent field; from different sides were heard the sounds of cymbals, drums, and merry songs. The leader of the sixth company sang out with full strength, and full of feeling and power the notes of his clear robust tenor were borne afar through the translucent evening air.

1852

RECOLLECTIONS OF A
BILLIARD-MARKER

Well, it happened about three o'clock. The gentlemen were playing. There was the tall visitor, as our men called him. The prince was there,—the two are always together. The mustached barin was there; also the little hussar, Oliver, who was an actor; there was the Polish *pan*.[1] It was a pretty good crowd.

The tall visitor and the prince were playing together. Now, here I was walking up and down around the billiard-table with my stick, keeping tally,—ten and forty-seven, twelve and forty-seven.

Everybody knows it's our business to score. You don't get a chance to get a bite of anything, and you don't get to bed till two o'clock o' nights, but you're always being screamed at to bring the balls.

I was keeping tally; and I look, and see a new barin comes in at the door. He gazed and gazed, and then sat down on the divan. Very good!

"Now, who can that be?" thinks I to myself. "He must be somebody."

His dress was neat,—neat as a pin,—checkered tricot pants, stylish little short coat, plush vest, and gold chain and all sorts of trinkets dangling from it.

He was dressed neat; but there was something about the man neater still; slim, tall, his hair brushed forward in style, and his face fair and ruddy,—well, in a word, a fine young fellow.

You must know our business brings us into contact with all sorts of people. And there's many that ain't of much consequence, and there's a good deal of

[1] Polish name for lord or gentleman.

poor trash. So, though you're only a scorer, you get used to telling folks; that is, in a certain way you learn a thing or two.

I looked at the barin. I see him sit down, modest and quiet, not knowing anybody; and the clothes on him are so brand-new that, thinks I, "Either he's a foreigner,—an Englishman maybe,—or some count just come. And though he's so young, he has an air of some distinction."

Oliver sat down next him, so he moved along a little.

They began a game. The tall man lost. He shouts to me. Says he, "You're always cheating. You don't count straight. Why don't you pay attention?"

He scolded away, then threw down his cue, and went out. Now, just look here! Evenings, he and the prince plays for fifty silver rubles a game; and here he only lost a bottle of Makon wine, and got mad. That's the kind of a character he is.

Another time he and the prince plays till two o'clock. They don't bank down any cash; and so I know neither of them's got any cash, but they are simply playing a bluff game.

"I'll go you twenty-five rubles," says he.

"All right."

Just yawning, and not even stopping to place the ball,—you see, he was not made of stone,—now just notice what he said. "We are playing for money," says he, "and not for chips."

But this man puzzled me worse than all the rest. Well, then, when the big man left, the prince says to the stranger, "Wouldn't you like," says he, "to play a game with me?"

"With pleasure," says he.

He sat there, and looked rather foolish, indeed he did. He may have been courageous in reality; but, at all events, he got up, went over to the billiard-table, and did not seem flustered as yet. But whether he was flustered or not, you couldn't help seeing that he was not quite at his ease.

Either his clothes were a little too new, or he was embarrassed because everybody was looking at him; at any rate, he seemed to have no energy. He sort of sidled up to the table, caught his pocket on the edge, began to chalk his cue, dropped his chalk.

Whenever he hit the ball, he always glanced around, and reddened. Not so the prince. He was used to it; he chalked and chalked his hand, tucked up his sleeve; he goes and sits down when he pockets the ball, even though he is such a little man.

They played two or three games; then I notice the prince puts up the cue, and says, "Would you mind telling me your name?"

"Nekhliudof," says he.

Says the prince, "Was your father commander in the corps of cadets?"

"Yes," says the other.

Then they began to talk in French, and I could not understand them. I suppose they were talking about family affairs.

"Au revoir," says the prince. "I am very glad to have made your acquaintance."

He washed his hands, and went to get a lunch; but the other stood by the billiard-table with his cue, and was knocking the balls about.

It's our business, you know, when a new man comes along, to be rather sharp;

it's the best way. I took the balls, and went to put them up. He reddened, and says, "Can't I play any longer?"

"Certainly you can," says I. "That's what billiards is for." But I don't pay any attention to him. I straighten the cues.

"Will you play with me?"

"Certainly, sir," says I.

I place the balls.

"Shall we play for odds?"

"What do you mean,—'play for odds'?"

"Well," says I, "you give me a half-ruble, and I crawl under the table."

Of course, as he had never seen that sort of thing, it seemed strange to him; he laughed.

"Go ahead," says he.

"Very well," says I, "only you must give me odds."

"What!" says he, "are you a worse player than I am?"

"Most likely," says I. "We have few players who can be compared with you."

We began to play. He certainly had the idea that he was a crack shot. It was a caution to see him shoot; but the Pole sat there, and kept shouting out every time:—

"Ah, what a chance! ah, what a shot!"

But what a man he was! His ideas were good enough, but he didn't know how to carry them out. Well, as usual I lost the first game, crawled under the table, and grunted.

Thereupon Oliver and the Pole jumped down from their seats, and applauded, thumping with their cues.

"Splendid! Do it again," they cried, "once more."

Well enough to cry "once more," especially for the Pole. That fellow would have been glad enough to crawl under the billiard-table, or even under the Blue bridge, for a half-ruble! Yet he was the first to cry, "Splendid! but you haven't wiped off all the dust yet."

I, Petrushka the marker, was pretty well known to everybody.

Only, of course, I did not care to show my hand yet. I lost my second game.

"It does not become me at all to play with you, sir," says I.

He laughed. Then, as I was playing the third game, he stood forty-nine and I nothing. I laid the cue on the billiard-table, and said, "Barin, shall we play off?"

"What do you mean by playing off?" says he. "How would you have it?"

"You make it three rubles or nothing," says I.

"Why," says he, "have I been playing with you for money?" The fool!

He turned rather red.

Very good. He lost the game. He took out his pocket-book,—quite a new one, evidently just from the English shop,—opened it; I see he wanted to make a little splurge. It was stuffed full of bills,—nothing but hundred-ruble notes.

"No," says he, "there's no small stuff here."

He took three rubles from his purse.

"There," says he, "there's your two rubles; the other pays for the games, and you keep the rest for vodka."

"Thank you, sir, most kindly."

I see that he is a splendid fellow. For such a one I would crawl under anything.

For one thing, it's a pity that he won't play for money. For then, thinks I, I should know how to work him for twenty rubles, and maybe I could stretch it out to forty.

As soon as the Pole saw the young barin's money, he says, "Wouldn't you like to try a little game with me? You play so admirably."

Such sharpers prowl around.

"No," says he, "excuse me; I have not the time."

And he went out.

I don't know who that man was, that Pole. Some one called him *Pan*, and it stuck to him. Every day he used to sit in the billiard-room, and always look on. He was no longer allowed to take a hand in any game whatever; but he always sat by himself, and got out his pipe, and smoked. But then he could play well.

Very good. Nekhliudof came a second time, a third time; he began to come frequently. He would come morning and evening. He learned to play French carom and pyramid pool,—everything, in fact. He became less bashful, got acquainted with everybody, and played tolerably well. Of course, being a young man of a good family, with money, everybody liked him. The only exception was the "tall visitor"; he quarreled with him.

And the whole thing grew out of a trifle.

They were playing pool,—the prince, the "tall visitor," Nekhliudof, Oliver, and some one else. Nekhliudof was standing near the stove-talking with some one. When it came the big man's turn to play, it happened that his ball was just opposite the stove. There was very little space there, and he liked to have elbow-room.

Now, either he didn't see Nekhliudof, or he did it on purpose; but, as he was flourishing his cue, he hit Nekhliudof in the chest, a tremendous rap. It actually made him groan. What then? He did not think of apologizing, he was so boorish. He even went farther: he didn't look at him; he walks off grumbling:—

"Who's jostling me there? It made me miss my shot. Why can't we have some room?"

Then the other went up to him, pale as a sheet, but quite self-possessed, and says so politely:—

"You ought first, sir, to apologize; you struck me," says he.

"Catch me apologizing now! I should have won the game," says he, "but now you have spoiled it for me."

Then the other one says:—

"You ought to apologize."

"Get out of my way! I insist upon it, I won't."

And he turned away to look after his ball.

Nekhliudof went up to him, and took him by the arm.

"You're a boor," says he, "my dear sir."

Though he was a slender young fellow, almost like a girl, still he was all ready for a quarrel. His eyes flashed fire; he looked as if he could eat him alive. The big guest was a strong, tremendous fellow, no match for Nekhliudof.

"Wha-at!" says he, "you call me a boor?"

Yelling out these words, he raises his hand to strike him.

Then everybody there rushed up, and seized them both by the arms, and separated them.

After much talk, Nekhliudof says:—

"Let him give me satisfaction; he has insulted me."

"Not at all," said the other. "I don't care a whit about any satisfaction. He's nothing but a boy, a mere nothing. I'll pull his ears for him."

"If you aren't willing to give me satisfaction, then you are no gentleman."

And, saying this, he almost cried.

"Well, and you, you are a little boy; nothing you say or do can offend me."

Well, we separated them,—led them off, as the custom is, to different rooms. Nekhliudof and the prince had become friends.

"Go," says the former; "for God's sake make him listen to reason.". . .

The prince went. The big man says:—

"I'm not afraid of any one," says he. "I am not going," says he, "to have any explanation with such a baby. I won't do it, and that's the end of it."

Well, they talked and talked, and then the matter died out, only the "tall visitor" ceased to come to us any more.

As a result of this,—this row, I might call it,—he was regarded as quite the cock of the walk. He was quick to take offense,—I mean Nekhliudof;—as to so many other things, however, he was as unsophisticated as a new-born babe.

I remember once, the prince says to Nekhliudof, "Whom do you keep here?"

"No one," says he.

"What do you mean,—'no one' !"

"Why should I?" says Nekhliudof.

"How so,—why should you?"

"I have always lived thus. Why shouldn't I continue to live the same way?"

"You don't say so! It is incredible!"

And saying this, the prince burst into a peal of laughter, and the mustached barin also roared. They couldn't get over it.

"What, never?" they asked.

"Never!"

They were dying with laughter. Of course I understood well enough what they were laughing at him for. I keep my eyes open. "What," thinks I, "will come of it?"

"Come," says the prince, "come with me now."

"No; not for anything," was his answer.

"Now, that is absurd," says the prince. "Come along!"

They went out.

They came back at one o'clock. They sat down to supper; quite a crowd of them were assembled. Some of our very best customers,—Atanof, Prince Razin, Count Shustakh, Mirtsof. And all congratulated Nekhliudof, laughing as they did so. They called me in; I saw that they were pretty jolly.

"Congratulate the barin," they shout.

"What on?" I ask.

How did he call it? His initiation or his enlightenment; I can't remember exactly.

"I have the honor," says I, "to congratulate you."

And he sits there very red in the face, yet he smiles. Didn't they have fun with him, though!

Well and good. They went afterward to the billiard-room, all very gay; and Nekhliudof went up to the billiard-table, leaned on his elbow, and said:—

"It's amusing to you, gentlemen," says he, "but it's sad for me. Why," says he, "why did I do it? Prince," says he, "I shall never forgive you or myself as long as I live."

And he actually burst into tears. Evidently he did not know himself what he was saying. The prince went up to him with a smile.

"Don't talk nonsense," says he. "Let's go home, Anatoli."

"I won't go anywhere," says the other. "Why did I do that?"

And the tears poured down his cheeks. He would not leave the billiard-table, and that was the end of it. That's what it means for a young and inexperienced man to . . .

In this way he used often to come to us. Once he came with the prince, and the mustached man who was the prince's crony; the gentlemen always called him "Fedotka." He had prominent cheek-bones, and was homely enough, to be sure; but he used to dress neatly and drove in a carriage. Why did the gentlemen like him so well? I really could not tell.

"Fedotka! Fedotka!" they'd call, and ask him to eat and to drink, and they'd spend their money paying up for him; but he was a thoroughgoing beat. If ever he lost, he would be sure not to pay; but if he won, you bet he wouldn't fail to collect his money. Often, too, he came to grief; yet there he was, walking arm in arm with the prince.

"You are lost without me," he would say to the prince.

"I am, Fedot,"[1] says he; "but not a Fedot of that sort."

And what jokes he used to crack, to be sure! Well, as I said, they had already arrived that time, and one of them says, "Let's have the balls for three-handed pool."

"All right," says the other.

They began to play at three rubles a stake. Nekhliudof and the prince chat about all sorts of things.

"Ah!" says one of them, "you mind only what a neat little ankle she has."

"Oh," says the other, "her ankle is well enough; but what beautiful hair."

Of course they paid no attention to the game, only kept on talking to one another.

As to Fedotka, that fellow was alive to his work; he played his very best, but they didn't do themselves justice at all.

And so he won six rubles from each of them. God knows how many games he had won from the prince, yet I never knew them to pay each other any money; but Nekhliudof took out two greenbacks, and handed them over to him.

"No," says he, "I don't want to take your money. Let's square it: play 'quits or double,'—either double or nothing."

I set the balls. Fedotka began to play the first hand. Nekhliudof seemed to play only for fun; sometimes he would come very near winning a game, yet just fail of it. Says he, "It would be too easy a move, I won't have it so." But Fedotka did not forget what he was up to. Carelessly he proceeded with the game, and thus, as if it were unexpectedly, won.

---

[1] An untranslatable play on the word.

"Let us play double stakes once more," says he.

"All right," says Nekhliudof.

Once more Fedotka won the game.

"Well," says he, "it began with a mere trifle. I don't wish to win much from you. Shall we make it once more or nothing?"

"Yes."

Say what you may, but fifty rubles is a pretty sum, and Nekhliudof himself began to propose, "Let us make it double or quit." So they played and played.

It kept growing worse and worse for Nekhliudof. Two hundred and eighty rubles were written up against him. As to Fedotka, he had his own method; he would lose a simple game, but when the stake was doubled, he would win sure.

But the prince sits by and looks on. He sees that the matter is growing serious.

"Enough!" says he, "hold on."

My! they keep increasing the stake.

At last it went so far that Nekhliudof was in for more than five hundred rubles. Fedotka laid down his cue, and said:—

"Aren't you satisfied for to-day? I'm tired," says he.

Yet I knew he was ready to play till dawn of day, provided there was money to be won. Stratagem, of course. And the other was all the more anxious to go on. "Come on! Come on!"

"No,—by God, I'm tired. Come," says Fedot; "let's go up-stairs; there you shall have your *revanche*."

Up-stairs with us meant the place where the gentlemen used to play cards.

From that very day, Fedotka wound his net round him so that he began to come every day. He would play one or two games of billiards, and then proceed up-stairs,—every day up-stairs.

What they used to do there, God only knows; but it is a fact that from that time he began to be an entirely different kind of man, and seemed hand in glove with Fedotka. Formerly he used to be stylish, neat in his dress, with his hair slightly curled even; but now it would be only in the morning that he would be anything like himself; but as soon as he had paid his visit up-stairs, he would not be at all like himself.

Once he came down from up-stairs with the prince, pale, his lips trembling, and talking excitedly.

"I cannot permit such a one as *he* is," says he, "to say that I am not . . ." How did he express himself? I cannot recollect, something like "not defined enough," or what,—"and that he won't play with me any more. I tell you I have paid him ten thousand, and I should think that he might be a little more considerate, before others, at least."

"Oh, bother!" says the prince, "is it worth while to lose one's temper with Fedotka?"

"No," says the other, "I will not let it go so."

"Why, old fellow, how can you think of such a thing as lowering yourself to have a row with Fedotka?"

"That is all very well; but there were strangers there, mind you."

"Well, what of that?" says the prince; "strangers? Well, if you wish, I will go and make him ask your pardon."

"No," says the other.

And then they began to chatter in French, and I could not understand what it was they were talking about.

And what would you think of it? That very evening he and Fedotka ate supper together, and they became friends again.

Well and good. At other times again he would come alone.

"Well," he would say, "do I play well?"

It's our business, you know, to try to make everybody contented, and so I would say, "Yes, indeed;" and yet how could it be called good play, when he would poke about with his cue without any sense whatever.

And from that very evening when he took in with Fedotka, he began to play for money all the time. Formerly he didn't care to play for stakes, even for a dinner or for champagne. Sometimes the prince would say:—

"Let's play for a bottle of champagne."

"No," he would say. "Let us rather have the wine by itself. Hollo, there! bring a bottle!"

And now he began to play for money all the time; he used to spend his entire days in our establishment. He would either play with some one in the billiard-room, or he would go "up-stairs."

Well, thinks I to myself, every one else gets something from him, why don't I get some advantage out of it?

"Well, sir," says I, one day, "it's a long time since you have had a game with me."

And so we began to play. Well, when I won ten half-rubles of him, I says:—

"Don't you want to make it double or quit, sir?"

He said nothing. Formerly, if you remember, he would call me *durak*, fool, for such a boldness. But now we went playing "quit or double."

I won eighty rubles of him.

Well, what would you think? Since that first time he used to play with me every day. He would wait till there was no one about, for of course he would have been ashamed to play with a mere marker in presence of others. Once he had got rather warmed up by the play (he already owed me sixty rubles), and so he says:—

"Do you want to stake all you have won?"

"All right," says I.

I won. "One hundred and twenty to one hundred and twenty?"

"All right," says I.

Again I won. "Two hundred and forty against two hundred and forty?"

"Isn't that too much?" I ask.

He made no reply. We played the game. Once more it was mine. "Four hundred and eighty against four hundred and eighty?"

I says, "Well, sir, I don't want to wrong you. Let us make it a hundred rubles that you owe me, and call it square."

You ought to have heard how he yelled at this, and yet he was not a proud man at all.

"Either play, or don't play!" says he.

Well, I see there's nothing to be done. "Three hundred and eighty, then, if you please," says I.

I really wanted to lose. I allowed him forty points in advance. He stood fifty-two to my thirty-six. He began to cut the yellow one, and missed eighteen points; and I was standing just at the turning-point. I made a stroke so as to knock the ball off of the billiard-table. No—so luck would have it. Do what I might, he even missed the doublet. I had won again.

"Listen," says he. "Piotr,"—he did not call me *Petrushka* then,—"I can't pay you the whole on the spot. In a couple of months I can pay three thousand even, if it were necessary."

And there he stood just as red, and his voice kind of trembled.

"Very good, sir," says I.

With this he laid down the cue. Then he began to walk up and down, up and down, the sweat running down his face.

"Piotr," says he, "let's try it again, double or quit."

And he almost burst into tears.

"What, sir, what! would you play against such luck?"

"Oh, let us play, I beg of you."

And he brought the cue, and put it in my hand.

I took the cue, and I threw the balls on the table so that they bounced over on to the floor; I could not help showing off a little, naturally. I say, "All right, sir."

But he was in such a hurry that he went and picked up the balls himself, and I thinks to myself, "Anyway, I'll never be able to get the seven hundred rubles from him, so I can lose them to him all the same."

I began to play carelessly on purpose. But no—he won't have it so.

"Why," says he, "you are playing badly on purpose."

But his hands trembled, and when the ball went toward a pocket, his fingers would spread out and his mouth would screw up to one side, as if he could by any means force the ball into the pocket. Even I couldn't stand it, and I say:—

"That won't do any good, sir."

Very well. As he won this game, I says:—

"This will make it one hundred and eighty rubles you owe me, and fifty games; and now I must go and get my supper."

So I put up my cue, and went off.

I went and sat down all by myself, at a small table opposite the door; and I look in and see, and wonder what he will do. Well, what would you think? He began to walk up and down, up and down, probably thinking that no one's looking at him; and then he would give a pull at his hair, and then walk up and down again, and keep muttering to himself; and then he would pull his hair again.

After that he wasn't seen for a week. Once he came into the dining-room as gloomy as could be, but he didn't enter the billiard-room.

The prince caught sight of him.

"Come," says he, "let's have a game."

"No," says the other, "I am not going to play any more."

"Nonsense! come along."

"No," says he, "I won't come, I tell you. For you it's all one whether I go or not, yet for me it's no good to come here."

And so he did not come for ten days more. And then, it being the holidays, he came dressed up in a dress suit: he'd evidently been into company. And he was here all day long; he kept playing, and he came the next day, and the third. . . .

And it began to go in the old style, and I thought it would be fine to have another trial with him.

"No," says he, "I'm not going to play with you; and as to the one hundred and eighty rubles that I owe you, if you'll come at the end of a month, you shall have it."

Very good. So I went to him at the end of a month.

"By God," says he, "I can't give it to you; but come back on Thursday."

Well, I went on Thursday. I found that he had a splendid suite of apartments.

"Well," says I, "is he at home?"

"He hasn't got up yet," I was told.

"Very good, I will wait."

For a body-servant he had one of his own serfs, such a gray-haired old man! That servant was perfectly single-minded, he didn't know anything about beating about the bush. So we got into conversation.

"Well," says he, "what is the use of our living here, master and I? He's squandered all his property, and it's mighty little honor or good that we get out of this Petersburg of yours. When he started from the country, he thought it would be as it was with the last barin (the kingdom of heaven be his!), I shall go about with princes and counts and generals; he thought to himself, 'I'll find a countess for a sweetheart, and she'll have a big dowry, and we'll live on a big scale.' But it's quite a different thing from what he expected; here we are, running about from one tavern to another as bad off as we could be! The Princess Rtishcheva, you know, is his own aunt, and Prince Borotintsef is his godfather. What do you think? He went to see them only once, that was at Christmas time; he never shows his nose there. Yes, and even their people laugh about it to me. 'Why,' says they, 'your barin is not a bit like his father!' And once I take it upon myself to say to him:—

" 'Why wouldn't you go, sir, and visit your aunt? They are feeling bad because you haven't been for so long.'

" 'It's stupid there, Demyanitch,' says he. Just to think, he found his only amusement here in the saloon! If he only would enter the service! yet, no; he has got entangled with cards and all the rest of it. When men get going that way, there's no good in anything; nothing comes to any good. . . . E-ekh! we are going to the dogs, and no mistake. . . . The late mistress (the kingdom of heaven be hers!) left us a rich inheritance: no less than a thousand souls, and about three hundred thousand rubles worth of timber lands. He has mortgaged it all, sold the timber, let the estate go to rack and ruin, and still no money on hand. When the master is away, of course, the overseer is more than the master. What does he care? He only cares to stuff his own pockets.

"A few days ago a couple of peasants brought complaints from the whole estate. 'He has wasted all the property,' they say. What do you think? he pondered over the complaints, and gave the peasants ten rubles apiece. Says he, 'I'll be there very soon. I shall have some money, and I will settle all accounts when I come,' says he.

"But how can he settle accounts when we are getting into debt all the time? Money or no money, yet the winter here has cost eighty thousand rubles, and now there isn't a silver ruble in the house. And allowing to his kind-heartedness. You see, he's such a simple barin that it would be hard to find his equal; that's the very reason that he's going to ruin,—going to ruin, all for nothing."

And the old man almost wept.

Nekhliudof woke up about eleven, and called me in.

"They haven't sent me any money yet," says he. "But it isn't my fault. Shut the door," says he.

I shut the door.

"Here," says he, "take my watch or this diamond pin, and pawn it. They will give you more than one hundred and eighty rubles for it, and when I get my money I will redeem it," says he.

"No matter, sir," says I. "If you don't happen to have any money, it's no consequence; let me have the watch, if you don't mind. I can wait for your convenience."

I can see that the watch is worth more than three hundred.

Very good. I pawned the watch for a hundred rubles, and carried him the ticket.

"You will owe me eighty rubles," says I, "and you had better redeem the watch."

And so it happened that he still owed me eighty rubles.

After that he began to come to us again every day. I don't know how matters stood between him and the prince, but at all events he kept coming with him all the time, or else they would go and play cards up-stairs with Fedotka. And what queer accounts those three men kept between them! this one would lend money to the other, the other to the third, yet who it was that owed the money you never could find out.

And in this way he kept on coming our way for well-nigh two years; only it was to be plainly seen that he was a changed man, such a devil-may-care manner he assumed at times. He even went so far at times as to borrow a ruble of me to pay a hack-driver; and yet he would still play with the prince for a hundred rubles' stake.

He grew gloomy, thin, sallow. As soon as he came he used to order a little glass of absinthe, take a bite of something, and drink some port wine, and then he would grow more lively.

He came one time before dinner; it happened to be carnival time, and he began to play with a hussar.

Says he, "Do you want to play for a stake?"

"Very well," says he. "What shall it be?"

"A bottle of Claude Vougeaux? What do you say?"

"All right."

Very good. The hussar won, and they went off for their dinner. They sat down at table, and then Nekhliudof says, "Simon, a bottle of Claude Vougeaux, and see that you warm it to the proper point."

Simon went out, brought in the dinner, but no wine.

"Well," says he, "where's the wine?"

Simon hurried out, brought in the roast.

"Let us have the wine," says he.

Simon makes no reply.

"What's got into you? Here we've almost finished dinner, and no wine. Who wants to drink with dessert?"

Simon hurried out.

"The landlord," says he, "wants to speak to you."

Nekhliudof turned scarlet. He sprang up from the table.

"What's the need of calling me?"

The landlord is standing at the door.

Says he, "I can't trust you any more, unless you settle my little bill."

"Well, didn't I tell you that I would pay the first of the month?"

"That will be all very well," says the landlord, "but I can't be all the time giving credit, and having no settlement. There are more than ten thousand rubles of debts outstanding now," says he.

"Well, that'll do, *monshoor*, you know that you can trust me! Send the bottle, and I assure you that I will pay you very soon."

And he hurried back.

"What was it? why did they call you out?" asked the hussar.

"Oh, some one wanted to ask me a question."

"Now it would be a good time," says the hussar, "to have a little warm wine to drink."

"Simon, hurry up!"

Simon came back, but still no wine, nothing. Too bad! He left the table, and came to me.

"For God's sake," says he, "Petrushka, let me have six rubles!"

He was pale as a sheet.

"No, sir," says I; "by God, you owe me quite too much now."

"I will give forty rubles for six, in a week's time."

"If only I had it," says I, "I should not think of refusing you, but I haven't."

What do you think! He rushed away, his teeth set, his fist doubled up, and ran down the corridor like one mad, and all at once he gave himself a knock on the forehead.

"O my God!" says he, "what has it come to?"

But he did not return to the dining-room; he jumped into a carriage, and drove away. Didn't we have our laugh over it! The hussar asks:—

"Where is the gentleman who was dining with me?"

"He has gone," said some one.

"Where has he gone? What message did he leave?"

"He didn't leave any; he just took to his carriage, and went off."

"That's a fine way of entertaining a man!" says he.

Now, thinks I to myself, it'll be a long time before he comes again after this; that is, on account of this scandal. But no. On the next day he came about evening. He came into the billiard-room. He had a sort of a box in his hand. Took off his overcoat.

"Now, let us have a game," says he.

He looked out from under his eyebrows, rather fierce like.

We played one game.

"That's enough now," says he; "go and bring me a pen and paper; I must write a letter."

Not thinking anything, not suspecting anything, I bring some paper, and put it on the table in the little room.

"It's all ready, sir," says I.

"Very good."

He sat down at the table. He kept on writing and writing, and muttering to himself all the time; then he jumps up, and, frowning, says:—

"Look and see if my carriage has come yet."

It was on a Friday, during carnival time, and so there weren't any of the customers on hand; they were all at some ball. I went to see about the carriage, and just as I was going out of the door, "Petrushka! Petrushka!" he shouted, as if something suddenly frightened him.

I turn round. I see he's pale as a sheet, standing there, and looking at me.

"Did you call me, sir?" says I.

He made no reply.

"What do you want?" says I.

He says nothing.

"Oh, yes!" says he. "Let's have another game."

Then, says he:—

"Haven't I learned to play pretty well?"

He had just won the game. "Yes," says I.

"All right," says he; "go now, and see about my carriage."

He himself walked up and down the room.

Without thinking anything, I went down to the door. I didn't see any carriage at all. I started to go up again.

Just as I was going up, I heard what sounded like the thud of a billiard-cue. I went into the billiard-room. I noticed a peculiar smell.

I looked around; and there he was, lying on the floor, in a pool of blood, with a pistol beside him. I was that scared that I could not speak a word.

He kept twitching, twitching his leg, and stretched himself a little. Then he sort of snored, and stretched out his full length in such a strange way.

And God knows why such a sin came about,—how it was that it occurred to him to ruin his own soul,—but as to what he left written on this paper, I don't understand it at all.

Truly, you can never account for what is going on in the world.

"God gave me all that a man can desire,—wealth, name, intellect, noble aspirations. I wanted to enjoy myself, and I trod in the mire all that was best in me.

"I have done nothing dishonorable, I am not unfortunate, I have not committed any crime; but I have done worse: I have destroyed my feelings, my intellect, my youth.

"I became entangled in a filthy net, from which I cannot escape, and to which I cannot accustom myself. I feel that I am falling lower and lower every moment, and I cannot stop my fall.

"And what ruined me? Was there in me some strange passion which I might plead as an excuse? No!

". . . My recollections are pleasant.

"One fearful moment of forgetfulness, which can never be erased from my mind, led me to come to my senses. I shuddered when I saw what a measureless abyss separated me from what I desired to be, and might have been. In my imagination arose the hopes, the dreams, and the thoughts of my youth.

"Where are those lofty thoughts of life, of eternity, of God, which at times filled my soul with light and strength? Where that aimless power of love which kindled my heart with its comforting warmth?

". . . But how good and happy I might have been, had I trodden that path which, at the very entrance of life, was pointed out to me by my fresh mind and true feelings! More than once did I try to go from the ruts in which my life ran, into that sacred path.

"I said to myself, Now I will use my whole strength of will; and yet I could not do it. When I happened to be alone, I felt awkward and timid. When I was with others, I no longer heard the inward voice; and I fell all the time lower and lower.

"At last I came to a terrible conviction that it was impossible for me to lift myself from this low plane. I ceased to think about it, and I wished to forget all; but hopeless repentance worried me still more and more. Then, for the first time, the thought of suicide occurred to me.

"I once thought that the nearness of death would rouse my soul. I was mistaken. In a quarter of an hour I shall be no more, yet my view has not in the least changed. I see with the same eyes, I hear with the same ears, I think the same thoughts; there is the strange incoherence, unsteadiness, and lightness in my thoughts."

1855

SEVASTOPOL IN DECEMBER 1854

The flush of morning has but just begun to tinge the sky above Sapun Mountain; the dark blue surface of the sea has already cast aside the shades of night and awaits the first ray to begin a play of merry gleams; cold and mist are wafted from the bay; there is no snow—all is black, but the morning frost pinches the face and crackles underfoot, and the far-off, unceasing roar of the sea, broken now and then by the thunder of the firing in Sevastopol, alone disturbs the calm of the morning. It is dark on board the ships; it has just struck eight bells.

Toward the north the activity of the day begins gradually to replace the nocturnal quiet; here the relief guard has passed clanking their arms, there the doctor is already hastening to the hospital, farther on the soldier has crept out of his earth hut and is washing his sunburnt face in ice-incrusted water, and, turning toward the crimsoning east, crosses himself quickly as he prays to God; here a tall and heavy camel-wagon has dragged creaking to the cemetery, to bury the bloody dead, with whom it is laden nearly to the top. You go to the wharf— a peculiar odor of coal, manure, dampness, and of beef strikes you; thousands of objects of all sorts—wood, meat, gabions, flour, iron, and so forth—lie in heaps about the wharf; soldiers of various regiments, with knapsacks and muskets, without knapsacks and without muskets, throng thither, smoke, quarrel, drag weights aboard the steamer which lies smoking beside the quay; unattached two-oared boats, filled with all sorts of people,—soldiers, sailors, merchants, women, —land at and leave the wharf.

"To the Grafsky, your excellency? be so good." Two or three retired sailors rise in their boats and offer you their services.

You select the one who is nearest to you, you step over the half-decomposed carcass of a brown horse, which lies there in the mud beside the boat, and reach the stern. You quit the shore. All about you is the sea, already glittering in the morning sun; in front of you is an aged sailor, in a camel's-hair coat, and a young, white-headed boy, who work zealously and in silence at the oars. You gaze at the motley vastness of the vessels, scattered far and near over the bay, and at the small black dots of boats moving about on the shining azure expanse, and at the bright and beautiful buildings of the city, tinted with the rosy rays of the morning sun, which are visible in one direction, and at the foaming white line of the quay, and the sunken ships from which black tips of masts rise sadly here and there, and at the distant fleet of the enemy faintly visible as they rock on the crystal horizon of the sea, and at the streaks of foam on which leap salt bubbles beaten up by the oars; you listen to the monotonous sound of voices which fly to you over the water, and the grand sounds of firing, which, as it seems to you, is increasing in Sevastopol.

It cannot be that, at the thought that you too are in Sevastopol, a certain feeling of manliness, of pride, has not penetrated your soul, and that the blood has not begun to flow more swiftly through your veins.

"Your excellency! you are steering straight into the Kistentin,"[1] says your old sailor to you as he turns round to make sure of the direction which you are imparting to the boat; "starboard the helm."

"And all the cannon are still on it," remarks the white-headed boy, casting a glance over the ship as we pass.

"Of course; it's new. Korniloff lived on board of it," said the old man, also glancing at the ship.

"See where it has burst!" says the boy, after a long silence, looking at a white cloud of spreading smoke which has suddenly appeared high over the South Bay, accompanied by the sharp report of an exploding bomb.

"He is firing to-day with his new battery," adds the old man, calmly spitting on his hands. "Now, give way, Mishka! we'll overtake the barge." And your boat moves forward more swiftly over the broad swells of the bay, and you actually do overtake the heavy barge, upon which some bags are piled, and which is unevenly rowed by awkward soldiers, and it touches the Grafsky wharf amid a multitude of boats of every sort which are landing.

Throngs of gray soldiers, common sailors, and a medley of women move noisily along the shore. The women are selling rolls, Russian peasants with samovars are crying hot sbiten[2]; and here upon the first steps are strewn rusted cannon-balls, bombs, grape-shot, and cast-iron cannon of various calibers; a little farther

[1] The vessel *Constantine*.

[2] A drink made of water, molasses, laurel-leaves or salvia, which is drunk like tea, especially by the lower classes.

on is a large square, upon which lie huge beams, gun-carriages, sleeping soldiers; there stand horses, wagons, green guns, ammunition-chests, and stacks of arms; soldiers, sailors, officers, women, children, and merchants are moving about; carts are arriving with hay, bags, and casks; here and there Cossacks make their way through, or officers on horseback, or a general in a drozhky. To the right, the street is hemmed in by a barricade, in whose embrasures stand some small cannon, and beside these sits a sailor smoking his pipe. On the left a handsome house with Roman ciphers on the pediment, beneath which stand soldiers and blood-stained litters—everywhere you behold the unpleasant signs of a war encampment. Your first impression is inevitably of the most disagreeable sort. The strange mixture of camp and town life, of a beautiful city and a dirty bivouac, is not only not beautiful, but seems repulsive disorder; it even seems to you that every one is thoroughly frightened, and is fussing about without knowing what he is doing. But look more closely at the faces of these people who are moving about you, and you will gain an entirely different idea. Look at this little soldier from the baggage-train, for example, who is leading a troïka of brown horses to water, and is purring something to himself so composedly that he evidently will not go astray in this motley crowd, which does not exist for him; but he is fulfilling his duty, whatever that may be,—watering horses or carrying arms,—with just as much composure, self-confidence, and equanimity as though it were taking place in Tula or Saransk. You will read the same expression on the face of this officer who passes by in immaculate white gloves, and in the face of the sailor who is smoking as he sits on the barricade, and in the faces of the working soldiers, waiting with their litters on the steps of the former Club, and in the face of yonder girl, who, fearing to wet her pink gown, skips across the street on the little stones.

Yes! disenchantment certainly awaits you, if you are entering Sevastopol for the first time. In vain will you seek, on even a single countenance, for traces of anxiety, discomposure, or even of enthusiasm, readiness for death, decision,—there is nothing of the sort. You will see every-day people quietly engaged in their every-day callings, so that, possibly, you may reproach yourself for superfluous raptures, you may entertain some doubt as to the justice of the ideas regarding the heroism of the defenders of Sevastopol which you have formed from stories, descriptions, and the sights and sounds on the northern side. But, before you doubt, go upon the bastions, observe the defenders of Sevastopol on the very scene of the defense; or, better still, go straight across into that house, which was formerly the Sevastopol Club,[3] and upon whose steps stand soldiers with litters,—there you will behold the defenders of Sevastopol, there you will behold frightful and sad, great and laughable, but wonderful sights, which elevate the soul.

You enter the great Hall of Assembly. You have but just opened the door when the sight and smell of forty or fifty seriously wounded men and of those who have undergone amputation—some in cots, the majority upon the floor—suddenly strike you. Trust not to the feeling which detains you upon the threshold of the hall; be not ashamed of having come to *look at* the sufferers, be not

[3] The "Club (or Assembly) of the Nobility"; a sort of casino which exists in all Russian cities.

ashamed to approach and address them: the unfortunates like to see a sympathizing human face, they like to tell of their sufferings and to hear words of love and interest. You walk along between the beds and seek a face less stern and suffering, which you decide to approach, with the object of conversing.

"Where are you wounded?" you inquire, timidly and with indecision, of an old, gaunt soldier, who, seated on his cot, is watching you with a good-natured glance, and seems to invite you to approach him. I say "you ask timidly," because these sufferings inspire you, over and above the feeling of profound sympathy, with a fear of offending and with a lofty reverence for the man who has undergone them.

"In the leg," replies the soldier; but at the same time, you perceive, by the folds of the coverlet, that he has lost his leg above the knee. "God be thanked now," he adds,—"I shall get my discharge."

"Were you wounded long ago?"

"It was six weeks ago, your honor."

"Does it still pain you?"

"No, there's no pain now; only there's a sort of gnawing in my calf when the weather is bad, but that's nothing."

"How did you come to be wounded?"

"On the fifth bastion, during the first bombardment, your honor. I had just trained a cannon, and was on the point of going away, so, to another embrasure, when *it* struck me in the leg, just as if I had stepped into a hole,—and behold, I had no leg."

"Was it not painful at the first moment?"

"Not at all; only as though something boiling hot had struck my leg."

"Well, and then?"

"And then—nothing; only when they began to draw the skin, it was as though it had been rubbed off. The first thing of all, your excellency, *is not to think at all*. If you don't think about a thing, it amounts to nothing. Men suffer from thinking more than from anything else."

At that moment, a woman in a gray striped dress and a black kerchief bound about her head approaches you.

She joins in your conversation with the sailor, and begins to tell about him, about his sufferings, his desperate condition for the space of four weeks, and how, when he was wounded, he made the litter halt that he might see the volley from our battery, how the Grand Duke spoke to him and gave him twenty-five rubles, and how he said to them that he wanted to go back to the bastion to direct the younger men, even if he could not work himself. As she says all this in a breath, the woman glances now at you, now at the sailor, who has turned away as though he did not hear her and plucks some lint from his pillow, and her eyes sparkle with peculiar enthusiasm.

"This is my housewife, your honor!" the sailor says to you, with an expression which seems to say, "You must excuse her. Every one knows it's a woman's way —she's talking nonsense."

You begin to understand the defenders of Sevastopol. For some reason, you feel ashamed of yourself in the presence of this man. You would like to say a very great deal to him, in order to express to him your sympathy and admiration; but you find no words, or you are dissatisfied with those which come into your head,—and you do reverence in silence before this taciturn, unconscious grandeur and firmness of soul, this modesty in the face of his own merits.

"Well, God grant you a speedy recovery," you say to him, and you halt before another invalid, who is lying on the floor and appears to be awaiting death in intolerable agony.

He is a blond man with pale, swollen face. He is lying on his back, with his left arm thrown out, in a position which is expressive of cruel suffering. His parched, open mouth with difficulty emits his stertorous breathing; his blue, leaden eyes are rolled up, and from beneath the coverlet the remains of his right arm, enveloped in bandages, protrude. The oppressive odor of a corpse strikes you forcibly, and the consuming, internal fire which has penetrated every limb of the sufferer seems to penetrate you also.

"Is he unconscious?" you inquire of the woman, who comes up to you and gazes at you tenderly as at a relative.

"No, he can still hear, but he's very bad," she adds in a whisper. "I gave him some tea to-day,—what if he is a stranger, one must still have pity!—and he hardly tasted it."

"How do you feel?" you ask him.

The wounded man turns his eyeballs at the sound of your voice, but he neither sees nor understands you.

"There's a gnawing at my heart."

A little farther on, you see an old soldier changing his linen. His face and body are of a sort of cinnamon-brown color, and gaunt as a skeleton. He has no arm at all; it has been cut off at the shoulder. He is sitting with an alert air, he is convalescent; but you see, by his dull, corpse-like gaze, his frightful gauntness, and the wrinkles on his face, that he is a being who has suffered for the best part of his life.

On the other side, you behold in a cot the pale, suffering, and delicate face of a woman, upon whose cheek plays a feverish flush.

"That's our little sailor lass who was struck in the leg by a bomb on the 5th," your guide tells you. "She was carrying her husband's dinner to him in the bastion."

"Has it been amputated?"

"They cut it off above the knee."

Now, if your nerves are strong, pass through the door on the left. In yonder room they are applying bandages and performing operations. There you will see doctors with their arms blood-stained above the elbow, and with pale, stern faces, busied about a cot, upon which, with eyes widely opened, and uttering, as in delirium, incoherent, sometimes simple and touching, words, lies a wounded man under the influence of chloroform. The doctors are busy with the repulsive but beneficent work of amputation. You see the sharp, curved knife enter the healthy, white body, you see the wounded man suddenly regain consciousness with a piercing cry and curses, you see the assistant surgeon fling the amputated arm into a corner, you see another wounded man, lying in a litter in the same apartment, shrink convulsively and groan as he gazes at the operation upon his comrade, not so much from physical pain as from the moral torture of anticipation.—You behold frightful, soul-stirring scenes; you behold war, not from its conventional, beautiful, and brilliant side, with music and drum-beat, with fluttering flags and prancing generals, but you behold war in its real aspect—in blood, in suffering, in death.

On emerging from this house of pain, you will infallibly experience a sensation of pleasure, you will inhale the fresh air more fully, you will feel satisfaction in the consciousness of your health; but, at the same time, you will draw from the sight of these sufferings a consciousness of your nothingness, and you will go calmly and without any indecision to the bastion.

"What do the death and sufferings of such an insignificant worm as I signify in comparison with so many deaths and such great sufferings?" But the sight of the clear sky, the brilliant sun, the fine city, the open church, and the soldiers moving about in various directions soon restores your mind to its normal condition of frivolity, petty cares, and absorption in the present alone.

Perhaps you meet the funeral procession of some officer coming from the church, with rose-colored coffin, and music and fluttering church banners; perhaps the sounds of firing from the bastion reaches your ear, but this does not lead you back to your former thoughts; the funeral seems to you a very fine military spectacle, and you do not connect with this spectacle, or with these sounds, any clear idea of suffering and death, as you did at the point where the bandaging was going on.

Passing the barricade and the church, you come to the part of the city most animated with inner life. On either hand hang the signs of shops and inns. Merchants, women in bonnets and kerchiefs, dandified officers,—everything speaks to you of the firmness of spirit, of the independence and the security, of the inhabitants.

Enter the public house on the right if you wish to hear the conversations of sailors and officers; stories of the preceding night are sure to be in progress there,—of Fenka, and the affair of the 24th, and of the dearness and badness of cutlets, and of such and such a comrade who has been killed.

"Devil take it, how bad things are with us to-day!" ejaculates the bass voice of a beardless naval officer, with white brows and lashes, in a green knitted sash.

"Where?" asks another.

"In the fourth bastion," replies the young officer, and you are certain to look at the white-lashed officer with great attention, and even with some respect, at the words, "in the fourth bastion." His excessive ease of manner, the way he flourishes his hands, his loud laugh, and his voice, which seem to you insolent, reveal to you that peculiar boastful frame of mind which some very young men acquire after danger; nevertheless, you think he is about to tell you how bad the condition of things on the fourth bastion is because of the bombs and balls. Nothing of the sort! things are bad because it is muddy. "It's impossible to pass through the battery," says he, pointing at his boots, which are covered with mud above the calf. "And my best gun-captain was killed to-day; he was struck plump in the forehead," says another. "Who's that? Mitiukhin?" "No! . . . What now, are they going to give me any veal? the villains!" he adds to the servant of the inn. "Not Mitiukhin, but Abramoff. Such a fine young fellow—he was in the sixth sally."

At another corner of the table, over a dish of cutlets with peas, and a bottle of sour Crimean wine called "Bordeaux," sit two infantry officers; one with a red collar, who is young and has two stars on his overcoat, is telling the other, with a black collar and no stars, about the affair at Alma. The former has already drunk a good deal, and it is evident, from the breaks in his narrative, from his undecided glance expressive of doubt as to whether he is believed, and chiefly from the altogether too prominent part which he has played in it all, and from the excessive horror of it all, that he is widely departing from a strict statement of the truth. But these tales, which you will hear for a long time to come in every corner of Russia, are nothing to you; you prefer to go to the bastions, especially to the fourth, of which you have been told so many and such diverse things. When any one says that he has been in the fourth bastion, he says it with a peculiar air of pride and satisfaction; when any one says, "I am going to the fourth bastion," either a little agitation or an excess of indifference is infallibly perceptible in him; when any one wants to jest about another, he says, "You must be stationed in the fourth bastion;" when you meet litters and inquire whence they come, the answer is generally, "From the fourth bastion." On the whole, two totally different opinions exist with regard to this terrible bastion: one is held by those who have never been in it, and who are convinced that the fourth bastion is a regular grave for every one who enters it; and the other by those who live in it, like the white-lashed midshipman, and who, when they mention the fourth bastion, will tell you whether it is dry or muddy there, whether it is warm or cold in the mud hut, and so forth.

During the half-hour which you have passed in the public house, the weather has changed; the fog which before spread over the sea has collected into damp, heavy, gray clouds, and has veiled the sun; a kind of melancholy, frozen mist sprinkles from above, and wets the roofs, the sidewalks, and the soldiers' overcoats.

Passing by yet another barricade, you emerge from the door at the right and ascend the principal street. Behind this barricade, the houses are unoccupied on both sides of the street, there are no sign-boards, the doors are covered with boards, the windows are broken in; here the corners of the wall are broken away, there the roofs are pierced. The buildings seem to be old, to have undergone every sort of vicissitude and deprivation characteristic of veterans, and appear to gaze proudly and somewhat scornfully upon you. You stumble over the cannonballs which strew the way, and into holes filled with water, which have been excavated in the stony ground by the bombs. In the street you may meet and overtake bodies of soldiers, scouts, officers; now and then you encounter a woman or a child, but it is no longer a woman in a bonnet, but a sailor's wife in an old fur cloak and soldier's boots. As you proceed along the street, and descend a small declivity, you observe that there are no longer any houses about you, but only some strange heaps of ruined stones, boards, clay, and beams; ahead of you, upon a steep hill, you perceive a black, muddy expanse, intersected by canals, and this that is in front is the fourth bastion. Here you meet still fewer people, no women are visible, the soldiers walk briskly, you come across drops of blood on the road, and you will certainly encounter there four soldiers with a stretcher and upon the stretcher a pale yellowish face and a blood-stained overcoat. If you inquire, "Where is he wounded?" the bearers will say angrily, without turning toward you, "In the leg," or "the arm," if he is slightly wounded; or they will preserve a gloomy silence if no head is visible on the stretcher and he is already dead or badly hurt.

The shriek of a cannon-ball or a bomb close by surprises you unpleasantly, as you ascend the hill. You understand all at once, and quite differently from what you have before, the significance of those sounds of shots which you heard in the city. A quietly cheerful memory flashes suddenly before your fancy; your own personality begins to occupy you more than your observations; your attention to all that surrounds you diminishes, and a certain disagreeable feeling of indecision suddenly overmasters you. In spite of this base voice, which suddenly speaks within you, at the sight of danger, you force it to be silent, especially when you glance at a soldier who runs laughing past you at a trot, waving his hands, and slipping down the hill in the mud, and you involuntarily expand your chest, throw up your head a little higher, and scramble up the slippery, clayey hill. As soon as you pick your way a short distance up the hill, rifle-balls begin to whiz to the right and left of you, and, possibly, you begin to reflect whether you will not take to the trench which runs parallel with the road; but this trench is full of such yellow, liquid, foul-smelling mud, more than knee-deep, that you will infallibly choose the path on the hill, the more so as you see that *every one uses the path.* After traversing a couple of hundred paces, you emerge upon a muddy expanse, all plowed up, and surrounded on all sides by gabions, earthworks, platforms, earth-huts, upon which great cast-iron guns stand, and cannon-balls lie in symmetrical heaps. All these seem to be heaped up without any aim, connection, or order. Here in the battery sit a knot of sailors; there in the middle of the square, half buried in mud, lies a broken cannon; farther on, a foot-soldier, with his gun, is marching through the battery, and dragging his feet with difficulty through the sticky soil. But everywhere, on all sides, in every spot, you see broken dishes, unexploded bombs, cannon-balls, signs of encampment, all sunk in the liquid, viscous mud. You seem to hear not far from you the thud of a cannon-ball; on all sides, you seem to hear the varied sounds of bullets humming like bees, whistling sharply, or in a whine like a cord— you hear the frightful roar of the fusillade, which shakes you all through and seems to you, in some way, horribly dreadful.

"So this is it, the fourth bastion! This is that terrible, really frightful place!" you think to yourself, and you experience a little sensation of pride, and a very large sensation of suppressed terror. But you are mistaken: this is not the fourth bastion. It is the Yazonoff redoubt—a place which is, in comparison, very safe, and not at all dreadful.

In order to reach the fourth bastion, you turn to the right, through this narrow trench, through which the foot-soldier, bent double, has gone. In this trench you will perhaps meet stretchers again, sailors, and soldiers with shovels; you will see the superintendent of the mines, mud huts, into which only two men can crawl by bending down, and there you will see scouts of the Black Sea battalions, who are changing their shoes, eating, smoking their pipes, and living; and you will still see everywhere that same stinking mud, traces of a camp, and cast-off iron *débris* in every possible form. Proceeding yet three hundred paces, you will emerge again upon a battery,—on an open space, all cut up into holes and surrounded by gabions, covered with earth, cannon on platforms, and earthworks. Here you will perhaps see five sailors playing cards under the shelter of the breastworks, and a naval officer, who, perceiving that you are a newcomer,

and curious, will with pleasure show you his household arrangements, and everything which may be of interest to you.

This officer rolls himself a cigarette of yellow paper, with so much composure
as he sits on a gun, walks so calmly from one embrasure to another, converses
with you so quietly, without the slightest affectation, that, in spite of the bullets
which hum above you even more thickly than before, you become cool yourself,
question attentively, and listen to the officer's replies.

This officer will tell you, but only if you ask him, about the bombardment on
the 5th; he will tell you how only one gun in his battery could be used, and out
of all the gunners who served it only eight remained, and how, nevertheless, on
the next morning, the 6th, he fired all the guns; he will tell you how a bomb fell
upon a sailor's earth hut on the 5th, and laid low eleven men; he will point out
to you, from the embrasures, the enemy's batteries and intrenchments, which are
not more than thirty or forty fathoms distant from this point. I fear, however,
that, under the influence of the whizzing bullets, you may thrust yourself out of
the embrasure in order to view the enemy; you will see nothing, and, if you do
see anything, you will be very much surprised that that white stony rampart,
which is so near you and from which white smoke rises in puffs,—that that white
is the enemy—*he*, as the soldiers and sailors say.

It is even quite possible that the naval officer will want to discharge a shot or
two in your presence, out of vanity or simply for his own pleasure. "Send the
captain and his crew to the cannon;" and fourteen sailors step up briskly and
merrily to the gun and load it—one thrusting his pipe into his pocket, another
one chewing a biscuit, still another clattering his heels on the platform.

Observe the faces, the bearing, the movements, of these men. In every wrinkle
of that sunburned face, with its high cheek-bones, in every muscle, in the
breadth of those shoulders, in the thickness of those legs shod in huge boots, in
every calm, firm, deliberate gesture, these chief traits which constitute the power
of Russia—simplicity and straightforwardness—are visible; but here, on every
face, it seems to you that the danger, animosity, and the sufferings of war have,
in addition to these principal characteristics, left traces of consciousness of personal worth, emotion, and exalted thought.

All at once a frightful roar, which shakes, not your organs of hearing alone,
but your whole being, startles you so that you tremble all over. Then you hear
the receding shriek of the shot as it pursues its course, and the dense smoke of
the powder envelops the platform and the black figures of the sailors who are
moving about upon it. You hear various remarks of the sailors in reference to
this shot, and you see their animation, and the exhibition of a feeling which
you had not expected to behold, perhaps—a feeling of malice, of revenge against
the enemy, which lies hidden in the soul of each man. "It landed in the embrasure itself; it seems to have killed two men—see, they've carried them off!"
you hear their joyful exclamation. "And now they are angry; they'll fire at us
directly," says some one; and, in fact, shortly after you see a flash in front and
smoke; the sentry, who is standing on the breastwork, shouts "Can-non!" And
then the ball shrieks past you, strikes the earth heavily, and scatters a shower
of dirt and stones about it.

The ball enrages the commander of the battery; he orders a second and a
third gun to be loaded, the enemy also begins to reply to us, and you experience

a sensation of interest, you hear and see interesting things. Again the sentry shouts, "Can-non!" and you hear the same report and blow, the same shower; or he shouts "Mortar!" and you hear the monotonous, even rather pleasant, whistle of the bomb, with which it is difficult to connect the thought of horror; you hear this whistle approaching you, and increasing in swiftness; then you see the black sphere, the impact on the ground, the resounding explosion of the bomb, which can be felt. With the whistle and shriek, splinters fly again, stones whiz through the air, and mud showers over you. At these sounds you experience a strange feeling of enjoyment, and, at the same time, of terror. At the moment when you know that the projectile is flying toward you, it will infallibly occur to you that this shot will kill you; but the feeling of self-love sustains you, and no one perceives the knife which is cutting your heart. But when the shot has flown past without touching you, you revive, and a certain cheerful, inexpressibly pleasant feeling overpowers you, but only for a moment, so that you discover a peculiar sort of charm in danger, in this game of life and death; you want cannon-balls or bombs to strike nearer and nearer round about you.

But again the sentry has shouted in his loud, thick voice, "Mortar!" again there is a shriek, and a bomb bursts, but with this noise the groan of a man startles you. You approach the wounded man at the same moment with the bearers; he has a strange, inhuman aspect, covered as he is with blood and mud. A part of the sailor's breast has been torn away. During the first moments, there is visible on his mud-stained face only fear and a certain simulated, premature expression of suffering, peculiar to men in that condition; but, at the moment when the stretcher is brought to him and he places himself upon it on his sound side, you observe that this expression is replaced by an expression of a sort of exaltation and lofty, inexpressible thought. His eyes shine more brilliantly, his teeth are clenched, his head is held higher with an effort, and, as they lift him up, he stops the bearers and says to his comrades, with difficulty and in a trembling voice, "Comrades, forgive!" He tries to say something more, and it is plain that he wants to say something touching, but he repeats once more, "Comrades, forgive!"

At that moment, one of his fellow-sailors steps up to him, puts the cap on the head which the wounded man holds toward him, and, waving his hand indifferently, returns calmly to his gun. "That's the way with seven or eight men every day," says the naval officer to you, in reply to the expression of horror which has appeared upon your countenance, as he yawns, and rolls a cigarette of yellow paper.

Thus you have seen the defenders of Sevastopol, on the very scene of the defense, and you go back paying no attention, for some reason or other, to the cannon-balls and bullets, which continue to shriek the whole way until you reach the ruined theater,—you proceed with composure, and with your soul in a state of exaltation.

The principal and cheering conviction which you have brought away is the conviction of the impossibility of the Russian people wavering anywhere whatever—and this impossibility you have discerned not in the multitude of traverses, breastworks, artfully interlaced trenches, mines, and ordnance, piled one upon the other, of which you have comprehended nothing; but you have discerned

it in the eyes, the speech, the manners, in what is called the spirit of the defenders of Sevastopol. What they are doing they do so simply, with so little
effort and exertion, that you are convinced that they can do a hundred times
more—that they can do anything. You understand that the feeling which makes
them work is not that feeling of pettiness, ambition, forgetfulness, which you
have yourself experienced, but a different sentiment, one more powerful, and
one which has made of them men who live with their ordinary composure under
the fire of cannon, amid hundreds of chances of death, instead of the one to
which all men are subject, and who live under these conditions amid incessant
labor, poverty, and dirt. Men cannot accept these frightful conditions for the
sake of a cross or a title, nor because of threats; there must be another, a lofty
incentive, as the cause. And this cause is the feeling which rarely appears, of
which a Russian is ashamed, that which lies at the bottom of each man's soul—
love for his country.

Only now have the tales of the early days of the siege of Sevastopol, when
there were no fortifications there, no army, no physical possibility of holding it,
and when, nevertheless, there was not the slightest doubt that it would not
surrender to the enemy,—of the days when that hero worthy of ancient Greece,
Korniloff, said as he made the rounds of the troops: "We will die, boys, but
we will not surrender Sevastopol"; and our Russians, who are not fitted to be
phrase-makers, replied: "We will die! hurrah!"—only now have tales of that
time ceased to be for you the most beautiful historical legends, and have become
real facts and worthy of belief. You comprehend clearly, you figure to yourself,
those men whom you have just seen, as the very heroes who, in those grievous
times, have not fallen, but have been exalted in spirit, and have joyfully prepared for death, not for the sake of the city, but of their native land. This epos
of Sevastopol, whose hero was the Russian people, will leave mighty traces in
Russia for a long time to come.

Night is already falling. The sun, just before its setting, has emerged from
the gray clouds which cover the sky, and has suddenly illuminated with a
crimson glow the purple vapors, the greenish sea covered with ships and boats
rocking on the regular swell, and the white buildings of the city, and the people
who are moving through its streets. Sounds of some old waltz played by the
regimental band on the boulevard, and the sounds of firing from the bastions,
which echo them strangely, are borne across the water.

1855

SEVASTOPOL IN MAY 1855

1

Six months have already passed since the first cannon-ball whistled from the
bastions of Sevastopol, and plowed the earth in the works of the enemy, and
since that day thousands of bombs, cannon-balls, and rifle-balls have been flying

incessantly from the bastions into the trenches and from the trenches into the bastions, and the angel of death has never ceased to hover over them.

Thousands of men have been disappointed in their ambitions; thousands have succeeded in satisfying theirs, in becoming swollen with pride; thousands repose in the embrace of death. How many red coffins and canvas palls there have been! And still the same sounds are echoed from the bastions, and still on clear evenings the French peer from their camp, with involuntary tremor, at the yellow, furrowed bastions of Sevastopol, at the black forms of our sailors moving about upon them, and count the embrasures and the iron cannon which project angrily from them; the pilot still gazes through his telescope, from the heights of the telegraph station, at the motley figures of the French at their batteries, at their tents, at the columns moving over the green hill, and at the puffs of smoke which issue forth from the trenches,—and a crowd of men, formed of divers races, still streams in throngs from various quarters, with the same ardor as ever, and with desires differing even more greatly than their races, toward this fateful spot. And the question, unsolved by the diplomats, has still not been solved by powder and blood.

2

On the boulevard of the besieged city of Sevastopol, not far from the pavilion, the regimental band was playing, and throngs of military men and of women moved gayly through the streets. The brilliant sun of spring had risen in the morning over the works of the English, had passed over the bastions, then over the city, over the Nikolaeff barracks, and, illuminating all with equal cheer, had now sunk into the blue and distant sea, which was lighted with a silvery gleam as it heaved in regular swells.

A tall, rather round-shouldered infantry officer, who was drawing upon his hand a glove which was presentable, if not entirely white, came out of the small door of one of the small naval huts, built on the left side of the Morskaya[1] Street, and, staring thoughtfully at the ground, took his way up the slope to the boulevard.

The expression of this officer's homely countenance did not indicate any great mental capacity, but rather simplicity, judgment, honor, and a tendency to steadiness. He was badly built, not quite graceful, and he seemed to be constrained in his movements. He was dressed in a little worn cap, a cloak of a rather peculiar shade of lilac, from beneath whose edge the gold of a watch-chain was visible; in trousers with straps, and brilliantly polished calfskin boots. He must have been either a German—if his features had not clearly indicated his purely Russian descent—or an adjutant, or a regimental quartermaster (only in that case he would have had spurs), or an officer who had exchanged from the cavalry for the period of the campaign, or possibly from the Guards. He was, in fact, an officer who had exchanged from the cavalry, and, as he ascended the boulevard, he was meditating upon a letter which he had just received from a former comrade, now retired; a landowner in the Government of T., and his wife, pale, blue-eyed Natasha, his great friend. He recalled one passage of the letter, in which his comrade said:—

[1] Sea.

"When our *Invalid*[2] arrives, Pupka [this was the name by which the retired uhlan called his wife] rushes headlong into the vestibule, seizes the paper, and runs with it to the *vis-à-vis* seat in *the arbor, in the drawing-room* (in which, if you remember, you and I passed such delightful winter evenings when the regiment was stationed in our town), and reads *your* heroic deeds with such ardor as it is impossible for you to imagine. She often speaks of you. 'There is Mikhaïloff,' she says, 'he's such a *love of a man*. I am ready to kiss him when I see him. He fights on the bastions, and will surely receive the Cross of St. George, and he will be talked about in the newspapers . . .' and so on, and so on . . . so that I am really beginning to be jealous of you."

In another place he writes: "The papers reach us frightfully late, and, although there is plenty of news conveyed by word of mouth, not all of it can be trusted. For instance, the *young ladies with the music*, acquaintances of yours, were saying yesterday that Napoleon was already captured by our Cossacks, and that he had been sent to Petersburg; but you will comprehend how much I believe of this. Moreover, a traveler from Petersburg told us (he has been sent on special business by the minister, is a very agreeable person, and, now that there is no one in town, he is more of a *resource* to us than you can well imagine . . .)—well, he declares it to be a fact that our troops have occupied Eupatoria, *so that the French have no communication whatever with Balaklava*, and that in this engagement two hundred of ours were killed, but that the French lost as many as fifteen thousand. My wife was in such raptures over this that she *caroused* all night, and she declares that her instinct tells her that you certainly took part in that affair, and that you distinguished yourself."

In spite of these words, and of the expressions which I have purposely put in italics, and the whole tone of the letter, Staff-Captain Mikhaïloff recalled, with inexpressibly sad delight, his pale friend in the provinces, and how she had sat with him in the arbor in the evening, and talked about *sentiment*, and he thought of his good comrade, the uhlan, and of how the latter had grown angry and had lost the game when they used to play cards for kopek stakes in his study, and how the wife had laughed at him . . . he recalled the friendship of these two people for himself (perhaps it seemed to him to lie chiefly on the side of his pale feminine friend); all these faces with their surroundings flitted before his mind's eye, in a wonderfully sweet, consolingly rosy light, and, smiling at his reminiscences, he placed his hand on the pocket which contained the letter so *dear* to him.

From reminiscences Captain Mikhaïloff involuntarily proceeded to dreams and hopes. "And what will be the joy and amazement of Natasha," he thought, as he paced along the narrow lane, ". . . when she suddenly reads in the *Invalid* a description of how I was the first to climb upon the cannon, and that I have received the George! I shall certainly be promoted to a full captaincy, by virtue of that old recommendation. Then I may very easily get the grade of major in the line, this very year, because many of our fellows have already been killed, and many more will be in this campaign. And after that there will be more affairs on hand, and a regiment will be intrusted to me, since I am an experienced man . . . lieutenant-colonel . . . the Order of St. Anna on my neck . . .

---

2 *Military Gazette.*

colonel! . . ." and he was already a general, granting an interview to Natasha, the widow of his comrade, who, according to his dreams, would die about that time, when the sounds of the music on the boulevard penetrated more distinctly to his ears, the crowds of people caught his eye, and he found himself on the boulevard, a staff-captain of infantry as before.

3

He went, first of all, to the pavilion, near which were standing the musicians, for whom other soldiers of the same regiment were holding the notes, in the absence of stands, and about whom a ring of cadets, nurses, and children had formed, intent rather on seeing than on hearing. Around the pavilion stood, sat, or walked sailors, adjutants, and officers in white gloves. Along the grand avenue of the boulevard paced officers of every sort, and women of every description, rarely in bonnets, mostly with kerchiefs on their heads (some had neither bonnets nor kerchiefs), but not one of them was old, and it was worthy of note that all were young. Beyond, in the shady and fragrant alleys of white acacia, isolated groups walked and sat.

No one was especially delighted to encounter Captain Mikhaïloff on the boulevard, with the exception, possibly, of Obzhogoff, a captain in his regiment, and Captain Suslikoff, who pressed his hand warmly; but the former was in camel's-hair trousers, without gloves, a threadbare coat, and his face was very red and covered with perspiration; and the second shouted so loudly and with so much freedom that it was mortifying to walk with them, particularly in the presence of the officers in white gloves (with one of whom, an adjutant, Staff-Captain Mikhaïloff exchanged bows; and he might have bowed to another staff-officer, since he had met him twice at the house of a mutual acquaintance). Besides, what pleasure was it to him to promenade with these two gentlemen, Obzhogoff and Suslikoff, when without that he met them and shook hands with them six times a day? It was not for this that he had come.

He would have liked to approach the adjutant with whom he had exchanged bows, and to enter into conversation with these officers, not for the sake of letting Captains Obzhogoff and Suslikoff and Lieutenant Pashtetzky and others see him talking with them, but simply because they were agreeable people, and, what was more, they knew all the news, and would have told it.

But why is Captain Mikhaïloff afraid, and why cannot he make up his mind to approach them? "What if they should, all at once, refuse to recognize me," he thinks, "or, having bowed to me, what if they continue their conversation among themselves, as though I did not exist, or walk away from me entirely, and leave me standing there alone among the *aristocrats*." The word aristocrats (in the sense of a higher, select circle, in any rank of life) has for some time past acquired great popularity with us, in Russia, where it would seem to have no reason for existing, and has penetrated into every locality and into every class of society whither vanity has penetrated (and into what conditions of time and circumstances does this wretched tendency not penetrate?)—among merchants, among officials, writers, and officers, to Saratoff, to Mamaduishi, to Vinnitzui, everywhere where men exist.

To Captain Obzhogoff, Staff-Captain Mikhaïloff was an *aristocrat*, To Staff-Captain Mikhaïloff, Adjutant Kalugin was an *aristocrat*, because he was an Ad-

jutant, and was on such a footing with the other adjutants as to call them "thou"!
To Adjutant Kalugin, Count Nordoff was an *aristocrat*, because he was an adjutant on the emperor's staff.

Vanity! vanity! and vanity everywhere, even on the brink of the grave, and among men ready to die for the highest convictions, vanity! It must be that it is a characteristic trait, and a peculiar malady of our century. Why was nothing ever heard among the men of former days, of this passion, any more than of the small-pox or the cholera? Why, in our age, are there but three sorts of people: those who accept the principle of vanity as a fact whose existence is inevitable, and, therefore, just; those who accept it as an unfortunate but invincible condition; and those who, unconsciously, act with slavish subservience under its influence? Why did Homer and Shakespeare talk of love, of glory, of suffering, while the literature of our age is nothing but an endless narrative of snobs and vanity?

The staff-captain twice walked in indecision past the group of *his aristocrats*, and the third time he exerted an effort over himself and went up to them. This group consisted of four officers: Adjutant Kalugin, an acquaintance of Mikhaïloff's, Adjutant Prince Galtzin, who was something of an aristocrat even for Kalugin himself, Colonel Neferdoff, one of the so-called *hundred and twenty-two* men of the world (who had entered the service for this campaign, from the retired list), and Captain of Cavalry Praskukhin, also one of the hundred and twenty-two. Luckily for Mikhaïloff, Kalugin was in a very fine humor (the general had just been talking to him in a very confidential way, and Prince Galtzin, who had just arrived from Petersburg, was stopping with him); he did not consider it beneath his dignity to give his hand to Captain Mikhaïloff, which Praskukhin, however, could not make up his mind to do, though he had met Mikhaïloff very frequently on the bastion, had drunk the latter's wine and vodka, and was even indebted to him twenty rubles and a half at preference. As he did not yet know Prince Galtzin very well, he did not wish to convict himself, in the latter's presence, of an acquaintance with a simple staff-captain of infantry. He bowed slightly to the latter.

"Well, Captain," said Kalugin, "when are we to go to the bastion again? Do you remember how we met each other on the Schvartz redoubt . . . it was hot there, hey?"

"Yes, it was hot," said Mikhaïloff, recalling how he had, that night, as he was making his way along the trenches to the bastion, encountered Kalugin, who was walking along like a hero, valiantly clanking his sword. "I really ought to go there to-morrow, according to present arrangements; but we have a sick man," pursued Mikhaïloff, "one officer, as . . ."

He was about to relate how it was not his turn, but, as the commander of the eighth company was ill, and the company had only a cornet left, he had regarded it as his duty to offer himself in the place of Lieutenant Nepshisetzky, and was, therefore, going to the bastion to-day. But Kalugin did not hear him out.

"I have a feeling that something is going to happen within a few days," he said to Prince Galtzin.

"And won't there be something to-day?" asked Mikhaïloff, glancing first at Kalugin, then at Galtzin.

No one made him any reply. Prince Galtzin merely frowned a little, sent his eyes past the other's cap, and, after maintaining silence for a moment, said:—

"That's a magnificent girl in the red kerchief. You don't know her, do you, Captain?"

"She lives near my quarters; she is the daughter of a sailor," replied the staff-captain.

"Come on; let's have a good look at her."

And Prince Galtzin linked one arm in that of Kalugin, the other in that of the staff-captain, being convinced in advance that he could afford the latter no greater gratification, which was, in fact, quite true.

The staff-captain was superstitious, and considered it a great sin to occupy himself with women before a battle; but on this occasion he feigned to be a vicious man, which Prince Galtzin and Kalugin evidently did not believe, and which greatly amazed the girl in the red kerchief, who had more than once observed how the staff-captain blushed as he passed her little window. Praskukhin walked behind, and kept touching Prince Galtzin with his hand, and making various remarks in the French tongue; but as a fourth person could not walk on the small path, he was obliged to walk alone, and it was only on the second round that he took the arm of the brave and well-known naval officer *Servyagin*, who had stepped up and spoken to him, and who was also desirous of joining the circle of *aristocrats*. And the gallant and famous man joyfully thrust his honest and muscular hand through the elbow of a man who was known to all, and even well known to *Servyagin* himself, as not too *nice*. When Praskukhin, explaining to the prince his acquaintance with *that sailor*, whispered to him that the latter was well known for his bravery, Prince Galtzin, who had been on the fourth bastion on the previous evening, had seen a bomb burst twenty paces from him, considered himself no less a hero than this gentleman, and thought that many a reputation is acquired undeservedly, paid no attention whatever to Servyagin.

It was so agreeable to Staff-Captain Mikhaïloff to walk about in this company that he forgot the *dear* letter from T——, and the gloomy thoughts which had assailed him in connection with his impending departure for the bastion. He remained with them until they began to talk exclusively among themselves, avoiding his glances, thereby giving him to understand that he might go, and finally deserted him entirely. But the staff-captain was content, nevertheless, and as he passed Yunker[1] Baron Pesth, who had been particularly haughty and self-conceited since the preceding night, which was the first that he had spent in the bomb-proof of the fifth bastion, and consequently considered himself a hero, he was not in the least offended at the suspiciously haughty expression with which the yunker straightened himself up and doffed his hat before him.

4

But as soon as the staff-captain crossed the threshold of his quarters, entirely different thoughts entered his mind. He looked around his little chamber, with its uneven earth floor, and saw the windows all awry, pasted over with paper,

---

[1] A civilian, without military training, attached to a regiment as a non-commissioned officer, who may eventually become a regular officer.

his old bed, with a rug nailed over it, upon which was depicted a lady on horseback, and over which hung two Tula pistols, the dirty couch of a cadet who lived with him, and which was covered with a chintz coverlet; he saw his Nikita, who, with untidy, tallowed hair, rose from the floor, scratching his head; he saw his ancient cloak, his extra pair of boots, and a little bundle, from which peeped a bit of cheese and the neck of a porter bottle filled with vodka, which had been prepared for his use on the bastion, and all at once he remembered that he was obliged to go with his company for the whole night to the fortifications.

"It is certainly foreordained that I am to be killed to-night," thought the staff-captain . . . "I feel it. And the principal point is that I need not have gone, but that I offered myself. And the man who thrusts himself forward is always killed. And what's the matter with that accursed Nepshisetsky? It is quite possible that he is not sick at all; and they will kill another man for his sake, they will infallibly kill him. However, if they don't kill me, I shall be promoted probably. I saw how delighted the regimental commander was when I asked him to allow me to go, if Lieutenant Nepshisetsky was ill. If I don't turn out a major, then I shall certainly get the Vladimir Cross. This is the thirteenth time that I have been to the bastion. Ah, the thirteenth is an unlucky number. They will surely kill me, I feel that I shall be killed; but some one had to go, it was impossible for the lieutenant of the corps to go. And, whatever happens, the honor of the regiment, the honor of the army, depends on it. It was my *duty* to go . . . yes, my sacred duty. But I have a foreboding."

The staff-captain forgot that this was not the first time that a similar foreboding had assailed him, in a greater or less degree, when it had been necessary to go to the bastion, and he did not know that every one who sets out on an affair experiences this foreboding with more or less force. Having calmed himself with this conception of duty, which was especially and strongly developed in the staff-captain, he seated himself at the table, and began to write a farewell letter to his father. Ten minutes later, having finished his letter, he rose from the table, his eyes wet with tears, and, mentally reciting all the prayers he knew, he set about dressing. His coarse, drunken servant indolently handed him his new coat (the old one, which the captain generally wore when going to the bastion, was not mended).

"Why is not my coat mended? You never do anything but sleep, you good-for-nothing!" said Mikhaïloff, angrily.

"Sleep!" grumbled Nikita. "You run like a dog all day long; perhaps you stop —but you must not sleep, even then!"

"You are drunk again, I see."

"I didn't get drunk on your money, so you needn't scold."

"Hold your tongue, blockhead!" shouted the captain, who was ready to strike the man. He had been absent-minded at first, but now he was at last out of patience, and embittered by the rudeness of Nikita, whom he loved, even spoiled, and who had lived with him for twelve years.

"Blockhead? Blockhead?" repeated the servant. "Why do you call me a blockhead, sir? Is this a time for that sort of thing? It is not good to curse."

Mikhaïloff recalled whither he was on the point of going, and felt ashamed of himself.

"You are enough to put a saint out of patience, Nikita," he said, in a gentle voice. "Leave that letter to my father on the table, and don't touch it," he added, turning red.

"Yes, sir," said Nikita, melting under the influence of the wine which he had drunk, as he had said, "at his own expense," and winking his eyes with a visible desire to weep.

But when the captain said, "Good-by, Nikita," on the porch, Nikita suddenly broke down into repressed sobs, and ran to kiss his master's hand. . . . "Farewell, master!" he exclaimed, sobbing. The old sailor's wife, who was standing on the porch, could not, in her capacity of a woman, refrain from joining in this touching scene, so she began to wipe her eyes with her dirty sleeve, and to say something about even gentlemen having their trials to bear, and that she, poor creature, had been left a widow. And she related for the hundredth time to drunken Nikita the story of her woes; how her husband had been killed in the first bombardment, and how her little house had been utterly ruined (the one in which she was now living did not belong to her), and so on. When his master had departed, Nikita lighted his pipe, requested the daughter of their landlord to go for some vodka, and very soon ceased to weep, but, on the contrary, got into a quarrel with the old woman about some small bucket, which, he declared, she had broken.

"But perhaps I shall only be wounded," meditated the captain, as he marched through the twilight to the bastion with his company. "But where? How? Here or here?" he thought, indicating his belly and his breast. . . . "If it should be here" (he thought of the upper portion of his leg), "it might run round. Well, but if it were here, and by a splinter, that would finish me."

The staff-captain reached the lodgments safely through the trenches, set his men to work, with the assistance of an officer of sappers, in the darkness, which was already complete, and seated himself in a pit behind the breastworks. There was not much firing; only once in a while the lightning flashed from our batteries, then from *his*, and the brilliant fuse of a bomb traced an arc of flame against the dark, starry heavens. But all the bombs fell far in the rear and to the right of the rifle-pits in which the captain sat. He drank his vodka, ate his cheese, lit his cigarette, and, after saying his prayers, he tried to get a little sleep.

5

Prince Galtzin, Lieutenant-Colonel Neferdoff, and Praskukhin, whom no one had invited, to whom no one spoke, but who never left them, all went to drink tea with Adjutant Kalugin.

"Well, you did not finish telling me about Vaska Mendel," said Kalugin, as he took off his cloak, seated himself by the window in a soft lounging-chair, and unbuttoned the collar of his fresh, stiffly starched cambric shirt: "How did he come to marry?"

"That's a joke, my dear fellow! There was a time, I assure you, when nothing else was talked of in Petersburg," said Prince Galtzin, with a laugh, as he sprang up from the piano at which he was sitting, and seated himself at the window beside Kalugin's window. "It is simply ludicrous, and I know all the details of the affair."

And he began to relate—in a merry and skilful manner—a love-story, which we will omit, because it possesses no interest for us. But it is worthy of note that not only Prince Galtzin, but all the gentlemen who had placed themselves here, one at the window, another with his legs coiled up under him, a third at at the piano, seemed totally different persons from what they had been when on the boulevard; there was nothing of that absurd arrogance and haughtiness which they had exhibited in public to the infantry officers; here they were among their own set, and natural, especially Kalugin and Prince Galtzin, and were very good, amiable, and merry fellows. The conversation turned on their comrades in the service in Petersburg, and on their acquaintances.

"What of Maslovsky?"

"Which? the uhlan of the body-guard or of the horse-guard?"

"I know both of them. The one in the horse-guards was with me when he was a little boy and had only just left school. What is the elder one? a captain of cavalry?"

"Oh, yes! long ago."

"And is he still going about with his gipsy maid?"

"No, he has deserted her . . ." and so forth, and so forth, in the same strain.

Then Prince Galtzin seated himself at the piano, and sang a gipsy song in magnificent style. Praskukhin began to sing second, although no one had asked him, and he did it so well that they requested him to accompany the prince again, which he gladly consented to do.

The servant came in with the tea, cream, and cracknels on a silver salver.

"Serve the prince," said Kalugin.

"Really, it is strange to think," said Galtzin, taking a glass, and walking to the window, "that we are in a beleaguered city; *pianofortes*, tea with cream, and such quarters as I should be only too happy to get in Petersburg."

"Yes, if it were not for that," said the old lieutenant-colonel, who was dissatisfied with everything, "this constant waiting for something would be simply unendurable . . . and to see how men are killed, killed every day, . . . and there is no end to it, and under such circumstances it would not be comfortable to live in the mud."

"And how about our infantry officers," said Kalugin; "who live in the bastions with the soldiers in the casemates, and eat beet soup with the soldiers . . . how about them?"

"How about them? They don't change their linen for ten days at a time, and they are heroes—wonderful men."

At this moment an officer of infantry entered the room.

"I . . . I was ordered . . . may I present myself to the gen . . . to his excellency from General N.?" he inquired, bowing with an air of embarrassment.

Kalugin rose, but, without returning the officer's salute, he asked him, with insulting courtesy and strained official smile, whether *they*[1] would not wait awhile and, without inviting him to be seated or paying any further attention to him, he turned to Prince Galtzin and began to speak to him in French, so that

---

[1] A polite way of referring to the general in the plural.

the unhappy officer, who remained standing in the middle of the room, absolutely did not know what to do with himself.

"It is on very important business, sir," said the officer, after a momentary pause.

"Ah! very well, then," said Kalugin, putting on his cloak, and accompanying him to the door.

"Well, gentlemen, I think there will be hot work to-night," said Kalugin, in French, on his return from the general's.

"Hey? What? A sortie?" They all began to question him.

"I don't know yet . . . you will see for yourselves," replied Kalugin, with a mysterious smile.

"And my commander is on the bastion . . . of course, I shall have to go," said Praskukhin, buckling on his sword.

But no one answered him; he must know for himself whether he had to go or not.

Praskukhin and Neferdoff went off, in order to betake themselves to their posts. "Farewell, gentlemen!" "Au revoir, gentlemen! We shall meet again to-night!" shouted Kalugin from the window when Praskukhin and Neferdoff trotted down the road, bending over the bows of their Cossack saddles. The trampling of their Cossack horses soon died away in the dusky street.

"No, tell me, is something really going to take place to-night?" said Galtzin, in French, as he leaned with Kalugin on the window-sill, and gazed at the bombs which were flying over the bastions.

"I can tell you; you see . . . you have been on the bastions, of course?" (Galtzin made a sign of assent, although he had been only once to the fourth bastion.) "Well, there was a trench opposite our lunette;" and Kalugin, who was not a specialist, although he considered his judgment on military affairs particularly accurate, began to explain the position of our troops and of the enemy's works, and the plan of the proposed affair, mixing up the technical terms of fortifications a good deal in the process.

"But they are beginning to hammer away at our lodgments. Oho! was that ours or *his*? there, it has burst," they said, as they leaned out of the window, gazing at the fiery lines of the bombs intersecting in the air, at the lightnings of the discharges, at the dark blue sky, momentarily illuminated, and at the white smoke of the powder, and listened to the sounds of the firing, which grew louder and louder.

"What a charming sight? is it not?" said Kalugin, in French, directing the attention of his guest to the really beautiful spectacle. "Do you know, you cannot distinguish the stars from the bombs at times."

"Yes, I was just thinking that that was a star; but it darted down . . . there, it has burst now. And that big star yonder, what is it called? It is just exactly like a bomb."

"Do you know, I have grown so used to these bombs that I am convinced that a starlight night in Russia will always seem to me to be all bombs; one gets so accustomed to them."

"But ought not I to go on this sortie?" inquired Galtzin, after a momentary silence.

"Enough of that, brother! Don't think of such a thing! I won't let you go!" replied Kalugin. "Your turn will come, brother!"

"Seriously? So you think that it is not necessary to go? Hey?" . . .

At that moment, a frightful crash of rifles was heard above the roar of the cannon in the direction in which these gentlemen were looking, and thousands of small fires, flaring up incessantly, without intermission, flashed along the entire line.

"That's it, when the real work has begun!" said Kalugin. . . . "That is the sound of the rifles, and I cannot listen to it with indifference; it takes a sort of hold on your soul, you know. And there is the hurrah!" he added, listening to the prolonged and distant roar of hundreds of voices, "A-a-aa!" which reached him from the bastion.

"What is this hurrah, theirs or ours?"

"I don't know; but it has come to a hand-to-hand fight, for the firing has ceased."

At that moment, an officer followed by his Cossack galloped up to the porch, and slipped down from his horse.

"Where from?"

"From the bastion. The general is wanted."

"Let us go. Well, now, what is it?"

"They have attacked the lodgments . . . have taken them . . . the French have brought up vast reserves . . . they have attacked our forces . . . there were only two battalions," said the panting officer, who was the same that had come in the evening, drawing his breath with difficulty, but stepping to the door with perfect unconcern.

"Well, have they retreated?" inquired Galtzin.

"No," answered the officer, angrily. "The battalion came up and beat them back; but the commander of the regiment is killed, and many officers, and I have been ordered to ask for reinforcements." . . .

And with these words he and Kalugin went off to the general, whither we will not follow them.

Five minutes later, Kalugin was mounted on the Cossack's horse (and with that peculiar, *quasi*-Cossack seat, in which, as I have observed, all adjutants find something especially captivating, for some reason or other), and rode at a trot to the bastion, in order to give some orders, and to await the news of the final result of the affair. And Prince Galtzin, under the influence of that oppressive emotion which the signs of a battle near at hand usually produce on a spectator who takes no part in it, went out into the street, and began to pace up and down there without any object.

6

The soldiers were bearing the wounded on stretchers, and supporting them by their arms. It was completely dark in the streets; now and then a rare light flashed in the hospital or from the spot where the officers were seated. The same thunder of cannon and exchange of rifle-shots was borne from the bastions, and the same fires flashed against the black sky. Now and then, you could hear the trampling hoofs of an orderly's horse, the groan of a wounded man, the footsteps and voices of the stretcher-bearers, or the conversation of some of the frightened female inhabitants, who had come out on their porches to view the cannonade.

Among the latter were our acquaintances, Nikita, the old sailor's widow, with whom he had already made his peace, and her ten-year-old daughter. "O Lord! O Most Holy Mother of God!" whispered the old woman to herself with a sigh, as she watched the bombs, which, like balls of fire, sailed incessantly from one side to the other. "How dreadful, how dreadful! I-i-hi-hi! It was not so in the first bombardment. See, there it has burst, the cursed thing! right above our house in the suburbs."

"No, it is farther off, in aunt Arinka's garden, that they all fall," said the little girl.

"And where, where is my master now!" said Nikita, with a drawl, for he was still rather drunk. "Oh, how I love that master of mine . . . I don't know myself! . . . I love him so that if, which God forbid, they should kill him in this sinful fight, then, if you will believe it, aunty, I don't know what I might do to myself in that case . . . by Heavens, I don't! He is such a master that words will not do him justice! Would I exchange him for one of those who play cards? That is simply . . . whew! that's all there is to say!" concluded Nikita, pointing at the lighted window of his master's room, in which, as the staff-captain was absent, Yunker Zhvadchevsky had invited his friends to a carouse, on the occasion of his receiving the cross: Sub-Lieutenant Ugrovitch and Sub-Lieutenant Nepshisetsky, who was ill with a cold in the head.

"Those little stars! They dart through the sky like stars, like stars!" said the little girl, breaking the silence which succeeded Nikita's words. "There, there! another has dropped! Why do they do it, mamma?"

"They will ruin our little cabin entirely," said the old woman, sighing, and not replying to the little girl's question.

"And when uncle and I went there to-day, mamma," continued the little girl, in a shrill voice, "there was such a bi-ig cannon-ball lying in the room, near the cupboard; it had broken through the wall and into the room . . . and it is so big that you couldn't lift it."

"Those who had husbands and money have gone away," said the old woman, "and now they have ruined the last little house. See, see how they are firing, the wretches. O Lord! O Lord!"

"And as soon as we came out, a bomb flew at us, and burst and scattered the earth about, and a piece of the shell came near striking uncle and me."

7

Prince Galtzin met more and more wounded men, in stretchers and on foot, supporting each other, and talking loudly.

"When they rushed up, comrades," said one tall soldier, who had two guns on his shoulder, in a bass voice, "when they rushed up and shouted, 'Allah, Allah!'[1] they pressed each other on. You kill one, and another takes his place . . . you can do nothing. You never saw such numbers as there were of them." . . .

But at this point in his story Galtzin interrupted him.

"You come from the bastion?"

[1] The Russian soldiers, who had been fighting the Turks, were so accustomed to this cry of the enemy that they always declared that the French also cried "Allah."—Author's Note.

"Just so, your honor!"

"Well, what has been going on there? Tell me."

"Why, what has been going on? They attacked in force, your honor; they climbed over the wall, and that's the end of it. They conquered completely, your honor."

"How conquered? You repulsed them, surely?"

"How could we repulse them when *his* whole force came up. They killed all our men, and there was no help given us."

The soldier was mistaken, for the trenches were behind our forces; but this is a peculiar thing, which any one may observe: a soldier who has been wounded in an engagement always thinks that the day has been lost, and that the encounter has been a frightfully bloody one.

"Then, what did they mean by telling me that you had repulsed them?" said Galtzin, with irritation. "Perhaps the enemy was repulsed after you left. Is it long since you came away?"

"I have this instant come from there, your honor," replied the soldier. "It is hardly possible. The trenches remained in his hands . . . he won a complete victory."

"Well, and are you not ashamed to have surrendered the trenches? This is horrible!" said Galtzin, angered by such indifference.

"What, when he was there in *force?*" growled the soldier.

"And, your honor," said a soldier on a stretcher, who had just come up with them, "how could we help surrendering, when nearly all of us had been killed? If we had been in force, we would only have surrendered with our lives. But what was there to do? I ran one man through, and then I was struck. . . . O-oh! softly, brothers! steady, brothers! go more steadily! . . . O-oh!" groaned the wounded man.

"There really seem to be a great many extra men coming this way," said Galtzin, again stopping the tall soldier with the two rifles. "Why are you walking off? Hey there, halt!"

The soldier halted, and removed his cap with his left hand.

"Where are you going, and why?" he shouted at him, sternly. "He . . ."

But, approaching the soldier very closely at that moment, he perceived that the latter's right arm was covered with blood from the coat-cuff to far above the elbow.

"I am wounded, your honor!"

"Wounded? how?"

"It must have been a bullet, here!" said the soldier, pointing at his arm; "and here also . . . I cannot tell what broke my head," and, bending over, he showed the hair upon the back of it all clotted together with blood.

"And whose gun is that second one you have?"

"A choice French one, your honor! I captured it. And I should not have come away if it had not been to accompany this soldier; he might fall down," he added, pointing at the soldier, who was walking a little in front, leaning upon his gun, and with difficulty dragging and moving his left foot.

Prince Galtzin all at once became frightfully ashamed of his unjust suspicions. He felt that he was growing crimson, and turned away, without questioning the wounded men further, and, without looking after them, he went to the place where the injured men were being cared for.

Having forced his way with difficulty to the porch, through the wounded men who had come on foot, and the stretcher-bearers, who were entering with the wounded and emerging with the dead, Galtzin entered the first room, glanced round, and involuntarily turned back, and immediately ran into the street. It was too terrible.

8

The vast, dark, lofty hall, lighted only by the four or five candles which the doctors were carrying about to inspect the wounded, was literally full. The stretcher-bearers incessantly brought in the wounded, ranged them one beside another on the floor, which was already so crowded that the unfortunate wretches jostled each other and sprinkled each other with their blood, and then went forth for more. The pools of blood which were visible on the unoccupied places, the hot breaths of several hundred men, and the steam which rose from those who were toiling with the stretchers produced a peculiar, thick, heavy, offensive atmosphere, in which the candles burned dimly in the different parts of the room. The dull murmur of diverse groans, sighs, death-rattles, broken now and again by a shriek, was borne throughout the apartment. Sisters of charity, with tranquil faces, and with an expression not of empty, feminine, tearfully sickly compassion, but of active, practical sympathy, flitted hither and thither among the blood-stained overcoats and shirts, stepping over the wounded, with medicine, water, bandages, lint.

Doctors, with their sleeves rolled up, knelt beside the wounded, beside whom the assistant surgeons held the candles, inspecting, feeling, and probing the wounds, in spite of the terrible groans and entreaties of the sufferers. One of the doctors was seated at a small table by the door, and, at the moment when Galtzin entered the room, he was just writing down "No. 532."

"Ivan Bogaeff, common soldier, third company of the S—— regiment, *fractura femoris complicata!*" called another from the extremity of the hall, as he felt of the crushed leg. . . . "Turn him over."

"O-oi, my fathers, good fathers!" shrieked the soldier, beseeching them not to touch him.

"*Perforatio capitis.*"

"Semyon Neferdoff, lieutenant-colonel of the N—— regiment of infantry. Have a little patience, colonel; otherwise it is impossible; I will let you alone!" said a third, picking away at the head of the unfortunate colonel, with some sort of a hook.

"Ai! stop! Oi! for God's sake, quick, quick, for the sake a-a-a-a!" . . .

"*Perforatio pectoris* . . . Sevastyan Sereda, common soldier . . . . of what regiment? however, you need not write that: *moritur.* Carry him away," said the doctor, abandoning the soldier, who was rolling his eyes, and already emitting the death-rattle.

Forty stretcher-bearers stood at the door, awaiting the task of transporting to the hospital the men who had been attended to, and the dead to the chapel, and gazed at this picture in silence, only uttering a heavy sigh from time to time. . . .

9

On his way to the bastion, Kalugin met numerous wounded men; but, knowing from experience that such a spectacle has a bad effect on the spirits of a man on the verge of an action, he not only did not pause to interrogate them, but, on the contrary, he tried not to pay any heed to them. At the foot of the hill he encountered an orderly, who was galloping from the bastion at full speed.

"Zobkin! Zobkin! Stop a minute!"

"Well, what is it?"

"Where are you from?"

"From the lodgments."

"Well, how are things there? Hot?"

"Ah, frightfully!"

And the orderly galloped on.

In fact, although there was not much firing from the rifles, the cannonade had begun with fresh vigor and greater heat than ever.

"Ah, that's bad!" thought Kalugin, experiencing a rather unpleasant sensation, and there came to him also a presentiment, that is to say, a very usual thought— the thought of death.

But Kalugin was an egotist and gifted with nerves of steel; in a word, he was what is called brave. He did not yield to his first sensation, and began to arouse his courage; he recalled to mind a certain adjutant of Napoleon, who, after having given the command to advance, galloped up to Napoleon, his head all covered with blood.

"You are wounded?" said Napoleon to him. "I beg your pardon, Sire, I am dead,"—and the adjutant fell from his horse, and died on the spot.

This seemed very fine to him, and he fancied that he somewhat resembled this adjutant; then he gave his horse a blow with the whip, and assumed still more of that dashing *Cossack seat*, glanced at his orderly, who was galloping behind him, standing upright in his stirrups, and thus in dashing style he reached the place where it was necessary to dismount. Here he found four soldiers, who were smoking their pipes as they sat on the stones.

"What are you doing here?" he shouted at them.

"We have been carrying a wounded man from the field, your honor, and have sat down to rest," one of them replied, concealing his pipe behind his back, and pulling off his cap.

"Resting indeed! March off to your posts!"

And, in company with them, he walked up the hill through the trenches, encountering wounded men at every step.

On attaining the crest of the hill, he turned to the left, and, after taking a few steps, found himself quite alone. Splinters whizzed near him, and struck in the trenches. Another bomb rose in front of him, and seemed to be flying straight at him. All of a sudden he felt terrified; he ran off five paces at full speed, and lay down on the ground. But when the bomb burst, and at a distance from him, he grew dreadfully vexed at himself, and glanced about as he rose, to see whether any one had perceived him fall, but there was no one about.

When fear has once made its way into the mind, it does not speedily give way to another feeling. He, who had boasted that he never bent, hastened along the trench with accelerated speed, and almost on his hands and knees. "Ah! this is very bad!" he thought, as he stumbled. "I shall certainly be killed!" And, conscious of how difficult it was for him to breathe, and that the perspiration was breaking out all over his body, he was amazed at himself, but he no longer strove to conquer his feelings.

All at once steps became audible in advance of him. He quickly straightened himself up, raised his head, and, boldly clanking his sword, began to proceed at a slower pace than before. He did not know himself. When he joined the officer of sappers and the sailor who were coming to meet him, and the former called to him, "Lie down," pointing to the bright speck of a bomb, which, growing ever brighter and brighter, swifter and swifter, as it approached, crashed down in the vicinity of the trench, he only bent his head a very little, involuntarily, under the influence of the terrified shout, and went his way.

"Whew! what a brave man!" ejaculated the sailor, who had calmly watched the exploding bomb, and, with practised glance, at once calculated that its splinters could not strike inside the trench; "he will not even lie down."

Only a few steps remained to be taken, across an open space, before Kalugin would reach the casemate of the commander of the bastion, when he was again attacked by dimness of vision and that stupid sensation of fear; his heart began to beat more violently, the blood rushed to his head, and he was obliged to exert an effort over himself in order to reach the casemate.

"Why are you so out of breath?" inquired the general, when Kalugin had communicated to him his orders.

"I have been walking very fast, your excellency!"

"Will you not take a glass of wine?"

Kalugin drank the wine, and lighted a cigarette. The engagement had already come to an end; only the heavy cannonade continued on both sides.

In the casemate sat General N., the commander of the bastion, and six other officers, among whom was Praskukhin, discussing various details of the conflict. As he sat in this comfortable apartment, with blue hangings, with a sofa, a bed, a table, covered with papers, a wall clock, and the holy picture, before which burned a lamp, and gazed upon these signs of habitation, and at the arshin-thick (twenty-eight inches) beams which formed the ceiling, and listened to the shots, which were deadened by the casemate, Kalugin positively could not understand how he had twice permitted himself to be overcome with such unpardonable weakness. He was angry with himself, and he longed for danger, in order that he might subject himself to another trial.

"I am glad that you are here, captain," he said to a naval officer, in the cloak of staff-officer, with a large mustache and the Cross of St. George, who entered the casemate at that moment, and asked the general to give him some men that he might repair the two embrasures on his battery, which had been demolished. "The general ordered me to inquire," continued Kalugin, when the commander of the battery ceased to address the general, "whether your guns can fire grape-shot into the trenches."

"Only one of my guns will do that," replied the captain, gruffly.

"Let us go and see, all the same."

The captain frowned, and grunted angrily: —

"I have already passed the whole night there, and I came here to try and get a little rest," said he. "Cannot you go alone? My assistant, Lieutenant Kartz, is there, and he will show you everything."

The captain had now been for six months in command of this, one of the most dangerous of the batteries—and even when there were no casemates he had lived without relief, in the bastion and among the sailors, from the beginning of the siege, and he bore a reputation among them for bravery. Therefore his refusal particularly struck and amazed Kalugin. "That's what reputation is worth!" he thought.

"Well, then, I will go alone, if you will permit me," he said in a somewhat bantering tone to the captain, who, however, paid not the slightest heed to his words.

But Kalugin did not reflect that he had passed, in all, at different times, perhaps fifty hours on the bastion, while the captain had lived there for six months. Kalugin was actuated, moreover, by vanity, by a desire to shine, by the hope of reward, of reputation, and by the charm of risk; but the captain had already gone through all that: he had been vain at first, he had displayed valor, he had risked his life, he had hoped for fame and guerdon, and had even obtained them, but these actuating motives had already lost their power over him, and he regarded the matter in another light; he fulfilled his duty with punctuality, but understanding quite well how small were the chances for his life which were left him, after a six months' residence in the bastion, he no longer risked these chances, except in case of stern necessity, so that the young lieutenant, who had entered the battery only a week previous, and who was now showing it to Kalugin, in company with whom he took turns in leaning out of the embrasure, or climbing out on the ramparts, seemed ten times as brave as the captain.

After inspecting the battery, Kalugin returned to the casemate, and ran against the general in the dark, as the latter was ascending to the watch-tower with his staff-officers.

"Captain Praskukhin!" said the general, "please to go to the first lodgment and say to the second battery of the M—— regiment, which is at work there, that they are to abandon their work, to evacuate the place without making any noise, and to join their regiment, which is standing at the foot of the hill in reserve. . . . Do you understand? Lead them to their regiment yourself."

"Yes, sir."

And Praskukhin set out for the lodgment on a run.

The firing was growing more infrequent.

10

"Is this the second battalion of the M—— regiment?" asked Praskukhin, hastening up to the spot, and running against the soldiers who were carrying earth in sacks.

"Exactly so, sir."

"Where is the commander?"

Mikhaïloff, supposing that the inquiry was for the commander of the corps, crawled out of his pit, and, taking Praskukhin for the colonel, he stepped up to him with his hand at his vizor.

"The general has given orders . . . that you . . . are to be so good as to go . . . as quickly as possible . . . and, in particular, as quietly as possible, to the rear, . . . not to the rear, but to the reserve," said Praskukhin, glancing askance at the enemy's fires.

On recognizing Praskukhin and discovering the state of things, Mikhaïloff dropped his hand, gave his orders, and the battalion started into motion, gathered up their guns, put on their overcoats, and set out.

No one who has not experienced it can imagine the delight which a man feels when he takes his departure, after a three hours' bombardment, from such a dangerous post as the lodgments. Several times in the course of those three hours, Mikhaïloff, who had, not without reason, considered his *end* as inevitable, had grown accustomed to the conviction that he should infallibly be killed, and that he no longer belonged to this world. In spite of this, however, he had great difficulty in keeping his feet from running away with him when he issued from the lodgments at the head of his corps, in company with Praskukhin.

"*Au revoir*," said the major, the commander of another battalion, who was to remain in the lodgments, and with whom he had shared his cheese, as they sat in the pit behind the breastworks—"a pleasant journey to you."

"Thanks, I hope you will get off luckily. The firing seems to be holding up."

But no sooner had he said this than the enemy, who must have observed the movement in the lodgments, began to fire faster and faster. Our guns began to reply to him, and again a heavy cannonade began. The stars were gleaming high, but not brilliantly, in the sky. The night was dark—you could hardly see your hand before you; only the flashes of the discharges and the explosions of the bombs illuminated objects for a moment. The soldiers marched on rapidly, in silence, involuntarily treading close on each other's heels; all that was audible through the incessant firing was the measured sound of their footsteps on the dry road, the noise of their bayonets as they came in contact, or the sigh and prayer of some young soldier, "Lord, Lord! what is this?" Now and then the groan of a wounded man arose, and the shout, "Stretcher!" (In the company commanded by Mikhaïloff, twenty-six men were killed in one night, by the fire of the artillery alone.) The lightning flashed against the distant horizon, the sentry in the bastion shouted, "Can-non!" and the ball, shrieking over the heads of the corps, tore up the earth, and sent the stones flying.

"Deuce take it! how slowly they march," thought Praskukhin, glancing back continually, as he walked beside Mikhaïloff. "Really, it will be better for me to run on in front; I have already given the order. . . . But no, it might be said later on that I was a coward. What will be will be; I will march alongside them."

"Now, why is he walking behind me?" thought Mikhaïloff, on his side. "So far as I have observed, he always brings ill-luck. There it comes, flying straight for us, apparently."

After traversing several hundred paces, they encountered Kalugin, who was going to the casemates, clanking his sword boldly as he walked, in order to learn, by the general's command, how the works were progressing there. But on meeting Mikhaïloff, it occurred to him that, instead of going thither, under that terrible fire, which he was not ordered to do, he could make minute inquiries of the officer who had been there. And, in fact, Mikhaïloff furnished him with a detailed account of the works. After walking a short distance with them, Kalugin turned into the trench which led to the casemate.

"Well, what news is there?" inquired the officer, who was seated alone in the room, and eating his supper.

"Well, nothing, apparently, except that there will not be any further conflict."

"How so? On the contrary, the general has but just gone up to the watch-tower. A regiment has already arrived. Yes, there it is. . . . do you hear? The firing has begun again. Don't go. Why should you?" added the officer, perceiving the movement made by Kalugin.

"But I must be there without fail, in the present instance," thought Kalugin, "but I have already subjected myself to a good deal of danger to-day; the firing is terrible."

"Well, after all, I had better wait for him here," he said.

In fact, the general returned, twenty minutes later, accompanied by the officers who had been with him; among their number was the yunker, Baron Pesth, but Praskukhin was not with them. The lodgments had been captured and occupied by our forces.

After receiving a full account of the engagement, Kalugin and Pesth went out of the casemates.

11

"There is blood on your cloak; have you been having a hand-to-hand fight?" Kalugin asked him.

"Oh, 'tis frightful! Just imagine. . . ."

And Pesth began to relate how he had led his company, how the commander of the company had been killed, how he had spitted a Frenchman, and how, if it had not been for him, the battle would have been lost.

The foundations for this tale, that the company commander had been killed, and that Pesth had killed a Frenchman, were correct; but, in giving the details, the yunker invented facts and bragged.

He bragged involuntarily, because, during the whole engagement, he had been in a kind of mist, and had forgotten himself to such a degree that everything which happened seemed to him to have happened somewhere, sometime, and with some one, and very naturally he had endeavored to bring out these details in a light which should be favorable to himself. But what had happened in reality was this:—

The battalion to which the yunker had been ordered for the sortie had stood under fire for two hours, near a wall; then the commander of the battalion in front said something, the company commanders made a move, the battalion got under way, issued forth from behind the breastworks, marched forward a hundred paces, and came to a halt in columns. Pesth had been ordered to take his stand on the right flank of the second company.

The yunker stood his ground, absolutely without knowing where he was, or why he was there, and, with restrained breath, and with a cold chill running down his spine, he had stared stupidly straight ahead into the dark beyond, in the expectation of something terrible. But, since there was no firing in progress, he did not feel so much terrified as he did queer and strange at finding himself outside the fortress, in the open plain. Again the battalion commander ahead said something. Again the officers conversed in whispers, as they communicated the orders, and the black wall of the first company suddenly disappeared. They had been ordered to lie down. The second company lay down also, and Pesth, in the act, pricked his hand on something sharp. The only man who did not lie down was the commander of the second company. His short form, with the naked sword which he was flourishing, talking incessantly the while, moved about in front of the troop.

"Boys! my brave lads! . . . look at me! Don't fire at them, but at them with your bayonets, the dogs! When I shout, 'Hurrah!' follow me close . . . the chief thing is to be as close together as possible . . . let us show what we are made of! Do not let us cover ourselves with shame—shall we, hey, my boys? For our father the Tzar!"

"What is our company commander's surname?" Pesth inquired of a yunker, who was lying beside him. "What a brave fellow he is!"

"Yes, he's always that way in a fight. . . ." answered the yunker. "His name is Lisinkovsky."

At that moment, a flame flashed up in front of the company. There was a crash, which deafened them all, stones and splinters flew high in the air (fifty seconds, at least, later a stone fell from above and tore off the leg of a soldier). This was a bomb from an elevated platform, and the fact that it fell in the midst of the company proved that the French had caught sight of the column.

"So they are sending bombs! . . . Just let us get at you, and you shall feel a three-cornered Russian bayonet, curse you!" shouted the commander of the company, in so loud a tone that the battalion commander was forced to order him to be quiet and not to make so much noise.

After this the first company rose to their feet, and after it the second. They were ordered to lower arms, and the battalion advanced. Pesth was so terrified that he absolutely could not recollect whether they advanced far, or whither, or who did what. He walked like a drunken man. But all at once millions of fires flashed from all sides, there was a whistling and a crashing. He shrieked and ran somewhere or other, because they were all shrieking and running. Then he stumbled and fell upon something. It was the company commander (who had been wounded at the head of his men and who, taking the yunker for a Frenchman, seized him by the leg). Then, when he had freed his leg, and risen to his feet, some man ran against his back in the dark and almost knocked him down again; another man shouted, "Run him through! what are you staring at?"

Then he seized a gun, and ran the bayonet into something soft. "Ah, Dieu!" exclaimed some one in a terribly piercing voice, and then only did Pesth discover that he had transfixed a Frenchman. The cold sweat started out all over his body. He shook as though in a fever, and flung away the gun. But this lasted only a moment; it immediately occurred to him that he was a hero. He seized the gun again, and, shouting "Hurrah!" with the crowd, he rushed away from the dead Frenchman. After having traversed about twenty paces, he came to the trench. There he found our men and the company commander.

"I have run one man through!" he said to the commander.

"You're a brave fellow, Baron."

12

"But, do you know, Praskukhin has been killed," said Pesth, accompanying Kalugin, on the way back.

"It cannot be!"

"But it can. I saw him myself."

"Farewell; I am in a hurry."

"I am well content," thought Kalugin, as he returned home; "I have had luck for the first time when on duty. That was a capital engagement, and I am alive and whole. There will be some fine presentations for promotion, and I shall certainly get a golden sword. And I deserve it, too."

After reporting to the general all that was necessary, he went to his room, in which sat Prince Galtzin, who had returned long before, and who was reading a book, which he had found on Kalugin's table, while waiting for him.

It was with a wonderful sense of enjoyment that Kalugin found himself at home again, out of all danger; and, having donned his night-shirt and lain down on his bed, he began to relate to Galtzin the particulars of the affair, communicating them, naturally, from a point of view which made it appear that he, Kalugin, was a very active and valiant officer, to which, in my opinion, it was superfluous to refer, seeing that every one knew it and that no one had any right to doubt it, with the exception, perhaps, of the deceased Captain Praskukhin, who, in spite of the fact that he had been accustomed to consider it a piece of happiness to walk arm in arm with Kalugin, had told a friend, only the evening before, in private, that Kalugin was a very fine man, but that, between you and me, he was terribly averse to going to the bastions.

No sooner had Praskukhin, who had been walking beside Mikhaïloff, taken leave of Kalugin, and, betaking himself to a safer place, had begun to recover his spirits somewhat, than he caught sight of a flash of lightning behind him flaring up vividly, heard the shout of the sentinel, "Mortar!" and the words of the soldiers who were marching behind, "It's flying straight at the bastion!"

Mikhaïloff glanced round. The brilliant point of the bomb seemed to be suspended directly over his head in such a position that it was absolutely impossible to determine its course. But this lasted only for a second. The bomb came faster and faster, nearer and nearer, the sparks of the fuse were already visible, and the fateful whistle was audible, and it descended straight in the middle of the battalion.

"Lie down!" shouted a voice.

Mikhaïloff and Praskukhin threw themselves on the ground. Praskukhin shut his eyes, and only heard the bomb crash against the hard earth somewhere in the vicinity. A second passed, which seemed an hour—and the bomb had not burst. Praskukhin was alarmed; had he felt cowardly for nothing? Perhaps the bomb had fallen at a distance, and it merely seemed to him that the fuse was hissing near him. He opened his eyes, and saw with satisfaction that Mikhaïloff was lying motionless on the earth, at his very feet. But then his eyes encountered for a moment the glowing fuse of the bomb, which was twisting about at a distance of an arshin [1] from him.

A cold horror, which excluded every other thought and feeling, took possession of his whole being. He covered his face with his hands.

Another second passed—a second in which a whole world of thoughts, feelings, hopes, and memories flashed through his mind.

"Which will be killed, Mikhaïloff or I? Or both together? And if it is I, where

[1] Twenty-eight inches.

will it strike? If in the head, then all is over with me; but if in the leg, they will cut it off, and I shall ask them to be sure to give me chloroform,—and I may still remain among the living. But perhaps no one but Mikhaïloff will be killed; then I will relate how we were walking along together, and how he was killed and his blood spurted over me. No, it is nearer to me . . . it will kill me!"

Then he remembered the twenty rubles which he owed Mikhaïloff, and recalled another debt in Petersburg, which ought to have been paid long ago; the gipsy air which he had sung the previous evening recurred to him. The woman whom he loved appeared to his imagination in a cap with lilac ribbons, a man who had insulted him five years before, and whom he had not paid off for his insult, came to his mind, though inextricably interwoven with these and with a thousand other memories the feeling of the moment—the fear of death—never deserted him for an instant.

"But perhaps it will not burst," he thought, and, with the decision of despair, he tried to open his eyes. But at that instant, through his still closed eyelids, his eyes were smitten with a red fire, and something struck him in the center of the breast, with a frightful crash; he ran off, he knew not whither, stumbled over his sword, which had got between his legs, and fell over on his side.

"Thank God! I am only bruised," was his first thought, and he tried to touch his breast with his hands; but his arms seemed fettered, and pincers were pressing his head. The soldiers flitted before his eyes, and he unconsciously counted them: "One, two, three soldiers; and there is an officer, wrapped up in his cloak," he thought. Then a flash passed before his eyes, and he thought that something had been fired off; was it the mortars, or the cannon? It must have been the cannon. And there was still another shot; and there were more soldiers; five, six, seven soldiers were passing by him. Then suddenly he felt afraid that they would crush him. He wanted to shout to them that he was bruised; but his mouth was so dry that his tongue clove to his palate and he was tortured by a frightful thirst.

He felt that he was wet about the breast; this sensation of dampness reminded him of water, and he even wanted to drink this, whatever it was. "I must have brought the blood when I fell," he thought, and, beginning to give way more and more to terror, lest the soldiers who passed should crush him, he collected all his strength, and tried to cry: "Take me with you!" but, instead of this, he groaned so terribly that it frightened him to hear himself. Then more red fires flashed in his eyes—and it seemed to him as though the soldiers were laying stones upon him; the fires danced more and more rarely, the stones which they piled on him oppressed him more and more.

He exerted all his strength, in order to cast off the stones; he stretched himself out, and no longer saw or heard or thought or felt anything. He had been killed on the spot by a splinter of shell, in the middle of the breast.

13

Mikhaïloff, on catching sight of the bomb, fell to the earth, and, like Praskukhin, he went over in thought and feeling an incredible amount during those two seconds while the bomb lay there unexploded. He prayed to God mentally, and kept repeating: "Thy will be done!"

"And why did I enter the military service?" he thought at the same time;

"and why, again, did I exchange into the infantry, in order to take part in this campaign? Would it not have been better for me to remain in the regiment of Uhlans, in the town of T——, and pass the time with my friend Natasha? And now this is what has come of it."

And he began to count, "One, two, three, four," guessing that if it burst on the even number, he would live, but if on the uneven number, then he would be killed. "All is over; killed," he thought, when the bomb burst (he did not remember whether it was on the even or the uneven number), and he felt a blow and a sharp pain in his head. "Lord, forgive my sins," he murmured, folding his hands, then rose, and fell back senseless.

His first sensation, when he came to himself, was the blood which was flowing from his nose, and the pain in his head, which had become much less powerful. "It is my soul departing," he thought. "What will it be like *there?* Lord, receive my soul in peace! But one thing is strange," he thought, . . . "and that is that, though dying, I can still hear so plainly the footsteps of the soldiers and the report of the shots."

"Fetch the stretcher . . . hey there . . . the captain is killed!" shouted a voice over his head, which he recognized as the voice of his drummer, Ignatieff.

Some one grasped him by the shoulders. He made an effort to open his eyes, and saw overhead the dark blue heavens, clusters of stars, and two bombs, which were flying over him, one after the other; he saw Ignatieff, the soldiers with the stretcher, the ramparts, the trenches, and all at once he became convinced that he was not yet in the other world.

He had been slightly wounded in the head with a stone. His very first impression was one resembling regret; he had so beautifully and so calmly prepared himself for transit *yonder* that a return to reality, with its bombs, its trenches, and its blood, produced a disagreeable effect on him; his second impression was an involuntary joy that he was alive, and the third a desire to leave the bastion as speedily as possible. The drummer bound up his commander's head with his handkerchief, and, taking him under the arm, he led him to the place where the bandaging was going on.

"But where am I going, and why?" thought the staff-captain, when he recovered his senses a little. "It is my duty to remain with my men and not to go on ahead, . . . the more so as they will soon be out of range of the shots," some voice whispered to him.

"Never mind, my boy," he said, pulling his arm away from the obliging drummer. "I will not go to the field-hospital; I will remain with my men."

And he turned back.

"You had better have your wound properly attended to, your honor," said Ignatieff. "In the heat of the moment, it seems as if it were a trifle; but it will be the worse if not attended to. There is some inflammation rising there . . . really, now, your honor."

Mikhaïloff paused for a moment in indecision, and would have followed Ignatieff's advice, in all probability, had he not called to mind how many severely wounded men there must needs be at the field-hospital. "Perhaps the doctor will smile at my scratch," thought the staff-captain, and he returned with decision to his men, wholly regardless of the drummer's admonitions.

"And where is orderly-officer Praskukhin, who was walking with me?" he asked the lieutenant, who was leading the corps when they met.

"I don't know . . . killed, probably," replied the lieutenant, reluctantly.

"How is it that you do not know whether he was killed or wounded? He was walking with us. And why have you not carried him with you?"

"How could it be done, brother, when the place was so hot for us!"

"Ah, how could you do such a thing, Mikhaïl Ivanitch!" said Mikhaïloff, angrily. "How could you abandon him if he was alive; and if he was dead, you should still have brought away his body."

"How could he be alive when, as I tell you, I went up to him and saw!" returned the lieutenant. "As you like, however! Only, his own men might carry him off. Here, the dogs are beginning to fire cannon-balls now!" he added. . . .

Mikhaïloff sat down, and clasped his head, which the motion caused to pain him terribly.

"Yes, they must go and get him, without fail; perhaps he is still alive," said Mikhaïloff. "It is your *duty*, Mikhaïl Ivanitch!"

Mikhaïl Ivanitch made no reply.

"He did not take him at the time, and now the soldiers must be sent alone . . . and how can they be sent? their lives may be sacrificed in vain, under that hot fire," thought Mikhaïloff.

"Boys! we must go back . . . and get the officer who was wounded there in the ditch," he said, in not too loud and commanding a tone, for he felt how unpleasant it would be to the soldiers to obey his order,—and, in fact, as he did not address any one in particular by name, no one set out to fulfil it.

"And really, it is quite possible that he is already dead, and it is *not worth while* to subject the men to unnecessary danger; I alone am to blame for not having seen to it. I will go myself and learn whether he is alive. It is my *duty*," said Mikhaïloff to himself.

"Mikhaïl Ivanitch! Lead the men forward, and I will overtake you," he said, and, pulling up his overcoat with one hand, and with the other constantly touching the image of Saint Mitrofaniy, in which he cherished a special faith, he set off on a run along the trench.

Having convinced himself that Praskukhin was dead, he dragged himself back, panting, and supporting with his hand the loosened bandage and his head, which began to pain him severely. The battalion had already reached the foot of the hill, and a place almost out of range of shots, when Mikhaïloff overtook it. I say *almost* out of range because some stray bombs struck here and there.

"At all events, I must go to the hospital to-morrow, and put down my name," thought the staff-captain, as the medical student assisting the doctors bound his wound.

14

Hundreds of bodies, freshly smeared with blood, of men who two hours previous had been filled with divers lofty or petty hopes and desires, now lay, with stiffened limbs, in the dewy, flowery valley which separated the bastion from the trenches, and on the level floor of the chapel for the dead in Sevastopol; hundreds of men crawled, twisted, and groaned, with curses and prayers on their parched lips, some amid the corpses in the flower-strewn vale, others on stretchers, on cots, and on the blood-stained floor of the field-hospital.

And still, as on the days preceding, the dawn glowed, over Sapun Mountain, the twinkling stars paled, the white mist spread abroad from the dark, sounding sea, the red glow illuminated the east, long crimson cloudlets darted across the blue horizon; and still, as on days preceding, the powerful, all-beautiful sun rose up, giving promise of joy, love, and happiness to all who dwell in the world.

15

On the following day, the band of the chasseurs was playing again on the boulevard, and again officers, cadets, soldiers, and young women were promenading in festive guise about the pavilion and through the low-hanging alleys of fragrant white acacias in bloom.

Kalugin, Prince Galtzin, and some colonel or other were walking arm-in-arm near the pavilion, and discussing the engagement of the day before. As always happens in such cases, the chief governing thread of the conversation was not the engagement itself, but the part which those who were narrating the story of the affair took in it.

Their faces and the sound of their voices had a serious, almost melancholy expression, as though the losses of the preceding day had touched and saddened them deeply; but, to tell the truth, as none of them had lost any one very near to him, this expression of sorrow was an official expression, which they merely felt it to be their duty to exhibit.

On the contrary, Kalugin and the colonel were ready to see an engagement of the same sort every day, provided that they might receive a gold sword or the rank of major-general—notwithstanding the fact that they were very fine fellows.

I like it when any warrior who destroys millions to gratify his ambition is called a monster. Only question any Ensign Petrushkoff, and Sub-Lieutenant Antonoff, and so on, on their word of honor, and every one of them is a petty Napoleon, a petty monster, and ready to bring on a battle on the instant, to murder a hundred men, merely for the sake of receiving an extra star of an order or an increase of a third in his pay.

"No, excuse me," said the colonel; "it began first on the left flank. I was there myself."

"Possibly," answered Kalugin. "I was farther on the right; I went there twice. Once I was in search of the general, and the second time I went merely to inspect the lodgments. It was a hot place."

"Yes, of course, Kalugin knows," said Prince Galtzin to the colonel. "You know that V. told *me* to-day that you were a brave fellow." . . .

"But the losses, the losses were terrible," said the colonel. "I lost four hundred men from my regiment. It's a wonder that I escaped from there alive."

At this moment, the figure of Mikhaïloff, with his head bandaged, appeared at the other extremity of the boulevard, coming to meet these gentlemen.

"What, are you wounded, captain?" said Kalugin.

"Yes, slightly, with a stone," replied Mikhaïloff.

"Has the flag been lowered yet?"[1] inquired Prince Galtzin, gazing over the staff-captain's cap, and addressing himself to no one in particular.

"*Non, pas encore*," answered Mikhaïloff, who wished to show that he understood and spoke French.

"Is the truce still in force?" said Galtzin, addressing him courteously in Russian, and thereby intimating—so it seemed to the captain—It must be difficult for you to speak French, so why is it not better to talk in your own tongue simply? . . . And with this the adjutants left him. The staff-captain again felt lonely, as on the preceding day, and, exchanging salutes with various gentlemen,—some he did not care, and others he did not dare, to join,—he seated himself near Kazarsky's monument, and lighted a cigarette.

Baron Pesth also had come to the boulevard. He had been telling how he had gone over to arrange the truce, and had conversed with the French officers, and he declared that one had said to him, "If daylight had held off another half-hour, these ambushes would have been retaken;" and that he had replied, "Sir, I refrain from saying no, in order not to give you the lie," and how well he had said it, and so on.

But, in reality, although he had had a hand in the truce, he had not dared to say anything very particular there, although he had been very desirous of talking with the French (for it is awfully jolly to talk with Frenchmen!). Yunker Baron Pesth had marched up and down the line for a long time, incessantly inquiring of the Frenchmen who were near him: "To what regiment do you belong?" They answered him; and that was the end of it.

When he walked too far along the line, the French sentry, not suspecting that this soldier understood French, cursed him. "He has come to spy out our works, the cursed . . ." said he; and, in consequence, Yunker Baron Pesth, taking no further interest in the truce, went home, and thought out on the way thither those French phrases, which he had now repeated. Captain Zoboff was also on the boulevard, talking loudly, and Captain Obzhogoff, in a very disheveled condition, and an artillery captain, who courted no one, and was happy in the love of the yunkers, and all the faces which had been there on the day before, and all still actuated by the same motives. No one was missing except Praskukhin, Neferdoff, and some others, whom hardly any one remembered or thought of now, though their bodies were not yet washed, laid out, and interred in the earth.

16

White flags are hung out from our bastion and from the trenches of the French, and in the blooming valley between them lie disfigured corpses, shoeless, in garments of gray or blue, which laborers are engaged in carrying off and heaping upon carts. The odor of the dead bodies fills the air. Throngs of people have poured out of Sevastopol and from the French camp, to gaze upon this spectacle, and they press one after the other with eager and benevolent curiosity.

Listen to what these people are saying.

Here, in a group of Russians and French who have come together, is a young officer, who speaks French badly, but well enough to make himself understood, examining a cartridge-box of the guards.

[1] This sentence is in French.

"And what is this bird here for?" says he.

"Because it is a cartridge-box belonging to a regiment of the guards, monsieur, and bears the imperial eagle."

"And do you belong to the guard?"

"Pardon, monsieur, I belong to the sixth regiment of the line."

"And this—bought where?" asks the officer, pointing to a cigar-holder of yellow wood, in which the Frenchman is smoking his cigarette.

"At Balaklava, monsieur. It is very plain, of palm-wood."

"Pretty!" says the officer, guided in his conversation not so much by his own wishes as by the words which he knows.

"If you will have the kindness to keep it as a souvenir of this meeting, you will confer an obligation on me."

And the polite Frenchman blows out the cigarette, and hands the holder over to the officer, with a little bow. The officer gives him his, and all the members of the group, Frenchmen as well as Russians, appear very much pleased and smile.

Then a bold infantryman, in a pink shirt, with his overcoat hanging from his shoulders, accompanied by two other soldiers, who, with their hands behind their backs, were standing behind him, with merry, curious countenances, stepped up to a Frenchman, and requested a light for his pipe. The Frenchman brightened his fire, stirred up his short pipe, and shook out a light for the Russian.

"Tobacco good!" says the soldier in the pink shirt; and the spectators smile.

"Yes, good tobacco, Turkish tobacco," says the Frenchman. "And your tobacco—Russian?—good?"

"Russian, good,"[1] says the soldier in the pink shirt; whereupon those present shake with laughter. "The French not good—*bon jour, monsieur,*" says the soldier in the pink shirt, letting fly his entire charge of knowledge in the language at once, as he laughs and taps the Frenchman on the stomach. The French join in the laugh.

"They are not handsome, these beasts of Russians," says a zouave, amid the crowd of Frenchmen.

"What are they laughing about?" says another black-complexioned one, with an Italian accent, approaching our men.

"Caftan good," says the audacious soldier, staring at the zouave's embroidered coat-skirts, and then there is another laugh.

"Don't leave your lines; back to your places, *sacré nom!*" shouts a French corporal, and the soldiers disperse with evident reluctance.

In the meantime, our young cavalry officer is making the tour of the French officers. The conversation turns on some Count Sazonoff, "with whom I was very well acquainted, monsieur," says a French officer, with one epaulet—"he is one of those real Russian counts, of whom we are so fond."

"There is a Sazonoff with whom I am acquainted," says the cavalry officer, "but he is not a count, so far as I know, at least; a little dark-complexioned man, of about your age."

"Exactly, monsieur, that is the man. Oh, how I should like to see that dear count! If you see him, pray present my compliments to him—Captain Latour," says he, bowing.

[1] He pronounces *bon—been.*

"Isn't this a terrible business that we are conducting here? It was hot work last night, wasn't it?" says the cavalry officer, wishing to continue the conversation, and pointing to the dead bodies.

"Oh, frightful, monsieur! But what brave fellows your soldiers are—what brave fellows! It is a pleasure to fight with such valiant fellows."

"It must be admitted that your men do not hang back, either," says the cavalryman, with a bow, and the conviction that he is very amiable.

But enough of this.

Let us rather observe this lad of ten, clad in an ancient cap, his father's probably, shoes worn on bare feet, and nankeen breeches, held up by a single suspender, who has climbed over the wall at the very beginning of the truce, and has been roaming about the ravine, staring with dull curiosity at the French, and at the bodies which are lying on the earth, and plucking the blue wild-flowers with which the valley is studded. On his way home with a large bouquet, he held his nose because of the odor which the wind wafted to him, and paused beside a pile of corpses, which had been carried off the field, and stared long at one terrible, headless body, which chanced to be the nearest to him. After standing there for a long while, he stepped up closer, and touched with his foot the stiffened arm of the corpse which protruded. The arm swayed a little. He touched it again, and with more vigor. The arm swung back, and then fell into place again. And at once the boy uttered a shriek, hid his face in the flowers, and ran off to the fortifications as fast as he could go.

Yes, white flags are hung out from the bastion and the trenches, the flowery vale is filled with dead bodies, the splendid sun sinks into the blue sea, and the blue sea undulates and glitters in the golden rays of the sun. Thousands of people congregate, gaze, talk, and smile at each other. And why do not Christian people, who profess the one great law of love and self-sacrifice, when they behold what they have wrought, fall in repentance upon their knees before Him who, when He gave them life, implanted in the soul of each of them, together with a fear of death, a love of the good and the beautiful, and, with tears of joy and happiness, embrace each other like brothers? No! But it is a comfort to think that it was not we who began this war, that we are only defending our own country, our fatherland. The white flags have been hauled down, and again the weapons of death and suffering are shrieking; again innocent blood is shed, and groans and curses are audible.

I have now said all that I wish to say at this time. But a heavy thought overpowers me. Perhaps it should not have been said; perhaps what I have said belongs to one of those evil truths which, unconsciously concealed in the soul of each man, should not be uttered, lest they become pernicious, as the lees of wine should not be shaken, lest it be thereby spoiled.

Where is the expression of evil which should be avoided? Where is the expression of good which should be imitated in this sketch? Who is the villain, who the hero? All are good, and all are evil.

Neither Kalugin, with his brilliant bravery—*bravoure de gentilhomme*—and his vanity, the instigator of all deeds; nor Praskukhin, the empty-headed, harmless man, though he fell in battle for the faith, the throne, and his native land; nor Mikhaïloff, with his shyness; nor Pesth, a child with no firm convictions or principles, can be either the heroes or the villains of the tale.

The hero of my tale, whom I love with all the strength of my soul, whom I have tried to set forth in all his beauty, and who has always been, is, and always will be most beautiful, is—the truth.

1855

SEVASTOPOL IN AUGUST 1855

1

At the end of August, along the rocky highway to Sevastopol, between Duvanka[1] and Bakhtchisaraï, through the thick, hot dust, at a foot-pace, drove an officer's light cart, that peculiar telyezhka, not now to be met with, which stands about halfway between a Jewish britchka, a Russian traveling-carriage, and a basket-wagon. In the front of the wagon, jerking the reins, squatted the servant, clad in a nankeen coat and an officer's cap, which had become quite limp; behind, on bundles and packages covered with a military coat, sat an infantry officer, in a summer overcoat.

As well as he could be judged in his sitting position, the officer was not tall of stature, but extremely thick, and that not so much from shoulder to shoulder as from chest to back he was broad and thick; and his neck and the base of the head were excessively developed and tense. His waist, so called—a receding strip in the center of his body—did not exist in his case; but neither had he any belly; on the contrary, he was rather thin than otherwise, particularly in the face, which was overspread with an unhealthy yellowish sunburn. His face would have been handsome had it not been for a certain bloated appearance, and the soft, yet not elderly, heavy wrinkles that flowed together and enlarged his features, imparting to the whole countenance a general expression of coarseness and of lack of freshness. His eyes were small, brown, extremely searching, even bold; his mustache was very thick, but the ends were kept constantly short by his habit of gnawing them; and his chin, and his cheek-bones in particular, were covered with a remarkably strong, thick, and black beard, of two days' growth.

The officer had been wounded on the 10th of May, by a splinter, in the head, on which he still wore a bandage, and, having now felt perfectly well for the last week, he had come out of the Simferopol Hospital to rejoin his regiment, which was stationed somewhere in the direction from which shots could be heard; but whether that was in Sevastopol itself, in the northern suburb, or at Inkerman, he had not so far succeeded in ascertaining with much accuracy from any one.

Shots were still audible near at hand, especially at intervals, when the hills did not interfere, or when borne on the wind with great distinctness and fre-

[1] The last station before Sevastopol.

quency, and apparently near at hand. Then it seemed as though some explosion shook the air, and caused an involuntary shudder. Then, one after the other, followed less resounding reports in quick succession, like a drum-beat, interrupted at times by a startling roar. Then, everything mingled in a sort of reverberating crash, resembling peals of thunder, when a thunderstorm is in full force, and the rain has just begun to pour down in floods; every one said, and it could be heard, that a frightful bombardment was in progress.

The officer kept urging on his servant, and seemed desirous of arriving as speedily as possible. They were met by a long train of Russian peasant carts, which had carried provisions into Sevastopol, and were now returning with sick and wounded soldiers in gray coats, sailors in black paletots, volunteers in red fezzes, and bearded militiamen. The officer's light cart had to halt in the thick, immovable cloud of dust raised by the train of wagons, and the officer, blinking and frowning with the dust that stuffed his eyes and ears, gazed at the faces of the sick and wounded as they passed.

"Ah, there's a weak young soldier from our company," said the servant, turning to his master, and pointing to the wagon full of wounded, which was just on a line with them at the moment.

On the cart, toward the front, a bearded Russian, in a lamb's-wool cap, was seated sidewise, and, holding the stock of his whip under his elbow, was tying on the lash. Behind him in the cart, about five soldiers, in different positions, were shaking about. One, though pale and thin, with his arm in a bandage, and his overcoat hanging, with sleeves unused, from his shoulders, over his shirt, was sitting up bravely in the middle of the cart, and tried to touch his cap on seeing the officer, but immediately afterward (recollecting, probably, that he was wounded) he pretended that he only wanted to scratch his head. Another, beside him, was lying flat on the bottom of the wagon; all that was visible was two hands, as they clung to the rails of the wagon, and his knees uplifted limp as mops, as they swayed about in various directions. A third, with a swollen face and a bandaged head, on which was placed his soldier's cap, sat on one side, with his legs dangling over the wheel, and, with his elbows resting on his knees, seemed immersed in thought. It was to him that the passing officer addressed himself.

"Dolzhnikoff!" he exclaimed.

"Here," replied the soldier, opening his eyes, and pulling off his cap, in such a thick and halting bass voice that it seemed as though twenty soldiers had uttered an exclamation at one and the same time.

"Where were you wounded, my boy?"

The leaden and swimming eyes of the soldier grew animated; he evidently recognized his officer.

"I wish yourhonor health!" he began again, in the same abrupt bass as before.

"Where is the regiment stationed now?"

"It was stationed in Sevastopol, but they were to move on Wednesday, yourhonor."

"Where to?"

"I don't know; it must have been to the Sivernaya, yourhonor! To-day, yourhonor," he added in a drawling voice, as he put on his cap, "they have begun to fire clear across, mostly with bombs, that even go as far as the bay; they are fighting horribly to-day, so that . . ."

It was impossible to hear what the soldier said further; but it was evident, from the expression of his countenance and from his attitude, that he was uttering discouraging remarks, with the touch of malice of a man who is suffering.

The traveling officer, Lieutenant Kozeltzoff, was no common officer. He was not one of those that live so and so and do thus and so because others live and do thus; he did whatever he pleased, and others did the same, and were convinced that it was well. He was rather richly endowed by nature with small gifts: he sang well, played on the guitar, talked very cleverly, and wrote very easily, particularly official documents, in which he had practised his hand in his capacity of adjutant of the battalion; but the most noticeable point in his character was his egotistical energy, which, although chiefly founded on this array of petty talents, constituted in itself a sharp and striking feature. His egotism was of the sort that is most frequently found developed in purely masculine and especially in military circles, and which had become a part of his life to such a degree that he understood no other choice than to domineer or to humiliate himself; and his egotism was the mainspring even of his private impulses; he liked to usurp the first place over people with whom he put himself on a level.

"Well! it's absurd of me to listen to what a Moskva[2] chatters!" muttered the lieutenant, experiencing a certain weight of apathy in his heart, and a dimness of thought, which the sight of the transport full of wounded and the words of the soldier, whose significance was emphasized and confirmed by the sounds of the bombardment, had left with him. "*That Moskva is ridiculous!* Drive on, Nikolaeff! go ahead! Are you asleep?" he added, rather fretfully, to the servant, as he rearranged the skirts of his coat.

The reins were tightened, Nikolaeff clacked his lips, and the wagon moved on at a trot.

"We will only halt a minute for food, and will proceed at once, this very day," said the officer.

2

As he entered the street of the ruined remains of the stone walls forming the Tartar houses of Duvanka, Lieutenant Kozeltzoff was stopped by a transport of bombs and cannon-balls, which were on their way to Sevastopol, and had accumulated on the road. Two infantry soldiers were seated in the dust, on the stones of a ruined garden-wall by the roadside, devouring a watermelon and bread.

"Have you come far, fellow-countryman?" said one of them, as he chewed his bread, to a soldier with a small knapsack on his back, who had halted near them.

"I have come from my government to join my regiment," replied the soldier, turning his eyes away from the watermelon, and readjusting the sack on his back. "There we were, two weeks ago, at work on the hay, a whole troop of us; but now they have drafted all of us, and we don't know where our regiment is

[2] In many regiments the officers call a soldier, half in scorn, half caressingly, *Moskva* (Moscovite).

at the present time. They say that our men went on the Korabelnaya last week. Have you heard anything, gentlemen?"

"It's stationed in the town, comrade, in the town," said the second, an old soldier of the reserves, digging away with his clasp-knife at the white, unripe melon. "We have just come from there, this afternoon. It's terrible, my boy!"

"How so, gentlemen?"

"Don't you hear? They are firing all around to-day, so that there is not a whole spot anywhere. It is impossible to say how many of our brethren have been killed." And the speaker waved his hand and adjusted his cap.

The passing soldier shook his head thoughtfully, gave a clack with his tongue, then pulled his pipe from his boot-leg, and, without filling it, stirred up the half-burned tobacco, lit a bit of tinder from the soldier who was smoking, and raised his cap.

"There is no one like God, gentlemen! I ask your pardon," said he, and, with a shake of the sack on his back, he went his way.

"Hey, there! you'd better wait," said the man who was digging out the watermelon, with an air of conviction.

"It makes no difference!" muttered the traveler, threading his way among the wheels of the assembled wagons.

3

The posting-station was full of people when Kozeltzoff drove up to it. The first person whom he encountered, on the porch itself, was a thin and very young man, the superintendent, who continued his altercation with two officers, who had followed him out.

"It's not three days only, but ten that you will have to wait. Even generals wait, my good sirs!" said the superintendent, with a desire to administer a prick to the travelers; "and I am not going to harness up for you."

"Then don't give anybody horses, if there are none! But why furnish them to some lackey or other with baggage?" shouted the elder of the two officers, with a glass of tea in his hand, and plainly avoiding the use of pronouns,[1] but giving it to be understood that he might very easily address the superintendent as "thou."

"Judge for yourself, now, Mr. Superintendent," said the younger officer, with some hesitation. "We don't want to go for our own pleasure. We must certainly be needed, since we have been called for. And I certainly shall report to the general. But this, of course, you know—that you are not paying proper respect to the military profession."

"You are always spoiling things," the elder man interrupted, with vexation. "You only hinder me; you must know how to talk to him. Here, now, he has lost his respect. Horses this very instant, I say!"

"I should be glad to give them to you, batiushka,[2] but where am I to get them?"

After a brief silence, the superintendent began to grow irritated, and to talk, flourishing his hands the while.

---

[1] This effect cannot be reproduced in English.

[2] "My good sir," literally, "little father," a familiarly respectful mode of address.

"I understand, batiushka. And I know all about it myself. But what are you going to do? Only give me"—here a ray of hope gleamed across the faces of the officers—"only give me a chance to live until the end of the month, and you won't see me here any longer. I'd rather go on the Malakhoff hill, by Heavens! than stay here. Let them do what they please about it! There's not a single sound team in the station this day, and the horses haven't seen a wisp of hay these three days." And the superintendent disappeared behind the gate.

Kozeltzoff entered the room in company with the officers.

"Well," said the elder officer, quite calmly, to the younger one, although but a second before he had appeared to be greatly irritated, "we have been traveling these three weeks, and we will wait a little longer. There's no harm done. We shall get there at last."

The dirty, smoky apartment was so filled with officers and trunks that it was with difficulty that Kozeltzoff found a place near the window, where he seated himself; he began to roll himself a cigarette, as he glanced at the faces and lent an ear to the conversations.

To the right of the door, near a crippled and greasy table, upon which stood two samovars, whose copper had turned green in spots, here and there, and where sugar was spread out in various papers, sat the principal group: a young officer, without mustache, in a new, short, wadded summer coat, was pouring water into the teapot; four such young officers were there, in different corners of the room. One of them had placed some sort of fur coat under his head, and was fast asleep on the divan. Another, standing by the table, was cutting up some roast mutton for an officer without an arm, who was seated at the table.

Two officers, one in an adjutant's overcoat, the other in an infantry overcoat, a thin one, however, and with a satchel strapped over his shoulder, were sitting near the oven-bench, and it was evident, from the very way in which they stared at the rest, and from the manner in which the one with the satchel smoked his cigar, that they were not line officers on duty at the front, and that they were glad of it.

Not that there was any scorn apparent in their manner, but there was a certain self-satisfied tranquillity, founded partly on money and partly on their close intimacy with generals,—a certain consciousness of superiority which even extended to a desire to hide it.

A thick-lipped young doctor and an officer of artillery, with a German cast of countenance, were seated almost on the feet of the young officer who was sleeping on the divan, and counting over their money.

There were four officer's servants, some dozing and others busy with the trunks and packages near the door.

Among all these faces, Kozeltzoff did not find a single familiar one; but he began to listen with curiosity to the conversation. The young officers, who, as he instantly decided from their looks alone, had but just come out of the military academy, pleased him, and, what was the principal point, they reminded him that his brother had also come from the military academy, and should have recently joined one of the batteries of Sevastopol.

But everything about the officer with the satchel, whose face he had seen before somewhere, seemed bold and repulsive to him. He even left the window, and, going to the stove-bench, seated himself on it, with the thought that he would "put the fellow down if he took it into his head to say anything." In general, purely as a brave "line" officer, he did not like "the staff," such as he had recognized these two officers to be at the first glance.

4

"But this is dreadfully annoying," said one of the young officers, "to be so near, and yet not be able to get there. Perhaps there will be an action this very day, and we shall not be there."

In the sharp voice and the mottled freshness of the color that swept across the youthful face of this officer as he spoke, there was apparent the sweet young timidity of the man who is constantly afraid lest his every word shall not turn out exactly right.

The one-armed officer glanced at him with a smile.

"You will get there soon enough, I assure you," he said.

The young officer looked with respect at the haggard face of the armless officer, so unexpectedly illuminated by a smile, held his peace for a while, and busied himself once more with his tea. In fact, the one-armed officer's face, his attitude, and, most of all, the empty sleeve of his coat, expressed much of that tranquil indifference which may be explained in this way—that he looked upon every conversation and every occurrence as though saying, "That is all very fine; I know all about that, and I can do a little of that myself, if I only choose."

"What is our decision to be?" said the young officer again to his companion in the short coat. "Shall we pass the night here, or shall we proceed with our own horse?"

His comrade declined to proceed.

"Just imagine, captain," said the one who was pouring the tea, turning to the one-armed man, and picking up the knife that the latter had dropped, "they told us that horses were frightfully dear in Sevastopol, so we bought a horse in partnership at Simferopol."

"They made you pay pretty high for it, I fancy."

"Really, I do not know, captain; we paid ninety rubles for it and the wagon. Is that very dear?" he added, turning to all the company, and to Kozeltzoff, who was staring at him.

"It was not dear, if the horse is young," said Kozeltzoff.

"Really? but they told us that it was dear. Only, she limps a little, but that will pass off. They told us that she was very strong."

"What military academy are you from?" asked Kozeltzoff, who wished to inquire for his brother.

"We are just from the regiment of the nobility; there are six of us, and we are on our way to Sevastopol at our own desire," said the talkative young officer. "But we do not know where our battery is; some say that it is in Sevastopol, others that it is at Odessa."

"Was it not possible to find out at Simferopol?" asked Kozeltzoff.

"They do not know there. Just imagine, one of our comrades went to the headquarters there, and they were impertinent to him. You can imagine how disagreeable that was! Would you like to have me make you a cigarette?" he said at that moment to the one-armed officer, who was just pulling out his cigarette-case.

He waited on the latter with a sort of servile enthusiasm.

"And are you from Sevastopol also?" he went on. "Oh, good heavens, how wonderful that is! How much we did think of you, and of all our heroes, in Petersburg," he said, turning to Kozeltzoff with respect and good-natured flattery.

"Really? And now, perhaps, you may have to go back?" inquired the lieutenant.

"That is just what we are afraid of. You can imagine that, after having bought the horse, and provided ourselves with all the necessaries,—a coffee-pot with a spirit-lamp, and other indispensable trifles,—we have no money left," he said, in a low voice, as he glanced at his companion; "so that, if we have to go back, we don't know what is to be done."

"Have you received no money for traveling expenses?" inquired Kozeltzoff.

"No," replied he, in a whisper; "they only promised to give it to us here."

"Have you the certificate?"

"I know that . . . the principal thing . . . is the certificate; but a senator in Moscow,—he's my uncle,—when I was at his house, said that they would give it to us here; otherwise, he would have given me some himself. So they will give it to us here?"

"Most certainly they will."

"I too think that they will," he said, in a tone which showed that, after having made the same identical inquiry in thirty posting-stations, and having everywhere received different answers, he no longer believed any one implicitly.

5

"Who ordered beet-soup?" called out the slatternly mistress of the house, a fat woman of forty, as she entered the room with a bowl of soup.

The conversation ceased at once, and all who were in the room fixed their eyes on the woman. One officer even instigated another officer, by a wink, to look at her.

"Ah, it was Kozeltzoff who ordered it," said the young officer. "He must be waked. Get up for your dinner," he said, approaching the sleeper on the divan, and jogging his elbow.

A young lad of seventeen, with merry black eyes and red cheeks, sprang energetically from the sofa, and stood in the middle of the room, rubbing his eyes.

"Ah, excuse me, please," he said to the doctor, whom he had touched in rising.

Lieutenant Kozeltzoff immediately recognized his brother, and stepped up to him.

"Don't you know me?" he said, with a smile.

"A-a-a-h!" exclaimed the younger brother; "this is astonishing!" And he began to kiss his brother.

They kissed twice, but hesitated at the third repetition, as though the thought had occurred to both of them:—

"Why is it necessary to do it exactly three times?"

"Well, *how* I am delighted!" said the elder, looking at his brother. "Let us go out on the porch; we can have a talk."

"Come, come. I don't want any soup, you eat it, Federsohn!" he said to his comrade.

"But you wanted something to eat."

"I don't want anything."

When they emerged on the porch, the younger kept asking his brother, "Well, how are you; tell me all about it." And still he kept on saying how glad he was to see him, but he told nothing himself.

When five minutes had elapsed, during which time they had succeeded in becoming somewhat silent, the elder brother inquired why the younger had not gone into the guards, as they had all expected him to do.

He wanted to get to Sevastopol as speedily as possible, he said; for if things turned out favorably there, he could get advancement more rapidly than in the guards. There it takes ten years to reach the grade of colonel, while here Todleben had risen in two years from lieutenant-colonel to general. Well, and if one did get killed, there was nothing to be done.

"What a fellow you are!" said his brother, smiling.

"But the principal thing, do you know, brother," said the younger, smiling and blushing as though he were preparing to say something very disgraceful, "all this is nonsense, and the principal reason why I asked it was that I was ashamed to live in Petersburg when men are dying for their country here. Yes, and I wanted to be with you," he added, with still greater shamefacedness.

"How absurd you are!" said the elder brother, pulling out his cigarette-case, and not even glancing at him. "It's a pity, though, that we can't be together."

"Now, honestly, is it so terrible in the bastions?" inquired the younger man, abruptly.

"It is terrible at first, but you get used to it afterward. It's nothing. You will see for yourself."

"And tell me still another thing. What do you think?—will Sevastopol be taken? I think that it will not."

"God knows!"

"But one thing is annoying. Just imagine what bad luck! A whole bundle was stolen from us on the road, and it had my shako in it, so that now I am in a dreadful predicament; and I don't know how I am to show myself."

The younger Kozeltzoff, Vladimir, greatly resembled his brother Mikhaïl, but he resembled him as a budding rose bush resembles a wild rose bush that is out of flower. His hair was chestnut also, but it was thick and lay in curls on his temples. On the soft white back of his neck there was a blond lock; a sign of good luck, so the nurses say. The full-blooded crimson of youth did not stand fixed on the soft, white hue of his face, but flashed up and betrayed all the movements of his mind. He had the same eyes as his brother, but they were more widely opened, and clearer, which appeared the more peculiar because they were veiled frequently by a slight moisture. A golden down was sprouting on his cheeks, and over his ruddy lips, which were very often folded into a shy smile, displaying teeth of dazzling whiteness. He was a well-formed and broad-shouldered fellow, in unbuttoned coat, from beneath which was visible a red shirt with a slanting collar. As he stood before his brother, leaning his elbows on the railing of the porch, with cigarette in hand and innocent joy in his face and gesture, he was so agreeable and comely a youth that any one would have gazed at him with delight. He was extremely pleased with his brother, he looked at him with respect and pride, fancying him his hero; but in some ways, so far as judgments on worldly culture, ability to talk French, behavior in the society of distinguished people, dancing, and so on, he was somewhat ashamed of him, looked down on him, and even cherished a hope of improving him if such a thing were possible.

All his impressions, so far, were from Petersburg, from the house of a lady who was fond of good-looking young fellows and who had had him spend his holidays with her, and from Moscow, from the house of a senator, where he had once danced at a great ball.

6

Having nearly talked their fill and having arrived at the feeling that you frequently experience, that there is little in common between you, though you love one another, the brothers were silent for a few moments.

"Pick up your things and we will set out at once," said the elder.

The younger suddenly blushed, stammered, and became confused.

"Are we to go straight to Sevastopol?" he inquired, after a momentary pause.

"Why, yes. You can't have many things, and we can manage to carry them, I think."

"Very good! we will start at once," said the younger, with a sigh, and he went inside.

But he paused in the vestibule without opening the door, dropped his head gloomily, and began to reflect.

"Straight to Sevastopol, on the instant, within range of the bombs . . . frightful! It's no matter, however; it must have come sometime. Now, at all events, with my brother . . ."

The fact was that it was only now, at the thought that, once seated in the cart, he would enter Sevastopol without dismounting from it, and that no chance occurrence could any longer detain him, that the danger which he was seeking clearly presented itself to him, and he was troubled at the very thought of its nearness. He managed to control himself after a fashion, and entered the room; but a quarter of an hour elapsed, and still he had not rejoined his brother, so that the latter opened the door at last, in order to call him. The younger Kozeltzoff, in the attitude of a naughty school-boy, was saying something to an officer named P. When his brother opened the door, he became utterly confused.

"Immediately. I'll come out in a minute!" he cried, waving his hand at his brother. "Wait for me there, please."

A moment later he emerged, in fact, and approached his brother, with a deep sigh.

"Just imagine! I cannot go with you, brother," he said.

"What? What nonsense is this?"

"I will tell you the whole truth, Misha! Not one of us has any money, and we are all in debt to that staff-captain whom you saw there. It is horribly mortifying!"

The elder brother frowned, and did not break the silence for a long while.

"Do you owe much?" he asked, glancing askance at his brother.

"A great deal . . . no, not a great deal; but I am dreadfully ashamed of it. He has paid for me for three stages, and all his sugar is gone, so that I do not know . . . yes, and we played at preference. I am a little in his debt there, too."

"This is bad, Volodya! Now, what would you have done if you had not met me?" said the elder, sternly, without looking at his brother.

"Why, I was thinking, brother, that I should get that traveling-money at Sevastopol, and that I would give him that. Surely, that can be done? And it will be better for me to go with him to-morrow."

The elder brother pulled out his purse, and, with fingers that shook a little, he took out two ten-ruble notes, and one for three rubles.

"This is all the money I have," said he. "How much do you owe?"

Kozeltzoff did not speak the exact truth when he said that this was all the money he had. He had, besides, four gold pieces sewn into his cuff, in case of an emergency; but he had taken a vow not to touch them.

It appeared that Kozeltzoff, what with preference and sugar, was in debt to the amount of eight rubles only. The elder brother gave him this sum, merely remarking that one should not play preference when one had no money.

"For what stakes did you play?"

The younger brother answered not a word. His brother's question seemed to him to cast a reflection on his honor. Vexation at himself, shame at his conduct, which could give rise to such a suspicion, and the insult from his brother, of whom he was so fond, produced upon his sensitive nature so deeply painful an impression that he made no reply. Conscious that he was not in a condition to restrain the sobs which rose in his throat, he took the money without glancing at it, and went back to his comrades.

7

Nikolaeff, who had fortified himself at Duvanka with two jugs of vodka, purchased from a soldier who was peddling it on the bridge, gave the reins a jerk, and the team jolted away over the stony road, shaded here and there, which led along the Belbek to Sevastopol; but the brothers, whose legs jostled each other, maintained a stubborn silence, although they were thinking of each other every instant.

"Why did he insult me?" thought the younger. "Could he not have held his tongue about that? It is exactly as though he thought that I was a thief; yes, and now he is angry, apparently, so that we have quarreled for good. And how splendid it would have been for us to be together in Sevastopol. Two brothers, on friendly terms, both fighting the foe! one of them, the elder, though not very cultivated, yet a valiant warrior, and the other younger, but a brave fellow too. In a week's time I would have shown every one that I am not such a young-ster after all! I shall cease to blush, there will be manliness in my countenance, and, though my mustache is not very large now, it would grow to a good size by that time;" and he pulled the down which was making its appearance round the edges of his mouth. "Perhaps we shall arrive to-day, and get directly into the conflict, my brother and I. He must be obstinate and very brave, one of those who do not say much, but act better than others. I should like to know," he continued, "whether he is squeezing me against the side of the wagon on purpose or not. He probably is conscious that I feel awkward, and he is pretending not to notice me. We shall arrive to-day," he went on with his argument, pressing close to the side of the wagon, and fearing to move lest his brother should observe that he was uncomfortable, "and, all at once, we shall go straight to the bastion. We shall both go together, I with the guns, and my brother with his company. All of a sudden, the French throw themselves on us. I begin to fire, and fire on them. I kill a terrible number; but they still continue to run straight at me. Now, it is impossible to fire any longer, and there is no hope for me; all at once my brother rushes out in front with his sword, and I grasp my gun, and we rush on with the soldiers. The French throw themselves on my brother. I hasten up; I kill one Frenchman, then another, and I save my brother. I am wounded in one arm; I seize my gun with the other, and continue my flight; but my brother is slain by my side by the bullets. I halt for a moment, and gaze at him so sorrowfully; then I straighten myself up and shout: 'Follow me! We will avenge him! I loved my brother more than any one in the world,' I shall say, 'and I have lost him. Let us avenge him! Let us annihilate the foe, or let us all die together there!' All shout, and fling themselves after me. Then the whole French army makes a sortie, including even Pélissier himself. We all fight; but, at last, I am wounded a second, a third time, and I fall, wounded unto death. Then, all rush up to me. Gortchakoff comes up and asks what I would like. I say that I want nothing—except that I may be laid beside my brother, that I wish to die with him. They carry me, and lay me down by the side of my brother's bloody corpse. Then I shall raise myself, and merely say: 'Yes, you did not understand how to value two men who really loved their fatherland; now they have both fallen,—and may God forgive you!' and I shall die."

Who knows in what measure these dreams will be realized?

"Have you ever been in a hand-to-hand fight?" he suddenly inquired of his brother, quite forgetting that he had not meant to speak to him.

"No, not once," answered the elder. "Our regiment has lost two thousand men, all on the works; and I, also, was wounded there. War is not carried on in the least as you fancy, Volodya."

The word "Volodya" touched the younger brother. He wanted to come to an explanation with his brother, who had not the least idea that he had offended Volodya.

"You are not angry with me, Misha?" he said, after a momentary silence.

"What about?"

"Why, because . . . because we had such a . . . nothing."

"Not in the least," replied the elder, turning to him, and slapping him on the leg.

"Then forgive me, Misha, if I have wounded you."

And the younger brother turned aside, in order to hide the tears that suddenly started to his eyes.

8

"Is this Sevastopol already?" asked the younger brother, as they ascended the hill.

And before them appeared the bay, with its masts of ships, its shipping, and the sea, with the hostile fleet in the distance; the white batteries on the shore, the barracks, the aqueducts, the docks, and the buildings of the town, and the white and lilac clouds of smoke rising incessantly over the yellow hills, which surrounded the town and stood out against the blue sky, in the rosy rays of the sun, which was reflected by the waves, and sinking toward the horizon of the shadowy sea.

Volodya, without the slightest shudder, gazed upon this terrible place of which he had thought so much; on the contrary, he did so with an esthetic enjoyment, and a heroic sense of self-satisfaction at the idea that he would be there in another half-hour, that he would behold that really charmingly original spectacle —and he stared with concentrated attention from that moment until they arrived at the north fortification, at the baggage-train of his brother's regiment, where they were to ascertain with certainty the situations of the regiment and the battery.

The officer in charge of the train lived near the so-called new town (huts built of boards by the sailors' families), in a tent, connecting with a tolerably large shed, constructed out of green oak boughs, that were not yet entirely withered.

The brothers found the officer seated before a greasy table, upon which stood a glass of cold tea, a tray with vodka, crumbs of dry sturgeon roe, and bread, clad only in a shirt of a dirty yellow hue, and engaged in counting a huge pile of bank-bills on a large abacus.

But before describing the personality of the officer, and his conversation, it is indispensable that we should inspect with more attention the interior of his shed, and become a little acquainted, at least, with his mode of life and his occupations. The new shed, like those built for generals and regimental commanders, was large, closely wattled, and comfortably arranged, with little tables and benches made of turf. The sides and roof were hung with three rugs, to keep the leaves from showering down, and, though extremely ugly, they were new, and certainly costly.

Upon the iron bed, which stood beneath the principal rug, with a young lady on horseback depicted on it, lay a plush coverlet, of a brilliant crimson, a torn and dirty pillow, and a racoon-lined cloak. On the table stood a mirror in a silver frame, a silver brush, frightfully dirty, a broken horn comb, full of greasy hair, a silver candlestick, a bottle of liqueur with a huge gold and red label, a gold watch with a portrait of Peter I., two gold pens, a small box containing pills of some sort, a crust of bread, and some old castaway cards, and there were bottles, both full and empty, under the bed.

This officer had charge of the commissariat of the regiment and the fodder of the horses. With him lived his great friend, the commissioner who had charge of the operations.

At the moment when the brothers entered, the latter was asleep in the tent, and the commissary officer was making up his accounts of the government money, in anticipation of the end of the month. The commissary officer had a very comely and warlike exterior. His stature was tall, his mustache huge, and he possessed a respectable amount of plumpness. The only disagreeable points about him were a certain perspiration and puffiness of the whole face, which almost concealed his small gray eyes (as though he was filled up with porter), and an excessive lack of cleanliness, from his thin, greasy hair, to his big, bare feet, thrust into some sort of ermine slippers.

"Money, money!" said Kozeltzoff number one, entering the shed, and fixing his eyes, with involuntary greed, upon the pile of bank-notes. "You might lend me half of that, Vasily Mikhaïlitch!"

The commissary officer cringed at the sight of his visitors, and, sweeping up his money, he bowed to them without rising.

"Oh, if it only belonged to me! It's government money, my dear fellow. And who is this you have with you?" said he, thrusting the money into a coffer which stood beside him, and staring at Volodya.

"This is my brother, who has just come from the military academy. We have both come to learn from you where our regiment is stationed."

"Sit down, gentlemen," said the officer, rising, and going into the tent, without paying any heed to his guests. "Won't you have something to drink? Some porter, for instance?" said he.

"Don't put yourself out, Vasily Mikhaïlitch."

Volodya was impressed by the size of the commissary officer, by his carelessness of manner, and by the respect with which his brother addressed him.

"It must be that this is one of their very fine officers, whom every one respects. Really, he is simple, but hospitable and brave," he thought, seating himself in a timid and modest manner on the divan.

"Where is our regiment stationed, then?" called out his elder brother across the tent.

"What?"

He repeated his query.

"Zeifer has been here to-day. He told me that they had removed to the fifth bastion."

"Is that true?"

"If I say so, it must be true; but the deuce only knows, anyway! He would think nothing of telling a lie. Won't you have some porter?" said the commissary officer, still from the tent.

"I will, if you please," said Kozeltzoff.

"And will you have a drink, Osip Ignatievitch?" went on the voice in the tent, apparently addressing the sleeping commissioner. "You have slept enough; it's five o'clock."

"Why do you worry me? I am not asleep," answered a shrill, languid little voice.

"Come, get up! we find it stupid without you."

And the commissary officer came out to his guests.

"Fetch some Simferopol porter!" he shouted.

A servant entered the booth, with a haughty expression of countenance, as it seemed to Volodya, and, having jostled Volodya, he drew forth the porter from beneath the bench.

The bottle of porter had already been emptied, and the conversation had proceeded in the same style for rather a long time, when the flap of the tent flew open, and out stepped a short, fresh-colored man, in a blue dressing-gown with tassels, in a cap with a red rim and a cockade. At the moment of his appearance, he was smoothing his small black mustache, and, with his gaze fixed on the rugs, he replied to the greetings of the officer by a barely perceptible movement of the shoulders.

"I will drink a small glassful too!" said he, seating himself by the table. "What is this, have you come from Petersburg, young man?" he said, turning courteously to Volodya.

"Yes, sir, I am on my way to Sevastopol."

"Did you make the application yourself?"

"Yes, sir."

"What queer tastes you have, gentlemen! I do not understand it!" continued the commissioner. "It strikes me that I should be ready just now to travel on foot to Petersburg, if I could get away. By Heavens, I am tired of this cursed life!"

"What is there about it that does not suit you?" said the elder Kozeltzoff, turning to him. "You're the very last person to complain of life here!"

The commissioner cast a look upon him, and then turned away.

"This danger, these privations, it is impossible to get anything here," he continued, addressing Volodya. "And why you should take such a freak, gentlemen, I really cannot understand. If there were any advantages to be derived from it, but there is nothing of the sort. It would be a nice thing, now, wouldn't it, if you, at your age, were to be left a cripple for life!"

"Some need the money, and some serve for honor's sake!" said the elder Kozeltzoff, in a tone of vexation, joining the discussion once more.

"What's the good of honor, when there's nothing to eat!" said the commissioner, with a scornful laugh, turning to the commissary, who also laughed at this. "Give us something from 'Lucia'; we will listen," he said, pointing to the music-box. "I love it."

"Well, is that Vasily Mikhaïlitch a fine man?" Volodya asked his brother when they emerged, at dusk, from the shed, and pursued their way to Sevastopol.

"Not at all, but such a niggard that it is a perfect terror! And I can't bear the sight of that commissioner. I shall give him a thrashing one of these days."

9

Volodya was not precisely out of sorts when, nearly at nightfall, they reached the great bridge over the bay, but he felt a certain heaviness at his heart. All that he had heard and seen was so little in consonance with the impressions which had recently passed away: the huge, light examination hall, with its polished floor, the kind and merry voices and laughter of his comrades, the new uniform, his beloved Tzar, whom he had been accustomed to see for the last seven years, and who, when he took leave of them had called them his children, with tears in his eyes,—and everything that he had seen so little resembled his very beautiful, rainbow-hued, magnificent dreams.

"Well, here we are at last!" said the elder brother, when they arrived at the Mikhaïloff battery, and dismounted from their cart. "If they let us pass the bridge, we will go directly to the Nikolaeff barracks. You stay there until morning, and I will go to the regiment and find out where your battery is stationed, and to-morrow I will come for you."

"But why? It would be better if we both went together," said Volodya; "I will go to the bastion with you. It won't make any difference; I shall have to get used to it. If you go, then I can too."

"Better not go."

"No, if you please; I shall find out, at least, that . . ."

"My advice is, not to go; but as you choose." . . .

The sky was clear and dark; the stars, and the incessantly moving fires of the bombs and discharges, gleamed brilliantly through the gloom. The large white building of the battery and the beginning of the bridge stood out in the darkness. Literally, every second several discharges of artillery and explosions, following each other in quick succession or occurring simultaneously, shook the air with increasing thunder and distinctness. Through this roar, and as though playing an accompaniment, the melancholy dash of the waves was audible. A faint breeze was drawing in from the sea, and the air was heavy with moisture. The brothers stepped upon the bridge. A soldier struck his gun awkwardly against his arm, and shouted:—

"Who goes there?"

"A soldier."

"The orders are not to let any one pass!"

"What of that! We have business! We must pass!"

"Ask the officer."

The officer, who was drowsing as he sat on an anchor, rose up and gave the order to let them pass.

"You can go that way, but not this. Where are you driving to, all in a heap!" he cried to the transport wagons, piled high with gabions, which had clustered about the entrance.

As they descended to the first pontoon, the brothers encountered soldiers who were coming thence, and talking loudly.

"If he has received his ammunition money, then he has squared his accounts in full . . . that's what it is!"

"Eh, comrades!" said another voice, "when you get over on the Syevernaya[1] you will see the world, by Heavens! The air is entirely different."

"You may say more!" said the first speaker. "A cursed shell flew in there the other day, and it tore the legs off of two sailors, so that . . ."

The brothers traversed the first pontoon, while waiting for the wagon, and halted on the second, which was already flooded with water in parts. The breeze, which had seemed weak inland, was very powerful here, and came in gusts; the bridge swayed to and fro, and the waves, beating noisily against the beams, and tearing at the cables and anchors, flooded the planks. At the right the gloomily hostile sea roared and darkled, as it lay separated by an interminable level black line from the starry horizon, which was light gray, in its gleam; lights flashed afar on the enemy's fleet; on the left towered the black masts of one of our vessels, and the waves could be heard as they beat against her hull; a steamer was visible, as it moved noisily and swiftly from the Syevernaya.

The flash of a bomb, as it burst near it, illuminated for a moment the lofty heaps of gabions on the deck, two men who were standing on it, and the white foam and the spurts of greenish waves, as the steamer plowed through them. On the edge of the bridge, with his legs dangling in the water, sat a man in his shirt-sleeves, who was repairing something connected with the pontoon. In front, over Sevastopol, floated the same fires, and the terrible sounds grew louder and

[1] The *northern* suburb.

louder. A wave rolled in from the sea, flowed over the right side of the bridge, and wet Volodya's feet; two soldiers passed them, dragging their feet through the water. Something suddenly burst with a crash and lighted up the bridge ahead of them, the wagon driving over it, and a man on horseback, and the splinters fell into the waves with a hiss, and sent up the water in splashes.

"Ah, Mikhaïlo Semyonitch!" said the rider, stopping, reining in his horse in front of the elder Kozeltzoff, "have you fully recovered already?"

"As you see. Whither is God taking you?"

"To the Syevernaya, for cartridges; I am on my way to the adjutant of the regiment . . . we expect an assault to-morrow, at any hour."

"And where is Martzoff?"

"He lost a leg yesterday; he was in the town, asleep in his room. . . . Is it possible that you know him?"

"The regiment is in the fifth bastion, isn't it?"

"Yes; it has taken the place of the M—— regiment. Go to the field-hospital; some of our men are there, and they will show you the way."

"Well, and are my quarters on the Morskaya still intact?"

"Why, my good fellow, they were smashed to bits long ago by the bombs. You will not recognize Sevastopol now; there's not a single woman there now, nor any public houses nor music; the last establishment took its departure yesterday. It has become horribly dismal there now. . . . Farewell!"

And the officer rode on his way at a trot.

All at once, Volodya became terribly frightened; it seemed to him as though a cannon-ball or a splinter of bomb would fly in their direction, and strike him directly on the head. This damp darkness, all these sounds, especially the angry splashing of the waves, seemed to be saying to him that he ought not to go any farther, that nothing good awaited him yonder, that he would never again set foot on the ground upon this side of the bay, that he must turn about at once, and flee somewhere or other, as far as possible from this terrible haunt of death. "But perhaps it is too late now, everything is settled," thought he, trembling partly at this thought and partly because the water had soaked through his boots and wet his feet.

Volodya heaved a deep sigh, and went a little apart from his brother.

"Lord, will they kill me—me in particular? Lord, have mercy on me!" said he, in a whisper, and he crossed himself.

"Come, Volodya, let us go on!" said the elder brother, when their little cart had driven upon the bridge. "Did you see that bomb?"

On the bridge, the brothers met wagons filled with the wounded, with gabions, and one loaded with furniture, which was driven by a woman. On the farther side no one detained them.

Clinging instinctively to the walls of the Nikolaeff battery, the brothers listened in silence to the noise of the bombs, exploding overhead, and to the roar of the fragments, showering down upon their heads, and came to that spot in the battery where the image was. There they learned that the fifth light battery, to which Volodya had been assigned, was stationed on the Korabelnaya, and they decided that he should go, in spite of the danger, and pass the night with the elder in the fifth bastion, and that he should from there join his battery the next day. They turned into the corridor, stepping over the legs of the sleeping soldiers, who were lying all along the walls of the battery, and at last they arrived at the field-hospital.

10

As they entered the first room, surrounded with cots on which lay the wounded, and permeated with the frightful and disgusting hospital odor, they met two Sisters of Mercy, who were coming to meet them.

One woman of fifty, with black eyes, and a stern expression of countenance, was carrying bandages and lint, and was giving strict orders to a young fellow, an assistant surgeon, who was following her; the other, a very pretty girl of twenty, with a pale and delicate little fair face, gazed in a peculiarly amiable and helpless way from beneath her white cap, held her hands in the pockets of her apron, as she walked beside the elder woman, and seemed to be afraid to quit her side.

Kozeltzoff addressed to them the question whether they knew where Martzoff was—the man whose leg had been torn off on the day before.

"He belonged to the P—— regiment, did he not?" inquired the elder. "Is he a relative of yours?"

"No, a comrade."

"Show them the way," said she, in French, to the young sister. "Here, this way," and she approached a wounded man, in company with the assistant.

"Come along; what are you staring at?" said Kozeltzoff to Volodya, who, with uplifted eyebrows and somewhat suffering expression of countenance, could not tear himself away, but continued to stare at the wounded. "Come, let us go."

Volodya went off with his brother, still continuing to gaze about him, however, and repeating unconsciously:—

"Ah, my God! Ah, my God!"

"He has probably not been here long?" inquired the sister of Kozeltzoff, pointing at Volodya, who, groaning and sighing, followed them through the corridor.

"He has but just arrived."

The pretty little sister glanced at Volodya, and suddenly burst out crying. "My God! my God! when will there be an end to all this?" she said, with the accents of despair. They entered the officers' ward. Martzoff was lying on his back, with his muscular arms, bare to the elbow, thrown over his head, and with the expression on his yellow face of a man who is clenching his teeth in order to keep from shrieking with pain. His whole leg, in its stocking, was thrust outside the coverlet, and it could be seen how he was twitching his toes convulsively inside it.

"Well, how goes it, how do you feel?" asked the sister, raising his partly bald head with her slender, delicate fingers, on one of which Volodya noticed a gold ring, and arranging his pillow. "Here are some of your comrades come to inquire after you."

"Badly, of course," he answered angrily. "Let me alone! it's all right,"—the toes in his stocking moved more rapidly than ever. "How do you do? What is your name? Excuse me," he said, turning to Kozeltzoff. . . . "Ah, yes, I beg your pardon! one forgets everything here," he said, when the latter had men-

tioned his name. "You and I lived together," he added, without the slightest
expression of pleasure, glancing interrogatively at Volodya.

"This is my brother, who has just arrived from Petersburg to-day."

"Hm! and here am I who have finished my service," he said, with a frown.
"Ah, how painful it is! . . . The best thing would be a speedy end."

He drew up his leg, and covered his face with his hands, continuing to move
his toes with redoubled swiftness.

"You must leave him," said the sister, in a whisper, while the tears stood in
her eyes; "he is in a very bad state."

The brothers had already decided in the Syevernaya (northern suburb) to go
to the fifth bastion; but, on emerging from the Nikolaeff battery, they seemed to
have come to a tacit understanding not to subject themselves to unnecessary
danger, and, without discussing the subject, they determined to go their ways
separately.

"Only, how are you to find your way, Volodya?" said the elder. "However,
Nikolaeff will conduct you to the Korabelnaya, and I will go my way alone, and
will be with you to-morrow."

Nothing more was said at this last leave-taking between the brothers.

11

The thunder of the cannon continued with the same power as before, but
Yekaterinskaya Street, along which Volodya walked, followed by the taciturn
Nikolaeff, was quiet and deserted. All that he could see through the thick darkness was the wide street, with the white walls of large houses, battered in many
places, and the stone sidewalk beneath his feet; now and then, he met soldiers
and officers. As he passed along the left side of the street, near the Admiralty
building, he perceived, by the light of a bright fire burning behind the wall, the
acacias planted along the sidewalk, with green guards beneath, and the wretch-
edly dusty leaves of these acacias.

He could plainly hear his own steps and those of Nikolaeff, who followed
him, breathing heavily. He thought of nothing; the pretty little Sister of Mercy,
Martzoff's leg with the toes twitching in its stocking, the bombs, the darkness,
the divers pictures of death, floated hazily through his mind. All his young and
sensitive soul shrank together, and ached by his consciousness of loneliness, and
the indifference of every one to his fate in the midst of danger!

"They will kill me, I shall be tortured, I shall suffer, and no one will weep."
And all this, instead of the hero's life, filled with energy and sympathy, of which
he had cherished such glorious dreams. The bombs burst and shrieked nearer
and ever nearer. Nikolaeff sighed more frequently, without breaking the silence.
As he crossed the bridge leading to the Korabelnaya, he saw something fly
screaming into the bay, not far from him, which lighted up the lilac waves for an
instant with a crimson glow, then disappeared, and then rose thence in a cloud
of foam.

"See there, it was not put out!" said Nikolaeff, hoarsely.

"Yes," answered Volodya, involuntarily, and quite unexpectedly to himself, in
a thin, piping voice.

They encountered litters with wounded men, then more regimental transports
with gabions; they met a regiment on Korabelnaya Street; men on horseback

passed them. One of them was an officer, with his Cossack. He was riding at a trot, but, on catching sight of Volodya, he reined in his horse near him, looked into his face, turned, and rode on, giving the horse a blow of his whip.

"Alone, alone; it is nothing to any one whether I am in existence or not," thought the lad, and he felt seriously inclined to cry.

After ascending the hill, past a high white wall, he entered a street of small ruined houses, incessantly illuminated by bombs. A drunken and disheveled woman, who was coming out of a small door in company with a sailor, ran against him.

"If he were only a fine man," she grumbled,—"pardon, your honor the officer."

The poor boy's heart sank lower and lower, and more and more frequently flashed the lightnings against the dark horizon, and the bombs screamed and burst about him with ever increasing frequency. Nikolaeff sighed, and all at once he began to speak, in what seemed to Volodya a frightened and constrained tone.

"What haste you made to get here from home. It was nothing but traveling. A pretty place to be in a hurry to get to!"

"That's nothing; if my brother were only well again," replied Volodya, in hope that he might banish by conversation the frightful feeling that was taking possession of him.

"Well, what sort of health is it when he is thoroughly ill! Those who are really well had better stay in the hospital at such a time. A vast deal of joy there is about it, isn't there? You will have a leg or an arm torn off, and that's all you will get! It's not far removed from a downright sin! And here in the town it's not at all like the bastion, and that is a perfect terror. You go and say your prayers the whole way. Eh, you beast, there you go whizzing past!" he added, directing his attention to the sound of a splinter of shell whizzing by near them. "Now, here," Nikolaeff went on, "I was ordered to show your honor the way. My business, of course, is to do as I am bid; but the cart has been abandoned to some wretch of a soldier, and the bundle is undone. . . . Go on and on; but if any of the property disappears, Nikolaeff will have to answer for it."

After proceeding a few steps farther, they came out on a square. Nikolaeff held his peace, but sighed.

"Yonder is your artillery, your honor!" he suddenly said. "Ask the sentinel; he will show you."

And Volodya, after he had taken a few steps more, ceased to hear the sound of Nikolaeff's sighs behind him.

All at once he felt himself entirely and finally alone. This consciousness of solitude in danger before death, as it seemed to him, lay upon his heart like a terribly cold and heavy stone.

He halted in the middle of the square, glanced about him, to see whether he could catch sight of any one, grasped his head, and uttered his thought aloud in his terror: "Lord! Can it be that I am a coward, a vile, disgusting, worthless coward . . . can it be that I so lately dreamed of dying with joy for my father-land, my Tzar? No, I am an unfortunate, wretched being!" And Volodya, with a genuine sentiment of despair and disenchantment with himself, inquired of the sentinel for the house of the commander of the battery, and set out in the direction indicated.

12

The residence of the commander of the battery, which the sentinel had pointed out to him, was a small, two-story house, with an entrance on the courtyard. In one of the windows, which was pasted over with paper, burned the feeble flame of a candle. A servant was seated on the porch, smoking his pipe; he went in and announced Volodya to the commander, and then led him in. In the room, between the two windows, and beneath a shattered mirror, stood a table, heaped with official documents, several chairs, and an iron bedstead with a clean pallet, and a small bed-rug by its side.

Near the door stood a handsome man, with a large mustache,—a sergeant, in saber and cloak, on the latter of which hung a cross and a Hungarian medal. Back and forth in the middle of the room paced a short staff-officer of forty, with a swollen cheek bound up, and dressed in a thin old overcoat.

"I have the honor to report myself, Ensign Kozeltzoff, 2d, ordered to the fifth light battery," said Volodya, uttering the phrase which he had learned by heart, as he entered the room.

The commander of the battery responded dryly to his greeting, and, without offering his hand, invited him to be seated.

Volodya dropped timidly into a chair, beside the writing-table, and began to twist in his fingers the scissors which his hand happened to light upon. The commander of the battery put his hands behind his back, and, dropping his head, pursued his walk up and down the room, in silence, only bestowing an occasional glance at the hands which were twirling the scissors, with the aspect of a man who is trying to recall something.

The battery commander was a rather stout man, with a large bald spot on the crown of his head, a thick mustache, which drooped straight down and concealed his mouth, and pleasant brown eyes. His hands were handsome, clean, and plump, his feet small and well turned, and they stepped out in a confident and rather dandified manner, proving that the commander was not a timid man.

"Yes," he said, coming to a halt in front of the sergeant; "to-morrow an extra measure must be added to the pair of our horses who are fed from boxes, because they are getting thin. What do you think?"

"Of course, it is possible to do so, your excellency! Oats are very cheap just now," replied the sergeant, twitching his fingers, which he held on the seams of his trousers, but which evidently liked to assist by gestures in the conversation. "Our forage-master, Frantchuk, sent me a note yesterday, from the transports, your excellency, saying that we should certainly be obliged to purchase oats there; they say they are cheap. Therefore, what are your orders?"

"Very well, you have money." And the commander resumed his tramp through the room. "And where are your things?" he suddenly inquired of Volodya, as he paused in front of him.

Poor Volodya was so overwhelmed by the thought that he was a coward, that he espied scorn for himself in every glance, in every word, as though they had been addressed to a pitiable poltroon. It seemed to him that the commander of the battery had already divined his secret, and was making sport of him. He answered, with embarrassment, that his effects were on the Grafskaya, and that his brother had promised to send them to him on the morrow.

But the lieutenant-colonel did not hear him out, and, turning to the sergeant, he inquired:—

"Where are we to put the ensign?"

"The ensign, sir?" said the sergeant, throwing Volodya into still greater confusion by the fleeting glance which he cast upon him, and which seemed to say, "What sort of an ensign is this?"—"He can be quartered down-stairs, with the staff-captain, your excellency," he continued, after a little reflection. "The captain is at the bastion just now, and his cot is empty."

"Will not that suit you, temporarily?" said the commander. "I think you must be tired, but we will lodge you better to-morrow."

Volodya rose and bowed.

"Will you not have some tea?" said the commander, when he had already reached the door. "The samovar can be brought in."

Volodya saluted and left the room. The lieutenant-colonel's servant conducted him down-stairs, and led him into a bare, dirty chamber, in which various sorts of rubbish were lying about, and where there was an iron bedstead without either sheets or coverlet. A man in a red shirt was fast asleep on the bed, covered over with a thick cloak.

Volodya took him for a soldier.

"Piotr Nikolaïtch!" said the servant, touching the sleeper on the shoulder. "The ensign is to sleep here.—This is our yunker," he added, turning to the ensign.

"Ah, don't trouble him, please," said Volodya; but the yunker, a tall, stout young man, with a handsome but very stupid face, rose from the bed, threw on his cloak, and, evidently not having had a good sleep, left the room.

"No matter; I'll lie down in the yard," he muttered.

13

Left alone with his own thoughts, Volodya's first sensation was a fear of the incoherent, forlorn state of his own soul. He wanted to go to sleep, and forget all his surroundings, and himself most of all. He extinguished the candle, lay down on the bed, and, taking off his overcoat, he wrapped his head up in it, in order to relieve his terror of the darkness, with which he had been afflicted since his childhood. But all at once the thought occurred to him that a bomb might come and crush in the roof and kill him. He began to listen attentively; directly overhead, he heard the footsteps of the battery commander.

"Anyway, if it does come," he thought, "it will kill any one who is up-stairs first, and then me; at all events, I shall not be the only one."

This thought calmed him somewhat.

"Well, and what if Sevastopol should be taken unexpectedly, in the night, and the French make their way hither? What am I to defend myself with?"

He rose once more, and began to pace the room. His terror of the actual danger outweighed his secret fear of the darkness. There was nothing heavy in the room except the samovar and a saddle. "I am a scoundrel, a coward, a miserable coward!" the thought suddenly occurred to him, and again he experienced that oppressive sensation of scorn, and even of disgust, for himself. Again he threw himself on the bed, and tried not to think.

Then the impressions of the day involuntarily penetrated his imagination, in consequence of the unceasing sounds, which made the glass in the solitary window rattle, and again the thought of danger recurred to him: now he saw visions of wounded men and blood, now of bombs and splinters flying into the room; then of the pretty little Sister of Mercy, who was applying a bandage to him, a dying man, and weeping over him; then of his mother, accompanying him to the provincial town, and praying, amid burning tears, before the wonder-working images, and once more sleep appeared an impossibility to him.

But suddenly the thought of Almighty God, who can do all things, and who hears every supplication, came clearly into his mind. He knelt down, crossed himself, and folded his hands as he had been taught to do in his childhood, when he prayed. This gesture, all at once, brought back to him a consoling feeling, which he had long since forgotten.

"If I must die, if I must cease to exist, 'Thy will be done, Lord,' " he thought, "let it be quickly; but if bravery is needed, and the firmness which I do not possess, give them to me; deliver me from shame and disgrace, which I cannot bear, but teach me what to do in order to fulfil Thy will."

His childish, frightened, narrow soul was suddenly encouraged; it was illuminated, and caught sight of broad, brilliant, and new horizons. During the brief period while this feeling lasted, he felt and thought many other things, and soon fell asleep quietly and unconcernedly, to the sounds of the continuous roar of the bombardment and the rattling of the window-panes.

Great Lord! Thou alone hast heard, and Thou alone knowest those ardent, despairing prayers of ignorance, of troubled repentance, those petitions for the healing of the body and the enlightenment of the mind, which have ascended to Thee from that terrible precinct of death, from the general who, a moment before, was thinking of his Cross of the George on his neck, and conscious in his terror of Thy near presence, to the simple soldier writhing on the bare earth of the Nikolaeff battery, and beseeching Thee to bestow upon him there the reward, which he unconsciously anticipates, for all his sufferings.

14

The elder Kozeltzoff, meeting on the street a soldier belonging to his regiment, betook himself at once, in company with the man, to the fifth bastion.

"Keep under the wall, your honor," said the soldier.

"What for?"

"It's dangerous, your honor; there's one passing over," said the soldier, listening to the sound of a screaming cannon-ball, which struck the dry road, on the other side of the street.

Kozeltzoff, paying no heed to the soldier, walked bravely along the middle of the street.

These were the same streets, the same fires, even more frequent now, the sounds, the groans, the encounters with the wounded, and the same batteries, breastworks, and trenches, which had been there in the spring, when he was last in Sevastopol; but, for some reason, all this was now more melancholy, and, at the same time, more energetic, the apertures in the houses were larger, there were no longer any lights in the windows, with the exception of the Kushtchin house (the hospital), not a woman was to be met with, the earlier tone of custom and freedom from care no longer rested over all, but, instead, a certain impress of heavy expectation, of weariness and earnestness.

But here is the last trench already, and here is the voice of a soldier of the P—— regiment, who has recognized the former commander of his company, and here stands the third battalion in the gloom, clinging close to the wall, and lighted up now and then, for a moment, by the discharges; and a sound is audible of subdued conversation, and the rattling of guns.

"Where is the commander of the regiment?" inquired Kozeltzoff.

"In the bomb-proofs with the sailors, your honor," replied an obliging soldier; "I will show you the way, if you like."

From trench to trench the soldier led Kozeltzoff, to a small ditch in the trench. In the ditch sat a sailor, smoking his pipe; behind him a door was visible, through whose cracks shone a light.

"Can I enter?"

"I will announce you at once," and the sailor went in through the door.

Two voices became audible on the other side of the door.

"If Prussia continues to observe neutrality," said one voice, "then Austria also . . ."

"What difference does Austria make," said the second, "when the Slavic lands . . . well, ask him to come in."

Kozeltzoff had never been in this casemate. He was struck by its elegance. The floor was of polished wood, screens shielded the door. Two bedsteads stood against the wall; in one corner stood a large ikon of the Mother of God, in a gilt frame, and before her burned a rose-colored lamp.

On one of the beds, a naval officer, fully dressed, was sleeping. On the other, by a table on which stood two bottles of wine, partly empty, sat the men who were talking—the new regimental commander and his adjutant.

Although Kozeltzoff was far from being a coward, and was certainly not guilty of any wrongdoing so far as his superior officers were concerned, nor toward the regimental commander, yet he felt timid before the colonel, who had been his comrade not long before, so proudly did this colonel rise and listen to him.

"It is strange," thought Kozeltzoff, as he surveyed his commander, "it is only seven weeks since he took the regiment, and how visible already is his power as regimental commander, in everything about him—his dress, his bearing, his look. Is it so very long," thought he, "since this Batrishtcheff used to carouse with us, and wore a plain white cotton shirt, without pattern, and ate by himself, never inviting any one to his quarters, his eternal meat-balls and curd-patties? But now! and that expression of cold pride in his eyes, which says to you, 'Though I am your comrade, because I am a regimental commander of the new school, yet, believe me, I am well aware that you would give half your life merely for the sake of being in my place!'"

"You have been a long time in recovering," said the colonel to Kozeltzoff, coldly, with a stare.

"I was ill, colonel! The wound has not closed well even now."

"Then there was no use in your coming," said the colonel, casting an incredulous glance at the captain's stout figure. "You are, nevertheless, in a condition to fulfil your duty?"

"Certainly I am, sir."

"Well, I'm very glad of that, sir. You will take the ninth company from Ensign Zaitzoff—the one you had before; you will receive your orders immediately." "I obey, sir."

"Please send me the regimental adjutant when you arrive," said the regimental commander, giving him to understand, by a slight nod, that his audience was at an end.

As he emerged from the casemate, Kozeltzoff muttered something several times, and shrugged his shoulders, as though pained, embarrassed, or vexed at something, and vexed, not at the regimental commander (there was no cause for that), but at himself, and he appeared to be dissatisfied with himself and with everything about him.

15

Before going to his officers, Kozeltzoff went to greet his company, and to see where it was stationed.

The breastwork of gabions, the shapes of the trenches, the cannons which he passed, even the fragments of shot, bombs, over which he stumbled in his path—all, incessantly illuminated by the light of the firing, were well known to him, all had engraved themselves in vivid colors on his memory, three months before, during the two weeks which he had spent in this very bastion without once leaving it. Although there was much that was terrible in these reminiscences, a certain charm of past things was mingled with it, and he recognized the familiar places and objects with pleasure, as though the two weeks spent there had been agreeable ones. The company was stationed along the defensive wall toward the sixth bastion.

Kozeltzoff entered the long casemate, utterly unprotected at the entrance side, in which they had told him that the ninth company was stationed. There was, literally, no room to set his foot in the casemate, so filled was it, from the very entrance, with soldiers. On one side burned a crooked tallow candle, which a recumbent soldier was holding to illuminate the book which another one was spelling out slowly. Around the candle, in the reeking half-light, heads were visible, eagerly raised in strained attention to the reader. The little book in question was a primer. As Kozeltzoff entered the casemate he heard the following:—

"Pray-er after lear-ning. I thank Thee, O Crea-tor . . ."

"Snuff that candle!" said a voice. "That's a splendid book." "O . . . my . . . God . . ." went on the reader.

When Kozeltzoff asked for the sergeant, the reader stopped, the soldiers began to move about, coughed, and blew their noses, as they always do after enforced silence. The sergeant rose near the group about the reader, buttoning up his coat as he did so, and, stepping over and on the legs of those who had no room to withdraw them, came forward to his officer.

"How are you, brother? Do all these belong to our company?"

"I wish you health! Welcome on your return, your honor!" replied the sergeant, with a cheerful and friendly look at Kozeltzoff. "Has your honor recovered your health? Well, God be praised! It has been very dull for us without you."

It was immediately apparent that Kozeltzoff was beloved in the company.

In the depths of the casemate, voices could be heard. Their old commander, who had been wounded, Mikhaïl Semyonitch Kozeltzoff, had arrived, and so forth; some even approached, and the drummer greeted him.

"How are you, Obantchuk?" said Kozeltzoff. "Are you all right? Good day, my boys!" he said, raising his voice.

"We wish you health!" sounded through the casemate.

"How are you getting on, boys?"

"Badly, your honor. The French are getting the better of us. . . . Fighting from behind the fortifications is bad work, and that's all there is about it! and they won't come out into the open field."

"Perhaps luck is with me, and God will grant that they shall come out into the field, my boys!" said Kozeltzoff. "It won't be the first time that you and I have taken a hand together; we'll beat them again."

"We'll be glad to try it, your honor!" exclaimed several voices.

"And how about them . . . are they really bold?"

"Frightfully bold!" said the drummer, not loudly, but so that his words were audible, turning to another soldier, as though justifying before him the words of the commander, and persuading him that there was nothing boastful or improbable in these words.

From the soldiers, Kozeltzoff proceeded to the defensive barracks and his brother officers.

16

In the large room of the barracks there was a great number of men,—naval, artillery, and infantry officers. Some were sleeping, others were conversing, seated on the shot-chest and gun-carriages of the cannon of the fortification; others still, who formed a very numerous and noisy group behind the arch, were seated upon two felt Cossack cloaks which had been spread on the floor, and were drinking porter and playing cards.

"Ah! Kozeltzoff, Kozeltzoff! Capital! it's a good thing that he has come! He's a brave fellow! . . . How's your wound?" rang out from various quarters. Here also it was evident that they loved him and were rejoiced at his coming.

After shaking hands with his friends, Kozeltzoff joined the noisy group of officers engaged in playing cards. There were some of his acquaintances among them. A slender, handsome, dark-complexioned man, with a long, sharp nose and a huge mustache, which began on his cheeks, was dealing the cards with his thin, white, taper fingers, on one of which there was a heavy gold seal-ring. He was dealing straight on, and carelessly, being evidently excited by something, —and merely desirous of making a show of heedlessness. On his right, and beside him, lay a gray-haired major, supporting himself on his elbow, and playing for half a ruble with affected coolness, and settling up immediately. On his left squatted an officer with a red, perspiring face, who was laughing and jesting in a constrained way. When his cards won, he moved one hand about incessantly in his empty trousers pocket. He was playing high, and evidently no longer for ready money, which displeased the handsome, dark-complexioned man. A thin and pallid officer with a bald head, and a huge nose and mouth, was walking about the room, holding a large package of bank-notes in his hand, staking ready money on the bank, and winning.

Kozeltzoff took a drink of vodka, and sat down by the players.

"Take a hand, Mikhaïl Semyonitch!" said the dealer to him; "you have brought lots of money, I suppose."

"Where should I get any money? On the contrary, I got rid of the last I had in town."

"The idea! Some one certainly must have fleeced you in Simferopol."

"I really have but very little," said Kozeltzoff, but he was evidently desirous that they should not believe him; then he unbuttoned his coat, and took the old cards in his hand.

"I don't care if I do try; there's no knowing what the devil will do! queer things do come about at times. But I must have a drink, to get up my courage."

And within a very short space of time he had drunk another glass of vodka and several of porter, and had lost his last three rubles.

A hundred and fifty rubles were written down against the little, perspiring officer.

"No, he will not bring them," said he, carelessly, drawing a fresh card.

"Please send it," said the dealer to him, pausing a moment in his occupation of laying out the cards, and glancing at him.

"Permit me to send it to-morrow," repeated the perspiring officer, rising, and moving his hand about vigorously in his empty pocket.

"Hm!" growled the dealer, and, throwing the cards angrily to the right and left, he completed the deal. "But this won't do," said he, when he had dealt the cards. "I'm going to stop. It won't do, Zakhar Ivanitch," he added; "we have been playing for ready money and not on credit."

"What, do you doubt me? That's strange, truly!"

"From whom is one to get anything?" muttered the major, who had won about eight rubles. "I have lost over twenty rubles, but when I have won—I get nothing."

"How am I to pay," said the dealer, "when there is no money on the table?"

"I won't listen to you!" shouted the major, jumping up, "I am playing with you, but not with them."

All at once the perspiring officer flew into a rage.

"I tell you that I will pay to-morrow; how dare you say such impertinent things to me?"

"I shall say what I please! This is not the way to do—that's the truth!" shouted the major.

"That will do, Feodor Feodoritch!" all chimed in, holding back the major.

But let us draw a veil over this scene. To-morrow, to-day, it may be, each one of these men will go cheerfully and proudly to meet his death, and he will die with firmness and composure; but the one consolation of life in these conditions, which terrify even the coldest imagination in the absence of all that is human, and the hopelessness of any escape from them,—the one consolation is forgetfulness, the annihilation of consciousness. At the bottom of the soul of each lies that noble spark, which makes of him a hero; but this spark wearies of burning clearly—when the fateful moment comes it flashes up into a flame, and illuminates great deeds.

17

On the following day, the bombardment proceeded with the same vigor. At eleven o'clock in the morning, Volodya Kozeltzoff was seated in a circle of battery officers, and, having already succeeded to some extent in habituating himself to them, he was surveying the new faces, taking observations, making inquiries, and telling stories.

The discreet conversation of the artillery officers, which made some pretensions to learning, pleased him and inspired him with respect. Volodya's shy, innocent, and handsome appearance disposed the officers in his favor.

The eldest officer in the battery, the captain, a short, sandy-complexioned man, with his hair arranged in a topknot, and smooth on the temples, educated in the old traditions of the artillery, a squire of dames, and a would-be learned man, questioned Volodya as to his acquirements in artillery and new inventions, jested caressingly over his youth and his pretty little face, and treated him, in general, as a father treats a son, which was extremely agreeable to Volodya.

Sub-Lieutenant Dyadenko, a young officer, who talked with a Little Russian accent, had a tattered overcoat and disheveled hair, although he talked very loudly, and constantly seized opportunities to dispute acrimoniously over some topic, and was very abrupt in his movements, pleased Volodya, who, beneath this rough exterior, could not help detecting in him a very fine and extremely good man. Dyadenko was incessantly offering his services to Volodya, and pointing out to him that not one of the guns in Sevastopol was properly placed, according to rule.

Lieutenant Tchernovitzky, with his brows elevated on high, though he was more courteous than any of the rest, and dressed in a coat that was tolerably clean, but not new, and carefully patched, and though he displayed a gold watch-chain on a satin waistcoat, did not please Volodya. He kept inquiring what the emperor and the minister of war were doing, and related to him, with unnatural triumph, the deeds of valor which had been performed in Sevastopol, complained of the small number of true patriots, and displayed a great deal of learning, and sense, and noble feeling in general; but, for some reason, all this seemed unpleasant and unnatural to Volodya. The principal thing which he noticed was that the other officers hardly spoke to Tchernovitzky.

Yunker Vlang, whom he had waked up on the preceding evening, was also there. He said nothing, but, seated modestly in a corner, laughed when anything amusing occurred, refreshed their memories when they forgot anything, handed the vodka, and made cigarettes for all the officers. Whether it was the modest, courteous manners of Volodya, who treated him exactly as he did the officers, and did not torment him as though he were a little boy, or his agreeable personal appearance which captivated Vlanga, as the soldiers called him, declining his name, for some reason or other, in the feminine gender, at all events, he never took his big, kind eyes from the face of the new officer. He divined and anticipated all his wishes, and remained uninterruptedly in a sort of lover-like ecstasy, which, of course, the officers perceived, and made fun of.

Before dinner, the staff-captain was relieved from the bastion, and joined their company. Staff-Captain Kraut was a light-complexioned, handsome, dashing officer, with a heavy, reddish mustache, and side-whiskers; he spoke Russian capitally, but too elegantly and correctly for a Russian. In the service and in his life, he was the same as in his language; he served very well, was a capital comrade, and the most faithful of men in money matters; but simply as a man something was lacking in him, precisely because everything about him was so excellent. Like all Russian-Germans, by a strange contradiction with the ideal German-Germans, he was "praktisch" to the highest degree.

"Here he is, our hero makes his appearance!" said the captain, as Kraut, flourishing his arms and jingling his spurs, entered the room. "Which will you have, Friedrich Kristyanitch, tea or vodka?"

"I have already ordered my tea to be served," he answered, "but I may take a little drop of vodka also, for the refreshing of the soul. Very glad to make your acquaintance; I beg that you will love us, and lend us your favor," he said to Volodya, who rose and bowed to him. "Staff-Captain Kraut. . . . The gunsergeant on the bastion informed me that you arrived last night."

"Much obliged for your bed; I passed the night in it."

"I hope you found it comfortable. One of the legs is broken; but no one can stand on ceremony . . . in time of siege . . . you must prop it up."

"Well, now, did you have a fortunate time on your watch?" asked Dyadenko.

"Yes, all right; only Skvortzoff was hit, and we mended one of the guncarriages last night. The cheek was smashed to atoms."

He rose from his seat, and began to walk up and down; it was plain that he was wholly under the influence of that agreeable sensation which a man experiences who has escaped a danger.

"Well, Dmitri Gavrilitch," he said, tapping the captain on the knee, "how are you getting on, my dear fellow? How about your promotion?—no word yet?"

"Nothing yet."

"No, and there will be nothing," interpolated Dyadenko; "I proved that to you before."

"Why won't there?"

"Because the story was not properly written down."

"Oh, you quarrelsome fellow, you quarrelsome fellow!" said Kraut, smiling gayly; "a regular obstinate Little Russian! Now, just to provoke you, he'll turn out your lieutenant."

"No, he won't."

"Vlang! fetch me my pipe, and fill it," said he, turning to the yunker, who at once hastened up obligingly with the pipe.

Kraut made them all lively; he told about the bombardment, he inquired what had been going on in his absence, and entered into conversation with every one.

18

"Well, how are things? Have you already got settled among us?" Kraut asked Volodya. . . . "Excuse me, what is your name and patronymic? that's the custom with us in the artillery, you know. Have you got hold of a saddle-horse?"

"No," said Volodya; "I do not know what to do. I told the captain that I had no horse, and no money, either, until I get some for forage and traveling expenses. I want to ask the battery commander for a horse in the meantime, but I am afraid that he will refuse me."

"Apollon Sergieitch, do you mean?" he produced with his lips a sound in-dicative of the strongest doubt, and glanced at the captain; "not likely."

"What of that? If he does refuse, there'll be no harm done," said the captain. "No horse is necessary, to tell the truth, but still one might try; I will inquire to-day."

"What! Don't you know him?" Dyadenko interpolated. "He might refuse anything else, but there is no reason for refusing this. Do you want to bet on it?" . . .

"Well, of course, everybody knows already that you always contradict."

"I contradict because I know. He is niggardly about other things, but he will give the horse because it is no advantage to him to refuse."

"No advantage, indeed, when it costs him eight rubles here for oats!" said Kraut. "Is there no advantage in not keeping an extra horse?"

"Ask Skvoretz yourself, Vladimir Semyonitch!" said Vlang, returning with Kraut's pipe. "It's a capital horse."

"The one you tumbled into the ditch with, on the festival of the Forty Martyrs, in March? Hey! Vlang?" remarked the staff-captain.

"No, and why should you say that it costs eight rubles for oats," pursued Dyadenko, "when there is inquiry for it at ten and a half? Of course, he has no object in it."

"Just as though he would have nothing left! So when you get to be battery commander, you won't let any horses go into the town?"

"When I get to be battery commander, my dear fellow, my horses will get four measures of oats to eat, and I shall not accumulate an income, never fear!"

"If we live, we shall see," said the staff-captain; "and you will act just so, and so will he when he commands a battery," he added, pointing at Volodya.

"Why do you think, Friedrich Kristyanitch, that he would turn it to his profit?" broke in Tchernovitzky. "Perhaps he has property of his own; then why should he turn it to profit?"

"No, sir, I . . . excuse me, captain," said Volodya, reddening up to his ears, "that strikes me as insulting."

"Oh, ho, ho! What a severe fellow he is!" said Kraut.

"That has nothing to do with it; I only think that if the money were not mine, I should not take it."

"Now, I'll tell you something right here, young man," began the staff-captain in a more serious tone: "you are to understand that when you command a battery, if you manage things well, that's sufficient; the commander of a battery does not meddle with provisioning the soldiers; that is the way it has been from time immemorial in the artillery. If you are a bad manager, you will have nothing left. Now, these are the expenditures in conformity with your position: for shoeing your horse,—one (he closed one finger); for the apothecary,—two (he closed another finger); for office work,—three (he shut a third); for extra horses, which cost five hundred rubles, my dear fellow,—that's four; you must change the soldiers' collars, you will use a great deal of coal, you must keep open table for your officers. If you are a battery commander, you must live decently; you need a carriage, and a fur coat, and this thing and that thing, and a dozen more . . . but what's the use of enumerating them all!"

"But this is the principal thing, Vladimir Semyonitch," interpolated the captain, who had held his peace all this time; "imagine yourself to be a man, who, like myself, for instance, has served twenty years, first for two hundred, then for three hundred rubles pay; why should he not be given in return for his service at least a bit of bread in his old age?"

"Eh! yes, there you have it!" spoke up the staff-captain again, "don't be in a hurry to pronounce judgment, but live on and serve your time."

Volodya was horribly ashamed and sorry for having spoken so thoughtlessly, and he muttered something and continued to listen in silence, when Dyadenko undertook, with the greatest zeal, to dispute it and to prove the contrary.

The dispute was interrupted by the arrival of the colonel's orderly, who summoned them to dinner.

"Tell Apollon Sergieitch that he must give us some wine to-day," said Tchernovitzky, to the captain, as he buttoned up his uniform.—"Why is he so stingy with it? He will be killed, and no one will get the good of it."

"Tell him yourself."

"Not a bit of it. You are my superior officer. Rank must be regarded in all things."

19

The table had been moved out from the wall, and spread with a soiled table-cloth, in the same room in which Volodya had presented himself to the colonel on the preceding evening. The battery commander now offered him his hand, and questioned him about Petersburg and his journey.

"Well, gentlemen, I beg the favor of a glass with any of you who drink vodka. The ensigns do not drink," he added, with a smile.

On the whole, the battery commander did not appear nearly so stern to-day as he had on the preceding evening; on the contrary, he had the appearance of a kindly, hospitable host, and an elder comrade among the officers. But, in spite of this, all the officers, from the old captain down to Ensign Dyadenko, by their very manner of speaking, and looking the commander straight in the eye, as they approached, one after the other, to drink their vodka, exhibited great respect for him.

The dinner consisted of a large wooden bowl of cabbage-soup, in which floated fat chunks of beef, and a huge quantity of pepper and laurel-leaves with mustard, and Polish meat-balls in a cabbage leaf, and turnover patties of chopped meat and dough, with butter which was not quite fresh. There were no napkins, the spoons were of pewter and wood, there were only two glasses, and on the table stood a decanter of water with a broken neck; but the dinner was not dull, the conversation never flagged.

At first, their talk turned on the battle of Inkerman, in which the battery had taken part, as to the causes of failure on which occasion each one gave his own impressions and ideas, and held his tongue as soon as the battery commander himself began to speak; then the conversation naturally changed to the insufficiency of caliber of the light guns, and the new light-weight ordnance, in which connection Volodya had an opportunity to display his knowledge of artillery.

But their talk did not dwell upon the present terrible position of Sevastopol, as though each of them had meditated too much on that subject to allude to it again. In the same way, to Volodya's great amazement and disappointment, not a word was said about the duties of the service which he was to fulfil, just as though he had come to Sevastopol merely for the purpose of telling about the new light-weight ordnance and dining with the commander of the battery.

While they were at dinner, a bomb fell not far from the house in which they were seated. The walls and the floor trembled, as though in an earthquake, and the window was obscured with the smoke of the powder.

"You did not see anything of this sort in Petersburg, I fancy; but these surprises often take place here," said the battery commander.

"Look out, Vlang, and see where it burst."

Vlang looked, and reported that it had burst on the square, and then nothing more was said about the bomb.

Just before the end of the dinner, an old man, the clerk of the battery, entered the room, with three sealed envelopes, and handed them to the commander.

"This is very important; a messenger has this moment brought these from the chief of the artillery."

All the officers gazed, with impatient curiosity, at the commander's practised fingers as they broke the seal of the envelope and drew forth the *very important* paper. "What can it be?" each one asked himself.

It might be that they were to march out of Sevastopol for a rest, it might be an order for the whole battery to betake themselves to the bastions.

"Again!" said the commander, flinging the paper angrily on the table.

"What's it about, Apollon Sergieitch?" inquired the eldest officer.

"An officer and crew are required for a mortar battery over yonder, and I have only four officers, and there is not a full gun-crew in the line," growled the commander, "and here more are demanded of me. But some one must go, gentlemen," he said, after a brief pause; "the order requires him to be at the barrier at seven o'clock. . . . Send the sergeant! Who is to go, gentlemen? decide," he repeated.

"Well, here's one who has never been yet," said Tchernovitzky, pointing to Volodya. The commander of the battery made no reply.

"Yes, I should like to go," said Volodya, as he felt the cold sweat start out on his back and neck.

"No; why should you? There's no occasion!" broke in the captain. "Of course, no one will refuse, but neither is it proper to ask any one; but if Apollon Sergieitch will permit us, we will draw lots, as we did once before."

All agreed to this. Kraut cut some paper into bits, rolled them up, and dropped them into a cap. The captain jested, and even plucked up the audacity, on this occasion, to ask the colonel for wine, to keep up their courage, he said. Dyadenko sat in gloomy silence, Volodya smiled at something or other, Tchernovitzky declared that it would infallibly fall to him, Kraut was perfectly composed.

Volodya was allowed to draw first; he took one slip, which was rather long, but it immediately occurred to him to change it; he took another, which was smaller and thinner, unfolded it, and read on it, "Go."

"It has fallen to me," he said, with a sigh.

"Well, God be with you. You will get your baptism of fire at once," said the commander of the battery, gazing at the perturbed countenance of the ensign with a kindly smile; "but you must get there as speedily as possible. And, to make it more cheerful for you, Vlang shall go with you as gun-sergeant."

20

Vlang was exceedingly well pleased with the duty assigned to him, and ran hastily to make his preparations, and, when he was dressed, he went to the assistance of Volodya, and tried to persuade the latter to take his cot and fur coat with him, and some old "Annals of the Fatherland," and a spirit-lamp coffee-pot, and other useless things. The captain advised Volodya to read up his "Manual,"[1] first, about mortar-firing, and immediately to copy the tables out of it.

Volodya set about this at once, and, to his amazement and delight, he perceived that, though he was still somewhat troubled with a sensation of fear of danger, and still more lest he should turn out a coward, yet it was far from being to that degree in which it had affected him on the preceding evening. The reason for this lay partly in the daylight and in active occupation, and partly, —principally, also,—in the fact that fear, like any powerful emotion, cannot long continue with the same intensity. In a word, he had already succeeded in recovering from his terror.

At seven o'clock, just as the sun had begun to hide itself behind the Nikolaeff barracks, the sergeant came to him, and announced that the men were ready and waiting for him.

"I have given the list to Vlang*a.* You will please to ask him for it, your honor!" said he.

Twenty artillerymen, with side-arms, but without loading-tools, were standing at the corner of the house. Volodya and the yunker stepped up to them.

"Shall I make them a little speech, or shall I simply say, 'Good day, boys!' or shall I say nothing at all?" thought he. "And why should I not say, 'Good day, boys!' Why, I ought to say that much!" And he shouted boldly, in his ringing voice:—

"Good day, boys!"

The soldiers responded cheerfully; the fresh, young voice sounded pleasant in the ears of all. Volodya marched vigorously on in front of the soldiers, and, although his heart beat as if he had run several versts at the top of his speed, his step was light and his countenance cheerful.

On arriving at the Malakoff mound, and climbing the slope, he perceived that Vlang, who had not lagged a single pace behind him, and who had appeared such a valiant fellow at home in the house, kept constantly swerving to one side, and ducking his head, as though all the cannon-balls and bombs, which whizzed by very frequently in that locality, were flying straight at him. Some of the soldiers did the same, and the faces of the majority of them betrayed, if not fear, at least anxiety. This circumstance put the finishing touch to Volodya's composure, and encouraged him.

"So here I am also on the Malakoff mound, which I imagined to be a thousand times more terrible! And I can walk along without ducking my head before the bombs, and am far less terrified than the rest! So I am not a coward, after

---

[1] "Manual for Artillery Officers," by Bezak.

all!" he thought with delight, and even with a somewhat enthusiastic self-sufficiency.

But this feeling was soon shaken by a spectacle upon which he stumbled in the twilight, on the Korniloff battery, in his search for the commander of the bastion. Four sailors standing near the breastworks were holding the bloody body of a man, without shoes or coat, by its arms and legs, and getting into swing in an effort to fling it over the ramparts.

(On the second day of the bombardment, it had been found impossible, in some localities, to carry off the corpses from the bastions, and so they were flung into the ditch, in order that they might not impede action in the batteries.)

Volodya stood petrified for a moment, as he saw the corpse waver on the summit of the breastworks, and then roll down into the ditch; but, luckily for him, the commander of the bastion met him there, communicated his orders, and furnished him with a guide to the battery and to the bomb-proofs designated for his service. We will not enumerate the remaining dangers and disenchantments which our hero underwent that evening: how, instead of the firing, such as he had seen on the Volkoff field, according to the rules of accuracy and precision, which he had expected to find here, he found two cracked mortars, one of which had been crushed by a cannon-ball in the muzzle, while the other stood upon the splinters of a ruined platform; how he could not obtain any workmen until the following morning in order to repair the platform; how not a single charge was of the weight prescribed in the "Manual"; how two soldiers of his command were wounded, and how he was twenty times within a hair's-breadth of death.

Fortunately there had been assigned for his assistant a gun-captain of gigantic size, a sailor, who had served on the mortars since the beginning of the siege, and who convinced him of the practicability of using them, conducted him all over the bastion, with a lantern, during the night, exactly as though it had been his own kitchen-garden, and promised to put everything in proper shape on the morrow.

The bomb-proof to which his guide conducted him was excavated in the rocky soil, and consisted of a long hole, two cubic fathoms in extent, covered with oaken planks an arshin in thickness. Here he took up his post, with all his soldiers. Vlang was the first, when he caught sight of the little door, twenty-eight inches high, of the bomb-proof, to rush headlong into it, in front of them all, and, after nearly cracking his skull on the stone floor, he huddled down in a corner, from which he did not again emerge.

But Volodya, when all the soldiers had placed themselves along the wall on the floor, and some had lighted their pipes, set up his bed in one corner, lighted a candle, and lay upon his cot, smoking a cigarette.

Shots were incessantly heard, over the bomb-proof, but they were not very loud, with the exception of those from one cannon, which stood close by and shook the bomb-proof with its thunder. In the bomb-proof itself all was still; the soldiers, who were a little shy, as yet, of the new officer, only exchanged a few words, now and then, as they requested each other to move out of the way or to furnish a light for a pipe. A rat scratched somewhere among the stones, or Vlang, who had not yet recovered himself, and who still gazed wildly about him, uttered a sudden vigorous sigh.

Volodya, as he lay on his bed, in his quiet corner, crowded with men, and illuminated only by a single candle, experienced that sensation of well-being which he had known as a child, when, in the course of a game of hide-and-seek, he used to crawl into a cupboard or under his mother's skirts, and listen, not daring to draw his breath, afraid of the dark, and yet conscious of enjoying himself. He felt a little oppressed, but cheerful.

21

After the lapse of about ten minutes, the soldiers began to grow bolder and to converse together. The most important personages among them—the two gun-sergeants—placed themselves nearest the officer's light and bed: one was old and gray-haired, with every possible medal and cross except the George; the other was young, a militia-man, who smoked cigarettes, which he was rolling. The drummer, as usual, assumed the duty of waiting on the officer. The bombardiers and cavalrymen sat next, and then farther away, in the shadow of the entrance, the *underlings* took up their post. They too began to talk among themselves. It was caused by the hasty entrance of a man into the bomb-proof.

"How now, brother! couldn't you stay in the street? Don't the girls sing merrily?" said a voice.

"They sing such marvelous songs as were never heard in the village," said the man who had fled into the bomb-proof, with a laugh.

"But Vasin does not love bombs—ah, no, he does not love them!" said one from the aristocratic corner.

"The idea! It's quite another matter when it's necessary," drawled the voice of Vasin, who made all the others keep silent when he spoke; "since the 24th, the firing has been going on desperately; and what is there wrong about it? You'll get killed for nothing, and your superiors won't so much as say 'Thank you!' for it."

At these words of Vasin, all burst into a laugh.

"There's Melnikoff, that fellow who will sit outside," said some one.

"Well, send him here, that Melnikoff," added the old gunner; "they will kill him, for a fact, and that to no purpose."

"Who is this Melnikoff?" asked Volodya.

"Why, your honor, he's a stupid young soldier of ours. He doesn't seem to be afraid of anything, and now he keeps walking about outside. Please to take a look at him; he looks like a bear."

"He knows a spell," said the slow voice of Vasin, from the corner.

Melnikoff entered the bomb-proof. He was fat (which is extremely rare among soldiers), and a sandy-complexioned, handsome man, with a huge, bulging forehead and prominent, light blue eyes.

"Are you afraid of the bombs?" Volodya asked him.

"What is there about the bombs to be afraid of!" replied Melnikoff, shrugging his shoulders and scratching his head, "I know that I shall not be killed by a bomb."

"So you would like to go on living here?"

"Why, of course I would. It's jolly here!" he said, with a sudden outburst of laughter.

"Oh, then you must be detailed for the sortie! I'll tell the general so, if you like," said Volodya, although he was not acquainted with a single general there.

"Why shouldn't I like? I do!"

And Melnikoff disappeared behind the others.

"Let's have a game of noski,[1] children! Who has cards?" rang out his brisk voice.

And, in fact, it was not long before a game was started in the back corner, and blows on the nose, laughter, and calling of trumps were heard.

Volodya drank some tea from the samovar, which the drummer served for him, treated the gunners, jested, chatted with them, being desirous of winning popularity, and felt very well content with the respect which was shown him. The soldiers, too, perceiving that the gentleman put on no airs, began to talk together.

One declared that the siege of Sevastopol would soon come to an end, because a trustworthy man from the fleet had said that the emperor's brother Constantine was coming to our relief with the 'Merican fleet, and there would soon be an agreement that there should be no firing for two weeks, and that a rest should be allowed, and if any one did fire a shot, every discharge would have to be paid for at the rate of seventy-five kopeks each.

Vasin, who, as Volodya had already noticed, was a little fellow, with large, kindly eyes, and side-whiskers, related, amid a general silence at first, and afterward amid general laughter, how, when he had gone home on leave, they had been glad at first to see him, but afterward his father had begun to send him off to work, and the lieutenant of the foresters' corps sent his drozhky for his wife.

All this amused Volodya greatly. He not only did not experience the least fear or inconvenience from the closeness and heavy air in the bomb-proof, but he felt in a remarkably cheerful and agreeable frame of mind.

Many of the soldiers were already snoring. Vlang had also stretched himself out on the floor, and the old gun-sergeant, having spread out his overcoat, was crossing himself and muttering his prayers, preparatory to sleep, when Volodya took a fancy to step out of the bomb-proof, and see what was going on outside.

"Take your legs out of the way!" cried one soldier to another, as soon as he rose, and the legs were pressed aside to make way for him.

Vlang, who appeared to be asleep, suddenly raised his head, and seized Volodya by the skirt of his coat.

"Come, don't go! how can you!" he began, in a tearfully imploring tone.

"You don't know about things yet; they are firing at us out there all the time; it is better here."

But, in spite of Vlang's entreaties, Volodya made his way out of the bomb-proof, and seated himself on the threshold, where Melnikoff was already sitting.

The air was pure and fresh,—particularly after the bomb-proof,—the night was clear and still. Through the roar of the discharges could be heard the sounds of cart-wheels, bringing gabions, and the voices of the men who were at work on the magazine. Above their heads was the lofty, starry sky, across which flashed the fiery streaks caused by the bombs; on the left, a tiny opening, twenty-eight inches in size, led to another bomb-proof, through which the feet and backs of

---

[1] A game in which the loser is rapped on the nose with the cards.

the soldiers who lived there were visible, and through which their voices were audible; in front, the elevation produced by the powder-vault could be seen, and athwart it flitted the bent figures of men, and upon it, at the very summit, amid the bullets and the bombs which whistled past the spot incessantly, stood a tall form in a black paletot, with his hands in his pockets, and feet treading down the earth, which other men were fetching in sacks. Often a bomb would fly over, and burst close to the cave. The soldiers engaged in bringing the earth bent over and ran aside; but the black figure never moved, went on quietly stamping down the dirt with his feet, and remained on the spot in the same attitude as before.

"Who is that black man?" inquired Volodya of Melnikoff.

"I don't know; I will go and see."

"Don't go! it is not necessary."

But Melnikoff, without heeding him, walked up to the black figure, and stood beside him for a tolerably long time, as calm and immovable as the man himself.

"That is the man who has charge of the magazine, your honor!" he said, on his return. "It has been pierced by a bomb, so the infantrymen are fetching more earth."

Now and then, a bomb seemed to fly straight at the door of the bomb-proof. On such occasions, Volodya shrank into the corner, and then peered forth again, gazing upward, to see whether another was not coming from some direction. Although Vlang, from the interior of the bomb-proof, repeatedly besought Volodya to come back, the latter sat on the threshold for three hours, and experienced a sort of satisfaction in thus tempting fate and in watching the flight of the bombs. By the end of the evening, he had learned from what point most of the firing proceeded, and where the shots struck.

22

On the following day, the 27th, after a ten hours' sleep, Volodya, fresh and active, stepped out on the threshold of the bomb-proof. Vlang also started to crawl out with him, but, at the first sound of a bullet, he flung himself backward through the opening of the bomb-proof, bumping his head as he did so, amid the general merriment of the soldiers, the majority of whom had also come out into the open air. Vlang, the old gun-sergeant, and a few others were the only ones who rarely went out into the trenches; it was impossible to restrain the rest; they all scattered about in the fresh morning air, escaping from the fetid bomb-proof, and, in spite of the fact that the bombardment was as vigorous as on the preceding evening, they disposed themselves around the door, and some even on the breastworks. Melnikoff had been strolling about among the batteries since daybreak, and staring up with perfect coolness.

Near the entrance sat two old soldiers and one young, curly-haired fellow, a Jew, who had been detailed from the infantry. This soldier picked up one of the bullets which were lying about, and, having smoothed it against a stone with a potsherd, with his knife he carved from it a cross, after the style of the order of St. George; the others looked on at his work as they talked. The cross really turned out to be quite handsome.

"Now, if we stay here much longer," said one of them, "then, when peace is made, the time of service will be up for all of us."

"Nothing of the sort; I have at least four years' service yet before my time is up, and I have been in Sevastopol these five months."

"It is not counted toward the discharge, do you understand," said another.

At that moment, a cannon-ball shrieked over the heads of the speakers, and struck only a little more than two feet away from Melnikoff, who was approaching them from the trenches.

"That came near killing Melnikoff," said one man.

"I shall not be killed," said Melnikoff.

"Here's a cross for you, for your bravery," said the young soldier who had made the cross, handing it to Melnikoff.

"No, brother, a month here counts for a year, of course . . . that was the order," the conversation continued.

"Think what you please, but when peace is declared, there will be an imperial review at Arshava,[1] and if we don't get our discharge, we shall be allowed to go on indefinite leave."

At that moment, a shrieking little bullet flew past the speakers' heads, and struck a stone.

"You'll get a *full* discharge before evening . . . see if you don't," said one of the soldiers.

They all laughed.

Not only before evening, but before the expiration of two hours, two of them received their full discharge, and five were wounded; but the rest jested on as before.

By morning, the two mortars had actually been brought into such a condition that it was possible to fire them. At ten o'clock, in accordance with the orders which he had received from the commander of the bastion, Volodya called out his command, and marched to the battery with it.

In the men, as soon as they proceeded to action, there was not perceptible a drop of that sentiment of fear which had been expressed on the preceding evening. Vlang alone could not control himself; he dodged and ducked just as before, and Vasin lost some of his composure, and fidgeted and squatted down incessantly.

But Volodya was in an extraordinary state of enthusiasm; the thought of danger did not even occur to him. Delight that he was fulfilling his duty, that he was not only not a coward, but even a valiant fellow, the feeling that he was in command, and the presence of twenty men, who, as he was aware, were surveying him with curiosity, made a thoroughly brave man of him. He was even vain of his valor, put on airs before his soldiers, climbed up on the banquette, and unbuttoned his overcoat expressly that he might render himself the more distinctly visible.

The commander of the bastion, who was going the rounds of his establishment, as he expressed it, at the moment, accustomed as he had become during his eight months' experience to all sorts of bravery, could not refrain from admiring this handsome lad, in the unbuttoned coat, beneath which a red shirt was visible, encircling his soft white neck, with his animated face and eyes, as he clapped his hands and shouted: "First! second!" and ran gayly along the ramparts, in order to see where his bomb would fall.

1 Warsaw.

At half-past eleven the firing ceased on both sides, and precisely at twelve o'clock the storming of the Malakoff mound,—of the second, third, and fifth bastions, began.

23

On this side of the bay, between Inkerman and the northern suburb, on the telegraph hill, about midday, stood two naval men; one was an officer, who was engaged in observing Sevastopol through a telescope, and the other had just arrived at the signal-station with his orderly.

The sun stood high and brilliant above the bay, and played with the ships which floated upon it, and with the moving sails and boats, with a warm and cheerful glow. The light breeze hardly moved the leaves of the dry oak shrubs which stood about the signal-pole, puffed out the sails of the boats, and ruffled the waves.

Sevastopol, with her unfinished church, her columns, her line of shore, her boulevard showing green against the hill, and her elegant library building, with her tiny azure inlets, filled with masts, with the picturesque arches of her aqueducts, and the clouds of blue smoke, lighted up now and then by red flashes of flame from the firing; the same beautiful, proud, festive Sevastopol, hemmed in on one side by yellow, smoke-crowned hills, on the other by the bright blue sea, which glittered in the sun, was visible the same as ever, on the other side of the bay.

Over the horizon-line of the sea, along which floated a long wreath of black smoke from some steamer, crept long white clouds, portending a gale. Along the entire line of the fortifications, especially over the hills on the left, rose columns of thick, dense, white smoke, suddenly, abruptly, and incessantly illuminated by flashes, lightnings, which shone even amid the light of high noon, and which constantly increased in volume, assuming divers forms, as they swept upward, and tinged the heavens with a darker hue. These puffs of smoke flashing now here, now there, took their birth on the hills, in the batteries of the enemy, in the city, and high against the sky. The sound of the discharges never ceased, but shook the air with their mingled roar.

At twelve o'clock the puffs of smoke began to occur less and less frequently, and the atmosphere quivered less with the roar.

"But the second bastion is no longer replying at all," said the officer of hussars, who sat there on horseback; "it is utterly destroyed! Horrible!"

"Yes, and the Malakoff only sends one shot to their three," replied the officer who was looking through his glass. "It enrages me to have them silent. They are firing straight on the Korniloff battery, and it is not answering at all."

"But you see that they always cease the bombardment at twelve o'clock, just as I said. It is the same to-day. Let us go and get some breakfast . . . they are already waiting for us . . . there's nothing to see."

"Stop, don't interfere," said the officer with the glass, gazing at Sevastopol with peculiar eagerness.

"What's going on there? What is it?"

"There is a movement in the trenches, and heavy columns are marching."

"Yes, that is evident," said the naval officer. "The columns are under way. We must give the signal."

"See, see! They have emerged from the trenches."

In truth, it was visible to the naked eye that dark masses were moving down the hill, across the narrow valley, from the French batteries to the bastions. In front of these specks, dark streaks were visible, which were already close to our lines. White puffs of smoke of discharges burst out at various points on the bastions, as though the firing were running along the line.

The breeze bore to them the sounds of musketry-shots, exchanged briskly, like rain beating upon the window-pane. The black streaks moved on, nearer and nearer, into the very smoke. The sounds of firing grew louder and louder, and mingled in a lengthened, resounding roar.

The smoke, rising more and more frequently, spread rapidly along the line, flowed together in one lilac-hued cloud, which dispersed and joined again, and through which, here and there, flitted flames and black points—and all sounds were commingled in one reverberating crash.

"An assault," said the officer, with a pale face, as he handed the glass to the naval officer.

Cossacks galloped along the road, officers on horseback, the commander-in-chief in a calash, and his suite passed by. Profound emotion and expectation were visible on all countenances.

"It cannot be that they have taken it!" said the mounted officer.

"By Heavens, there's the standard! Look, look!" said the other, sighing and abandoning the glass. "The French standard on the Malakoff!"

"It cannot be!"

24

The elder Kozeltzoff, who had succeeded in winning back his money and losing it all again that night, including even the gold pieces which were sewed into his cuffs, had fallen, just before daybreak, into a heavy, unhealthy, but profound slumber, in the fortified barracks of the fifth battalion, when the fateful cry, repeated by various voices rang out:—

"The alarm!"

"Why are you sleeping, Mikhaïl Semyonitch! There's an assault!" a voice shouted to him.

"That is probably some school-boy," he said, opening his eyes, but putting no faith in it.

But all at once he caught sight of an officer running aimlessly from one corner to the other, with such a pale face that he understood it all. The thought that he might be taken for a coward, who did not wish to go out to his company at a critical moment, struck him with terrible force. He ran to his corps at the top of his speed. Firing had ceased from the heavy guns; but the crash of musketry was at its height. The bullets whistled, not singly like rifle-balls, but in swarms, like a flock of birds in autumn, flying past overhead. The entire spot on which his battalion had stood the night before was veiled in smoke, and the shouts and cries of the enemy were audible. Soldiers, both wounded and unwounded, met him in throngs. After running thirty paces farther, he caught sight of his company, which was hugging the wall.

"They have captured Schwartz," said a young officer. "All is lost!"

"Nonsense!" said he, angrily, grasping his blunt little iron sword, and he began to shout:—

"Forward, boys! Hurrah!"

His voice was strong and ringing; it roused even Kozeltzoff himself. He ran forward along the traverse; fifty soldiers rushed after him, shouting as they went. From the traverse he ran out upon an open square. The bullets fell literally like hail. Two struck him,—but where, and what they did, whether they bruised or wounded him, he had not the time to decide.

In front, he could already see blue uniforms and red trousers, and could hear shouts which were not Russian; one Frenchman was standing on the breastworks, waving his cap, and shouting something. Kozeltzoff was convinced that he was about to be killed; this gave him courage.

He ran on and on. Some soldiers overtook him; other soldiers appeared from somewhere at one side, also running. The blue uniforms remained at the same distance from him, fleeing back from him to their own trenches; but beneath his feet were the dead and wounded. When he had run to the outermost ditch, everything became confused before Kozeltzoff's eyes, and he was conscious of a pain in the breast.

Half an hour later, he was lying on a stretcher, near the Nikolaeff barracks, and knew that he was wounded, though he felt hardly any pain; all he wanted was something cooling to drink, and to be allowed to lie still in peace.

A plump little doctor, with large black side-whiskers, approached him, and unbuttoned his coat. Kozeltzoff stared over his chin at what the doctor was doing to his wound, and at the doctor's face, but he felt no pain. The doctor covered his wound with his shirt, wiped his fingers on the skirts of his coat, and without a word or glance at the wounded man, went off to some one else.

Kozeltzoff's eyes mechanically took note of what was going on before him, and, recalling the fact that he had been in the fifth bastion, he thought, with an extraordinary feeling of self-satisfaction, that he had fulfilled his duty well, and that, for the first time in all his service, he had behaved as handsomely as it was possible for any one, and had nothing with which to reproach himself. The doctor, after bandaging the other officer's wound, pointed to Kozeltzoff, and said something to a priest, with a huge reddish beard and a cross, who was standing near by.

"What! am I dying?" Kozeltzoff asked the priest, when the latter approached him.

The priest, without making any reply, recited a prayer and handed the cross to the wounded man.

Death had no terrors for Kozeltzoff. He grasped the cross with his weak hands, pressed it to his lips, and burst into tears.

"Well, were the French repulsed?" he inquired of the priest, in firm tones.

"The victory has remained with us at every point," replied the priest, in order to comfort the wounded man, concealing from him the fact that the French standard had already been unfurled on the Malakoff mound.

"Thank God!" said the wounded man, without feeling the tears which were trickling down his cheeks.

The thought of his brother occurred to his mind for a single instant. "May God grant him the same good fortune," he said to himself.

25

But the same fate did not await Volodya. He was listening to a tale which Vasin was in the act of relating to him, when there was a cry,—"The French are coming!" The blood fled for a moment to Volodya's heart, and he felt his cheeks turn cold and pale. For one second he remained motionless; but, on glancing about him, he perceived that the soldiers were buttoning up their coats with tolerable equanimity, and crawling out, one after the other. One even, probably Melnikoff, remarked, in a jesting way:—

"Go out and offer them the bread and salt of hospitality, boys!"

Volodya, in company with Vlang, who never separated from him by so much as a step, crawled out of the bomb-proof, and ran to the battery.

There was no artillery firing whatever in progress on either side. It was not so much the sight of the soldiers' composure which aroused his courage as the pitiful and undisguised cowardice of Vlang. "Is it possible for me to be like him?" he said to himself, and he ran on gayly up to the breastworks, near which his mortars stood. It was clearly apparent to him that the French were making straight for him through an open space, and that masses of them, with their bayonets glistening in the sun, were moving in the nearest trenches.

One, a short, broad-shouldered fellow, in zouave uniform, and armed with a sword, ran on in front and leaped the ditch.

"Fire grape-shot!" shouted Volodya, hastening from the banquette; but the soldiers had already made their preparations without waiting for his orders, and the metallic sound of the grape-shot which they discharged shrieked over his head, first from one and then from the other mortar.

"First! second!" commanded Volodya, running from one mortar to the other, and utterly oblivious of danger.

On one side, and near at hand, the crash of musketry from our men under shelter, and anxious cries, were heard.

All at once a startling cry of despair, repeated by several voices, was heard on the left: "They are surrounding us! They are surrounding us!"

Volodya looked round at this shout. Twenty Frenchmen made their appearance in the rear. One of them, a handsome man with a black beard, was in front of all; but, after running up to within ten paces of the battery, he halted, and fired straight at Volodya, and then ran toward him once more.

For a second, Volodya stood as though turned to stone, and did not believe his eyes. When he recovered himself and glanced about him, there were blue uniforms in front of him on the ramparts; two Frenchmen were even spiking a cannon not ten paces distant from him.

There was no one near him, with the exception of Melnikoff, who had been killed by a bullet beside him, and Vlang, who, with a handspike clutched in his hand, had rushed forward, with an expression of wrath on his face, and with eyes lowered.

"Follow me, Vladimir Semyonitch! Follow me!" shouted the desperate voice of Vlang, as he brandished his handspike over the French, who were pouring in from the rear. The yunker's ferocious countenance startled them. He struck the one who was in advance on the head; the others involuntarily paused, and Vlang continued to glare about him, and to shout in despairing accents: "Follow me, Vladimir Semyonitch! Why do you stand there? Run!" and ran toward the trenches in which lay our infantry, firing at the French. After leaping into the trench, he came out again to see what his adored ensign was doing. Something in an overcoat was lying prostrate where Volodya had been standing, and the whole place was filled with Frenchmen, who were firing at our men.

26

Vlang found his battery on the second line of defense. Out of the twenty soldiers who had been in the mortar battery, only eight survived.

At eight o'clock in the evening, Vlang crossed over with the battery on a steamer loaded down with soldiers, cannon, horses, and wounded men, to the northern suburb.

There was no firing anywhere. The stars shone brilliantly in the sky, as on the preceding night; but a strong wind tossed the sea. On the first and second bastions, lightnings flashed along the earth; explosions rent the atmosphere, and illuminated strange black objects in their vicinity, and the stones which flew through the air.

Something was burning near the docks, and the red glare was reflected in the water. The bridge, covered with people, was lighted up by the fire from the Nikolaeff battery. A vast flame seemed to hang over the water, from the distant promontory of the Alexandroff battery, and illuminated the clouds of smoke beneath, as it rose above them; and the same tranquil, insolent, distant lights as on the preceding evening gleamed over the sea, from the hostile fleet.

The fresh breeze raised billows in the bay. By the red light of the conflagrations, the masts of our sunken ships, which were slowly settling deeper and deeper into the water, were visible. Not a sound of conversation was heard on deck; there was nothing but the regular swish of the parted waves, and the steam, the neighing and pawing of the horses, the words of command from the captain, and the groans of the wounded. Vlang, who had had nothing to eat all day, drew a bit of bread from his pocket, and began to chew it; but all at once he recalled Volodya, and burst into such loud weeping that the soldiers who were near him heard it.

"See how our Vlanga is eating his bread and crying too," said Vasin.

"Wonderful!" said another.

"And see, they have fired our barracks," he continued, with a sigh. "And how many of our comrades perished there; and the French got it for nothing!"

"At all events, we have got out of it alive—thank God for that!" said Vasin.

"But it's provoking, all the same!"

"What is there provoking about it? Do you suppose they are enjoying themselves there? Not exactly! You wait, our men will take it away from them again. And however many of our brethren perish, as God is holy, if the emperor commands, they will win it back. Can ours leave it to them thus? Never! There you have the bare walls; but they have destroyed all the breastworks. Even if they have planted their standard on the hill, they won't be able to make their way into the town."

"Just wait, we'll have a hearty reckoning with you yet, only give us time," he concluded, addressing himself to the French.

"Of course we will!" said another, with conviction.

Along the whole line of bastions of Sevastopol, which, for so many months, had seethed with remarkably vigorous life, which, for so many months, had seen dying heroes relieved one after another by death, and which, for so many months, had awakened the terror, the hatred, and finally the admiration of the enemy, —on the bastions of Sevastopol, there was no longer a single man. All was dead, wild, horrible,—but not silent.

Destruction was still in progress. On the earth, furrowed and strewed with the recent explosions, lay bent gun-carriages, crushing down the bodies of Russians and of the foe; heavy iron cannons silenced forever, bombs and cannon-balls hurled with horrible force into pits, and half-buried in the soil, then more corpses, pits, splinters of beams, bomb-proofs, and still more silent bodies in gray and blue coats. All these were still frequently shaken and lighted up by the crimson glow of the explosions, which continued to shake the air.

The foe perceived that something incomprehensible was going in that menacing Sevastopol. Those explosions and the death-like silence on the bastions made them shudder; but they dared not yet believe, being still under the influence of the calm and forcible resistance of the day, that their invincible enemy had disappeared, and they awaited motionless and in silence the end of that gloomy night.

The army of Sevastopol, like the gloomy, surging sea, quivering throughout its entire mass, wavering, plowing across the bay, on the bridge, and at the northern suburb, moved slowly through the impenetrable darkness of the night, away from the place where it had left so many of its brave brethren, from the place all steeped in its blood, from the place which it had defended for eleven months against a foe twice as powerful as itself, and which it was now ordered to abandon without a battle.

The first impression produced on every Russian by this command was inconceivably sad. The second feeling was a fear of pursuit. The men felt that they were defenseless as soon as they abandoned the places on which they were accustomed to fight, and they huddled together uneasily in the dark, at the entrance to the bridge, which was swaying about in the heavy breeze.

The infantry pressed forward, with a clash of bayonets, and a thronging of regiments, equipages, and arms; cavalry officers made their way about with orders; the inhabitants and the military servants accompanying the baggage, which was not permitted to cross, wept and entreated; while the artillery, in haste to get off, forced their way to the bay with a thunder of wheels.

In spite of the diversions created by the varied and anxious demands on their attention, the instinct of self-preservation and the desire to escape as speedily as possible from that dread place of death were present in every soul. This instinct existed also in a soldier mortally wounded, who lay among the five hundred other wounded, upon the stone pavement of the Pavloff quay, and prayed God to send death; and in the militiaman who, with his last remaining strength, pressed into the compact throng, in order to make way for a general who rode by; and in the general in charge of the transportation, who was engaged in restraining the haste of the soldiers; and in the sailor who had become entangled in the moving battalion, and who, crushed by the surging throng, had lost his breath; and in the wounded officer who was being borne along in a litter by four soldiers, who, stopped by the crowd, had placed him on the ground by the

Nikolaeff battery; and in the artilleryman who had served his gun for sixteen years, and who, at his superior's command, to him incomprehensible, to throw overboard the guns, had, with the aid of his comrades, sent them over the steep bank into the bay; and in the men of the fleet, who had just let down the gang-ways of the ships, and had rowed lustily away in their boats. On stepping upon the farther end of the bridge, nearly every soldier pulled off his cap and crossed himself.

But behind this instinct there was another, oppressive and far deeper, existing along with it; this was a feeling which resembled repentance, shame, and hatred. Almost every soldier, as he gazed on abandoned Sevastopol, from the northern suburb, sighed with inexpressible bitterness of heart, and menaced the foe.

1856

THE WOOD-CUTTING
EXPEDITION

1

In midwinter, in the year 185–, a division of our battery was engaged in an expedition on the Great Chechen River. On the evening of February 26, having been informed that the platoon which I commanded in the absence of its regular officer was detailed for the following day to help cut down the forest, and having that evening obtained and given the necessary directions, I betook myself to my tent earlier than usual; and as I had not got into the bad habit of warming it with burning coals, I threw myself, without undressing, on my bed made of branches, and, drawing my Circassian cap over my eyes, I rolled myself up in my shuba, and fell into that peculiarly deep and heavy sleep which one obtains at the moment of tumult and disquietude on the eve of a great peril. The anticipation of the morrow's action brought me to such a state.

At three o'clock in the morning, while it was still perfectly dark, my warm sheepskin was pulled off from me, and the red light of a candle was unpleasantly flashed upon my sleepy eyes.

"It's time to get up," said some one's voice.

I shut my eyes, without knowing what I was doing, wrapped my sheepskin around me again, and dropped off into slumber.

"It's time to get up," repeated Dmitri, relentlessly, shaking me by the shoulder. "The infantry are starting."

I suddenly came to a sense of the reality of things, started up, and sprang to my feet.

Having hastily swallowed a glass of tea, and washed in ice-water, I crept out from my tent, and went to the artillery park.

It was dark, misty, and cold. The night fires, burning here and there through-out the camp, lighted up the forms of drowsy soldiers scattered around them, and made the darkness deeper by their ruddy flickering flames. Near at hand one could hear monotonous, tranquil snoring; in the distance, movement, the babble of voices, and the jangle of arms, as the foot-soldiers got in readiness for the expedition. There was an odor of smoke, manure, wicks, and fog. The morning frost crept down my back, and my teeth chattered in spite of all my efforts to prevent it.

Only by the snorting and occasional stamping of horses could one make out in the impenetrable darkness where the harnessed limbers and caissons were drawn up, and, by the flashing points of the linstocks, where the cannon were. With the words *s Bogom*,—God speed it,—the first gun moved off with a clang, followed by the rumbling caisson, and the platoon got under way.

We all took off our caps, and made the sign of the cross. Taking its place in the interval between the infantry, our platoon halted, and waited from four o'clock until the muster of the whole force was made, and the commander came.

"There's one of our men missing, Nikolaï Petrovitch," said a black form coming to me. I recognized him by his voice only as the platoon-artillerist Maksimof.

"Who?"

"Velenchuk is missing. When we hitched up he was here, I saw him; but now he's gone."

As it was entirely unlikely that the column would move immediately, we determined to send Corporal Antonof to find Velenchuk. Shortly after this, the sound of several horses riding by us in the darkness was heard; this was the commander and his suite. In a few moments the head of the column stirred and started,—finally we also moved,—but Antonof and Velenchuk had not appeared.

However, we had not gone a hundred paces when the two soldiers overtook us.

"Where was he?" I asked of Antonof.

"In the 'park,' asleep."

"What! he was drunk, wasn't he?"

"No, not at all."

"What made him go to sleep, then?"

"I don't know."

During three hours of darkness we slowly defiled in monotonous silence across uncultivated, snowless fields and low bushes which crackled under the wheels of the ordnance.

At last, after we had crossed a shallow but phenomenally rapid brook, a halt was called, and from the vanguard were heard desultory musket-shots. These sounds, as always, created the most extraordinary excitement in us all. The division had been almost asleep; now the ranks became alive with conversation, repartees, and laughter. Some of the soldiers wrestled with their mates; others played hop, skip, and jump; others chewed on their hardtack, or, to pass away the time, engaged in drumming the different roll-calls. Meantime the fog slowly began to lift in the east, the dampness became more palpable, and the surrounding objects gradually made themselves manifest emerging from the darkness.

I already began to make out the green caissons and gun-carriages, the brass cannon wet with mist, the familiar forms of my soldiers whom I knew even to the least details, the sorrel horses, and the files of infantry, with their bright bayonets, their knapsacks, ramrods, and canteens on their backs.

We were quickly in motion again, and, after going a few hundred paces where there was no road, were shown the appointed place. On the right were seen the steep banks of a winding river and the high wooden posts of a Tartar burying-ground. At the left and in front of us, through the fog, appeared the black belt. The platoon got under way with the limbers. The eighth company, which was protecting us, stacked their arms; and a battalion of soldiers with muskets and axes started for the forest.

Not five minutes had elapsed when on all sides piles of wood began to crackle and smoke; the soldiers were swarming about, fanning the fires with their hands and feet, lugging brushwood and logs; and in the forest were heard the incessant strokes of a hundred axes and the crash of falling trees.

The artillery, with not a little spirit of rivalry with the infantry, heaped up their pile,—although the fire was already burning so fiercely that it was impossible to get within six feet of it, and the dense black smoke was pouring up through the icy branches, from which the water dropped hissing into the flames, as the soldiers heaped them on the fire; and the glowing coals dropped down on the dead white grass exposed by the heat. Still it was all mere boy's play to the soldiers; they dragged great logs, threw on the tall steppe grass, and fanned the fire more and more.

As I came near a bonfire to light a cigarette, Velenchuk, always officious, but, now that he had been found napping, showing himself more actively engaged about the fire than any one else, in an excess of zeal seized a coal with his naked hand from the very middle of the fire, tossed it from one palm to the other two or three times, and flung it on the ground.

"Light a match and give it to him," said one man. "Bring a linstock, fellows," said another.

When I at last lighted my cigarette without the aid of Velenchuk, who tried to bring another coal from the fire, he rubbed his burnt fingers on the back of his sheepskin coat, and, doubtless for the sake of doing something, seized a great plane-tree stump, and with a mighty swing flung it on the fire. When at last it seemed to him that he might rest, he went close to the fire, spread out his cloak, which he wore like a mantle fastened at the back by a single button, stretched his legs, folded his great black hands in his lap, and, opening his mouth a little, closed his eyes.

"O dear! I forgot my pipe! What a shame, fellows!" he said, after a short silence, and not addressing anybody in particular.

2

In Russia there are three predominating types of soldiers, which embrace the soldiers of all arms,—those of the Caucasus, of the line, the guards, the infantry, the cavalry, the artillery, and the rest.

These three types, with many subdivisions and combinations, are as follows:—
(1) The obedient,
(2) The domineering or dictatorial, and
(3) The desperate.

The obedient are subdivided into (*a*) the apathetic-obedient and (*b*) the energetic-obedient.

The domineering are subdivided into(*a*) the gruffly domineering and (*b*) the diplomatically domineering.

The desperate are subdivided into (*a*) the humorously desperate and (*b*) the criminally desperate.

The type more frequently encountered than the rest—the type most gentle, most sympathetic, and for the most part endowed with the Christian virtues of meekness, devotion, patience, and submission to the will of God—is that of the obedient.

The distinctive character of the apathetic-obedient is a certain invincible indifference and disdain of all the turns of fortune that may overtake him.

The characteristic trait of the drunken obedient is a mild poetical tendency and sensitiveness.

The characteristic trait of the energetic-obedient is his limitation in intellectual faculties, united with an endless assiduity and fervor.

The type of the domineering is to be found more especially in the higher spheres of the army: corporals, non-commissioned officers, sergeants, and others. In the first division of the gruffly domineering are the highborn, the energetic, and especially the martial type, not excepting those who are stern in a lofty poetic way (to this category belonged Corporal Antonof, with whom I intend to make the reader acquainted).

The second division is composed of the diplomatically domineering, and this class has for some time been making rapid advances. The diplomatically domineering is always eloquent, knows how to read, goes about in a pink shirt, does not eat from the common kettle, often smokes Musatof tobacco, considers himself immeasurably higher than the simple soldier, and is himself rarely as good a soldier as the gruffly domineering of the first class.

The type of the desperate is almost the same as that of the domineering, that is, it is good in the first division,—the humorously desperate, the characteristic features of whom are an invariable jollity, a mighty aptitude for everything, a wealth of nature and boldness.

The second division is, in the same way, detestable: the criminally desperate, but these, it must be said for the honor of the Russian army, are very rarely met with, and, if they are met with, then they are quickly drummed out of comradeship with the true soldier. Atheism, and a certain audacity in crime, are the chief traits of this character.

Velenchuk came under the head of the energetically obedient. He was a Little Russian by birth, had been fifteen years in the service; and, while he was uncomely and none too capable as a soldier, still he was simple-hearted, kind, and extraordinarily full of zeal, though for the most part misdirected zeal, and he was extraordinarily honest.

I say extraordinarily honest, because the year before there had been an occurrence in which he had given a remarkable exhibition of this characteristic. You must know that almost every soldier has his own trade. The greater number are tailors and shoemakers. Velenchuk himself practised the trade of tailoring; and, judging from the fact that Sergeant Mikhaïl Dorofeïtch gave him his custom, it is safe to say that he had reached a famous degree of accomplishment. The year before, it happened that, while in camp, Velenchuk took an elegant cloak to make for Mikhaïl Dorofeïtch. But that very night, after he had cut the cloth, and stitched on the trimmings, and put it under his pillow in his tent, a misfortune befell him: the cloth, which was worth seven rubles, disappeared during the night. Velenchuk, with tears in his eyes, with pale quivering lips, and with stifled lamentations, confessed the circumstance to the sergeant.

Mikhaïl Dorofeïtch fell into a passion. In the first moment of his indignation he threatened the tailor; but afterward, like a kindly man with plenty of means, he waved his hand, and did not exact from Velenchuk the value of the cloak. In spite of the fussy tailor's endeavors, and the tears that he shed while telling about his misfortune, the thief was not detected. Although strong suspicions were attached to a criminally desperate soldier named Chernof, who slept in the same tent with him, still there were no decisive proofs. The diplomatically dictatorial Mikhaïl Dorofeïtch, as a man of means, having various arrangements with the inspector of arms and steward of the mess, the aristocrats of the battery, quickly forgot all about the loss of that particular cloak.

Velenchuk, on the contrary, did not forget his unhappiness. The soldiers declared that at this time they were apprehensive about him, lest he should make way with himself, or flee to the mountains, so heavily did his misfortune weigh upon him. He neither ate nor drank, was not able to work, and wept all the time. At the end of three days he appeared before Mikhaïl Dorofeïtch, and without any color in his face, and with a trembling hand, drew out of his sleeve a gold piece and gave it to him.

"Faith, and here's all that I have, Mikhaïl Dorofeïtch; and this I got from Zhdanof," he said, beginning to sob again. "I will give you two more rubles, truly I will, when I have earned them. He [who the *he* was, Velenchuk himself did not know] made me seem like a rascal in your eyes. He, the beastly viper, stole from a brother soldier his hard earnings; and here I have been in the service fifteen years." . . .

To the honor of Mikhaïl Dorofeïtch, it must be said that he did not require of Velenchuk the last two rubles, though Velenchuk brought them to him at the end of two months.

3

Five other soldiers of my platoon besides Velenchuk were warming themselves around the bonfire.

In the best place, away from the wind, on a cask, sat the platoon artillerist Maksimof, smoking his pipe. In the posture, the gaze, and all the motions of this man, it could be seen that he was accustomed to command, and was conscious of his own worth, even if nothing were said about the cask whereon he sat, which during the halt seemed to become the emblem of power, or the nankeen short-coat he wore.

When I approached, he turned his head round toward me; but his eyes remained fixed on the fire, and only after some time did they follow the direction of his face, and rest on me. Maksimof came from a semi-noble family. He had property, and in the school brigade he obtained rank, and acquired some learning. According to the reports of the soldiers, he was fearfully rich and fearfully learned.

I remember how one time, when they were making practical experiments with the quadrant, he explained, to the soldiers gathered around him, that the motions of the spirit level arise from the same causes as those of the atmospheric quicksilver. In reality Maksimof was far from stupid, and knew his business admirably; but he had the bad habit of speaking, sometimes on purpose, in such a way that it was impossible to understand him, and I think he did not understand his own words, He had an especial fondness for the words "arises" and "to proceed";.and whenever he said "it arises," or "now let us proceed," then I knew in advance that I should not understand what would follow. The soldiers, on the contrary, as I had a chance to observe, enjoyed hearing his "arises," and suspected it of containing deep meaning, though, like myself, they could not understand his words. But this incomprehensibility they ascribed to their own stupidity, and they worshiped Feodor Maksimuitch accordingly. In a word, Maksimof was diplomatically dictatorial.

The second soldier near the fire, engaged in drawing on his sinewy red legs a fresh pair of stockings, was Antonof, the same bombardier Antonof who, as early as 1837, together with two others stationed by one gun without shelter, was returning the shot of the enemy, and with two bullets in his thigh continued still to serve his gun and load it.

"He would have been artillerist long before, had it not been for his character," said the soldiers; and it was true that his character was odd. When he was sober, there was no man more calm, more peaceful, more correct in his deportment; but when he had been drinking he became an entirely different man: not recognizing authority, he became quarrelsome and turbulent, and was wholly valueless as a soldier. Not more than a week before this time he got drunk at Shrovetide; and, in spite of all threats and exhortations, and his attachment to his cannon, he kept on drinking and brawling till the first Monday in Lent. Throughout the fast, notwithstanding the order for all in the division to eat meat, he lived on hardtack alone, and in the first week he did not even take the prescribed allowance of vodka.

However, it was necessary to see this man, with short figure, tough as iron, with his stumpy bow-legs, his shiny, whiskered face, when in his cups he would take the balalaïka into his strong hands, and, carelessly glancing to this side and that, play some love-song; or, with his cloak thrown over his shoulders, and the orders dangling from it, and his hands thrust into the pockets of his blue nankeen trousers, would roll along the street; it was necessary to see how his face at such a time was enlivened with an expression of martial pride, and scorn for all that did not pertain to the military,—to comprehend how absolutely impossible it was for him to compare himself at such moments with the rude or the simply insinuating servant, the Cossack, the infantry soldier, or the volunteer, or any one else who did not belong to the artillery. He quarreled and was turbulent, not so much for his own pleasure as for the sake of upholding the spirit of all soldierhood, of which he felt himself to be the representative.

The third soldier, with ear-rings in his ears, with bristling mustaches, goose-flesh, and a porcelain pipe between his teeth, crouching on his heels in front of the bonfire, was the artillery-rider Chikin. The dear man Chikin, as the soldiers called him, was a buffoon. In bitter cold, up to his knees in the mud, going without food two days at a time, on the march, on parade, undergoing instruction, the dear man always and everywhere screwed his face into grimaces, executed flourishes with his legs, and poured out such a flood of nonsense that the whole platoon would go into fits of laughter. During a halt or in camp Chikin had always around him a group of young soldiers, whom he either played fil'ka[1] with, or amused by telling stories about the sly soldier and the English milord, or by imitating the Tartar and the German, or simply by making his jokes, at which everybody nearly died with laughter.

It was a fact that his reputation as a joker was so widespread in the battery, that he had only to open his mouth and wink, and he would be rewarded with a universal burst of guffaws; but he really had a great gift for the comic and unexpected. In everything he had the cleverness to see something remarkable, such as never came into anybody else's head; and, what is more important, this talent for seeing something ridiculous never failed under any trial.

The fourth soldier was an awkward young fellow, a recruit of the last year's draft, and he was now serving in an expedition for the first time. He was standing in the very smoke, and so close to the fire that it seemed as if his well-worn short-coat would catch on fire; but notwithstanding this, by the way in which he had flung open his coat, by his calm self-satisfied pose, with his calves arched out, it was evident that he was enjoying perfect happiness.

And finally, the fifth soldier, sitting at some little distance from the fire, and whittling a stick, was Uncle Zhdanof. Zhdanof had been in service the longest of all the soldiers in the battery,—knew all the recruits; and every one, from force of habit, called him *dy'adenka*, or little uncle. It was said that he never drank, never smoked, never played cards (not even noski), and never indulged in bad talk. All the time when military duties did not engross him he worked at his trade of shoemaking; on holidays he went to church wherever it was possible, or placed a kopek candle before the image, and read the psalter, the only book in which he cared to read. He had little to do with the other soldiers,—with those higher in rank, even though they were younger, he was coldly respectful. With his equals, since he did not drink, he had little reason for social intercourse; but he was extremely fond of recruits and young soldiers; he always protected them, read them their lessons, and often helped them. All in the battery considered him a capitalist, because he had twenty-five rubles, which he willingly loaned to any soldier who really needed it. That same Maksimof who was now artillerist used to tell me that when, ten years before, he had come as a recruit, and the old topers among the soldiers helped him to drink up the money that he had, Zhdanof, pitying his unhappy situation, took him home with him, severely upbraided him for his behavior, even administered a beating, read him the lesson about the duties of a soldier's life, and sent him away after presenting him with a shirt (for Maksimof hadn't one to his back) and a half-ruble piece.

"He made a man of me," Maksimof used to say, always with respect and gratitude in his tone. He had also taken Velenchuk's part always, ever since he came as a recruit, and had helped him at the time of his misfortune about the lost cloak, and had helped many, many others during the course of his twenty-five years' service.

[1] *Fil'ka*, a game of cards played by soldiers.—Author's Note.

In the service it was impossible to find a soldier who knew his business better, who was braver or more obedient; but he was too meek and mean-looking to be chosen as an artillerist, though he had been bombardier fifteen years. Zhdanof's one pleasure, and even passion, was music. He was exceedingly fond of some songs, and he always gathered round him a circle of singers from among the young soldiers; and, though he himself could not sing, he stood with them, and, putting his hands into the pockets of his short-coat, and shutting his eyes, expressed his contentment by the motions of his head and cheeks. I know not why it was, that in that regular motion of the cheeks under the mustache, a peculiarity which I never saw in any one else, I found unusual expression. His head white as snow, his mustache dyed black, and his brown, wrinkled face, gave him at first sight a stern and gloomy appearance; but as you looked more closely into his great round eyes, especially when they smiled (he never laughed with his lips), something extraordinarily sweet and almost childlike suddenly struck you.

4

"Dear me! I have forgotten my pipe; that's a misfortune, fellows," repeated Velenchuk.

"But you should smoke *cikarettes*, dear man," urged Chikin, screwing up his mouth, and winking. "I always smoke *cikarettes* at home; it's sweeter."

Of course, all joined in the laugh.

"So you forgot your pipe?" interrupted Maksimof, proudly knocking out the ashes from his pipe into the palm of his left hand, and not paying any attention to the universal laughter, in which even the officers joined. "You lost it somewhere here, didn't you, Velenchuk?"

Velenchuk wheeled to right face at him, started to lift his hand to his cap, and then dropped it again.

"You see, you haven't woke up from your last evening's spree, so that you didn't get your sleep out. For such work you deserve a good raking."

"May I drop dead on this very spot, Feodor Maksimovitch, if a single drop passed my lips. I myself don't know what happened to me," replied Velenchuk. "How glad I should have been to get drunk!" he muttered to himself.

"All right. But one is responsible to the chief for one's conduct, and when you behave this way it's perfectly abominable," said the eloquent Maksimof, in a more gentle tone.

"Well, here is something strange, fellows," continued Velenchuk after a moment's silence, scratching the back of his head, and not addressing any one in particular; "fact, it's strange, fellows. I have been sixteen years in the service, and have not had such a thing happen to me. As we were told to get ready for a march, I got up, as my duty behooved. There was nothing at all, when suddenly in the 'park' *it* came over me . . . came over me more and more; laid me out . . . laid me out on the ground . . . and everything. . . . And when I got asleep, I did not hear a sound, fellows. It must have been sheer drowsiness," he said in conclusion.

"At all events, it took all my strength to wake you up," said Antonof, as he pulled on his boot. "I pushed you, and pushed you. You slept like a log."

"See here," remarked Velenchuk, "if I had been drunk . . ."

"Like a peasant woman we had at home," interrupted Chikin. "For almost two years running she did not get down from the big oven. They tried to wake her up one time, for they thought she was asleep; but there she was, lying just as if she was dead; the same kind of sleep you had—isn't that so, dear man?"

"Just tell us, Chikin, how you led the fashion the time when you had leave of absence," said Maksimof, smiling, and winking at me as much as to say, "Don't you like to hear what the foolish fellow has to say?"

"How led the fashion, Feodor Maksimuitch?" asked Chikin, casting a quick side glance at me. "Of course, I merely told what kind of people we are here in the Kapkas."[1]

"Well, then, that's so, that's so. You are not a fashion leader . . . but just tell us how you made them think you were commander."

"You know how I became commander for them. I was asked how we live," began Chikin, speaking rapidly, like a man who has often told the same story. "I said, 'We live well, dear man; we have plenty of victuals. At morning and night, to our delight, all we soldiers get our choco*let*; and then at dinner, every sinner has his imperial soup of barley groats, and instead of vodka, Modeira at each plate, genuine old Modeira in the cask, '42!' "

"Fine Modeira!" replied Velenchuk, louder than the others and with a burst of laughter. "Let's have some of it."

"Well, then, what did you have to tell them about the *Esiatics?*" said Maksimof, carrying his inquiries still farther as the general merriment subsided.

Chikin bent down to the fire, picked up a coal with his stick, put it on his pipe, and, pretending not to notice the discreet curiosity aroused in his hearers, puffed for a long time in silence.

When at last he had raised a sufficient cloud of smoke, he threw away the coal, pushed his cap still farther on the back of his head, and, making a grimace, and with an almost imperceptible smile, he continued: "They asked," said he, " 'What kind of a person is the little Cherkes yonder? or is it the Turk that you are fighting with in the Kapkas country?' I tell 'em, 'The Cherkes here with us is not of one sort, but of different sorts. Some are like the mountaineers who live on the rocky mountain-tops, and eat stones instead of bread. The biggest of them,' I say, 'are exactly like big logs, with one eye in the middle of the forehead, and they wear red caps, they glow like fire,'—just like yours, my dear fellow," he added, addressing a young recruit, who, in fact, wore an odd little cap with a red crown.

The recruit, at this unexpected sally, suddenly sat down on the ground, slapped his knees, and burst out laughing and coughing so that he could hardly command his voice to say, "That's the kind of mountaineers we have here."

" 'And,' says I, 'besides, there are the *mumri*,' " continued Chikin, jerking his head so that his hat fell forward on his forehead; " 'they go out in pairs like little twins,—these others. Everything comes double with them,' says I, 'and they cling hold of each other's hands, and run so *queek* that I tell you you couldn't catch up with them on horseb•ck.'—'Well,' says he, 'these *mumri* who are so small as you say, I suppose they are born hand in hand?' " said

[1] Caucasus.

Chikin, endeavoring to imitate the deep throaty voice of the peasant. " 'Yes,' says I, 'my dear man, they are so by nature. You try to pull their hands apart, and it makes 'em bleed, just as with the Chinese: when you pull their caps off, the blood comes.'—'But tell us,' says he, 'how they kill any one.'—'Well, this is the way,' says I: 'they take you and they rip you all up, and they reel out your bowels in their hands. They reel 'em out and you defy them and defy them—till your soul . . .' "

"Well, now, did they believe anything you said, Chikin?" asked Maksimof, with a slight smile, when those standing round had stopped laughing.

"And indeed it is a strange people, Feodor Maksimuitch: they believe every one; by God, they do. But still, when I began to tell them about Mount Kazbek, and how the snow does not melt all summer there, they all burst out laughing at the absurdity of it. 'What a story!' they said. 'Could such a thing be possible, —a mountain so big that the snow does not melt on it?' And I say, 'With us when the thaw comes, there is such a heap; and even after it begins to melt, the snow lies in the hollows.'—'Go away,' " said Chikin, with a concluding wink.

5

The bright disk of the sun, gleaming through the milk-white mist, had now got well up; the purple-gray horizon gradually widened; but, though the view became more extended, still it was sharply defined by the delusive white wall of the fog.

In front of us, on the other side of the forest, opened out a good-sized field. Over the field there spread from all sides the smoke from the bonfires, here black, here milk-white, here purple; and the white folds of the mist as it arose assumed strange forms. Far in the distance, from time to time, groups of mounted Tartars showed themselves; and the occasional reports from our rifles, and from their guns and cannon, were heard.

"It wasn't anything at all of an action—mere boys' play," as the worthy Captain Khlopof said.

The commander of the ninth company of Jägers, who was with us as escort, rode up to our cannon, and pointing to three mounted Tartars who were just then riding under cover of the forest, more than six hundred sazhens from us, asked me to give them a shot or a shell. His request was an illustration of the love universal among all infantry officers for artillery practice.

"You see," said he, with a kindly and convincing smile, stretching his hand across my shoulder, "where those two big trees are, right in front of us: one is on a white horse, and dressed in a black cherkeska; and directly behind him are two more. Do you see? If you please, we must . . ."

"And there are three others riding along under the lee of the forest," interrupted Antonof, who was distinguished for his sharp eyes, and had now joined us with the pipe that he had been smoking concealed behind his back. "The front one has just taken his carbine from its case. It's easy to see, your excellency."

"Ha! he fired then, fellows. See the white puff of smoke," said Velenchuk, who was standing in a group of soldiers a little back of us.

"He must be aiming at us, the blackguard!" remarked some one else.

"See, those fellows only come out a little way from the forest. We see the place; we want to aim a cannon at it," suggested a third. "If we could only *blant* a *krenade* into the midst of 'em, it would scatter 'em." . . .

"And what makes you think you could shoot to such a *tistance*, dear man?" asked Chikin.

"Only five hundred or five hundred and twenty sazhens—it can't be less than that," said Maksimof, coolly, as if he were speaking to himself; but it was evident that he, like the others, was terribly anxious to bring the guns into play. "If the howitzer is aimed up at an angle of forty-five degrees, then it will be possible to reach that spot; that is perfectly possible."

"You know, now, that if you aim at that group, it would infallibly hit some one. There, there! as they are riding along now, please hurry up and order the gun to be fired," continued the infantry commander, beseeching me.

"Will you give the order to unlimber the gun?" asked Antonof, suddenly, in a jerky bass voice, with a slight touch of surliness in his manner.

I confess that I myself felt a strong desire for this, and I commanded the second cannon to be unlimbered.

The words had hardly left my mouth ere the bomb was powdered and rammed home; and Antonof, clinging to the gun-cheek, and leaning his two fat fingers on the carriage, was already giving directions for getting the gun into position.

"A little . . . little more to the left . . . now a little to the right . . . now, now the least bit more . . . there, that's right," said he, with a proud face, turning from the gun.

The infantry officer, myself, and Maksimof in turn sighted along the gun, and all gave expression to various opinions.

"By God! it will miss," said Velenchuk, clicking with his tongue, although he could only see over Antonof's shoulder, and therefore had no basis for such a surmise.

"By-y-y God! it will miss; it will hit that tree right in front, fellows."

"Two!" I commanded.

The men about the gun scattered. Antonof ran to one side, so as to follow the flight of the ball. There was a flash and a ring of brass. At the same instant we were enveloped in gunpowder smoke; and, after the startling report, was heard the metallic, whizzing sound of the ball rushing off quicker than lightning, amid a general silence dying away in the distance.

Just a little behind the group of horsemen a white puff of smoke appeared; the Tartars scattered in all directions, and then the sound of a crash came to us.

"Capitally done!" . . . "Ah! they take to their heels." . . . "See! the devils don't like it."

Such were the exclamations and jests heard among the ranks of the artillery and infantry.

"If the aim had been a trifle lower, 'twould have hit right in the midst of *him*," remarked Velenchuk. "I said it would strike the tree: it did; it took the one at the right."

6

Leaving the soldiers to argue about the Tartars taking to flight when they saw the shell, and why it was that they came there, and whether there were many in the forest, I went with the company commander a few steps aside, and sat down under a tree, waiting for some warmed chops which he had offered me. The company commander, Bolkhof, was one of the officers that are called in the regiment *bonjour-ui*. He had property, had previously served in the guards, and spoke French. But, in spite of this, his comrades liked him. He was rather intellectual, had tact enough to wear his Petersburg overcoat, to eat a good dinner, and to speak French without too much offending the sensibilities of his brother officers.

As we talked about the weather, about the events of the war, about the officers known to us both, and as we became convinced, by our questions and answers, by our views of things in general, that we were mutually sympathetic, we involuntarily fell into more intimate conversation. Moreover, in the Caucasus, among men who meet in one circle, the question invariably arises, though it is not always expressed, "Why are you here?" and it seemed to me that my companion was desirous of satisfying this inarticulate question.

"When will this expedition end?" he asked lazily; "it's tiresome."

"It isn't tiresome to me," I said; "it's much more so serving on the staff."

"Oh, on the staff it's ten thousand times worse!" said he, fiercely. "No, I mean when will this sort of thing end altogether?"

"What! do you wish that it would end?" I asked.

"Yes, all of it, altogether! . . . Well, are the chops ready, Nikolaïef?" he inquired of his servant.

"Why do you serve in the Caucasus, then," I asked, "if the Caucasus does not please you?"

"You know why," he replied, with an outburst of frankness; "on account of tradition. In Russia, you see, there exists a strange tradition about the Caucasus, that it is a sort of promised land for all kinds of unfortunate people."

"Well," said I, "that is pretty nearly true; the majority of us here . . ."

"But what is better than all," said he, interrupting me, "is that all of us who on account of this tradition come to the Kavkas are fearfully deceived in our calculations; and really, I don't see why, in consequence of disappointment in love or disorder in one's affairs, one should come to serve in the Caucasus rather than in Kazan or Kaluga. You see, in Russia they imagine the Kavkas as something immense,—everlasting virgin ice-fields, with impetuous streams, with daggers, cloaks, Circassian girls,—all that is strange and wonderful; but in reality there is nothing gay in it at all. If they only knew, for example, that we have never been on the virgin ice-fields, and that there was nothing gay in it at all, and that the Caucasus was divided into the districts of Stavropol, Tiflis, and so forth . . ."

"Yes," said I, laughing, "when we are in Russia we look on the Caucasus in an absolutely different way from what we do here. Haven't you ever noticed it: when you read poetry in a language that you don't know very well, you imagine it much better than it really is, don't you?" . . .

"I don't know how that is, but this Kavkas disgusts me awfully," he said, interrupting me.

"It isn't so with me," I said; "the Caucasus is delightful to me now, only in a different way." . . .

"Maybe it is delightful," he continued, with a touch of asperity, "but I know that it is not delightful to me."

"Why so?" I asked, with a view of saying something.

"In the first place, it has deceived me—all that which I expected, from tradition, to be delivered of in the Caucasus, I find in me just the same here, only with this distinction, that before, it was all on a large scale, but now on a small and nasty scale; at every step I find millions of petty annoyances, worriments, and miseries; in the second place, because I feel that each day I am falling morally lower and lower; and principally because I feel myself incapable of service here . . . I cannot endure to face the danger . . . simply, I am a coward." . . .

He got up and looked at me earnestly.

Though this unbecoming confession completely took me by surprise, I did not contradict him, as my messmate evidently expected me to do; but I awaited from the man himself the refutation of his words, which is always ready in such circumstances.

"You know to-day's expedition is the first time that I have taken part in action," he continued, "and you can imagine what my evening was. When the sergeant brought the order for my company to join the column, I became as pale as a sheet, and could not utter a word from emotion; and if you knew how I spent the night! If it is true that people turn gray from fright, then I ought to be perfectly white-headed to-day, because no man condemned to death ever suffered so much from terror in a single night as I did; even now, though I feel a little more at my ease than I did last night, still it goes here in me," he added, pressing his hand to his heart. "And what is absurd," he went on to say, "while this fearful drama is playing here, I myself am eating chops and onions, and trying to persuade myself that it is very gay. . . . Is there any wine, Nikolaïef?" he added, with a yawn.

"There he is, fellows!" shouted one of the soldiers at this moment in a tone of alarm, and all eyes were fixed upon the edge of the far-off forest.

In the distance a puff of bluish smoke took shape, and, rising up, drifted away on the wind.

When I realized that the enemy were firing at us, everything that was in the range of my eyes at that moment, everything suddenly assumed a new and majestic character. The stacked muskets, and the smoke of the bonfires, and the blue sky, and the green gun-carriages, and Nikolaïef's sunburned, whiskered face, —all this seemed to tell me that the shot which had already emerged from the smoke, and was at that instant flying through space, might be directed straight at my breast.

"Where did you get the wine?" I meanwhile asked Bolkhof carelessly, while in the depths of my soul two voices were speaking with equal distinctness: one said, "Lord, take my soul in peace;" the other, "I hope I shall not duck my head, but smile while the ball is coming." And at that instant something horribly unpleasant whistled above our heads, and the shot came crashing to the ground not two paces away from us.

"Now, if I were Napoleon or Frederick the Great," said Bolkhof at this time, with perfect composure, turning to me, "I should certainly have said something graceful."

"But that you have just done," I replied, hiding with some difficulty the panic which I felt at being exposed to such a danger.

"Why, what did I say? No one will put it on record."

"I'll put it on record."

"Yes: if you put it on record, it will be in the way of criticism, as Mishchenkof says," he replied, with a smile.

"Tful you devils!" exclaimed Antonof in vexation just behind us, and spitting to one side; "it just missed my leg."

All my solicitude to appear cool, and all our refined phrases, suddenly seemed to me unendurably stupid after this artless exclamation.

7

The enemy, in fact, had posted two cannon on the spot where the Tartars had been scattered, and every twenty or thirty minutes sent a shot at our wood-choppers. My division was sent out into the field, and ordered to reply to him. At the skirt of the forest a puff of smoke would show itself, the report would be heard, then the whiz of the ball, and the shot would bury itself behind us or in front of us. The enemy's shots were placed fortunately for us, and no loss was sustained.

The artillerists, as always, behaved admirably, loaded rapidly, aimed carefully wherever the smoke appeared, and jested unconcernedly with each other. The infantry escort, in silent inactivity, were lying around us, awaiting their turn. The wood-cutters were busy at their work; their axes resounded through the forest more and more rapidly, more and more eagerly, save when the "svist" of a cannon-shot was heard: then suddenly the sounds ceased, and amid the deathlike still-ness a voice, not altogether calm, would exclaim, "Stand aside, boys!" and all eyes would be fastened upon the shot ricochetting on the woodpiles and the brush.

The fog was now completely lifted, and, taking the form of clouds, was dis-appearing slowly in the dark blue vault of heaven. The unclouded orb of the sun shone bright and threw its cheerful rays on the steel of the bayonets, the brass of the cannon, on the thawing ground, and the glittering points of the icicles. The atmosphere was brisk with the morning frost and the warmth of the spring sun. Thousands of varying shades and tints mingled in the dry leaves of the forest; and on the hard shining level of the road could be seen the regular tracks of wheel-tires and horseshoes.

The action between the troops grew more and more violent and more striking. In all directions the bluish puffs of smoke from the firing became more and more frequent. The dragoons, with bannerets waving from their lances, kept riding to the front. In the infantry companies songs resounded, and the train loaded with wood began to form itself as the rear-guard. The general rode up to our division, and ordered us to be ready for the return. The enemy took up their position in the bushes over against our left flank, and began to pour a heavy musketry fire into us. From the left-hand side a ball came whizzing from the forest, and buried itself in a gun-carriage; then a second, a third. . . .

The infantry guard, scattered around us, jumped up with a shout, seized their muskets, and took aim. The cracking of the musketry was redoubled, and the bullets began to fly thicker and faster. The retreat had begun, and the present attack was the result, as is always the case in the Caucasus.

It was perfectly manifest that the artillerists did not like the bullets so well as the infantry had liked the solid shot. Antonof put on a deep frown. Chikin imitated the sound of the bullets, and fired his jokes at them; but one could see that he did not like them. In regard to one he said, "What a hurry it's in!" another he called a "honey-bee"; a third, which flew over us with a sort of slow and lugubrious drone, he called an "orphan,"—a term which raised general amusement.

The recruit, who had the habit of bending his head to one side and stretching out his neck, every time he heard a bullet, was also a source of amusement to the soldiers, who said, "Who is it? some acquaintance that you are bowing to?"

Even Velenchuk, who always showed perfect equanimity in time of danger, was now in an alarming state of mind; he was manifestly vexed because we did not send some canister in the direction from which the bullets came. He more than once exclaimed in a discontented tone, "What is *he* allowed to shoot at us with impunity for? If we could only answer with some grape, that would silence him, take my word for it."

In fact, it was time to do this. I ordered the last shell to be fired, and to load with grape.

"Grape!" shouted Antonof, bravely, in the midst of the smoke, coming up to the gun with his sponge as soon as the discharge was made.

At this moment, not far behind us, I heard the swift buzzing sound of a bullet suddenly stop as it buried itself in something with a dry thud. My heart sank within me.

"Some one of our men must have been struck," I said to myself; but at the same time, under the influence of this powerful presentiment I did not dare to turn round. In fact, immediately after this sound, the heavy fall of a body was heard, and "o-o-o-oï,"—the heart-rending groan of the wounded man.

"I'm hit, fellows," exclaimed a voice which I knew.

It was Velenchuk.

He was lying on his back between the limbers and the gun. The cartridge-box which he carried was flung to one side. His forehead was all bloody, and down from his right eye and his nose flowed a thick red stream. The wound was in his abdomen, but it bled very little; he had hit his forehead on something when he fell.

All this I perceived after some little time. At the first instant I saw only a sort of obscure mass, and a terrible quantity of blood as it seemed to me.

None of the soldiers who were loading the gun said a word,—only the recruit muttered between his teeth, "See, how bloody!" and Antonof, frowning still blacker, snorted angrily; but all the time it was evident that the thought of death presented itself to the mind of each. All took hold of their work with great activity. The gun was loaded in one instant; and the gun-captain, in getting the canister, went two steps around the place where lay the wounded man, now groaning constantly.

8

Every one who has been in action has doubtless experienced the strange although illogical but still powerful feeling of repulsion for the place in which any one has been killed or wounded. My soldiers were noticeably affected by this feeling at the first moment when it became necessary to lift Velenchuk and carry him to the wagon which had driven up. Zhdanof sternly went to the sufferer, and, notwithstanding his cry of anguish, took him under his arms and lifted him. "What are you standing there for? Help lug him!" he shouted; and instantly a dozen men sprang to his assistance, some of whom could not do any good at all. But they had scarcely started to move him from the place when Velenchuk began to scream fearfully and to struggle.

"What are you screeching for, like a rabbit?" said Antonof, clutching him roughly by the leg. "If you don't stop, we'll drop you."

And the sufferer really calmed down, and only occasionally cried out, "Okh! I'm dead! o-okh, fellows! I'm dead!"

As soon as they laid him in the wagon, he ceased to groan, and I heard how he said something to his comrades—it must have been a farewell—in a weak but audible voice.

Indeed, no one likes to look at a wounded man; and I, instinctively hastening to get away from this spectacle, ordered the men to take him as soon as possible to a suitable place, and then return to the guns. But in a few minutes I was told that Velenchuk was asking for me, and I returned to the ambulance.

The wounded man lay on the wagon bottom, holding the sides with both hands. His healthy, broad face had in a few seconds entirely changed; he had, as it were, grown gaunt, and older by several years. His lips were pinched and white, and tightly compressed, with evident effort at self-control. In place of the quick and anxious expression in his eyes had come a peculiarly clear and tranquil gleam, and on his blood-stained forehead and nose already lay the seal of death.

In spite of the fact that the least motion caused him unendurable anguish, he was trying to take from his left leg his purse, which contained money.

A fearfully burdensome thought came into my mind when I saw his bare, white, and healthy-looking leg as he was taking off his boot and untying his purse.

"There are three silver rubles and a fifty-kopek piece," he said, when I took the girdle-purse. "You keep them."

The ambulance had started to move, but he stopped it.

"I was working on a cloak for Lieutenant Sulimovsky. He had paid me two-o-o silver rubles. I spent one and a half on buttons, but half a ruble lies with the buttons in my bag. Give them to him."

"Very good, I will," said I. "Keep up good hopes, brother."

He did not answer me; the wagon moved away, and he began once more to groan, and to cry in the same terribly heartrending tone. As if he had done with earthly things, he felt that he had no longer any pretext for self-restraint, and he now considered this alleviation permissible.

9

"Where are you off to? Come back! Where are you going?" I shouted to the recruit, who, carrying in his arms his reserve linstock, and a sort of cane in his hand, was calmly marching off toward the ambulance in which the wounded man was carried.

But the recruit lazily looked up at me, and kept on his way, and I was obliged to send a soldier to bring him back. He took off his red cap, and looked at me with a stupid smile.

"Where were you going?" I asked.

"To camp."

"Why?"

"Because—they have wounded Velenchuk," he replied, smiling again.

"What has that to do with you? It's your business to stay here."

He looked at me in amazement, then coolly turned round, put on his cap, and went to his place.

The result of the action had been fortunate on the whole. The Cossacks, it was reported, had made a glorious attack, and had captured three Tartars; the infantry had laid in a store of firewood, and had suffered in all a loss of six men wounded. In the artillery, from the whole array, only Velenchuk and two horses were put *hors du combat*. Moreover, they had cut the forest for three versts, and cleared a place, so that it was impossible to recognize it; now, instead of a seemingly impenetrable forest girdle, a great field was opened up, covered with heaps of smoking bonfires, and lines of infantry and cavalry on their way to camp. Notwithstanding the fact that the enemy incessantly harassed us with cannonade and musketry fire, and followed us down to the very river where the cemetery was, that we had crossed in the morning, the retreat was successfully managed.

I was already beginning to dream of the cabbage soup and rib of mutton with kasha gruel that were awaiting me at the camp, when the word came that the general had commanded a redoubt to be thrown up on the river bank, and that the third battalion of regiment K, and a division of the fourth battery, should stay behind till the next day for that purpose. The wagons with the firewood and the wounded, the Cossacks, the artillery, the infantry with muskets and fagots on their shoulders,—all with noise and songs passed by us. On the faces of all shone enthusiasm and content, caused by the return from peril, and hope of rest; only we and the men of the third battalion were obliged to postpone these joyful feelings till the morrow.

10

While we of the artillery were busy about the guns, disposing the limbers and caissons, and picketing the horses, the foot-soldiers had stacked their arms, piled up bonfires, made shelters of boughs and cornstalks, and were cooking their porridge.

It began to grow dark. Across the sky swept bluish white clouds. The mist, changing into fine drizzling fog, began to wet the ground and the soldiers' cloaks. The horizon became contracted, and all our surroundings took on gloomy shadows. The dampness which I felt through my boots and on my neck, the incessant motion and chatter in which I took no part, the sticky mud with which my legs were covered, and my empty stomach, all combined to arouse in me a most uncomfortable and disagreeable frame of mind after a day of physical and moral fatigue. The thought of Velenchuk did not leave my mind. The whole simple story of his military life kept repeating itself before my imagination.

His last moments were as unclouded and peaceful as all the rest of his life. He had lived too honestly and simply for his artless faith in the heavenly life to come to be shaken at the decisive moment.

"Your health," said Nikolaïef, coming to me. "The captain begs you to be so kind as to come and drink tea with him."

Managing to make my way between stacks of arms and the camp-fires, I followed Nikolaïef to where Captain Bolkhof was, and felt a glow of satisfaction in dreaming about the glass of hot tea and the gay converse which should drive away my gloomy thoughts.

"Well, has he come?" said Bolkhof's voice from his cornstalk wigwam, in which the light was gleaming.

"He is here, your honor," replied Nikolaïef in his deep bass.

In the hut, on a dry *burka*, or Cossack mantle, sat the captain in négligé, and without his cap. Near him the samovar was singing, and a drum was standing loaded with luncheon. A bayonet stuck into the ground held a candle.

"How is this?" he said with some pride, glancing around his comfortable habitation. In fact, it was so pleasant in his wigwam, that while we were at tea I absolutely forgot about the dampness, the gloom, and Velenchuk's wound. We talked about Moscow and subjects that had no relation to the war or the Caucasus.

After one of the moments of silence which sometimes interrupt the most lively conversations, Bolkhof looked at me with a smile.

"Well, I suppose our talk this morning must have seemed very strange to you?" said he.

"No. Why should it? It only seemed to me that you were very frank; but there are things which we all know, but which it is not necessary to speak about."

"Oh, you are mistaken! If there were only some possibility of exchanging this life for any sort of life, no matter how tame and mean, but free from danger and service, I should not hesitate a minute."

"Why, then, don't you go back to Russia?" I asked.

"Why?" he repeated. "Oh, I have been thinking about that for a long time. I can't return to Russia until I have won the Anna and Vladimir, wear the Anna ribbon around my neck, and am major, as I expected when I came here."

"Why not, pray, if you feel that you are so unfitted as you say for the service here?"

"Simply because I feel still more unfitted to return to Russia the same as I came. That also is one of the traditions existing in Russia which were handed down by Passek, Sleptsof, and others,—that you must go to the Caucasus, so as to come home loaded with rewards. And all of us are expecting and working for this; but I have been here two years, have taken part in two expeditions, and haven't won anything. But still, I have so much vanity that I shall not go away from here until I am major, and have the Vladimir and Anna around my neck. I am already accustomed to having everything avoid me, when even Gnilokishkin gets promoted, and I don't. And so how could I show myself in Russia, before the eyes of my elder, the merchant Kotelnikof, to whom I sell wheat, or to my aunty in Moscow, and all those people, if I had served two years in the Caucasus without getting any reward? It is true that I don't wish to know these people, and, of course, they don't care very much about me; but a man is so constituted, that though I don't wish to know them, yet on account of them I am wasting my best years, and destroying all the happiness of my life, and all my future."

11

At this moment the voice of the battalion commander was heard on the outside, saying:—

"Who is it with you, Nikolaï Feodorovitch?"

Bolkhof mentioned my name, and in a moment three officers came into the wigwam,—Major Kirsanof, the adjutant of his battalion, and company commander Trosenko.

Kirsanof was a short, thick-set fellow, with black mustaches, ruddy cheeks, and little oily eyes. His little eyes were the most noticeable features of his physiognomy. When he laughed, there remained of them only two moist little stars; and these little stars, together with his pursed-up lips and long neck, sometimes gave him a peculiar expression of insipidity. Kirsanof considered himself better than any one else in the regiment. The non-commissioned officers did not dispute this; and the chiefs esteemed him, although the general impression about him was that he was very dull-witted. He knew his duties, was accurate and zealous, was always in funds, kept a carriage and a cook, and, naturally enough, managed to get a fair reputation for pride.

"What are you gossiping about, Nikolaï Feodorovitch?" he asked, as he came in.

"Oh, about the delights of the service here."

But at this instant Kirsanof caught sight of me, a mere yunker; and in order to make me feel his importance, as if he had not heard Bolkhof's answer, and glancing at the drum, he asked:—

"What, were you tired, Nikolaï Feodorovitch?"

"No. You see, we . . ." began Bolkhof.

But once more, and it must have been the battalion commander's dignity that caused him to interrupt the answer, he put a new question:—

"Well, didn't we have a glorious action to-day?"

The adjutant of the battalion was a young ensign who had only lately been promoted from the yunker service. He was a modest and gentle young fellow, with a sensitive and good-natured face. I had met him before at Bolkhof's. The young man often came to see him. Having made him a bow, he would sit down in a corner, and for hours at a time say nothing, and only make cigarettes and smoke them; and then he would get up, make another bow, and go away.

He was the type of the poor son of a Russian noble family, who has chosen the profession of arms as the only one open to him in his circumstances, and who values above everything else in the world his official calling,—an ingenuous and lovable type, notwithstanding his absurd, indefeasible peculiarities: his tobacco-pouch, his dressing-gown, his guitar, and his mustache-brush, with which we used to picture him to ourselves. In the regiment they used to say of him that he boasted of being just but stern with his servant, and quoted him as saying, "I rarely punish; but when they drive me to it, then let 'em beware;" and they say that once, when his servant got drunk, and plundered him, and began to rail at his master, he took him to the guard-house, and commanded them to have everything ready for the chastisement; but when he saw the preparations, he was so confused, that he could only stammer a few meaningless words: "Well, now you see, . . . I might," and, thoroughly upset, he set off home, and from that time never dared to look into the eyes of his man. His comrades gave him no peace, but were always nagging him about this; and I often heard how the ingenuous lad tried to defend himself, and, blushing to the roots of his hair, avowed that it was not true, but absolutely false.

The third character, Captain Trosenko, was an old Caucasian in the full acceptation of the word: that is, he was a man for whom the company under his command stood for his family; the fortress where the staff was, his home; and the song-singers his only pleasure in life,—a man for whom everything that was not Kavkas was worthy of scorn, yes, was almost unworthy of belief; everything that was Kavkas was divided into two halves, ours and not ours. He loved the first, the second he hated with all the strength of his soul. And, above all, he was a man of iron nerve, of serene bravery, of rare goodness and devotion to his comrades and subordinates, and of desperate frankness, and even insolence in his bearing, toward those who did not please him; that is, adjutants and *bonjourists*.

As he came into the wigwam, he almost bumped his head on the roof, then suddenly sank down and sat on the ground.

"Well, how is it?" said he; and suddenly becoming cognizant of my presence, and recognizing me, he got up, turning on me a troubled, serious gaze.

"Well, why were you talking about it?" asked the major, taking out his watch and consulting it, though I verily believe there was not the slightest necessity of his doing so.

"Well, he asked me why I served here."

"Of course, Nikolaï Feodorovitch wants to win distinction here, and then go home."

"Well, now, you tell us, Abram Ilyitch, why you serve in the Caucasus."

"I? Because, as you know, in the first place we are all in duty bound to serve. What?" he added, though no one spoke. "Yesterday evening I received a letter from Russia, Nikolaï Feodorovitch," he continued, eager to change the conversation. "They write me that . . . what strange questions are asked!"

"What sort of questions?" asked Bolkhof.

He turned red.

"Really, now, strange questions . . . they write me, asking, 'Can there be jealousy without love?' . . . What?" he asked, looking at us all.

"How so?" said Bolkhof, smiling.

"Well, you know, in Russia it's a good thing," he continued, as if his phrases followed one another in perfectly logical sequence. "When I was at Tambof in '52 I was invited everywhere, as if I were on the emperor's suite. Would you believe me, at a ball at the governor's, when I got there . . . well, don't you know, I was received very cordially. The governor's wife herself, you know, talked with me, and asked about the Caucasus; and so did all the rest . . . why, I don't know . . . they looked at my gold cap as if it were some sort of curiosity, and they asked me how I had won it, and how about the Anna and the Vladimir; and I told them all about it. . . . What? . . . That's why the Caucasus is good, Nikolaï Feodorovitch," he continued, not waiting for a response. "There they look on us Caucasians very kindly. A young man, you know, a staff-officer with the Anna and Vladimir,—that means a great deal in Russia. . . . What?"

"You boasted a little, I imagine, Abram Ilyitch," said Bolkhof.

"He-he," came his silly laugh in reply. "You know, you have to. Yes, and didn't I feed royally those two months!"

"So it is fine in Russia, is it?" asked Trosenko, asking about Russia as if it were China or Japan.

"Yes, indeed! We drank so much champagne there in those two months, that it was a terror!"

"The idea! you? You drank lemonade probably. I should have died to show them how the Kavkazets drinks. The glory has not been won for nothing. I would show them how we drink. . . . Hey, Bolkhof?" he added.

"Yes, you see, you have been already ten years in the Caucasus, uncle," said Bolkhof, "and you remember what Yermolof said; but Abram Ilyitch has been here only six."

"Ten years, indeed! almost sixteen."

"Let us have some sage-brandy, Bolkhof; it's raw, b-rr! Well?" he continued, smiling, "shall we drink, major?"

But the major was out of sorts, on account of the old captain's behavior to him at first; and now he evidently retired into himself, and took refuge in his own greatness. He began to hum some song, and again looked at his watch.

"Well, I shall never go there again," continued Trosenko, paying no heed to the peevish major. "I have got out of the habit of going about and speaking Russian. They'd ask, 'What is this wonderful creature who's come?' and the answer'd be, 'Asia.' Isn't that so, Nikolaï Feodoruitch? And so what is there for me in Russia? It's all the same, you'll get shot here sooner or later. They'll ask, 'Where is Trosenko?' 'Shot!' And down you go! What will you do then in the eighth company—heh?" he added, continuing to address the major.

"Send the officer of the day to the battalion," shouted Kirsanof, not answering the captain, though I was again compelled to believe that there was no need of his giving any orders.

"But, young man, I think that you are glad now that you are having double pay?" said the major, after a few moments' silence, addressing the adjutant of the battalion.

"Why, yes, very."

"I think that our pay is now very large, Nikolaï Feodoruitch," he went on to say. "A young man can live very comfortably, and even allow himself some little luxury."

"No, truly, Abram Ilyitch," said the adjutant, timidly: "even though we get double pay, it's only so much; and you see one must keep a horse." . . .

"What is that you say, young man? I myself have been an ensign, and I know. Believe me, with care, one can live very well. But you must calculate," he added, tapping his left palm with his little finger.

"We pledge all our salary before it's due: this is the way to economize," said Trosenko, drinking down a glass of vodka.

"Well, now, you see that's the very thing. . . . What?"

At this instant at the door of the wigwam appeared a white head with a flattened nose; and a sharp voice with a German accent said:—

"You there, Abram Ilyitch? The officer of the day is hunting for you."

"Come in, Kraft," said Bolkhof.

A tall form in the coat of the general's staff entered the door, and with re-markable zeal endeavored to shake hands with every one.

"Ah, my dear captain, you here too?" said he, addressing Trosenko.

The new guest, notwithstanding the darkness, rushed up to the captain and kissed him on the lips, to his extreme astonishment, and displeasure as it seemed to me.

"This is a German who wishes to be a hail fellow well met," I said to myself.

12

My presumption was immediately confirmed. Captain Kraft called for some vodka, which he called corn-brandy, and threw back his head, and made a terrible noise like a duck, in draining the glass.

"Well, gentlemen, we rolled about well to-day on the plains of the Chechen," he began; but, catching sight of the officer of the day, he immediately paused to allow the major to give his directions.

"Well, you have made the tour of the lines?"

"I have."

"Are the pickets posted?"

"They are."

"Then you may order the captain of the guard to be as alert as possible."

"I will."

The major blinked his eyes, and went into a brown study.

"Well, tell the boys to get their supper."

"That's what they're doing now."

"Good! then you may go. Well," continued the major, with a conciliating smile, addressing us, "we were reckoning what an officer needed; let us finish the calculation."

"We need one uniform and trousers, don't we?"

"Yes."

"That, let us suppose, would amount to fifty rubles every two years; say, twenty-five rubles a year for dress. Then for eating we need every day at least forty kopeks, don't we?"

"Yes, certainly as much as that."

"Well, I'll call it so. Now, for a horse and saddle for remount, thirty rubles; that's all. Twenty-five and a hundred and twenty and thirty make a hundred and seventy-five rubles. All the rest stands for luxuries,—for tea and for sugar and for tobacco,—twenty rubles. Will you look it over? . . . It's right, isn't it, Nikolaï Feodoruitch?"

"Not quite. Excuse me, Abram Ilyitch," said the adjutant, timidly, "nothing is left for tea and sugar. You reckon one suit for every two years, but here in field-service you can't get along with one pair of pantaloons! And boots? Why, I wear out a new pair almost every month. And then linen, shirts, handkerchiefs, and leg-wrappers; all that sort of thing one has to buy. And when you have accounted for it, there isn't anything left at all. That's true, by God! Abram Ilyitch."

"Yes, it's splendid to wear leg-wrappers," said Kraft, suddenly, after a mo-ment's silence, with a loving emphasis on the word *podviortki*, "leg-wrappers"; "you know it's simply Russian fashion."

"I will tell you," remarked Trosenko, "however you reckon it, it all amounts to this, that our brother imagines that we have nothing to eat; but the fact is, that we all live, and drink tea, and smoke tobacco, and drink our vodka. If you served with me," he added, addressing the ensign, "you would soon learn how to live. I suppose you gentlemen know how he treated his denshchik?"

And Trosenko, dying with laughter, told us the whole story of the ensign and his man, though we had all heard it a thousand times.

"What makes you look so rosy, brother?" he continued, pointing to the ensign, who turned red, broke into a perspiration, and smiled with such constraint that it was painful to look at him.

"It's all right, brother. I used to be just like you; but now, you see, I have become hardened. Just let any young fellow come here from Russia,—we have seen 'em,—and here they would get all sorts of rheumatism and spasms; but look at me sitting here: it's my home, and bed, and all. You see" . . . here he drank still another glass of vodka. "Hah?" he continued, looking straight into Kraft's eyes.

"That's what I like in you. He's a genuine old Kavkazets. Kive us your hant."

And Kraft pushed through our midst, rushed up to Trosenko, and, grasping his hand, shook it with remarkable feeling.

"Yes, we can say that we have had all sorts of experiences here," he continued. "In '45 you must have been there, captain? Do you remember the night of the 24th and 25th, when we camped in mud up to our knees, and the next day went against the intrenchments? I was then with the commander-in-chief, and in one day we captured fifteen intrenchments. Do you remember, captain?"

Trosenko nodded assent, and, pushing out his lower lip, closed his eyes.

"You ought to have seen," Kraft began, with extraordinary animation, making awkward gestures with his arms, and addressing the major.

But the major, who must have more than once heard this tale, suddenly threw such an expression of muddy stupidity into his eyes, as he looked at his comrade, that Kraft turned from him, and addressed Bolkhof and me, alternately looking at each of us. But he did not once look at Trosenko, from one end of his story to the other.

"You ought to have seen how, in the morning, the commander-in-chief came to me, and says,'Kraft, take those intrenchments.' You know our military duty,—no arguing, hand to vizor. 'It shall be done, your excellency,' and I started. As soon as we came to the first intrenchment, I turn round, and shout to the soldiers, 'Poys, show your mettle! Pe on your guard! The one who stops I shall cut down with my own hand.' With Russian soldiers you know you have to be plain-spoken. Then suddenly comes a shell . . . I look . . . one soldier, two soldiers, tree soldiers, then the bullets . . . vz-zhin! vz-zhin! vz-zhin! I shout, 'Forward, poys, follow me!' As soon as we reach it, you know, I look and see . . . how it . . . you know: what do you call it?" and the narrator waved his hands in his search for the word.

"Rampart," suggested Bolkhof.

"No. . . . Ach! what is it? Mein Gott, now, what is it? . . . Yes, rampart," said he, quickly. "Then, clubbing their guns! . . . hurrah! ta-ra-ta-ta-ta! The enemy—not a soul was left. Do you know, they were amazed. All right. We rush on . . . the second intrenchment. This was quite a different affair. Our hearts poiled within us, you know. As soon as we got there, I look, and I see the second intrenchment—impossible to mount it. There . . . what was it . . . what was it we just called it? Ach! what was it?" . . .

"Rampart," again I suggested.

"Not at all," said he, with some heat. "Not rampart. Ah, now, what is it called?" and he made a sort of despairing gesture with his hand. "Ach! mein Gott! what is it?" . . .

He was evidently so troubled, that one could not help offering suggestions.

"Moat, perhaps," said Bolkhof.

"No; simply rampart. As soon as we reached it, if you will believe me, there was a fire poured in upon us . . . it was hell." . . .

At the crisis, some one behind the wigwam inquired for me. It was Maksimof. As there still remained thirteen of the intrenchments to be taken in the same monotonous detail, I was glad to have an excuse to go to my division. Trosenko went with me.

"It's all a pack of lies," he said to me when we had gone a few steps from the wigwam. "He wasn't at the intrenchments at all;" and Trosenko laughed so good-naturedly, that I could not help joining him.

13

It was already dark night, and the camp was lighted only by the flickering bonfires, when I, after giving my orders, rejoined my soldiers. A great smoldering log was lying on the coals. Around it were sitting only three of the men,— Antonof, who had set his kettle on the fire to boil his *ryabko*[1]; Zhdanof, thoughtfully poking the ashes with a stick; and Chikin, with his pipe, which was forever in his mouth.

The rest had already turned in, some under gun-carriages, others in the hay, some around the fires. By the faint light of the coals I recognized the backs, the legs, and the heads of those whom I knew. Among the latter was the recruit, who, curled up close to the fire, seemed to be already fast asleep. Antonof made room for me. I sat down by him, and began to smoke a cigarette. The odor of the mist and of the smoke from the wet branches spreading through the air made one's eyes smart, and the same penetrating drizzle fell from the gloomy sky.

Behind us could be heard regular snoring, the crackling of wood in the fire, muffled conversation, and occasionally the clank of muskets among the infantry. Everywhere about us the watch-fires were glowing, throwing their red reflections within narrow circles on the dark forms of the soldiers. Around the nearer fires, I distinguished, in places where it was light, the figures of naked soldiers waving their shirts in the very flames. Many of the men had not yet gone to bed, but were wandering around, and talking over a space of fifteen square sazhens;[2] but the thick, gloomy night imparted a peculiarly mysterious tone to all this movement, as if each felt this gloomy silence, and feared to disturb its peaceful harmony. When I spoke, it seemed to me that my voice sounded strange. On the faces of all the soldiers sitting by the fire I read the same mood.

[1] A military mess—soaked hardtack and tallow.—Author's Note.

[2] A *sazhen* is seven feet.

I thought that, when I joined them, they were talking about their wounded comrade; but it was nothing of the sort. Chikin was telling about the condition of things at Tiflis, and about school-children there.

Always and everywhere, especially in the Caucasus, I have remarked in our soldiery at the time of danger peculiar tact in ignoring or avoiding those things that might have a depressing effect on their comrades' spirits. The spirit of the Russian soldier is not constituted like the courage of the Southern nations, for quickly kindled and quickly cooling enthusiasm; it is as hard to set him on fire as it is to cause him to lose courage. For him it is not necessary to have accessories, speeches, martial shouts, songs, and drums; on the contrary, he wants calmness, order, and avoidance of everything unnatural. In the Russian, the genuine Russian soldier, you never find braggadocio, bravado, or the tendency to get demoralized or excited in time of danger; on the contrary, discretion, simplicity, and the faculty of seeing in peril something quite distinct from the peril, constitute the distinguishing traits of his character.

I have seen a soldier wounded in the leg, at the first moment mourning only over the hole in his new sheepskin polushubok; a messenger thrown from his horse, which was killed under him, unbuckling the girth so as to save the saddle. Who does not recollect the incident at the siege of Hergebel when the fuse of a loaded bomb was on fire in the powder-room, and the artillerist ordered two soldiers to take the bomb and fling it over the wall, and how the soldiers did not take it to the most convenient place, which was near the colonel's tent on the rampart, but carried it farther, lest it should wake the gentlemen who were asleep in the tent, and both of them were blown to pieces?

I remember that, during this same expedition of 1852, one of the young soldiers, during action, said to some one that he did not believe the division would come out of it, and how the whole division in scorn went for him for saying such shameful words that they would not even repeat them.

Here, when now the thought of Velenchuk must have been in the mind of each, and when any second might bring on us the broadside of the stealthy Tartars, all were listening to Chikin's lively story, and no one mentioned the events of the day, nor the present danger, nor their wounded friend, as if it had happened God knows how long ago, or had never been at all. But still, it seemed to me their faces were more serious than usual; they listened with too little attention to Chikin's tale, and even Chikin himself felt that they were not listening to him, but that he was talking to himself.

Maksimof came to the bonfire, and sat down by me. Chikin made room for him, stopped talking, and again began to suck at his pipe.

"The infantry have sent to camp for some vodka," said Maksimof, after a considerably long silence. "They'll be back with it very soon." He spat into the fire. "A subaltern was saying that he had seen our comrade."

"Was he still alive?" asked Antonof, turning his kettle round.

"No, he is dead."

The recruit suddenly raised above the fire his graceful head within his red cap, for an instant gazed intently at Maksimof and me, then quickly dropped it, and rolled himself up in his cloak.

"You see, it was death that was coming on him this morning when I woke him in the gun-park," said Antonof.

"Nonsense!" said Zhdanof, turning over the smoldering log; and all were silent.

Amid the general silence a shot was heard behind us in the camp. Our drummers took it up immediately, and beat the tattoo. When the last roll had ceased, Zhdanof was already up, and the first to take off his cap. The rest of us followed his example.

Amid the deep silence of the night a choir of harmonious male voices resounded:—

"Our Father who art in heaven, hallowed be thy name. Thy kingdom come; thy will be done, as on earth, so in heaven. Give us this day our daily bread, and forgive us our debts as we forgive our debtors. And lead us not into temptation, but deliver us from the evil one."

"It was just so with us in '45; one man was contused in this place," said Antonof, when we had put on our hats and were sitting round the fire again, "and so we carried him two days on the gun. . . . Do you remember Shevchenko, Zhdanof? . . . We left him there under a tree."

At this time a foot-soldier with enormous whiskers and mustaches, carrying a gun and a knapsack, came to our fire.

"Please give a fellow-countryman a coal for his pipe," said he.

"Of course, smoke away; there is plenty of fire," remarked Chikin.

"You were talking about Dargi, weren't you, friend?" asked the soldier, addressing Antonof.

The soldier shook his head, frowned, and squatted down near us on his heels.

"There were all sorts of things there," he remarked.

"Why did you leave him?" I asked of Antonof.

"He had awful pains in his belly. When we stood still, he did not feel it; but when we moved, he screeched and screeched. He besought us by all that was holy to leave him; it was pitiful. Well, and when *he* began to vex us sorely, and had killed three of our men at the guns and one officer, then our batteries opened on him, and did some execution too. We weren't able to drag out the guns . . . there was such mud."

"It was worse under the Indian mountains than anywhere else," remarked one of the soldiers.

"Well, but indeed it kept growing worse and worse for him and Anoshenka— he was an old artillerist—and I decided that indeed there was no chance for him but to say a prayer, and so we left him there. And so we decided. A tree grew there, welcome enough. We left some hardtack for him,—Zhdanof had some,—put him against the tree, put a clean shirt on him, said good-by to him, and so we left him."

"Was he a man of importance?"

"Not at all; he was a soldier," remarked Zhdanof.

"And what became of him, God knows," added Antonof. "Many of our brothers were left there."

"At Dargi?" asked the infantryman, standing up and picking up his pipe, and again frowning and shaking his head. . . . "There were all sorts of things there."

And he left us.

"Say, are there many of the soldiers in our battery who were at Dargi?" I asked.

"Let us see; here is Zhdanof, myself, Patsan,—who is now on furlough,— and there's some six men more. There wouldn't be any others."

"Why has our Patsan gone off on furlough?" asked Chikin, shaking out his legs, and laying his head on a log. "It's almost a year since he went."

"Well, haven't you had your year's furlough?" I asked of Zhdanof.

"No, I've not," he replied reluctantly.

"I tell you it's a good thing to go," said Antonof, "when you come from a rich home, or when you are able to work; and it's rather flattering to go and have the folks glad to see you."

"But how about going when you have a brother," asked Zhdanof, "and would have to be supported by him? They have enough for themselves, but there's nothing for a poor fellow who's a soldier. Wretched kind of help after serving twenty-five years. Besides, whether they are alive or no, who knows?"

"But why haven't you written?" I asked.

"Written? I did send two letters, but they don't reply. Either they are dead, or they don't reply because, of course, they are poor. It's so everywhere."

"Have you written lately?"

"When we left Dargi I wrote my last letter."

"You had better sing that song about the little birch tree," said Zhdanof to Antonof, who at this moment was on his knees, and purring some song. Antonof sang his "Song of the White Birch."

"That's Uncle Zhdanof's very most favorite song," said Chikin to me, in a whisper, pulling me by my coat. "The other day, as Filipp Antonuitch was singing it, he actually cried."

Zhdanof at first sat absolutely motionless, with his eyes fastened on the smoldering embers, and his face, shining in the ruddy glow, seemed extraordinarily gloomy; then his cheek under his mustaches began to move quicker and quicker; and at last he got up, and, spreading out his cloak, he lay down in the shadow behind the fire. Either he tossed about and groaned as he got ready for bed, or the death of Velenchuk and this wretched weather had completely upset me; but it certainly seemed to me that he was weeping.

The bottom of the log, which had been rolled on the fire, occasionally blazing up, threw its light on Antonof's form, with his gray mustache, his red face, and the ribbons on the cloak flung over his shoulders, and brought into relief the boots, heads, or backs of other sleeping soldiers.

From above the same melancholy drizzle was falling; in the atmosphere was the same odor of dampness and smoke; around us could be seen the same bright dots of the dying fires, and amid the general silence the melancholy notes of Antonof's song rang out. And when this ceased for a moment, the faint nocturnal sounds of the camp, the snoring, the clank of the sentinel's musket, and quiet conversation, seemed to repeat it.

"Second watch! Makatiuk and Zhdanof," shouted Maksimof.

Antonof ceased to sing; Zhdanof arose, drew a deep sigh, stepped across the log, and went off quietly to the guns.

AN OLD ACQUAINTANCE

PRINCE NEKHLIUDOF RELATES HOW, DURING
AN EXPEDITION IN THE CAUCASUS, HE MET
AN ACQUAINTANCE FROM MOSCOW

Our division was out in the field.

The work in hand was accomplished; we had made a clearing in the forest, and each day we were expecting from headquarters orders for our return to the fort. Our division of field-pieces was stationed at the top of a steep mountain crest which was terminated by the swift mountain river Mechik, and had to sweep with cannon-shot the plain that stretched before us. Here and there on this picturesque plain, out of the reach of gunshot, now and then, especially at evening, harmless groups of mounted mountaineers showed themselves, attracted by curiosity to ride up and view the Russian camp.

The evening was clear, mild, and fresh, as it generally is in December in the Caucasus; the sun was setting behind the steep spur of the mountains at the left, and threw rosy rays on the tents scattered over the slope, on the soldiers moving about, and on our two guns, which seemed to crane out their necks as they rested, motionless, on the earthwork two paces from us. The infantry picket, stationed on the knoll at the left, stood in perfect silhouette against the light of the sunset; no less distinct were the stacks of muskets, the form of the sentry, the groups of soldiers, and the smoke of the smoldering camp-fire.

At the right and left of the slope, on the black, sodden earth, the tents gleamed white; and behind the tents, black stood the bare trunks of the chinar trees, which rang with the incessant sound of axes, the crackling of the bonfires, and the crashing of the trees as they fell under the axes. The bluish smoke arose from tobacco-pipes on all sides, and vanished into the transparent azure of the frosty sky.

Past the tents, and on the lower ground around the arms, rushed the Cossacks, dragoons, and artillerists, with great galloping and snorting of horses, as they returned from getting water. It began to freeze; all sounds were heard with extraordinary distinctness, and one could see an immense distance across the plain through the clear, rare atmosphere.

The groups of the enemy, no longer arousing the curiosity of the soldiers, quietly galloped off across the fields, still yellow with the golden corn-stubble, toward their *auls*, or villages, which were visible beyond the forest, with the tall posts of the cemeteries, and the smoke, rising in the air.

Our tent was pitched not far from the guns, on a place high and dry, from which we had a remarkably extended view. Near the tent, on a cleared space, around the battery itself, we had our games of chushki and skittles. The obliging soldiers had made for us rustic benches and tables. On account of all these conveniences the artillery officers, our comrades, and a few infantrymen liked to come together at our battery, and they called the place the club.

The evening was fine, the best players had collected, and we were amusing ourselves with *gorodki*, or skittles. Ensign D., Lieutenant O., and I had played two games in succession; and to the common satisfaction and amusement of all the spectators,—officers, soldiers, and servants,—who were watching us from their tents, we had twice carried the winning party on our backs from one end of the ground to the other. Especially droll was the situation of the huge, fat Captain S., who, puffing and smiling good-naturedly, with legs dragging on the ground, rode pickapack on the feeble little Lieutenant O.

But when it was now somewhat later, the servants brought three glasses of tea for the six men of us, and not a saucer; and we who had finished our game came to the plaited benches.

There was standing near them a small bow-legged man, a stranger to us, in a sheepskin tulup, and a *papakha*, or Circassian cap, with long, overhanging white crown. As soon as we came near where he stood, he several times irresolutely took off his cap, and put it on again; and several times he seemed to make up his mind to come to meet us, and then stopped again. But after deciding, probably, that it was impossible to remain unobserved, the stranger took off his cap, and, going in a circuit around us, approached Captain S.

"Ah, Guskantini, how is it, old man?" said S., still smiling good-naturedly under the influence of his ride.

Guskantini, as S. called him, instantly replaced his cap, and made a motion to thrust his hands into the pockets of his jacket; but on the side toward me there was no pocket in the jacket, and his small red hand hung in an awkward position. I felt a strong desire to make out who this man was—was he a yunker, or a degraded officer?—and, not realizing that my gaze—that is, the gaze of a strange officer—disconcerted him, I continued to stare at his dress and appearance.

I judged that he was about thirty. His small, round, gray eyes had a sleepy expression, and at the same time gazed restlessly out from under the dirty white lambskin of his cap, which hung down over his face. His thick, irregular nose, standing out between his sunken cheeks, gave evidence of emaciation that was the result of illness, and not natural. His lips, barely covered by a sparse, soft, whitish mustache, were constantly changing their shape, as if they were trying to assume now one expression, now another. But all these expressions seemed to be endless; yet his face retained one predominating expression of haste and fright. Around his thin neck, where the veins stood out, was tied a green woolen scarf tucked into his jacket. His short *polushubok*, or jacket, was worn bare, and had dog-fur sewed on the collar and on the false pockets. The trousers were checkered, of ash-gray color, and his shoes had short, unblacked military bootlegs.

"I beg of you, do not disturb yourself," said I, when he, for the second time, timidly glancing at me, had taken off his cap.

He bowed to me with an expression of gratitude, replaced his hat, and, drawing from his pocket a dirty calico tobacco-pouch with lacings, began to roll a cigarette.

I myself had not been long a yunker, an elderly yunker; and as I was incapable, as yet, of being good-naturedly serviceable to my younger comrades, and as I had no means, I well knew all the moral difficulties of this situation for a proud man no longer young and I sympathized with all men who found themselves in such a situation, and I endeavored to make clear to myself their character and rank, and the tendencies of their intellectual peculiarities, in order to judge of the degree of their moral sufferings. This yunker or degraded officer, judging by his restless eyes and that expectant and perpetual variation of expression which I noticed in him, was a man very far from stupid, and extremely egotistical, and therefore much to be pitied.

Captain S. invited us to play another game of gorodki, the stakes to consist, not only of the usual pickapack ride of the winning party, but also of a few bottles of red wine, rum, sugar, cinnamon, and cloves for the mulled wine which that winter, on account of the cold, was greatly popular in our division.

Guskantini, as S. again called him, was also invited to take part; but before the game began, the man, struggling between the gratification afforded him by the invitation and a certain timidity, drew Captain S. aside, and began to say something in a whisper. The good-natured captain punched him in the ribs with his big, fat hand, and replied, loud enough to be heard:—

"Not at all, old fellow, I assure you."

When the game was over, and that side in which the stranger whose rank was so low had taken part, had come out winners, and it fell to his lot to ride on one of our officers, Ensign D., the ensign grew red in the face; he went to the little divan and offered the stranger a cigarette by way of a compromise.

While they were ordering the mulled wine, and in the steward's tent were heard assiduous preparations on the part of Nikita, who had sent an orderly for cinnamon and cloves, and the shadow of his back was alternately lengthening and shortening on the dingy sides of the tent, we men, seven in all, sat around on the benches; and while we took turns in drinking tea from the three glasses, and gazed out over the plain, which was now beginning to glow in the twilight, we talked and laughed over the various incidents of the game.

The stranger in the sheepskin took no share in the conversation, obstinately refused to drink the tea which I several times offered him, and as he sat there on the ground in Tartar fashion, occupied himself in making cigarettes of fine-cut tobacco, and smoking them one after another, evidently not so much for his own satisfaction as to give himself the appearance of a man with something to do.

When it was remarked that the summons to return was expected on the morrow, and that there might be an engagement, he got up on his knees, and, addressing Captain S. only, said that he was now living at the adjutant's, and had himself written the order for the return on the next day. We all said nothing while he was speaking; and, notwithstanding the fact that he seemed so bashful, we begged him to repeat this most interesting piece of news. He repeated what he had said, adding only that he had been staying at the adjutant's (since he made it his home there) when the order came.

"Look here, old fellow, if you are not telling us a lie, I shall have to go to my company and give some orders for to-morrow," said Captain S.

"No . . . why . . . it may be, I am sure . . ." stammered the stranger, but suddenly stopped, and, apparently feeling himself affronted, contracted his brows unnaturally, and, muttering something between his teeth, began to roll another cigarette. But he found that he had emptied his calico bag of the fine-cut tobacco and that there was not enough, so he asked S. to favor him with a little cigarette.

We kept on for a considerable time with that monotonous military chapter which every one who has ever been on an expedition will appreciate; all of us, with one and the same expression, complaining of the dullness and length of the expedition, in one and the same fashion sitting in judgment on our superiors, and all of us likewise, as we had done many times before, praising one comrade, pitying another, wondering how much this one had gained, how much that one had lost, and so on, and so on.

"Here, fellows, this adjutant of ours is completely broken up," said Captain S. "At headquarters he was everlastingly on the winning side; no matter whom he sat down with, he'd rake in everything; but now for two months past he has been losing all the time. The present expedition hasn't been lucky for him. I think he has got away with two thousand silver rubles and five hundred rubles' worth of articles,—the carpet that he won at Mukhin's, Nikitin's pistols, Sada's gold watch which Vorontsof gave him. He has lost it all."

"He's got his deserts," said Lieutenant O.: "he used to cheat everybody; it was impossible to play with him."

"He's cheated every one, but now it's all gone up in his pipe;" and here Captain S. laughed good-naturedly, "Our friend Guskof here lives with him. He hasn't gambled *him* away yet; that's so, isn't it, old fellow?" he asked, addressing Guskof.

Guskof laughed. It was a melancholy, sickly laugh, which completely changed the expression of his countenance. Till this moment it had seemed to me that I had seen and known this man before; and, besides, the name Guskof, by which Captain S. called him, was familiar to me; but how and when I had seen and known him, I really could not remember.

"Yes," said Guskof, who kept putting his hand to his mustaches, but instantly dropping it again without touching them. "Pavel Dmitrievitch's luck has been against him in this expedition, such a *veine de malheur*," he added, in a careful but pure French pronunciation, again giving me to think that I had seen him, and seen him often, somewhere. "I know Pavel Dmitrievitch very well. He has great confidence in me," he proceeded to say; "he and I are old friends; that is, he is fond of me," he explained, evidently fearing that it might be taken as presumption for him to claim old friendship with the adjutant. "Pavel Dmitrievitch plays admirably; but now, strange as it may seem, it's all up with him, he is just about perfectly ruined; *la chance a tourné*," he added, addressing himself particularly to me.

At first we had listened to Guskof with condescending attention; but as soon as he made use of that second French phrase, we all involuntarily turned from him.

"I have played with him a thousand times, and we agreed then that it was strange," said Lieutenant O., with peculiar emphasis on the word *strange*. "I never once won a ruble from him. Why was it, when I used to win of others?"

"Pavel Dmitrievitch plays admirably; I have known him for a long time," said I.

In fact, I had known the adjutant for several years; more than once I had seen him in the full swing of a game, surrounded by officers, and I had remarked his handsome, rather gloomy and always passionless, calm face, his deliberate Malo-Russian pronunciation, his handsome equipment and horses, his bold, manly figure, and above all his skill and self-restraint in carrying on the game accurately and agreeably. More than once, I am sorry to say, as I looked at his plump white hands, with a diamond ring on the index-finger, dealing out one card after another, I grew angry with that ring, with his white hands, with the whole of the adjutant's person, and evil thoughts on his account arose in my mind.

But as I afterwards reconsidered the matter coolly, I persuaded myself that he played more skilfully than all with whom he happened to play; the more so, because as I heard his general observations concerning the game,—how one ought not to back out when one had laid the smallest stake, how one ought not to leave off in certain cases as the first rule for honorable men, and so forth, and so forth,—it was evident that he was always on the winning side merely from the fact that he played more sagaciously and coolly than the rest of us. And now it seemed that this self-reliant, careful player had been stripped not only of his money but of his effects, which marks the lowest depths of loss for an officer.

"He always had devilish good luck with me," said Lieutenant O. "I made a vow never to play with him again."

"What a marvel you are, old fellow!" said S., nodding at me, and addressing O. "You lost three hundred silver rubles, that's what you lost to him."

"More than that," said the lieutenant, savagely.

"And now you have come to your senses; it is rather late in the day, old man, for the rest of us have known for a long time that he was the cheat of the regiment," said S., with difficulty restraining his laughter, and feeling very well satisfied with his fabrication. "Here is Guskof right here,—he *fixes* his cards for him. That's the reason of the friendship between them old man." . . .

And Captain S., shaking all over, burst out into such a hearty "ha, ha, ha!" that he spilt the glass of mulled wine which he was holding in his hand. On Guskof's pale, emaciated face there showed something like a color; he opened his mouth several times, raised his hands to his mustaches and once more dropped them to his side where the pockets should have been, stood up, and then sat down again, and finally in an unnatural voice said to S.:—

"It's no joke, Nikolaï Ivanovitch, for you to say such things before people who don't know me and who see me in this unlined jacket . . . because . . ."

His voice failed him, and again his small red hands with their dirty nails went from his jacket to his face, touching his mustache, his hair, his nose, rubbing his eyes, or needlessly scratching his cheek.

"As to saying that, everybody knows it, old fellow," continued S., thoroughly satisfied with his jest, and not heeding Guskof's emotion.

Guskof was still trying to say something; and, placing the palm of his right hand on his left knee in a most unnatural position, and gazing at S., he had an appearance of smiling contemptuously.

"No," said I to myself, as I noticed that smile of his, "I have not only seen him, but have spoken with him somewhere."

"You and I have met somewhere," said I to him, when, under the influence of the common silence, S.'s laughter began to calm down. Guskof's mobile face suddenly lighted up, and his eyes for the first time, with a truly joyous expression, rested on me.

"Why, I recognized you immediately," he replied in French. "In '48 I had the pleasure of meeting you quite frequently in Moscow at my sister's, Madame Ivashin's."

I apologized for not recognizing him at first in that costume and in that new garb. He arose, came to me, and with his moist hand irresolutely and weakly seized my hand, and sat down by me. Instead of looking at me, though he apparently seemed so glad to see me, he gazed with an expression of unfriendly bravado at the officers.

Either because I recognized in him a man whom I had met a few years before in a dress-coat in a drawing-room, or because he was suddenly raised in his own opinion by the fact of being recognized,—at all events it seemed to me that his face and even his motions completely changed: they now expressed lively intelligence, a childish self-satisfaction in the consciousness of such intelligence, and a certain contemptuous indifference; so that I confess, notwithstanding the pitiable position in which he found himself, my old acquaintance did not so much excite sympathy in me as it did a sort of hostile sentiment.

I now vividly remembered our first meeting. In 1848, while I was staying at Moscow, I frequently went to the house of Ivashin, who had been an old friend of mine from childhood. His wife was an agreeable hostess, a charming woman, as everybody said; but she never pleased me. . . .

The winter I knew her, she often spoke with hardly concealed pride of her brother, who had shortly before completed his course, and promised to be one of the most cultivated and popular young men in the best society of Petersburg. As I knew by reputation the father of the Guskofs, who was very rich and occupied an important position, and as I knew also the sister's ways, I felt some prejudice against meeting the young man.

One evening when I was at Ivashin's, I saw a short, thoroughly pleasant-looking young man, in a black dress-coat, white waistcoat and necktie. My host hastened to make me acquainted with him. The young man, evidently dressed for a ball, with his hat in his hand, was standing before Ivashin, and was eagerly but politely arguing with him about a common friend of ours, who had distinguished himself at the time of the Hungarian campaign. He said that this acquaintance was not at all a hero or a man born for war, as was said of him, but was simply a clever and cultivated man. I recollect, I took part in the argument against Guskof, and went to the extreme of declaring even that intellect and cultivation always bore an inverse relation to bravery; and I recollect how Guskof pleasantly and cleverly pointed out to me that bravery was necessarily the result of intellect and a decided degree of development,—a statement which I, who considered myself an intellectual and cultivated man, could not in my heart of hearts agree with.

I recollect that toward the close of our conversation Madame Ivashin introduced me to her brother; and he, with a condescending smile, offered me his little hand on which he had not yet had time to draw his lavender kid glove, and weakly and irresolutely pressed my hand as he did now. Though I had been prejudiced against Guskof, I could not help granting that he was in the right, and agreeing with his sister that he was really a clever and agreeable young man, who ought to have great success in society.

He was extraordinarily neat, beautifully dressed, and fresh, and had self-confidently modest manners, and a thoroughly youthful, almost childish appearance, on account of which, you could not help pardoning him for an expression of conceit and a desire to temper his superiority over you, which were constantly manifested in his intellectual face and especially his smile.

It was said that he had enjoyed great success that winter with the ladies of Moscow. As I saw him at his sister's I could only infer how far this was true by the look of happiness and satisfaction which he constantly wore, and by his sometimes indiscreet anecdotes.

He and I met half a dozen times, and talked a good deal; or, rather, he talked a good deal, and I listened. He spoke for the most part in French, with a thoroughly good accent, very fluently and ornately; and he had the skill of drawing others gently and politely into the conversation. As a general thing, he behaved toward all, and toward me, somewhat condescendingly, and I felt that he was perfectly right in this way of treating people. I always feel that way in regard to men who are firmly convinced that they ought to treat me condescendingly, and who are comparative strangers to me.

Now, as he sat with me, and gave me his hand, I distinctly recognized in him that same old haughtiness of expression; and it seemed to me that he did not properly appreciate his position of official inferiority before an officer, he asked me with such nonchalance what I had been doing in all that time, and how I happened to be there. In spite of the fact that I invariably made my replies in Russian, he kept talking in French, expressing himself remarkably well, but not so fluently as in days gone by. About himself he remarked casually that after his unhappy, wretched story (what the story was, I did not know, and he had not told me), he had been three months under arrest, and then had been sent to the Caucasus to the N. regiment, and had now been serving three years as a soldier in that regiment.

"You would not believe," said he to me in French, "how much I have to suffer in these regiments from the society of the officers. Still, it is a pleasure to me that I used to know the adjutant of whom we were just speaking; he is a good man . . . it's a fact," he remarked condescendingly. "I live with him, and that's something of a relief for me. Yes, my dear, the days fly by, but they aren't all alike," he added; and suddenly hesitated, reddened, and stood up, as he caught sight of the adjutant himself coming toward us.

"It is such a pleasure to meet such a man as you," said Guskof to me in a whisper, as he turned from me; "I should like very, very much to have a long talk with you."

I said that I should be very happy to talk with him, but in reality I confess that Guskof excited in me a sort of dull pity which was not akin to sympathy.

I had a presentiment that I should feel a constraint in a private conversation with him; but still I was anxious to learn from him several things, and, above all, why it was, when his father had been so rich, that he was in poverty, as was evident by his dress and appearance.

The adjutant greeted all of us, except Guskof, and sat down by me in the seat which the cashiered officer had just vacated. Pavel Dmitrievitch, who had always been calm and leisurely, a genuine gambler, and a man of means, was now very different from what I had known him in the flowery days of his success; he seemed to be in haste to go somewhere, kept constantly glancing at every one, and although he had sworn off from playing, it was not five minutes before he proposed to Lieutenant O. to set up a small faro-bank.

Lieutenant O. refused, under the pretext of having to attend to his duties, but in reality because, as he knew how few possessions and little money Pavel Dmitrievitch had left, he did not feel himself justified in risking his three hundred rubles against a hundred or even less which the adjutant might stake.

"Well, Pavel Dmitrievitch," said the lieutenant, anxious to avoid a repetition of the invitation, "is it true, what they tell us, that we return to-morrow?"

"I don't know," replied Pavel Dmitrievitch. "Orders came, to be in readiness; but if it's true, then you'd better play a game. I would wager my Kabarda."

"No, to-day I've . . ."

"He's a gray. Don't count that once; but if you prefer, play for money. How is that?" . . .

"Yes, but . . . I should be willing . . . pray don't think that . . ." said Lieutenant O., answering the implication; "but as there may be a raid or some movement, I must go to bed early."

The adjutant stood up, and, thrusting his hands into his pockets, started to go across the grounds. His face assumed its ordinary expression of coldness and pride, which I admired in him.

"Won't you have a glass of mulled wine?" I asked him.

"That might be acceptable," and he came back to me; but Guskof hastily snatched the glass from me, and handed it to the adjutant, striving at the same time not to look at him. But as he did not notice the tent-rope, Guskof stumbled over it, and fell on his hands, dropping the glass.

"What a bungler!" exclaimed the adjutant, still holding out his hand for the glass. Everybody burst out laughing, not excepting Guskof, who was rubbing his hand over his bruised knee, which he had somehow struck as he fell. "That's the way the bear waited on the hermit," continued the adjutant. "It's the way he waits on me every day. He has pulled up all the tent-pins; he's always tripping up."

Guskof, not hearing him, apologized to us, and glanced toward me with a smile of almost noticeable melancholy as if saying that I alone could understand him. He was pitiable to see; but the adjutant, his protector, seemed, for some reason, to be severe on his messmate, and did not try to put him at his ease.

"Well, you're a graceful lad! Where did you think you were going?"

"Well, who can help tripping over these pins, Pavel Dmitrievitch?" said Guskof. "You tripped over them yourself the other day."·

"I, batyushka,—I am not of the rank and file, and gracefulness is not expected of me."

"He can be a laggard," said Captain S., keeping the ball rolling, "but low-rank men have to make their legs fly."

"Strange jests," said Guskof, almost in a whisper, and casting down his eyes.

The adjutant was evidently vexed with his messmate; he listened with inquisitive attention to every word he said.

"He'll have to be sent out into ambuscade again," said he, addressing S., and pointing to the cashiered officer.

"Well, there'll be some more tears," said S., laughing.

Guskof no longer looked at me, but acted as if he were going to take some tobacco from his pouch, though there had been none there for some time.

"Get ready for the ambuscade, old man," said S., addressing him amid shouts of laughter. "To-day the scouts have brought the news, there'll be an attack on the camp to-night, so it's necessary to designate the trusty lads."

An irresolute smile crossed Guskof's face as if he were preparing to make some reply, and several times he cast a supplicating look at S.

"Well, you know I have been, and I'm ready to go again if I am sent," he said hastily.

"Then you'll be sent."

"Well, I'll go. Isn't that all right?"

"Yes, as at Arguna you deserted the ambuscade and threw away your gun," said the adjutant; and, turning from him, he began to tell us the orders for the next day.

As a matter of fact, we expected from the enemy a cannonade of the camp that night, and the next day some sort of diversion. While still chatting about various subjects of general interest, the adjutant, as if from a sudden and unexpected impulse, proposed to Lieutenant O. to have a little game. The lieutenant most unexpectedly consented; and, together with S. and the ensign, they went off to the adjutant's tent, where there was a folding green table with cards on it. The captain, the commander of our division, went to his tent to sleep; the other gentlemen also took their departure, and Guskof and I were left alone. My presentiment was right: it was really very uncomfortable for me to have a *tête-à-tête* with him; I arose involuntarily, and began to promenade up and down on the battery. Guskof walked in silence by my side, hastily and awkwardly wheeling around so as not to delay or incommode me.

"I do not annoy you?" he asked in a soft, mournful voice. As well as I could see by his face in the dim light, he seemed deeply thoughtful and melancholy.

"Not at all," I replied; but as he did not immediately begin to speak, and as I did not know what to say to him, we walked in silence a considerably long time.

The twilight had now absolutely changed into dark night; over the black profile of the mountains gleamed the bright evening heat-lightning; over our heads in the light-blue frosty sky twinkled the little stars; on all sides gleamed the ruddy flames of the smoking watch-fires; near us the white tents stood out in contrast to the frowning blackness of our earthworks. The light from the nearest watch-fire, around which our servants, engaged in quiet conversation, were warming themselves, occasionally flashed on the brass of our heavy guns, and fell on the form of the sentry, who, wrapped in his cloak, paced with measured tread along the battery.

"You cannot imagine what a delight it is for me to talk with such a man as you are," said Guskof, although as yet he had not spoken a word to me. "Only one who had been in my position could appreciate it."

I did not know how to reply to him, and we again relapsed into silence, although, evidently, he wanted to talk and I to listen to him.

"Why were you . . . why did you suffer this?" I inquired at last, not being able to invent any better way of starting a conversation.

"Why, didn't you hear about this wretched business from Metvenin?"

"Yes, a duel, I believe; I did not hear much about it," I replied. "You see, I have been for some time in the Caucasus."

"No, it wasn't a duel, but it was a stupid and horrid story. I will tell you all about it, if you don't know. It happened the same year that I met you at my sister's; I was living then at Petersburg. I must tell you I had then what they call *une position dans le monde,*—a position good enough if it was not brilliant. *Mon père me donnait* 10,000 *par an.* In '49 I was promised a place in the embassy at Turin; my uncle on my mother's side had influence, and was always ready to do a great deal for me. That sort of thing is all past now. *J'étais reçu dans la meilleure société de Petersbourg;* I might have aspired to any girl in the city. I was well educated, as we all are who come from the school, but was not especially cultivated; to be sure, I read a good deal afterward, *mais j'avais surtout,* you know, *ce jargon du monde,* and, however it came about, I was looked on as one of the leading young men of Petersburg. What raised me more than all in common estimation, *c'est cette liaison avec Madame D.,* about which a great deal was said in Petersburg; but I was frightfully young at that time, and did not prize these advantages very highly. I was simply young and stupid. What more did I need? Just then that Metyenin had some notoriety . . ."

And Guskof went on in the same fashion to relate to me the history of his misfortunes, which I will omit, as it would not be at all interesting.

"Two months I remained under arrest," he continued, "absolutely alone; and what thoughts did I not have during that time? But you know, when it was all over, as if every tie had been broken with the past, then it became easier for me. *Mon père*—you have heard tell of him, of course, a man of iron will and strong convictions,—*il m'a déshérité,* and has broken off all intercourse with me. According to his convictions he had to do as he did, and I don't blame him at all. *Il a été conséquent*—perfectly consistent. Consequently I have not taken a step to induce him to change his mind. My sister was abroad. Madame D. is the only one who wrote to me when I was released, and she sent me assistance; but you understand that I could not accept it, so that I had none of those little things which make one's position a little easier, you know,—books, linen, food, or anything. At this time I thought things over and over, and began to look at life with different eyes. For instance, this noise, this society gossip about me in Petersburg, did not interest me, did not flatter me; it all seemed to me ridiculous. I felt that I myself had been to blame; I was young and indiscreet; I had spoiled my career, and I only thought how I might get into the right track again. And I felt that I had strength and energy enough for it. After my arrest, as I told you, I was sent here to the Caucasus to the N. regiment.

"I thought," he went on to say, all the time becoming more and more animated,—"I thought that here in the Kavkas, *la vie de camp*, the simple, honest men with whom I should associate, and war and danger, would all admirably agree with my state of mind, so that I might begin a new life. They will see me under fire. I shall make myself liked; I shall be respected for my real self,—the cross—non-commissioned officer; they will relieve me of my fine; and I shall get up again, *et, vous savez, avec ce prestige du malheur!* But, *quel désenchantement!* You can't imagine how I have been deceived! . . . You know what sort of men the officers of our regiment are."

He did not speak for some little time, waiting, as it appeared, for me to tell him how bad I knew the society of our officers here was; but I made him no reply. It went against my grain that he should expect me, because I knew French, forsooth, to take issue with the society of the officers, which, during my long residence in the Caucasus, I had had time enough to appreciate fully, and which I respected a thousandfold more than the society from which Mr. Guskof had sprung. I wanted to tell him so, but his position constrained me.

"In the N. regiment the society of the officers is a thousand times worse than it is here," he continued. "I hope that it is saying a good deal; that is, you cannot imagine what it is. I am not speaking of the yunkers and the soldiers. That is horrible, it is so bad. At first they received me very kindly, that is absolutely the truth; but when they saw that I could not help despising them, you know, in these inconceivably small circumstances, they saw that I was a man absolutely different, standing far above them, they got angry with me, and began to put various little humiliations on me. You haven't an idea what I had to suffer. Then this forced relationship with the yunkers, and especially with the small means that I had . . . I lacked everything; I had only what my sister used to send me. And here's a proof for you! As much as it made me suffer, I, with my character, *avec ma fierté, j'ai écris à mon père*, I begged him to send me something. I understand how living four years of such a life may make a man like our cashiered Dromof, who drinks with soldiers, and writes notes to all the officers asking them to lend him three rubles, and signing it, *tout à vous*, Dromof. One must have such a character as I have not to be mired in the least by such a horrible position."

For some time he walked in silence by my side.

"Have you a cigarette?" he asked me.

"And so I stayed right where I was? Yes. I could not endure it physically, because I lived like a common soldier, and we were wretched, cold, and ill-fed . . . but still the officers had some sort of consideration for me. I had still some prestige, which they regarded. I wasn't sent out on guard, nor for drill. I could not have stood that. But morally my sufferings were frightful; and especially because I saw no escape from my position. I wrote my uncle, begged him to get me transferred to my present regiment, which, at least, sees some service; and I thought that here Pavel Dmitrievitch, *qui est le fils de l'intendant de mon père*, might be of some use to me. My uncle did this for me; I was transferred. After that regiment this one seemed to me a collection of chamberlains. Then Pavel Dmitrievitch was here; he knew who I was, and I was splendidly received. At my uncle's request . . . a Guskof, *vous savez*; but I observed that with these men, without cultivation, and undeveloped, . . . they can't appreciate a man, and show him marks of esteem, unless he has that aureole of wealth, of friends; and I noticed how, little by little, when they saw that I was poor, their behavior to me showed more and more indifference, until they have come almost to despise me. It is horrible, but it is absolutely the truth.

"Here I have been in action, I have fought, they have seen me under fire," he continued; "but when will it all end? I think, never. And my strength and energy have already begun to flag. Then I had imagined *la guerre, la vie de camp*; but it isn't at all what I expected: in a sheepskin jacket, dirty linen, soldier's boots, you go out in ambuscade, and the whole night long lie in the ditch with some Antonof reduced to the ranks for drunkenness, and any minute, from behind the bush, may come a rifle-shot, and hit you or Antonof,—it's all the same. That is not bravery; it's horrible, *c'est affreux*, it's killing!"

"Well, you may be promoted a non-commissioned officer for this campaign, and next year an ensign," said I.

"Yes, it may be; they promised me that, but in two years, and it's not up yet. What would those two years amount to, if I knew any one! You can imagine this life with Pavel Dmitrievitch; cards, low jokes, drinking all the time; if you wish to tell anything that is weighing on your mind, you are not understood, or you are laughed at; they talk with you, not for the sake of sharing a thought, but to get something funny out of you. Yes . . . and so it has gone . . . in a brutal, beastly way, and you are always conscious that you belong to the rank and file; they always make you feel that. Hence you can't realize what an enjoyment it is to talk à *cœur ouvert* to such a man as you are."

I had never imagined what kind of a man I was, and consequently I did not know what answer to make him.

"Will you have your supper now?" asked Nikita at this juncture, approaching me unseen in the darkness, and, as I could perceive, vexed at the presence of a guest. "Nothing but curd dumplings; there's none of the roast beef left."

"Has the captain had his supper yet?"

"He went to bed long ago," replied Nikita, gruffly. "According to my directions, I was to serve your supper here and your brandy."

He muttered something else discontentedly, and sauntered off to his tent. After grumbling a little more, he brought us, nevertheless, a bottle-case; he placed a candle on the bottle-case, and shielded it from the wind with a sheet of paper. He brought a saucepan, some mustard in a jar, a tin dipper with a handle, and a bottle of absinthe. After he had arranged all these things, Nikita lingered around us for some moments, and looked on with great disapprobation as Guskof and I were drinking the liqueur. By the feeble light shed by the candle through the paper, amid the encircling darkness, could be seen the sealskin cover of the bottle-case, the supper arranged on it, Guskof's sheepskin jacket, his face, and his small red hands which he used in lifting the dumplings from the pan. Everything round us was black; and only by straining the sight could be seen the dark battery, the dark form of the sentry moving along the breastwork, on all sides the watch-fires, and on high the ruddy stars.

Guskof wore a melancholy, almost guilty smile, as if it were awkward for him to look into my face after his confession. He drank still another glass of the liqueur, and ate ravenously, emptying the saucepan.

"Yes; for you it must be a relief all the same," said I, for the sake of saying something,—"your acquaintance with the adjutant. He is a very good man, I have heard."

"Yes," replied the cashiered officer, "he is a kind man; but he can't help being what he is, with his education, and it is useless to expect it." A flush seemed suddenly to cross his face. "You remarked his coarse jest this evening about the ambuscade."

And Guskof, though I tried several times to interrupt him, began to justify himself before me, and to show that he had not run away from the ambuscade, and that he was not a coward as the adjutant and Captain S. tried to make him out.

"As I was telling you," he went on to say, wiping his hands on his sheepskin jacket, "such people can't show any delicacy toward a man, a common soldier, who hasn't much money either. That's beyond their strength. And here recently, since I haven't received anything at all from my sister for five months, I have noticed how they have changed toward me. This sheepskin jacket, which I bought of a soldier, and which hasn't any warmth in it, because it's all worn out,"—and here he showed me where the wool was gone from the inside, —"it doesn't arouse in him any sympathy or consideration for my unhappiness, but scorn, which he does not take pains to hide. Whatever my necessities may be, as now when I have nothing to eat except soldiers' kasha-gruel, and nothing to wear," he continued, casting down his eyes, and pouring out for himself still another glass of the liqueur, "he does not even offer to lend me some money, though he knows perfectly well that I would give it back to him; but he waits till I am obliged to ask him for it. But you appreciate how it is for me to go to *him*. In your case I should say square and fair, *Vous êtes au dessus de cela, mon cher, je n'ai pas le sou.* And you know," said he, looking straight into my eyes with an expression of desperation, "I am going to tell you square and fair, I am in terrible straits: *pouvez-vous me prêter dix rubles argent?* My sister ought to send me some by the next mail, *et mon père . . ."*

"Why, most willingly," said I, although, on the contrary, it was trying and unpleasant, especially because the evening before, having lost at cards, I had left only about five rubles in Nikita's care. "In a moment," said I, arising; "I will go and get it at the tent."

"No, by and by; *ne vous dérangez pas.*"

Nevertheless, not heeding him, I hastened to the closed tent, where stood my bed, and where the captain was sleeping.

"Alekseï Ivanuitch, let me have ten rubles, please, for rations," said I to the captain, shaking him.

"What! have you been losing again? But this very evening you were not going to play any more," murmured the captain, still half asleep.

"No, I have not been playing; but I want the money; let me have it, please."

"Makatiuk!" shouted the captain to his servant, "hand me my bag with the money."

"Hush, hush!" said I, hearing Guskof's measured steps near the tent.

"What? Why hush?"

"Because that cashiered fellow has asked to borrow it of me. He's right there."

"Well, if you knew him, you wouldn't let him have it," remarked the captain. "I have heard about him. He's a dirty, low-lived fellow."

Nevertheless, the captain gave me the money, ordered his man to put away the bag, pulled the flap of the tent neatly to, and, again saying, "If you only knew him, you wouldn't let him have it," drew his head down under the coverlet. "Now you owe me thirty-two, remember," he shouted after me.

When I came out of the tent, Guskof was walking near the settees; and his slight figure, with his crooked legs, his shapeless cap, his long white hair, kept appearing and disappearing in the darkness, as he passed in and out of the candle-light. He pretended not to see me.

I handed him the money. He said, "*Merci,*" and, crumpling the bank-bill, thrust it into his trousers-pocket.

"Now I suppose the game is in full swing at the adjutant's," was his very next remark.

"Yes, I suppose so."

"He's a wonderful player, always bold, and never backs out. When he's in luck, it's fine; but when it does not go well with him, he can lose frightfully. He has given proof of that. During this expedition, if you reckon his valuables, he has lost more than fifteen hundred rubles. But, as he played discreetly before, that officer of yours seemed to have some doubts about his honor."

"Well, that's because he . . . Nikita, haven't we any of that red wine left?" I asked, very much relieved by Guskof's readiness of speech. Nikita still kept muttering; but he brought us the chikhir, and again looked on angrily as Guskof drained his glass. The free and easy ways formerly characteristic of Guskof were still noticeable. I wished that he would go as soon as possible; it seemed as if his only reason for not going was because he did not wish to go immediately after receiving the money. I said nothing.

"How could you, who have means, and were under no necessity, simply *de gaiété de cœur,* make up your mind to come and serve in the Caucasus? That's what I don't understand," said he to me.

I endeavored to explain this act of renunciation, which seemed so strange to him.

"I can imagine how disagreeable the society of these officers—men without any comprehension of culture—must be for you. You could not understand one another. You see, you might live ten years, and not see anything, and not hear about anything, except cards, wine, and gossip about rewards and campaigns."

It was unpleasant for me, that he wished me to put myself on a par with him in his position; and, with absolute honesty, I assured him that I was very fond of cards and wine, and gossip about campaigns, and that I did not care to have any better comrades than those with whom I was associated. But he would not believe me.

"Well, you may say so," he continued; "but the lack of women's society, —I mean, of course, *femmes comme il faut,*—is that not a terrible deprivation? I don't know what I would give now to go into a drawing-room, if only for a moment, and to have a look at a pretty woman, even though it were through a crack."

He said nothing for a little, and drank still another glass of the chikhir.

"Oh, my God, my God! If it only might be our fate to meet again, somewhere in Petersburg, to live and move among men, among ladies!"

He drank up the dregs of the wine still left in the bottle, and when he had finished it, he said, "*Akh! pardon*, maybe you wanted some more. I was awfully heedless. However, I suppose I must have taken too much, and my head isn't very strong. There was a time when I lived on Morskaya Street, *au rez-de-chaussée*, and had marvelous apartments, furniture, you know, and I was able to arrange it all beautifully, not so very expensively though; my father, to be sure, gave me porcelains, flowers, and silver,—a wonderful lot. *Le matin je sortais*, visits, *à cinq heures régulièrement*. I used to go and dine with *her*; often she was alone. *Il faut avouer que c'était une femme ravissante!* You didn't know her at all, did you?"

"No."

"You see, there was such a high degree of womanliness in her, and such tenderness, and what love! Lord! I did not know how to appreciate my happiness then. We would return after the theater, and have a little supper together. It was never dull where she was, *toujours gaie toujours aimante.* Yes, and I never realized what rare happiness it was. *Et j'ai beaucoup à me reprocher* in regard to her. *Je l'ai fait souffrir et souvent.* I was outrageous. Oh! What a marvelous time that was! Do I bore you?"

"No, not at all."

"Then I will tell you about our evenings. I used to go . . . that stairway, every flower-pot I knew, . . . the door-handle, all was so lovely, so familiar; then the vestibule, her room. . . . No, it will never, never come back to me again! Even now she writes to me; if you will let me, I will show you her letters. But I am not what I was; I am ruined; I am no longer worthy of her. . . . Yes, I am ruined forever. *Je suis cassé.* There's no energy in me, no pride, nothing . . . nor even any rank. . . . Yes, I am ruined; and no one will ever guess what I have suffered. Every one is different. I am a lost man. Never any chance for me to rise, because I have fallen morally . . . into the mire . . . I have fallen." . . .

At this moment there was evident in his words a genuine, deep despair; . . . he did not look at me, but sat motionless.

"Why are you in such despair?" I asked.

"Because I am abominable. This life has degraded me, all that was in me, all is crushed out. It is not through pride that I hold out, but through abjectness: there's no *dignité dans le malheur*. I am humiliated every moment. I endure it all; it is my own fault that I fell into this abasement. This mire *a éteint sur moi*,—it has soiled me. I myself have become coarse; I have forgotten what I used to know; I can't speak French any more; I am conscious that I am base and low. I cannot tear myself away from these surroundings, indeed I cannot. I might have been a hero; give me a regiment, gold epaulets, a trumpeter, but to march in the ranks with some wild Anton Bondarenko or the like, and feel that between me and him there was no difference at all—that he might be killed or I might be killed—all the same, that thought is maddening. You understand how horrible it is to think that some ragamuffin may kill me, a man who has thoughts and feelings, and that it would make no difference if alongside of me some Antonof were killed,—a creature not different from an animal—and that it might easily happen that I and not this Antonof should be killed; death is always *une fatalité* for every lofty and good man. I know that they call me a coward; grant that I am a coward, I certainly am a coward, and can't be anything else. Not only am I a coward, but I am in my way a low and despicable man. Here I have just been borrowing money of you, and you have the right to despise me. No, take back your money." And he held out to me the crumpled bank-bill. "I want you to have a good opinion of me." He covered his face with his hands, and burst into tears. I really did not know what to say or do.

"Calm yourself," I said to him. "You are too sensitive; don't take everything so to heart; don't indulge in self-analysis, look at things more simply. You yourself say that you have character. Keep up good heart, you won't have long to wait."

I said this to him, but not very consistently, because I was much stirred both by a feeling of sympathy and a feeling of repentance, because I had allowed myself mentally to criticize a man truly and deeply unhappy.

"Yes," he began, "if I had heard even once, at the time when I was in that hell, one single word of sympathy, of advice, of friendship—one humane word such as you have just spoken, perhaps I might have calmly endured all; perhaps I might have struggled, and been a soldier. But now this is horrible. . . . When I think soberly, I long for death. Why should I love my despicable life and my own self, now that I am ruined for all that is worth while in the world? And at the least danger, I suddenly, in spite of myself, begin to pray for my miserable life, and to watch over it as if it were precious, and I cannot, *je ne puis pas*, control myself.— That is, I can," he continued again after a minute's silence, "but it is too hard work for me, a monstrous work, when I am alone. With others, under special circumstances, when you are going into action, I am brave, *j'ai fait mes preuves*, because I am vain and proud; that is my weakness, and in presence of others. . . . Do you know, let me spend the night with you; with us, they will play all night long; it makes no difference, anywhere, on the ground."

While Nikita was making the bed, we got up, and once more began to walk up and down in the darkness on the battery. Certainly Guskof's head must have been very weak, because two glasses of liqueur and two of wine made him dizzy. As we got up and moved away from the candles, I noticed that he again thrust the ten-ruble bill into his pocket, trying to do so without my seeing it. During all the foregoing conversation, he had held it in his hand. He continued to reiterate how he felt that he might regain his old station if he had a man such as I was to take some interest in him.

We were just going in to the tent to go to bed when suddenly a cannon-ball whistled over us, and buried itself in the ground not far from us. So strange it was,—that peacefully sleeping camp, our conversation, and suddenly the hostile cannon-ball which flew from God knows where, into the midst of our tents,— so strange that it was some time before I could realize what it was. Our sentinel, Andreyef, walking up and down on the battery, moved toward me.

"Ha! he's crept up to us. It was the fire here that he aimed at," said he.

"We must rouse the captain," said I, and gazed at Guskof.

He crouched cowering close to the ground, and stammered, trying to say something, "Th-that's th-the enemy's . . . f-f-fire . . . th-that's . . . hidi . . ."

Further he could not say a word, and I did not see how and where he disappeared so instantaneously.

In the captain's tent a candle gleamed; his cough, which always troubled him when he was awake, was heard; and he himself soon appeared, asking for a linstock to light his little pipe.

"What does this mean, old man?" he asked, with a smile. "Aren't they willing to give me a little sleep to-night? First it's you with your cashiered friend, and then it's Shamyl. What shall we do, answer him or not? There was nothing about this in the instructions, was there?"

"Nothing at all. There he goes again," said I. "Two of them!"

Indeed, in the darkness, directly in front of us, flashed two fires, like two eyes; and quickly over our heads flew a cannon-ball and an empty shell which must have been one of ours returned. It came with a loud and penetrating hum. From the neighboring tents the soldiers hastened. We could hear them hawking and talking and stretching themselves.

"Hist! the fuse sings like a nightingale," remarked the artillerist.

"Send for Nikita," said the captain, with his habitually benevolent smile. "Nikita, don't hide yourself, but listen to the mountain nightingales."

"Well, your honor," said Nikita, who was standing near the captain, "I have seen them—these nightingales. I am not afraid of 'em; but there was that stranger who was here, drinking up your red wine, when he heard how lively that shot dashed by our tents, and the shell rolled by, he cowered down like some wild beast."

"Well, we must send to the commander of the artillery," said the captain to me, in a serious tone of authority, "and ask whether we shall reply to the fire or not. It will probably be nothing at all, but still it may. Have the goodness to go and ask him. Have a horse saddled. Do it as quickly as possible, even if you take my Polkan."

In five minutes they brought me a horse, and I galloped off to the commander of the artillery. "Look you, return on foot," whispered the punctilious captain, "else they won't let you through the lines."

It was half a verst to the artillery commander's. All along the road the tents were pitched. As soon as I rode away from our fire, it became so black that I could not see even the horse's ears, but only the watch-fires, now seeming very near, now very far off, as they flashed into my eyes. After I had ridden some distance, trusting to the intelligence of the horse, which I allowed free rein, I began to distinguish the white four-cornered tents and then the black ruts in the road. After a half-hour, having asked my way three times, and twice stumbled over the tent-stakes, causing each time a volley of curses from the tents, and twice been detained by the sentinels, I reached the artillery commander's.

While I was on the way, I had heard two more cannon-shot in the direction of our camp; but the projectiles did not reach to the place where the headquarters were. The artillery commander ordered not to reply to the firing, the more as the enemy did not stick to the same place; and I went back, leading the horse by the bridle, making my way on foot between the infantry tents.

More than once I delayed my steps, as I went by some soldier's tent where a light was shining, and some merry-andrew was telling a story; or I listened to some educated soldier reading from some book to the whole division, which had poured into the tent, or hung around it, occasionally interrupting the reading with various remarks; or I simply listened to the talk about the expedition, about the fatherland, or about their chiefs.

As I came around one of the tents of the third battalion, I heard Guskof's loud voice; he was speaking hilariously and rapidly. Young voices replied no less hilariously to him, not those of soldiers, but gay gentlemen. It was evidently the tent of some yunker or sergeant-major. I stopped short.

"I've known him a long time," Guskof was saying. "When I lived in Petersburg, he used to come to my house often; and I went to his. He moved in the best society."

"Whom are you talking about?" asked a drunken voice.

"About the prince," said Guskof. "We are relatives, you see, but more than all, we are old friends. It's a mighty good thing, you know, gentlemen, to have such an acquaintance. You see, he's fearfully rich. To him a hundred silver rubles is a mere bagatelle. Here, I just got a little money out of him, enough to last me till my sister sends."

"Send for some more wine."

"In a moment.— Savelyitch, my dear," said Guskof, coming to the door of the tent, "here's ten rubles for you; go to the sutler, get two bottles of Kakhetinski. Anything else, gentlemen? What do you say?" and Guskof, with unsteady gait, with disheveled hair, without his cap, came out of the tent. Throwing open his jacket, and thrusting his hands into the pockets of his gray trousers, he stood at the door of the tent. Though he was in the light, and I in darkness, I trembled with fear lest he should see me, and I went on, trying to make no noise.

"Who goes there?" shouted Guskof after me in a thoroughly drunken voice. Apparently, the cold took hold of him. "Who the devil is going off with that horse?"

I made no answer, and silently went on my way.

1856

LOST ON THE STEPPE;

OR,

THE SNOWSTORM

A TALE

1

At seven o'clock in the evening, having taken my tea, I started from a station, the name of which I have quite forgotten, though I remember that it was somewhere in the region of the Don Cossacks, not far from Novocherkask. It was already dark when I took my seat in the sledge next to Alyoshka, and wrapped myself in my fur coat and the robes. Back of the station-house it seemed warm and calm. Though it was not snowing, not a single star was to be seen overhead, and the sky seemed remarkably low and black, in contrast with the clear snowy expanse stretching out before us.

We had scarcely passed by the black forms of the windmills, one of which was awkwardly waving its huge vans, and had left the station behind us, when I perceived that the road was growing rougher and more drifted; the wind began to blow more fiercely on the left, it tossed the horses' manes and tails to one side, and it kept lifting and carrying away the snow stirred up by the runners and hoofs. The little bell rang with a muffled sound; a draught of cold air forced its way through some opening in my sleeves, to my very back; and the inspector's advice came into my head, that I had better stay where I was lest I should wander all night, and freeze to death on the road.

"Won't you get us lost?" said I to the *yamshchik*, or driver, but, as I got no answer, I put the question more distinctly: "Say, shall we reach the station, driver? We shan't lose our way?"

"God knows," was his reply; but he did not turn his head. "You see what kind of going we have. No road to be seen. Lord save us!"

"Be good enough to tell me, do you hope to reach the station, or not?" I insisted. "Shall we get there?"

"Must get there," said the driver; and he muttered something else, which I could not hear on account of the wind.

I did not wish to turn about, but the idea of wandering all night in the cold and snow over the perfectly shelterless steppe, which made up this part of the Don Cossack land, was very disagreeable. Moreover, notwithstanding the fact that I could not, by reason of the darkness, see him very well, my driver, somehow, did not please me, nor inspire any confidence. He sat exactly in the middle, with his legs in, and not on one side; his stature was too great; his voice expressed indolence; his cap, not like those usually worn by yamshchiks, was large and loose on all sides. Besides, he did not manage his horses in the proper way, but held the reins in both hands, just like the lackey who sat on the box behind the coachman; and, chiefly, I did not believe in him, because he had his ears wrapped up in a handkerchief. In a word, he did not please me; and it seemed as if that crooked, sinister back looming before me boded nothing good.

"In my opinion, it would be better to turn about," said Alyoshka to me: "fine thing it would be to be lost!"

"Lord save us! see how the snow blows! No road in sight. It blinds one's eyes. . . . Gospodi-batyushka!" repeated the driver.

We had not been a quarter of an hour on our way when the driver stopped the horses, handed the reins to Alyoshka, awkwardly liberated his legs from the seat, and went to search for the road, crunching over the snow in his great boots.

"What is it? Where are you going? Are we lost?" I asked, but the driver made no reply; turning his face away from the wind, which cut his eyes, he marched off from the sledge.

"Well, how is it?" I repeated, when he returned.

"Nothing at all," said he to me impatiently and with vexation, as if I were to blame for his missing the road; and, again slowly wrapping up his big legs in the robe, he gathered the reins in his frozen mittens.

"What shall we do?" I asked, as we started off again.

"What shall we do? We shall go where God takes us."

And we drove along in the same slow trot over what was evidently an untrodden waste, sometimes sinking in deep, mealy snow, sometimes gliding over crisp, smooth crust.

Although it was cold, the snow melted very quickly on my collar. The low-flying snow-clouds increased, and occasionally dry snowflakes began to fall.

It was clear that we were going out of our way, because, after keeping on for a quarter of an hour more, we saw no sign of a verst-post.

"Well, what do you think about it now?" I asked of the driver once more. "Shall we get to the station?"

"Which one? We should go back if we let the horses have their way; they will take us. But, as for the next one, that's a problem. . . . Only we might perish."

"Well, then, let us go back," said I. "And indeed . . ."

"How is it? Shall we turn back?" repeated the driver.

"Yes, yes; turn back."

The driver shook the reins. The horses started off more rapidly; and, though I did not notice that we had turned around, the wind changed, and soon through the snow appeared the windmills. The driver's good spirits returned, and he began to be communicative.

"Lately," said he, "in just such a snowstorm some people coming from that same station lost their way. Yes; they spent the night in the hayricks, and barely managed to get here in the morning. Thanks to the hayricks, they were rescued. If it had not been for them, they would have frozen to death, it was so cold. And one froze his legs, and died three weeks afterward in consequence."

"But now, you see, it's not cold; and it's growing less windy," I said. "Couldn't we go on?"

"It's warm enough, but it's snowing. Now, going back, it seems easier. But it's snowing hard. Might go on, if you were a coulier or something; but this is on your own account. What kind of a joke would that be if a passenger froze to death? How, then, could I be answerable to your grace?"

2

At this moment we heard behind us the bells of several troïkas which were rapidly overtaking us.

"A coulier's bell," said my driver. "There's one such for every station."

And, in fact, the bell of the courier's troïka, the sound of which now came clearly to me on the wind, was peculiarly beautiful,—clear, sonorous, deep, and jangling a little. As I then knew, this was a huntsman's team; three bells, —one large one in the center, with the *crimson* tone, as it is called, and two small ones tuned in thirds. The sound of this triad and the tinkling fifth, ringing through the air, was extraordinarily effective and strangely pleasant in this dark desert steppe.

"The posht is coming," said my driver, when the foremost of the three troïkas drew up in line with ours.

"Say, how is the road? is it possible to go on?" he cried to the last of the drivers. But the man only shouted to his horses, and made no reply.

The sound of the bells quickly died away on the wind, almost as soon as the post-team passed us.

Of course my driver felt ashamed.

"Well, let us try it again, barin," he said to me. "People have made their way through, now their tracks will be fresh."

I agreed; and once more we faced the wind, and began to crawl along on the deep snow. I kept my eyes on one side on the road, so that we should not get off the track that had been made by the other sledges. For two versts the tracks were plainly visible, then there began to be only a slight irregularity where the runners had gone; and soon I really could no longer distinguish whether it was the track, or merely a layer of drifted snow.

My eyes grew weary of gazing at the monotonous stretch of snow under the runners, and I began to look ahead. The third verst-post we had already seen, but the fourth we could not find at all. As before, we went in the teeth of the wind, and with the wind, and to the right and to the left; and finally we reached such a state that the driver declared that we must have turned off to the right. I declared that we must have turned off to the left, and Alyoshka was sure that we were going back all the time.

Again we stopped a number of times, the driver uncoiled his long legs, and crawled along trying to find the road. But all in vain. I also got out once to see whether it were the road or something else that attracted my attention. But I had scarcely taken six steps with difficulty against the wind, and convinced myself that we were surrounded by the same monotonous white heaps of snow, and that the road existed only in my imagination, when I lost sight of the sledge. I shouted, "Yamshchik! Alyoshka!" but,—I felt how the wind tore my voice right out of my mouth, and carried it in a twinkling far from me.

I went in the direction where the sledge had been—the sledge was not there. I went to the right—not there either. I am ashamed to recollect in what a loud, penetrating, and even rather despairing voice I shouted once more, "Yamshchik!" and there he was two steps away. His black figure, with his whip, and his huge cap hanging down on one side, suddenly loomed up before me. He led me to the sledge.

"Thank the Lord, it's still warm!" said he. "To perish with the cold— awful! Lord save us!"

"Let the horses find their own way, let us turn back," said I, as I took my place in the sledge. "Won't they take us back? hey, driver?"

"They ought to."

He gave the horses the reins, cracked his whip three times over the saddle of the shaft-horse, and again we started off at haphazard. We went for half an hour. Suddenly before us again I heard the easily recognized bell of the hunting establishment, and the other two. But now they were coming toward us. It was the same three troïkas, which had already deposited the mail, and, with a change of horses attached behind, were returning to the station. The courier's troïka of powerful horses with the hunting-bell quickly dashed ahead. A single driver sat on the driver's seat, and was shouting vigorously. Behind him, in the middle one of the empty sledges, were two other drivers; and their loud and hilarious talk could be heard. One of them was smoking a pipe; and the spark, brightened by the wind, lighted up a part of his face.

As I looked at them, I felt ashamed that I was afraid to go on; and my driver doubtless had the same feeling, because we both said with one voice:—

"Let us follow them."

3

My driver, without waiting for the last troïka to pass, began awkwardly to turn around; and the thills hit the horses attached behind. One of the troïka teams shied, tore away the reins, and galloped off.

"Hey there, you squint-eyed devil! Don't you see where you are turning? Running people down, you devil!" in a hoarse, discordant voice scolded one of the drivers, a short, little old man, as I judged by his voice and temperament. He sprang hastily out of the hindmost sledge, where he had been sitting, and started to run after the horses, still continuing roughly and violently to vilify my yamshchik.

But the horses did not come back. The driver ran after them, and in one instant both horses and driver were lost from sight in the white mist of the storm.

"Vasi-i-i-li! bring the bay horse here, else I can't ke-e-etch him," rang his voice in the distance.

One of the drivers, a very tall muzhik, got out of his sledge, silently un-hitched his troïka, mounted one of the horses by the breeching, and, crunching over the snow in a clumsy gallop, disappeared in the same direction.

Our own troïka, with the two others, followed on over the steppe, behind the courier's, which dashed ahead in full trot, jingling its bell, and sticking closely to the road.

"How is it? He'll get 'em," said my driver, referring to the one who had gone to catch the horses. "If that mare didn't find the horses she wouldn't be good for much, you know: she'd wander off, so that . . . she'd get lost."

From the moment that my driver had the company of other teams he became more hilarious and talkative; and, as I had no desire to sleep, I did not fail, as a matter of course, to make the most of it. I took pains to ask him about his home and his family, and soon learned that he was from the same government that I was,—from Tula,—a peasant, belonging to a noble family from the village of Kirpitchnoye; that they had very little land, and the grain had entirely ceased to grow, since the time of the cholera; that he and one of his brothers had stayed at home, and a third had gone as a soldier; that up to Christmas they had lacked bread, and had been obliged to work out; that his younger brother had looked out for things at home because he was married, but that he himself was a widower; that his villagers every year came here to exercise the trade of yamshchik, or driver; that, though he did not go out as a regular driver, yet he was in the post-service, so as to help his brother; that he earned there, thanks to God, a hundred and twenty paper rubles a year, of which he sent a hundred to his family; and that it would be good living, "but the couliers were very wild beasts, and the people here were all impudent."

"Now, what was that driver scolding about? Lord save us! did I mean to lose his horses for him? Did I treat him in a mean way? And why did he go galloping off after 'em? They'd have come in of their own accord. Anyway, 'twould be better for the horses to freeze to death than for him to get lost," said the pious muzhik.

"What is that black thing I see coming?" I asked, pointing to some dark object in front of us.

"That's a baggage-train. Splendid wheeling!" he went on to say, as we came up with the huge mat-covered vans on wheels, following one after the other. "See, not a soul to be seen . . . all asleep. The wise horse knows: you won't drive her from the road, never. . . . We've driven in that same way . . . so we know," he added.

It was indeed strange to see the huge vans covered with snow from the matted tops to the wheels, moving along, absolutely alone. Only the front corner of the snow-covered mat would be lifted by two fingers; and, for a moment, a cap would peer out as our bells jingled past the train. A great piebald horse, stretching out his neck, and straining his back, walked with measured pace over the drifted road, monotonously shaking his shaggy head under the whitened bell-bow,[1] and pricking up one snow-covered ear as we went by.

After we had gone still another half-hour, the driver once more turned to me:—

"Well, what do you think, barin? Are we getting along well?"

"I don't know," I said.

"Before, the wind blew in our faces, but now we go right along with it. No, we shan't get there; we are off the track," he said in conclusion, with perfect equanimity.

It was evident that, though he was very timid, yet, as "death in company with others is pleasant," he was perfectly content to die now that there were a number of us, and he was not obliged to take the lead, and be responsible. He coolly made observations on the mistake of the head driver, as if it were not of the least consequence to himself. In fact, I had noticed that sometimes the front troïka appeared on my right, and again on my left. It seemed to me, too, that we were making a circle in very small space. However, it might be that it was an ocular deception, just as sometimes it seemed as if the front troïka were climbing up a mountain or were going along a slope or down a mountain, even when the steppe was everywhere perfectly level.

After we had gone on a little while longer, I saw, as it seemed to me, at a distance, on the very horizon, a long, black, moving line; but it quickly became plain to me that it was the same baggage-train which we had passed. In exactly the same way, the snow covered the creaking wheels, several of which did not turn; in exactly the same way, the men were sleeping under the matted tops; and likewise the piebald leader, swelling out his nostrils, snuffed out the road, and pricked back his ears.

"See, we've gone round in a circle; we've gone round in a circle! Here's the

---

[1] *Duga*, the distinctive part of the Russian harness, rising high above the horse, carrying the bells.

same baggage-train again!" exclaimed my driver, in a discontented tone. "The coulier's horses are good ones, so it makes no difference to him, even if he does go on a wild-goose chase. But ours will get tired out if we have to spend the whole night here."

He had an attack of coughing.

"Should we go back, barin, owing to the mistake?"

"No! Why? We shall come out somewhere."

"Come out where? We shall have to spend the night on the steppe. How it is snowing! . . . Lord save us!"

Although it was clear to me that the head driver, who had lost both the road and the direction, was not hunting for the road, but singing at the top of his voice, still drove on at a full trot, I did not like to part company from them.

"Follow them," said I.

The yamshchik drove on, but followed them even less willingly than before, and no longer had anything to say to me.

4

The storm became more and more violent, and the snow fell dry and fine; it seemed as if it were beginning to grow colder. My nose and cheeks felt as if they were freezing, more frequently the draught of cold air insinuated itself under my shuba, and it became necessary to bundle up warmer. Sometimes the sledge bumped on the bare, icy crust from which the snow had been blown away. As I had already gone six hundred versts without sleeping under roof, and though I felt great interest in the outcome of our wanderings, my eyes closed in spite of me, and I drowsed.

Once, when I opened my eyes, I was struck, as it seemed to me at the first moment, by a bright light, gleaming over the white plain: the horizon widened considerably, the lowering black sky suddenly lifted up on all sides, the white slanting lines of the falling snow became visible, the shapes of the head troïkas stood out clearly; and, when I looked up, it seemed to me at the first moment that the clouds had scattered, and that only the falling snow veiled the stars.

Just as I awoke from my drowse, the moon had come out, and was casting her cold bright beams through the tenuous clouds and the falling snow. I saw clearly my sledge, horses, driver, and the three troïkas, plowing on in front: the first was the courier's sledge, in which still sat on the box the one yamshchik, driving at a hard trot; the second, in which rode the two drivers, who had dropped the reins and made a shelter out of a camel's-hair coat behind which they still smoked their pipes, as could be seen by the sparks glowing in their direction; and the third, in which no one was visible, for the yamshchik was comfortably sleeping in the middle.

The leading driver, however, while I was awake, had several times brought his horses to a half halt and attempted to find the road. Then while we stopped the howling of the wind became more audible, and more noticeable the enormous heaps of snow afloat in the air. By the aid of the moonlight which made its way through the storm, I could see the driver's short figure, whip in hand, examining the snow before him, moving back and forth in the misty light, again coming back to the sledge, and springing sidewise on the seat; and then again I heard above the monotonous whistling of the wind, the comfortable, clear jingling and melody of the bells.

When the head driver crept out to find the marks of the road or the hay-ricks, each time was heard the lively, self-confident voice of one of the yam-shchiks in the second sledge, shouting:—

"Hey, Ignashka! you turned off too much to the left. Strike off to the right into the storm." Or, "Why are you going round in a circle? Keep straight ahead as the snow flies. Follow the snow, then you'll hit it." Or, "Take the right, take the right, old man. There's something black, it must be a post." Or, "What are you getting lost for? why are you getting lost? Unhitch the piebald horse, and let him find the road for you. He'll do it every time. That would be the best way."

The man who was so free with his advice not only did not offer to unhitch his off horse, or go himself across the snow to hunt for the road, but did not even put his nose outside of his shelter-coat; and when Ignashka, the leader, in reply to one of his proffers of advice, shouted to him to come and take the forward place, since he knew the road so well, the mentor replied that when he came to drive a courier's sledge, then he would take the lead, and never once miss the road. "But our horses wouldn't go straight through a snowdrift," he shouted; "they aren't the right kind."

"Then don't you worry," replied Ignashka, gayly whistling to his horses.

The yamshchik who sat in the same sledge with the mentor said nothing at all to Ignashka, and paid no attention to the difficulty, though he was not yet asleep, as I concluded by his pipe which still glowed, and because, when we halted, I heard his measured voice in uninterrupted flow. He was telling a story. Once only, when Ignashka for the sixth or seventh time came to a stop, it seemed to vex him because his comfort in traveling was disturbed, and he shouted:—

"Stopping again? He's missing the road on purpose. This is a regular blizzard! The surveyor himself could not find the road! he would let the horses find it. We shall freeze to death here; . . . just let him go on regardless!"

"What! Don't you know a poshtallion froze to death last winter?" shouted my driver.

All this time the driver of the third troïka had not been heard from. But once, while we were stopping, the advice-giver shouted, "Filipp! ha! Filipp!" and, not getting any response, remarked:—

"Can he have frozen to death? Ignashka, you go and look."

Ignashka, who was responsible for all, went to his sledge, and began to shake the sleeper.

"See how a teaspoonful of brandy makes him tipsy! If you are frozen to death, tell us so!" said he, shaking him.

The sleeper grunted a little, and then began to scold.

"He's alive, fellows!" said Ignashka, and again started ahead, and once more we drove on; and with such rapidity that the little brown off horse, in my three-span, which was constantly whipping his tail, did not once intermit his awkward gallop.

5

It was already about midnight, I judge, when the little old man and Vasili, who had gone in search of the runaway horses, rejoined us. They had caught the horses, and had now overtaken us; but how in the world they had accomplished this in the thick, blinding snowstorm, in the midst of the bare steppe, has always remained a mystery to me. The little old man, with his elbows and legs flying, came trotting up on the shaft-horse (the two other horses were fastened to the collars; in such a snowstorm, it was impossible to let them go). When they had caught up with me, he again began to scold at my driver.

"You see, you cross-eyed devil! you . . ."

"Oh, Uncle Mitritch,"[1] cried the talkative fellow in the second sledge, "are you alive? Come in with us."

The old man did not answer him, but continued to scold. When he had satisfied himself, he rode up to the second sledge.

"Get 'em all?" was asked him.

"Why, of course we did."

And his small figure shook up and down on the horse's back as he went off at full trot, then sprang down into the snow, and without stopping caught up with the sledge, and sat in it with his legs hanging over the side. The tall Vasili, just as before, took his place in perfect silence in the front sledge with Ignashka; and then the two began to look for the road together.

"What a spitfire! Lord save us!" muttered my driver.

For a long time after this we drove on without stopping, over the white waste, in the cold, pellucid, and wavering light of the snowstorm.

When I opened my eyes, there before me rose the same clumsy, snow-covered cap and back; the same low *duga*, or bell-bow, under which, between the leathern reins tightly stretched, there moved always at the same distance the head of the shaft-horse with the black mane blown to one side by the wind. And I could see, above his back, the brown off horse on the right, with his short braided tail, and the whiffletree sometimes knocking against the dasher of the sleigh. If I looked below, then I saw the scurrying snow stirred up by the runners, and constantly tossed and borne by the wind to one side. In front of me, always at the same distance, glided the other troïkas. To left and right, all was white and bewildering. Vainly the eye sought for any new object: no verst-post, or hayrick, or fence was to be seen, nothing at all. Everywhere, all was white, white and fluctuating: now the horizon seemed to be indistinguishably distant, then it would come down within two steps on every side; now suddenly a high white wall would grow up on the right, and accompany the course of the sledges, then it would suddenly vanish, and grow up in front, only to glide on in advance, farther and farther away, and disappear again.

When I looked up it would seem light. At the first moment, I imagined that through the haze I saw the stars; but the stars, as I gazed, seemed to flee into deeper and deeper depths, and I could see only the snow falling into my face and eyes, and the collar of my fur shuba; the sky had everywhere one tone of light, one tone of white,—colorless, monotonous, and constantly shifting.

[1] Condensed form for Dmitriyevitch, "son of Dmitri." The peasants often call each other by the patronymic.

The wind seemed to vary: at one moment it would blow into my face, and fling the snow into my eyes; the next it would go to one side, and peevishly toss the collar of my shuba over my head, and insultingly slap me in the face with it; then find some crevice behind, and play a tune on it.

I heard the soft, incessant crunching of the hoofs and the runners on the snow, and the muffled tinkling of the bells, as we sped over the deep snow. Only occasionally when we drove against the wind, and glided over the bare frozen crust, I could clearly distinguish Ignat's energetic whistling, and the full chords of the chime, with the resounding jarring fifth; and these sounds would break suddenly and comfortingly on the melancholy character of the desert; and then again ring monotonously, with unendurable fidelity of execution, the whole of that motive which involuntarily coincided with my thoughts.

One of my feet began to feel cold, and when I turned round so as to protect it better, the snow that covered my collar and my cap sifted down my neck, and made me shiver; but still I was, for the most, comfortable in my warm shuba, and drowsiness overcame me.

6

Things remembered and things conceived mixed and mingled with wonderful quickness in my imagination.

"The advice-giver who is always shouting from the second sledge, what kind of a muzhik must he be? Probably red-haired, thick-set, with short legs, a man somewhat like Feodor Filippuitch, our old butler," is what I say to myself.

And here I see the staircase of our great house, and five of the house-servants who, with towels, with heavy steps, carry the pianoforte from the wing; I see Feodor Filippuitch with the sleeves of his nankeen coat tucked up, carrying one of the pedals, and going in advance, unbolting the door, taking hold of the door-knob here, there pushing a little, now crawling under the legs; he is here, there, and everywhere, crying with an anxious voice continually:—

"Look out, take more weight, you there in front! Be careful, you there at the tail-end! Up—up—up—don't hit the door. There, there!"

"Excuse me, Feodor Filippuitch! There ain't enough of us," says the gardener, timidly, crushed up against the balustrade, and all red with exertion, lifting one end of the grand with all his remaining strength. But Feodor Filippuitch does not hold his peace.

"And what does it mean?" I ask myself. "Does he think that he is of any use, that he is indispensable for the work in hand? or is he simply glad that God has given him this self-confident persuasive eloquence, and takes enjoyment in squandering it? It must be so."

And I somehow see the pond, the weary servants, who, up to their knees in the water, drag the heavy net; and again Feodor Filippuitch with a watering-pot, shouting to everybody, walking up and down on the bank, and only now and then venturing to the brink, taking with his hand the golden carp, and letting the dirty water run out from his watering-pot, so as to fill it up with fresh.

But here it is midday, in the month of July. Across the newly mown turf of the lawn, under the burning perpendicular rays of the sun, I seem to be going somewhere. I am still very young; I am full of yearnings, full of desires. I go to the pond, to my own favorite spot between the wild rose bush and the birch-tree alley; and I lie down and nap. Keen is the sensation that I have, as I lie down, and look across the red thorny stems of the rose bush on the dark ground with its dry grass and on the gleaming bright blue mirror of the pond. It is a sensation of a naïve self-contentment and melancholy. All around me is so lovely, and this loveliness has such a powerful effect on me, that it seems to me as if I myself were good; and the one thing that vexes me is that no one is there to admire me.

It is hot. I try to go to sleep so as to console myself; but the flies, the unendurable flies, even here, give me no peace. They begin to swarm around me, and obstinately, insolently, as it were, heavy as cherry-stones, jump from my forehead to my hands. A bee buzzes near me in the sunbeams. Yellow-winged butterflies fly languidly from flower to flower.

I gaze up. It pains my eyes. The sun shines too bright through the light foliage of the bushy birch tree, gracefully waving its branches high above my head, and it seems hotter than ever. I cover my face with my handkerchief. It becomes stifling; and the flies stick to my hands, on which the perspiration stands. In the rose bush the sparrows twitter under the thick leaves. One hops to the ground almost within my reach, makes two or three feints to peck energetically at the ground, and, after making the little twigs crackle, chirping gayly it flies away from the bush; another also hops to the ground, wags his little tail, looks around, and, like an arrow, flies off twittering after the first.

At the pond are heard the blows of the pounder on the wet linen; and the noise reëchoes, and is carried far away down along the shore. I hear laughter and talking, and the splashing of bathers. The breath of the wind sweeps the tops of the birches far above my head, and bends them down again. I hear it moving the grass, and now the leaves of the rose bush toss and rustle on their stems. And now, lifting the corner of my handkerchief, it tickles my sweaty face, and pours in on me in a cooling draught. Through the opening where the handkerchief is lifted a fly finds his way, and timidly buzzes around my moist mouth. A dry twig begins to make itself felt under my back. No; it is unendurable to lie so; I must go and bathe.

But now, around the clump of bushes, I hear the sound of footsteps, and the frightened voice of a woman:—

"Mercy on me! what's to be done? And no man anywhere!"

"What's the matter?" I ask, running out into the sun, as a serving-woman, screaming, hurries past me. She merely glances at me, wrings her hands, and hurries along faster. And here comes also the seventy-year-old Matriona, holding her handkerchief to her head, with her hair all in disorder, and hopping along with her lame leg in a woolen stocking, hurrying to the pond. Two girls come running, hand in hand; and a ten-year-old boy in his father's jacket runs behind, clinging to the linen petticoat of one of them.

"What has happened?" I ask of them.

"A muzhik drowned!"

"Where?"

"In the pond."

"Who is he? one of ours?"

"No, a tramp."

The coachman Ivan, sliding in his big boots over the mown grass, and the fat overseer Yakof, all out of breath, come hurrying to the pond; and I follow after them.

I recall the feeling which said to me, "Now jump in, and pull the muzhik out, and save him; and all will admire you," for that was exactly what I wanted.

"Where is he? where?" I asked of the throng of domestics gathered on the shore.

"Over there in the deepest part, on the other shore, almost at the bath-house," says the laundress, stowing away the wet linen on her yoke. . . . "I see him dive; then he came up again, then he sank a second time, and came up again, and cried, 'I'm drowning, help!' And then he went down again—and up came a lot of bubbles. And while I was looking on, the muzhik got drowned. And so I give the alarm: 'Help! a muzhik is drowning!' "

And the laundress, lifting the yoke upon her shoulder, turning to one side, went along the narrow foot-path away from the pond.

"See! what a shame," says Yakof Ivanof, the overseer, in a despairing voice; "now there'll be a rumpus with the police court . . . we'll have enough of it."

One muzhik with a scythe makes his way through the throng of peasant women, children, and old men gathered round the shore, and, hanging the scythe on the limb of a willow, leisurely takes off his clothes.

"Where was it? where was he drowned?" I keep asking, having still the desire to jump in, and do something extraordinary.

They point out to me the smooth surface of the pond, which is now and then just ruffled by the puffs of the breeze. It is incomprehensible how he came to drown; for the water lies so smooth, beautiful, and calm above him, shining golden in the midday sun, and I realize that I cannot do anything or surprise any one, the more as I am a very poor swimmer; but the muzhik is now pulling his shirt over his head, and instantly throws himself into the water. All look at him with hope and anxiety. But after going into the water up to his neck, the muzhik slowly turns back, and puts on his shirt again; he cannot swim.

People keep coming down to the shore, the throng grows larger and larger, the women cling to one another; but no one brings any help. Those that have just come, offer advice, and groan; fear and despair are stamped on all faces. Of those who had come first, some have sat down on the grass, weary of standing, others have gone back to their work. The old Matriona asks her daughter whether she shut the oven door. The small boy in his father's jacket industriously flings stones into the water.

And now from the house down the hill comes Trezorka, the butler's dog, barking, and looking back in perplexity. And lo! there is Feodor Filippuitch's tall figure hurrying from the hilltop, and shouting something as he comes out from behind the wild rose bush.

"What are you standing there for?" he shouts, taking off his coat as he runs. "A man drowning, and there you are standing around! Get a rope."

All look at Feodor Filippuitch with hope and fear while he, leaning his hand on the shoulder of one of the men-servants, pries off his left boot with the toe of the right.

"There it was, where the people are standing, there at the right of the willows, Feodor Filippuitch, right there," says some one to him.

"I know it," he replies; and, knitting his brows, probably as a rebuke to the manifestations of prudery visible among the women, he takes off his shirt and baptismal cross, handing them to the gardener boy who stands officiously near him, and then stepping energetically across the mown grass, comes to the pond.

Trezorka, in doubt as to the reason for his master's rapid motions, stands irresolute near the crowd, and noisily nibbles a few grass-blades on the shore, then looks questioningly at his master, and suddenly with a joyous bark plunges with him into the water. At first nothing can be seen except foam, and splashing water, which reached even to us. But soon Feodor Filippuitch, gracefully spreading his arms in long strokes, and with regular motion lifting and sinking his back, swims across to the other shore. Trezorka, however, gurgling in the water, hastily returns, shakes himself near the crowd, and rolls over on his back on the shore.

While Feodor Filippuitch is swimming to the other side, two coachmen hasten to the willows with a net fastened to a stake. Feodor Filippuitch for some reason lifts up his hands, dives once, twice, three times, each time spewing from his mouth a stream of water, gracefully shaking his long hair, and paying no heed to the questions which are showered on him from all sides. At last he comes to the shore, and, as well as I can make out, arranges for the disposition of the net.

They haul out the net, but it contains nothing except slime and a few small carp flopping in it. They are just casting the net once more as I reach that side.

The voice of the butler giving directions, the water dripping from the wet rope, and sighs of dismay, alone break the silence. The wet rope attached to the right wing covers up more and more of the grass, and slowly emerges farther and farther out of the water.

"Now all together, with a stronger pull once more!" cries the butler's voice. The net appears, dripping with water.

"There's something! it comes heavy, fellows," says some one's voice.

And here the wings, with two or three carp flapping in them, are drawn to shore, wetting and crushing down the grass. And now, through the fine wavering bed of agitated water, something white gleams in the tightly stretched net. Not loud, but plainly audible amid the dead silence, a sigh of horror passes over the throng.

"Pull it up on the dry land! pull all together!" says the butler's resolute voice; and the drowned man is pulled up across the mown burdocks and other weeds, to the willows.

And here I see my good old auntie in her silk dress. I see her lilac sunshade with its fringe,—which somehow is incongruous with this picture of death terrible in its very simplicity,—and her face ready this moment to be convulsed with sobs. I recall the disappointment expressed on her face, because it was idle to use the arnica; and I recall the sickening melancholy feeling I have when she said with the simple egoism of love:—

"Let us go, my dear. Ah! how terrible this is! And here you always go in swimming by yourself."

I remember how bright and hot the sun shone on the dry ground crumpling under our feet; how it played on the mirror of the pond; how the plump carp flapped on the bank; how the schools of fish stirred the smooth surface in the middle of the pond; how a hawk hung high in the air, watching the ducklings quacking and spattering, as they swam through the reeds toward the center; how the white tumulous thunder-clouds gathered on the horizon; how the mud, brought up on the bank by the net, melted away; and how, as I came to the dike, I again heard the blows of the clothes-pounders at work along the pond.

But the clothes-pounder has a ringing sound; two clothes-pounders, as it were, ring together, making a chord; and this sound torments, pains me, the more as I know that this clothes-pounder is a bell, and Feodor Filippuitch could not succeed in stopping it. And this clothes-pounder, like an instrument of torture, squeezes my leg, which is freezing.—I fall into deep sleep.

I was waked by what seemed to me our very rapid progress, and by two voices speaking close to me.

"Say, Ignat, Ignat," says the voice of my driver. "You take my passenger; you've got to go anyway; it's only wasted labor for me, you take him."

Ignat's voice near me replies, "What fun would it be for me to answer for a passenger? . . . Will you treat me to a half-pint of brandy?"

"Now! a half-pint! Call it a glass."

"The idea, a glass!" cries the other voice; "bother my horses for a glass of vodka!"

I open my eyes. Still the same unendurable whirling snowflakes dazzling me, the same drivers and horses, but next me I see some sledge or other. My driver had caught up with Ignat, and for some time we have been going side by side.

Notwithstanding the fact that the voice from the other sledge advises not to take less than the half-pint, Ignat suddenly reins up his troïka.

"Change the things; just your good luck! You'll give me the brandy when we meet to-morrow. Have you got much luggage?"

My driver, with unwonted liveliness, leaps into the snow, makes me a bow, and begs me to change into Ignat's sledge. I am perfectly willing. But evidently the God-fearing little muzhik is so delighted that he must needs pour out to some one his gratitude and delight. He bows to me, to Alyoshka, to Ignasha, and thanks us.

"Well, now, glory to God! What a scheme this is! Lord save us! we have been going half the night. Don't know ourselves where we are. He will take you, sir; but my horses are all beat out."

And he transfers the luggage with vigorous activity.

When it was moved, I got into the other sledge in spite of the wind which almost carried me away. The sledge, especially on that side on which was spread the coat as a protection against the wind, for the two yamshchiks, was a quarter buried in the snow; but behind the coat, it was warm and cozy. The little old man was lying as before with his legs hanging over, and the story-teller was still spinning his yarn: "At that very same time when the general in the king's name, you know, comes to Marya, you know, in the darkness, at this same time, Marya says to him, 'General, I do not need you, and I cannot love you; and, you know, you are not my lover, but my lover is the prince himself.'—At this very time," he was going on to say; but, catching sight of me, he kept silence for a time, and began to puff at his pipe.

"Well, barin, have you come to hear the story?" said the other, whom I have called the advice-giver.

"Yes; but you are having a gay time, a splendid time behind here," said I.

"Out of sheer dullness,—have to keep ourselves from thinking."

"But, say, don't you know where we are now?"

This question, as it seemed to me, did not please the yamshchiks.

"Who can tell where we are? Maybe we are going to the Kalmucks," replied the advice-giver.

"But what are we going to do?" I asked.

"What are we going to do? Well, we are going, and will keep on going," he said, in a fretful tone.

"Well, what will keep us from getting lost? Besides, the horses will get tired in the snow. What then?"

"Well, nothing."

"But we may freeze to death."

"Of course we may, because we don't see any hayricks just now; but we may come, you know, to the Kalmucks. First thing, we must look at the snow."

"But you aren't afraid of freezing to death, are you, barin?" asked the little old man, with quavering voice.

Notwithstanding that he was making sport of me, as it were, it was plain that he was trembling all over.

"Yes; it is growing very cold," I replied.

"Ekh! barin! You ought to do like me. No, no; stamp up and down,—that will warm you up."

"Do it the first thing when you get to the sledge," said the advice-giver.

7

"If you please, all ready!" shouted Alyoshka from the front sledge.

The storm was so fierce that only by main force, leaning far forward and holding down the folds of my cloak with both hands, was I able to make my way through the whirling snow, drifting before the wind under my very feet, over the short distance between me and the sledge. My former driver was still on his knees in the middle of the empty sledge; but when he saw me going he took off his big cap, the wind angrily tossing up his hair, and asked me for vodka money. Evidently he did not expect me to give it to him, because my refusal did not affront him in the least. He even thanked me, waved his cap, and said, "Well, good luck to you, sir!" and picking up the reins, and clucking to the horses, turned from us.

Immediately Ignashka straightened his back, and shouted to his horses. Again the sound of crunching hoofs, voices, bells, took the place of the howling wind, which was chiefly audible when we stood still. For a quarter of an hour after my transfer I did not sleep, and I diverted my mind by contemplating the form of my new driver and horses. Ignashka was youthful in appearance, was constantly jumping up, cracking his whip over the horses, shouting out, changing from one leg to the other, and leaning forward to fix the breeching for the shaft-horse, which kept slipping to one side. He was not tall in stature, but well-built, as it seemed. Over his unlined sheepskin coat he wore an ungirdled cloak, the collar of which was almost turned back; his neck was perfectly bare; his boots were of leather, not felt; and he wore a small cap which he kept taking off and straightening. His ears were protected only by his hair. In all his motions was manifest not only energy, but much more, as it seemed to me, the desire to keep his energy alive.

However, the farther we went, the more frequently he settled himself on his seat, changed the position of his legs, and addressed himself to Alyoshka and me; it seemed to me that he was afraid of losing his spirits. And there was good reason; though the horses were excellent, the road each step grew heavier and heavier, and it was noticeable that the horses' strength was flagging. It was already necessary to use the whip; and the shaft-horse, a good, big, shaggy animal, stumbled once or twice, though immediately, as if frightened, it sprang forward and tossed up its shaggy head almost to the bell itself.

The right off horse, which I could not help watching, had a long leather breeching adorned with tassels, slipping and sliding to the left, and kept dropping the traces, and required the whip; but like a good and even zealous horse, seemed to be vexed at its own weakness, and angrily tossed its head, as if asking to be driven.

Indeed, it was terrible to see how, as the storm and cold increased, the horses grew weak, the road became worse; and we really did not know where we were, or where we were going, whether to a station or to any shelter whatever. And strange and ridiculous it was to hear the bells jingling so merrily and carelessly, and Ignatka shouting so energetically and delightfully as if it were a sunny Christmas noon, and we were hurrying to a festival along the village street; and stranger than all it was to think that we were all the time riding and riding rapidly away from the place where we had been.

Ignat began to sing some song in a horrible falsetto, but so loud and with such intervals, during which he whistled, that it was weird to listen to, and made one melancholy.

"Hey-y-y! Why are you splitting your throat, Ignat? Hold on a bit!" said the voice of the advice-giver.

"What?"

"Hold o-o-o-o-n!"

Ignat reined up. Again silence, only broken by the wailing and whistling of the wind, while the snow began to pile up, rustling on the sledge. The advice-giver drove up to us.

"Well, what is it?"

"Say! where are you going?"

"Who knows?"

"Are your feet frozen, that you stamp so?"

"They're frozen off."

"Well, you ought to go this way. The way you were going means starvation, —not even a Kalmuck there. Get out, and it will warm your legs."

"All right. Hold the horses—there."

And Ignat stumped off in the direction indicated.

"Have to keep looking all the time, have to get out and hunt; then you find the way. But this way's a crazy way to go," said the advice-giver. "See how tired the horses are."

All the time Ignat was gone, and it was so long that I actually began to be afraid that he had lost his way, the advice-giver kept talking to me in a self-confident, easy tone, telling me how one ought to behave in a snowstorm; how the best thing of all was to unhitch one of the horses, and let her go as God Almighty should direct; how sometimes you can see the stars; and how, if he had taken the front place, we should have been at the station long before.

"Well, how is it?" he asked, as Ignat came back, plowing with difficulty knee-deep in snow.

"Not so bad. I found a Kalmuck camp," replied Ignat, out of breath. "Still, I don't know where we are. It must be that we have been going toward the Prolgovsky datcha. We must bear off to the left."

"Why worry? It must be the camp just behind our station," replied the advice-giver.

"I tell you it isn't."

"Well, I've seen it, and so I know. If it isn't that, then it's Tamuishevsko. You must bear more to the right; and soon we'll be on the big bridge,—eight versts."

"Say what you will, 't ain't so. I have seen it," said Ignat, angrily.

"Eh! what's that? I am a yamshchik as much as you are."

"Fine yamshchik! you go ahead, then."

"Why should I go ahead? But I know."

Ignat was evidently angry. Without replying, he climbed to his seat, and drove on.

"You see how cold one's feet get. No way to warm them," said he to Alyoshka, pounding his feet more and more frequently, and brushing and shaking off the snow which had got into his boot-legs.

I felt an uncontrollable desire to sleep.

8

"Can it be that I am going to freeze to death?" I asked myself, as I dropped off. "Death, they say, always begins with drowsiness. It's much better to drown than freeze to death, then they would pull me out in the net. However, it makes no difference whether one drowns or freezes to death. If only this stake did not stick into my back so, I might forget myself."

For a second I lost consciousness.

"How will all this end?" I suddenly asked myself in thought, for a moment opening my eyes, and gazing at the white expanse,—"how will it end? If we don't find some hayricks, and the horses get winded, as it seems likely they will be very soon, we shall all freeze to death."

I confess that, though I was afraid, I had a desire for something extraordinary, something rather tragic, to happen to us; and this was stronger than the small fear. It seemed to me that it would not be a bad thing if at morning the horses themselves should bring us, half-frozen, to some far-off, unknown village, where some of us might even perish of the cold.

And while I have this thought, my imagination works with extraordinary clearness and rapidity. The horses become weary, the snow grows deeper and deeper, and now only the ears and the bell-bow are visible; but suddenly Ignashka appears on horseback, driving his troïka past us. We beseech him, we shout to him, to take us; but the wind carries away our voices; we have no voices left. Ignashka laughs at us, shouts to his horses, whistles, and passes out of our sight in some deep snow-covered ravine. A little old man climbs up on a horse, flaps his elbows, and tries to gallop after him; but he cannot stir from the place. My former driver, with his great cap, throws himself on him, drags him to the ground, and tramples him into the snow.

"You're a wizard—a koldun!" he cries. "You're a spitfire. We are all lost on your account."

But the little old man flings a snowball at his head. He is no longer a little old man, but only a hare, and bounds away from us. All the dogs bound after him. The advice-giver, who is now Feodor Filippuitch, tells us to sit around in a circle, that nothing will happen to us if we protect ourselves with snow; it will be warm.

In fact, it is warm and cozy; our only trouble is thirst. I get out my traveling-case; I offer every one rum and sugar, and I myself drink with great satisfaction. The story-teller spins some yarn about the rainbow, and over our heads is a ceiling of snow and a rainbow.

"Now each of you," I say, "make a chamber in the snow, and go to sleep."

Snow is as soft and warm as wool. I make myself a room, and am just going into it; but Feodor Filippuitch, who has caught a glimpse of my money in my traveling-case, says, "Hold! give me your money, you won't need it when you're dead," and seizes me by the leg. I hand him the money, asking him only to let me go; but they will not believe that it is all the money I have, and they are going to kill me. I seize the old man's hand and with indescribable pleasure kiss it; the old man's hand is tender and soft. At first he takes it away from me, but afterward he lets me have it, and even caresses me with his other hand.

Nevertheless, Feodor Filippuitch comes near and threatens me. I hasten to my chamber; it is not a chamber, but a long white corridor, and some one pulls back on my leg. I tear myself away. In the hand of the man who holds me back, remain my trousers and a part of my skin; but I feel only cold and ashamed,— all the more ashamed because my auntie with her sunshade, and homeopathic pellets, comes arm in arm with the drowned man to meet me. They smile, but do not understand the signs that I make to them. I fling myself on the sledge; my feet drag over the snow, but the little old man follows after me, flapping his elbows. He comes close to me. But I hear just in front of me two church-bells, and I know that I shall be safe when I reach them. The church-bells ring louder and louder; but the little old man has caught up with me, and falls with his body across my face, so that I can scarcely hear the bells. Once more I seize his hand, and begin to kiss it; but the little old man is no longer the little old man, but the drowned man, and he cries:—

"Ignashka, hold on! here are Akhmet's hayricks! just look!"

That is too terrible! no, I had better wake up. I open my eyes. The wind is flapping the tails of Alyoshka's cloak into my face; my knees are uncovered. We are going over the bare crust, and the triad of the bells rings pleasantly through the air with its clashing fifth.

I look, expecting to see the hayricks; but instead of hayricks, now that my

eyes are wide open, I see something like a house with a balcony, and the crenel-
ated walls of a fortress. I feel very little interest in seeing this house and fortress;
my desire is much stronger to see the white corridor where I had been walking,
to hear the sound of the church-bell, and to kiss the little old man's hand.
Again I close my eyes and fall asleep.

9

I slept soundly. But all the time I could hear the chords of the bells, and
in my dream I could see, now a dog barking and jumping after me; then the
organ, one stop of which I seemed to draw out; then the French poem which
I am composing. Then it seemed to me that this triad was some instrument
of torture with which my right foot was constantly compressed. This was so
severe that I woke up, and opening my eyes I rubbed my leg. It was beginning
to grow numb with cold.

The night was, as before, light, melancholy, white. The same motion kept
shaking me and the sledge; Ignashka was still sitting on one side and stamping
his feet. There was the off horse as before, straining her neck, lifting her feet,
as she trotted over the deep snow; the tassel slipping along the reins, and
whipping against the horse's belly; the head of the shaft-horse, with the waving
mane, alternately pulling and loosening the reins attached to the bell-bow as
it nodded up and down.

But all this was covered and hidden with snow far more than before. The
snow was whirled about in front of us, and covered up our runners, and reached
above the horses' knees, and fell thick and fast on our collars and caps. The
wind blew now from the right, now from the left, and played with the collar
and tails of Ignashka's cloak, the manes of the horses, and howled above the
bell-bow and the shafts.

It had become fearfully cold; and I had scarcely lifted my head out of my
collar ere the frosty dry snow made its way, rustling, into my eyelids, my nose,
and my mouth, and ran down my neck. Looking around, all was white, light,
and snowy; nothing anywhere except a melancholy light and the snow. In good
earnest I can say it was terrible to me.

Alyoshka was sleeping as he sat cross-legged in the very depths of the sledge;
his whole back was covered with a thick deposit of snow.

Ignashka did not become dejected; he kept pulling at the reins, shouting,
and stamping his feet. The bell also sounded strangely. The horses sometimes
snorted, but plunged along more quietly, though they stumbled more and more
often. Ignashka again sprang up, swung his mittens, and began to sing in his
clear, strong voice. Without finishing his song he stopped the troïka, tossed the
reins on the dasher, and got out. The wind howled madly; the snow, as if
shoveled down, was dashed upon the folds of my furs.

I looked around. The third troïka was nowhere to be seen (it had stopped
somewhere). Next the second troïka, in a mist of snow, could be seen the little
old man making his way with long strides. Ignashka went three steps from the
sledge, sat down in the snow, took off his girdle, and began to remove his boots.

"What are you doing?" I asked.

"Must change my boots; otherwise this leg will be frozen solid," he replied,
and went on with his work.

It was cold for me to keep my neck out of my collar to watch how he did it. I sat straight, looking at the off horse, which, with legs spread, stood feebly switching its snow-covered tail. The thump which Ignat gave the sledge as he clambered to his place startled me.

"Well, where are we now?" I asked. "Are we getting anywhere in the world?"

"Don't you worry. We shall get there," he replied. "Now my feet are thoroughly warm, since I changed them."

And he drove on; the bells jingled, the sledge again began to rock, and the wind whistled under the runners, and once more we struggled to swim through the limitless ocean of snow.

10

I sank into a sound sleep. When Alyoshka awoke me by punching me in the leg and I opened my eyes, it was already morning. It seemed even colder than it had been during the night. It was no longer snowing; but a strong dry wind still swept the powdery snow across the plain, and especially under the hoofs of the horses, and the runners of the sledge.

The sky on the right toward the east was of a deep purple color, but bright oblique stripes of reddish orange kept growing more and more clearly defined in it; above our heads, behind the hurrying, white clouds, scarcely tinged as yet, gleamed the pallid blue of the sky; in the west the clouds were bright, light, and shifting.

Everywhere around, as far as the eye could see, lay the snow, white and deep, in sharply defined strata. Here and there could be seen gray mounds where lay the fine, dry, powdery snow. Not a track was to be seen,—not that of a sledge, or of a human being, or of a beast. The outline and color of the driver's back, and of the horses, began to stand out clear and sharp against the white background. . . .

The rim of Ignashka's dark blue cap, his collar, his hair, and even his boots, were white. The sledge was perfectly covered. The whole right side and the mane of the brown shaft-horse were plastered with snow. The legs of my off horse were thick with it up to the knee, and the whole of the shaggy right flank where the sweat had dampened it had the same sticky covering. The tassel as before leaped up and down in a sort of rhythm, the structure of which it would not be easy to represent; and the off horse kept galloping on; only by the gaunt belly rising and sinking, and by the hanging ears, could it be seen how tired she was.

Only one new object attracted the attention; this was a verst-post, from which the snow had been blown away, leaving it clear to the ground, and around which the wind had drifted a perfect mountain on one side and was still sweeping the friable snow across, and drifting it from one side to the other.

I was greatly amazed that we had gone the whole night without change of horses, not knowing for twelve hours where we were, and not coming to our destination, and yet not really missing the road. Our bells seemed to sound more cheerfully than ever. Ignat buttoned his coat up, and began to shout again. Behind us snorted the horses and jingled the bells of the troïka that carried the little old man and the advice-giver; but the man who was asleep had wandered away from us somewhere on the steppe.

After going half a verst farther, we struck the fresh, and as yet unobliterated, track of a sledge and troïka; and occasionally pink spots of blood, caused apparently by the whip on the horses' side, could be seen.

"That was Filipp. See, he's got in ahead of us," said Ignashka.

But here appears a little house with a sign, alone by itself, near the road, standing in the midst of the snow, which covers it almost to the roof. Near the inn stands a troïka of gray horses, their hair rough with sweat, with widespread legs and drooping heads. At the door the snow is shoveled away, and the shovel is standing in it; but it still blows down from the roof, and the roaring wind whirls the snow around.

Out from the door at the sound of our bells comes a big, ruddy, red-headed driver, with a glass of wine in his hand, and shouts something. Ignashka turns to me, and asks permission to stop. Then for the first time I fairly see his face.

11

His features were not dark, dry, and regular, as I had reason to expect from his hair and build. His face was round, jolly, with a snub nose and a big mouth, and clear-shining eyes, blue and round. His cheeks and neck were like well-worn cloth. His eyebrows, his long eyelashes, and the beard which evenly covered the lower part of his face, were crusted thick with snow, and perfectly white.

The distance to the station was all of a half-verst, and we stopped.

"Only be quick about it," I said.

"Just a minute," replied Ignashka, springing down from his seat, and going up to Filipp.

"Let us have it, brother," said he, taking the glass in his right hand; and, throwing his mitten and whip down on the snow, tipping back his head, he drank down at a gulp the glass of vodka.

The innkeeper, who must have been a discharged Cossack, came, with a bottle in his hand, out of the door.

"Who have you got there?" he asked.

The tall Vasili, a lean, blond muzhik with a goatee, and the fat councilor, with white eyebrows, and a thick white beard framing his ruddy face, came up and also drank a glass. The little old man joined the group of drinkers; but no one offered him anything, and he went off again to his horses, fastened behind, and began to stroke one of them on the back and side.

The little old man was pretty much what I had imagined him to be: small, ugly, with wrinkled, strongly marked features, a thin little beard, a sharp nose, and worn yellow teeth. He wore a driver's cap, perfectly new; but his sheepskin jacket was old, soiled with oil, and torn on the shoulders and flaps, and did not cover his knees or his hempen trousers tucked into his huge felt boots. He himself was bent, and he kept frowning, and, with trembling lips and limbs, tramped around his sledge, evidently trying to keep warm.

"Well, Mitritch, you ought to have a drink; it would warm you up," said the advice-giver to him.

Mitritch gave a start. He arranged the horses' harness, straightened the bell-bow, and then came to me.

"Say, barin," said he, taking his cap off from his white hair and bowing very low, "all night long we have been wandering together; we have found the road. We would seem to deserve a bit of a drink. Isn't that so, sir, your eminence? just enough to get warmed," he added, with an obsequious smile.

I gave him a quarter-ruble. The innkeeper brought out a glass of vodka, and handed it to the old man. He laid aside his mitten and whip, and took the glass in his small, dark hand, bony and somewhat bluish; but strangely enough he could not control his thumb. He could not hold the glass, but dropped it in the snow, spilling the wine.

All the drivers burst out laughing.

"See, Mitritch-to is half-frozen like; he can't hold his wine."

But Mitritch was greatly vexed because he had spilt the wine.

They brought him, however, another glass, and poured it into his mouth. He immediately became jolly, went into the inn, lighted his pipe, began to show his yellow worn teeth, and to scold at every word. After they had taken their last drinks, the drivers came back to their troïkas, and we set off.

The snow kept growing whiter and brighter, till it made one's eyes ache to look at it. The orange-colored reddish streaks stretched brighter and brighter, higher and higher, across the heavens; now the red circle of the sun appeared on the horizon through dove-colored clouds; the blue sky kept growing brighter and deeper. On the road around the station the tracks were clear, distinct, and yellow; in some places were cradle-holes. In the frosty, bracing atmosphere, there was a pleasant exhilaration and freshness.

My troïka glided along very swiftly. The head of the shaft-horse, and the neck with the mane tossing up to the bell-bow, constantly made the same quick, swinging motions under the hunting-bell, the tongue of which no longer struck, but scraped around the rim. The good side horses, in friendly rivalry tugging at the frozen, twisted traces, energetically galloped on, the tassels striking against their ribs and necks. Occasionally the off horse would plunge into some drift, and kick up the snow, filling our eyes with the fine powder. Ignashka kept shouting in his gay tenor. The runners creaked over the dry, frosty snow. Behind us, with a loud festival sound, rang the two sledge-chimes; and the voices of the drivers, made jolly by wine, could be heard.

I looked back; the gray, shaggy side horses, arching their necks, regularly puffing out the breath, with their curved bits, galloped over the snow. Filipp was flourishing his whip and adjusting his cap. The little old man, with his legs hanging out, was reclining as before in the middle of his sledge.

At the end of two minutes the sledge scraped against the boards of the well-cleared entrance of the station-house; and Ignashka turned to me, his jolly face covered with snow, where his breath had turned to ice, and said:—

"Here we are, barin!"

1856

LUCERNE

FROM THE RECOLLECTIONS OF PRINCE

NEKHLIUDOF

JULY 20, 1857.

Yesterday evening I arrived at Lucerne, and put up at the best inn there, the Schweitzerhof.

"Lucerne, the chief city of the canton, situated on the shore of the Vierwaldstätter See," says Murray, "is one of the most romantic places of Switzerland: here cross three important highways, and it is only an hour's distance by steamboat to Mount Righi, from which is obtained one of the most magnificent views in the world."

Whether that be true or no, other Guides say the same thing, and consequently at Lucerne there are throngs of travelers of all nationalities, especially the English.

The magnificent five-storied building of the Hotel Schweitzerhof is situated on the quay, at the very edge of the lake, where in olden times there used to be the crooked covered wooden bridge with chapels on the corners and pictures on the roof. Now, thanks to the tremendous inroad of Englishmen, with their necessities, their tastes, and their money, they have torn down the old bridge, and in its place erected a granite quay, straight as a stick. On the quay they have built straight, quadrangular five-storied houses; in front of the houses they have set out two rows of lindens and provided them with supports, and between the lindens is the usual supply of green benches.

This is the promenade; and here back and forth stroll the Englishwomen in their Swiss straw hats, and the Englishmen in simple and comfortable attire, and rejoice in their work. Possibly these quays and houses and lindens and Englishmen would be excellent in their way anywhere else, but here they seem discordant amid this strangely magnificent, and at the same time indescribably harmonious and smiling nature.

As soon as I went up to my room, and opened the window facing the lake, the beauty of the sheet of water, of the mountains, and of the sky, at the first moment literally dazzled and overwhelmed me. I experienced an inward unrest, and the necessity of expressing in some manner the feelings that suddenly filled my soul to overflowing. I felt a desire to embrace, powerfully to embrace, some one, to tickle him, or to pinch him; in short, to do to him and to myself something extraordinary.

It was seven o'clock in the evening. The rain had been falling all day, but now it had cleared.

The lake, iridescent as melted sulphur, and dotted with boats, which left behind them vanishing trails, spread out before my windows smooth, motionless as it were, between the variegated green shores. Farther away it was contracted between two monstrous headlands, and, darkling, set itself against and disappeared behind a confused pile of mountains, clouds, and glaciers. In the foreground stretched a panorama of moist, fresh green shores, with reeds, meadows, gardens, and villas. Farther away, the dark green wooded heights, crowned with the ruins of feudal castles; in the background, the rolling, pale lilac-colored vista of mountains, with fantastic peaks built up of crags and pallid snow-capped summits. And everything was bathed in a fresh, transparent azure atmosphere, and kindled by the warm rays of the setting sun, bursting forth through the riven skies.

Not on the lake or on the mountains or in the skies was there a single completed line, a single unmixed color, a single moment of repose; everywhere motion, irregularity, fantasy, endless conglomeration and variety of shades and lines; and above all, a calm, a softness, a unity, and the inevitability of beauty.

And here amid this indeterminate, kaleidoscopic, unfettered loveliness, before my very window, stretched stupidly, compelling the gaze, the white line of the quay, the lindens with their supports, and the green seats,—miserable, tasteless creations of human ingenuity, not subordinated, like the distant villas and ruins, to the general harmony of the beautiful scene, but on the contrary brutally opposed to it. . . .

Constantly, though against my will, my eyes were attracted to that horribly straight line of the quay; and mentally I should have liked to get rid of it, to demolish it like a black spot which should disfigure the nose beneath one's eye.

But the quay with the sauntering Englishmen remained where it was, and I involuntarily tried to find a point of view where it would be out of my sight. I succeeded in finding such a view; and till dinner was ready I took delight, alone by myself, in this incomplete and therefore the more enjoyable feeling of oppression that one experiences in the solitary contemplation of natural beauty.

About half-past seven I was called to dinner. Two long tables, accommodating at least a hundred persons, were spread in the great, magnificently decorated dining-room on the first floor. The silent gathering of the guests lasted three minutes,—the rustle of women's gowns, the soft steps, the softly spoken words addressed to the courtly and elegant waiters. And all the places were occupied by ladies and gentlemen dressed elegantly, even richly, and for the most part in perfect taste.

As is apt to be the case in Switzerland, the majority of the guests were English, and this gave the ruling characteristics of the common table: that is, a strict decorum regarded as an obligation, a reserve founded not in pride but in the absence of any necessity for social relationship, and finally a uniform sense of satisfaction felt by each in the comfortable and agreeable gratification of his wants.

On all sides gleamed the whitest laces, the whitest collars, the whitest teeth, —natural and artificial,—the whitest complexions and hands. But the faces, many of which were very handsome, bore the expression merely of individual prosperity, and absolute absence of interest in all that surrounded them unless it bore directly on their own individual selves; and the white hands, glittering with rings or protected by mitts, moved only for the purpose of straightening collars, cutting meat, or filling wine-glasses; no soul-felt emotion was betrayed in these actions.

Occasionally members of some one family would exchange remarks in subdued voices, about the excellence of such and such a dish or wine, or about the beauty of the view from Mount Righi.

Individual tourists, whether men or women, sat beside one another in silence, and did not even seem to see one another. If it happened occasionally that, out of this five-score human beings, two spoke to each other, the topic of their conversation was certain to be the weather, or the ascent of the Righi.

Knives and forks scarcely rattled on the plates, so perfect was the observance of propriety; and no one dared to convey pease and vegetables to the mouth otherwise than on the fork. The waiters, involuntarily subdued by the universal silence, asked in a whisper what wine you would be pleased to order.

Such dinners always depress me: I dislike them, and before they are over I become blue. It always seems to me as if I had done something wrong; just as when I was a boy I was set upon a chair in consequence of some naughtiness, and bidden ironically, "Now rest a little while, my dear young fellow." And all the time my young blood was pulsing through my veins, and in the other room I could hear the merry shouts of my brothers.

I used to try to rebel against this feeling of being choked down, which I experienced at such dinners, but in vain. All these dead-and-alive faces have an irresistible influence over me, and I myself become also as one dead. I have no desires, I have no thoughts; I do not even observe.

At first I attempted to enter into conversation with my neighbors; but I got no response beyond the phrases which had probably been repeated in that place a hundred thousand times, a hundred thousand times by the same persons.

And yet these people were by no means all stupid and feelingless; but evidently many of them, though they seemed so dead, led self-centered lives, just as I did, and in many cases far more complicated and interesting ones than my own. Why, then, should they deprive themselves of one of the greatest enjoyments of life,—the enjoyment that comes from the intercourse of man with man?

How different it used to be in our *pension* at Paris, where twenty of us, belonging to as many different nationalities, professions, and individualities, met together at a common table, and, under the influence of the Gallic sociability, found the keenest zest!

There, immediately, from one end of the table to the other, the conversation, sandwiched with witticisms and puns, though often in a broken speech, became general. There every one, without being solicitous for the proprieties, said whatever came into his head. There we had our own philosopher, our own disputant, our own *bel esprit*, our own butt,—all common property.

There, immediately after dinner, we would move the table to one side, and, without paying too much attention to rhythm, take to dancing the polka on the dusty carpet, and often keep it up till evening. There, though we were rather flirtatious, and not overwise or dignified, still we were human beings.

And the Spanish countess with romantic proclivities, and the Italian *abbate* who insisted on declaiming from the "Divine Comedy" after dinner, and the American doctor who had the *entrée* into the Tuileries, and the young dramatic author with his long hair, and the pianist who, according to her own account, had composed the best polka in existence, and the unhappy widow who was a beauty, and wore three rings on every finger,—all of us enjoyed this society, which, though somewhat superficial, was human and pleasant. And we each carried away from it hearty recollections of the others, superficial or serious, as the case might be.

But at these English *table-d'hôte* dinners, as I look at all these laces, ribbons, jewels, pomaded locks, and silken gowns, I often think how many living women would be happy, and would make others happy, with these adornments.

Strange to think how many friends and lovers—most fortunate friends and lovers—are, perhaps, sitting side by side without knowing it! And God knows why they never come to this knowledge, and never give each other this happiness, which they might so easily give, and which they so long for.

I began to feel depressed, as usual, after such a dinner; and, without waiting for dessert, I sallied out in the most gloomy frame of mind for a constitutional through the city. My melancholy frame of mind was not relieved, but was rather confirmed, by the narrow, muddy streets without lanterns, the shuttered shops, the encounters with drunken workmen, and with women hastening after water, or in bonnets, glancing around them as they glided down the alleys or along the walls.

It was perfectly dark in the streets when I returned to the hotel without casting a glance about me, or having an idea in my head. I hoped that sleep would put an end to my melancholy. I experienced that horrible spiritual chill, loneliness, and heaviness, which sometimes, without any reason, beset those who are just arrived in any new place.

Looking down at my feet, I walked along the quay to the Schweitzerhof, when suddenly my ear was struck by the strains of a peculiar but thoroughly agreeable and sweet music.

These strains had an immediately enlivening effect on me. It was as if a bright, cheerful light had poured into my soul. I felt contented, gay. My slumbering attention was awakened again to all surrounding objects; and the beauty of the night and the lake, to which, till then, I had been indifferent, suddenly came over me with quickening force like something new.

I involuntarily took in at a glance the dark sky with gray clouds flecking its deep blue, now lighted by the rising moon, the glassy, dark green lake, with its surface reflecting the lighted windows, and far away the snowy mountains; and I heard the croaking of the frogs over on the Fröschenburg shore, and the dewy fresh call of the quail.

Directly in front of me, in the spot whence the sounds of music had first come, and which still especially attracted my attention, I saw, amid the semi-darkness on the street, a throng of people standing in a semicircle, and in front of the crowd, at a little distance, a small man in dark clothes.

Behind the throng and the man, there stood out harmoniously against the blue, ragged sky, gray and blue, the black tops of a few Lombardy poplars in some garden, and, rising majestically on high, the two stern spires that stand on the towers of the ancient cathedral.

I drew nearer, and the strains became more distinct. At some distance I could clearly distinguish the full accords of a guitar, sweetly swelling in the evening air, and several voices, which, while taking turns with one another, did not sing any definite theme, but gave suggestions of one in places wherever the melody was most pronounced.

The theme was in somewhat the nature of a mazurka, sweet and graceful. The voices sounded now near at hand, now far distant; now a bass was heard, now a tenor, now a falsetto such as the Tyrolese warblers are wont to sing.

It was not a song, but the graceful, masterly sketch of a song. I could not comprehend what it was, but it was beautiful.

Those voluptuous, soft chords of the guitar, that sweet, gentle melody, that solitary figure of the man in black, amid the fantastic environment of the dark lake, the gleaming moon, and the twin spires of the cathedral rising in majestic silence, and the black tops of the poplars,—all was strange and perfectly beautiful, or at least seemed so to me.

All the confused, arbitrary impressions of life suddenly became full of meaning and beauty. It seemed to me as if a fresh fragrant flower had sprung up in my soul. In place of the weariness, dullness, and indifference toward everything in the world, which I had been feeling the moment before, I experienced a necessity for love, a fullness of hope, and an unbounded enjoyment of life.

"What dost thou desire, what dost thou long for?" an inner voice seemed to say. "Here it is. Thou art surrounded on all sides by beauty and poetry. Breathe it in, in full, deep draughts, as long as thou hast strength. Enjoy it to the full extent of thy capacity. 'Tis all thine, all blessed!" . . .

I drew nearer. The little man was, as it seemed, a traveling Tyrolese. He stood before the windows of the hotel, one leg advanced, his head thrown back; and as he thrummed on the guitar, he sang his graceful song in all those different voices.

I immediately felt an affection for this man, and a gratefulness for the change which he had brought about in me.

The singer, as far as I was able to judge, was dressed in an old black coat. He had short black hair, and he wore a civilian's hat which was no longer new. There was nothing artistic in his attire, but his clever and youthfully gay motions and pose, together with his diminutive stature, formed a pleasing and at the same time pathetic spectacle.

On the steps, in the windows, and on the balconies of the brilliantly lighted hotel, stood ladies handsomely decorated and attired, gentlemen with polished collars, porters and lackeys in gold-embroidered liveries; in the street, in the semicircle of the crowd, and farther along on the sidewalk, among the lindens, were gathered groups of well-dressed waiters, cooks in white caps and aprons, and young girls wandering about with arms about each others' waists.

All, it seemed, were under the influence of the same feeling as I myself experienced. All stood in silence around the singer, and listened attentively. Silence reigned, except in the pauses of the song, when there came from far away across the waters the regular click of a hammer, and from the Fröschenburg shore rang in fascinating monotone the voices of the frogs, interrupted by the mellow, monotonous call of the quail.

The little man in the darkness, in the midst of the street, poured out his heart like a nightingale, in couplet after couplet, song after song. Though I had come close to him, his singing continued to give me greater and greater gratification.

His voice, which was of great power, was extremely pleasant and tender; the taste and feeling for rhythm which he displayed in the control of it were extraordinary, and proved that he had great natural gifts.

After he sung each couplet, he invariably repeated the theme in variation, and it was evident that all his graceful variations came to him at the instant, spontaneously.

Among the crowd, and above on the Schweitzerhof, and near by on the boulevard, were heard frequent murmurs of approval, though generally the most respectful silence reigned.

The balconies and the windows kept filling more and more with handsomely dressed men and women leaning on their elbows, and picturesquely illuminated by the lights in the house.

Promenaders came to a halt, and in the darkness on the quay stood men and women in little groups. Near me, at some distance from the common crowd, stood an aristocratic cook and lackey, smoking their cigars. The cook was forcibly impressed by the music, and at every high falsetto note enthusiastically nodded his head to the lackey, and nudged him with his elbow with an expression of astonishment which seemed to say, "How he sings! hey?"

The lackey, by whose undissimulated smile I could mark the depth of feeling he experienced, replied to the cook's nudges by shrugging his shoulders, as if to show that it was hard enough for him to be made enthusiastic, and that he had heard much better music.

In one of the pauses of his song, while the minstrel was clearing his throat, I asked the lackey who he was, and if he often came there.

"Twice in the summer he comes here," replied the lackey. "He is from Aargau; he gets his livelihood by begging."

"Tell me, do many like him come round here?" I asked.

"Oh, yes," replied the lackey, not comprehending the full force of what I asked; but, immediately after recollecting himself, he added, "Oh, no. This one is the only one I ever heard here. No one else."

At this moment the little man had finished his first song, was briskly twanging his guitar, and said something in his German *patois*, which I could not understand, but which brought forth a hearty round of laughter from the surrounding throng.

"What was that he said?" I asked.

"He said his throat is dried up, he would like some wine," replied the lackey, who was standing near me.

"What? is he rather fond of the glass?"

"Yes, all that sort of people are," replied thé lackey, smiling and pointing at the minstrel.

The minstrel took off his cap, and swinging his guitar went toward the hotel. Raising his head, he addressed the ladies and gentlemen standing by the windows and on the balconies, saying in a half-Italian, half-German accent, an¹ with the same intonation as jugglers use in speaking to their audiences:—

"*Messieurs et mesdames, si vous croyez que je gagne quelque chose, vous vous trompez: je ne suis qu'un pauvre tiaple.*"

He stood in silence a moment, but as no one gave him anything, he once more took up his guitar, and said:—

"A présent, messieurs et mesdames, je vous chanterai l'air du Righi."

His hotel audience made no response, but stood in expectation of the coming song. Below on the street a laugh went round, probably in part because he had expressed himself so strangely, and in part because no one had given him anything.

I gave him a few centimes, which he deftly changed from one hand to the other, and bestowed them in his vest-pocket; and then, replacing his cap, began once more to sing; it was the graceful, sweet Tyrolese melody which he had called l'air du Righi.

This song, which formed the last on his programme, was even better than the preceding, and from all sides in the wondering throng were heard sounds of approbation.

He finished. Again he swung his guitar, took off his cap, held it out in front of him, went two or three steps nearer to the windows, and again repeated his stock phrase: "Messieurs et mesdames, si vous croyez que je gagne quelque chose," which he evidently considered to be very shrewd and witty; but in his voice and motions I perceived now a certain irresolution and childish timidity which were especially touching in a person of such diminutive stature.

The elegant public, still picturesquely grouped in the lighted windows and on the balconies, were shining in their rich attire; a few conversed in soberly discreet tones, apparently about the singer who was standing there below them with outstretched hand; others gazed down with attentive curiosity on the little black figure; on one balcony could be heard a young girl's merry, ringing laughter.

In the crowd below the talk and laughter kept growing louder and louder.

The singer for the third time repeated his phrase, but in a still weaker voice, and did not even end the sentence; and again he stretched his hand with his cap, but instantly drew it back. Again, not one of those brilliantly dressed scores of people standing to listen to him threw him a penny.

The crowd laughed heartlessly.

The little singer, so it seemed to me, shrunk more into himself, took his guitar into his other hand, lifted his cap, and said:—

"Messieurs et mesdames, je vous remercie, et je vous souhais une bonne nuit."

Then he put on his hat.

The crowd cackled with laughter and satisfaction. The handsome ladies and gentlemen, calmly exchanging remarks, withdrew gradually from the balconies. On the boulevard the promenading began once more. The street, which had been still during the singing, assumed its wonted liveliness; a few men, however, stood at some distance, and, without approaching the singer, looked at him and laughed.

I heard the little man muttering something between his teeth, as he turned away; and I saw him, apparently growing more and more diminutive, start toward the city with brisk steps. The promenaders, who had been looking at him, followed him at some distance, still making merry at his expense. . . .

My mind was in a whirl; I could not comprehend what it all meant; and still standing in the same place, I gazed abstractedly into the darkness after the little man, who was fast disappearing, as he went with ever increasing swiftness with long strides into the city, followed by the merrymaking promenaders.

I was overmastered by a feeling of pain, of bitterness, and, above all, of shame for the little man, for the crowd, for myself, as if it were I who had asked for money and received none; as if it were I who had been turned to ridicule.

Without looking any longer, feeling my heart oppressed, I also hurried with long strides toward the entrance of the Schweitzerhof. I could not explain the feeling that overmastered me; only there was something like a stone, from which I could not free myself, weighing down my soul and oppressing me.

At the stately, well-lighted entrance I met the Swiss, who politely made way for me. An English family was also at the door. A portly, handsome, tall gentleman, with black side-whiskers, in a black hat, and with a plaid on one arm, while in his hand he carried a costly cane, came out slowly, and full of importance. Leaning on his arm was a lady, who wore a raw silk gown and a bonnet with bright ribbons and the most charming laces. With them was a pretty, fresh-looking young lady, in a graceful Swiss hat, with a feather, à la mousquetaire; from under it escaped long, light yellow curls, softly encircling her fair face. In front of them skipped a buxom girl of ten, with round, white knees which showed from under her thin embroideries. "What a lovely night!" the lady was saying in a sweet, happy voice, as I passed them.

"Oh, yes," growled the Englishman, lazily; and it was evident that he found it so enjoyable to be alive in the world, that it was too much trouble even to speak.

And it seemed as if all of them alike found it so comfortable and easy, so light and free, to be alive in the world, their faces and motions expressed such perfect indifference to the lives of every one else, and such absolute confidence, that it was to them that the Swiss made way, and bowed so profoundly, and that when they returned they would find clean, comfortable beds and rooms, and that all this was bound to be, and was their indefeasible right, that I could not help contrasting them with the wandering minstrel, who, weary, perhaps hungry, full of shame, was retreating before the laughing crowd. And then, suddenly, I comprehended what it was that oppressed my heart with such a load of heaviness, and I felt an indescribable anger against these people.

Twice I walked up and down past the Englishman, and each time, without turning out for him, my elbow punched him, which gave me a feeling of indescribable satisfaction; and then, darting down the steps, I hastened through the darkness in the direction taken by the little man on his way to the city.

Overtaking three men, walking together, I asked them where the singer was; they laughed, and pointed straight ahead. There he was, walking alone with brisk steps; no one was with him; all the time, as it seemed to me, he was indulging in bitter monologue.

I caught up with him, and proposed to him to go somewhere with me and drink a bottle of wine. He kept on with his rapid walk, and looked at me indignantly; but when it dawned on him what I meant, he halted.

"Well, I will not refuse, if you are so kind," said he; "here is a little café, we can go in there. It's very ordinary," he added, pointing to a drinking-saloon that was still open.

His expression "very ordinary" involuntarily suggested to my mind the idea of not going to a very ordinary *café*, but to go to the Schweitzerhof, where those who had been listening to him were. Notwithstanding the fact that several times he showed a sort of timid disquietude at the idea of going to the Schweitzerhof, declaring that it was too fashionable for him there, still I insisted on carrying out my purpose; and he, already pretending that he was not in the least abashed, and gayly swinging his guitar, went back with me across the quay.

A few loiterers who had happened along as I was talking with the minstrel, and had stopped to hear what I had to say, now, after arguing among themselves, followed us to the very entrance of the hotel, evidently expecting from the Tyrolese some further demonstration.

I ordered a bottle of wine of a waiter whom I met in the hall. The waiter smiled and looked at us, and went by without answering. The head waiter, to whom I addressed myself with the same order, listened to me and, measuring the minstrel's modest little figure from head to foot, sternly ordered the waiter to take us to the room at the left.

The room at the left was a bar-room for simple people. In the corner of this room a hunchbacked maid was washing dishes. The whole furniture consisted of bare wooden tables and benches.

The waiter who came to serve us looked at us with a supercilious smile, thrust his hands in his pockets, and exchanged some remarks with the humpbacked dish-washer. He evidently tried to give us to understand that he felt himself immeasurably higher than the minstrel, both in dignity and social position, so that he considered it not only an indignity, but actually ridiculous, that he was called on to serve us.

"Do you wish *vin ordinaire?*" he asked, with a knowing look, winking toward my companion and switching his napkin from one hand to the other.

"Champagne, and your very best," said I, endeavoring to assume my haughtiest and most imposing appearance.

But neither my champagne, nor my endeavor to look haughty and imposing, had the least effect on the servant; he smiled incredulously, loitered a moment or two gazing at us, took time enough to glance at his gold watch, and with leisurely steps, as if going out for a walk, left the room.

Soon he returned with the wine, bringing two other waiters with him. These two sat down near the dish-washer, and gazed at us with amused attention and a bland smile, just as parents gaze at their children when they are gently playing. Only the humpbacked dish-washer, it seemed to me, did not look at us scornfully but sympathetically.

Though it was trying and awkward to lunch with the minstrel, and to play the entertainer, under the fire of all these waiters' eyes, I tried to do my duty with as little constraint as possible. In the lighted room I could see him better. He was a small but symmetrically built and muscular man, though almost a dwarf in stature; he had bristly black hair, teary big black eyes, bushy eyebrows, and a thoroughly pleasant, attractively shaped mouth. He had little side-whiskers, his hair was short, his attire was very simple and mean. He was not over-clean, was ragged and sunburnt, and in general had the look of a laboring-man. He was far more like a poor tradesman than an artist.

Only in his ever humid and brilliant eyes, and in his firm mouth, was there any sign of originality or genius. By his face it might be conjectured that his age was between twenty-five and forty; in reality, he was thirty-seven.

Here is what he related to me, with good-natured readiness and evident sincerity, of his life. He was a native of Aargau. In early childhood he had lost father and mother; other relatives he had none. He had never owned any property. He had been apprenticed to a carpenter; but twenty-two years previously one of his arms had been attacked by caries, which had prevented him from ever working again.

From childhood he had been fond of singing, and he began to be a singer. Occasionally strangers had given him money. With this he had learned his profession, bought his guitar, and now for eighteen years he had been wandering about through Switzerland and Italy, singing before hotels. His whole luggage consisted of his guitar, and a little purse in which, at the present time, there was only a franc and a half. That would have to suffice for supper and lodgings this night.

Every year now for eighteen years he had made the round of the best and most popular resorts of Switzerland,—Zurich, Lucerne, Interlaken, Chamonix, etc.; by the way of the St. Bernard he would go down into Italy, and return over the St. Gotthard, or through Savoy. Just at present it was rather hard for him to walk, as he had caught a cold, causing him to suffer from some trouble in his legs,—he called it *Gliederzucht*, or rheumatism,—which grew more severe from year to year; and, moreover, his voice and eyes had grown weaker. Nevertheless, he was on his way to Interlaken, Aix-les-Bains, and thence over the little St. Bernard to Italy, which he was very fond of. It was evident that on the whole he was well content with his life.

When I asked him why he returned home, if he had any relatives there, or a house and land, his mouth parted in a gay smile, and he replied, "*Oui, le sucre est bon, il est doux pour les enfants!*" and he winked at the servants.

I did not catch his meaning, but the group of servants burst out laughing.

"No, I have nothing of the sort, but still I should always want to go back," he explained to me. "I go home because there is always a something that draws one to one's native place."

And once more he repeated with a shrewd, self-satisfied smile, his phrase, "*Oui, le sucre est bon*," and then laughed good-naturedly.

The servants were very much amused, and laughed heartily; only the hunch-backed dish-washer looked earnestly from her big kindly eyes at the little man, and picked up his cap for him, when, as we talked, he once knocked it off the bench. I have noticed that wandering minstrels, acrobats, even jugglers, delight in calling themselves artists, and several times I hinted to my comrade that he was an artist; but he did not at all accept this designation, but with perfect simplicity looked on his work as a means of existence.

When I asked him if he had not himself written the songs which he sang, he showed great surprise at such a strange question, and replied that the words of whatever he sang were all of old Tyrolese origin.

"But how about that song of the Righi? I think that cannot be very ancient," I suggested.

"Oh, that was composed about fifteen years ago. There was a German in Basle; he was a clever man; it was he who composed it. A splendid song. You see he composed it especially for travelers."

And he began to repeat the words of the Righi song, which he liked so well, translating them into French as he went along.

> *"If you wish to go to Righi,*
> *You will not need shoes to Wegis*
> *(For you go that far by steamboat),*
> *But from Wegis take a stout staff,*
> *Also on your arm a maiden;*
> *Drink a glass of wine on starting,*
> *Only do not drink too freely,*
> *For if you desire to drink here,*
> *You must earn the right to, first."*

"Oh! a splendid song!" he exclaimed, as he finished.

The servants, evidently, also found the song much to their mind, because they came up closer to us.

"Yes, but who was it composed the music?" I asked.

"Oh, no one at all; you know you must have something new when you are going to sing for strangers."

When the ice was brought, and I had given my comrade a glass of champagne, he seemed somewhat ill at ease, and, glancing at the servants, he turned and twisted on the bench.

We touched our glasses to the health of all artists; he drank half a glass, then he seemed to be collecting his ideas, and knit his brows in deep thought.

"It is long since I have tasted such wine, *je ne vous dis que ça.* In Italy the *vino d'Asti* is excellent, but this is still better. Ah! Italy; it is splendid to be there!" he added.

"Yes, there they know how to appreciate music and artists," said I, trying to bring him round to the evening's mischance before the Schweitzerhof.

"No," he replied. "There, as far as music is concerned, I cannot give anybody satisfaction. The Italians are themselves musicians,—none like them in the world; but I know only Tyrolese songs. They are something of a novelty to them, though."

"Well, you find rather more generous gentlemen there, don't you?" I went on to say, anxious to make him share in my resentment against the guests of the Schweitzerhof. "There it would not be possible to find a big hotel frequented by rich people, where, out of a hundred listening to an artist's singing, not one would give him anything."

My question utterly failed of the effect that I expected. It did not enter his head to be indignant with them; on the contrary, he saw in my remark an implied slur on his talent which had failed of its reward, and he hastened to set himself right before me. "It is not every time that you get anything," he remarked; "sometimes one isn't in good voice, or you are tired; now to-day I have been walking ten hours, and singing almost all the time. That is hard.

And these important aristocrats do not always care to listen to Tyrolese songs."

"But still, how can they help giving?" I insisted. He did not comprehend my remark.

"That's nothing," he said; "but here the principal thing is, *on est tres serré pour la police*, that's what's the trouble. Here, according to these republican laws, you are not allowed to sing; but in Italy you can go wherever you please, no one says a word. Here, if they want to let you, they let you; but if they don't want to, then they can throw you into jail."

"What? That's incredible!"

"Yes, it is true. If you have been warned once, and are found singing again, they may put you in jail. I was kept there three months once," he said, smiling as if that were one of his pleasantest recollections.

"Oh! that is terrible!" I exclaimed. "What was the reason?"

"That was in consequence of one of the new laws of the republic," he went on to explain, growing animated. "They cannot comprehend here that a poor fellow must earn his living somehow. If I were not a cripple, I would work. But what harm do I do to any one in the world by my singing? What does it mean? The rich can live as they wish, but *un pauvre tiaple* like myself can't live at all. What does it mean by laws of the republic? If that is the way they run, then we don't want a republic. Isn't that so, my dear sir? We don't want a republic, but we want . . . we simply want . . . we want" . . . he hesitated a little, . . . "we want natural laws."

I filled up his glass.

"You are not drinking," I said.

He took the glass in his hand, and bowed to me.

"I know what you wish," he said, blinking his eyes at me, and threatening me with his finger. "You wish to make me drunk, so as to see what you can get out of me; but no, you shan't have that gratification."

"Why should I make you drunk?" I inquired. "All I wished was to give you a pleasure."

He seemed really sorry that he had offended me by interpreting my insistence so harshly. He grew confused, stood up, and touched my elbow.

"No, no," said he, looking at me with a beseeching expression in his moist eyes. "I was only joking."

And immediately after he made use of some horribly uncultivated slang expression, intended to signify that I was, nevertheless, a fine young man.

"*Je ne vous dis que ça,*" he said in conclusion.

In this fashion the minstrel and I continued to drink and converse; and the waiters continued to stare at us unceremoniously, and, as it seemed, to ridicule us.

In spite of the interest which our conversation aroused in me, I could not avoid taking notice of their behavior; and I confess I began to grow more and more angry.

One of the waiters arose, came up to the little man, and, looking at the top of his head, began to smile. I was already full of wrath against the inmates of the hotel, and had not yet had a chance to pour it out on any one; and now I confess I was in the highest degree irritated by this audience of waiters.

The Swiss, not removing his hat, came into the room, and sat down near me, leaning his elbows on the table. This last circumstance, which was so insulting to my dignity or my vainglory, completely enraged me, and gave an outlet for all the wrath which the whole evening long had been boiling within me. Why had he so humbly bowed when he had met me before, and now, because I was sitting with the traveling minstrel, did he come and take his place near me so rudely? I was entirely overmastered by that boiling, angry indignation which I enjoy in myself, which I sometimes endeavor to stimulate when it comes over me, because it has an exhilarating effect on me, and gives me, if only for a short time, a certain extraordinary flexibility, energy, and strength in all my physical and moral faculties.

I leaped to my feet.

"Whom are you laughing at?" I screamed at the waiter; and I felt my face turn pale, and my lips involuntarily set together.

"I am not laughing, I only . . ." replied the waiter, moving away from me.

"Yes, you are; you are laughing at this gentleman. And what right have you to come, and to take a seat here, when there are guests? Don't you dare to sit down!"

The Swiss, muttering something, got up and turned to the door.

"What right have you to make sport of this gentleman, and to sit down by him, when he is a guest, and you are a waiter? Why didn't you laugh at me this evening at dinner, and come and sit down beside me? Because he is meanly dressed, and sings in the streets? Is that the reason? and because I have better clothes? He is poor, but he is a thousand times better than you are; that I am sure of, because he has never insulted any one, but you have insulted him."

"I didn't mean anything," replied my enemy, the waiter. "Did I disturb him by sitting down?"

The waiter did not understand me, and my German was wasted on him. The rude Swiss was about to take the waiter's part; but I fell upon him so impetuously that the Swiss pretended not to understand me, and waved his hand.

The hunchbacked dish-washer, either because she perceived my wrathful state, and feared a scandal, or possibly because she shared my views, took my part, and, trying to force her way between me and the porter, told him to hold his tongue, saying that I was right, but at the same time urging me to calm myself.

"*Der Herr hat Recht; Sie haben Recht,*" she said over and over again. The minstrel's face presented a most pitiable, terrified expression; and evidently he did not understand why I was angry, and what I wanted; and he urged me to let him go away as soon as possible.

But the eloquence of wrath burned within me more and more. I understood it all,—the throng that had made merry at his expense, and his auditors who had not given him anything; and not for all the world would I have held my peace.

I believe that, if the waiters and the Swiss had not been so submissive, I should have taken delight in having a brush with them, or striking the defenseless English girl on the head with a stick. If at that moment I had been at Sevastopol, I should have taken delight in devoting myself to slaughtering and killing in the English trench.

"And why did you take this gentleman and me into this room, and not into the other? What?" I thundered at the Swiss, seizing him by the arm\so that he could not escape from me. "What right had you to judge by his appearance that this gentleman must be served in this room, and not in that? Have not all guests who pay equal rights in hotels? Not only in a republic, but in all the world! Your scurvy republic! . . . Equality, indeed! You would not dare to take an Englishman into this room, not even those Englishmen who have heard this gentleman free of cost; that is, who have stolen from him, each one of them, the few centimes which ought to have been given to him. How did you dare to take us to this room?"

"That room is closed," said the porter.

"No," I cried, "that isn't true; it isn't closed."

"Then you know best."

"I know . . . I know that you are lying."

The Swiss turned his back on me.

"Eh! What is to be said?" he muttered.

"What is to be said?" I cried. "Now conduct us instantly into that room!"

In spite of the dish-washer's warning, and the entreaties of the minstrel, who would have preferred to go home, I insisted on seeing the head waiter, and went with my guest into the big dining-room. The head waiter, hearing my angry voice, and seeing my menacing face, avoided a quarrel, and, with contemptuous servility, said that I might go wherever I pleased. I could not prove to the Swiss that he had lied, because he had hastened out of sight before I went into the hall.

The dining-room was, in fact, open and lighted; and at one of the tables sat an Englishman and a lady, eating their supper. Although we were shown to a special table, I took the dirty minstrel to the very one where the Englishman was, and bade the waiter bring to us there the unfinished bottle.

The two guests at first looked with surprised, then with angry, eyes at the little man, who, more dead than alive, was sitting near me. They talked together in a low tone; then the lady pushed back her plate, her silk dress rustled, and both of them left the room. Through the glass doors I saw the Englishman saying something in an angry voice to the waiter, and pointing with his hand in our direction. The waiter put his head through the door, and looked at us. I waited with pleasurable anticipation for some one to come and order us out, for then I could have found a full outlet for all my indignation. But fortunately, though at the time I felt injured, we were left in peace. The minstrel, who before had fought shy of the wine, now eagerly drank all that was left in the bottle, so that he might make his escape as quickly as possible.

He, however, expressed his gratitude with deep feeling, as it seemed to me, for his entertainment. His teary eyes grew still more humid and brilliant, and he made use of a most strange and complicated phrase of gratitude. But still very pleasant to me was the sentence in which he said that if everybody treated artists as I had been doing, it would be very good, and ended by wishing me all manner of happiness. We went out into the hall together. There stood the servants, and my enemy the Swiss apparently airing his grievances against me before them. All of them, I thought, looked at me as if I were a man who had lost his wits. I treated the little man exactly like an equal, before all that audience of servants; and then, with all the respect that I was able to express in my behavior, I took off my hat, and pressed his hand with its dry and hardened fingers.

The servants pretended not to pay the slightest attention to me. Only one of them indulged in a sarcastic laugh.

As soon as the minstrel had bowed himself out, and disappeared in the darkness, I went up-stairs to my room, intending to sleep off all these impressions and the foolish, childish anger which had come upon me so unexpectedly. But, finding that I was too much excited to sleep, I once more went down into the street with the intention of walking until I should have recovered my equanimity, and, I must confess, with the secret hope that I might accidentally come across the porter or the waiter or the Englishman, and show them all their rudeness, and, most of all, their unfairness. But beyond the Swiss, who when he saw me turned his back, I met no one; and I began to promenade in absolute solitude back and forth along the quay.

"This is an example of the strange fate of poetry," said I to myself, having grown a little calmer. "All love it, all are in search of it; it is the only thing in life that men love and seek, and yet no one recognizes its power, no one prizes this best treasure of the world, and those who give it to men are not rewarded. Ask any one you please, ask all these guests of the Schweizerhof, what is the most precious treasure in the world, and all, or ninety-nine out of a hundred, putting on a sardonic expression, will say that the best thing in the world is money.

" 'Maybe, though, this does not please you, or coincide with your elevated ideas,' it will be urged; 'but what is to be done if human life is so constituted that money alone is capable of giving a man happiness? I cannot force my mind not to see the world as it is,' it will be added, 'that is, to see the truth.'

"Pitiable is your intellect, pitiable the happiness which you desire! And you yourselves, unhappy creatures, not knowing what you desire, . . . why have you all left your fatherland, your relatives, your money-making trades and occupations, and come to this little Swiss city of Lucerne? Why did you all this evening gather on the balconies, and in respectful silence listen to the little beggar's song? And if he had been willing to sing longer, you would have been silent and listened longer. What! could money, even millions of it, have driven you all from your country, and brought you all together in this little nook of Lucerne? Could money have gathered you all on the balconies to stand for half an hour silent and motionless? No! One thing compels you to do it, and will forever have a stronger influence than all the other impulses of life: the longing for poetry which you know, which you do not realize, but feel, always will feel as long as you have any human sensibilities. The word 'poetry' is a mockery to you; you make use of it as a sort of ridiculous reproach; you regard the love for poetry as something meet for children and silly girls, and you make sport of them for it. For yourselves you must have something more definite.

"But children look upon life in a healthy way; they recognize and love what man ought to love, and what gives happiness. But life has so deceived and perverted you, that you ridicule the only thing that you really love, and you seek for what you hate and for what gives you unhappiness.

"You are so perverted that you did not perceive what obligations you were under to the poor Tyrolese who rendered you a pure delight; but at the same time you feel needlessly obliged to humiliate yourselves before some lord, which gives you neither pleasure nor profit, but rather causes you to sacrifice your comfort and convenience. What absurdity! what incomprehensible lack of reason!

"But it was not this that made the most powerful impression on me this evening. This blindness to all that gives happiness, this unconsciousness of poetic enjoyment, I can almost comprehend, or at least I have become wonted to it, since I have almost everywhere met with it in the course of my life; the harsh, unconscious churlishness of the crowd was no novelty to me; whatever those who argue in favor of popular sentiment may say, the throng is a conglomeration of very possibly good people, but of people who touch each other only on their coarse animal sides, and express only the weakness and harshness of human nature. But how was it that you, children of a free, humane people, you Christians, you simply as human beings, repaid with coldness and ridicule the poor beggar who gave you a pure enjoyment? But no, in your country there are asylums for beggars. There are no beggars, there must be none; and there must be no feelings of sympathy, since that would be a confession that beggary existed.

"But he labored, he gave you enjoyment, he besought you to give him something of your superfluity in payment for his labor of which you took advantage. But you looked on him with a cool smile as on one of the curiosities in your lofty brilliant palaces; and though there were a hundred of you, favored with happiness and wealth, not one man or one woman among you gave him a *sou*. Abashed he went away from you, and the thoughtless throng, laughing, followed and ridiculed not you, but him, because you were cold, harsh, and dishonorable; because you robbed him in receiving the entertainment which he gave you; for this you jeered *him*.

" '*On the 19th of July, 1857, in Lucerne, before the Schweitzerhof Hotel, in which were lodging very opulent people, a wandering beggar minstrel sang for half an hour his songs, and played his guitar. About a hundred people listened to him. The minstrel thrice asked all to give him something. No one person gave him a thing, and many made sport of him.*'

"This is not an invention, but an actual fact, as those who desire can find out for themselves by consulting the papers for the list of those who were at the Schweitzerhof on the 19th of July.

"This is an event which the historians of our time ought to describe in letters of inextinguishable flame. This event is more significant and more serious, and fraught with far deeper meaning, than the facts that are printed in newspapers and histories. That the English have killed several thousand Chinese because the Chinese would not sell them anything for money while their land is overflowing with ringing coins; that the French have killed several thousand Kabyles because the wheat grows well in Africa, and because constant war is essential for the drill of an army; that the Turkish ambassador in Naples must not be a Jew; and that the Emperor Napoleon walks about in Plombières, and gives his people the express assurance that he rules only in direct accordance with the will of the people,—all these are words which darken or reveal something long known. But the episode that took place in Lucerne on the

19th of July seems to me something entirely novel and strange, and it is connected not with the everlastingly ugly side of human nature, but with a well-known epoch in the development of society. This fact is not for the history of human activities, but for the history of progress and civilization.

"Why is it that this inhuman fact, impossible in any German, French, or Italian country, is quite possible here where civilization, freedom, and equality are carried to the highest degree of development, where there are gathered together the most civilized travelers from the most civilized nations? Why is it that these cultivated human beings, generally capable of every honorable human action, had no hearty, human feeling for one good deed? Why is it that these people who, in their palaces, their meetings, and their societies, labor warmly for the condition of the celibate Chinese in India, about the spread of Christianity and culture in Africa, about the formation of societies for attaining all perfection,—why is it that they should not find in their souls the simple, primitive feeling of human sympathy? Has such a feeling entirely disappeared, and has its place been taken by vainglory, ambition, and cupidity, governing these men in their palaces, meetings, and societies? Has the spreading of that reasonable, egotistical association of people, which we call civilization, destroyed and rendered nugatory the desire for instinctive and loving association? And is this that boasted equality for which so much innocent blood has been shed, and so many crimes have been perpetrated? Is it possible that nations, like children, can be made happy by the mere sound of the word 'equality'?

"Equality before the law? Does the whole life of a people revolve within the sphere of law? Only the thousandth part of it is subject to the law; the rest lies outside of it, in the sphere of the customs and intuitions of society.

"But in society the lackey is better dressed than the minstrel, and insults him with impunity. I am better dressed than the lackey, and insult him with impunity. The Swiss considers me higher, but the minstrel lower, than himself; when I made the minstrel my companion, he felt that he was on an equality with us both, and behaved rudely. I was impudent to the Swiss, and the Swiss acknowledged that he was inferior to me. The waiter was impudent to the minstrel, and the minstrel accepted the fact that he was inferior to the waiter.

"And is that government free, even though men seriously call it free, where a single citizen can be thrown into prison, because, without harming any one, without interfering with any one, he does the only thing he can to prevent himself from dying of starvation?

"A wretched, pitiable creature is man with his craving for positive solutions, thrown into this everlastingly tossing, limitless ocean of *good* and *evil*, of facts, of combinations and contradictions. For centuries men have been struggling and laboring to put the *good* on one side, the *evil* on the other. Centuries will pass, and no matter how much the unprejudiced mind may strive to decide where the balance lies between the *good* and the *evil*, the scales will refuse to tip the beam, and there will always be equal quantities of the *good* and the *evil* on each scale.

"If only man would learn to form judgments, and not indulge in rash and arbitrary thoughts, and not to make reply to questions that are propounded merely to remain forever unanswered! If only he would learn that every thought is both a lie and a truth!—a lie from the one-sidedness and inability of man to recognize all truth; and true because it expresses one side of mortal endeavor. There are divisions in this everlastingly tumultuous, endless, endlessly confused chaos of the *good* and the *evil*. They have drawn imaginary lines over this ocean, and they contend that the ocean is really thus divided.

"But are there not millions of other possible subdivisions from absolutely different standpoints, in other planes? Certainly these novel subdivisions will be made in centuries to come, just as millions of different ones have been made in centuries past.

"Civilization is *good*, barbarism is *evil*; freedom, *good*, slavery, *evil*. Now this imaginary knowledge annihilates the instinctive, beatific, primitive craving for the *good* which is in human nature. And who will explain to me what is freedom, what is despotism, what is civilization, what is barbarism?

"Where are the boundaries that separate them? And whose soul possesses so absolute a standard of good and evil as to measure these fleeting, complicated facts? Whose intellect is so great as to comprehend and weigh all the facts in the irretrievable past? And who can find any circumstance in which *good* and *evil* do not exist together? And because I know that I see more of one than of the other, is it not because my standpoint is wrong? And who has the ability to separate himself so absolutely from life, even for a moment, as to look upon it independently from above?

"One, only one infallible Guide we have,—the universal Spirit which penetrates all collectively and as units, which has endowed each of us with the craving for the right; the Spirit which commands the tree to grow toward the sun, which commands the flower in autumn-tide to scatter its seed, and which commands each one of us unconsciously to draw closer together. And this one unerring, inspiring voice rings out louder than the noisy, hasty development of civilization.

"Who is the greater man, and who the greater barbarian,—that lord, who, seeing the minstrel's well-worn clothes, angrily left the table, who gave him not the millionth part of his possessions in payment of his labor, and now lazily sitting in his brilliant, comfortable room, calmly expresses his opinion about the events that are happening in China, and justifies the massacres that have been done there; or the little minstrel, who, risking imprisonment, with a franc in his pocket, and doing no harm to any one, has been going about for a score of years, up hill and down dale, rejoicing men's hearts with his songs, though they have jeered at him, and almost cast him out of the pale of humanity; and who, in weariness and cold and shame, has gone off to sleep, no one knows where, on his filthy straw?"

At this moment, from the city, through the dead silence of the night, far, far away, I caught the sound of the little man's guitar and his voice.

"No," something involuntarily said to me, "you have no right to commiserate the little man, or to blame the lord for his well-being. Who can weigh the inner happiness which is found in the soul of each of these men? There he stands somewhere in the muddy road, and gazes at the brilliant moonlit sky, and gayly sings amid the smiling, fragrant night; in his soul there is no reproach, no anger, no regret. And who knows what is transpiring now in the hearts of all these men within those opulent, brilliant rooms? Who knows if they all have as much unencumbered, sweet delight in life, and as much satisfaction with the world, as dwells in the soul of that little man?

"Endless are the mercy and wisdom of Him who has permitted and formed all these contradictions. Only to thee, miserable little worm of the dust, audaciously, lawlessly attempting to fathom His laws, His designs,—only to thee do they seem like contradictions.

"Full of love He looks down from His bright, immeasurable height, and rejoices in the endless harmony in which you all move in endless contradictions. In thy pride thou hast thought thyself able to separate thyself from the laws of the universe. No, thou also, with thy petty, ridiculous anger against the waiters,—thou also hast disturbed the harmonious craving for the eternal and the infinite." . . .

1857

ALBERT

1

Five rich young men went at three o'clock in the morning to a ball in Petersburg to have a good time.

Much champagne was drunk; a majority of the gentlemen were very young; the girls were pretty; a pianist and a fiddler played indefatigably one polka after another; there was no cessation to the noise of conversation and dancing. But there was a sense of awkwardness and constraint; every one felt somehow or other—and this is not unusual—that all was not as it should be.

There were several attempts made to make things more lively, but the simulated liveliness was much worse than melancholy.

One of the five young men, who was more discontented than any one else, with himself and with the others, and with the whole evening, got up with a feeling of disgust, took his hat, and went out noiselessly, intending to go home.

There was no one in the anteroom, but in the next room at the door he heard two voices disputing. The young man paused, and listened.

"It is impossible, there are guests in there," said a woman's voice.

"Come, let me in, please. I will not do any harm," urged a man, in a gentle voice.

"Indeed, I will not let you in without the madame's permission," said the woman. "Where are you going? Oh, what a man you are!" . . .

The door was flung open, and on the threshold appeared the figure of a strange-looking man. Seeing a guest, the maid ceased to detain him; and the stranger, timidly bowing, with a somewhat unsteady gait, came into the room.

He was a man of medium stature, with a lank, crooked back, bow legs, and long disheveled hair. He wore a short paletot, and tight ragged trousers over coarse dirty boots. His necktie, twisted into a string, exposed his long white neck. His shirt was filthy, and the sleeves came down over his lean hands.

But, notwithstanding his excessively emaciated body, his face was attractive and fair; and a fresh color even mantled his cheeks under his thin dark beard and side-whiskers. His disheveled locks, thrown back, exposed a low and remarkably pure forehead. His dark, languid eyes looked unswervingly forward with an expression of serenity, submission, and sweetness, which made a fascinating combination with the expression of his fresh, curved lips, visible under his thin mustache.

Advancing a few steps, he paused, turned to the young man, and smiled. He found it apparently rather hard to smile. But his face was so lighted up by it, that the young man, without knowing why, smiled in return.

"Who is that man?" he asked of the maid in a whisper, as the stranger walked toward the room where the dancing was going on.

"A crazy musician from the theater," replied the maid. "He sometimes comes to call upon the madame."

"Where are you going, Delyesof?" some one at this moment called from the drawing-room.

The young man who was called Delyesof returned to the drawing-room. The musician was now standing at the door; and, as his eyes fell on the dancers, he showed by his smile and by the beating of his foot how much pleasure this spectacle afforded him.

"Won't you come and have a dance, too?" said one of the guests to him.

The musician bowed, and looked at the madame inquiringly.

"Come, come. Why not, since the gentlemen have invited you?" said the madame.

The musician's thin, weak features suddenly began to work; and smiling and winking, and shuffling his feet, he awkwardly, clumsily, proceeded to prance through the room.

In the midst of a quadrille a jolly officer, who was dancing very beautifully and with great liveliness, accidentally hit the musician in the back. His weak, weary legs lost their equilibrium; and the musician, staggering several steps to one side, measured his length on the floor.

Notwithstanding the sharp, hard sound made by his fall, almost every one at the first moment laughed.

But the musician did not rise. The guests grew silent, even the piano ceased to sound. Delyesof and the madame were the first to reach the prostrate musician. He was lying on his elbow, and gloomily looking down. When he had been lifted to his feet, and set in a chair, he threw back his hair from his forehead with a quick motion of his bony hand, and began to smile without replying to the questions that were put.

"Mr. Albert! Mr. Albert!" exclaimed the madame. "Were you hurt? Where? Now, I told you that you had better not try to dance. . . . He is so weak," she added, addressing her guests. "It takes all his strength."

"Who is he?" some one asked the madame.

"A poor man, an artist. A very nice young fellow; but he's a sad case, as you can see."

She said this undeterred by the musician's presence. He suddenly opened his eyes, and, as if he were frightened at something, shrank away, and pushed aside those who were standing about him.

"It's nothing at all," said he, suddenly, arising from the chair with evident effort.

And in order to show that he had suffered no injury, he went into the middle of the room, and was going to dance; but he tottered, and would have fallen again, had he not been supported.

Everybody felt awkward. All looked at him, and no one spoke.

The musician's glance again lost its vivacity; and, apparently forgetting that any one was looking, he began to rub his knee with his hand. Suddenly he raised his head, advanced one faltering foot, and, with the same awkward gesture as before, tossed back his hair, and went to a violin-case, and took out the instrument.

"It was nothing at all," said he again, waving the violin. "Gentlemen, we will have a little music."

"What a strange face!" said the guests among themselves.

"Maybe there is great talent lurking in that unfortunate creature," said one of them.

"Yes; it's a sad case,—a sad case," said another.

"What a lovely face! . . . There is something extraordinary about it," said Delyesof. "Let us have a look at him." . . .

2

Albert by this time, not paying attention to any one, had raised his violin to his shoulder, and was slowly crossing over to the piano, and tuning his instrument. His lips were drawn into an expression of indifference, his eyes were almost shut; but his lank, bony back, his long white neck, his crooked legs, and shaggy black hair presented a strange but somehow not entirely ridiculous spectacle. After he had tuned the violin, he struck a quick chord, and, throwing back his head, turned to the pianist, who was waiting to accompany him.

"Mélancolie, G dur," he said, turning to the pianist with a peremptory gesture.

And immediately after, as if in apology for his peremptory gesture, he smiled sweetly, and with the same smile turned to his audience again.

Tossing back his hair with his right hand, Albert stood at one side of the piano, and, with a flowing motion of his arm, drew the bow across the strings. Through the room there swept a pure, harmonious sound, which instantly brought absolute silence.

At first there seemed to be a clear light. The notes of the theme poured forth in full abundance and exquisitely beautiful, after the dawn of the first light so unexpectedly clear and serene, suddenly illuminating the inner world of each hearer's consciousness.

Not one discordant or imperfect note distracted the attention. All the tones were clear, beautiful, and full of meaning. All silently, with trembling expectation, followed the development of the theme. From the state of tedium, of noisy gayety, or of spiritual drowsiness, into which these people had fallen, they were suddenly transported to a world the existence of which they had wholly forgotten.

There arose in their souls, now a sense of quiet contemplation of the past, now of passionate remembrance of some happiness, now the boundless longing for power and glory, now feelings of humility, of unsatisfied love, and of melancholy.

Now bitter-sweet, now vehemently despairing, the notes, freely intermingling, poured forth and poured forth, so sweetly, so powerfully, and so spontaneously, that it was not so much that sounds were heard, as that some sort of beautiful stream of poetry, long known, but now for the first time expressed, gushed through the soul.

At each note he played, Albert grew taller and taller. At a little distance, he had no appearance of being either crippled or peculiar. Pressing the violin to his chin, and with an expression of listening with passionate attention to the tones he produced, he convulsively moved his feet. Now he straightened himself up to his full height, now eagerly bent his back.

His left hand, bent intensely over the strings, seemed as it had swooned in its position, while only the bony fingers changed about spasmodically; the right hand moved smoothly, gracefully, without effort.

His face shone with absolute, enthusiastic delight; his eyes gleamed with a radiant, steely light; his nostrils quivered, his red lips were parted in rapture.

Sometimes his head bent down closer to his violin, his eyes almost closed, and his face, half shaded by his long locks, lighted up with a smile of genuine bliss. Sometimes he quickly straightened himself up, changed from one leg to the other, and his pure forehead and the radiant look which he threw around the room were alive with pride, greatness, and the consciousness of power.

Once the pianist made a mistake and struck a false chord. Physical pain was apparent in the whole form and face of the musician. He paused for a second, and with an expression of childish anger stamped his foot, and cried, "Moll, ce moll!" The pianist corrected his mistake; Albert closed his eyes, smiled, and, again forgetting himself and every one else and the whole world, gave himself up with beatitude to his work.

All who were in the room while Albert was playing preserved an attentive silence, and seemed to live and breathe only in the music.

The gay officer sat motionless in a chair by the window, with his lifeless eyes fixed on the floor, and breathing slowly and heavily long, heavy sighs. The girls, in perfect silence, sat along by the walls, only occasionally exchanging glances expressive of approval, or occasionally becoming perplexity.

The madame's fat, smiling face was radiant with happiness. The pianist kept his eyes fixed on Albert's face, and while his whole figure from head to foot showed his solicitude lest he should make some mistake, he did his best to follow him. One of the guests, who had been drinking more heavily than the rest, lay at full length on a divan, and tried not to move lest he should betray his emotion.

Delyesof experienced an unusual sensation. It seemed as if an icy band, now contracting, now expanding, were pressed on his head. The roots of his hair seemed endued with consciousness; the cold shivers ran down his back, something rose higher and higher in his throat, his nose and palate were full of little needles, and the tears stole down his cheeks.

He shook himself, tried to swallow them back and wipe them away without attracting attention, but fresh tears followed and streamed down his face. By some sort of strange association of impressions, the first tones of Albert's violin carried Delyesof back to his early youth.

Old before his time, weary of life, a broken man, he suddenly felt as if he were a boy of seventeen again, self-satisfied and handsome, blissfully dull, unconsciously happy. He remembered his first love for his cousin who wore a pink dress; he remembered his first confession of it in the linden alley; he remembered the warmth and the inexpressible charm of the fortuitous kiss; he remembered the immensity and enigmatical mystery of Nature as it surrounded them then.

In his imagination, as it went back in its flight, *she* gleamed in a mist of indefinite hopes, of incomprehensible desires, and the indubitable faith in the possibility of impossible happiness. All the priceless moments of that time, one after the other, arose before him, not like unmeaning instants of the fleeting present, but like the immutable, full-formed, reproachful images of the past.

He contemplated them with rapture, and wept,—wept not because the time had passed and he might have spent it more profitably (if that time had been given to him again, he would not have spent it any more profitably), but he wept because it had passed and would never return. His recollections evolved themselves without effort, and Albert's violin was their interpreter. It said, "They have passed, forever passed, the days of thy strength, of love, and of happiness; passed forever, and never will return. Weep for them, shed all thy tears, let thy life pass in tears for these days; this is the only and best happiness that remains to thee."

At the end of the next variation, Albert's face grew serene, his eyes flushed, great, clear drops of perspiration poured down his cheeks. The veins swelled on his forehead; his whole body swayed more and more; his lips had grown pale and were parted, and his whole figure expressed an enthusiastic craving for enjoyment.

Despairingly swaying with his whole body, and throwing back his hair, he laid down his violin, and with a smile of proud satisfaction and happiness gazed at his audience. Then his back assumed its ordinary curve, his head sank, his lips grew set, his eyes lost their fire; and, as if he were ashamed of himself, timidly glancing round, and stumbling, he went into the next room.

3

Something strange came over all the audience, and something strange was noticeable in the dead silence that succeeded Albert's playing. Apparently, each desired, and yet was not able, to express what it all meant.

What did it mean,—this brightly lighted, warm room, these brilliant women, the dawn just appearing at the windows, these hurrying pulses, and the pure impressions made by the fleeting sounds. But no one attempted to acknowledge the meaning of it all; on the contrary, almost all, feeling incapable of going wholly in the direction of that which the new impression concealed from them, rebelled against it.

"Well, now, he plays mighty well," said the officer.

"Wonderfully," replied Delyesof, stealthily wiping his cheek with his sleeve.

"One thing sure, it's time to be going, gentlemen," said he who had been lying on the divan, straightening himself up a little. "We'll have to give him something, gentlemen. Let us make a collection."

At this time, Albert was sitting alone in the next room on a divan. As he leaned his elbows on his bony knees, he smoothed his face with his dirty, sweaty hands, tossed back his hair, and smiled at his own happy thoughts.

A large collection was taken up, and Delyesof was chosen to present it.

Aside from this, Delyesof, who had been so keenly and unusually affected by the music, had conceived the thought of conferring some benefit on this man.

It came into his head to take him home with him, to feed him, to establish him somewhere,—in other words, to lift him from his vile position.

"Well, are you tired?" asked Delyesof, approaching him. Albert replied with a smile. "You have creative talent; you ought seriously to devote yourself to music, to play in public."

"I should like to have something to drink," exclaimed Albert, as if suddenly waking up.

Delyesof brought him some wine, and the musician greedily drained two glasses.

"What splendid wine!" he exclaimed.

"What a lovely thing that *Mélancolie* is!" said Delyesof.

"Oh, yes, yes," replied Albert, with a smile. "But pardon me, I do not know with whom I have the honor to be talking; maybe you are a count or a prince. Couldn't you let me have a little money?" He paused for a moment. "I have nothing—I am a poor man; I couldn't pay it back to you."

Delyesof flushed, grew embarrassed, and hastily handed the musician the money that had been collected for him.

"Very much obliged to you," said Albert, seizing the money. "Now let us have some more music; I will play for you as much as you wish. Only let me have something to drink, something to drink," he repeated, as he started to his feet.

Delyesof gave him some more wine, and asked him to sit down by him.

"Pardon me if I am frank with you," said Delyesof. "Your talent has interested me so much. It seems to me that you are in a wretched position."

Albert glanced now at Delyesof, now at the madame, who just then came into the room.

"Permit me to help you," continued Delyesof. "If you need anything, then I should be very glad if you would come and stay with me for a while. I live alone, and maybe I could be of some service to you."

Albert smiled, and made no reply.

"Why don't you thank him?" said the madame. "It seems to me that this would be a capital thing for you.— Only I would advise you not," she continued, turning to Delyesof, and shaking her head warningly.

"Very much obliged to you," said Albert, seizing Delyesof's hand with both his moist ones. "Only now let us have some music, please."

But the rest of the guests were already making their preparations to depart; and as Albert had not addressed them, they came out into the anteroom.

Albert bade the madame farewell; and, having put on his worn hat with wide brim, and a last summer's *alma viva*, which composed his only protection against the winter, he went with Delyesof down the steps.

As soon as Delyesof took his scat in his carriage with his new friend, and became conscious of that unpleasant odor of intoxication and filthiness exhaled by the musician, he began to repent of the step he had taken, and to curse himself for his childish softness of heart and lack of reason. Moreover, all that Albert said was so foolish and in such bad taste, and now that he was out in the open air he seemed suddenly so disgustingly intoxicated, that Delyesof was disgusted.

"What shall I do with him?" he asked himself.

After they had been driving for a quarter of an hour, Albert relapsed into silence, his hat slipped off his head and fell to his feet, he himself sprawled out in a corner of the carriage, and began to snore.

The wheels crunched monotonously over the frozen snow, the feeble light of dawn scarcely made its way through the frosty windows.

Delyesof glanced at his companion. His long body, wrapped in his mantle, lay almost lifeless near him. It seemed to him that a long head with large black nose was swaying on his trunk; but on examining more closely he perceived that what he took to be nose and face was the man's hair, and that his actual face was lower down.

He bent over and studied the features of Albert's face. Then the beauty of his brow and of his peacefully closed mouth once more charmed him. Under the influence of nervous excitement caused by the sleepless hours of the long night and the music, Delyesof, as he looked at that face, was once more carried back to the blessed world of which he had caught a glimpse once before that night; again he remembered the happy and *magnanimous* time of his youth, and he ceased to repent of his impulsive act. At that moment he loved Albert truly and warmly, and firmly resolved to be a benefactor to him.

4

The next morning, when Delyesof was awakened to go to his office, he saw, with an unpleasant feeling of surprise, his old screen, his old servant, and his clock on the table.

"What did I expect to see if not the usual objects that surround me?" he asked himself.

Then he recollected the musician's black eyes and happy smile; the motive of the *Mélancolie* and all the strange experiences of the night came back into his consciousness. It was never his way, however, to reconsider whether he had done wisely or foolishly in taking the musician home with him. After he had dressed, he carefully laid out his plans for the day; he took some paper, wrote out some necessary directions for the house, and hastily put on his cloak and galoshes.

As he went by the dining-room he glanced in at the door. Albert, with his face buried in the pillow and lying at full length in his dirty, tattered shirt, was buried in the profoundest slumber on the morocco divan, where in absolute unconsciousness he had been deposited some hours before.

Delyesof could not help feeling that something was not right.

"Please go for me to Boriuzovsky, and borrow his violin for a day or two," said he to his man; "and when he wakes up, bring him some coffee, and get him some clean linen and some old suit or other of mine. Fit him out as well as you can, please."

When he returned home in the afternoon, Delyesof, to his surprise, found that Albert was not there.

"Where is he?" he asked of his man.

"He went out immediately after dinner," replied the servant. "He took the violin, and went out, saying that he would be back again in an hour; but since that time we have not seen him."

"Ta, ta! how provoking!" said Delyesof. "Why did you let him go, Zakhar?"

Zakhar was a Petersburg lackey, who had been in Delyesof's service for eight years. Delyesof, as a bachelor, living alone, could not help intrusting him with his plans, and liked to get his judgment in regard to each of his undertakings.

"How should I have ventured to detain him?" replied Zakhar, playing with his watch-charms. "If you had intimated, Dmitri Ivanovitch, that you wished me to keep him here, I might have kept him at home. But you only spoke of his wardrobe."

"Ta! how vexatious! Well, what has he been doing while I was out?"

Zakhar smiled.

"Indeed, he's a real artist, as one may say, Dmitri Ivanovitch. As soon as he woke up he asked for some Madeira; then he began to keep the cook and me pretty busy. Such an absurd . . . However, he's a very interesting character. I brought him some tea, got some dinner ready for him; but he would not eat alone, so he asked me to sit down with him. But when he began to play on the fiddle, then I knew that you would not find many such artists at Izler's. One might well keep such a man. When he played 'Down the Little Mother Volga' for us, why, it was enough to make a man weep. It was too good for anything! The people from the floors came down into our entry to listen." . . .

"Well, did you give him some clothes?" asked the barin, interrupting.

"Certainly I did; I gave him your night-shirt, and I put on him a paletot of my own. You want to help such a man as that, he's a fine fellow." Zakhar smiled. "He kept asking me what rank you were, and if you had important acquaintances, and how many souls of peasantry you had."

"Very good; but now we must send and find him; and henceforth don't give him anything to drink, otherwise you'll do him more harm than good."

"That is true," said Zakhar, in assent. "He doesn't seem in very robust health; my former barin used to have an overseer who, like him . . ."

Delyesof, who had already long ago heard the story of the drunken overseer, did not give Zakhar time to finish, but bade him make everything ready for the night, and then go out and bring the musician back.

He threw himself down on his bed, and put out the candle; but it was long before he fell asleep, for thinking about Albert.

"This may seem strange to some of my friends," said Delyesof to himself, "but it is so seldom I can do anything for any one besides myself, that I ought to thank God for a chance when one presents itself, and I will not lose it. I will do everything. I certainly will do everything I can to help him. Maybe he is not absolutely crazy, but only inclined to get drunk. It certainly will not cost me very much. Where one is, there is always enough to satisfy two. Let him live with me awhile, and then we will find him a place, or get him up a concert; we'll help him off the shoals, and then there will be time enough to see what will come of it."

An agreeable sense of self-satisfaction came over him after making this resolution.

"Certainly I am not a bad man; I might say I am far from being a bad man," he thought. "I might go so far as to say that I am a good man, when I compare myself with others." . . .

He had just dropped off to sleep when the sound of opening doors, and steps in the anteroom, roused him again.

"Well, shall I treat him rather severely?" he asked himself; "I suppose that is best, and I ought to do it."

He rang.

"Well, did you find him?" he asked of Zakhar, who answered his call.

"He's a poor, wretched fellow, Dmitri Ivanovitch," said Zakhar, shaking his head significantly, and closing his eyes.

"What! is he drunk?"

"Very weak."

"Had he the violin with him?"

"I brought it; the lady gave it to me."

"All right. Now please don't bring him to me tonight; let him sleep it off; and to-morrow don't under any circumstances let him out of the house."

But before Zakhar had time to leave the room, Albert came in.

5

"You don't mean to say that you've gone to bed at this time!" said Albert, with a smile. "I was there again, at Anna Ivánovna's. I spent a very pleasant evening. We had music,—fine sport; there was a very pleasant company there. Please let me have a glass of something to drink," he added, seizing a carafe of water that stood on the table, "only not water."

Albert was just as he had been the night before,—the same lovely, smiling eyes and lips, the same fresh, inspired brow, and weak features. Zakhar's paletot fitted him as if it had been made for him, and the clean, wide, unstarched collar of the night-shirt picturesquely fitted around his slender white neck, giving him a peculiarly childlike and innocent appearance.

He sat down on Delyesof's bed, smiling with pleasure and gratitude, and looked at him without speaking. Delyesof gazed into Albert's eyes, and suddenly felt himself once more under the sway of that smile. All desire for sleep vanished from him, he forgot his resolution to be stern; on the contrary, he felt like having a gay time, to hear some music, and to talk confidentially with Albert till morning.

Delyesof bade Zakhar bring a bottle of wine, cigarettes, and the violin.

"This is excellent," said Albert. "It's early yet, we'll have a little music. I will play whatever you like."

Zakhar, with evident satisfaction, brought a bottle of Lafitte, two glasses, some mild cigarettes such as Albert smoked, and the violin. But, instead of going off to bed as his barin bade him, he lighted a cigar, and sat down in the next room.

"Let us talk instead," said Delyesof to the musician, who was beginning to tune the violin.

Albert sat down submissively on the bed, and smiled pleasantly.

"Oh, yes!" said he, suddenly striking his forehead with his hand, and putting on an expression of anxious curiosity. The expression of his face always gave an intimation of what he was going to say. "I wanted to ask you,"—he hesitated a little,—"that gentleman who was there with you last evening. . . . You called him N. Was he the son of the celebrated N.?"

"His own son," replied Delyesof, not understanding at all what Albert could find of interest in him.

"Indeed!" he exclaimed, smiling with satisfaction. "I instantly noticed that there was something peculiarly aristocratic in his manners. I love aristocrats. There is something splendid and elegant about an aristocrat. And that officer who danced so beautifully," he went on to ask. "He also pleased me very much, he was so gay and noble-looking. He is called Adjutant N. N."

"Who?" asked Delyesof.

"The one who ran into me when we were dancing. He must be a splendid man."

"No, he is a silly fellow," replied Delyesof.

"Oh, no! it can't be," rejoined Albert, hotly. "There's something very, very pleasant about him. And he's a glorious musician," he added. "He played something from an opera. It's a long time since I have seen any one who pleased me so much."

"Yes, he plays very well; but I don't like his playing," said Delyesof, wishing to bring his companion to talk about music. "He does not understand classic music, but only Donizetti and Bellini; and that's no music, you know. You agree with me, don't you?"

"Oh, no, no! Pardon me," replied Albert, with a gentle expression of opposition. "The old music is music; but modern music is music, too. And in the modern music there are extraordinarily beautiful things. Now, 'Somnambula,' and the *finale* of 'Lucia,' and Chopin, and 'Robert'! I often think,"—he hesitated, apparently collecting his thoughts,—"that if Beethoven were alive, he would weep tears of joy to hear 'Somnambula.' It's so beautiful all through. I heard 'Somnambula' first when Viardot and Rubini were here. That was something worth while," he said, with shining eyes, and making a gesture with both hands, as if he were casting something from his breast. "I'd give a good deal, but it would be impossible, to bring it back."

"Well, but how do you like the opera nowadays?" asked Delyesof.

"Bosio is good, very good," was his reply, "exquisite beyond words; but she does not touch me here," he said, pointing to his sunken chest. "A singer must have passion, and she hasn't any. She is enjoyable, but she doesn't torture you."

"Well, how about Lablache?"

"I heard him in Paris, in 'The Barber of Seville.' Then he was the only one, but now he is old. He can't be an artist, he is old."

"Well, supposing he is old, still he is fine in *morceaux d'ensemble,*" said Delyesof, still speaking of Lablache.

"How can he be old?" said Albert, severely. "He can't be old. The artist can never be old. Much is needed in an artist, the fire most of all," he declared with glistening eyes, and raising both hands in the air. And, indeed, a terrible inner fire seemed to glow throughout his whole frame. "Ah, my God!" he exclaimed suddenly. "You don't know Petrof, do you,—Petrof, the artist?"

"No, I don't know him," replied Delyesof, with a smile.

"How I wish that you and he might become acquainted! You would enjoy talking with him. How he does understand art! He and I often used to meet at Anna Ivanovna's, but now she is vexed with him for some reason or other. But I really wish that you might make his acquaintance. He has great, great talent."

"Oh! Does he paint pictures?" asked Delyesof.

"I don't know. No, I think not; but he was an artist of the Academy. What thoughts he had! Whenever he talks, it is wonderful. Oh, Petrof has great talent, only he leads a very gay life! . . . It's too bad," said Albert, with a smile. The next moment he got up from the bed, took the violin, and began to tune it.

"Have you been at the opera lately?" asked Delyesof.

Albert looked round and sighed.

"Oh, I have not been able to!" he said, clutching his head. Again he sat down by Delyesof. "I will tell you," he went on to say, almost in a whisper. "I can't go; I can't play there. I have nothing, nothing at all . . . no clothes, no home, no violin. It's a wretched life . . . a wretched life!" he repeated several times. "Yes, and why have I got into such a state? Why, indeed? It ought not to have been," said he, smiling. "*Akh! Don Juan.*"

And he struck his head.

"Now let us have something to eat," said Delyesof.

Albert, without replying, sprang up, seized the violin, and began to play the *finale* of the first act of "Don Juan," accompanying it with a description of the scene in the opera.

Delyesof felt the hair stand up on his head, when he played the voice of the dying commander.

"No, I cannot play to-night," said Albert, laying down the instrument. "I have been drinking too much."

But, immediately afterward, he went to the table, poured out a brimming glass of wine, drank it at one gulp, and again sat down on the bed near Delyesof.

Delyesof looked steadily at Albert. The latter occasionally smiled, and Delyesof returned his smile. Neither of them spoke, but the glance and smile brought them close together into a reciprocity of affection. Delyesof felt that he was growing constantly fonder and fonder of this man, and he experienced an inexpressible pleasure.

"Were you ever in love?" he asked suddenly. Albert remained sunk in thought for a few seconds, then his face lighted up with a melancholy smile. He bent over toward Delyesof, and gazed straight into his eyes.

"Why did you ask me that question?" he whispered. "But I will tell you all about it.—I like you," he added, after a few moments of thought, and glancing around. "I will not deceive you, I will tell you all, just as it was, from the beginning." He paused, and his eyes took on a strange, wild appearance. "You know that I am weak in judgment," he said suddenly. "Yes, yes," he continued. "Anna Ivanovna has told you about it. She tells everybody that I am crazy. It isn't true, she says it for a joke; she is a good woman, but I really have not been quite well for some time." Albert paused again, and stood up, gazing with wide-opened eyes at the dark door. "You asked me if I had ever been in love. Yes, I have been in love," he whispered, raising his brows. "That happened long ago; it was at a time when I still had a place at the theater. I went to play second violin at the opera, and she came into a parquet box at the left."

Albert stood up, and bent over to Delyesof's ear.

"But no," said he, "why should I mention her name? You probably know her, everybody knows her. I said nothing, but simply looked at her; I knew that I was a poor artist, and she an aristocratic lady. I knew that very well. I only looked at her, and had no thoughts."

Albert paused for a moment, as if making sure of his recollections.

"How it happened, I know not, but I was invited once to accompany her on my violin. . . . Now I was only a poor artist!" he repeated, shaking his head, and smiling. "But no, I cannot tell you, I cannot!" he exclaimed, again clutching his head. "How happy I was!"

"What? did you go to her house often?" asked Delyesof.

"Once, only once. . . . But it was my own fault; I wasn't in my right mind. I was a poor artist, and she an aristocratic lady. I ought not to have spoken to her. But I lost my senses, I committed a folly. Petrof told me the truth: 'It would have been better only to have seen her at the theater.' "

"What did you do?" asked Delyesof.

"Ah! wait, wait, I cannot tell you that."

And, hiding his face in his hands, he said nothing for some time.

"I was late at the orchestra. Petrof and I had been drinking that evening, and I was excited. She was sitting in her box, and talking with a general. I don't know who that general was. She was sitting at the very edge of the box, with her arm resting on the rim. She wore a white dress, with pearls on her neck. She was talking with him, but she looked at me. Twice she looked at me. She had arranged her hair in such a becoming way! I stopped playing, and stood near the bass, and gazed at her. Then, for the first time, something strange took place in me. She smiled on the general, but she looked at me. I felt certain that she was talking about me; and suddenly, I seemed to be not in my place in the orchestra, but was standing in her box, and seizing her hand in that place. What was the meaning of that?" asked Albert, after a moment's silence.

"That is the power of the imagination," said Delyesof.

"No, no, . . . I cannot tell," said Albert, frowning. "Even then I was poor. I had no home; and when I went to the theater, I sometimes used to sleep there."

"What, in the theater? in the dark, empty auditorium?" asked Delyesof.

"Ah! I am not afraid of these stupid things. Ah! just wait a moment. As soon as everybody was gone, I went to that box where she had been sitting, and slept there. That was my only pleasure. How many nights I spent there!

Only once again did I have that experience. At night many things seemed to come to me. But I cannot tell you much about them." Albert squinted his eyes, and looked at Delyesof. "What did it mean?" he asked.

"It was strange," replied the other.

"No, wait, wait!" He bent over to his ear, and said in a whisper:—

"I kissed her hand, wept there before her, and said many things to her. I heard the fragrance of her sighs, I heard her voice. She said many things to me that one night. Then I took my violin, and began to play softly. And I played beautifully. But it became terrible to me. I am not afraid of such stupid things, and I don't believe in them, but my head felt terribly," he said, smiling sweetly, and moving his hand over his forehead. "It seemed terrible to me on account of my poor mind; something happened in my head. Maybe it was nothing; what do you think?"

Neither spoke for several minutes.

> *"Und wenn die Wolken sie verhüllen,*
> *Die Sonne bleibt doch ewig klar."* [1]

hummed Albert, smiling gently. "That is true, isn't it?" he asked.

> *"Ich auch habe gelebt und genossen."*[2]

"Ah, old man Petrof! how this would have made things clear to you!"

Delyesof, in silence and with dismay, looked at his companion's excited and colorless face.

"Do you know the Juristen waltzes?" suddenly asked Albert, in a loud voice; and, without waiting for an answer, jumped up, seized the violin, and began to play the lively waltz. In absolute self-forgetfulness, and evidently imagining that a whole orchestra was playing for him, Albert smiled, danced, shuffled his feet, all the time playing admirably.

"Hey, we will have some sport!" he exclaimed, as he ended, and waved his violin. "I am going," said he, after sitting down in silence for a little. "Won't you come along, too?"

"Where?" asked Delyesof, in surprise.

"Let us go to Anna Ivanovna's again. It's gay there,—bustle, people, music."

Delyesof for a moment was almost persuaded. However, coming to his senses, he tried to prevent Albert from going that day.

"I should like to go this minute."

"Indeed, I wouldn't go."

Albert sighed, and laid down the violin.

"Shall I stay, then?"

He looked over at the table, but the wine was gone; and so, wishing him good-night, he left the room.

Delyesof rang.

"See here," said he to Zakhar, "don't let Mr. Albert go anywhere without asking me about it first."

[1] E'en though the clouds may veil it,
   The sun shines ever clear.

[2] I also have lived and enjoyed.

6

The next day was a holiday. Delyesof, on waking, sat in his parlor, drinking his coffee and reading a book. Albert, who was in the next room, had not yet moved.

Zakhar discreetly opened the door, and looked into the dining-room.

"Would you believe it, Dmitri Ivanovitch, there he lies asleep on the bare divan. I would not send him away for anything, God knows. He's like a little child. Indeed, he's an artist!"

At twelve o'clock, there was a sound of yawning and coughing on the other side of the door.

Zakhar again went into the dining-room; and Delyesof heard his wheedling voice, and Albert's gentle, beseeching voice.

"Well, how is he?" asked Delyesof, when Zakhar came out.

"He is in low spirits, Dmitri Ivanovitch. He doesn't want to get dressed. He's so cross. All he asks for is something to drink."

"Now, if we are to get hold of him, we must strengthen his character," said Delyesof, to himself. And, forbidding Zakhar to give him any wine, he again devoted himself to his book; in spite of himself, however, listening all the time to what was going on in the dining-room.

But there was no movement there, only occasionally were heard a heavy chest cough and spitting. Two hours passed. Delyesof, after dressing to go out, resolved to look in upon his guest. Albert was sitting motionless at the window, leaning his head on his hands.

He looked round. His face was sallow, morose, and not only melancholy but deeply unhappy. He tried to welcome his host with a smile, but his face assumed a still more woebegone expression. It seemed as if he were on the point of tears.

With effort he stood up and bowed.

"If I might have just a little glass of simple vodka," he exclaimed, with a supplicating expression. "I am so weak. If you please!"

"Coffee will be more strengthening, I would advise you."

Albert's face instantly lost its childish expression; he gazed coldly, sadly, out of the window, and fell back feebly into the chair.

"Wouldn't you like some breakfast?"

"No, thank you, I haven't any appetite."

"If you want to play on the violin, you will not disturb me," said Delyesof, laying the instrument on the table.

Albert looked at the violin with a contemptuous smile.

"No, I am too weak, I cannot play," he said, and pushed the instrument from him.

After that, in reply to all Delyesof's propositions to go to walk, to go to the theater in the evening, or anything else, he only shook his head mournfully, and preserved an obstinate silence.

Delyesof went out, made a few calls, dined with some friends, and before the theater hour, he returned to his rooms to change his attire and find out how the musician was getting along.

Albert was sitting in the dark anteroom, and, with his head resting on his hand, was gazing at the heated stove. He was neatly dressed, washed, and combed; but his eyes were sad and vacant, and his whole form expressed even more weakness and debility than in the morning.

"Well, have you had dinner, Mr. Albert?" asked Delyesof.

Albert nodded his head affirmatively, and, after looking with a terrified expression at Delyesof, dropped his eyes. It made Delyesof feel uncomfortable.

"I have been talking to-day with a manager," said he, also dropping his eyes. "He would be very glad to make terms with you, if you would like to accept an engagement."

"I thank you, but I cannot play," said Albert, almost in a whisper; and he went into his room, and closed the door as softly as possible. After a few minutes, lifting the latch as softly as possible, he came out of the room, bringing the violin. Casting a sharp, angry look at Delyesof, he laid the instrument on the table, and again disappeared.

Delyesof shrugged his shoulders, and smiled.

"What am I to do now? Wherein am I to blame?" he asked himself.

"Well, how is the musician?" was his first question when he returned home late that evening.

"Bad," was Zakhar's short and ringing reply. "He sighs all the time, and coughs, and says nothing at all, only he has asked for vodka four or five times, and once I gave him some. We shall be killing him this way, Dmitri Ivanovitch. That was the way the overseer . . ."

"Well, hasn't he played on the fiddle?"

"Didn't even touch it. I carried it to him twice . . . Well, he took it up slowly, and brought it out," said Zakhar, with a smile. "Do you still bid me refuse him something to drink?"

"Don't give him anything to-day; we'll see what'll come of it. What is he doing now?"

"He has shut himself into the drawing-room."

Delyesof went into his library, took down a few French books and the Testament in German.

"Put these books to-morrow in his room; and look out, don't let him get away," said he to Zakhar.

The next morning Zakhar informed his barin that the musician had not slept a wink all night. "He kept walking up and down his rooms, and going to the sideboard to try to open the cupboard and door; but everything, in spite of his efforts, remained locked."

Zakhar told how, while pretending to go to sleep, he heard Albert muttering to himself in the darkness and gesticulating.

Each day Albert grew more gloomy and taciturn. It seemed as if he were afraid of Delyesof, and his face expressed painful terror whenever their eyes met. He did not touch either book or violin, and made no replies to the questions put to him.

On the third day after the musician came to stay with him, Delyesof returned home late in the evening, tired and worried. He had been on the go all day, attending to his duties. Though they had seemed very simple and easy, yet, as is often the case, he had not made any progress at all, in spite of his strenuous endeavors. Afterward he had stopped at the club, and lost at whist. He was out of spirits.

"Well, God be with him," he replied to Zakhar, who had been telling him of Albert's pitiable state. "To-morrow I shall be really worried about him. Is he willing or not to stay with me, and follow my advice? No? Then it's idle. I have done the best that I could."

"That's what comes of trying to be a benefactor to people," said he to himself. "I am putting myself to inconvenience for him. I have taken this filthy creature into my rooms, which keeps me from receiving strangers in the morning; I work and am kept on the run; and yet he looks on me as some enemy who, against his will, would keep him in pound. But the worst is that he is not willing to take a step in his own behalf. That's the way with them all."

That word *all* referred to people in general, and especially to those with whom he had been associated in business that day. "But what is to be done for him now? What is he contemplating? Why is he melancholy? Is he melancholy because of the debauch from which I rescued him? on account of the degradation in which he has been? the humiliation from which I saved him? Can it be that he has fallen so low that it is a burden for him to look on a pure life? . . .

"No, this was a childish action," reasoned Delyesof. "Why should I undertake to direct others, when it is as much as I can do to manage my own affairs?"

The impulse came over him to let him go immediately, but after a little deliberation he postponed it till the morning.

During the night Delyesof was aroused by the noise of a falling table in the anteroom, and the sound of voices and stamping feet. He lighted a candle, and began to listen with amazement.

"Just wait a little, I will tell Dmitri Ivanovitch," said Zakhar's voice; Albert's voice replied passionately and incoherently.

Delyesof leaped up, and went with his candle into the anteroom. Zakhar, in his night-dress, was standing against the door; Albert, in cap and *alma viva*, was trying to pull him away, and was screaming at him in a pathetic voice:—

"You have no right to detain me; I have a passport; I have not stolen anything from you. You must let me go. I will go to the police."

"I beg of you, Dmitri Ivanovitch," said Zakhar, turning to his barin, and continuing to stand guard at the door. "He got up in the night, found the key in my paletot, and he has drunk up the whole decanter of sweet vodka. Was that good? And now he wants to go. You ordered me not to let him out, and so I could not let him go."

Albert, seeing Delyesof, began to pull still more violently on Zakhar.

"No one has the right to detain me! He cannot do it," he screamed, raising his voice more and more.

"Let him go, Zakhar," said Delyesof. "I do not wish to detain you, and I have no right to, but I advise you to stay till to-morrow," he added, addressing Albert.

"No one has the right to detain me. I am going to the police," screamed Albert, more and more furiously, addressing only Zakhar, and not heeding Delyesof. "Guard!" he suddenly shouted at the top of his voice.

"Now, what are you screaming like that for? You see you are free to go," said Zakhar, opening the door.

Albert ceased screaming.

"How did they dare? They were going to murder me! No!" he muttered to himself, as he put on his galoshes. Not bidding them good-by, and still muttering something unintelligible, he went out of the door. Zakhar accompanied him to the gate, and came back.

"Thank the Lord, Dmitri Ivanovitch! Any longer would have been a sin," said he to his barin. "And now we must verify the silver."

Delyesof only shook his head, and made no reply. There came over him a lively recollection of the first two evenings which he and the musician had spent together; he remembered the last wretched days which Albert had spent there; and, above all, he remembered the sweet but absurd sentiment of wonder, of love, and of sympathy which had been aroused in him by the very first sight of this strange man; and he began to pity him.

"What will become of him now?" he asked himself. "Without money, without warm clothing, alone at midnight!"

He thought of sending Zakhar after him, but now it was too late.

"Is it cold outdoors?" he asked.

"A healthy frost, Dmitri Ivanovitch," replied the man. "I forgot to tell you that you will have to buy some more firewood to last till spring."

"But what did you mean by saying that it would last?"

7

Out of doors it was really cold; but Albert did not feel it, he was so excited by the wine that he had taken and by the quarrel.

As he entered the street, he looked around him, and rubbed his hands with pleasure. The street was empty, but the long lines of lights were still brilliantly gleaming; the sky was clear and beautiful. "What!" he cried, addressing the lighted window in Delyesof's apartments; and then, thrusting his hands into his trousers pockets under his paletot, and looking straight ahead, he walked with heavy and uncertain steps straight up the street.

He felt an extraordinary heaviness in his legs and abdomen, something hummed in his head, some invisible power seemed to hurl him from side to side; but he still plunged ahead in the direction of where Anna Ivanovna lived.

Strange, disconnected thoughts rushed through his head. Now he remembered his quarrel with Zakhar, now something recalled the sea, and his first voyage in the steamboat to Russia; now the merry night that he had spent with some friend in the wine-shop by which he was passing; then suddenly there came to him a familiar air, singing itself in his recollections, and he seemed to see the object of his passion and the terrible night in the theater.

But notwithstanding their incoherence, all these recollections presented themselves before his imagination with such distinctness that when he closed his eyes he could not tell which was nearer to the reality,—what he was doing, or what he was thinking. He did not realize and he did not feel how his legs moved, how he staggered and hit against a wall, how he looked around him, and how he made his way from street to street. He realized and felt only that which presented itself to him, fantastically changing and confusing him.

As he went along the Little Morskaya, Albert tripped and fell. Collecting himself in a moment, he saw before him a huge and magnificent edifice, and he went toward it.

In the sky not a star was to be seen, nor sign of dawn, nor moon, neither were there any street-lights there; but all objects were perfectly distinguishable. The windows of the edifice, which loomed up at the corner of the street, were brilliantly lighted, but the lights wavered like reflections. The building kept coming nearer and nearer, clearer and clearer, to Albert.

But the lights vanished the moment Albert entered the wide portals. Inside it was dark. He took a few steps under the vaulted ceiling, and something like shadows glided by and fled at his approach.

"Why did I come here?" wondered Albert; but some irresistible power dragged him forward into the depths of the immense hall. . . .

There stood some lofty platform, and around it in silence stood what seemed like little men. "Who is going to speak?" asked Albert. No one answered, but some one pointed to the platform. There stood now on the platform a tall, thin man, with bushy hair and dressed in a variegated khalat. Albert immediately recognized his friend Petrof.

"How strange! what is he doing here?" said Albert to himself.

"No, brethren," said Petrof, pointing to something, "you did not appreciate the man while he was living among you; you did not appreciate him! He was not a cheap artist, not a merely mechanical performer, not a crazy, ruined man. He was a genius, a great musical genius, who perished among you unknown and unvalued."

Albert immediately understood of whom his friend was speaking; but not wishing to interrupt him, he hung his head modestly.

"He, like a sheaf of straw, was wholly consumed by the sacred fire which we all serve," continued the voice. "But he has completely fulfilled all that God gave him; therefore he ought to be considered a great man. You may despise him, torture him, humiliate him," continued the voice, more and more energetically, "but he has been, is, and will be immeasurably higher than you all. He is happy, he is good. He loved you all alike, or cared for you, it is all the same; but he has served only that with which he was so highly endowed. He loved one thing,—beauty, the only infinite good in the world. Oh, yes, what a man he is! Fall all of you before him. On your knees!" cried Petrof, in a thundering voice.

But another voice mildly answered from another corner of the hall. "I do not wish to bow my knee before him," said the voice.

Albert instantly recognized that it was Delyesof's voice.

"Why is he great? And why should we bow before him? Has he conducted himself in an honorable and righteous manner? Has he brought society any advantage? Do we not know how he borrowed money, and never returned it; how he carried off a violin that belonged to a brother artist, and pawned it?" . . .

"My God! how did he know all that?" said Albert to himself, dropping his head still lower.

"Do we not know," the voice went on, "how he pandered to the lowest of the low, pandered to them for money?" continued Delyesof. "Do we not know how he was driven out of the theater? How Anna Ivanovna threatened to hand him over to the police?"

"My God! that is all true, but protect me," cried Albert. "You are the only one who knows why I did so."

"Stop, for shame!" cried Petrof's voice again. "What right have you to accuse him? Have you lived his life? Have you experienced his enthusiasms?"

"Right! right!" whispered Albert.

"Art is the highest manifestation of power in man. It is given only to the favored few, and it lifts the chosen to such an eminence that the head swims, and it is hard to preserve its integrity. In art, as in every struggle, there are heroes who bring all under subjection to them, and perish if they do not attain their ends."

Petrof ceased speaking; and Albert lifted his head, and tried to shout in a loud voice, "Right! right!" but his voice died without a sound.

"That is not the case with you. This does not concern you," sternly said the artist Petrof, addressing him. "Yes, humble him, despise him," he continued, "for he is better and happier than all the rest of you."

Albert, with rapture in his heart at hearing these words, could not contain himself, but went up to his friend, and was about to kiss him.

"Get you gone, I do not know you," replied Petrof. "Go your own way, you cannot come here."

"Here, you drunken fellow, you cannot come here," cried a policeman at the crossing.

Albert hesitated, then collected all his forces, and, endeavoring not to stumble, crossed over to the next street.

It was only a few steps to Anna Ivanovna's. From the hall of her house a stream of light fell on the snowy dvor, and at the gate stood sledges and carriages.

Clinging with both hands to the balustrade, he made his way up the steps, and rang the bell.

The maid's sleepy face appeared at the open door, and looked angrily at Albert.

"It is impossible," she cried; "I have been forbidden to let you in," and she slammed the door.

The sounds of music and women's voices floated down to him.

Albert sat down on the ground, and leaned his head against the wall, and shut his eyes. At that very instant a throng of indistinct but correlated visions took possession of him with fresh force, mastered him, and carried him off into the beautiful and free domain of fancy.

"Yes! he is better and happier," involuntarily the voice repeated in his imagination.

From the door were heard the sounds of a polka. These sounds also told him that he was better and happier. In a neighboring church was heard the sound of a prayer bell; and the prayer bell also told him that he was better and happier.

"Now I will go back to that hall again," said Albert to himself. "Petrof must have many things still to tell me."

There seemed to be no one now in the hall; and, in the place of the artist

Petrof, Albert himself stood on the platform, and was playing on his violin all that the voice had said before.

But his violin was a strange make: it was composed of nothing but glass, and he had to hold it with both hands, and slowly rub it on his breast to make it give out sounds. The sounds were so sweet and delicious, that Albert felt he had never before heard anything like them. The more tightly he pressed the violin to his breast, the more sweet and consoling they became. The louder the sounds, the more swiftly the shadows vanished, and the more brilliantly the walls of the hall were illuminated. But it was necessary to play very cautiously on the violin, lest it should break.

Albert played on the instrument of glass cautiously and well. He played things the like of which he felt no one would ever hear again.

He was growing tired, when a heavy distant sound began to annoy him. It was the sound of a bell, but this sound seemed to have a language.

"Yes," said the bell, with its notes coming from somewhere far off and high up, "yes, he seems to you wretched; you despise him, but he is better and happier than you. No one ever will play more on that instrument!"

These words which he understood seemed suddenly so wise, so novel, and so true to Albert, that he stopped playing, and, while trying not to move, lifted his eyes and his arms toward heaven. He felt that he was beautiful and happy. Although no one was in the hall, Albert expanded his chest, and proudly lifted his head, and stood on the platform so that all might see him.

Suddenly some one's hand was gently laid on his shoulder; he turned around, and in the half-light saw a woman. She looked pityingly at him, and shook her head. He immediately became conscious that what he was doing was wrong, and a sense of shame came over him.

"Where shall I go?" he asked her.

Once more she gazed long and fixedly at him, and bent her head pityingly. She was the one, the very one whom he loved, and her dress was the same; on her full white bosom was the pearl necklace, and her lovely arms were bare above the elbows.

She took him in her arms, and bore him away from the hall. "The exit is on that side," said Albert, but she, not answering, smiled, and bore him away from the hall. At the entrance of the hall, Albert saw the moon and water. But the water was not below as is usually the case, and the moon was not above; there was a white circle in one place as sometimes happens. The moon and the water were together,—everywhere, above and below, and on all sides and around them both. Albert and his love darted off toward the moon and the water, and he now realized that she whom he loved more than all in the world was in his arms: he embraced her, and felt inexpressible felicity.

"Is not this a dream?" he asked himself. But no, it was the reality, it was more than reality; it was reality and recollection combined.

Then he felt that the indescribable pleasure which he had felt during the last moment was gone, and would never be renewed.

"Why am I weeping?" he asked of her. She looked at him in silence, with pitying eyes. Albert understood what she desired to say in reply. "Just as when I was alive," he went on to say. She, without replying, looked straight forward.

"This is terrible! How can I explain to her that I *am* alive?" he asked himself in horror. "My God, I am alive! Do understand me," he whispered.

"He is better and happier," said a voice.

But something kept oppressing Albert ever more powerfully. Whether it was the moon or the water, or her embrace or his tears, he could not tell, but he was conscious that he could not say all that he ought to say, and that all would be quickly over.

Two guests coming out from Anna Ivanovna's rooms stumbled against Albert lying on the threshold. One of them went back to Anna Ivanovna, and called her. "That was heartless," he said. "You might let a man freeze to death that way."

"Why, that is my Albert. See where he was lying!" exclaimed the madame. "Annushka, have him brought into the room; find a place for him somewhere," she added, addressing the maid.

"Oh! I am alive, why do you bury me?" muttered Albert, as they brought him unconscious into the room.

1858

THREE DEATHS

1

It was autumn.

Along the highway came two equipages at a brisk pace. In the first carriage sat two women. One was a lady, thin and pale; the other, her maid, with a brilliant red complexion, and plump. Her short, dry locks escaped from under a faded cap; her red hand, in a torn glove, put them back with a jerk. Her full bosom, incased in a tapestry shawl, breathed of health; her keen black eyes now gazed through the window at the fields hurrying by them, now rested on her mistress, now peered solicitously into the corners of the coach.

Before the maid's face swung the lady's bonnet on the rack; on her knees lay a puppy; her feet were raised by packages lying on the floor, and could almost be heard drumming upon them above the noise of the creaking of the springs and the rattling of the windows.

The lady, with her hands resting in her lap and her eyes shut, feebly swayed on the cushions which supported her back, and, slightly frowning, tried to suppress her cough.

She wore a white nightcap, and a blue neckerchief twisted around her delicate pale neck. A straight line, disappearing under the cap, parted her perfectly smooth blond hair, which was pomaded; and there was a dry, deathly appearance about the whiteness of the skin, in this wide parting. The withered and rather sallow skin was loosely drawn over her delicate and pretty features, and there was a hectic flush on the cheeks and cheek-bones. Her lips were dry and restless, her thin eyelashes had lost their curve, and a cloth traveling capote made straight folds over her sunken chest. Although her eyes were closed, her face gave the impression of weariness, irascibility, and habitual suffering.

The lackey, leaning back, was napping on the coach-box. The *yamshchik*, or hired driver, shouting in a clear voice, urged on his four powerful and sweaty horses, occasionally looking back at the other driver, who was shouting just behind them in an open barouche. The tires of the wheels, in their even and rapid course, left wide parallel tracks on the limy mud of the highway.

The sky was gray and cold, a moist mist was falling over the fields and the road. It was suffocating in the carriage, and smelt of eau-de-Cologne and dust. The invalid leaned back her head, and slowly opened her eyes. Her great eyes were brilliant, and of a beautiful dark color.

"Again!" said she, nervously, pushing away with her beautiful attenuated hand the end of her maid's cloak, which occasionally hit against her leg. Her mouth contracted painfully.

Matriosha raised her cloak in both hands, lifting herself up on her strong legs, and then sat down again, farther away. Her fresh face was suffused with a brilliant scarlet.

The invalid's beautiful dark eyes eagerly followed the maid's motions; and then with both hands she took hold of the seat, and did her best to raise herself a little higher, but her strength was not sufficient.

Again her mouth became contracted, and her whole face took on an expression of unavailing, angry irony.

"If you would only help me . . . ah! It's not necessary. I can do it myself. Only have the goodness not to put those pillows behind me. . . . On the whole, you had better not touch them, if you don't understand!"

The lady closed her eyes, and then again, quickly raising the lids, gazed at her maid.

Matriosha looked at her, and gnawed her red lower lip. A heavy sigh escaped from the sick woman's breast; but the sigh was not ended, but was merged in a fit of coughing. She scowled, and turned her face away, clutching her chest with both hands. When the coughing fit was over, she once more shut her eyes, and continued to sit motionless. The coach and the barouche rolled into a village. Matriosha drew her fat hand from under her shawl, and made the sign of the cross.

"What is this?" demanded the lady.

"A post-station, madame."

"Why did you cross yourself, I should like to know?"

"The church, madame."

The invalid lady looked out of the window, and began slowly to cross herself, gazing with all her eyes at the great village church, in front of which her carriage was now passing.

The two vehicles came to a stop together at the post-house. The sick woman's husband and the doctor dismounted from the barouche, and came to the coach.

"How are you feeling?" asked the doctor, taking her pulse.

"Well, my dear, aren't you fatigued?" asked the husband, in French. "Wouldn't you like to get out?"

Matriosha, gathering up the bundles, squeezed herself into the corner, so as not to interfere with the conversation.

"No matter, it's all the same thing," replied the invalid. "I will not get out."

The husband, after standing there a little, went into the post-house. Matriosha, jumping from the coach, tiptoed across the muddy road into the inclosure.

"If I am miserable, there is no reason why the rest of you should not have breakfast," said the sick woman, smiling faintly to the doctor, who was standing by her window.

"It makes no difference to them how I am," she remarked to herself as the doctor, turning from her with slow step, started to run up the steps of the station-house. "They are well, and it's all the same to them. O my God!"

"How now, Edouard Ivanovitch?" said the husband, as he met the doctor, and rubbing his hands with a gay smile. "I have ordered my traveling-case brought; what do you say to that?"

"That's worth while," replied the doctor.

"Well, now, how about *her?*" asked the husband, with a sigh, lowering his voice and raising his brows.

"I have told you that she cannot reach Moscow, much less Italy, especially in such weather."

"What is to be done, then? Oh! my God! my God!"

The husband covered his eyes with his hand. . . . "Give it here," he added, addressing his man, who came bringing the traveling-case.

"You'll have to stop somewhere on the route," replied the doctor, shrugging his shoulders.

"But tell me, what can I do?" rejoined the husband. "I have employed every argument to keep her from going; I have spoken to her of our means, and of our children whom we should have to leave behind, and of my business. She would not hear a word. She has made her plans for living abroad, as if she were well. But if I should tell her what her real condition is, it would kill her."

"Well, she is a dead woman now; you may as well know it, Vasili Dmitritch. A person cannot live without lungs, and there is no way of making lungs grow again. It is melancholy, it is hard, but what is to be done about it? It is my business and yours to make her last days as easy as possible. The confessor is the person needed here."

"Oh, my God! Now just perceive how I am situated, in speaking to her of her last will. Let come whatever may, yet I cannot speak of that. And yet you know how good she is."

"Try at least to persuade her to wait until the roads are frozen," said the doctor, shaking his head significantly; "something might happen during the journey." . . . .

"Aksiusha, oh, Aksiusha!" cried the superintendent's daughter, throwing a cloak over her head, and tiptoeing down the muddy back steps. "Come along. Let us have a look at the Shirkinskaya lady; they say she's got lung trouble, and they're taking her abroad. I never saw how any one looked in consumption."

Aksiusha jumped down from the door-sill; and the two girls, hand in hand, hurried out of the gates. Shortening their steps, they walked by the coach, and stared in at the lowered window. The invalid bent her head toward them; but, when she saw their inquisitiveness, she frowned and turned away.

"Oh, de-e-ar!" said the superintendent's daughter, vigorously shaking her head. . . . "How wonderfully pretty she used to be, and how she has changed! It is terrible! Did you see? Did you see, Aksiusha?"

"Yes, and how thin she is!" assented Aksiusha. "Let us go by and look again; we'll make believe go to the well. Did you see, she turned away from us; still I got a good view of her. Isn't it too bad, Masha?"

"Yes, but what terrible mud!" replied Masha, and both of them started to run back within the gates.

"It's evident that I have become a fright," thought the sick woman. . . . "But we must hurry, hurry, and get abroad, and there I shall soon get well."

"Well, and how are you, my dear?" inquired the husband, coming to the coach with still a morsel of something in his mouth.

"Always one and the same question," thought the sick woman, "and he's even eating!"

"It's no consequence," she murmured, between her teeth.

"Do you know, my dear, I am afraid that this journey in such weather will only make you worse. Edouard Ivanovitch says the same thing. Hadn't we better turn back?"

She maintained an angry silence.

"Maybe the weather will improve, the roads will become good, and that would be better for you; then at least we could start all together."

"Pardon me. If I had not listened to you so long, I should at this moment be at Berlin and have entirely recovered."

"What's to be done, my angel? it was impossible, as you know. But now if you would wait a month, you would be ever so much better; I could finish up my business, and we could take the children with us." . . .

"The children are well, and I am not."

"But just see here, my love, if in this weather you should grow worse on the road . . . At least we should be at home."

"What is the use of being at home? . . . *Die* at home?" replied the invalid, peevishly.

But the word *die* evidently startled her, and she turned on her husband a supplicating and inquiring look. He dropped his eyes, and said nothing.

The sick woman's mouth suddenly contracted in a childish fashion, and the tears sprang to her eyes. Her husband covered his face with his handkerchief, and silently turned from the coach.

"No, I will go," cried the invalid; and, lifting her eyes to the sky, she clasped her hands, and began to whisper incoherent words. "My God! why must it be?" she said, and the tears flowed more violently.

She prayed long and fervently, but still there was just the same sense of constriction and pain in her chest, just the same gray melancholy in the sky and the fields and the road; just the same autumnal mist, neither thicker nor more tenuous, but ever the same in its monotony, falling on the muddy highway, on the roofs, on the carriage, and on the sheepskin coats of the drivers, who were talking in strong, gay voices, as they were oiling and adjusting the carriage.

2

The coach was ready, but the driver loitered. He had gone into the drivers' room. In the izba it was warm, close, dark, and suffocating, smelling of human occupation, of cooking bread, of cabbage, and of sheepskin garments.

Several drivers were in the room; the cook was engaged near the oven, on top of which lay a sick man wrapped up in his sheepskins.

"Uncle Khveodor! hey! Uncle Khveodor," called a young man, the driver, in a tulup, and with his knout in his belt, coming into the room, and addressing the sick man.

"What do you want, rattlepate? What are you calling to Fyedka for?" asked one of the drivers. "There's your carriage waiting for you."

"I want to borrow his boots. Mine are worn out," replied the young fellow, tossing back his curls and straightening his mittens in his belt. "Why? is he asleep? Say, Uncle Khveodor!" he insisted, going to the oven.

"What is it?" a weak voice was heard saying, and an emaciated face was lifted up from the oven.

A broad, gaunt hand, bloodless and covered with hairs, pulled up his overcoat over the dirty shirt that covered his bony shoulder. "Give me something to drink, brother; what is it you want?"

The young fellow handed him a small dish of water.

"I say, Fyedya," said he, hesitating, "I reckon you won't want your new boots now; let me have them? Probably you won't need them any more."

The sick man, dropping his weary head down to the lacquered bowl, and dipping his thin, hanging mustache in the brown water, drank feebly and eagerly.

His tangled beard was unclean; his sunken, clouded eyes were with difficulty raised to the young man's face. When he had finished drinking, he tried to raise his hand to wipe his wet lips, but his strength failed him, and he wiped them on the sleeve of his overcoat. Silently, and breathing with difficulty through his nose, he looked straight into the young man's eyes, and tried to collect his strength.

"Maybe you have promised them to some one else?" said the young driver. "If that's so, all right. The worst of it is, it is wet outside, and I have to go out to my work, and so I said to myself, 'I reckon I'll ask Fyedka for his boots; I reckon he won't be needing them.' But maybe you will need them,—just say." . . .

Something began to bubble up and rumble in the sick man's chest; he bent over, and began to strangle with a cough that rattled in his throat.

"Now I should like to know where he would need them?" unexpectedly snapped out the cook, angrily addressing the whole hovel. "This is the second month that he has not crept down from the oven. Just see how he is all broken up! and you can hear how it must hurt him inside. Where would he need boots? They would not think of burying him in new ones! And it was time long ago, God pardon me the sin of saying so. Just see how he chokes! He ought to be taken from this room to another, or somewhere. They say there's hospitals in the city; but what's you going to do? he takes up the whole room, and that's too much. There isn't any room at all. And yet you are expected to keep neat."

"Hey! Seryoha, come along, take your place, the people are waiting," cried the head man of the station, coming to the door.

Seryoha started to go without waiting for his reply, but the sick man during his cough intimated by his eyes that he was going to speak.

"You take the boots, Seryoha," said he, conquering the cough, and getting his breath a little. "Only, do you hear, buy me a stone when I am dead," he added hoarsely.

"Thank you, uncle; then I will take them, and as for the stone,—yei-yei!—I will buy you one."

"There, children, you are witnesses," the sick man was able to articulate, and then once more he bent over and began to choke.

"All right, we have heard," said one of the drivers. "But run, Seryoha, or else the starosta will be after you again. You know Lady Shirkinskaya is sick."

Seryoha quickly pulled off his ragged, unwieldy boots, and flung them under the bench. Uncle Feodor's new ones fitted his feet exactly, and the young driver could not keep his eyes off them as he went to the carriage.

"Ek! what splendid boots! Here's some grease," called another driver with the grease-pot in his hand, as Seryoha mounted to his box and gathered up the reins. "Get them for nothing?"

"So you're jealous, are you?" cried Seryoha, lifting up and tucking around his legs the tails of his overcoat. "Off with you, my darlings," he cried to the horses, cracking his knout; and the coach and barouche, with their occupants, trunks, and other belongings, were hidden in the thick autumnal mist, and rapidly whirled away over the wet road.

The sick driver remained on the oven in the stifling hovel, and, not being able to throw off the phlegm, by a supreme effort turned over on the other side, and stopped coughing.

Till evening there was a continual coming and going, and eating of meals in the room, and the sick man was not noticed. Before night came on, the cook climbed up on the oven, and got the sheepskin coat from the farther side of his legs.

"Don't be angry with me, Nastasya," exclaimed the sick man. "I shall soon leave your room."

"All right, all right, it's of no consequence," muttered the woman. "But what is the matter with you, uncle? Tell me."

"All my inwards are gnawed out. God knows what it is!"

"And I don't doubt your gullet hurts you when you cough so!"

"It hurts me all over. My death is at hand, that's what it is. Okh! okh! okh!" groaned the sick man.

"Now cover up your legs this way," said Nastasya, comfortably arranging the overcoat so that it would cover him, and then getting down from the oven.

During the night the room was faintly lighted by a single taper. Nastasya and a dozen drivers were sleeping, snoring loudly, on the floor and the benches. Only the sick man feebly hawked and coughed, and tossed on the oven.

In the morning no sound was heard from him.

"I saw something wonderful in my sleep," said the cook, as she stretched herself in the early twilight the next morning. "I seemed to see Uncle Khveodor get down from the oven an go out to cut wood. 'Look here,' says he, 'I'm going to help you, Nastya;' and I says to him, 'How can you split wood?' but he seizes the hatchet, and begins to cut so fast, so fast that nothing but chips fly. 'Why,' says I, 'haven't you been sick?'—'No,' says he, 'I am well,' and he kind of lifted up the ax, and I was scared; and I screamed and woke up. He can't be dead, can he?—Uncle Khveodor! hey, uncle!"

Feodor did not move.

"Now he can't be dead, can he? Go and see," said one of the drivers, who had just waked up.

The emaciated hand, covered with reddish hair, that hung down from the oven, was cold and pale.

"Go tell the superintendent; it seems he is dead," said the driver.

Feodor had no relatives. He was a stranger. On the next day they buried him in the new burying-ground behind the grove; and Nastasya for many days had to tell everybody of the vision which she had seen, and how she had been the first to discover that Uncle Feodor was dead.

3

Spring had come.

Along the wet streets of the city swift streamlets ran purling between heaps of dung-covered ice; bright were the colors of people's dresses and the tones of their voices, as they hurried along. In the walled gardens, the buds on the trees were burgeoning, and the fresh breeze swayed their branches with a soft gentle murmur. Everywhere transparent drops were forming and falling. . . .

The sparrows chattered incoherently, and fluttered about on their little wings. On the sunny side, on the walls, houses, and trees, all was full of life and brilliancy. The sky, and the earth, and the heart of man overflowed with youth and joy.

In front of a great seignorial mansion, in one of the principal streets, fresh straw had been laid down; in the house lay that same moribund invalid whom we saw hastening abroad.

Near the closed doors of her room stood the sick lady's husband, and a lady well along in years. On a divan sat the confessor, with cast-down eyes, holding something wrapped up under his stole. In one corner, in a Voltaire easy-chair, reclined an old lady, the sick woman's mother, weeping violently.

Near her stood the maid, holding a clean handkerchief, ready for the old lady's use when she should ask for it. Another maid was rubbing the old lady's temples, and blowing on her gray head underneath her cap.

"Well, Christ be with you, my dear," said the husband to the elderly lady who was standing with him near the door: "she has such confidence in you; you know how to talk with her; go and speak with her a little while, my darling, please go!"

He was about to open the door for her; but his cousin held him back, putting her handkerchief several times to her eyes, and shaking her head.

"There, now she will not see that I have been weeping," said she, and, opening the door herself, went to the invalid.

The husband was in the greatest excitement, and seemed quite beside himself. He started to go over to the old mother, but, after taking a few steps, he turned around, walked the length of the room, and approached the priest.

The priest looked at him, raised his brows toward heaven, and sighed. The thick gray beard also was lifted and fell again.

"My God! my God!" said the husband.

"What can you do?" exclaimed the confessor, sighing and again lifting up his brows and beard, and letting them drop.

"And the old mother there!" exclaimed the husband, almost in despair. "She will not be able to endure it. You see, she loved her so, she loved her so, that she . . . I don't know. You might try, father, to calm her a little, and persuade her to go away."

The confessor arose and went over to the old lady.

"It is true, no one can appreciate a mother's heart," said he, "but God is compassionate."

The old lady's face was suddenly convulsed, and a hysterical sob shook her frame.

"God is compassionate," repeated the priest, when she had grown a little calmer. "I will tell you, in my parish there was a sick man, and much worse than Marya Dmitrievna, and he, though he was only a shopkeeper, was cured in a very short time, by means of herbs. And this very same shopkeeper is now in Moscow. I have told Vasili Dmitrievitch about him; it might be tried, you know. At all events, it would satisfy the invalid. With God, all things are possible."

"No, she won't get well," persisted the old lady. "Why should God have taken her, and not me?"

And again the hysterical sobbing overcame her, so violently that she fainted away.

The invalid's husband hid his face in his hands, and rushed from the room.

In the corridor the first person whom he met was a six-year-old boy, who was chasing his little sister with all his might and main.

"Do you bid me take the children to their mamasha?" inquired the nurse.

"No, she does not like to see them. They distract her."

The lad stopped for a moment, and, after looking eagerly into his father's face, he cut a dido with his leg, and with merry shouts ran on.

"I'm playing she's a horse, papasha," cried the little fellow, pointing to his sister.

Meantime, in the next room, the cousin had taken her seat near the sick woman, and was skilfully bringing the conversation by degrees round so as to prepare her for the thought of death. The doctor stood by the window, mixing some draught.

The invalid, in a white capote, all surrounded by cushions, was sitting up in bed, and gazed silently at her cousin.

"Ah, my dear!" she exclaimed, unexpectedly interrupting her, "don't try to prepare me; don't treat me like a little child! I am a Christian woman. I know all about it. I know that I have not long to live; I know that if my husband had heeded me sooner, I should have been in Italy, and possibly, yes probably, should have been well by this time. They all told him so. But what is to be done? it's as God saw fit. We all of us have sinned, I know that; but I hope in the mercy of God, that all will be pardoned, ought to be pardoned. I am trying to sound my own heart. I also have committed many sins, my love. But how much I have suffered in atonement! I have tried to bear my sufferings patiently." . . .

"Then shall I have the confessor come in, my love? It will be all the easier for you, after you have been absolved," said the cousin.

The sick woman dropped her head in token of assent. "O God! pardon me, a sinner," she whispered.

The cousin went out, and beckoned to the confessor. "She is an angel," she said to the husband, with tears in her eyes. The husband wept. The priest went into the sick-room; the old lady still remained unconscious, and in the room beyond all was perfectly quiet. At the end of five minutes the confessor came out, and, taking off his stole, arranged his hair.

"Thanks be to the Lord, she is calmer now," said he. "She wishes to see you."

The cousin and the husband went to the sick-room. The invalid, gently weeping, was gazing at the images.

"I congratulate you, my love," said the husband.

"Thank you. How well I feel now! what ineffable joy I experience!" said the sick woman, and a faint smile played over her thin lips. "How merciful God is! Is He not? He is merciful and omnipotent!"

And again with an eager prayer she turned her tearful eyes toward the holy images.

Then suddenly something seemed to occur to her mind. She beckoned to her husband.

"You are never willing to do what I desire," said she, in a weak and querulous voice.

The husband, stretching his neck, listened to her submissively.

"What is it, my love?"

"How many times I have told you that these doctors don't know anything! There are simple women doctors; they make cures. That's what the good father said. . . . A shopkeeper . . . send for him." . . .

"For whom, my love?"

"Good heavens! you can never understand me." And the dying woman frowned, and closed her eyes.

The doctor came to her, and took her hand. Her pulse was evidently growing feebler and feebler. He made a sign to the husband. The sick woman remarked this gesture, and looked around in fright. The cousin turned away to hide her tears.

"Don't weep, don't torment yourselves on my account," said the invalid. "That takes away from me my last comfort."

"You are an angel!" exclaimed the cousin, kissing her hand.

"No, kiss me here. They only kiss the hands of those who are dead. My God! my God!"

That same evening the sick woman was a corpse, and the corpse in the coffin lay in the parlor of the great mansion. In the immense room, the doors of which were closed, sat the clerk, and with a monotonous voice read the Psalms of David through his nose.

The bright glare from the wax candles in the lofty silver candelabra fell on the white brow of the dead, on the heavy waxen hands, on the stiff folds of the cerement which brought out into awful relief the knees and the feet.

The clerk, not varying his tones, continued to read on steadily, and in the silence of the chamber of death his words rang out and died away. Occasionally from distant rooms came the voice of children and their romping.

"*Thou hidest thy face, they are troubled; thou takest away their breath, they die and return to their dust.*

"*Thou sendest forth thy Spirit, they are created; and thou renewest the face of the earth.*

"*The glory of the Lord shall endure forever.*" . . .

The face of the dead was stern and majestic. But there was no motion either on the pure cold brow, or the firmly closed lips. She was all attention! But did she perhaps now understand these majestic words?

4

At the end of a month, over the grave of the dead a stone chapel was erected. Over the driver's there was as yet no stone, and only the fresh green grass sprouted over the mound which served as the sole record of the past existence of a man.

"It will be a sin and a shame, Seryoha," said the cook at the station-house one day, "if you don't buy a gravestone for Khveodor. You kept saying, 'It's winter, winter,' but now why don't you keep your word? I heard it all. He has already come back once to ask why you don't do it; if you don't buy him one, he will come again, he will choke you."

"Well, now, have I denied it?" urged Seryoha. "I am going to buy him a stone, as I said I would. I can get one for a ruble and a half. I have not forgotten about it; I'll have to get it. As soon as I happen to be in town, then I'll buy him one."

"You ought at least to put up a cross, that's what you ought to do," said an old driver. "It isn't right at all. You're wearing those boots now."

"Yes. But where could I get him a cross? You wouldn't want to make one out of an old piece of stick, would you?"

"What is that you say? Make one out of an old piece of stick? No; take your ax, go out to the wood a little earlier than usual, and you can hew him out one. Take a little ash tree, and you can make one. You can have a covered cross. If you go then, you won't have to give the watchman a little drink of vodka. One doesn't want to give vodka for every trifle. Now, yesterday I broke my axletree, and I go and hew out a new one of green wood. No one said a word."

Early the next morning, almost before dawn, Seryoha took his ax, and went to the wood.

Over all things hung a cold, dead veil of falling mist, as yet untouched by the rays of the sun.

The east gradually grew brighter, reflecting its pale light over the vault of heaven still covered by light clouds. Not a single grass-blade below, not a single leaf on the topmost branches of the tree-top, waved. Only from time to time could be heard the sounds of fluttering wings in the thicket, or a rustling on the ground broke in on the silence of the forest.

Suddenly a strange sound, foreign to this nature, resounded and died away at the edge of the forest. Again the noise sounded, and was monotonously repeated again and again, at the foot of one of the ancient, immovable trees. A tree-top began to shake in an extraordinary manner; the juicy leaves whispered something; and the warbler, sitting on one of the branches, flew off a couple of times with a shrill cry, and, wagging its tail, finally perched on another tree.

The ax rang more and more frequently; the white chips, full of sap, were scattered upon the dewy grass, and a slight cracking was heard beneath the blows.

The tree trembled with all its body, leaned over, and quickly straightened itself, shuddering with fear on its base.

For an instant all was still, then once more the tree bent over; a crash was heard in its trunk; and, tearing the thicket, and dragging down the branches, it plunged toward the damp earth.

The noise of the ax and of footsteps ceased.

The warbler uttered a cry, and flew higher. The branch which she grazed with her wings shook for an instant, and then came to rest like all the others with their foliage.

The trees, more joyously than ever, extended their motionless branches over the new space that had been made in their midst.

The first sunbeams, breaking through the cloud, gleamed in the sky, and shone along the earth and heavens.

The mist, in billows, began to float along the hollows; the dew, gleaming, played on the green foliage; translucent white clouds hurried along their azure path.

The birds hopped about in the thicket, and, as if beside themselves, voiced their happiness; the juicy leaves joyfully and contentedly whispered on the tree-tops; and the branches of the living trees slowly and majestically waved over the dead and fallen tree.

1859

DESIRE STRONGER THAN NECESSITY

We were on a bear hunt. My comrade had succeeded in shooting a bear; he had wounded him in some tender spot. There was a little blood on the snow, but the bear had escaped.

We went into the forest and began to plan what to do,—whether we should make a search then and there for the bear, or wait two or three days until he showed himself.

We began to ask the peasant bear-drivers whether it were possible now to get on the track of this bear. An old bear-driver said:—

"It is impossible! you must give the bear a chance to recover: in five days you can get round him; but now if you follow him it will only frighten him, and he won't go to his lair."

But a young bear-driver disagreed with the old peasant, and said that now was the time to get round the bear.

"In such deep snow as this the bear can't go a great distance—he is a fat bear.

He won't go into his lair to-day. And if he does not go into his lair, I can track him on my snow-shoes."

My comrade also was disinclined to track the bear, and advised waiting till another time.

But said I:—

"What is the use of discussing it? You do as you please, but I am going with Demyan after the bear. If we track him, all right; if we don't track him, it's all the same whether we do anything more to-day or not: it is still early."

That was what we did.

The others got into the sledge and returned to the village, while Demyan and I took some bread with us and remained in the woods.

As soon as the rest were gone from us, Demyan and I inspected our arms, belted our shubas, and started after the bear.

The weather was fine,—frosty and still. But it was laborious traveling on snow-shoes, for the snow was deep and mealy. The snow had not yet settled in the forest, and the evening before there had been a fresh fall, so that the snow-shoes sank over the edge, and in some places even deeper. The bear's tracks were visible for a long distance. We could see how the bear had made off; how in some places he had sunk up to his belly, and had scratched away the snow.

At first we followed the tracks over the deep snow through tall forest trees, but at last they turned into a fir thicket. Demyan halted.

"Now," said he, "we must abandon the trail. He must have his lair here. Here he stopped to rest; you can see by the snow. We will turn away from the trail, and make a circuit. Only we must go quietly, and not shout or cough, else we shall scare him."

We turned away from the trail abruptly to the left. After going five hundred paces, we discovered the bear's tracks again, right in front of us. Again we followed the trail, and this time the trail led us to the road. We stopped on the road and tried to decide what direction the bear had taken.

In one place on the road we could see where the bear's whole paw, with its toes, was imprinted; and here in another place a peasant had walked along the road in his bark shoes. Apparently it had gone toward the village.

We went along the road, and Demyan said:—

"We shan't find his trail on the road; but if he has turned off anywhere to the right or the left, then we shall see it in the snow. He will turn off somewhere; he won't go to the village."

Thus we walked along the road for a verst,[1] and then we discovered the trail turning from the road. We examined it, and wonder of wonders! the bear's tracks were not running from the road to the forest, but from the forest to the road, as we could see by the claws turned toward the road.

Said I, "This is another bear."

Demyan scrutinized it carefully, and thought for a moment.

"No," said he, "it is the same one, but he has been playing us a trick. He backed off the road."

We followed this trail, and it proved to be the case. The bear had evidently

[1] 3500 feet.

walked backward ten steps from the road, then gone behind a fir tree, turned about, and made straight off.

Demyan paused, saying:—

"Now we have really caught him. He probably would not make his lair anywhere else than in this marsh. We will encircle him."

We started on our circuit through thick fir forest. I was already weary, and the going became harder and harder. Sometimes I would stumble over a juniper bush or a young fir would get between my legs, or my snow-shoes would slide away from me without any reason, and sometimes I would trip over a stump or a log hidden under the snow. And I began to be tired out. I took off my shuba, for the sweat was pouring off from me. But Demyan glided along as if he were in a boat. His snow-shoes seemed of their own accord to bear him along. He never stumbled or slipped. He took my shuba also, and threw it over his shoulders, and kept encouraging me to come on.

We made a circuit of three versts, entirely inclosing the swamp. I had already begun to lag behind. I lost control of my snow-shoes; my legs gave way under me. Suddenly Demyan stopped in front of me and waved his arm. I caught up with him. Demyan bent over, and said in a whisper, pointing with his hand:—

"Hear the magpie screaming on yonder stump; the bird scents the bear from a long distance. He is there."

We set out again, and, after going another verst, we came upon our old track. Thus we had made a complete circuit around the bear, and the bear remained in the middle of our ring.

We paused.

I took off my cap also, and unbuttoned my coat. I was as hot as if I had been in a Russian bath, and my clothes were just as wet as a drowned rat. Demyan also was red with exertion, and wiped his face with his sleeve.

"Well," says he, "barin, we have finished the job; now we must rest."

The twilight was already beginning to throw its purple glow across the trees. We squatted down on our snow-shoes to get breath.

We took out the bread and salt from our bag; first I ate a little snow, and then my bread. And that bread was more delicious than anything I had ever eaten before in my life.

Thus we rested, and the nightfall was already beginning. I asked Demyan if it was far to the village.

"It will be about a dozen versts. We can get there to-night; but now we must rest. Put on your shuba, barin, or you will get cold."

Demyan broke off some fir boughs, brushed away the snow, made a bed, and he and I lay down together, side by side, with our arms for pillows. I don't remember how I fell off to sleep. But I woke up about two hours later. Something snapped.

I had been so sound asleep that I had forgotten where I was. I looked about me—what a marvelous spectacle! Where was I? I was in a strange white palace; there were white columns, and above all spangles were sparkling. I gazed up, and saw white arabesques, and beyond the arabesques an inky black vault, and variegated fires flashing.

As I gazed around I remembered that we were in the forest and that what had seemed to me a palace was the trees covered with snow and frost, and the fires were the stars beyond the branches, twinkling in the sky.

During the night the hoar-frost had fallen; there was frost on the branches, and frost on my shuba, and Demyan was all covered by frost, and the air was full of falling hoar-frost.

I awakened Demyan. We got up on our snow-shoes and started on our way. It was silent in the forest. The only sound was what we made gliding over the soft snow, and the occasional cracking of a tree under the frost, and the echo of it dying away through the aisles.

Once only some living creature rustled out from under our feet, and scurried away. I immediately thought it might be the bear. We went to the spot which the animal had left, and found the trail of a hare. The aspens were girdled. Hares had been nibbling there.

When we reached the road, we took off our snow-shoes and fastened them behind, and marched along the road. It was easy going. The snow-shoes behind us slipped along, clattering over the smooth road; the snow creaked under our boots, and the cold hoar-frost clung to our faces like down. And the stars above the tree-tops ran along apparently racing with us, flashing and disappearing, just as if the whole heaven were in motion.

My comrade was asleep; I awakened him.

We told him how we had surrounded the bear, and we told the landlord to collect the peasant whippers-in early in the morning. We got something to eat and turned in.

I was so weary that I should have been glad to sleep till dinner-time, but my comrade roused me. I leaped out of bed, and found him already dressed, and doing something to his gun.

"Where is Demyan?"

"He went long ago into the woods. He has already verified the circuit, and came running back, and now he has gone out to show the whippers-in the way."

After washing and dressing, I loaded my gun. We took our places in the sledge and set off.

The temperature still continued low; the air was motionless; the sun was not visible; heavy clouds had risen and the hoar-frost was falling.

We drove three versts along the road, and reached the forest. We could see in the valley columns of blue smoke, and people standing around—peasant men and women, with cudgels.

We leaped out, and joined the throng. The peasants were sitting around, roasting potatoes, and jesting with the women.

Demyan also was among them. The people got up. Demyan posted them on the circular trail that we had made the evening before. The men and women formed the line,—thirty of them in all,—buried in snow up to their waists, and made their way into the woods. Then my comrade and I followed after them.

Although the path was somewhat trodden, it was hard walking; still there was no possibility of falling; you walk as it were between two walls.

Thus we proceeded half a verst, and then we caught sight of Demyan on the other side, hurrying on snow-shoes to meet us, beckoning us to come to him.

We joined him; he showed us our places. As soon as I reached my station, I looked around me.

On my left there was a high fir tree; beyond it there was a wide view, and behind the trees stood a peasant whipper-in making a black spot. Opposite me there was a growth of young fir trees as tall as a man. The branches of the little firs were weighed down and stuck together by the snow. Through the clump led a footpath trodden through the snow. This path led straight to me. On my right was another clump of firs, and then began a clearing. And I saw that Demyan had posted my comrade on this clearing.

I examined my two muskets, cocking them, and tried to decide where would be the best place for me to take my position. Just behind me, three paces distant, was a tall pine tree.

"Let me stand by this pine and rest my second musket against it."

I made my way over to the pine, through snow that reached above my knees, and then under the pine I trampled down a little space and established myself in it. I held one musket across my arm; the other I leaned against the tree, ready cocked. I took out my dagger and put it in its sheath again, so as to see if in case of necessity it would come out easily.

I had just finished my preparations when I heard Demyan shouting in the woods:—

"He has started out! he has started! he has started!"

And in reply to Demyan's call, the peasants on all sides began to shout in various voices. "Pashol! u-u-u-u-u!" shouted the peasants. "Aï, i-i-ikh!" screamed the women, in their sharp voices.

The bear was inside the circle. Demyan was driving him. On all sides the people were shouting; only my comrade and I were standing silent and motionless, awaiting the bear. I stood and listened, and my heart within me was beating like a sledge-hammer. I had my musket in position; I trembled a little.

"Now, now," I thought to myself, "He will come leaping by; I will aim, I will fire my gun at him, and down he will go." . . .

Suddenly, on my left, I heard something rushing through the snow; only it was at some distance. I gazed at the tall fir; fifty paces away, behind the trees, stood something black and big. I raised my gun and waited. I asked myself:—

"Won't it come any nearer?"

As I looked, it moved its ears and started to retreat. As it turned around and presented its side, I got a full view of it. The tremendous beast! I took aim in hot haste.

Bang! I could hear my bullet bury itself in a tree. I gazed through the smoke; my bear was galloping back under cover, and disappeared in the forest.

"Well," I said to myself, "I have spoiled my game; now there's no hope of his coming back to me; either my comrade will hit him, or he will make his escape through the peasants; but I shall not have another chance at him."

Nevertheless I reloaded my musket, and stood there, listening. The peasants were shouting on all sides; but on my right, not far from where my comrade stood, I heard a woman screaming at the top of her voice:—

"Here he is! here he is! here he is! This way! this way! oï! oï! aï! aï! aï!"

Evidently she saw the bear. I no longer had any expectations of its coming my way, so I fixed my eyes on my comrade. I saw Demyan, with a cudgel, and not wearing his snow-shoes, running along the trodden path toward my comrade, crouching down behind him, and calling his attention to something, as if he were urging him to fire. I saw my comrade lift his musket and aim in the direction indicated by Demyan with his stick.

Bang! The gun went off.

"Well," said I to myself, "he has killed him!"

But when I saw that my comrade was not hurrying to the bear, I said to myself:—

"Missed, evidently; he could not have got a good aim. Now the bear will retreat, and there's no hope of his coming in my direction."

But what was this?

Suddenly I heard, directly in front of me, some one rushing along like a tornado, scattering the snow and puffing close to me. I looked up the path, and there he was, coming straight down upon me, over the little path between the thick fir bushes, galloping along with head down, and evidently frightened out of his wits.

He was now only five paces away from me. I could see his black breast, and his huge head covered with red hair. He was rushing directly at me, scattering the snow in every direction. I could see by his eyes that he did not perceive me, but was so terrified that he was dashing off full tilt, no matter where. But his course was bringing him directly toward the tree near which I was standing. I raised my musket—I fired—he was directly upon me. I perceived that I missed; the bullet glanced off, but the bear did not notice; he dashed at me, and not even yet did he see me.

I aimed my gun, and almost touched him. Bang! I could see that I hit him, but that the shot had failed to kill him.

He lifted his head, put back his ears, and thrust his snout straight into my face.

I tried to snatch my second musket; but no sooner had I put out my hand, than he dashed at me, knocked me over into the snow, and sprang away.

"Well," said I to myself, "lucky for me that he left me."

I was just picking myself up, when I discovered that something was pressing me down, keeping me from rising. His momentum had carried him along, he had fallen beyond me; and then, coming back to me, he had fallen upon me with his full weight. I was conscious of something heavy resting upon me, I was conscious of something warm on my face, and I was conscious that he had taken my whole face into his jaws. My nose was already in his mouth, and I could smell the warm odor of his blood. He had planted his paws on my shoulders, and it was impossible for me to move.

I managed, however, to extricate my head from his jaws on to his breast, and I turned away my eyes and nose. But a second time he succeeded in setting his tusks into my face and eyes. I became conscious that he was setting the tusks of his upper jaw into my forehead, under the hair, and those of his lower jaw in the flesh under my eyes; he shut his teeth together and began to crush me Like knives they cut into my head. I struggled, I pulled myself out of his clutches; but he made haste, and, snapping like a dog, hugged me closer and closer.

I got away from him, and again he clutched me.

"Well," said I to myself, "my end has come."

Suddenly I perceived that his pressure on me became less. I looked, and he had gone! he had bounded away from me, and was making off.

When my comrade and Demyan saw that the bear had knocked me down into the snow, and was gnawing me, they rushed toward me. My comrade, in his eagerness to get to me as speedily as possible, made a mistake; instead of running along the beaten path, he tried to cut across and fell. While he was struggling out of the deep snow, the bear was all the time biting me. But Demyan, though he was not armed with a musket, and had only a dry branch, ran along the path, and kept shouting:—

"He is killing the barin! he is eating up the barin!"

And then, as he approached the bear, he cried:—

"Oh, you beast! what are you doing? Let go! Let go!"

The bear heard, let go of me, and made off.

When I picked myself up, there was as much blood on the snow as if they had been killing a wild boar, and the flesh under my eyes hung in shreds; but I was so excited that I felt no pain.

My comrade came to me; the people gathered together; they examined my wounds; they wet them with snow. But as for me I forgot all about my wounds; I asked:—

"Where is the bear? Where has he gone?"

Suddenly we heard them shouting:—

"Here he is! here he is!"

And we saw the bear rushing back in our direction. We seized our muskets but before any one had time to fire, he had already dashed by. The bear was maddened; he wanted to finish devouring me; but when he saw that a crowd had collected, he was afraid. By the trail we could see that the blood came from the bear's head; they wanted to go in pursuit of him; but my head began to pain me, and we returned to the village, to the doctor.

The doctor sewed up my wounds with silk, and they began to heal.

At the end of a month we again went out in pursuit of this bear; but I did not have the chance of finishing him. The bear did not come out of his lair, but kept moving around and around, and roaring in a terrible voice.

Demyan put an end to him. The lower jaw of this bear had been broken by my shot, and a tooth knocked out.

This bear was huge, and he had a splendid black skin.

I had him stuffed, and he lies in my sleeping-room. The wounds in my face got well, so that there is scarcely any scar where they were made.

c. 1872

THE LONG EXILE;

OR,

GOD SEES THE TRUTH, BUT
BIDES HIS TIME

Once upon a time there lived in the city of Vladimir a young tradesman named Aksenof. He had two shops and a house.

Aksenof had a ruddy complexion and curly hair; he was a very jolly fellow and a good singer. When he was young he used to drink too much, and when he was tipsy he was turbulent; but after his marriage he ceased drinking, and only occasionally had a spree.

One summer Aksenof was going to Nizhni to the great Fair. As he was about to bid his family good-by, his wife said to him:—

"Ivan Dmitrievitch, do not start to-day; I dreamed that some misfortune befell you."

Aksenof laughed at her, and said:—

"Are you still afraid that I shall go on a spree at the Fair?"

His wife said:—

"I myself know not what I am afraid of, but I had such a bad dream; you seemed to be coming home from town, and you took off your hat, and I looked, and your head was all gray."

Aksenof laughed.

"That means good luck. See, I am going now. I will bring you some rich remembrances."

And he bade his family farewell and set off.

When he had gone half his journey, he fell in with a tradesman who was an acquaintance of his, and the two stopped at the same tavern for the night. They took tea together, and went to sleep in adjoining rooms.

Aksenof did not care to sleep long; he awoke in the middle of the night, and in order that he might get a good start while it was cool he aroused his driver and bade him harness up, went down into the smoky hut, settled his account with the landlord, and started on his way.

After he had driven forty versts,[1] he again stopped to get something to eat; he rested in the vestibule of the inn, and when it was noon, he went to the doorstep and ordered the samovar[2] got ready; then he took out his guitar and began to play.

Suddenly a troïka[3] with a bell dashed up to the inn, and from the equipage leaped an official with two soldiers; he came directly up to Aksenof, and asked:—

[1] Nearly twenty-six and a half miles.

[2] Water-boiler for making Russian tea.

[3] A team of three horses harnessed abreast; the outside two gallop, the shaft-horse trots.

"Who are you? Where did you come from?"

Aksenof answered without hesitation, and asked him if he would not like to have a glass of tea with him.

But the official kept on with his questions:—

"Where did you spend last night? Were you alone or with a merchant? Have you seen the merchant this morning? Why did you leave so early this morning?"

Aksenof wondered why he was questioned so closely; but he told everything just as it was, and asked:—

"Why do you put so many questions to me? I am not a thief or a murderer. I am on my own business; there is nothing to question me about."

Then the official called up the soldiers, and said:—

"I am the police inspector, and I have made these inquiries of you because the merchant with whom you spent last night has been stabbed. Show me your things, and you men search him."

They went into the tavern, brought in the trunk and bag, and began to open and search them. Suddenly the police inspector pulled out from the bag a knife, and demanded:—

"Whose knife is this?"

Aksenof looked, and saw a knife covered with blood taken from his bag, and he was frightened.

"And whose blood is that on the knife?"

Aksenof tried to answer, but he could not articulate his words:—

"I . . . I . . . don't . . . know . . . I . . . That knife . . . it is . . . not mine. . . ."

Then the police inspector said:—

"This morning the merchant was found stabbed to death in his bed. No one except you could have done it. The tavern was locked on the inside, and there was no one in the tavern except yourself. And here is the bloody knife in your bag, and your guilt is evident in your face. Tell me how you killed him and how much money you took from him."

Aksenof swore that he had not done it, that he had not seen the merchant after he had drunk tea with him, that the only money that he had with him— eight thousand rubles—was his own, and that the knife was not his.

But his voice trembled, his face was pale, and he was all quivering with fright, like a guilty person.

The police inspector called the soldiers, and commanded them to bind Aksenof, and take him to the wagon.

When they took him to the wagon with his feet tied, Aksenof crossed himself and burst into tears.

They confiscated Aksenof's things and his money, and took him to the next city, and threw him into prison.

They sent to Vladimir to make inquiries about Aksenof's character, and all the merchants and citizens of Vladimir declared that Aksenof, when he was young, used to drink and was wild, but that now he was a worthy man. Then he was brought up for judgment.

He was sentenced for having killed the merchant and for having robbed him of twenty thousand rubles.

Aksenof's wife was dumfounded by the event, and did not know what to think. Her children were still small, and there was one at the breast. She took them all with her and journeyed to the city where her husband was imprisoned.

At first they would not grant her admittance, but afterward she got permission from the nachalniks and was taken to her husband.

When she saw him in his prison garb, in chains, together with murderers, she fell to the floor, and it was a long time before she recovered from her swoon. Then she placed her children around her, sat down amid them, and began to tell him about their domestic affairs, and to ask him about everything that had happened to him.

He told her the whole story.

She asked:—

"What is to be done now?"

He said:—

"We must petition the Tsar. It is impossible that an innocent man should be condemned."

The wife said that she had already sent in a petition to the Tsar, but that the petition had not been granted. Aksenof said nothing, but was evidently very much downcast.

Then his wife said:—

"You see the dream I had, when I dreamed that you had become gray-headed, meant something, after all. Already your hair has begun to turn gray with trouble. You ought to have stayed at home that time."

And she began to tear her hair, and she said:—

"Vanya, my dearest husband, tell your wife the truth: Did you commit that crime?"

Aksenof said:—

"So you, too, have no faith in me!"

And he wrung his hands and wept.

Then a soldier came and said that it was time for the wife and children to go. And Aksenof for the last time bade his family farewell.

When his wife was gone, Aksenof began to think over all that they had said. When he remembered that his wife had also distrusted him, and had asked him if he had murdered the merchant, he said to himself:—

"It is evident that no one but God can know the truth of the matter, and He is the only one to ask for mercy, and He is the only one from whom to expect it."

And from that time Aksenof ceased to send in petitions, ceased to hope, and only prayed to God. Aksenof was sentenced to be knouted, and then to exile with hard labor.

And so it was done.

He was flogged with the knout, and then, when the wounds from the knout were healed, he was sent with other exiles to Siberia.

Aksenof lived twenty-six years in the mines. The hair on his head had become white as snow, and his beard had grown long, thin, and gray. All his gayety had vanished. He was bent, his gait was slow, he spoke little, he never laughed, and he spent much of his time in prayer.

Aksenof had learned while in prison to make boots, and with the money that he earned he bought the "Book of Martyrs," and used to read it when it was light enough in prison, and on holidays he would go to the prison church, read the Gospels, and sing in the choir, for his voice was still strong and good.

The authorities liked Aksenof for his submissiveness, and his prison associates respected him and called him "Grandfather" and the "man of God." Whenever they had petitions to be presented, Aksenof was always chosen to carry them to the authorities; and when quarrels arose among the prisoners, they always came to Aksenof as umpire.

Aksenof never received any letters from home, and he knew not whether his wife and children were alive.

One time some new convicts came to the prison. In the evening all the old convicts gathered around the newcomers, and began to ply them with questions as to the cities or villages from which this one or that one had come, and what their crimes were.

At this time Aksenof also was sitting on his bunk, near the strangers, and, with bowed head, was listening to what was said.

One of the new convicts was a tall, healthy-looking old man of sixty years, with a close-cropped gray beard. He was telling why he had been arrested. He said:—

"And so, brothers, I was sent here for nothing. I unharnessed a horse from a postboy's sledge, and they caught me with it, and insisted that I was stealing it. But I said, 'I only wanted to go a little faster, so I whipped up the horse. And, besides, the driver was a friend of mine. It's all right,' I said. 'No,' said they; 'you were stealing it.' But they did not know what and where I had stolen. I have done things which long ago would have sent me here, but I was not found out; and now they have sent me here without any justice in it. But what's the use of grumbling? I have been in Siberia before. They did not keep me here very long, though." . . .

"Where did you come from?" asked one of the convicts.

"Well, we came from the city of Vladimir; we are citizens of that place. My name is Makar, and my father's name was Semyon."

Aksenof raised his head and asked:—

"Tell me, Semyonuitch, have you ever heard of the Aksenofs, merchants in Vladimir city? Are they alive?"

"Indeed, I have heard of them! They are rich merchants, though their father is in Siberia. It seems he was just like any of the rest of us sinners. And now tell me, grandfather, what you were sent here for?"

Aksenof did not like to speak of his misfortunes; he sighed, and said:—

"Twenty-six years ago I was condemned to hard labor on account of my sins."

Makar Semyonof said:—

"But what was your crime?"

Aksenof replied, "So I must have deserved this."

But he would not give any further particulars; the other convicts, however, related why Aksenof had been sent to Siberia. They told how on the road some one had killed a merchant, and put the knife into Aksenof's luggage, and how he had been unjustly punished for this.

When Makar heard this, he glanced at Aksenof, slapped himself on the knees, and said:—

"Well, now, this is wonderful! This is really wonderful! You have been growing old, grandfather!"

They began to ask him what he thought was wonderful, and where he had seen Aksenof. But Makar did not answer; he only repeated:—

"A miracle, boys! how wonderful that we should meet again here!"

And when he said these words, it came over Aksenof that perhaps this man might know who had killed the merchant. And he said:—

"Did you ever hear of that crime, Semyonuitch, or did you ever see me before?"

"Of course I heard of it! The country was full of it. But it happened a long time ago. And I have forgotten what I heard," said Makar.

"Perhaps you heard who killed the merchant?" asked Aksenof.

Makar laughed, and said:—

"Why, of course the man who had the knife in his bag killed him. It would have been impossible for any one to put the knife in your things and not have been caught doing it. For how could the knife have been put into your bag? Was it not standing close by your head? And you would have heard it, wouldn't you?"

As soon as Aksenof heard these words he felt convinced that this was the very man who had killed the tradesman. He stood up and walked away. All that night he was unable to sleep. Deep melancholy came upon him, and he began to call back the past in his imagination.

He imagined his wife as she had been when for the last time she had accompanied him to the Fair. She seemed to stand before him exactly as if she were alive, and he saw her face and her eyes, and he seemed to hear her words and her laugh.

Then his imagination brought up his children before him; one a boy in a little fur coat, and the other at his mother's breast.

And he imagined himself as he was at that time, young and happy. He remembered how he had sat on the steps of the tavern when they arrested him, and how he had played on his guitar, and how his soul was full of joy at that time.

And he remembered the place of execution where they had flogged him, and the executioner, and the people standing around, and the chains and the convicts, and all his twenty-six years of prison life, and he remembered his old age.

And such melancholy came upon Aksenof that he was tempted to put an end to himself.

"And all on account of this criminal!" said Aksenof to himself.

And then he began to feel such anger against Makar Semyonof that he almost lost himself, and was crazy with desire to pay off the load of vengeance. He repeated prayers all night, but could not recover his calm. When day came, he walked by Makar and did not look at him.

Thus passed two weeks. At night Aksenof was not able to sleep, and such melancholy had come over him that he did not know what to do.

One time during the night, as he happened to be passing through the prison, he saw that the soil was disturbed under one of the bunks. He stopped to examine it. Suddenly Makar crept from under the bunk, and looked at Aksenof with a startled face.

Aksenof was about to pass on so as not to see him, but Makar seized his arm, and told him how he had been digging a passage under the wall, and how every day he carried the dirt out in his boot-legs and emptied it in the street when they went out to work. He said:—

"If you only keep quiet, old man, I will get you out too. But if you tell on me, they will flog me; but afterward I will make it hot for you. I will kill you."

When Aksenof saw the man who had injured him, he trembled all over with rage, twitched away his arm, and said:—

"I have no reason to make my escape, and to kill me would do no harm; you killed me long ago. But as to telling on you or not, I shall do as God sees fit to have me."

On the next day, when they took the convicts out to work, the soldiers discovered where Makar Semyonof had been digging in the ground; they began to make a search, and found the hole. The chief came into the prison and asked every one, "Who was digging that hole?"

All denied it. Those who knew did not name Makar, because they were aware that he would be flogged half to death for such an attempt.

Then the chief came to Aksenof. He knew that Aksenof was a truthful man, and he said:—

"Old man, you are truthful; tell me before God who did this."

Makar Semyonof was standing near, in great excitement, and he looked at the nachalnik, but he dared not look at Aksenof.

Aksenof's hands and lips trembled, and it was some time before he could speak a word. He said to himself:—

"If I shield him . . . but why should I forgive him when he has been my ruin? Let him pay for my sufferings! But shall I tell on him? They will surely flog him. But what difference does it make what I think of him? Will it be any the easier for me?"

Once more the chief demanded:—

"Well, old man, tell the truth! Who dug the hole?"

Aksenof glanced at Makar Semyonof, and then said:—

"I cannot tell, your honor. God does not bid me tell. I will not tell. Do with me as you please; I am in your power."

In spite of all the chief's efforts, Aksenof would say nothing more. And so they failed to find out who dug the hole.

On the next night, as Aksenof was lying on his bunk, and was almost asleep, he heard some one come along and sit down at his feet.

He peered through the darkness and saw that it was Makar. Aksenof asked:—

"What do you wish of me? What are you doing here?"

Makar Semyonof remained silent. Aksenof arose, and said:—

"What do you want? Go away, or else I will call the guard."

Makar Semyonof bent close to Aksenof, and said in a whisper:—

"Ivan Dmitrievitch, forgive me!"

Aksenof said:—

"What have I to forgive you?"

"I killed the merchant and put the knife in your bag. And I was going to kill you too, but there was a noise in the yard; I thrust the knife in your bag, and slipped out of the window."

Aksenof said nothing, and he did not know what to say. Makar got down from the bunk, knelt on the ground, and said:—

"Ivan Dmitrievitch, forgive me, forgive me for God's sake. I will confess that I killed the merchant—they will pardon you. You will be able to go home."

Aksenof said:—

"It is easy for you to say that, but how could I endure it? Where should I go now? . . . My wife is dead! my children have forgotten me. . . . I have nowhere to go." . . .

Makar did not rise; he beat his head on the ground, and said:—

"Ivan Dmitritch, forgive me! When they flogged me with the knout, it was easier to bear than it is now to look at you. . . . And you had pity on me after all this . . . you did not tell on me. . . . Forgive me for Christ's sake! Forgive me, though I am a cursed villain!"

And the man began to sob.

When Aksenof heard Makar Semyonof sobbing, he himself burst into tears, and said:—

"God will forgive you; maybe I am a hundred times worse than you are!"

And suddenly he felt a wonderful peace in his soul. And he ceased to mourn for his home, and had no desire to leave the prison, but only thought of his last hour.

Makar Semyonof would not listen to Aksenof, and confessed his crime.

When the orders came to let Aksenof go home, he was dead.

c. 1872

A PRISONER IN THE CAUCASUS

1

A Russian gentleman was serving as an officer in the army of the Caucasus. His name was Zhilin.

One day a letter from his home came to him. His old mother wrote him:—

I am now getting along in years, and I should like to see my beloved son before I die. Come and bid me farewell, lay me in the ground, and then with my blessing return again to your service. And I have been finding a bride for you, and she is intelligent and handsome and has property. If she pleases you, why then you can marry and settle down together.

Zhilin thought the matter over.

"It is very true: the old lady has been growing feeble; maybe I shall not have a chance to see her again. I'll go, and if the girl is pretty—then I might marry."

He went to his colonel, got his leave of absence, bade his comrades farewell, gave the soldiers of his command nine gallons of vodka as a parting treat, and made his arrangements to leave.

There was war at that time in the Caucasus. The roads were not open for travel either by day or night. If any Russian rode or walked outside of the fortress, the Tartars were likely either to kill him or carry him off to the mountains. And it was arranged that twice a week an escort of soldiers should go from fortress to fortress. In front and behind marched the soldiers, and the travelers rode in the middle.

It was now summer-time. At sunrise the baggage train was made up behind the fortification; the guard of soldiery marched ahead, and the procession moved along the road.

Zhilin was on horseback, and his effects were on a cart which formed part of the train.

They had twenty-five versts[1] to travel. The train proceeded slowly; sometimes the soldiers halted; sometimes a wagon-wheel came off, or a horse balked, and all had to stop and wait.

The sun was already past the zenith, but the train had only gone halfway. It was dusty and hot, the sun was fierce, and there was no shelter. A bald steppe; not a tree or a shrub along the road.

Zhilin rode on ahead, occasionally stopping and waiting till the train caught up with him. He would listen, and hear the signal on the horn to halt again. And Zhilin thought, "Had I now better go on alone without the soldiers? I have a good horse under me; if I fall in with the Tartars, I can escape. Or shall I wait?"

He kept stopping and pondering. And just then another officer, also on horseback, rode up to him; his name was Kostuilin, and he had a musket.

He said:—

"Zhilin, let us ride on ahead together. I am so hungry that I cannot stand it any longer, and the heat too,—you could wring my shirt out!"

Kostuilin was a heavy, stout, ruddy man, and the sweat was dripping from him.

Zhilin reflected, and said:—

"And your musket is loaded?"

"It is."

"All right, let us go. Only one condition: not to separate."

And they started on up the road. They rode along the steppe, talking and looking on each side. There was a wide sweep of view in all directions. As soon as the steppe came to an end, the road went into a pass between two mountains.

And Zhilin said:—

"I must ride up on that mountain, and reconnoiter; otherwise you see they might come down from the mountain and surprise us."

But Kostuilin said:—

"What is there to reconnoiter? Let us go ahead."

Zhilin did not heed him.

[1] Sixteen and a half miles.

"No," says he, "you wait for me here below. I'll just glance around."

And he spurred his horse up the mountain to the left.

The horse that Zhilin rode was a hunter; he had bought her out of a drove of colts, paying a hundred rubles for her, and he had himself trained her. She bore him up the steep slope as if on wings. He had hardly reached the summit when before him, on a place a little less than three acres, mounted Tartars were standing. There were thirty of them.

He saw them, and started to turn back, but the Tartars had caught sight of him; they set out in pursuit of him, unstrapping their weapons as they galloped. Zhilin dashed down the precipice with all the speed of his horse, and cried to Kostuilin:—

"Fire your gun!" and to his horse he said, though not aloud:—

"Little mother, carry me safely, don't stumble; if you trip up, I am lost. If we get back to the gun, we won't fall into their hands."

But Kostuilin, as soon as he saw the Tartars, instead of waiting for him, galloped on with all his might toward the fortress. With his whip he belabored his horse, first on one side, then on the other; all that could be seen through the dust was the horse switching her tail.

Zhilin saw that his case was desperate. The gun was gone; nothing was to be done with a saber alone. He turned his horse back toward the train; he thought he might escape that way.

But in front of him he saw that six were galloping down the slope. His horse was good, but theirs were better; and besides, they had got the start of him. He attempted to wheel about, and was going to dash ahead again, but his horse had got momentum, and could not be held back; he flew straight down toward them.

He saw a red-bearded Tartar approaching him on a gray horse. He was gaining on him; he was gnashing his teeth; he was getting his gun ready.

"Well," thought Zhilin, "I know you devils; if you should take me prisoner, you would put me into a hold, and flog me with a whip. I won't give myself up alive."

Now, Zhilin was not of great size, but he was a uhlan. He drew his saber, spurred his horse straight at the red-bearded Tartar. He said to himself, "Either I will crush him with my horse, or I will hack him down with my saber."

Zhilin, however, did not reach the place on horseback; suddenly, from behind him, gunshots were fired at the horse. The horse fell headlong, and pinned Zhilin's leg to the ground.

He tried to arise; but already two ill-smelling Tartars were sitting on him, and pinioning his hands behind his back.

He burst from them, knocking the Tartars over; but three others had leaped from their horses, and began to beat him on the head with their gun-stocks.

His sight failed him, and he staggered.

The Tartars seized him, took from their saddles extra saddle-girths, bent his arms behind his back, fastened them with a Tartar knot, and lifted him up.

They took his saber from him, pulled off his boots, made a thorough search of him, relieved him of his money and his watch, and tore his clothes in pieces.

Zhilin glanced at his horse. The poor beast lay as she had fallen, on her side, and was kicking, vainly trying to rise. In her head was a hole, and from the hole the black blood was pouring; the dust for an arshin around was wet with it.

A Tartar went to the horse to remove the saddle. She was still kicking, so the man took out his dagger and cut her throat. The throat gave a whistling sound, a trembling ran over the body, and all was over.

The Tartars took off the saddle and the other trappings. The one with the red beard mounted his horse, and the others lifted Zhilin behind him; and, in order to keep him from falling, they fastened him with the reins to the Tartar's belt, and thus they carried him off to the mountains.

Zhilin sat behind, swaying, and bumping his face against the stinking Tartar's back.

All that he could see before him was the healthy Tartar back, and the sinewy neck, and a smooth-shaven nape, showing blue beneath the cap.

Zhilin's head ached; the blood trickled into his eyes. And it was impossible for him to get a more comfortable position on the horse, or wipe away the blood. His arms were so tightly bound that his collar-bones ached.

They rode along from mountain to mountain; they forded a river; then they entered a highway, and rode along a valley.

Zhilin tried to follow the route that they took him; but his eyes were glued together with blood, and it was impossible for him to turn round.

It began to grow dark; they crossed still another river, and began to climb a rocky mountain. There was an odor of smoke. The barking of dogs was heard.

They had reached an *aul* (a Tartar village).
The Tartars dismounted. The Tartar children came running up, and surrounded Zhilin, whistling and exulting. Finally they began to hurl stones at him.

The Tartar drove away the children, lifted Zhilin from the horse, and called a menial.

A Nogayets, with prominent cheek-bones, came at the call. He wore only a shirt. The shirt was torn; his whole breast was bare. The Tartar gave him some order. The menial brought a foot-stock. It consisted of two oaken blocks provided with iron rings, and in one of the rings was a clamp with a lock. They unfastened Zhilin's arms, put on the clog, and took him to a shed, pushed him in, and shut the door.

Zhilin fell on the manure. As he lay there, he felt round in the darkness, and when he had found a place that was less foul, he stretched himself out.

2

Zhilin scarcely slept that night. The nights were short. He saw through a crack that it was growing light. Zhilin got up, widened the crack, and managed to look out.

Through the crack he could see a road leading down from the mountain; at the right, a Tartar hut with two trees near it. A black dog was lying on the road; a she-goat with her kids was walking by; they were shaking their tails.

He saw coming down the mountain a young Tartar girl in a variegated shirt, ungirdled, in pantalettes and boots; her head was covered with a kaftan, and on it she bore a great tin water-jug.

She walked along, swaying and bending her back, and holding by the hand a little shaven-headed Tartar urchin, who wore a single shirt.

After the Tartar maiden had gone into the saklia with her water-jug, the red-bearded Tartar of the evening before came out, wearing a silk beshmet, a silver dagger in his belt, and *bashmaks*, or sandals, on his bare feet. On the back of his head was a high cap of sheepskin, dyed black. He came out, stretched himself, stroked his red beard. He paused, gave some order to the menial, and went off somewhere.

Then two children on horseback came along on their way to the watering-trough. The snouts of the horses were wet.

Other shaven-headed youngsters, with nothing but shirts on, and nothing on their legs, formed a little band, and came to the shed; they got a dry stick, and stuck it through the crack.

Zhilin growled "ukh" at them. The children began to squeal, and scatter in every direction as fast as their legs would carry them; only their bare knees glistened. But Zhilin began to be thirsty; his throat was parched. He said to himself:—

"I wonder if they won't come to look after me?"

While he was listening, the barn doors were thrown open.

The red Tartar came in, and with him another, of slighter stature and of dark complexion. His eyes were bright and black, his cheeks ruddy, his little beard well trimmed, his face jolly and always enlivened with a grin.

The dark man's clothing was still richer,—a beshmet of blue silk, embroidered with gold lace. In his belt, a great silver dagger; red morocco bashmaks, embroidered with silver, and over the fine bashmaks he wore a larger pair of stout ones. His cap was tall, of white lamb's-wool.

The red Tartar came in, muttered something, gave vent to some abusive language, and then stood leaning against the wall, fingering his dagger, and scowling under his brows at Zhilin, like a wolf.

But the dark Tartar, nervous and active, and always on the go, as if he were made of springs, came straight up to Zhilin, squatted down on his heels, showed his teeth, tapped him on the shoulder, began to gabble something in his own language, winked his eyes, and, clucking his tongue, kept saying:—

"A fine Russ, a fine Russ!"

Zhilin did not understand him, and said:—

"Drink; give me some water."

The dark one grinned, and all the time he kept babbling:—

"A fine Russ!"

Zhilin signified by his hands and lips that they should give him water.

The dark one understood, grinned, put his head out of the door, and cried:—

"Dina!"

A young girl came running in,—a slender, lean creature of thirteen, with a face like the dark man's. Evidently she was his daughter. She also had black, luminous eyes, and she was very pretty.

She was dressed in a long, blue shirt, with wide sleeves and without a belt. On the bottom, on the breast, and on the cuffs it was relieved with red trimmings. She wore on her legs pantalettes and bashmaks, and over the bashmaks another pair with high heels. On her neck was a necklace wholly composed of

Russian half-ruble pieces. Her head was uncovered; she had her hair in a black braid, and on the braid was a ribbon, and to the ribbon were attached various ornaments and a silver ruble.

Her father gave her some command. She ran out, and quickly returned, bringing a little tin pitcher. After she had handed him the water, she also squatted on her heels in such a way that her knees were higher than her shoulders.

She sat that way, and opened her eyes, and stared at Zhilin while he was drinking, as if he were some wild beast.

Zhilin offered to return the pitcher to her. She darted away like a wild goat. Even her father laughed.

He sent her after something else. She took the pitcher, ran out, and brought back some unleavened bread on a small, round board, and again squatted down, and stared without taking her eyes from him.

The Tartars went out, and again bolted the door.

After a while the Nogayets also came to Zhilin, and said:—

"Aï-da, khozyaïn, aï-da!"

But he did not know Russian either. Zhilin, however, perceived that he wished him to go somewhere.

Zhilin hobbled out with his clog; it was impossible to walk, so he had to drag one leg. The Nogayets led the way for him.

He saw a Tartar village, a dozen houses, and the native mosque with its minaret.

In front of one house stood three horses saddled. Lads held them by their bridles. From this house came the dark Tartar, and beckoned with his hand, signifying that Zhilin was to come to him. He grinned, and kept saying something in his own tongue, and went into the house.

Zhilin followed him.

The room was decent; the walls were smoothly plastered with clay. Against the front wall were placed feather-beds; on the sides hung costly rugs; on the rugs were guns, pistols, and sabers, all silver-mounted.

On one side a little oven was set in, on a level with the floor.

The floor was of earth, clean as a threshing-floor, and the whole of the front part was covered with felt; rugs were distributed over the felt, and on the rugs were down pillows.

On the rugs were sitting some Tartars with bashmaks only on their feet— the dark Tartar, the red-bearded one, and three guests. Behind their backs, down cushions were placed; and before them on wooden plates were pancakes of millet flour, and melted butter in a cup, and the Tartar beer, called *buza*, in a pitcher. They ate with their fingers and all dipped into the butter.

The dark man leaped up, bade Zhilin sit on one side, not on a rug but on the bare floor; going back again to his rug, he served his guests with cakes and buza.

The menial showed Zhilin his place; he himself took off his outside bashmaks, placed them by the door in a row with the bashmaks of the other guests, and took his seat on the felt as near as possible to his masters; and while they ate he looked at them, and his mouth watered.

After the Tartars had finished eating the pancakes, a Tartar woman entered, dressed in the same sort of shirt as the girl wore, and in pantalettes; her head was covered with a handkerchief. She carried out the butter and the cakes, and brought a handsome finger-bowl, and a pitcher with a narrow nose.

The Tartars proceeded to wash their hands, then they folded their arms, knelt down, and puffed on all sides, and said their prayers. Then they talked together in their own tongue.

Finally one of the guests, a Tartar, approached Zhilin, and began to speak to him in Russian.

"Kazi Muhamet made you prisoner," said he, pointing to the red-bearded Tartar; "and he has given you to Abdul Murat," indicating the dark one. "Abdul Murat is now your master."

Zhilin said nothing.

Abdul Murat began to talk, all the time pointing toward Zhilin, and grinned as he talked:—

"*Soldat Urus, korosho Urus.*"

The dragoman went on to say:—

"He commands you to write a letter home, and have them send money to ransom you. As soon as money is sent, he will set you free."

Zhilin pondered a little, and then said:—

"Does he wish a large ransom?"

The Tartars took counsel together, and then the dragoman said:—

"Three thousand silver rubles."

"No," replied Zhilin, "I can't pay that."

Abdul leaped up, began to gesticulate and talk to Zhilin; he seemed all the time to think that Zhilin understood him.

The dragoman translated his words.

"He means," says he, "how much will you give?"

Zhilin, after pondering a little, said:—

"Five hundred rubles."

Then the Tartars all began to talk at once. Abdul began to scream at the red-bearded Tartar. He grew so excited as he talked that the spittle flew from his mouth.

But the red-bearded Tartar only frowned, and clucked with his tongue.

When all became silent again, the dragoman said:—

"Five hundred rubles is not enough to buy you of your master. He himself has paid two hundred for you. Kazi Muhamet was in debt to him. He took you for the debt. Three thousand rubles; it is no use to send less. But if you don't write, they will put you in a hole, and flog you with a whip."

"Ekh!" said Zhilin to himself, "the more cowardly one is, the worse it is for him."

He leaped to his feet, and said:—

"Now you tell him, dog that he is, that if he thinks he is going to frighten me, then I will not give him a single kopek nor will I write. I am not afraid of you, and you will never make me afraid of you, you dog!" The dragoman interpreted this to them, and again they all began to talk at once.

They gabbled a long time, then the dark one got up and came to Zhilin.

"*Urus,*" says he, "*jigit, jigit Urus!*"

The word *jigit* in their language signifies a brave young man. And he grinned, said something to the dragoman, and the dragoman said:—

"Give a thousand rubles."

Zhilin would not give in:—

"I will not pay more than five hundred. But if you kill me, you will get nothing at all."

The Tarters consulted together, sent out the menial, and they themselves looked first at the door, then at Zhilin.

The menial returned, followed by a rather stout man in bare feet and almost stripped. His feet also were fastened to a clog.

Zhilin uttered an exclamation; he saw it was Kostuilin. So they had captured him too.

They placed him next his comrade; the two began to talk together, and the Tartars looked on and listened in silence.

Zhilin told how it had gone with him; Kostuilin told how his horse had stood stock-still, and his gun had missed fire, and that this same Abdul had overtaken him and captured him.

Abdul sprang to his feet, pointed to Kostuilin, and made some remark. The dragoman translated his words to mean that they now both belonged to the same master, and that the one who paid the ransom first would be freed first.

"Now," said he to Zhilin, "you lose your temper so easily, but your comrade is calm; he has written a letter home; they will send five thousand silver rubles. And so he will be well fed, and he won't be hurt."

And Zhilin said:—

"Let my comrade do as he pleases. Maybe he is rich. But I am not rich; I will do as I have already told you. Kill me if you wish, but it would not do you any good, and I will not pay you more than five hundred rubles."

They were silent.

Suddenly Abdul leaped up, brought a little chest, took out a pen, a sheet of paper, and ink, and pushed them into Zhilin's hands, then tapped him on the shoulder and said by signs:—

"Write."

He had agreed to take the five hundred rubles.

"Wait a moment," said Zhilin to the dragoman. "Tell him that he must feed us well, clothe us, and give us good decent foot-wear, and let us stay together so that it may be pleasanter for us. And lastly, that he take off these clogs."

He looked at his Tartar master, and smiled. The master also smiled, and when he learned what was wanted, said:—

"I will give you the very best clothes; a cloak and boots, fit for a wedding. And I will feed you like princes. And if you want to live together, why, you can live in the shed. But it won't do to take away the clogs; you would run away. Only at night will I have them taken off." Then he jumped up and tapped him on the shoulder: "You good, me good."

Zhilin wrote his letter, but he put on it the wrong address so that it might never reach its destination. He said to himself:—

"I shall run away."

They took Zhilin and Kostuilin to the shed, strewed corn-stalks, gave them water in a pitcher, and bread, two old cherkeski, and some worn-out military boots. It was evident that they had been stolen from some dead soldier. When night came they took off their clogs, and locked them up in the shed.

3

Thus Zhilin and his comrade lived a whole month. Their master was always on the grin.

"You, Ivan, good—me, Abdul, good."

But he gave them wretched food,—unleavened bread made of millet flour, cooked in the form of cakes, but often not heated through.

Kostuilin wrote home again, and was anxiously awaiting the arrival of the money, and lost his spirits. Whole days at a time he sat in the shed, and counted the days till his money should arrive, or else he slept.

But Zhilin knew that his letter would not reach its destination, and he did not write another.

"Where," he asked himself,—"where would my mother get so much money for my ransom? And besides, she lived for the most part on what I used to send her. If she made out to raise five hundred rubles, she would be in want till the end of her days. If God wills it, I may escape."

And all the time he kept his eyes open, and made plans to elude his captors.

He walked about the aul; he amused himself by whistling; or else he sat down and fashioned things, either modeling dolls out of clay or plaiting baskets of osiers, for Zhilin was a master at all sorts of handiwork.

One time he made a doll with nose and hands and feet, and dressed in a Tartar shirt, and he set the doll on the roof. The Tartar women were going for water. Dina, the master's daughter, caught sight of the doll.

She called the Tartar women. They set down their jugs, and looked and laughed.

Zhilin took the doll, and offered it to them. They kept laughing, but did not dare to take it.

He left the doll, went to the barn, and watched what would take place.

Dina ran up to the doll, looked around, seized the doll, and fled.

The next morning at dawn he saw Dina come out on the doorstep with the doll. And she had already dressed it up in pieces of red cloth, and was rocking it like a little child, and singing a lullaby in her own language.

The old woman came out, gave her a scolding, snatched the doll away, broke it in pieces, and sent off Dina to work.

Zhilin made another doll, a still better one, and gave it to Dina.

One time Dina brought a little jug, put it down, took a seat, and looked at him. Then she laughed, and pointed to the jug.

"What is she so gay about?" wondered Zhilin.

He took the jug, and began to drink. He supposed that it was water, but it was milk.

He drank up the milk.

"Good," says he.

How delighted Dina was! "Good, Ivan, good!"

And she jumped up, clapped her hands, snatched the jug, and ran away.

And from that time she began to bring him secretly fresh milk every day.

Now, sometimes the Tartars would make cheesecakes out of goat's milk, and dry them on their roofs; so she used to carry some of these cakes secretly to him. And another time, when her father had killed a sheep, she brought him a piece of mutton in her sleeve. She threw it down, and ran away.

One time there was a heavy shower, and for a whole hour the rain poured as from buckets; and all the brooks grew roily. Wherever there had been a ford, the depth of the water increased to a fathom, and boulders were rolled along by it. Everywhere torrents were rushing, the mountains were full of the roaring.

Now, when the shower was over, streams were pouring all through the village. Zhilin asked his master for a knife, whittled out a cylinder and some paddles, and made a water-wheel, and fastened manikins at the two ends.

The little girls brought him some rags, and he dressed up the manikins, one like a man, the other like a woman. He fastened them on, and put the wheel in a brook. The wheel revolved, and the dolls danced.

The whole village collected; the little boys and the little girls, the women, and even the Tartars, came and clucked with their tongues:—

"Aï, Urus! aï, Ivan!"

Abdul had a Russian watch, which had been broken. He took it, and showed it to Zhilin, and clucked with his tongue. Zhilin said:—

"Let me have it, I will mend it."

He took it, opened the penknife, took it apart. Then he put it together again, and gave it back. The watch ran.

The Tartar was delighted, brought him his old beshmet, which was all in rags, and gave it to him. Nothing else was to be done,—he took it, and used it as a covering at night.

From that time, Zhilin's fame went abroad, that he was a "master." Even from distant villages, they came to him. One brought him a gun-lock or a pistol to repair, another a watch.

His master furnished him with tools,—a pair of pincers and gimlets and a little file.

One time a Tartar fell ill; they came to Zhilin: "Come, cure him!"

Zhilin knew nothing of medicine. He went, looked at the sick man, said to himself, "Perhaps he will get well, anyway." He went into the shed, took water and sand, and shook them up together. He whispered a few words to the water in presence of the Tartars, and gave it to the sick man to drink.

Fortunately for him, the Tartar got well.

Zhilin had by this time learned something of their language. And some of the Tartars became accustomed to him; when they wanted him, they called him by name, "Ivan, Ivan;" but others always looked at him as if he was a wild beast.

The red-bearded Tartar did not like Zhilin; when he saw him, he scowled and turned away, or else insulted him.

There was another old man among them; he did not live in the aul, but came from down the mountain. Zhilin never saw him except when he came to the mosque to prayer. He was of small stature; on his cap he wore a white towel as an ornament. His beard and mustaches were trimmed; they were white as wool, and his face was wrinkled and brick-red. His nose was hooked like a hawk's, and his eyes were gray and cruel, and he had no teeth except two tusks.

He used to come in his turban, leaning on his staff, and glare like a wolf; whenever he saw Zhilin, he would snort, and turn his back.

One time Zhilin went down the mountain to see where the old man lived. He descended a narrow path, and saw a little stone-walled garden. On the other side of the wall were cherry trees, peach trees, and a little hut with a flat roof.

He went nearer; he saw beehives made of straw, and bees flying and humming around them. And the old man was on his knees busy doing something to one of the hives.

Zhilin raised himself up, so as to get a better view, and his clog made a noise.

The old man looked up,—squealed; he whipped his pistol from his belt, and fired at Zhilin, who had barely time to hide behind the wall.

The old man came to make his complaint to Zhilin's master. Abdul called him in, grinned, and asked him:

"Why did you go to the old man's?"

"I didn't do him any harm. I wanted to see how he lived."

Abdul explained it to the old man; but he was angry, hissed, mumbled something, showed his tusks, and threatened Zhilin with his hands.

Zhilin did not understand it all; but he made out that the old man wished Abdul to kill the two Russians, and not keep them in the aul.

The old man went off.

Zhilin began to ask his master:—

"Who is that old man?"

And the master replied:—

"He is a great man. He used to be our first jigit; he has killed many Russians. He used to be rich. He had three wives and eight sons. All lived in one village. The Russians came, destroyed his village, and killed seven of his sons. One son was left, and surrendered to the Russians. The old man went and gave himself up to the Russians also. He lived among them three months, found his son, killed him with his own hand, and escaped. Since that time he has stopped fighting. He went to Mecca to pray to God, and that's why he wears a turban. Whoever has been to Mecca is called a hadji, and wears a chalma. But he does not love you Russians. He has bade me kill you, but I don't intend to kill you. I have paid out money for you, and besides, Ivan, I have come to like you. And so far from wishing to kill you, I would rather not let you go from me at all, if I had not given my word."

He laughed, and began to repeat in broken Russian:—

"*Tvoya Ivan, khorosh, moya, Abdul, khorosh*—Ivan, you good; Abdul, me good."

4

Thus Zhilin lived a month. In the daytime he walked about the aul or did some handiwork, but when night came, and it grew quiet in the aul, he burrowed in his shed. It was hard work digging because of the stones, and he sometimes had to use his file on them; and thus he dug a hole under the wall big enough to crawl through.

"Only," he thought, "I must know the region a little first, so as to escape in the right direction. And the Tartars wouldn't tell me anything."

He chose a time when his master was absent, then he went after dinner behind the aul to a mountain. His idea was to reconnoiter the country.

Now when Abdul went away he commanded his little son to follow Zhilin, and not take his eyes from him. The little fellow tagged after Zhilin, and kept crying:—

"Don't go there. Father won't allow it. I will call the men if you go!"

Zhilin began to reason with him.

"I am not going far," says he, "only to that hill; I want to find some herbs so as to cure your people. Come with me; I can't run away with this clog. If you will I will make you a bow and arrows to-morrow."

He persuaded the lad, they went together. To look at, the mountain was not far, but it was hard work with the clog; he went a little distance at a time, pulling himself up by main strength.

Zhilin sat down on the summit, and began to survey the ground.

To the south behind the shed lay a valley through which a herd was grazing, and another aul was in sight at the foot of it. Back of the village was another mountain still steeper, and back of that still another. Between the mountains lay a further stretch of forest, and then still other mountains rising ever higher and higher. And higher than all, stood snow-capped peaks white as sugar, and one snowy peak rose like a dome above them all.

To the east and west also were mountains. In every direction the smoke of auls was to be seen in the ravines.

"Well," he said to himself, "this is all their country."

He began to look in the direction of the Russian possessions. At his very feet was a little river, his aul surrounded by gardens. By the river some women, no larger in appearance than little dolls, were standing and washing. Behind the aul was a lower mountain, and beyond it two other mountains covered with forests. And between the two mountains a plain stretched far, far away in the blue distance; and on the plain lay what seemed like smoke.

Zhilin tried to remember in what direction, when he lived at home in the fortress, the sun used to rise, and where it set. He looked.

"Just about there," says he, "in that valley, our fortress ought to be. There, between those two mountains, I must make my escape."

The little sun began to slope toward the west. The snowy mountains changed from white to purple; the wooded mountains grew dark; a mist arose from the valley; and the valley itself, where the Russian fortress must be, glowed in the sunset as if it were on fire. Zhilin strained his gaze. Something seemed to hang waving in the air, like smoke arising from chimneys.

And so it seemed to him that it must be from the fortress itself,—the Russian fortress.

It was already growing late. The voice of the mulla calling to prayer was heard. The herds began to return; the kine were lowing. The little lad kept repeating, "Let us go!" but Zhilin could not tear himself away.

They returned home.

"Well," thinks Zhilin, "now I know the place; I must make my escape."

He proposed to make his escape that very night. The nights were dark; it was the wane of the moon.

Unfortunately the Tartars returned in the evening. Usually they came in

272 A PRISONER IN THE CAUCASUS

driving the cattle with them, and came in hilarious. But this time they had no
cattle; but they brought a Tartar, dead, on his saddle. It was the red-headed
Tartar's brother who had been killed. They rode in solemnly, and all collected
for the burial.

Zhilin also went out to look.

They did not put the dead body in a coffin, but wrapped it in linen, and
placed it under a plane tree behind the village, where it lay on the sward.

The mulla came; the old men gathered together, their caps bound around
with towels. They took off their shoes, and sat in rows on their heels before
the dead.

In front was the mulla, behind him three old men in turbans, and behind
them the rest of the Tartars. They sat there, with their heads bent low and
kept silence. Long they kept silence. The mulla lifted his head and said:
"Allah!" (That means God.) He said this one word, and again they hung their
heads, and were silent a long time; they sat motionless.

Again the mulla lifted his head, saying, "Allah!" and all repeated it after
him:—

"Allah!"

Then silence again.

The dead man lay on the sward; he was motionless, and they sat as if they
were dead. Not one made a motion. The only sound was the rustling of
the foliage of the plane tree, stirred by the breeze.

Then the mulla offered a prayer. All got to their feet; they took the dead
body in their arms, and carried it away.

They brought it to a pit. The pit was not a mere hole, but was hollowed out
under the earth like a cellar.

They took the body under the armpits and by the legs, doubled it up, and
let it down gently, shoved it forcibly under the ground, and laid the arms along
the belly. The Nogayets brought a green osier. They laid it in the pit; then
they quickly filled it up with earth, and over the dead man's head they placed
a gravestone. They smoothed the earth over, and again sat around the grave
in rows. There was a long silence.

"Allah! Allah! Allah!"

They sighed and got up.

The red-bearded Tartar gave money to the old men, then he got up, struck
his forehead three times with a whip, and went home.

The next morning Zhilin saw the red-haired Tartar leading a mare through
the village, and three Tartars following him. They went behind the village.
Kazi Muhamet took off his beshmet, rolled up his sleeves,—his hands were
powerful,—took out his dagger, and sharpened it on a whetstone. The Tartars
held back the mare's head. Kazi Muhamet approached, and cut the throat;
then, he turned the animal over, and began to flay it, pulling away the hide
with his mighty fists.

The women and maidens came, and began to wash the intestines and the
viscera. Then they cut up the mare, and carried the meat to the hut. And
the whole village collected at the Kazi Muhamet's to celebrate the dead.

For three days they feasted on the mare and drank buza, and they celebrated
the dead. All the Tartars were at home.

On the fourth day about noon, Zhilin saw that they were collecting for some expedition. Their horses were brought out. They put on their gear, and started off, ten men of them, under the command of the red-headed Tartar; only Abdul stayed at home. There was a new moon, but the nights were still dark.

"Now," said Zhilin to himself, "we must escape today." And he told Kostuilin.

But Kostuilin was afraid. "How can we escape? We don't know the way."

"I know the way."

"But we should not get there during the night."

"Well, if we don't get there we will spend the night in the woods. I have some cakes. What are you going to do? It will be all right if they send you the money, but you see, your friends may not collect so much. And the Tartars are angry now because the Russians have killed one of their men. They say they are thinking of killing us."

Kostuilin thought and thought. "All right, let us go!"

5

Zhilin crept down into his hole, and widened it so that Kostuilin also could get through, and then they sat and waited till all should be quiet in the aul.

As soon as the people were quiet in the aul, Zhilin crept under the wall, and came out on the other side. He whispered to Kostuilin:—

"Crawl under."

Kostuilin also crept under, but in doing so he hit a stone with his leg, and it made a noise.

Now, the master had a brindled dog as a watch,—a most ferocious animal; they called him Ulyashin.

Zhilin had been in the habit of feeding him. Ulyashin heard the noise, and began to bark and jump about, and the other dogs joined in.

Zhilin gave a little whistle, threw him a piece of cake. Ulyashin recognized him, began to wag his tail, and ceased barking.

Abdul had heard the disturbance, and cried from within the saklia:—

"Haït! haït! Ulyashin."

But Zhilin scratched the dog behind the ears. The dog made no more sound, rubbed against his legs, and wagged his tail.

They waited behind the corner.

All became silent again; the only sound was the bleating of a sheep in the fold, and far below them the water roaring over the boulders.

It was dark, but the sky was studded with stars. Over the mountain the young moon hung red, with its horns turned upward.

In the valleys a mist was rising, white as milk. Zhilin started up, and said to his comrade, "Well, brother, aï-da!"

They set out again.

But as they got under way, they heard the call of the mulla on the minaret:—

"Allah! Bis'm Allah! el Rakhman!"

"That means, the people will be going to the mosque."

Again they sat down and hid under the wall.

They sat there long, waiting until the people should pass. Again it grew still.

"Now God be with us!"

They crossed themselves, and started.

They went across the dvor, and down the steep bank to the stream, crossed the stream, and proceeded along the valley. The mist was thick, and closed in all around them, but above their heads the stars could still be seen.

Zhilin used the stars to guide him which way to go. It was cool in the mist, it was easy walking, only their boots were troublesome,—they were worn at the heels. Zhilin took his off, threw them away, and walked barefoot. He sprang from stone to stone, and kept glancing at the stars.

Kostuilin began to grow weary.

"Go slower," said he; "my boots chafe me, my whole foot is raw."

"Then take them off, it will be easier."

Kostuilin began to go barefoot, but that was still worse; he kept scraping his feet on the stones and having to stop.

Zhilin said to him:—

"You may cut your feet, but you will save your life; but if you are caught they will kill you, which would be worse."

Kostuilin said nothing, but crept along, groaning. For a long time they went down the valley. Suddenly they heard dogs barking at the right. Zhilin halted, looked around, climbed up the bank, and felt about with his hands.

"Ekh!" said he, "we have made a mistake; we have gone too far to the right. Here is a strange aul. I could see it from the hill. We must go back to the left, up the mountain. There must be a forest there."

But Kostuilin objected:—

"Just wait a little while, let us get breath. My feet are all blood."

"Eh, brother! they will get well. You should walk more lightly. This way."

And Zhilin turned back toward the left, and uphill toward the forest.

Kostuilin kept halting and groaning. Zhilin tried to hush him up, and still hastened on.

They climbed the mountain. And there they found the forest. They entered it; their clothes were all torn to pieces on the thorns. They found a little path through the woods. They walked along it.

"Halt!"

There was the sound of hoofs on the path. They stopped to listen. It sounded like the tramping of a horse: then it also stopped. They set out once more; again the tramping hoofs. When they stopped, it stopped.

Zhilin crept ahead, and investigated a light spot on the path.

Something was standing there. Whether it was a horse or not, on it there was something strange, not at all like a man.

It snorted—plainly!

"What a strange thing!"

Zhilin gave a slight whistle. There was a dash of feet from the path into the forest, a crackling in the underbrush, and something rushed along like a hurricane, with a crashing of dry boughs.

Kostuilin almost fell to the ground in fright. But Zhilin laughed, and said:—

"That was a stag. Do you hear how it crashes through the woods with its horns? We were afraid of him, and he is afraid of us."

They went on their way. Already the Great Bear was beginning to set: the dawn was not distant. And they were in doubt whether they should come out right or not. Zhilin was inclined to think that they were on the right track, and that it would be about ten versts farther before they reached the Russian fortress, but there was no certain guide; you could not tell in the night.

They came to a little clearing. Kostuilin sat down and said:—

"Do as you please, but I will not go any farther; my legs won't carry me." Zhilin tried to persuade him.

"No," said he, "I won't go, I can't go."

Zhilin grew angry; he threatened him, he scolded him.

"Then I will go on without you. Good-by!"

Kostuilin jumped up and followed. They went four versts farther. The fog began to grow thicker in the forest. Nothing could be seen before them; the stars were barely visible.

Suddenly they heard the tramping of a horse just in front of them; they could hear his shoes striking on the stones.

Zhilin threw himself down on his belly, and tried to listen by laying his ear to the ground.

"Yes, it is,—it is some one on horseback coming in our direction."

They slipped off to one side of the road, crouched down in the bushes, and waited. Zhilin crept close to the path, and looked.

He saw a mounted Tartar riding along, driving a cow, and muttering to himself. When the Tartar had ridden by, Zhilin returned to Kostuilin.

"Well, God has saved us. Up with you! Come along!"

Kostuilin tried to rise, and fell back.

"I can't; by God, I can't. My strength is all gone."

The man was staggered, and was bloated, and the sweat poured from him; and as they were caught in the forest in the midst of the cold fog, and his feet were torn, he lost all courage. Zhilin tried to lift him by main force. Then Kostuilin cried:—

"Aï! it hurts."

Zhilin was frightened to death.

"What are you screaming for? Don't you know that Tartar is near? He will hear you." But he said to himself, "Now, if he is really played out, what can I do with him? I can't abandon a comrade. Now," says he, "get up; climb on my back. I will carry you if you can't walk any longer." He took Kostuilin on his shoulders, holding him by the thighs, and went along the path with his burden. "Only," says he, "don't put your hands on my throat, for Christ's sake! Hold on by my shoulders."

It was hard for Zhilin. His feet were also bloody, and he was weary. He stopped, and made it a little easier for himself by setting Kostuilin down, and getting him higher up on his shoulders. Then he went on again.

Evidently the Tartar had heard Kostuilin scream. Zhilin caught the sound of some one following them, and shouting in his language. Zhilin hid among the bushes. The Tartar aimed his gun; he fired it off but missed; began to whine in his native tongue, and galloped up the path.

"Well," said Zhilin, "we are lost, brother. The dog . . . he will be right back with a band of Tartars on our track. . . . If we don't succeed in putting three versts between us, we are lost." And he thinks to himself, "The devil take it, that I had to bring this clod along with me! Alone, I should have got there long ago."

Kostuilin said:—

"Go alone. Why should you be lost on my account?"

"No, I will not go; it would not do to abandon a comrade."

He lifted him again on his shoulders, and started on. Thus he made a verst. It was forest all the way, and no sign of outlet. But the fog was now beginning to lift, and seemed to be floating away in little clouds; not a star was any longer to be seen. Zhilin was tired out.

A little spring gushed out by the road; it was walled in with stones. There he stopped, and dropped Kostuilin.

"Let me rest a little," said he, "and get a drink. We will eat our cakes. It can't be very far now."

He had just stretched himself out to drink, when the sound of hoofs was heard behind them. Again they hid in the bushes at the right under the crest, and crouched down.

They heard Tartar voices. The Tartars stopped at the very spot where they had turned in from the road. After discussing awhile, they seemed to be setting dogs on the scent.

The refugees heard the sound of a crashing through the bushes; a strange dog came directly to them. He stopped and barked.

The Tartars followed on their track. They also were strangers.

They seized them, bound them, lifted them on horses, and carried them off.

After they had ridden three versts, Abdul, their master, with two Tartars, met them. He said something to their new captors. They were transferred to Abdul's horses, and were brought back to the aul.

Abdul was no longer grinning, and he said not a word to them.

They reached the village at daybreak; the prisoners were left in the street. The children gathered around them, tormenting them with stones and whips, and howling.

The Tartars gathered around them in a circle, and the old man from the mountain was among them. They began to discuss. Zhilin made out that they were deciding on what should be done with them. Some said that they ought to be sent farther into the mountains, but the old man declared that they must be killed. Abdul argued against it.

"I have paid out money for them," said he. "I shall get a ransom for them."

But the old man said:—

"They won't pay anything; they will only be an injury to us. And it is a sin to feed Russians. Kill them, and that is the end of it."

They separated. Abdul came to Zhilin, and reported the decision.

"If," says he, "the ransom is not sent in two weeks, I will flog you. And if you try to run away again, I will kill you like a dog. Write your letter, and write it good!"

Paper was brought them; they wrote their letters. Clogs were put on their feet again; they were taken behind the mosque. There was a pit twelve feet deep, and they were thrust down into this pit.

6

Life was made utterly wretched for them. Their clogs were not taken off even at night, and they were not let out at all.

Unbaked dough was thrown down to them as if they were dogs, and water was let down in a jug. In the pit it was damp and suffocating.

Kostuilin became ill, and swelled up, and had rheumatism all over his body, and he groaned or slept all the time.

Even Zhilin lost his spirits; he saw that they were in desperate straits. And he did not know how to get out of it.

He had begun to make an excavation, but there was nowhere to hide the earth; Abdul discovered it, and threatened to kill him.

He was squatting down one time in the pit, and thinking about liberty, and he grew sad.

Suddenly a cake fell directly into his lap, then another, and some cherries followed.

He looked up, and there was Dina. She peered down at him, laughed, and then ran away. And Zhilin began to conjecture, "Couldn't Dina help me?"

He cleared out a little place in the pit, picked up some clay, and made some dolls. He made men and women, horses and dogs; he said to himself:—

"When Dina comes, I will toss them up to her."

But Dina did not make her appearance on the next day. And Zhilin heard the trampling of horses' hoofs; men came riding up; the Tartars collected at the mosque, arguing, shouting, and talking about the Russians.

And he also heard the voice of the old man. Zhilin could not understand very well, but he gathered that the Russians were somewhere near, and the Tartars were afraid that they would attack the aul, and they did not know what to do with the prisoners.

They talked awhile, and went away.

Suddenly Zhilin heard a rustling at the edge of the pit.

He saw Dina squatting on her heels, with her knees higher than her head; she leaned over, her necklace hung down, and swung over the pit. And her little eyes twinkled like stars. She took from her sleeve two cheese-cakes, and threw them down to him. Zhilin accepted them, and said:—

"Why did you stay away so long? I have been making you some dolls. Here they are."

He began to toss them up to her, one at a time.

But she shook her head, and would not look at them. "I can't take them," said she. She was silent for a while, but sat there; then she said, "Ivan, they want to kill you."

She made a significant motion across her throat.

"Who wants to kill me?"

"Father. The old men have ordered him to. But I am sorry for you."

And Zhilin said:—

"Well, then, if you are sorry for me, bring me a long pole."

She shook her head, meaning that it was impossible.

He clasped his hands in supplication to her.

"Dina, please! Bring one to me, Dinushka!"

278 A PRISONER IN THE CAUCASUS

"I can't," said she. "They would see me; they are all at home."

And she ran away.

Afterward, Zhilin was sitting there in the evening, and wondering what was going to happen. He kept looking up. He could see the stars, but the moon had not yet risen. The mulla uttered his call, then all became silent.

Zhilin began already to doze, thinking to himself, "The little maid is afraid."

Suddenly a piece of clay fell on his head; he glanced up; a long pole was sliding over the edge of the pit, it slid out, began to descend toward him, it reached the bottom of the pit. Zhilin was delighted. He seized it, pulled it along,—it was a strong pole. He had noticed it before on his master's roof.

He gazed up; the stars were shining high in the heavens, and Dina's eyes, at the edge of the pit, gleamed in the darkness like a cat's.

She craned her head over, and whispered, "Ivan, Ivan." And she waved her hands before her face, meaning, "Softly, please."

"What is it?" said Zhilin.

"All have gone, there are only two at home."

And Zhilin said:—

"Well, Kostuilin, let us go, let us make our last attempt. I will help you."

Kostuilin, however, would not hear to it.

"No," says he, "it is not meant for me to get away from here. How could I go when I haven't even strength to turn over?"

"All right, then. Good-by. Don't think me unkind."

He kissed Kostuilin.

He clasped the pole, told Dina to hold it firmly, and tried to climb up. Twice he fell back,—his clog so impeded him. Kostuilin pushed him from below; he managed to get to the top; Dina pulled on the sleeves of his shirt with all her might, laughing heartily.

Zhilin pulled up the pole, and said:—

"Carry it back to its place, Dina, for if they found it they would flog you."

She dragged off the pole, and Zhilin began to go down the mountain. When he had reached the bottom of the cliff he took a sharp stone and tried to break the padlock of his clog. But the lock was strong; he could not strike it fairly.

He heard some one hurrying down the hill, with light, skipping steps. He said to himself:—

"That is probably Dina again."

Dina ran to him, took a stone, and said:—

"*Daï ya.*—Let me try it."

She knelt down, and began to work with all her might. But her hands were as delicate as osiers. She had no strength. She threw down the stone, and burst into tears.

Zhilin again tried to break the lock, and Dina squatted by his side, and leaned against his shoulder. Zhilin glanced up, and saw at the left behind the mountain a red glow like a fire; it was the moon just rising.

"Well," he said to himself, "I must cross the valley and get into the woods before the moon rises." He stood up and threw away the stone. He would have to go as he was, even with the clog.

"Good-by," says he. "Dinushka, I shall always remember you."

Dina clung to him; searched with her hands for a place to stow away some cakes. He took the cakes.

"Thank you," said he; "you are a thoughtful darling. Who will make you dolls after I am gone?" and he stroked her hair.

Dina burst into tears, hid her face in her hands, and scrambled up the hillside like a kid. He could hear, in the darkness, the jingling of the coins on her braids.

Zhilin crossed himself, picked up the lock of his clog so that it might not make a noise, and started on his way, dragging his leg all the time, and keeping his eyes all the time on the glow where the moon was rising.

He knew the way. He had eight versts to go in a direct course, but he would have to strike into the forest before the moon became entirely visible. He crossed the stream, and now the light was increasing behind the mountain.

He proceeded down the valley; and as he walked along, he kept glancing around; still the moon was not visible. The glow was now changing to white light, and one side of the valley grew brighter and brighter. The shadow kept creeping nearer and nearer to the mountain, till it reached its very foot.

Zhilin still hurried along, all the time keeping in the shadow.

He hurried as fast as he could, but the moon rose still faster; and now, at the right, the mountain tops began to be illuminated.

He struck into the forest just as the moon rose above the mountains. It became as light and white as day. On the trees all the leaves were visible. It was warm and bright on the mountain side; everything seemed as if it were dead. The only sound was the roaring of a torrent far below. He walked along in the forest and met no one. Zhilin found a little spot in the forest where it was still darker, and sat down to rest.

While he rested he ate one of his cakes. He procured a stone and once more tried to break the padlock, but he only bruised his hands, and failed to break the lock.

He arose and went on his way. When he had gone a verst his strength gave out, his sore feet tortured him. He had to walk ten steps at a time and then stop.

"There's nothing to be done for it," says he to himself. "I will push on as long as my strength holds out; for if I sit down, then I shall not get up again. If I do not reach the fortress before it is daylight, then I will lie down in the woods and spend the day, and start on to-morrow night again."

He walked all night. Once he passed two Tartars on horseback, but he heard them at some distance, and hid behind a tree.

Already the moon was beginning to pale, the dew had fallen, it was near dawn, and Zhilin had not reached the end of the forest.

"Well," said he to himself, "I will go thirty steps farther, strike into the forest, and sit down."

He went thirty steps, and saw the end of the forest. He went to the edge; it was broad daylight. Before him, as on the palm of his hand, were the steppe and the fortress; and on the left, not far away on the mountain side, fires were burning, or dying out; the smoke rose, and men were moving around the watch-fires.

He looked, and saw the gleaming of firearms; Cossacks, soldiers!

Zhilin was overjoyed.

He gathered his remaining strength, and walked down the mountain. And he said to himself:—

"God help me, if a mounted Tartar should get sight of me on this bare field! I should not escape him, even though I am so near."

Even while these thoughts were passing through his mind, he saw at the left, on a hillock not fourteen hundred feet away, three Tartars on the watch. They caught sight of him—bore down upon him. Then his heart failed within him. Waving his arms, he shouted at the top of his voice:—

"Brothers! help, brothers!"

Our men heard him—mounted Cossacks dashed out toward him. They spurred their horses so as to outstrip the Tartars.

The Cossacks were far off, the Tartars near. And now Zhilin collected his last remaining energies, seized his clog in his hand, ran toward the Cossacks, and, without any consciousness of feeling, crossed himself and cried, "Brothers, brothers, brothers!"

The Cossacks were fifteen in number.

The Tartars were dismayed. Before they reached him, they stopped short. And Zhilin was running toward the Cossacks.

The Cossacks surrounded him, and questioned him: "Who are you?" "What is your name?" "Where did you come from?"

But Zhilin was almost beside himself; he wept, and kept shouting, "Brothers, brothers!"

The soldiers hastened up, and gathered around him; one brought him bread, another kasha-gruel, another vodka, another threw a cloak around him, still another broke off his clog.

The officers recognized him, they brought him into the fortress. The soldiers were delighted, his comrades pressed into Zhilin's room.

Zhilin told them what had happened to him, and he ended his tale with the words:—

"That's the way I went home and got married! No, I see such is not to be my fate."

And he remained in the service in the Caucasus.

At the end of a month Kostuilin was ransomed for five thousand rubles. He was brought home scarcely alive.

c. 1872

WHAT MEN LIVE BY

"We know that we have passed out of death into life, because we love the brethren. He that loveth not abideth in death."—1 EPISTLE OF ST. JOHN, iii. 14.

"But whoso hath the world's goods, and beholdeth his brother in need, and shutteth up his compassion from him, how doth the love of God abide in him?

"My little children, let us not love in word, neither with the tongue, but in deed and truth."—iii. 17, 18.

"Love is of God; and every one that loveth is begotten of God and knoweth God.

"He that loveth not knoweth not God; for God is love." —iv 7,8.

"No man hath beheld God at any time: if we love one another, God abideth in us."—iv. 12.

"God is love; and he that abideth in love abideth in God, and God abideth in him."—iv. 16.

"If a man say, I love God, and hateth his brother, he is a liar; for he that loveth not his brother whom he hath seen cannot love God whom he hath not seen."—iv. 20.

1

A cobbler and his wife and children had lodgings with a peasant. He owned neither house nor land, and he supported himself and his family by shoemaking.

Bread was dear and labor was poorly paid, and whatever he earned went for food.

The cobbler and his wife had one shuba[1] between them, and this had come to tatters, and for two years the cobbler had been hoarding in order to buy sheepskins for a new shuba.

When autumn came, the cobbler's hoard had grown; three paper rubles lay in his wife's box, and five rubles and twenty kopeks more were due the cobbler from his customers.

One morning the cobbler betook himself to the village to get his new shuba. He put on his wife's wadded nankeen jacket over his shirt, and outside of all a woolen kaftan. He put the three-ruble note in his pocket, broke off a staff, and after breakfast he set forth.

He said to himself:—

"I will get my five rubles from the peasant, and that with these three will buy pelts for my shuba."

The cobbler reached the village and went to one peasant's; he was not at home, but his wife promised to send her husband with the money the next week, but she could not give him any money. He went to another, and this peasant swore that he had no money at all; but he paid him twenty kopeks for cobbling his boots.

The cobbler made up his mind to get the pelts on credit. But the fur-dealer refused to sell on credit.

"Bring the money," said he; "then you can make your choice; but we know how hard it is to get what is one's due."

And so the cobbler did not do his errand, but he had the twenty kopeks for cobbling the boots, and he took from a peasant an old pair of felt boots to mend with leather.

At first the cobbler was vexed at heart; then he spent the twenty kopeks for vodka, and started to go home. In the morning he had felt cold, but after having drunk the brandy he was warm enough even without the shuba.

The cobbler was walking along the road, striking the frozen ground with the

[1] Fur or sheepskin outside garment.

staff which he had in one hand, and swinging the felt boots in the other, and thus he talked to himself:—

"I am warm even without a shuba," said he. "I drank a glass, and it dances through all my veins. And so I don't need a sheepskin coat. I walk along, and all my vexation is forgotten. What a fine fellow I am! What do I need? I can get along without the shuba. I don't need it at all. There's one thing: the wife will feel bad. Indeed, it is too bad; here I have been working for it, and now to have missed it! You just wait now! if you don't bring the money, I will take your hat, I vow I will! What a way of doing things! He pays me twenty kopeks at a time! Now what can you do with twenty kopeks? Get a drink; that's all! You say, 'I am poor!' But if you are poor, how is it with me? You have a house and cattle and everything; I have nothing but my own hands. You raise your own grain, but I have to buy mine, when I can, and it costs me three rubles a week for food alone. When I get home now, we shall be out of bread. Another ruble and a half of outgo! So you must give me what you owe me."

By this time the cobbler had reached the chapel at the cross-roads, and he saw something white behind the chapel.

It was already twilight, and the cobbler strained his eyes, but he could not make out what the object was.

"There never was any such stone there," he said to himself. "A cow? But it does not look like a cow! The head is like a man's; but what is that white? And why should there be any man there?"

He went nearer. Now he could see plainly. What a strange thing! It was indeed a man, but was he alive or dead? sitting there stark naked, leaning against the chapel, and not moving.

The cobbler was frightened. He said to himself:—

"Some one has killed that man, stripped him, and flung him down there. If I go near, I may get into trouble."

And the cobbler hurried by.

In passing the chapel he could no longer see the man; but after he was fairly beyond it, he looked back, and saw that the man was no longer leaning against the chapel, but was moving, and apparently looking after him.

The cobbler was still more scared by this, and he said to himself:—

"Shall I go back to him or go on? If I go back to him, there might something unpleasant happen; who knows what sort of a man he is? He can't have gone there for any good purpose. If I went to him, he might spring on me and choke me, and I could not get away from him; and even if he did not choke me, why should I try to make his acquaintance? What could be done with him, naked as he is? I can't take him with me, and give him my own clothes! That would be absurd."

And the cobbler hastened his steps. He had already gone some distance beyond the chapel, when his conscience began to prick him.

He stopped short.

"What is this that you are doing, Semyon?" he asked himself. "A man is perishing of cold, and you are frightened, and hurry by! Are you so very rich? Are you afraid of losing your money? Aï, Sema! That is not right!"

Semyon turned and went back to the man.

2

Semyon went back to the man, looked at him, and saw that it was a young man in the prime of life; there were no bruises visible on him, but he was evidently freezing and afraid; he was sitting there, leaning back, and he did not look at Semyon; apparently he was so weak that he could not lift his eyes.

Semyon went up close to him, and suddenly the man seemed to revive; he lifted his head and fastened his eyes on Semyon.

And by this glance the man won Semyon's heart.

He threw the felt boots down on the ground, took off his belt and laid it on the boots, and pulled off his kaftan.

"There's nothing to be said," he exclaimed. "Put these on! There now!"

Semyon put his hand under the man's elbow, to help him, and tried to lift him. The man got up.

And Semyon saw that his body was graceful and clean, that his hands and feet were comely, and that his face was agreeable. Semyon threw the kaftan over his shoulders. He could not get his arms into the sleeves. Semyon found the place for him, pulled the coat up, wrapped it around him, and fastened the belt.

He took off his tattered cap, and was going to give it to the stranger, but his head felt cold, and he said to himself:—

"The whole top of my head is bald, but he has long curly hair."

So he put his hat on again.

"I had better let him put on my boots."

He made him sit down and put the felt boots on him.

After the cobbler had thus dressed him, he says: "There now, brother, just stir about, and you will get warmed up. All these things are in other hands than ours. Can you walk?"

The man stood up, looked affectionately at Semyon, but was unable to speak a word.

"Why don't you say something? We can't spend the winter here. We must get to shelter. Now, then, lean on my stick, if you don't feel strong enough. Bestir yourself!"

And the man started to move. And he walked easily, and did not lag behind. As they walked along the road Semyon said:—

"Where are you from, if I may ask?"

"I do not belong hereabouts."

"No; I know all the people of this region. How did you happen to come here and get to that chapel?"

"I cannot tell you."

"Some one must have treated you outrageously."

"No one has treated me outrageously. God has punished me."

"God does all things, but you must have been on the road bound for somewhere. Where do you want to go?"

"It makes no difference to me."

Semyon was surprised. The man did not look like a malefactor, and his speech was gentle, but he seemed reticent about himself.

And Semyon said to himself:—

"Such things as this do not happen every day." And he said to the man, "Well, come to my house, though you will find it very narrow quarters."

As Semyon approached the yard, the stranger did not lag behind, but walked abreast of him. The wind had arisen, and searched under Semyon's shirt, and as the effect of the wine had now passed away, he began to be chilled to the bone. He walked along, and began to snuffle, and he muffled his wife's jacket closer around him, and he said to himself:—

"That's the way you get a shuba! You go after a shuba, and you come home without your kaftan! yes, and you bring with you a naked man—besides, Matriona won't take kindly to it!"

And as soon as the thought of Matriona occurred to him, he began to feel downhearted.

But as soon as his eyes fell on the stranger, he remembered what a look he had given him behind the chapel, and his heart danced with joy.

3

Semyon's wife had finished her work early. She had chopped wood, brought water, fed the children, taken her own supper, and was now deliberating when it would be best to mix some bread, "to-day or to-morrow?"

A large crust was still left. She said to herself:—

"If Semyon gets something to eat in town, he won't care for much supper, and the bread will last till to-morrow."

Matriona contemplated the crust for some time, and said:—

"I am not going to mix any bread. There's just enough flour to make one more loaf. We shall get along till Friday."

Matriona put away the bread, and sat down at the table to sew a patch on her husband's shirt.

She sewed, and thought how her husband would be buying sheepskins for the shuba.

"I hope the fur-dealer will not cheat him. For he is as simple as he can be. He, himself, would not cheat anybody, but a baby could lead him by the nose. Eight rubles is no small sum. You can get a fine shuba with it. Perhaps not one tanned, but still a good one. How we suffered last winter without any shuba! Could not go to the river nor anywhere! And whenever he went out-doors, he put on all the clothes, and I hadn't anything to wear. He is late in getting home. He ought to be here by this time. Can my sweetheart have got drunk?"

Just as these thoughts were passing through her mind the door-steps creaked: some one was at the door. Matriona stuck in the needle, and went to the entry. There she saw that two men had come in,—Semyon, and with him a strange peasant, without a cap and in felt boots.

Matriona perceived immediately that her husband's breath smelt of liquor.

"Now," she said to herself, "he has gone and got drunk."

And when she saw that he had not his kaftan on, and wore only her jacket, and had nothing in his hands, and said nothing, but only simpered, Matriona's heart failed within her.

"He has drunk up the money, he has been on a spree with this miserable beggar; and, worse than all, he has gone and brought him home!"

Matriona let them pass by her into the cottage; then she herself went in; she saw that the stranger was young, and that he had on their kaftan. There was no shirt to be seen under the kaftan; and he wore no cap.

As soon as he went in, he paused, and did not move and did not raise his eyes.

And Matriona thought:—

"He is not a good man; his conscience troubles him."

Matriona scowled, went to the oven, and watched to see what they would do. Semyon took off his cap and sat down on the bench good-naturedly.

"Well," said he, "Matriona, can't you get us something to eat?"

Matriona muttered something under her breath.

She did not offer to move, but as she stood by the oven she looked from one to the other and kept shaking her head.

Semyon saw that his wife was out of sorts and would not do anything, but he pretended not to notice it, and took the stranger by the arm.

"Sit down, brother," says he; "we'll have some supper."

The stranger sat down on the bench.

"Well," says Semyon, "haven't you cooked anything?"

Matriona's anger blazed out.

"I cooked," said she, "but not for you. You are a fine man! I see you have been drinking! You went to get a shuba, and you have come home without your kaftan. And, then, you have brought home this naked vagabond with you. I haven't any supper for such drunkards as you are!"

"That'll do, Matriona; what is the use of letting your tongue run on so? If you had only asked first: 'What kind of a man . . .'"

"You just tell me what you have done with the money!"

Semyon went to his kaftan, took out the bill, and spread it out.

"Here's the money, but Trifonof did not pay me; he promised it to-morrow."

Matriona grew still more angry:—

"You didn't buy the new shuba, and you have given away your only kaftan to this naked vagabond whom you have brought home!"

She snatched the money from the table, and went off to hide it away, saying:—

"I haven't any supper. I can't feed all your drunken beggars!"

"Hey there! Matriona, just hold your tongue! First you listen to what I have to say . . ."

"Much sense should I hear from a drunken fool! Good reason I had for not wanting to marry such a drunkard as you are. Mother gave me linen, and you have wasted it in drink; you went to get a shuba, and you spent it for drink."

Semyon was going to assure his wife that he had spent only twenty kopeks for drink; he was going to tell her where he had found the man; but Matriona would not give him a chance to speak a word; it was perfectly marvelous, but she managed to speak two words at once! Things that had taken place ten years before—she called them all up.

Matriona scolded and scolded; then she sprang at Semyon, and seized him by the sleeve.

"Give me back my jacket! It's the only one I have, and you took it from me and put it on yourself. Give it here, you miserable dog! bestir yourself, you villain!"

Semyon began to strip off the jacket. As he was pulling his arms out of the sleeves, his wife gave it a twitch and split the jacket up the seams. Matriona snatched the garment away, threw it over her head, and started for the door. She intended to go out, but she paused, and her heart was pulled in two directions,—she wanted to vent her spite, and she wanted to find what kind of a man the stranger was.

4

Matriona paused, and said:—

"If he were a good man, then he would not have been naked; why, even now, he hasn't any shirt on; if he had been engaged in decent business, you would have told where you discovered such an elegant fellow!"

"Well, I was going to tell you. I was walking along, and there, behind the chapel, this man was sitting, stark naked, and half frozen to death. It is not summer, mind you, for a naked man! God brought me to him, else he would have perished. Now what could I do? Such things don't happen every day. I took and dressed him, and brought him home with me. Calm your anger. It's a sin, Matriona; we must all die."

Matriona was about to make a surly reply, but her eyes fell on the stranger, and she held her peace.

The stranger was sitting motionless on the edge of the bench, just as he had sat down. His hands were folded on his knees, his head was bent on his breast, his eyes were shut, and he kept frowning, as if something stifled him.

Matriona made no reply.

Semyon went on to say:—

"Matriona, can it be that God is not in you?"

Matriona heard his words, and glanced again at the stranger, and suddenly her anger vanished. She turned from the door, went to the corner where the oven was, and brought the supper.

She set a bowl on the table, poured out the kvas,[1] and put on the last of the crust. She gave them the knife and the spoons.

"Have some victuals," she said.

Semyon touched the stranger.

"Draw up, young man," said he.

Semyon cut the bread and crumbled it into the bowl, and they began to eat their supper. And Matriona sat at the end of the table, leaned on her hand, and gazed at the stranger. And Matriona began to feel sorry for him, and she took a fancy to him.

And suddenly the stranger brightened up, ceased to frown, lifted his eyes to Matriona, and smiled.

After they had finished their supper, the woman cleared off the things, and began to question the stranger:—

"Where are you from?"

"I do not belong hereabouts."

---

[1] Fermented drink made of rye meal or soaked bread-crumbs.

"How did you happen to get into this road?"

"I cannot tell you."

"Who maltreated you?"

"God punished me."

"And you were lying there stripped?"

"Yes; there I was lying all naked, freezing to death, when Semyon saw me, had compassion on me, took off his kaftan, put it on me, and bade me come home with him. And here you have fed me, given me something to eat and to drink, and have taken pity on me. May the Lord requite you!"

Matriona got up, took from the window Semyon's old shirt which she had been patching, and gave it to the stranger; then she found a pair of drawers and gave them also to him.

"There now," said she, "I see that you have no shirt. Put these things on, and then lie down wherever you please, in the loft or on the oven."

The stranger took off the kaftan, put on the shirt, and went to bed in the loft. Matriona put out the light, took the kaftan, and lay down beside her husband.

Matriona covered herself up with the skirt of the kaftan, but she lay without sleeping; she could not get the thought of the stranger out of her mind.

When she remembered that he had eaten her last crust, and that there was no bread for the morrow, when she remembered that she had given him the shirt and the drawers, she felt disturbed; but then came the thought of how he had smiled at her, and her heart leaped within her.

Matriona lay a long time without falling asleep, and when she heard that Semyon was also awake, she pulled up the kaftan, and said:—

"Semyon!"

"Ha?"

"You ate up the last of the bread, and I did not mix any more. I don't know how we shall get along to-morrow. Perhaps I might borrow some of neighbor Malanya."

"We shall get along; we shall have enough."

The wife lay without speaking. Then she said:—

"Well, he seems like a good man; but why doesn't he tell us about himself?"

"It must be because he can't."

"Siom!"[1]

"Ha?"

"We are always giving; why doesn't some one give to us?"

Semyon did not know what reply to make. He said:—

"You have talked enough!"

Then he turned over and went to sleep.

5

In the morning Semyon woke up.

His children were still asleep; his wife had gone to a neighbor's to get some bread. The stranger of the evening before, dressed in the old shirt and drawers,

[1] Diminutive of Semyon, or Simon.

was sitting alone on the bench, looking up. And his face was brighter than it had been the evening before. And Semyon said:—

"Well, my dear, the belly asks for bread, and the naked body for clothes. You must earn your own living. What do you know how to do?"

"There is nothing that I know how to do."

Semyon was amazed, and he said:—

"If one has only the mind to, men can learn anything."

"Men work, and I will work."

"What is your name?"

"Mikhaïla."

"Well, Mikhaïla, if you aren't willing to tell about yourself, that is your affair; but you must earn your own living. If you will work as I shall show you, I will keep you."

"The Lord requite you! I am willing to learn; only show me what to do."

Semyon took a thread, drew it through his fingers, and showed him how to make a waxed end.

"It does not take much skill . . . look . . ."

Mikhaïla looked, and then he also twisted the thread between his fingers; he instantly imitated him, and finished the point.

Semyon showed him how to make the welt. This also Mikhaïla immediately understood. The shoemaker likewise showed him how to twist the bristle into the thread, and how to use the awl; and these things also Mikhaïla immediately learned to do.

Whatever part of the work Semyon showed him he imitated him in, and in two days he was able to work as if he had been all his life a cobbler. He worked without relaxation, he ate little, and when his work was done he would sit silent, looking up. He did not go on the street, he spoke no more than was absolutely necessary, he never jested, he never laughed.

The only time that he was seen to smile was on the first evening, when the woman got him his supper.

6

Day after day, week after week, rolled by for a whole year.

Mikhaïla lived on in the same way, working for Semyon. And the fame of Semyon's apprentice went abroad; no one, it was said, could make such neat, strong boots as Semyon's apprentice, Mikhaïla. And from all around people came to Semyon to have boots made, and Semyon began to lay up money.

One winter's day, as Semyon and Mikhaïla were sitting at their work, a sleigh drawn by a troïka drove up to the cottage, with a jingling of bells.

They looked out of the window; the sleigh stopped in front of the cottage; a footman jumped down from the box and opened the door. A barin[1] in a fur coat got out of the sleigh, walked up to Semyon's cottage, and mounted the steps. Matriona hurried to throw the door wide open.

The barin bent his head and entered the cottage; when he drew himself up to his full height, his head almost touched the ceiling; he seemed to take up nearly all the room.

[1] The ordinary title of any landowner or noble.

Semyon rose and bowed; he was surprised to see the barin. He had never before seen such a man.

Semyon himself was thin, the stranger was spare, and Matriona was like a dry chip; but this man seemed to be from a different world. His face was ruddy and full, his neck was like a bull's; it seemed as if he were made out of cast-iron.

The barin got his breath, took off his shuba, sat down on the bench, and said:—

"Which is the master shoemaker?"

Semyon stepped out, saying:—

"I, your honor."

The barin shouted to his footman:—

"Hey, Fedka,[2] bring me the leather."

The young fellow ran out and brought back a parcel. The barin took the parcel and laid it on the table.

"Open it," said he.

The footman opened it.

The barin touched the leather with his finger, and said to Semyon:—

"Now listen, shoemaker. Do you see this leather?"

"I see it, your honor," says he.

"Well, do you appreciate what kind of leather it is?"

Semyon felt of the leather, and said:—

"That's good leather."

"Indeed it's good! Fool that you are! you never in your life saw such before! German leather. It cost twenty rubles."

Semyon was startled. He said:—

"Where, indeed, could we have seen anything like it?"

"Well, that's all right. Can you make from this leather a pair of boots that will fit me?"

"I can, your honor."

The barin shouted at him:—

" 'Can' is a good word. Now just realize whom you are making those boots for, and out of what kind of leather. You must make a pair of boots, so that when the year is gone they won't have got out of shape, or ripped. If you can, then take the job and cut the leather; but if you can't, then don't take it and don't cut the leather. I will tell you beforehand, if the boots rip or wear out of shape before the year is out, I will have you locked up; but if they don't rip or get out of shape before the end of the year, then I will give you ten rubles for your work."

Semyon was frightened, and was at a loss what to say.

He glanced at Mikhaïla. He nudged him with his elbow, and whispered:—

"Had I better take it?"

Mikhaïla nodded his head, meaning:—

"You had better take the job."

Semyon took Mikhaïla's advice; he agreed to make a pair of boots that would not rip or wear out of shape before the year was over.

2 Diminutive of Feodor, Theodore.

The barin shouted to his footman, ordered him to take the boot from his left foot; then he stretched out his leg:—

"Take the measure!"

Semyon cut off a piece of paper seventeen inches long, smoothed it out, knelt down, wiped his hands nicely on his apron, so as not to soil the barin's stockings, and began to take the measure.

Semyon took the measure of the sole, he took the measure of the instep; then he started to measure the calf of the leg, but the paper was not long enough. The leg at the calf was as thick as a beam.

"Look out; don't make it too tight around the calf!"

Semyon was going to cut another piece of paper. The barin sat there, rubbing his toes together in his stockings, and looking at the inmates of the cottage; he caught sight of Mikhaïla.

"Who is that yonder?" he asked; "does he belong to you?"

"He is a master workman. He will make the boots."

"Look here," says the barin to Mikhaïla, "remember that they are to be made so as to last a whole year."

Semyon also looked at Mikhaïla; he saw that Mikhaïla was paying no attention, but was standing in the corner, as if he saw some one there behind the barin. Mikhaïla gazed and gazed, and suddenly smiled, and his whole face lighted up.

"What a fool you are, showing your teeth that way! You had better see to it that the boots are ready in time."

And Mikhaïla replied:—

"They will be ready as soon as they are needed."

"Very well."

The barin drew on his boot, wrapped his shuba round him, and went to the door. But he forgot to stoop, and so struck his head against the lintel.

The barin stormed and rubbed his head; then he got into his sleigh and drove off. After the barin was gone Semyon said:—

"Well, he's as solid as a rock! You could not kill him with a mallet. His head almost broke the door-post, but it did not seem to hurt him much."

And Matriona said:—

"How can they help getting fat, living as they do? Even death does not carry off such a nail as he is."

7

And Semyon said to Mikhaïla:—

"Now, you see, we have taken this work, and we must do it as well as we can. The leather is expensive, and the barin gruff. We must not make any blunder. Now, your eye has become quicker, and your hand is more skilful, than mine; there's the measure. Cut out the leather, and I will be finishing up those vamps."

Mikhaïla did not fail to do as he was told; he took the barin's leather, stretched it out on the table, doubled it over, took the knife, and began to cut.

Matriona came and watched Mikhaïla as he cut, and she was amazed to see what he was doing. For she was used to cobbler's work, and she looked and saw that Mikhaïla was not cutting the leather for boots, but in rounded fashion.

Matriona wanted to speak, but she thought in her own mind:—

"Of course I can't be expected to understand how to make boots for gentlemen; Mikhaïla must understand it better than I do; I will not interfere."

After he had cut out the work, he took his waxed ends and began to sew, not as one does in making boots, with double threads, but with one thread, just as slippers are made.

Matriona wondered at this also, but still she did not like to interfere. And Mikhaïla kept on steadily with his work.

It came time for the nooning; Semyon got up, looked, and saw that Mikhaïla had been making slippers out of the barin's leather. Semyon groaned.

"How is this?" he asked himself. "Mikhaïla has lived with me a whole year, and never made a mistake, and now he has made such a blunder! The barin ordered thick-soled boots, and he has been making slippers without soles! He has ruined the leather. How can I make it right with the barin? We can't find such leather."

And he said to Mikhaïla:—

"What is this you have been doing? . . . My dear fellow, you have ruined me! You know the barin ordered boots, and what have you made?"

He was in the midst of his talk with Mikhaïla when a knock came at the rapper; some one was at the door. They looked out of the window, some one had come on horseback, and was fastening the horse. They opened the door. The same barin's footman came walking in.

"Good-day."

"Good-day to you; what is it?"

"My mistress sent me in regard to a pair of boots."

"What about the boots?"

"It is this. My barin does not need the boots; he has gone from this world."

"What is that you say?"

"He did not live to get home from your house; he died in the sleigh. When the sleigh reached home, we went to help him out, but there he had fallen over like a bag, and there he lay stone dead, and it took all our strength to lift him out of the sleigh. And his lady has sent me, saying: 'Tell the shoemaker of whom your barin just ordered boots from leather which he left with him—tell him that the boots are not needed, and that he is to make a pair of slippers for the corpse out of that leather just as quick as possible.' And I was to wait till they were made, and take them home with me. And so I have come."

Mikhaïla took the rest of the leather from the table and rolled it up; he also took the slippers, which were all done, slapped them together, wiped them with his apron, and gave them to the young man. The young man took them.

"Good-by, friends! Good luck to you!"

8

Still another year, and then two more passed by, and Mikhaïla had now been living five years with Semyon. He lived in just the same way as before. He never went anywhere, he kept his own counsels, and in all that time he smiled only twice,—once when Matriona gave him something to eat, and the other time when he smiled on the barin.

Semyon was more than contented with his workman, and he no longer asked him where he came from; his only fear was lest Mikhaïla should leave him.

One time they were all at home. The mother was putting the iron kettles on the oven, and the children were playing on the benches and looking out of the window. Semyon was pegging away at one window, and Mikhaïla at the other was putting lifts on a heel.

One of the boys ran along the bench toward Mikhaïla, leaned over his shoulder, and looked out of the window.

"Uncle Mikhaïla, just look! a merchant's wife is coming to our house with some little girls. And one of the little girls is a cripple."

The words were scarcely out of the boy's mouth before Mikhaïla threw down his work, leaned over toward the window, and looked out-of-doors. And Semyon was surprised. Never before had Mikhaïla cared to look out, but now his face seemed soldered to the window; he was looking at something very intently.

Semyon also looked out of the window: he saw a woman coming straight through his yard; she was neatly dressed; she had two little girls by the hand; they wore shubkas,[1] and kerchiefs over their heads. The little girls looked so much alike that it was hard to tell them apart, except that one of the little girls was lame in her foot; she limped as she walked.

The woman came into the entry, felt about in the dark, lifted the latch, and opened the door. She let the two little girls go before her into the cottage, and then she followed.

"How do you do, friends?"

"Welcome! What can we do for you?"

The woman sat down by the table; the two little girls clung to her knee; they were bashful.

"These little girls need to have some goatskin shoes made for the spring."

"Well, it can be done. We don't generally make such small ones; but it's perfectly easy, either with welts or lined with linen. This here is Mikhaïla; he's my master workman."

Semyon glanced at Mikhaïla, and saw that he had thrown down his work, and was sitting with his eyes fastened on the little girls.

And Semyon was amazed at Mikhaïla. To be sure the little girls were pretty; they had dark eyes, they were plump and rosy, and they wore handsome shubkas and kerchiefs; but still Semyon could not understand why he gazed so intently at them, as if they were friends of his.

Semyon was amazed, and he began to talk with the woman, and to make his bargain. After he had made his bargain, he began to take the measures. The woman lifted on her lap the little cripple, and said:—

"Take two measures from this one; make one little shoe from the twisted foot, and three from the well one. Their feet are alike; they are twins."

Semyon took his tape, and said in reference to the little cripple:—

---

[1] Little fur garments.

"How did this happen to her? She is such a pretty little girl. Was she born so?"

"No; her mother crushed it."

Matriona joined the conversation; she was anxious to learn who the woman and children were, and so she said:—

"Then you aren't their mother?"

"No, I am not their mother; I am no relation to them, good wife, and they are no relation to me at all; I adopted them."

"If they are not your children, you take good care of them."

"Why shouldn't I take good care of them? I nursed them both at my own breast. I had a baby of my own, but God took him. I did not take such good care of him as I do of these."

"Whose children are they?"

9

The woman became confidential, and began to tell them about it.

"Six years ago," said she, "these little ones were left orphans in one week; the father was buried on Tuesday, and the mother died on Friday. Three days these little ones remained without their father, and then their mother followed him. At that time I was living with my husband in the country: we were neighbors; we lived in adjoining yards. Their father was a peasant, and worked in the forest at wood-cutting. And they were felling a tree, and it caught him across the body. It hurt him all inside. As soon as they got him out, he gave his soul to God, and that same week his wife gave birth to twins—these are the little girls here. There they were, poor and alone, no one to take care of them, either grandmother or sister.

"She must have died soon after the children were born. For when I went in the morning to look after my neighbor, as soon as I entered the cottage, I found the poor thing dead and cold. And when she died she must have rolled over on this little girl. . . . That's the way she crushed it, and spoiled this foot.

"The people got together, they washed and laid out the body, they had a coffin made, and buried her. The people were always kind. But the two little ones were left alone. What was to be done with them? Now I was the only one of the women who had a baby. For eight weeks I had been nursing my first-born, a boy. So I took them for the time being. The peasants got together; they planned and planned what to do with them, and they said to me:—

" 'Marya, you just keep the little girls for a while, and give us a chance to decide.'

"So I nursed the well one for a while, but did not think it worth while to nurse the deformed one. I did not expect that she was going to live. And, then, I thought to myself, why should the little angel's soul pass away? and I felt sorry for it. I tried to nurse her, and so I had my own and these two besides; yes, I had three children at the breast. But I was young and strong, and I had good food! And God gave me so much milk in my breasts that I had enough and to spare. I used to nurse two at once and let the third one wait. When one had finished, I would take up the third. And so God let me nurse all three; but when my boy was in his third year, I lost him. And God never gave me any more children. But we began to be in comfortable circumstances.

And now we are living with the trader at the mill. We get good wages and live well. But we have no children of our own. And how lonely it would be, if it were not for these two little girls! How could I help loving them? They are to me like the wax in the candle!"

And the woman pressed the little lame girl to her with one arm, and with the other hand she tried to wipe the tears from her cheeks.

And Matriona sighed, and said:—

"The old saw isn't far wrong, 'Men can live without father and mother, but without God one cannot live.'"

While they were thus talking together, suddenly a flash of lightning seemed to irradiate from that corner of the cottage where Mikhaïla was sitting. All looked at him; and, behold! Mikhaïla was sitting there with his hands folded in his lap, and looking up and smiling.

10

The woman went away with the children, and Mikhaïla arose from the bench and laid down his work; he took off his apron, made a low bow to the shoemaker and his wife, and said:—

"Farewell, friends; God has forgiven me. Do you also forgive me?"

And Semyon and Matriona perceived that it was from Mikhaïla that the light had flashed. And Semyon arose, bowed low before Mikhaïla, and said to him:—

"I see, Mikhaïla, that you are not a mere man, and I have no right to detain you nor to ask questions of you. But tell me one thing: when I had found you and brought you home, you were sad; but when my wife gave you something to eat, you smiled on her, and after that you became more cheerful. And then when the barin ordered the boots, why did you smile a second time, and after that become still more cheerful; and now when this woman brought these two little girls, why did you smile for the third time and become perfectly radiant? Tell me, Mikhaïla, why was it that such a light streamed from you, and why you smiled three times?"

And Mikhaïla said:—

"The light blazed from me because I had been punished, but now God has forgiven me. And I smiled the three times because it was required of me to learn three of God's truths, and I have now learned the three truths of God. One truth I learned when your wife had pity on me, and so I smiled; the second truth I learned when the rich man ordered the boots, and I smiled for the second time; and now that I have seen the little girls, I have learned the third and last truth, and I smiled for the third time."

And Semyon said:—

"Tell me, Mikhaïla, why God punished you, and what were the truths of God, that I, too, may know them."

And Mikhaïla said:—

"God punished me because I disobeyed Him. I was an angel in heaven, and I was disobedient to God. I was an angel in heaven, and the Lord sent me to bring back the soul of a certain woman. I flew down to earth and I saw the woman lying alone—she was sick—she had just borne twins, two little girls. The little ones were sprawling about near their mother, but their mother was unable to lift them to her breast. The mother saw me; she perceived that God had sent me after her soul; she burst into tears, and said:—

" 'Angel of God, I have just buried my husband; a tree fell on him in the forest and killed him. I have no sister, nor aunt, nor mother to take care of my little ones; do not carry off my soul; let me bring up my children myself, and nurse them and put them on their feet. It is impossible for children to live without father or mother.'

"And I heeded what the mother said; I put one child to her breast, and laid the other in its mother's arms, and I returned to the Lord in heaven. I flew back to the Lord, and I said:—

" 'I cannot take the mother's soul. The father has been killed by a tree, the mother has given birth to twins, and begs me not to take her soul; she says:—

" ' "Let me bring up my little ones; let me nurse them and put them on their feet. It is impossible for children to live without father and mother." I did not take the mother's soul.'

"And the Lord said:—

" 'Go and take the mother's soul, and thou shalt learn three lessons: Thou shalt learn *what is in men*, and *what is not given unto men*, and *what men live by*. When thou shalt have learned these three lessons, then return to heaven.'

"And I flew down to earth and took the mother's soul. The little ones fell from her bosom. The dead body rolled over on the bed, and fell on one of the little girls and crushed her foot. I rose above the village and was going to give the soul to God, when a wind seized me, my wings ceased to move and fell off, and the soul arose alone to God, and I fell back to earth."

11

And Semyon and Matriona now knew whom they had clothed and fed, and who it was that had been living with them, and they burst into tears of dismay and joy; and the angel said:—

"I was there in the field naked and alone. Hitherto I had never known what human poverty was; I had known neither cold nor hunger, and now I was a man. I was famished, I was freezing, and I knew not what to do. And I saw across the field a chapel made for God's service. I went to God's chapel, thinking to get shelter in it. But the chapel was locked, and I could not enter. And I crouched down behind the chapel, so as to get shelter from the wind. Evening came; I was hungry and chill, and ached all over. Suddenly I hear a man walking along the road, with a pair of boots in his hand, and talking to himself. I now saw for the first time since I had become a man the face of a mortal man, and it filled me with dismay, and I tried to hide from him. And I heard this man asking himself how he should protect himself from cold during the winter, and how get food for his wife and children. And I thought:—

" 'I am perishing with cold and hunger, and here is a man whose sole thought is to get a shuba for himself and his wife and to furnish bread for their sustenance. It is impossible for him to help me.'

"The man saw me and scowled; he seemed even more terrible than before; then he passed on. And I was in despair. Suddenly I heard the man coming back. I looked up, and did not recognize that it was the same man as before; then there was death in his face, but now it had suddenly become alive, and I saw that God was in his face. He came to me, put clothes on me, and took me home with him.

"When I reached his house, a woman came out to meet us, and she began to scold. The woman was even more terrible to me than the man; a dead soul seemed to proceed forth from her mouth, and I was suffocated by the stench of death. She wanted to drive me out into the cold, and I knew that she would die if she drove me out. And suddenly her husband reminded her of God. And instantly a change came over the woman. And when she had prepared something for me to eat, and looked kindly on me, I looked at her, and there was no longer anything like death about her; she was now alive, and in her also I recognized God.

"And I remembered God's first lesson: *'Thou shalt learn what is in men.'*

"And I perceived that LOVE was in men. And I was glad because God had begun to fulfil His promise to me, and I smiled for the first time. But I was not yet ready to know the whole. I could not understand what was not given to men, and what men lived by.

"I began to live in your house, and after I had lived with you a year the man came to order the boots which should be strong enough to last him a year without ripping or wearing out of shape. And I looked at him, and suddenly perceived behind his back my comrade, the Angel of Death. No one besides myself saw this angel; but I knew him, and I knew that before the sun should go down he would take the rich man's soul. And I said to myself: 'This man is laying his plans to live another year, and he knows not that ere evening comes he will be dead.'

"And I realized suddenly the second saying of God: *'Thou shalt know what is not given unto men.'*

"And now I knew what was in men. And now I knew also what was not given unto men. It is not given unto men to know what is needed for their bodies. And I smiled for the second time. I was glad because I saw my comrade, the angel, and because God had revealed unto me the second truth.

"But I could not yet understand all. I could not understand what men live by, and so I lived on, and waited until God should reveal to me the third truth also. And now in the sixth year the little twin girls have come with the woman, and I recognized the little ones, and I remembered how they had been left. And after I had recognized them, I thought:—

" 'The mother besought me in behalf of her children, because she thought that it would be impossible for children to live without father and mother, but another woman, a stranger, has nursed them and brought them up.'

"And when the woman caressed the children that were not her own, and wept over them, then I saw in her THE LIVING GOD, and knew *what people live by.* And I knew that God had revealed to me the last truth, and had pardoned me, and I smiled for the third time."

12

And the angel's body became manifest, and he was clad with light so bright that the eyes could not endure to look on him, and he spoke in clearer accents, as if the voice proceeded not from him, but came from heaven.

And the angel said:—

"I have learned that every man lives, not through care of himself, but by love.

"It was not given to the mother to know what her children needed to keep them alive. It was not given the rich man to know what he himself needed, and it is not given to any man to know whether he will need boots for daily living, or slippers for his burial.

"When I became a man, I was kept alive, not by what thought I took for myself, but because a stranger and his wife had love in their hearts, and pitied and loved me. The orphans were kept alive, not because other people deliberated about what was to be done with them, but because a strange woman had love for them in her heart, and pitied them and loved them. And all men are kept alive, not by their own forethought, but because there is LOVE IN MEN.

"I knew before that God gave life to men, and desired them to live; but now I know something above and beyond that.

"I have learned that God does not wish men to live each for himself, and therefore He has not revealed to them what they each need for themselves, but He wishes them to live in union, and therefore He has revealed to them what is necessary for each and for all together.

"I have now learned that it is only in appearance that they are kept alive through care for themselves, but that in reality they are kept alive through love. *He who dwelleth in love dwelleth in God, and God in him, for God is love.*"

And the angel sang a hymn of praise to God, and the cottage shook with the sound of his voice.

And the ceiling parted, and a column of fire reached from earth to heaven. And Semyon and his wife and children fell prostrate on the ground. And pinions appeared on the angel's shoulders, and he soared away to heaven.

And when Semyon opened his eyes, the cottage was the same as it had ever been, and there was no one in it save himself and his family.

1881

A CANDLE

"Ye have heard that it hath been said, An eye for an eye, and a tooth for a tooth:

"But I say unto you, That ye resist not evil: but whosoever shall smite thee on thy right cheek, turn to him the other also."—MATT. v. 38, 39.

This affair took place in the days when there were masters. There used to be all kinds of masters. There were those who remembered God, and that they must die, and took pity on people; and there were dogs,—excuse the use of the term. But there was nothing worse than the *nachalniks*, or stewards, who had risen from serfdom. As it were, out of the mud, they became princes! And they made life worse than anything else.

There happened to be such a *prikashchik,* or overseer, on a proprietor's estate. The peasants worked their share for the estate. There was plenty of land, and the land was good,—there was water, and meadows, and woodland. There was enough, and to spare, for master and peasants; but the master made one of his house-serfs from another estate the overseer.

This overseer took the power into his hands, and sat upon the necks of the muzhiks. He himself had a family,—a wife, and two married daughters,—and he had made money. He might easily have lived without sin; but he was a covetous man, and fell into sin. He began to compel the muzhiks to work on the barin's estate more than their regular allotment. He started a brickyard; he wore out all the peasants, both women and men, and sold the bricks.

The muzhiks went to complain to the proprietor at Moscow, but they had no success. He dismissed the muzhiks without any satisfaction, and did not curb the overseer's power. The prikashchik learned that the muzhiks had been to complain of him, and he began to vent his spite on them so that they were worse off than before. There happened to be false men among the muzhiks, who used to carry stories about one another. And all the people were in a ferment, and the overseer kept growing worse and worse.

As time went on, the overseer became so bad that the people came to fear him worse than a terrible wild beast. When he passed through the village, all would keep out of his way as from a wolf, hiding wherever they could, so as to keep away from his eyes. The overseer saw it; and the fact that they were afraid of him made him still fiercer. He persecuted the people, both by blows and hard work; and the muzhiks suffered terribly at his hands.

Sometimes such evil-doers were put out of the way, and the muzhiks began to plan this way of escape. They would meet in some retired spot, and the boldest among them would say:—

"Must we go on suffering forever from our persecutor?—We are lost anyhow—to kill such a man is no sin."

The muzhiks were at one time gathered in the forest; it was before Holy Week. The overseer had sent them out to clear up the proprietor's forest. They gathered at dinner, and began to talk.

"How can we live now?" they said. "He will destroy us root and branch. He tortures us with work; neither we nor the women have any rest day or night any more. The least thing not to his mind, and he finds fault, he lashes us. Semyon died under his whip. Anisim was tortured in the stocks. What else can we expect? He will come here this evening; he will be making trouble again; let's just pull him off from his horse, give him a blow with the ax, and that'll be the end of it. We'll bury him somewhere like a dog, and no one will be any wiser. Only one condition: we must all stand together and not give it away."

Thus spoke Vasili Minayef. He was more than all the rest incensed against the prikashchik, for he had whipped him every week and robbed him of his wife, by taking her as his cook.

Thus talked the muzhiks; in the evening the overseer came; he was on horseback; as soon as he came, he began to find fault with their work. They had not cut the wood in the right way. He discovered a little linden in the pile.

He said, "I did not tell you to cut the lindens. Who cut it down? Confess, or I'll flog you all!"

He began to inquire in whose pile the linden was. They told him it was Sidor's. The prikashchik beat Sidor's face till it bled. Then he lashed Vasili like a Tartar because his pile was small; then he started home.

In the evening the muzhiks met again, and Vasili was the spokesman.

"Ekh! What people you are! Not men, but sparrows. 'We'll stand together, we'll stand together!' but when it comes to the point, all rush under the pent-roof. Thus sparrows try to fight a hawk: 'Don't give it away, don't give it away, we'll stand together!' But when he swooped down on us, all scattered in the grass! And so the hawk caught the one he wanted, carried it off. The sparrows hopped out: 'Cheeveek! cheeveek!' There is one missing! 'Who is gone?' Vanka, eh! 'That's his road, let him go! He deserves it.' The same way with you. If you aren't going to give it away, then don't give it away. When he seized Sidor, you should have clubbed together, and put an end to him. But still it is, 'Don't peach, don't peach! we'll stand together!' But when he swooped down, all flew into the bushes!"

Thus they spoke more and more often, and at last the muzhiks determined to do away with the prikashchik. On Good Friday the overseer announced to the muzhiks that they must be ready to plow for the barin at Easter, so as to sow the oats. This seemed to the muzhiks an insult; and on Good Friday they gathered at Vasili's, in the back yard, and began to talk again.

"Since he has forgotten God," say they, "and wants to do such things, we must really kill him. We are ruined anyway."

Piotr Mikhyeyef also came with them. Piotr Mikhyeyef was a peace-loving muzhik, and did not agree with the others. Mikhyeyef came, heard their talk, and said:—

"You are meditating a great sin, brethren. To destroy a soul is a great crime. To destroy another man's soul is easy, but how about your own? He does wrong; it is bad for him. Brethren, we must bear it."

Vasili was angry at these words.

"He keeps repeating the same thing over and over," says he: " 'It's a sin to kill a man! You know it is a sin to kill such a man,' says he. It is a sin to kill a good man, but even God has commanded to kill such a dog. You must kill a mad dog, out of pity for men; and not to kill him would be a greater sin. Why does he ruin people? But though we should suffer for it, we ought to do it for others. People will thank us. And to get rid of such spittle! He is ruining everybody. You talk nonsense, Mikhyeyitch. Why, it would be less of a sin than for all to go to work on Easter Sunday. You yourself would not go."

And Mikhyeyitch replied:—

"Why not go?" he asked. "They will send us, and I am going to plow. Not for myself. But God knows whose sin it is, only we should not forget Him. I, brethren," says he, "don't speak my own thoughts. If we had been commanded to do evil for evil, there would have been a law from God to that effect; but just the opposite is commanded us. You will do evil, but it will come back on you. It is not even clever to kill a man. His blood will stick in your soul. Kill a man—you stain your own soul with blood. You think, 'I have killed a bad man.' You think, 'I have destroyed a pest.' On the contrary, look, you have been led into doing a much worse sin to yourself. Yield to evil, and evil will yield to you."

And so the muzhiks did not agree; they were divided by their thoughts. Some had the same opinion as Vasilyef; others coincided with the views of Piotr, that they should not attempt the sin, but bear it.

The muzhiks were celebrating the first of the holidays, which was Sunday. At evening the *starosta,* or village elder, came with attendants from the master's country-seat, and said:—

"Mikhaïl Semyonovitch, the overseer, has given orders that all the muzhiks perpare on the morrow to plow in the oat-field."

The village elder went round with his attendants through the village, gave the orders for all to go out and plow the next day, calling to this one from over the river, this one from the highroad. The muzhiks wept, but dared not disobey. In the morning they went out with their wooden plows and began to work.

At church the early morning mass was going on, the people everywhere else were celebrating the festival; but those muzhiks were plowing!

Mikhaïl Semyonovitch, the overseer, woke up not very early, and went out on his place; his people—his wife and his widowed daughter, who had come for the festival—were dressed, and had on their finery; a laborer harnessed for them the little cart; they went off to mass and came home again; the serving-woman put on the samovar; Mikhaïl Semyonovitch came in, and they began their tea-drinking.

After Mikhaïl Semyonovitch had drunk enough tea, he lighted his pipe and called the village elder.

"Well, then, did you set the muzhiks to plowing?"

"I did, Mikhaïl Semyonovitch."

"What! did they all go?"

"All went; I myself set them at it."

"Setting them at work is all very well, but are they plowing? Go out and look, and tell them that I am coming after dinner to see if they have been plowing a desyatin to every two plows, and plowing it well, besides. If I find any mistake, I shan't hear to any festival."

"I will do so."

The village elder had started, but Mikhaïl Semyonovitch called him back; he hesitated, tried to say something, but could not.

He hesitated and hesitated, and at last he said:—

"Now, here, I want you to listen to what those villains are saying about me. Who is grumbling, and what they say,—tell me all about it. I know those villains; they don't like to work; all they care for is to be at their ease or go wandering about. They like to gormandize and have holidays, but they don't realize that if you put off the plowing it gets to be too late. So now, you just listen to what they say, and report it all to me. I must know about it. Go along and notice, and tell me all, and don't hide anything."

The village elder turned round, went off, mounted his horse, and rode off to the muzhiks in the field.

The overseer's wife had heard her husband's talk with the village elder, and came to her husband, and began to question him. She was a peace-loving woman, and kind-hearted. Where it was possible, she restrained her husband, and took the part of the muzhiks.

She came to her husband, and began to question him:—

"Mishenka, my love," says she, "on the great day, the festival of the Lord, don't commit a sin; for Christ's sake, let the muzhiks off!"

Mikhaïl Semyonovitch did not heed his wife's words; he only began to laugh at her.

"It's a long time, isn't it," said he, "since you had a little taste of the whip, that you dare mix yourself up with other people's affairs?"

"Mishenka, my love, I had a bad dream about you; heed me; let the muzhiks off!"

"All right," said he; "I tell you, you've been living too high of late and think the whip won't reach you. Look out!"

Semyonovitch got angry, thrust his lighted pipe into his wife's teeth, drove her away, and ordered his dinner brought.

Mikhaïl Semyonovitch ate some cold meat, a pirog, cabbage-soup with pork, roast shoat, vermicelli cooked in milk; he drank some cherry wine and tasted a sweet tart; then he called up the cook and set her to performing some songs, while he himself took his guitar and began to play the accompaniments.

Mikhaïl Semyonovitch was sitting in a gay frame of mind, belching, thrumming on the strings, and jesting with the cook.

The village elder came in, bowed low, and began to report what he had seen in the field.

"How is it? are they plowing? Will they finish their stint?"

"They have already done more than half of the plowing."

"None left undone?"

"I did not see any; they plow very well; they are afraid."

"Well, does the ground break up well?"

"The ground breaks up easily, it is as soft as poppy seed."

The overseer was silent.

"Well, and what are they saying about me? do they revile me?"

The starosta began to stammer, but Mikhaïl Semyonovitch bade him tell the whole truth.

"Tell me everything; you won't be speaking your own words, but those of others. If you tell the truth, I will reward you; but if you deceive me, look out! I will pickle you! Hé, Katyusha,[1] give him a glass of vodka to keep his courage up."

The cook came and brought the starosta the brandy. He thanked her, drank it up, wiped his lips, and began to speak:—

"All the same," he said to himself, " 'tisn't my fault that they don't praise him. I will tell the truth, since he tells me to."

And the starosta plucked up courage, and began to speak:—

"They grumble, Mikhaïl Semyonovitch, they grumble."

"Yes; but what do they say? Tell me."

"They say one thing: 'He does not believe in God.' "

1 Katyusha, diminutive of Katya

The overseer laughed:—

"Who says that?"

"They all say it. They say, 'He has sold himself to the devil.'"

The overseer laughed.

"That," says he, "is excellent; now tell me individually who says that. Does Vaska say so?"

The starosta did not want to tell on his own people, but there had been a quarrel between him and Vasili for a long time.

"Vasili," say he, "scolds worse than any one else."

"Yes; what does he say? Speak it out."

"But it is terrible even to tell it. He says, 'You won't escape a violent death.'"

"Ay! the smart fellow! Why does he wait—why doesn't he kill me? He can't because his arms aren't long enough to reach me! Just wait!" said he. "Vaska! we'll be quits with you! Now, how about Tishka? That dog also, I suppose?"

"Yes; they all speak bad."

"Yes; but what do they say?"

"Well, they say something abominable."

"What was abominable? Don't be afraid to tell."

"Well, they say that your belly will break open, and your bowels gush out."

Mikhaïl Semyonovitch was delighted; he burst into a laugh.

"We will see whose does first! Who says that? Tishka?"

"No one said anything good; all growl, all are full of threats."

"Well, but how about Petrushka Mikheyef? What does he say? The gobbler! he reviles me, too, I suppose?"

"No, Mikhaïlo Semyonovitch. Piotr does not revile you."

"What does he do?"

"He is the only one of all the muzhiks that says nothing. He is a clever muzhik. I wondered at him, Mikhaïl Semyonuitch."

"But why?"

"At what he did; and all the muzhiks wondered at him."

"But what did he do?"

"Yes, it was very queer. I tried to get near him. He is plowing the sloping field on Turkin height. As I came near him, I heard him singing; he was carrying something gingerly, carefully; and on his plow, between the handles, something was shining."

"Well?"

"It was exactly like a little fire, shining. I went nearer and looked; it was a little wax candle—cost five kopeks—was stuck on to the cross-bar, and was lighted; and the wind didn't blow it out. And he, in his clean shirt, went up and down, plowing, and singing Sunday songs. And he turned back, and shook, and still the candle didn't go out. He shook it as I stood there, shifted the plowshare, lifted the plow, and all the time the candle was burning, and it did not go out."

"And what did he say?"

"Well, he didn't say anything; he only looked at me, gave me the Easter salutation, and began to sing again."

"But what did you say to him?"

"I did not speak; but the muzhiks came up, and began to make sport of him; here they say, 'Mikhyeyitch, you will say enough prayers to atone for the sin of plowing on Easter Sunday.'"

"What did he say to that?"

"He only said, '*On earth, peace, good-will to men.*' Then he took hold of the plow again, started up the horse, and sang in a low voice; but the candle burned, and didn't go out."

The overseer ceased to laugh, laid down the guitar, hung his head, and fell into thought.

He sat there, and sat there; then he sent out the cook and the starosta, and went behind the partition; lay down on the bed, and began to sigh, and groan, like a cart-load of sheaves going by. His wife came to him, began to talk with him; he gave her no reply. Only he said:—

"He has conquered me. Now it's my turn."

His wife said to him:—

"Yes, go and let them off. Perhaps no harm is done. No matter what you have done, you have never feared before; what is there to be afraid of now?"

"I am lost," he said; "he has conquered me;" and he kept repeating, "He has conquered, conquered!"

His wife cried:—

"You keep repeating: 'He has conquered me, he has conquered me.' Go on! let the muzhiks off, then it will be all right. Go on, I will have the horse saddled."

They brought the horse; and the overseer's wife persuaded her husband to go out to the field and let the muzhiks go.

Mikhaïl Semyonuitch mounted his horse, and rode out to the field. He came to the inclosure; a peasant woman opened the gate for him; he rode into the village. As soon as the people saw him, they all hid themselves from him, one in a yard, another behind a corner, another in an orchard.

The overseer rode through the whole village; he came to the gates at the farther end. The gates were shut, and he could not open them on horseback. He shouted and shouted for some one to open them for him, but no one came. Getting down from his horse, he opened the gates himself, and tried to mount again from the gate-post. He lifted his foot to the stirrup, lifted himself, and was just going to swing himself into the saddle, when the horse took fright at a pig, sprang against the paling; and the man was heavy; he did not reach the saddle, but was thrown on his belly against the paling. There was one sharp pole that stood out above the paling, and this was higher than the others. And he fell on his belly straight on this pole. And it ripped open his belly, and he fell on the ground.

The muzhiks were coming from the plowing; the horses snorted and refused to pass through the turn into the gates; the muzhiks looked to see what the matter was, and there Mikhaïl Semyonovitch was lying on his back, his arms stretched out, and his eyes fixed, and his insides had gushed out over the ground, and his blood made a pool—the earth would not drink it.

The muzhiks were frightened; they drove the horses in by another way; only Piotr Mikhyeyitch dismounted and went to the overseer, and, seeing that he was dead, closed his eyes, harnessed the telyega, helped the dead man's son to put him in a box, and carried him back to the manor-house.

The barin learned about all these things, and on account of the sin forgave the muzhiks their tax.

And the muzhiks learned that God's power works not by sin, but by goodness.

1885

THE DEVIL'S PERSISTENT, BUT GOD IS RESISTANT

There lived in olden times a good master. He had plenty of everything, and many slaves served him. And the slaves used to praise their master. They said:—

"There is not a better master under heaven, than ours. He not only feeds us and clothes us well, and gives us work according to our strength, but he never insults any of us, and never gets angry with us; he is not like other masters, who treat their slaves worse than cattle, and put them to death whether they are to blame or not, and never say a kind word to them. Our master wishes us well, and treats us kindly, and says kind things to us. We couldn't have a better life than ours."

Thus the slaves praised their master.

And here the Devil began to get vexed because the slaves lived in comfort and love with their master.

And the Devil got hold of one of this master's slaves named Alyeb. He got hold of him and commanded him to entice the other slaves.

And when all the slaves were taking their rest, and were praising their master, Alyeb raised his voice, and said:—

"It's all nonsense your praising our master's goodness. Try to humor the Devil, and the Devil will be good. We serve our master well, we humor him in all things. As soon as he thinks of anything, we do it; we divine his thoughts. How make him be not good to us? Just stop humoring him, and do bad work for him, and he will be like all the others, and he will return evil for evil worse than the crossest of masters."

And the other slaves began to argue with Alyeb. And they argued, and laid a wager. Alyeb undertook to make their kind master angry. He undertook it on the condition that, if he did not make him angry, he should give his holiday clothes; but if he should make him angry, then they agreed to give him, each one of them, their holiday clothes; and, moreover, they agreed to protect him from their master, if he should be put in irons, or, if thrown in prison, to free him. They laid the wager, and Alyeb promised to make their master angry the next morning.

Alyeb served his master in the sheep-cote; he had charge of the costly breeding-rams.

And here in the morning the good master came with some guests to the sheep-cote, and began to show them his beloved, costly rams. The Devil's accomplice winked to his comrades:—

"Look! I'll soon get the master angry."

All the slaves had gathered. They peered in at the door and through the fence; and the Devil climbed into a tree, and looked down into the dvor, to see how his accomplice would do his work.

The master came round the dvor, showed his guests his sheep and lambs, and then was going to show his best ram.

"The other rams," says he, "are good; but this one here, the one with the twisted horns, is priceless; he is more precious to me than my eyes."

The sheep and rams were jumping about the dvor to avoid the people, and the guests were unable to examine the valuable ram. This ram would scarcely come to a stop before the Devil's accomplice, as if accidentally, would scare the sheep, and again they would get mixed up.

The guests were unable to make out which was the priceless ram.

Here the master became tired. He said:—

"Alyeb, my dear, just try to catch the best ram with the wrinkled horns, and hold him. Be careful."

And, as soon as the master said this, Alyeb threw himself, like a lion, amid the rams, and caught the priceless ram by the wool. He caught him by the wool, and instantly grabbed him with one hand by the left hind leg, lifted it up, and, right before the master's eyes, bent his leg, and it cracked like a dry stick. Alyeb broke the precious ram's leg below the knee. The ram bleated, and fell on his fore knees. Alyeb grabbed him by the right leg; but the left turned inside out, and hung down like a whip. The guests and all the slaves groaned, and the Devil rejoiced when he saw how cleverly Alyeb had done his job.

The master grew darker than night, frowned, hung his head, and said not a word. The guests and slaves were also silent. . . . They waited to see what would happen.

The master kept silent awhile; then he shook himself, as if trying to throw off something, and raised his head, and turned his eyes heavenward. Not long he gazed before the wrinkles on his brow disappeared; he smiled, and fixed his eyes on Alyeb. He looked at Alyeb, smiled again, and said:—

"O Alyeb, Alyeb! Thy master told thee to make me angry. But my master is stronger than thine, and thou hast not led me into anger; but I shall make thy master angry. Thou wert afraid that I would punish thee, and hast wished to be free, Alyeb. Know, then, that thy punishment will not come from me; but as thou art anxious for thy freedom, here, in the presence of my guests, I give thee thy freedom. Go wherever it may please thee, and take thy holiday clothes."

And the kind master went back to the house with his guests. But the Devil gnashed his teeth, fell from the tree, and sank through the earth.

1885

ILYAS

There lived in the government of Ufa a Bashkir by the name of Ilyas. When his father died, Ilyas was left by no means rich, but the year before his father had got him a wife, and at that time Ilyas's possessions consisted of seven mares, two cows, and a score of sheep. Now Ilyas was a good manager, and he began to gain; from morning till night he and his wife worked; he got up earlier than any one else, and went to bed later than any one else, and each year he kept getting richer.

Thus Ilyas toiled for thirty-five years, and he made a great fortune. He had two hundred head of horse, a hundred and fifty head of horned cattle, and twelve hundred sheep. The servants pastured the flocks and herds; and the maid-servants milked the mares and cows, and made kumys, butter, and cheese.

Ilyas had plenty of everything, and every one round about envied Ilyas's life. Men said:—

"Lucky man, Ilyas. He has plenty of everything; he doesn't need to die."

Fine people began to get acquainted with Ilyas, and associated with him. And guests came to visit him from far and near. And Ilyas received them all, and gave them all food and drink. Whoever came had kumys; all had tea, chowder, and mutton. As soon as guests came, he would immediately have a ram or two killed: and if many came, they would have a mare also killed.

Ilyas had two sons and a daughter. He married off his sons, and got his daughter a husband. When Ilyas was poor, his sons worked with him, and they themselves pastured the flocks and herds; but as they became rich, the sons began to get spoiled, and one took to drinking.

One, the elder, was killed in a brawl; and the other, the younger, got a proud wife; and this son began to be disobedient to his father, and Ilyas was compelled to banish him.

Ilyas banished him, but gave him a house and cattle; and Ilyas's wealth was diminished. And soon after this a distemper fell upon Ilyas's sheep, and many perished. Then there came a year of famine; the hay did not ripen; many cattle died during the winter. Then the Kirgiz carried off his best horses, and Ilyas's property was still further diminished.

Ilyas began to fall lower and lower. And his strength was less than it had been. And at the age of seventy years, Ilyas had come to such a pass that he began to sell out his furs, his carpets, saddles, and kibitkas; and then he had to dispose of his last cattle, and Ilyas came to nothing.

He himself did not realize how he had nothing left; but he and his wife were obliged, in their old age, to hire out as servants. All Ilyas's possessions consisted of the clothes on his body, his shuba, a hat, shoes, and slippers—yes, and his wife, Sham-Shemagi, now an old woman. His banished son had gone to a far-off land, and his daughter died. And then there was no one to help the old people.

Their neighbor, Muhamedshah, felt sorry for the old people. Muhamedshah himself was neither poor nor rich, but lived in medium circumstances; and he was a good man.

He remembered Ilyas's hospitality, and pitied him, and said to Ilyas:—

"Come, Ilyas," says he, "and live with me—you and your old woman. In summer you can work for me in the garden, and in winter take care of the cattle; and Sham-Shemagi may milk the mares, and make kumys. I will feed and clothe you both; and whatever you need, tell me; I will give it."

Ilyas thanked his neighbor, and he and his wife began to live with Muhamedshah as servants. At first it came hard to them, but afterward they got used to it; and the old people went on living and working as much as their strength permitted.

The khozyaïn found it profitable to keep such people, because they had been masters themselves, and knew how to keep things orderly, and were not lazy, and worked according to their strength; only Muhamedshah felt sorry to see how people of such high station should have fallen to such a low condition.

Once it came to pass that some guests, some kinsmen from a distance, came to visit Muhamedshah; a Mulla[1] came with them.

Muhamedshah gave orders to have a ram caught and killed. Ilyas dressed the ram, cooked it, and served it to the guests. The guests ate the mutton, drank some tea, and took some kumys.

While the guests were sitting with the khozyaïn on down pillows, on carpets, and were drinking kumys out of cups, and chatting, Ilyas had finished his chores, and was passing in front of the door.

Muhamedshah saw him, and asked a guest:—

"Did you see that old man who went by the door?"

"I saw him," said the guest; "but what is there remarkable about him?"

"This is remarkable,—he was once our richest man. His name is Ilyas; maybe you have heard of him?"

"Certainly I have," said the guest. "I never saw him before, but his fame has been widespread."

"Now he has nothing at all left, and lives out at service with me; he and his old woman milk the cows."

The guest was amazed, clucked with his tongue, shook his head, and said:—

"Yes, this shows how fortune turns round like a wheel; he who is on top gets to the bottom. Well, I suppose the old man feels pretty bad about it?"

"Who can tell about him? He lives quietly, peacefully; works well."

The guest said:—

"May I have a talk with him? I should like to ask him about his life."

"Well, you can," says the khozyaïn, and shouts toward the kibitka, "Babaï,[2] come in; bring some kumys, and call your old woman."

So Ilyas came with his wife. He greeted the guests and his master, repeated a prayer, and squatted down by the door. But his wife went behind the curtain, and sat with her mistress.

Ilyas was given a cup of kumys. Ilyas wished the health of the guests and of his master, bowed, sipped a little, and set it down.

[1] *Mulla* or *Molla*, a sort of title given to priest and teachers among the Mohammedans.
[2] Little grandfather,

"Well, dyedushka," says the guest, "I suppose you feel rather blue looking at us, to remember your past life,—how you used to be in luck, and how now your life is spent in sorrow?"

And Ilyas smiled and said:—

"If I told you about my fortune and misfortune, you would not believe me. Better ask my wife. She is a woman,—what's in her heart's on her tongue also. She will tell you the whole truth about this matter."

And the guest spoke to her behind the curtain: "Well, now, babushka, tell us what you think about your former luck, and your present misfortune."

And Sham-Shemagi spoke from behind the curtain:—

"This is what I think about it: my old man and I have lived fifty years. We sought for happiness, and did not find it; and now here it is two years since we lost everything, and have been living out at service; and we have found real happiness, and ask for nothing better."

The guests were amazed; and the khozyaïn was amazed, and even rose from his seat, lifted the curtain to look at the old woman; and the old woman was standing, with folded arms. She smiled as she looked at her old man, and the old man smiled back.

The old woman went on:—

"I am speaking the truth, not jesting. We sought for happiness for half a century, and as long as we were rich we did not find it; but now that we have nothing left, and have to go out to service, we have found such happiness that we ask for nothing better."

"But wherein consists your happiness now?"

"Well, in this: while we were rich, my old man and I never had an hour's rest. We never had time to talk, nor to think about our souls, nor to pray to God. There was nothing for us but care. When we had guests, it was a bother how to treat them, what to give them, so that they might not talk ill about us. Then, when guests went away, we had to look after our work-people; they would have to rest, they would have to be furnished with enough to eat, and we would have to see to it that nothing that was ours got lost. So we sinned. Then, again, there was worry lest the wolf should kill a colt or a calf, or lest thieves should drive off our horses. We would lie down to sleep, but could not sleep for fear the sheep should trample the lambs. We would go out, we would walk in the night; and at last, when we would get ourselves calmed down, then, again, there would be anxiety about getting food for the winter. Besides this, my old man and I never agreed. He would say we must do so, and I would say we must do so; and we would begin to quarrel; so we sinned. So we lived in worry and care, in worry and care, and never knew the happiness of life."

"Well, and now?"

"Now, when my old man and I get up in the morning, we always have a talk, in love and sympathy, we have nothing to quarrel about, nothing to worry about; our only care is to serve our khozyaïn. We work according to our strength, we work willingly, so that our khozyaïn may not lose, but gain. When we come in, we have dinner, we have supper, we have kumys. If it is cold, we have our kizyak[1] to warm us, and a sheepskin shuba. And we have time to talk and

[1] Brick made of dried dung.

think about our souls, and to pray to God. For fifty years we sought for happiness, and only now we have found it!"

The guests began to laugh.

But Ilyas said:—

"Don't laugh, brothers; this thing is no jest, but human life. And the old woman and I were foolish when we wept over the loss of our property, but now God has revealed the truth to us; and it is not for our own consolation, but for your good, that we reveal it to you."

And the Mulla said:—

"This is a wise saying, and Ilyas has told the exact truth; and this is written also in the Scriptures."

And the guests ceased laughing, and were lost in thought.

1885

LITTLE GIRLS WISER THAN
THEIR ELDERS

Easter was early. Folks had just ceased going in sledges. The snow still lay in the courtyards, and little streams ran through the village. In an alley between two dvors a large pool had collected from the dung-heaps. And near this pool were standing two little girls from either dvor,—one of them younger, the other older.

The mothers of the two little girls had dressed them in new sarafans,—the younger one's blue, the elder's of yellow flowered damask. Both wore red handkerchiefs. The little girls, after mass was over, had gone to the pool, shown each other their dresses, and begun to play. And the whim seized them to splash in the water. The younger one was just going to wade into the pool with her little slippers on; but the older one said:—

"Don't do it, Malashka . . . your mother will scold. I'm going to take off my shoes and stockings . . . you take off yours."

The little girls took off their shoes and stockings, held up their clothes, and went into the pool so as to meet. Malashka waded in up to her ankles, and said:—

"It's deep, Akulyushka[1] . . . I am afraid."

"Nonsense! It won't be any deeper. Come straight toward me."

They approached nearer and nearer to each other. And Akulka said:—

"Be careful, Malashka, don't splash, but go more slowly."

But the words were hardly out of her mouth, when Malashka put her foot down into the water; it splashed directly on Akulka's sarafan. The sarafan was well spattered, and the water flew into her nose and eyes.

Akulka saw the spots on her sarafan; she became angry with Malashka, scolded her, ran after her, tried to slap her.

[1] Akulka and Akulyushka, diminutives of Akulina.

Malashka was frightened when she saw what mischief she had done; she sprang out of the pool, and hastened home.

Akulka's mother happened to pass by and saw her little daughter's sarafan spattered, and her shirt bedaubed.

"How did you get yourself all covered with dirt, you good-for-nothing?"

"Malashka spattered me on purpose."

Akulka's mother caught Malashka, and struck her on the back of the head. Malashka howled along the whole street. Malashka's mother came out:—

"What are you striking my daughter for?"

She began to scold her neighbor. A word for a word; the women got into a quarrel. The muzhiks hastened out, a great crowd gathered on the street. All were screaming. No one would listen to any one. They quarreled, and the one jostled the other; there was a general row imminent: but an old woman, Akulka's grandmother, interfered.

She came out into the midst of the muzhiks, and began to speak.

"What are you doing, neighbors? What day is it? We ought to rejoice. And you are doing such wrong things!"

They did not heed the old woman; they almost struck her. And the old woman would never have succeeded in persuading them, had it not been for Akulka and Malashka. While the women were keeping up the quarrel, Akulka cleaned her sarafanchik, and came out again to the pool in the alley. She picked up a little stone, and began to clear away the earth by the pool, so as to let the water run into the street.

While she was cleaning it out, Malashka also came along and began to help her—to make a little gutter with a splinter.

The muzhiks were just coming to blows when the water reached the street, flowing through the gutter made by the little girls; and it went straight to the very spot where the old woman was trying to separate the muzhiks.

The little girls were chasing it, one on one side, the other on the other, of the runnel.

"Hold it back, Malashka! hold it!" cried Akulka. Malashka also tried to say something, but she laughed so that she could not speak.

Thus the little girls were chasing it, and laughing as the splinter swam down the runnel.

They ran right into the midst of the muzhiks. The old woman saw them, and she said to the muzhiks:—

"You should fear God, you muzhiks! It was on account of these same little girls that you picked a quarrel, but they forgot all about it long ago; dear little things, they are playing together lovingly again."

The muzhiks looked at the little girls, and felt ashamed. Then the muzhiks laughed at themselves, and went home to their dvors.

"If ye are not like little children, ye cannot enter into the kingdom of God."

1885

NEGLECT A FIRE AND IT
SPREADS

"Then came Peter to him, and said, Lord, how oft shall my brother sin against me, and I forgive him? till seven times?

Jesus saith unto him, I say not unto thee, Until seven times: but, Until seventy times seven.

Therefore is the kingdom of heaven likened unto a certain king which would take account of his servants.

And when he had begun to reckon, one was brought unto him, which owed him ten thousand talents.

But forasmuch as he had not to pay, his lord commanded him to be sold, and his wife, and children, and all that he had, and payment to be made.

The servant therefore fell down, and worshiped him, saying, Lord, have patience with me, and I will pay thee all.

Then the lord of that servant was moved with compassion, and loosed him, and forgave him the debt.

But the same servant went out, and found one of his fellow-servants, which owed him an hundred pence: and he laid hands on him, and took him by the throat, saying, Pay me that thou owest.

And his fellow-servant fell down at his feet, and besought him, saying, Have patience with me, and I will pay thee all.

And he would not: but went and cast him into prison, till he should pay the debt.

So when his fellow-servants saw what was done, they were very sorry, and came and told unto their lord all that was done.

Then his lord, after that he had called him, said unto him, O thou wicked servant, I forgave thee all that debt, because thou desiredst me:

Shouldest not thou also have had compassion on thy fellow-servant even as I had pity on thee?

And his lord was wroth, and delivered him to the tormentors, till he should pay all that was due unto him.

So likewise shall my heavenly Father do also unto you, if ye from your hearts forgive not every one his brother their trespasses."—
MATT. xviii. 21–35.

Ivan Shcherbakof, a peasant, lived in the country. He lived well. He had perfect health, he was the best laborer in the village, and he had three sons grown up: one was married, one was engaged, and the third was a lad who was just beginning to tend the horses and plows. His old wife, Ivanova, was a clever woman, and a good housekeeper; and the daughter-in-law was peaceful and industrious. Ivan lived comfortably with his family. The only one of his household who ate the bread of idleness was his infirm old father. For six years he had been lying on the oven, suffering from asthma. Ivan had plenty of everything; he had three horses and a colt, a cow with a calf, and fifteen sheep. The women not only mended their husbands' clothes, and made them, and also worked in the field: the muzhiks worked like true peasants. The old grain held out till the new came. They paid their taxes, and supplied all their necessities, with their oat-crop. Ivan lived comfortably with his children.

But in the next dvor lived Ivan's neighbor, Gavrilo, a cripple, the son of Gordyeï Ivanof. And a quarrel arose between him and Ivan.

As long as the old Gordyeï was alive, and Ivan's father was manager, the muzhiks lived like exemplary neighbors. If the women needed a sifter or a tub, or the muzhiks needed a corn-cloth or to borrow a wheel, they would send from one yard to the other, and, like good neighbors, accommodate each other. If a calf broke into the threshing-floor, they would drive it out, and only say, "Look out, don't let him come in again; we have not moved the corn yet." But as for hiding or locking things up either at the threshing-floor or in the shed, or quarreling, such things never happened.

Thus they got along while the old folks were alive. But when the next generation took the reins, a new state of things came about.

The whole trouble arose from a trifle.

A little hen belonging to Ivan's daughter-in-law took to laying early in the season. The young wife began to collect the eggs for Easter. Every day she went after the eggs to the wagon-box that stood in the shed. But the children, it seems, scared the hen, which flew over the fence into the neighbor's yard, and there began to lay. The young woman heard the little hen cackling; she said to herself:—

"I haven't time now; I must clean up the izba against the holidays. I'll go and get it by and by."

In the evening she went to the shed, to the wagon-box; not a sign of an egg. The young woman began to ask her mother-in-law and her brother-in-law if they had taken any out.

"No," say they, "we haven't."

But Taraska, the smallest brother-in-law, said:—

"Your bantam has been laying over in the next yard. She was cackling over there, and she came flying back from there."

And the young woman looked at her bantam; she was sitting next the cockerel on the roost; her eyes were already shut; she was just going to sleep. And she would have asked her where she had been laying, if the hen could only have answered.

And the young woman went over to her neighbor's. The old woman came to the door.

"What do you want, young woman?"

"Well," says she, "baushka,[1] my little hen flew over into your yard to-day. I wonder if she didn't lay an egg?"

"We haven't seen it at all. Our own hens, thank God, have been laying this long time. We gathered up our own, but we don't need other folks's. We, my little girl, never go into strangers' yards to collect eggs."

This was an insult to the young woman, she said a word too much; the neighbor replied in the same way, and the women began to berate each other. Ivan's wife came out after water, and she also took a hand. Gavrilo's wife rushed out of the room and began to blame her neighbor: she recalled things

---

[1] *Baushka*, for *babushka*, old woman or grandmother.

that had happened, and added things that had never happened. A regular
cackle ensued.

All screamed at once, and tried to say two words at a time. Yes, and the
words were all bad: "You are such and such,"—"you are another,"—"you are a
thief,"—"you are a trollop,"—"you starve your old father-in-law,"—"you are
a beast."

"And you, mean little beggar that you are, you made a hole in my sieve!"
—"And you've got our bucket-yoke. I want it back again."

They caught hold of the bucket-yoke, spilt the water, tore off each other's
shawls, and began to fight.

Just here Gavrilo came in from the field, and took his wife's part. Ivan and
his son rushed over, and they all fell in a heap. Ivan was a strong muzhik,
and threw them all in different directions. He tore out a handful of Gavrilo's
whiskers. A crowd collected, and it was hard to separate them.

That was the beginning of it.

Gavrilo wrapped up his bunch of whiskers in a piece of writing-paper and
brought suit in the district court.

"I did not grow my beard," says he, "for the sake of letting that pigheaded
Vanka pull it out."

And his wife kept telling her neighbors that now they would try Ivan at court,
and send him to Siberia; and so the quarrel went on.

From the very first day the old man, as he lay on the oven, tried to pacify
them; but the young people would not listen to him. He said to them:—

"Children, you are acting foolishly; and the whole thing started from a piece
of foolishness. Just think, the whole trouble is about an egg! Suppose the children did pick up the little egg. Why, let them have it. One egg isn't worth much.
God has plenty for all. Well, suppose she did say a bad word; you ought to
have corrected it; you ought to have taught her to say better things. Well,
you've had your fight—we are all sinners! Such things happen. Now go and
make it up, and all will be forgotten! But, if you act out of spite, things will
go from bad to worse for you."

The younger ones did not listen; they thought the old man was talking nonsense, and was only grumbling, as old men are apt to do.

Ivan did not give in to his neighbor.

"I did not pull out his whiskers," said he, "he pulled them out himself; but
his son tore out all my eye-hooks, and tore the shirt off my back. Just look
at it!"

And Ivan also went to court. The case was tried before the magistrate
and at the district court. While they were at law, a bolt was missing from
Gavrilo's cart. Gavrilo's women folk accused Ivan's son of stealing it.

"We ourselves saw him go by the window at night," they said, "on his way
to the cart; and some one said he stopped at the tavern, and tried to sell the
bolt to the tavern-keeper."

Another suit was begun; and at home, every day, there was a new quarrel,
a new fight. The little children, imitating their elders, quarreled; and the
women, when they met at the river, did not pound so much with their paddles
as they clacked with their tongues, and all to no good.

At first the muzhiks only accused each other, but in course of time they

314 NEGLECT A FIRE AND IT SPREADS

actually began to steal whatever happened to be lying round. And the women and children also learned to do the same. Their lives grew constantly worse and worse.

Ivan Shcherbakof and Gavrilo the cripple had their cases tried before the commune, and in the district court, and before the arbiter of the peace, until all the judges were weary of it; Gavrilo would have Ivan fined and put into jail, or Ivan would do the same to Gavrilo. And the more harm they did to each other the angrier they became. When dogs get to fighting, the more they tear each other, the more desperate they become. If some one pounds the dog from behind, he thinks it is the other dog that is biting, and grows madder still. So it was with these muzhiks. They went ahead with their lawsuits: either one or the other would get punished by fine or arrest; and for all that, their hearts were filled with still greater hatred.

"Just wait! I'll get even with you yet!"

Thus their affairs dragged on for six years. Still the old man on the oven kept saying the same thing. He used to try to reason with them:—

"What are you doing, children? Drop all these doings; don't neglect your business, and don't bear malice; it will be much better. For the angrier you get, the worse it becomes."

Still they paid no attention to the old man.

On the seventh year it came to pass that, at a wedding, Ivan's daughter-in-law insulted Gavrilo in the presence of the people. She began to accuse him of horse-stealing. Gavrilo was drunk; he could not control his temper, and he struck the woman; he hit her so hard that she was confined to her bed for a whole week; but she was in a delicate condition. Ivan was glad of the occurrence, and he went for a warrant at the magistrate's. . . .

"Now," said he to himself, "I shall square accounts with my neighbor; he shall not escape prison or Siberia."

But again Ivan lost his case. The magistrate did not accept his petition; the woman was examined; when she got up, there were no marks at all on her. Ivan went to the arbiter of the peace, and the latter transferred the case to the district court. Ivan began to bother the volost;[2] he drank up two or three gallons of mead with the secretary and the elder, and he succeeded in having Gavrilo sentenced to be whipped. They read the sentence to Gavrilo in court. The secretary read it:—

"The court has decided that the peasant Gavrilo Gordyeyef be punished with twenty lashes in presence of the officers of the volost."

Ivan also listened to the sentence, and looked at Gavrilo: "Now, what will he do about it?" Gavrilo listened to it, turned as white as a sheet, turned around, and went out into the vestibule. Ivan followed him and started to go to his horse; but he heard Gavrilo saying:—

"All right," says he; "he will lash my back; it will burn; but something of his may burn worse."

Ivan heard these words, and immediately turned to the judges.

"Just judges! he has threatened to set my house on fire! Listen: he said it in the presence of witnesses!"

2 The *volost* is a district comprising several villages.

Gavrilo was called back.

"Is it true you said so?"

"I said nothing. Lash me, since you have the power. It seems that I am the only one to suffer, though I am right; but he's allowed to do anything."

Gavrilo wanted to say more, but his lips and cheeks began to tremble. And he turned his face to the partition. Even the judges were frightened as they looked at Gavrilo. "Now," they think, "suppose he actually makes up his mind to do some harm to his neighbor or himself." And the little old judge began to speak:—

"See here, brothers! you had better make up your minds to become friends again. You, brother Gavrilo, did you do right in striking a woman with child? It is fortunate for you that God spared her, else what a sin you would have committed. Was it right? Confess, and ask his pardon, and he will forgive you. Then we'll change the sentence."

When the secretary heard it, he said:—

"That cannot be done, because, according to the 117th article, there was no peaceful settlement; but the judge's sentence was passed, and the sentence must be carried out."

But the judge did not heed the secretary.

"That will do . . . hold your tongue! There is only one article, brother, and that is the first, Remember God; and God has commanded you to become reconciled."

And again the judge tried to persuade the muzhiks, but his words were in vain. Gavrilo would not heed him.

"I am almost fifty years old," he said. "I have a married son, and I was never beaten in all my life; but now this pig-headed Vanka has brought me under the lash, and yet I am to ask his forgiveness, am I? Well, that will do! Only let Vanka look out for me!"

Gavrilo's voice trembled again; he could talk no longer. He turned around and went out.

It was ten versts from the court-house to the dvor, and it was late when Ivan reached home. The women had already gone to get the cattle. He unharnessed his horses, put things away, and went into the izba. There was no one in the izba. The children had not yet returned from the field, and the women were after the cattle. Ivan went in, sat down on the bench, and became lost in thought.

He remembered how the sentence was read to Gavrilo, and how he turned pale, and faced the partition; and his heart felt oppressed. He imagined himself in the same position, about to receive the punishment of lashes. And he began to pity Gavrilo. And he heard the old man coughing on the oven, then shifting from side to side, stretching out his legs, and then clambering down to the floor. The old man clambered down, dragged himself to the bench, and sat down. The old man found it hard to drag himself to the bench; he coughed and coughed; and when his coughing fit was over, he leaned his elbows on the table, and said:—

"Well, was he sentenced?"

Ivan says:—

"Sentenced to twenty lashes."

The old man shook his head.

"You are doing wrong, Ivan!" says he. "Oh, very wrong! Not to him, but to yourself, you are doing wrong. Now, suppose they lash his back; will it do you any good?"

"He won't do it any more," said Ivan.

"What won't he do any more? Is he doing anything worse than you do?"

"Do you want to know what he has done to me?" asked Ivan. "Why, he nearly killed the woman, and even now he threatened to set the house on fire! Why must I beg his pardon for it?"

The old man sighed, and said:—

"This whole free world is open for you, Ivan, to come and go upon; and because I have been lying on the oven for these last few years, do you think that you see all, and I see nothing. No, young man, you see nothing at all; anger has blinded your eyes. The faults of others are before you, but your own are behind your back. You say he did wrong; if he were the only man to do wrong, then there would be no wickedness in the world. Does wrong arise among people on account of one man? There must be two in a quarrel. You can see his sins, but you can't see your own. Had he been the only one to do wrong, and you had done right, there would have been no quarrel. Who pulled out his beard? Who threw down his hayrick? Who dragged him around in the courts? and yet you blame him for everything! Your own life is wrong, and that is bad. That isn't the way I used to live, brother; that isn't what I taught you. Is that the way the old man, his father, and I used to live? How did we live? Like good neighbors. If he was out of flour, the wife would come —'Uncle Frol, we are out of flour.'—'Just go to the closet, young woman, and get what you need.' He had no one to tend to the horses—'Go, Vanyatka,[8] and take care of his horses.' And whatever I was short of, I would go to him— 'Uncle Gordyeï, I need such and such a thing.'—'Take it, Uncle Frol!' And so it used to go with us. And it used to be the same nice way with you. And how is it now? Here, lately, a soldier was telling about Plevna; well, your quarrel is worse than that of Plevna. Is this living? It's a sin! You are a muzhik, you are master of a house. You will have to answer for it. What are you teaching your women and children to do? To fight like dogs! The other day, Taraska, that dirty-nosed rascal, was abusing Aunt Arina before his mother, and his mother was laughing at it. Is that good? You'll have to answer for it. Just think about your soul. Ought things to go on this way? You give me a word—I give you two back; you give me a slap—I give back two. No, my dear. Christ went about on earth, but He did not teach us fools such things. If a word is said to you, hold your peace: his own conscience will accuse him. That is the way He taught us, batyushka. If any one slap you, turn the other cheek: 'Here, strike, if I am worth it.' And his conscience will prick him. He will grow humble, and hear what you have to say. That is the way He commanded us, but not to be stiff-necked. Why don't you say something? am I not telling you the truth?"

Ivan said nothing—he was listening.

The old man had a fit of coughing, raised some phlegm, and began to speak again.

"Do you think that what Christ taught us is wrong? It was intended for us

8 Diminished diminutive of Ivan.

for our good. Think about your earthly life: has it been good, or bad, for you since this Plevna began between you? Just count up how much you have lost by these lawsuits, your traveling expenses, and all you have spent in eating. Those sons of yours are growing like young eagles: you ought to be living and enjoying life, and 'climb the mountain'; and here you are losing what you have! And why is it? It is all for nothing! All because of your pride! You ought to go with your children, and work in the field, and do the planting yourself; but the devil drives you off, either to the judge or to some pettifogger. You don't plow at the right time, you don't plant at the right time, and our little mother does not bring forth her fruit. Why were there no oats this year? When did you sow them? When you came from town! And what did you gain at law? You got in up to your neck! Ekh! you foolish fellow! just attend to business. Work with your boys in the field and house; and if any one insults you, then forgive them in God's name; and you will be far better off, and your heart will feel much easier."

Ivan said nothing.

"Just see here, Vanya! Listen to me: I am an old man. Go and harness the roan, go right back to court again, have all your cases dismissed, and in the morning go to Gavrilo, beg his forgiveness in God's name, invite him to the house,—to-morrow is a holiday"—this happened to be in September, just before the Birthday of the Virgin,—"light the samovarchik,[4] bring out a bottle and clear up all the sins so that they may not happen again, and tell the babas and the children to do the same."

Ivan sighed, and thought, "The old man says right," and his heart softened; only he did not know how to begin, how to become reconciled now.

And the old man began again, as if he read his thoughts.

"Go ahead, Vanya! don't put it off. Put out the fire when it first begins; but when it burns up, it is hard to do it."

The old man started to say something more, but he did not finish; the women came into the izba, and chattered like magpies. All the news had reached them, —how Gavrilo had been sentenced to be lashed, and how he had threatened to set their house on fire. They had heard everything, and they made their own additions; and they had already succeeded in getting into a new quarrel with Gavrilo's women folks in the pasture.

They began to tell how Gavrilo's daughter-in-law had threatened to set the marshal on them. The marshal, it seemed, took Gavrilo's part. He would reverse the whole case; and the school-teacher, it seemed, had written a second petition to the Tsar himself, against Ivan, and put in the petition all the things, about the bolt, and about the garden, and half of the farm would now be given to them.

As Ivan listened to their speeches, his heart grew hard again, and he changed his mind about becoming reconciled with Gavrilo.

The farmer always has many things to do about his place. Ivan did not stop to talk to the women, but he got up and left the izba; he went to the threshing-floor and to the shed. Before he had finished his work and returned to the yard, the little sun was already set; the boys, too, had come in from the field. The two had been plowing for the spring corn. Ivan met them, asked them

4 Little tea-urn.

about their work; he helped them put away their tools, laid aside the torn horse-collar; he was going also to put away the poles under the shed, but it had already become quite dark.

Ivan left the poles till the next day, but he fed the cattle; he opened the gates, and let Taraska and his horses out into the street to go to the pasture for the night, and shut them again, and put the board under the gate.

"Now for supper and bed," thought Ivan, as he picked up the torn collar and went into the izba.

By this time he had forgotten all about Gavrilo, and all that his father had said to him. Before he had taken hold of the door-knob, and entered the vestibule, he heard his neighbor from behind the fence scolding against some one, in a hoarse voice. "For this I call him a devil," cried Gavrilo, addressing some one.

"He ought to be killed!"

When Ivan heard these words, all his former anger against his neighbor flamed up in him. He stood for a while and listened while Gavrilo was scolding. When Gavrilo became quiet, Ivan went into the izba. When he entered, the room was lighted up. The young woman was sitting in one corner with her spinning-wheel, the old woman was getting supper, the oldest son was twisting cloth around his lapti.[5] The second one was sitting by the table with a little book. Taraska was going out for the night.

In the izba, all had been pleasant, comfortable, if it had not been for this annoyance—a bad neighbor.

Ivan came in angry, pushed the cat from the bench, scolded the women because the slop-pail was not in the right place. Ivan felt discouraged; he sat down, frowned, and began to mend the horse-collar; and Gavrilo's words kept rising in his mind, how he threatened him at court, and how he just shouted in a hoarse voice about some one, "He ought to be killed!"

The old woman prepared supper for Taraska; he ate it, put on his sheepskin shubyonka and his kaftan, tightened his belt, took some bread, and went out to the horses. His older brother intended to see him out; but Ivan rose, and went to the front steps.

It was already beginning to grow quite dark out of doors; the clouds covered the sky, and a wind sprang up. Ivan descended the steps, helped his son to mount, stirred up the little colt, then he stood for a while looking and listening as Taraska galloped down through the village, as he greeted the other boys, and as they all went out of hearing distance. Ivan stood long at the gate, and Gavrilo's words did not leave his mind:—

"Something of his may burn worse."

"He would not take pity on himself," thought Ivan. "Everything is dried up, and there is a wind besides. He might get in from the rear, start a fire, and all would be up with us; the villain might burn us up, and not get caught. Now, if I could only catch him, he would not get off so easy."

And thus it occurred to Ivan not to go back by the front way, but to go straight into the street, and behind the gate.

"No, I'll go round the dvor. Who knows what he's up to now?"

And Ivan crept quietly alongside of the gates. Just as he turned around the

[5] Wooden sandals.—Ed.

corner, and looked in the direction of the fence, it seemed to him that he saw something move in the corner, as if some one stuck his head out and then hid again.

Ivan stood still, and held his breath. He listened, and strained his eyes; all was quiet; only the wind was rustling the little leaves on the twigs, and whistling in the straw-heap. At first it was as dark as a pocket. But soon his eyes got accustomed to the darkness; and Ivan could see the whole corner, and the sokha-plow, and the sloping roof. He stood for a while, and gazed, but there was no one to be seen.

"It must have been a deception," thought Ivan; "still, I will make a turn around."

And he went stealthily alongside the shed. Ivan crept softly, in his lapti, so that he could not hear his own steps. He reached the corner, and lo! at the very farther end something near the plow flashed up and instantly vanished again. A pang seized Ivan's heart, and he stood still. He had scarcely stopped before a brighter light flashed up in the same place, and a man with a cap on was plainly seen squatting down with his back turned, and was trying to kindle a bundle of straw that he held in his hand.

Ivan's heart began to flutter in his breast like a bird; and he braced himself up, and advanced with long steps, but so cautiously that he himself could not hear them.

"There," says he to himself, "I've got him now; I've caught him in the very act."

But before Ivan had gone two more steps, suddenly something flared up brightly,—brightly, but in an entirely different place; and it was no small fire, either; and the staw blazed up under the pent-roof, and began to spread toward the house; and then Gavrilo was seen standing in the light.

Like a hawk on a sparrow, Ivan threw himself on the cripple.

"I'll choke the life out of him! he won't escape me this time," he says to himself.

But the cripple must have heard his steps; he looked around, and, in spite of his lameness, leaped like a rabbit along by the shed.

"You shan't escape!" shouted Ivan, and he flew after him.

But just as he was about to get him by the collar, Gavrilo slipped from under his hand, and Ivan caught him by the coat-tail. The coat-tail tore out, and Ivan fell. Ivan leaped to his feet. "Help! Catch him!" And he started after him again.

But, by the time he got to his feet, Gavrilo was already at his own dvor; but Ivan caught up with him, even then. But, as he tried to lay hands on him, something struck him on the head, as if a stone had hit his temple. It was Gavrilo, who had picked up an oak stave; and when Ivan came up to him, he struck him on the head with all his force.

Ivan saw stars; everything grew dark; he staggered, and fell senseless.

When he came to, Gavrilo was gone; it was as light as day; in the direction of his yard there was a noise like a machine, a crackling and roaring. Ivan turned around, and saw that the back shed was already gone, that the side shed was on fire, and the flame and smoke and burning straw were drifting toward the izba.

"What does this mean? Bratsui!"[6] exclaimed Ivan, lifting his hand and slapping his thigh. "All it needs, is to pull down the pent-roof, and trample it out. What does it mean, bratsui?" he repeated.

He tried to shout, but he had no breath; his voice stuck in his throat. He tried to run, but his feet refused to move; they tripped each other up. He merely walked and staggered; again his breath failed him. He stood for a moment, got his wind, and then started again. While he was making his way round to the shed, and getting to the fire, the side shed also burned to the ground, and the corner of the izba and the gates caught fire. The flames poured up from the izba, and all entrance to the yard was cut off. A great crowd gathered, but nothing could be done. The neighbors were carrying out their own effects, and driving their cattle out of their yards.

After Ivan's dvor had burned up, Gavrilo's took fire; the wind arose, and carried the fire across the street. Half the village was destroyed.

From Ivan's house the old man was rescued with difficulty, and his people rushed out with only the clothes they had on. Everything else was burned, with the exception of the horses which had gone to the night-pasture. All the cattle were destroyed. The poultry were burned on their roosts; the carts, the plows, the harrows, the women's boxes, the corn and wheat in the granary,—everything was destroyed.

Gavrilo's cattle were rescued, and a few of his effects were removed in safety.

The fire lasted all night long. Ivan stood by his dvor, and gazed, and kept repeating, "What does this mean? Bratsui! All it needs, is to pull it down, and trample it out."

But when the ceiling of his izba fell in, he crept up close to the fire, caught hold of a burning beam, and tried to pull it out. The women saw him, and began to call him back; but he pulled the beam out, and went back after another, but staggered, and fell into the fire.

Then his son dashed in after him, and pulled him out. Ivan's beard and hair were burned off, his clothes were scorched, his hands were ruined, and yet he did not notice it.

"He has lost his wits from grief," said the crowd.

The fire began to die down; and Ivan still stood in the same place, and kept repeating, "Bratsui! Only pull it down!"

In the morning the starosta sent his son after Ivan.

"Uncle Ivan, your father is dying; he wants you to come and say good-by."

Ivan had forgotten all about his father, and did not comprehend what they said to him.

"What father?" says he; "wants whom?"

"He wants you to come and bid him good-by; he is dying in our izba. Come, let us go, Uncle Ivan," said the village elder's son, and took him by the arm. Ivan followed the starosta's son.

The old man, when he was rescued, was surrounded by burning straw, and was badly burned. He was taken to the starosta's, at the farther end of the village. That part of the village was not burned.

When Ivan came to his father, there was no one in the izba except a little old woman,—the starosta's wife,—and some children on the oven. All the rest

[6] *Bratsui*, brothers! an exclamation.

were at the fire. The old man was lying on the bench with a little candle in his hand, and was gazing at the door. When his son entered, he started. The old woman went to him, and told him that his son had come. He asked him to come nearer. Ivan approached, and the old man said:—

"Well, Vanyatka," he said, "I told you so. Who burned up the village?"

"He did, batyushka," said Ivan. "He did! I myself caught him at it. Right before my eyes he touched off the roof. All I needed to do was to pull out the bunch of burning straw, trample it down, and it would never have happened."

"Ivan," said the old man, "my death has come; you, too, will have to die. Whose sin was it?"

Ivan looked at his father, and said nothing. He could not utter a word.

"Tell me in God's presence! Whose sin was it? What did I tell you?"

Only at this moment Ivan came to himself, and comprehended all. He began to snuffle with his nose, and said:—

"Mine, batyushka!" and he fell on his knees before his father, began to weep, and said:—

"Forgive me, batyushka; I am guilty before you and before God."

The old man waved his arms, took the candle in his left hand, and pointed with his right to his forehead; tried to cross himself, but failed to lift it high enough, and stopped short.

"Glory to Thee, O Lord, glory to Thee, O Lord!" he said, and then he turned his eyes on his son.

"But Vanka, Vanka!"

"What is it, batyushka?"

"What ought you to do now?"

Ivan kept on weeping.

"I don't know, batyushka," he said. "How are we going to live now, batyushka?"

The old man shut his eyes, moved his lips, as if he were trying to gather his strength; and then he opened his eyes again, and said:—

"You will get along! if you live with God—you will get along."

The old man stopped speaking, and smiled, and said:—

"Look here, Vanya! don't tell who set the fire. Hide your neighbor's sin, and God will forgive two."

The old man took the candle in both his hands, held them crossed on his breast, sighed, stretched himself, and died.

Ivan did not expose Gavrilo, and no one knew what was the cause of the fire.

And Ivan's heart grew soft toward Gavrilo, and Gavrilo was surprised because Ivan did not tell any one about him.

At first Gavrilo was afraid of him, but afterward he got accustomed to it. The muzhiks ceased to quarrel, their families also. While they were rebuilding, both families lived in one dvor; and when the village was restored, and the dvors were put at a greater distance apart, Ivan and Gavrilo again became neighbors in one nest.

And Ivan and Gavrilo lived in neighborly fashion, just as the old men had formerly lived. And Ivan Shcherbakof remembered the old man's advice, and God's proof that a fire ought to be quenched at the beginning.

And if any one ever did him any harm, he made no attempt to retaliate, but tried to arrange things; and if any one ever called him a bad name, he did not try to outdo him in his reply, but he tried to teach him not to say bad things; and thus he taught the women and children of his household; and thus Ivan Shcherbakof reformed, and began to live better than before.

1885

SKAZKA

1

Once on a time a rich muzhik lived in a certain empire, in a certain kingdom. And the rich muzhik had three sons,—Semyon the warrior, Taras the pot-bellied, and Ivan the fool,—and a deaf and dumb daughter, Malanya the spinster.

Semyon the warrior went to war, to serve the Tsar; Taras the pot-bellied went to the city, to a merchant's, to engage in trade; but Ivan the fool stayed at home with the girl, to work, and grow round-shouldered.

Semyon won high rank and an estate, and married a nobleman's daughter. His pay was large, and his estate large, and yet he did not make ends meet: what the husband made, his wife, the lady, squandered with lavish hand; and they never had any money!

And Semyon went to his estate to collect his revenues. And the steward said to him:—

"We have no way of getting any revenue; we have neither cattle nor tools, nor horses nor cows, nor plows nor harrows. All these must be got; then there will be an income."

And Semyon went to his father.

"Father," said he, "you are rich; and yet you have given me nothing. Give me my third, and I will improve my estate with it."

And the old man said:—

"You have brought nothing to my house: why should I give you a third part. It would be unfair to Ivan and the girl."

But Semyon said:—

"Now, look here; he is a fool, and she is a deaf and dumb old maid; what do they need?"

And the old man replied:—

"Be it as Ivan shall say."

But Ivan says:—

"All right, let him have it."

Semyon took his share from home, spent it on his estate, and went off again to the Tsar, to serve him.

The pot-bellied Taras also made much money; he married into the merchant family, but still he had not enough. He went to his father, and said:—

"Give me my portion."

The old man did not want to give Taras his portion either.

Said he: "You have brought nothing to us; but whatever is in the house, that Ivan has saved. And so we must not wrong him and the girl."

But Taras said:—

"What good does it do him? he is a fool. He cannot marry, no one would have him. And the dumb girl doesn't need anything either.—Ivan," said he, "give me half the grain,—I won't take the tools,—and of the live-stock I will take only the gray stallion; he's no good to you for plowing."

Ivan laughed, and said:—

"All right; I will make a new start."

So they gave Taras his share.

Taras took the grain to the city; he took the gray stallion; and Ivan was left with one old mare, to toil like a peasant, as before, and support his father and mother.

2

The old devil was angry because the brothers had not quarreled over the division, but had parted amicably; and he summoned three devilkins.

"Look here," says he: "there are three brothers, Semyon the warrior, Taras the pot-bellied, and Ivan the fool. They all ought to be quarreling, but they live peaceably; they visit one another. The fool has ruined the whole business for me. Now you three go and get hold of the three brothers, and stir them up, so that they will scratch one another's eyes out. Can you do this?"

"We can," said they.

"How will you do it?"

"Well, we shall do it this way: first, we'll ruin them, so that they'll have nothing to eat, and then tie them all together; and they will fall to fighting."

"Now, that's capital," says he. "I see you know your business. Make haste, and don't you come back to me until you have set the three by the ears, otherwise I'll skin you all alive."

The devilkins all went to a bog and began to plan how to undertake their task. They wrangled and wrangled, for each one wished to have the easiest part of the job to do; and at last they decided to cast lots for which one each should take; and if any of them should accomplish his work first, he should come to the aid of the others.

So the devilkins cast lots, and set a time to meet again in a bog, to learn who had succeeded, and who needed help.

The time appointed came, and the devilkins met in the bog according to agreement. They proceeded to describe how matters stood. The first devilkin began to tell about Semyon the warrior.

"My work," said he, "is getting along well. To-morrow," said he, "my Semyon is going to his father."

His comrades began to ask:—

"How did you bring it about?"

"Well," said he, "in the first place, I inspired Semyon with such courage that he promised his Tsar to conquer the whole world; and the Tsar made Semyon his general-in-chief, and sent him to conquer the Tsar of India. They met for battle. That very night I wet all the powder in Semyon's army, and I went to the Tsar of India and I made a countless multitude of straw soldiers. Semyon's soldiers saw the straw soldiers surrounding them on all sides, and they were frightened. Semyon ordered them to fire but their cannon and guns did not go off. Semyon's soldiers were panic-struck, and ran like sheep; and the Tsar of India slaughtered them. Semyon was disgraced: his estate was confiscated, and to-morrow they intend to execute him. But I have only one day's work more with him. I have let him out of prison, so that he may run home. To-morrow I shall finish with him; so tell us which of you two needs help."

And the second devilkin—Taras's—began to tell about his affairs.

"I need no help," said he; "my job also has gone smoothly, and Taras will not hold out more than a week. In the first place," said he, "I caused his belly to grow, and filled him with envy. So covetous has he become of others' goods, that he wishes to buy everything he sees. He has spent all his money on a host of things, and still he keeps on buying. Now he has already begun to buy on credit. His debts hang already round his neck like a weight, and he has entangled himself so that he can't get out of the tangle. At the end of a week his obligations will fall due, and I shall make rubbish of all of his wares. . . . He won't be able to pay, and he will go home to his father."

They turned now to ask the third devilkin—Ivan's:—

"And how are you getting along?"

"Well," said he, "my affair does not get on well. In the first place, I spat into his jug of kvas, so as to give him the belly-ache; and I went to his field, stamped the ground as hard as a stone, so that he could not work it. I thought that he would not plow it; but he, the fool, came with his wooden plow, began to work at it. His belly-ache made him groan, but he went on plowing. I broke one plow for him: he went home, exchanged it for another, bound with new withs, and took up his plowing again. I crept under the soil and tried to hold back his plowshares; you couldn't hold them back at all. He lays out all his strength on the plow, and the plowshares were sharp and cut my hands all up. He plowed almost the whole; only one little strip was left. Come, brothers, to my aid; for if we don't get the better of him, all our labor will be lost. If the fool is left, and is going to farm it, they won't know want; he will support both his brothers."

Semyon's devilkin promised to come to his aid the next day, and the devilkins separated.

3

Ivan had plowed the whole fallow; only one narrow strip remained. He went out to finish it. His belly ached, but the plowing had to be done. He straightened the ropes, turned his plow, and started to plow. He had made only one furrow and was coming back, when it seemed to catch on a root and dragged. Now this was the devilkin, who had suddenly twisted his legs around the plowshare and was holding it.

"What a strange thing!" said Ivan to himself. "There were no roots here, but here's a root."

Ivan put his hand down into the furrow and felt something soft. He seized it, and pulled it out.

It was black, like a root; but on the root, something was wriggling. Lo! a live devilkin!

"Hey, there," said Ivan, "what a nasty thing!" and he lifted up his hand to dash it against the plow, when the devilkin began to whine.

"Don't strike me," said he, "but I will do for you whatever you wish."

"What will you do for me?"

"Only tell me what you wish."

Ivan scratched his head.

"My belly aches," said he; "can you cure it?"

"I can," said he.

"All right, cure it."

The devilkin bent down to the furrow; scratched about, scratched about with his claws; pulled out a little root,—a three-pronged root,—and gave it to Ivan.

"Here," said he; "whoever swallows this one little root, every pain will disappear."

Ivan took it, broke off the little root, and swallowed it. Immediately his belly [-ache] went away.

Again the devilkin begged.

"Let me go now," said he. "I will dive into the earth; I will never come again."

"All right. God be with you."

And the moment Ivan spoke of God, the devilkin plunged suddenly under the earth, like a stone in the water; only the hole was left.

Ivan put the two other little roots into his cap, and went on with his plowing. He plowed the strip to the end, turned over the sokha, and went home. He unharnessed, went into the izba, and found his elder brother Semyon the warrior and his wife sitting at supper. His estate had been confiscated; he had broken out of prison, and had hurried home to his father to live.

Semyon saw Ivan.

"I have come," said he, "to live with you. Feed me and my wife until we find a new place."

"All right," said he; "live with us."

But as Ivan was about to sit down on the bench, the lady found the odor from him disgusting. She even said to her husband:—

"I cannot endure," said she, "to eat with a stinking muzhik."

And Semyon said:—

"My lady says you smell bad; you had better go out and eat in the entry."

"Very well," said he; "I must go out anyway to pasture the mare for the night."

Ivan took some bread and his kaftan, and went out for the night.

4

That night Semyon's devilkin, having finished his job, went according to agreement to find Ivan's devilkin to help him subdue the fool.

He came to the field and there he searched and he searched for his comrade, but there was no sign of him anywhere—all he found was a hole.

"Well," he thought, "some ill has certainly befallen my comrade. I must take his place. The fallow has been all plowed. I shall have to subdue the fool in his hay-field."

The devilkin went to the meadow, and flooded Ivan's grass; all the hay-field was matted with mud. Ivan returned at dawn from the pasture, whetted his scythe, and went to mow the meadow. He began to mow. He swung his scythe once—he swung it twice—the scythe became so dull it would not cut at all— he had to sharpen it. Ivan struggled and struggled. "It's no use," said he; "I am going home to get a whetstone and a slice of bread. Though I have to work a week, I won't give in till I mow it all."

The devilkin was listening; he said to himself:—

"This fool is a tough one; I shall not get him this way. We must try some other trick on him."

Ivan came back, sharpened his scythe, and began to mow. The devilkin crept into the grass, and kept catching the scythe by the heel, and thrusting the point into the ground. It was hard for Ivan, yet he kept on with his mowing; there remained only one patch in the marsh. The devilkin crept into the marsh; thinks to himself: "Though I cut my paws, still I will not let him mow."

Ivan came to the marsh; the grass did not look thick, but it resisted the scythe. Ivan grew angry, began to mow with all his might; the devilkin had to give it up—he hadn't time to leap away—he saw it was a bad business, and he jumped into a bush. Ivan was swinging his scythe, and, as he grazed the bush, he clipped off half of the devilkin's tail. Ivan finished mowing his field, bade the girl rake it up, and went off to mow the rye.

He went out with his sickle, but the dock-tailed devilkin was there before him, and tangled up the rye, so that the sickle was useless. Ivan turned round, took his pruning-hook, and set about reaping; he reaped all the rye.

"Well, now," said he, "I must take hold of the oats."

The dock-tailed devilkin was listening; he thinks, "I did not get the better of him on the rye, so I must catch him on the oats; only wait till morning."

The devilkin hurried out in the morning to the oat-field, but the oats were already mowed. Ivan had mowed the field by night, in order that less grain might shake out.

The devilkin was enraged.

"The fool," said he, "has hacked me and tortured me! I never saw such ill luck, even in war. The cursed fellow does not sleep; I can't get ahead of him. I am going now," said he, "to the grain-ricks; I will make them all rot for him."

And the devilkin went to the ricks of rye; he crept among the sheaves and they began to rot. He heated them, and got warm himself, and fell asleep.

But Ivan harnessed the mare, and went with the dumb girl to get them. They came to the ricks, began to pitch them up; he had pitched up two sheaves, and vas just thrusting in his fork again, when the fork stuck straight into the devilkin's back; he lifted his fork—and lo! on the prongs was a live devilkin; yea, verily, with his tail cut short, and sprawling, wriggling, and trying to wriggle off.

"Hallo, there!" says he, "you nasty thing! Are you here again?"

"I," says he, "am another one; that was my brother. But I have been with your brother Semyon."

"Well," says Ivan, "whoever you are, you shall have the same treatment."

He was just going to dash him against the cart-rail, but the devilkin began to beseech him.

"Let me off," said he. "I won't do so any more, but I will do whatever you want me to."

"Well, what can you do?"

"Well," said he, "I can make soldiers out of anything you please."

"But what are they good for?"

"You can do anything with them you wish," said he. "They can do all things."

"Can they sing?"

"They can."

"Very good," said Ivan; "make some."

And the devilkin said:—

"Here, take this sheaf of rye; drag it over the ground, set it up, and merely say, ' 'Tis my slave's decree that thou shalt be a sheaf no more. Let every straw there is in thee a soldier be.' "

Ivan took the sheaf, dragged it over the ground, and repeated what the devilkin bade him say. And the sheaf fell asunder, and soldiers were created, with the drummer and the trumpeter playing at their head. Ivan burst out laughing.

"I declare," said he, "that's clever! How it will amuse the girls!"

"Well," said the devilkin, "let me go now."

"No," says he, "I am going to make them out of chaff; else good seed will be wasted. Show me how to change them back to the sheaf again. I'm going to thresh it."

And the devilkin said:—

"Repeat, 'Let every soldier be a straw. 'Tis my slave's decree that a sheaf thou be.' "

Ivan said this and the sheaf came back. And again the devilkin began to plead.

"Now let me go," said he.

"All right!"

Ivan seized him by the legs, held him in his hand, and pulled him from the fork.

"God be with you!" said Ivan; and as soon as he said "s Bogom," the devilkin plunged into the earth like a stone into water; only the hole was left.

Ivan went home; and at home he found his other brother, Taras, and his wife, sitting down to supper. Taras had failed to pay his debts, had fled from his creditors, and come home to his father. As soon as he saw Ivan, he said:—

"Well, now that I'm dead broke, keep me and my wife."

"All right," said Ivan, "stay with us."

Ivan took off his kaftan, and sat down to table.

But the merchant's wife said:—

"I can't eat with a fool. He smells of perspiration!"

So Taras said:—

"Ivan, you smell strong; go and eat in the entry."

"Well, all right," said Ivan; and, taking some bread, he went out into the yard: "It's about time for me to go to pasture, anyway."

5

That night Taras's devilkin, who also accomplished his job, came, according to agreement, to help his comrades to get the better of Ivan the fool. He came to the fallow; he searched and searched for his comrades. No sign of them anywhere; he found only a hole. So he went to the meadow; in the swamp he found the tail, and in the rye-stubble-field he found the other hole.

"Well," he said to himself, "some ill must have befallen my comrades. I must take their places and tackle the fool."

The devilkin went to look for Ivan. But Ivan had already left the field for the woods, to cut down trees.

The brothers had begun to find it crowded living together, and they bade the fool prepare lumber and build them new houses.

The devilkin hastened to the forest, crept into the knots, and began to hinder Ivan from falling the trees. Ivan under-cut a tree so that it should fall in a clear space; it began to fall. The mischief got into the tree; it fell in the wrong direction and became entangled in the branches.

Ivan got his cant-hook and tried to free the tree, and at last brought it to the ground. He tried to fall another; again the same thing occurred. He struggled and struggled, and with great difficulty succeeded. He took hold of a third; again the same story. Ivan had expected to cut down a half-hundred saplings, and he had not hewed down a dozen; and it was already night, and Ivan was tired out. The steam arose from him, spread through the forest like a fog; but still he would not leave off. He under-cut still another tree; his back was almost broken; and, as he had no more strength, he drove the ax into the tree, and sat down to rest.

The devilkin perceived that Ivan had ceased working; and he rejoiced.

"Well," he said to himself, "he is tired out; he will give it up. I, too, will rest now."

He seated himself astride of a limb, and chuckled. But Ivan got up, pulled out the ax, swung it, and as he hacked on the other side, the tree all at once began to crack, and fell heavily. The devilkin was not prepared for this, and had no time to get his leg out of the way; the branch broke, and nipped the devilkin by the paw. Ivan began to lop away the branches, and lo! there was a live devilkin! He was amazed.

"Hallo!" said he, "what a nasty thing! Are you here again?"

"I am another one," said he; "I have been at your brother Taras's."

"Well, whoever you are, it will be all the same with you."

Ivan flourished his ax and was about to strike him with the ax-head, but the devilkin begged for mercy.

"Don't strike me," said he, "and I will do for you whatever you wish."

"Well, then, what can you do?"

"I can make you as much money," says he, "as you wish."

"All right," says he; "do so."

And the devilkin began to show him how:—

"Take some oak leaves from this oak, and rub them in your hands. Gold will fall to the ground."

Ivan took the leaves, rubbed them, and gold fell out.

"This is good," says he, "to amuse children with, when they have leisure time."

"Let me go," says the devilkin.

"All right!"

Ivan took his cant-hook and set the devilkin free.

"God be with you!" said he, and as soon as he said the words, "*Bog s Toboï,*" the devilkin plunged under the earth, like a stone into the water; only the hole was left.

6

The brothers built houses, and began to live apart. But Ivan got in his crops, brewed beer, and invited his brothers to a revel; but they refused to come as Ivan's guests.

"Haven't we seen a peasant revel?" they said.

Ivan entertained the peasant men and women; and he himself drank till he grew tipsy, and went into the street to the singers. Ivan went up to the singers, and bade the women sing a song in his honor.

"I will give you," says he, "what you never saw in your lives before."

The women laughed, and began to sing a song in his honor. They finished their song and dance in his praise, and said:—

"Now, then, give it to us."

"I will bring it to you immediately," said he. He took his seed-basket and hastened out to the forest. The women made sport of him. "What a fool!" they cried and they forgot all about him.

But lo! Ivan came running back, bringing his seed-basket full of something. "Shall I distribute it, or not?"

"Distribute it!"

Ivan took a handful of gold, and flung it among the women. Batyushki! The women sprang to pick it up; the muzhiks scrambled after it—they each tried to snatch it from the other—they carry it off. One old woman was almost crushed to death. Ivan burst out laughing.

"Oh, you fools!" said he, "why have you crushed the old grandmother? Be calmer, and I will give you more."

He began to scatter more. The people crowded around; Ivan emptied his whole seed-basket. They still begged for more.

But Ivan said:—

"That's all; another time I'll give you some more. Now for a dance. Sing us your songs!"

The women began to sing their songs.

"Your songs," said he, "are no good."

"What kind of ones are better?" they asked.

"Well, I'll show you," says he, "in a little while."

He went to the barn, pulled out a sheaf, threshed it, stood it up, dragged it on the ground.

"Now," said he, "slave, now decree that it shall be a sheaf no more, but every straw a soldier."

The sheaf fell apart, the soldiers stood forth, the drums and trumpets played.

Ivan commanded the soldiers to sing some songs; he came with them up the street. The people were amazed. The soldiers sang their songs, and then Ivan led them back to the barn; but he commanded that no one should follow him, and turned the soldiers into a sheaf again, and flung it on the pile.

He went home, and lay down to sleep in the stable.

7

In the morning the elder brother, Semyon the warrior, who had heard about these doings, came to Ivan.

"Show me," said he, "where you got soldiers, and where you have taken them."

"But what good," says he, "will it do you?"

"Why do you ask? With soldiers, everything can be done. One can win a kingdom for one's self."

Ivan was amazed.

"Really?" said he; "why didn't you say so long ago? I will make you as many as you wish. It's well the girl and I put aside a good many."

Ivan took his brother to the barn, and said:—

"Look, I will make them; but you must march them away, for, if we have to feed them, then they will eat up the whole village in a day."

Semyon promised to march the soldiers away, and Ivan began to make them. He thumped a sheaf on the barn floor—a squad appeared! He thumped another —another squad. He made so many of them that they filled the whole field.

"Well, will that be enough?"

Semyon was delighted, and said:—

"That'll be enough. Thank you, Ivan."

"All right," says he; "if you need any more, come back, and I will make some more. We have a great deal of straw this season."

Semyon the warrior immediately gave orders to his army, drew them up in proper order, and went off to make war.

Hardly had Semyon gone when Taras the pot-bellied made his appearance —he also had heard of yesterday's doings, and he began to beg his brother.

"Show me where you get gold money. If I had such an abundance of free money, I would with that money get in money from all over the world."

Ivan was amazed.

"Really? You should have told me long ago. I will make you as much as you like."

His brother was delighted.

"Give me only three basketfuls."

"All right," said he, "let us go to the woods; but put in the horse—it'll be too much for you to lug."

They went to the forest; Ivan began to rub the oak leaves. He made a great heap.

"Is that enough, or not?"

Taras was delighted.

"Enough for now," says he. "Thanks, Ivan."

"All right," says he. "If you need more, come to me, and I will rub some more for you; plenty of leaves are left."

Taras gathered up a whole cartful, and went off to trade.

Both brothers went off, and Semyon began to make war, and Taras to trade. And Semyon conquered for himself a tsardom, and Taras made a vast heap of money in trade.

The brothers met, and told each other whence Semyon got his soldiers, and Taras his money.

And Semyon said to his brother:—

"I," said he, "have conquered for myself a tsardom; and I might live well, only—I have not enough money to keep my soldiers."

And Taras said:—

"And I," said he, "have gathered together a great heap of money; but," said he, "there's one trouble, there is no one to guard my money."

And Semyon said:—

"Let us go," said he, "to our brother. I will bid him make some more soldiers—I will give you enough to guard your money, but you must bid him rub enough money for me to sustain my soldiers."

And they went to Ivan.

They went to Ivan, and Semyon said:—

"I haven't enough soldiers, brother," said he; "make me some more soldiers; change at least two ricks into soldiers."

Ivan shook his head.

"No use," said he; "I am not going to make you any more soldiers."

"But how is that?" said he. "You promised me you would."

"I know I promised," said he; "but I will not make any more."

"But why, you fool, won't you make any more?"

"Well, because your soldiers killed a man. The other day I was plowing by the road, and I saw a baba carrying along the road a coffin, and she was wailing. I asked her, 'Who is dead?' She said, 'Semyon's soldiers have killed my husband in the war.' I thought that soldiers were for singing songs, but they have put a man to death. I will give you no more."

And thus he persisted, and refused to make any more soldiers.

Taras now began to implore Ivan to make some more gold money for him. Ivan shook his head.

"No use," said he, "I will not rub any more."

"Well, but how is this?" said Taras. "You promised me you would."

"I promised," said he, "but I will not make any more."

"But why, you fool, will you not make any more?"

"Well, because your gold pieces have robbed Mikhaïlovna of her cow!"

"How have they robbed her?"

"In this way they have robbed her: Mikhaïlovna had a cow, her children drank milk; but lately her children have come to me to beg milk. And I said to them, 'Where is your cow?' They said, 'Taras, the pot-bellied overseer, came along, gave our mamushka three gold pieces, and she let him have the cow; now we have no milk to drink.' I thought that you wanted to play with the gold pieces, but you have robbed the children of their cow; I will not give you any more."

And the fool was firm, and would give no more. And so the brothers went away.

The brothers went away, and began to plan how to help their misfortune. Semyon said:—

"See here, this is what we'll do: you give me money to maintain my soldiers, and I will give you half my tsardom, with soldiers to guard your money."

Taras agreed. So the brothers went shares, and both became tsars, and both were rich.

8

But Ivan lived at home, supported his father and mother, worked with the dumb girl in the field.

Now, it happened one day that Ivan's old watch-dog fell sick, grew mangy, and almost died. Ivan was sorry for him; got some bread from the dumb girl, put it in his cap, carried it to the dog, and threw it to him. But the cap was torn, and a little root fell with the bread.

The old dog swallowed it with the bread. And as soon as the dog had swallowed the root, he jumped up, began to frisk around, to bark, to wag his tail, and got well.

The father and mother saw this and were amazed.

"How," said they, "did you cure the dog?"

And Ivan said:—

"I had two little roots,—they will cure any pain,—and the dog swallowed one of them."

And it happened about this time that the Tsar's daughter fell ill; and the Tsar published through all cities and towns, that whoever should cure her should be rewarded; and, if he were unmarried, that he should receive, in addition, the Tsar's daughter in marriage. The proclamation was made also in Ivan's village.

Ivan's father and mother called him in, and said to him, "Have you heard what the Tsar proclaims? You have said that you have a little root; make haste, and cure the Tsar's daughter. You will win good luck for life."

"All right," said he.

And Ivan got ready to start; they spruced him up.

Ivan went out on the door-step; he sees standing there a beggar woman, with a crippled hand.

"I have heard," said she, "that you can cure folks. Cure my hand, for now I cannot put on my own shoes."

And Ivan said:—

"All right."

He took out the little root and gave it to the beggar woman and bade her swallow it. The beggar woman swallowed it and became cured; she began at once to use her hand.

Ivan's father and mother came out to go with him to the Tsar. When they learned that Ivan had given away his last rootlet, and had nothing to cure the Tsar's daughter with, his father and mother began to upbraid him.

"You had pity on the beggar woman," said they, "but on the Tsar's daughter you had no pity."

Ivan began to feel sorry for the Tsar's daughter also. He harnessed the horse, spread straw in the cart, and started.

"Now, where are you going, fool?"

"To cure the Tsar's daughter."

"Yes, but see here: you have nothing to cure her with."

"It's all right," said he; and he started up the horse.

He came to the Tsar's palace; and, as soon as he mounted the steps, the Tsar's daughter got well.

The Tsar was overjoyed, commanded Ivan to be brought to him. He clothed him and decorated him. "Be my son-in-law!" said he.

"All right," said Ivan.

And Ivan married the Tsarevna. And soon the Tsar died, and Ivan became Tsar.

Thus all three of the brothers were tsars.

9

The three brothers lived and reigned.

The eldest brother, Semyon the warrior, got along well. With his straw soldiers he collected real soldiers. He commanded that every ten houses throughout his whole tsardom should furnish a soldier, and that this soldier should be tall in stature, and white in body, and clean in face. And he collected many such soldiers, and drilled them all. And when any one contradicted him in anything, he immediately sent these soldiers, and he did whatever he pleased. And all began to fear him.

And life was pleasant to him. Whatever he fancied, and whatever his eyes rested on, became his. He would send soldiers, and they would seize and bring to him all he wanted.

Taras the pot-bellied also got along well. He did not waste the money he had got from Ivan, but he made great additions to it. He also set up fine arrangements in his tsardom. He kept his money in coffers, and he exacted money from the people. He exacted money for their serfs, and for their walking and driving, and for their bark shoes, and for their leg-wrappers, and for their flounces. And whatever he fancied was his. For money they would bring him anything; and they were glad to work for him because every one must have money.

And Ivan the fool did not live poorly. As soon as he had buried his father-in-law, he took off all his royal raiment and gave it to his wife to lock up in the chest; he dressed in his hempen shirt again, put on his drawers and bark shoes, and betook himself to work.

"It is tiresome to me," said he; "I am growing fat, and I have no appetite, and I can't sleep."

He brought his father and mother, and the dumb girl, and began once more to work.

And they said to him:—

"But, don't you see, you are the Tsar!"

"Well," said he, "even a Tsar must eat."

The minister came to him, and said:—

"We have no money to pay salaries."

"All right," said he; "if you have none, then don't pay them."

"But they won't serve."

"All right," said he; "let them not serve. They will have all the more time to work. Let them carry out manure; they have heaped up a lot."

They came to Ivan to hold a trial. One said, "He stole my money."

And Ivan said:—

"All right! that shows he needed it."

All perceived that Ivan was a fool; and his wife said to him:—

"They say you are a fool."

"All right!" said he.

Ivan's wife thought and thought; but she also was a fool.

"What is the use," she asked herself, "for me to go against my husband? Where the needle goes the thread follows."

She took off her royal raiment, locked it up in the chest, went to the dumb girl, and learned how to work. When she had learned how to work, she began to help her husband.

And all the wise left Ivan's tsardom; only fools were left. No one had money. They lived, they worked, they supported themselves, and supported good men.

10

The old devil waited and waited for tidings from the devilkins, about their success in destroying the three brothers; but no tidings came. He himself went to investigate. He searched and searched, but could find nothing of them except the three holes.

"Well," says he to himself, "plainly they did not get the better of them. I must tackle it myself."

He started to find the brothers, but they were not in their old places. He found them in their different kingdoms. All three are alive, reigning as tsars. This seemed outrageous to the old devil.

"Well," says he, "I had better take hold of this job myself."

He went first of all to Tsar Semyon. He went not in his own shape, but changed into a vaïvode,[1] came to Tsar Semyon.

"Tsar Semyon, I have heard," said he, "that you are a great warrior; and I know that business well. I wish to enter your service."

The Tsar Semyon began to question him, and, seeing that he was a man of sense, took him into his service.

The new vaïvode began to show Tsar Semyon how to collect a powerful army.

"First," said he, "it is necessary to collect more soldiers; and now," said he, "many people are idly wandering up and down your tsardom. It is necessary," said he, "to recruit all the young men, without exception; then you will have an army five times as large as before. Secondly, it is necessary to get new rifles and cannon. I will get for you rifles which will shoot a hundred bullets at a time so that they will fly about like peas. And I will get cannon which will consume with fire either man, or horse, or wall—they will burn everything up."

Tsar Semyon listened to his new vaïvode, and ordered all the young men, without distinction, to be taken as soldiers; and he established new manufactories. He made new rifles and cannon, and immediately went to war with a neighboring Tsar.

[1] Army leader.

As soon as the army came out to meet them, Tsar Semyon ordered his soldiers to let fly at it with bullets, and to hurl fire at it from the cannon, and at one blow he disabled and burned up half the army. The neighboring Tsar was frightened, he humbled himself and surrendered his tsardom. Tsar Semyon was overjoyed.

"Now," said he, "I am going to attack the Tsar of India."

But the Tsar of India had heard about Tsar Semyon, and had adopted all of his inventions; yes, and, moreover, added some of his own. The Tsar of India not only began to take as soldiers young men, but also enlisted all the single women as soldiers; and his army became even larger than Tsar Semyon's. And he copied from Tsar Semyon all his rifles and cannon, and, moreover, invented a method of flying through the air, and launching explosive bombshells from above.

Tsar Semyon went to war against the Tsar of India—he thought to win in battle as before; but the scythe that once cut was dulled; the Tsar of India did not let Semyon's army come within gunshot, but he sent his women soldiers up into the air to lunch explosive bombshells upon Semyon's army. The women began to shower bombs from above upon Semyon's army, like borax on cockroaches; all Semyon's army took to flight, and Tsar Semyon was left alone. The Tsar of India took Semyon's tsardom, and Semyon barely escaped with his life.

The old devil finished with this brother, and went to Tsar Taras. He changed into a merchant, and settled in Taras's tsardom; he established a business house, began to pay out his money. The merchant began by paying high prices for every sort of thing, and all the people flocked to the merchant—to make money. And the people made so much money that they all paid their debts, and began to pay their taxes promptly.

Tsar Taras was delighted.

"Thanks to the merchant," said he to himself, "now I shall get still more money—my life will be still better."

And Tsar Taras endeavored to make new plans; he began to build a new palace for himself. He notified the people to bring him lumber and stone and to set to work for him; he offered high prices for everything. Tsar Taras thought that, judging by the past, the people would come to work for him in crowds for the money. But lo! they brought all the lumber and stone to the merchant, and all the working-people flocked to him. Tsar Taras raised his offer, but the merchant went still higher. Tsar Taras had much money, but the merchant still more; and the merchant's price was better than the Tsar's. The Tsar's palace was at a standstill; building stopped.

A park had been laid out for Tsar Taras. The autumn came. Taras invited the people to come to him to work in the park—no one came—all the people were engaged in digging a pond for the merchant.

Winter came. Tsar Taras wanted to buy sable furs for a new shuba; he sent out to buy them—his messenger came back, saying:—

"There are no sable furs. The merchant has them all; he gave a higher price, and he has made a carpet out of the sable skins."

Tsar Taras wanted to buy some stallions; he sent out to buy them—his agents returned, saying:—

"The merchant has all the good stallions; they are carrying water to fill up his pond."

All the Tsar's affairs came to a standstill; no one would do anything for him, but they did everything for the merchant; and all they bring him is the merchant's money, which they pay for their taxes.

And the Tsar collected so much money that he had nowhere to put it, and life became wretched. The Tsar had now ceased to make plans—his only concern was to live at all—even this was impossible. He ran short of everything. His cooks and coachmen left him and took service with the merchant. It had now gone so far that he had nothing to eat. If he sent to the bazaar to buy anything—there was nothing to be got; the merchant had bought up everything, and the people brought him only money for taxes!

Tsar Taras was angry, and banished the merchant beyond the frontier; but the merchant settled down on the very frontier and went on as before, all exactly the same; for the sake of the merchant's money they carry everything away from the Tsar to the merchant. It became utterly wretched for the Tsar; for days at a time, there was nothing to eat; the report spread even that the merchant was boasting that he was going to buy the Tsar himself. Tsar Taras became alarmed, and did not know what to do.

Semyon the warrior came to him, and said:—

"Help me! the Tsar of India has conquered me."

But the affairs of Taras the Tsar himself were in a knot.

"I myself," said he, "have not had anything to eat for two days."

11

The old devil had finished with two of the brothers, and he came to Ivan. The old devil changed into a vaïvode and came to Ivan, and tried to persuade him to form an army.

Said he, "It does not become a Tsar to live without an army. Only give me orders, and I will gather soldiers from your people, and form an army."

Ivan listened to him.

"All right," said he, "form an army; but teach them to sing songs most cleverly. I like that."

The old devil set to work to enlist volunteer soldiers throughout Ivan's dominion. He bade them take service: each recruit would have a measure of vodka and a red cap.

The fools burst into a laugh.

"We have enough brandy," said they, "we make it ourselves; and as for caps, our women will make us as many as you like, even striped ones; yes, and with tassels too!"

And so he got no recruits. The old devil came to Ivan and said:—

"Your fools will not enlist as volunteers; they must be made to enlist."

"All right," said he, "make them enlist."

And the old devil gave orders that all the fools should be enrolled as soldiers, and whoever did not come, Ivan would put to death.

The fools came to the vaïvode, and said:—

"You tell us that if we will not go as soldiers, the Tsar will put us to death;

but you do not tell us what will happen to us in the army. They say that even soldiers are killed."

"Yes, but not without reason."

The fools heard this, and were obstinate.

"We will not go," they said. "It is better for us to wait for death at home. Even thus it is not to be escaped."

"You are fools, fools!" said the old devil; "soldiers may get killed, or may not; but if you don't come, Ivan the Tsar will assuredly put you to death."

The fools pondered a little; they went to Ivan the fool to ask him.

"A vaïvode," said they, "appeared and commanded us all to go as soldiers. 'If you go as soldiers,' said he, 'you may be killed, or may not; but if you don't come, then the Tsar Ivan will assuredly put you to death.' Is this true?"

Ivan burst into a laugh.

"How," said he, "can I, who am one, put you all to death? If I were not a fool, I would explain it for you; but now I don't understand it myself."

"Then," say they, "we will not go."

"All right," says he, "don't go."

The fools went to the vaïvode, and refused to enlist.

The old devil saw that his work was not prospering. He went to the Tarakan-tsar: he went in disguise.

"Come on," said he, "let us make war on Ivan the Tsar. He has not much money, but he has grain and cattle, and all sorts of good things."

The Tarakan-tsar prepared to make war; he collected a great army; procured rifles and cannon and crossed the frontier, began to march into Ivan's dominion.

Folks came to Ivan and said:—

"The Tarakan-tsar is marching to make war upon us."

"All right," says he, "let him come."

The Tarakan-tsar crossed the frontier with his army, and sent out scouts to reconnoiter and find Ivan's army. They searched and searched; but there was no army! They waited and waited for one to appear somewhere! But there was no sign of an army—nobody to fight with! The Tarakan-tsar sent to seize the villages. The soldiers came to one village. The fools—men and women—ran out and gazed at the soldiers—in astonishment.

The soldiers began to rob the fools of their grain and their cattle. The fools gave them up, and no one offered resistance.

The soldiers came to another village—the same thing happened there. The soldiers went on for one day; they went on for another day; everywhere always the same thing: everything was given up, no one offered to resist, but instead they invited the soldiers to live with them.

"If life is so wretched over on your side, dear friends," they say, "come and live with us!"

The soldiers marched and marched,—still no army! And all the people lived by feeding themselves and others; and they offered no resistance, but invited the soldiers to live with them.

It became dull work to the soldiers; they returned to their Tarakan-tsar, and said:—

"We cannot fight here; lead us to some other place. The war would have been good, good; but this is like cutting kissel-jelly. We cannot make war any longer here."

The Tarakan-tsar was angry, and commanded the soldiers to overrun the whole tsardom; to pick quarrels; to set villages, houses, grain, on fire; to kill the cattle.

"If you do not obey my command," said he, "all of you," said he, "I will put you to death."

The soldiers were frightened; they began to carry out the ukase on the tsardom. They began to burn houses, grain; to kill the cattle. Still the fools offered no resistance, but only wept. The old men wept, the old women wept, the young children wept.

"Why," said they, "do you injure us? Why," said they, "do you waste good things? If you need anything, you had better take it for yourselves!"

It seemed outrageous to the soldiers. They went no farther, and the whole army took to its heels.

12

So the old devil also went off—he could not catch Ivan by his soldiers.

The old devil changed into a fine gentleman, and came to live in Ivan's dominions; he made up his mind to catch him by means of money, as he had Taras.

"I wish," said he, "to do you a good turn,—to teach you how to be wise. I am going to build a house among you, and establish a business."

"All right," says Ivan, "live here."

The fine gentleman spent the night, and in the morning went to the public square, took a great bag of gold, and sheets of paper, and said:—

"You live, all of you," said he, "like swine; I want to teach you how you ought to live. Build me," said he, "a house on this plan. You work, and I will show you how; and I will pay you in gold coin."

And he showed them the gold. The fools wondered. They had no money in manufactures, and they bartered among themselves one thing for another, and paid in labor. They wondered at the gold, and said:—

"They are pretty little trinkets."

And they began to exchange their produce and work for the gentleman's gold pieces. The old devil began to be free with his gold, as he had in Taras's case; and they began to exchange all sorts of things for his gold, and to do all sorts of work for it.

The old devil was overjoyed; he said to himself: "My scheme is coming on excellently. Now I am going to ruin the fool as I did Taras; and I shall buy him absolutely, body and soul."

As soon as the fools got their gold coins, they gave them to their women for necklaces; all the girls twined them into their tresses. And even the children in the streets began to use them as toys to play with. All had a quantity, and they ceased taking any more. But still the fine gentleman's mansion was not half completed, and he had not as yet provided enough grain and cattle for the year. And the gentleman publicly invited the people to work for him, to cart him grain, to bring him cattle; for all kinds of things, and for all kinds of work, he would give much gold.

But no one came to work, and no one brought anything. Only now and then a lad or a little girl happened along to exchange an egg for a gold piece, but no one else came, and he soon had nothing to eat.

The fine gentleman began to get famished; went through a village to buy himself a dinner. He made his way into one dvor; offered gold for a hen; the woman of the house refused it, saying:—

"I have a lot of these things."

He made his way into a poor peasant woman's hut, to buy a herring, and offered a gold piece.

"I don't need it, kind sir," said she. "I have no children," said she, "to play with such a thing; and I have already got three pieces as curiosities."

He made his way into a muzhik's to get bread; the muzhik also refused the money.

"I don't need it," said he. "But if you are begging in Christ's name, just wait till I tell my woman to cut you off a slice of bread."

The devil spat, and hastened away from the muzhik. He could not stomach that *For Christ's sake*; even to hear the words hurt him worse than a knife.

And so he got no bread.

All had sufficient; wherever the old devil went, no one would give him anything for money; but all said: *"Bring something else,"* or *"Come and work,"* or *"Take it, in Christ's name."*

But the devil had nothing except money, and no desire to work; and the *Christ's sake* he cannot stomach. The old devil grew angry.

"What do you need more," he asked, "when I offer you money? You can buy everything for gold, and hire every kind of workman."

The fools would not listen to him.

"No," said they, "we don't need it. No one here pays taxes or wages. What should we want of money?"

The old devil went to bed without any supper.

This affair was reported to Ivan the fool. Folks came to ask him:—

"What are we to do? This fine gentleman appeared among us: he likes to eat and drink good things; he likes to dress neatly; but he does not like to work, and he does not ask alms in Christ's name; but he offers only gold pieces everywhere. Until we got enough of them, we gave him what he wanted for them; but now we don't give him any more. What are we to do with him? He will be dying of starvation."

Ivan listened.

"All right," said he. "We must support him. Let him go from dvor to dvor as the shepherd goes."

No help for it: the old devil began to go from dvor to dvor. He came in due time to Ivan's house.

The old devil came in to dinner; and at Ivan's the dumb girl was getting it ready.

Those who were the laziest had often deceived her. They would leave their work unfinished and hurry in to dinner before the rest, and eat up all the kasha-gruel. And the dumb girl had learned to recognize the sluggard by his hands. Any one who had callous places on his hands, she would seat at the table; but the one who had not, she gave the scraps to.

The old devil slipped in behind the table; but the dumb girl seized him by the hands and examined them closely; there were no callous places, and the hands were clean, smooth, and the nails were long. The dumb girl grunted, and pulled the devil away from the table.

But Ivan's wife said to him:—

"Do not be offended, my fine gentleman; my sister-in-law does not allow those who have not callous hands to come to table. . . . Here, have patience; the men are almost done eating, then you shall have what is left."

The old devil was affronted because at the Tsar's they wanted him to feed like the pigs. He said to Ivan:—

"It is a foolish law you have in your dominions—that all people must work with their hands. You invented it in your stupid way. Why should people work with their hands alone? Do you realize in what way men of intellect work?"

But Ivan said:—

"How should we fools know? We always do the most of our work with our hands and with our backs."

"That is because you are fools. But I," said he, "will teach you how to work with your brains; then you will know that head-work is more profitable than hand-work."

Ivan was amazed.

"Well," said he, "we are not called fools for nothing."

And the old devil said, "But it is not easy," says he, "to work with the brain. Here you did not allow me to eat with you because my hands were not calloused, but you do not understand that it is a hundred times more difficult to work with the brain. Sometimes the head even splits."

Ivan grew thoughtful.

"Why, then, friend," said he, "do you torment yourself so? Is it pleasant when the head splits? You would much better do easy work—with the hands and the back."

But the devil said:—

"Why should I bother myself to take pity on you fools? If I did not bother myself, you would be fools forever. But I have worked with my brains, and now I am going to teach you."

Ivan was amazed.

"Teach us," said he, "and then when the hands get tired out, then change them for head-work."

And the devil promised to teach them.

And Ivan proclaimed throughout all his dominions, that a fine gentleman had come who would teach all how to work with the brains, and said that more could be produced with their brains than with their hands, and that the people should come and be taught.

There was in Ivan's tsardom a high tower, and steep stairs led up to it; and on the top there was a platform. And Ivan took the gentleman there, so that he might be in sight of all.

The gentleman stood on the tower, and began to speak from it. And the fools gathered to see him. The fools thought that the gentleman was going to show them how to work with the brain apart from the hands. But the old devil only taught them in words how it was possible to live without work.

The fools could not understand at all. They gazed and gazed, and then went in different directions to their labors.

The old devil stood one day on the tower, stood for another day, and talked all the time. He began to get hungry. But the fools thought it needless to bring bread to the tower. They thought that if he could work better with his head than with his hands, then it would be mere play for the head to provide bread.

And the old devil stood for still another day on the platform, talking all the time. And the people would come up and look and stare, and then go away again.

And Ivan asked: "Well, has the gentleman begun to work with his head yet?"

"Not yet," said the people; "he is still spouting away." The old devil stood a second day on the platform, and he began to grow weak. He staggered once, and thumped his head against the post. One fool noticed it, and told Ivan's wife; and Ivan's wife hurried out to her husband, in the fallow field.

"Let us go," says she, "and look; they say that the gentleman is beginning to work with his head."

Ivan was surprised.

"Really?" said he. He turned the horse round and went to the tower.

By the time he reached the tower the old devil was thoroughly weak from hunger, and began to totter and whacked his head against the post. And just as Ivan came, the devil stumbled, fell with a thundering noise down the stairs, heels over head; he counted all the steps.

"Well," says Ivan, "the fine gentleman told the truth when he said that sometimes the head splits; that's its kind of callosities. From such work the head gets covered with bumps."

The old devil came bumping down the stairs, and thumped against the ground. Ivan was just going to see whether he had accomplished much work, when, suddenly, the earth opened, and the old devil fell through the earth; only the hole was left.

Ivan scratched his head. "Ah, ha!" says he. "What a nasty thing! There he was again! Must have been the father. What a healthy one!"

Ivan is still living, and all the people are thronging to his dominions; and his brothers have come to him, and he supports them. Whoever comes, and says, "Give us food,"—"All right," says he; "you're welcome! we have plenty of everything."

There is only one regulation in his tsardom: Whoever has callous hands, comes to the table; and who has not, gets what is left.

1885

TWO BROTHERS AND GOLD

Once upon a time, there lived, not far from Jerusalem, two brothers, the elder Afanasi, and the younger one Ioann. They lived on a mountain, not far from the city, and subsisted on what men gave them. The brothers spent all their time in work. They did not work for themselves, but for the poor. Wherever there were people worn out by work, wherever they were ill, or orphans or widows, there the brothers would go, and there they would work, and on their departure take no pay. Thus the brothers would spend a whole week at a time, and only on Saturday evening would they come back to their dwelling. Only on Sunday they stayed at home, praying and talking. And the angel of the Lord came to them and blessed them. On Monday they parted, each going his own way.

Thus the brothers lived many summers; and every week the angel of the Lord came to them, and blessed them.

One Monday, when the brothers were going out to work, and had already started in different directions, the elder, Afanasi, began to feel sorry to part from his beloved brother; and he halted, and looked back. Ioann was walking on his way, with head bent, and not looking back.

But suddenly Ioann also stopped, and, as if he saw something, began to gaze back intently, shading his eyes with his hand. Then he approached what he was looking at; then suddenly he leaped to one side, and, without looking round, ran to the base of the mountain, and up the mountain, away from that place, as if a wild beast were pursuing him.

Afanasi was surprised, and turned back to the place to see what had scared his brother so.

As he approached nearer, he saw something glistening in the sun. He came still nearer. On the grass, as if thrown out from a measure, a heap of gold was lying. . . .

And Afanasi was still more astonished, both at the gold and at his brother's flight.

"What scared him? and why did he run away?" Afanasi asked himself. "There is no sin in gold: sin is in man. Gold can do no harm: it may do good. How many widows and orphans this gold can nourish! how many naked it can clothe! how many poor and sick it can heal! We are now serving-men; but our service is small, just as our strength is small. But with this gold, we can be of better service to people."

Thus reasoned Afanasi, and he wanted to tell all this to his brother; but Ioann was already gone out of hearing, and could only be seen now like a little beetle on the other mountain.

And Afanasi took off his coat, filled it with as much gold as he had strength to lug, put it on his shoulder, and carried it to the city. He came to a hotel, deposited the gold with the hotel-keeper, and went for the rest of it.

And when he had got all the gold, he went to the merchants, bought land in the city, bought stone and lumber, engaged laborers, and began to build three houses.

And Afanasi lived in the city three months. He built in the city three houses,—one house, an asylum for widows and orphans; the second house, a hospital for the sick and poverty-stricken; the third house, for pilgrims and beggars.

And Afanasi found three pious old men; and one of them he placed over the asylum, the other over the hospital, and the third over the pilgrims' home.

And still Afanasi had left three thousand gold pieces. And he gave to each of the old men a thousand to distribute among the poor.

And all three of the houses began to fill with people, and men began to praise Afanasi for all that he had done. And Afanasi was so delighted at this, that he did not care to leave the city.

But Afanasi loved his brother; and, having said good-by to the people, and not leaving himself any money at all, and wearing the very same old clothes in which he had come, he went back to his house.

And as Afanasi was approaching his mountain, he kept thinking:—

"My brother reasoned wrong when he jumped away from the gold and fled. Haven't I done better?"

And this thought had scarcely occurred to Afanasi, when suddenly he saw standing, directly in his path, the same angel who had blessed them; he looked sternly at him.

And Afanasi was stupefied, and could only say:—

"What is it, Lord?"

And the angel opened his lips, and said:—

"Get thee hence! Thou art unworthy to live with thy brother. Thy brother's one leap is worth more than all those things that thou hast done with thy gold."

And Afanasi began to tell how many poor and wanderers he had fed, how many orphans he had cared for.

And the angel said to him:—

"The Devil, who put down the gold to seduce thee, also taught thee these words."

And then Afanasi felt the prick of conscience, and understood that he had not done these deeds for God's sake; and he burst into tears, and began to repent.

Then the angel stepped out of the road, and allowed him to pass; and there stood Ioann, waiting for his brother. And from that time Afanasi did not yield to the temptation of the Devil who had scattered the gold; and he learned that God and men can be served, not by gold, but only by labor.

And the brothers continued to live as before.

1885

THE TWO OLD MEN

1

"The woman saith unto him, Sir, I perceive that thou art a prophet.

Our fathers worshiped in this mountain; and ye say that in Jerusalem is the place where men ought to worship.

Jesus saith unto her, Woman, believe me, the hour cometh, when *ye shall neither in this mountain, nor yet at Jerusalem, worship the Father.*

Ye worship ye know not what: we know what we worship: for salvation is of the Jews.

*But the hour cometh, and now is, when the true worshipers shall worship the Father in spirit and in truth: for the Father seeketh such to worship him."—*JOHN iv. 19–23.

Two aged men resolved to worship God in old Jerusalem. One was a rich muzhik; his name was Yefim Tarasuitch Shevelef: the other—Yeliseï Bodrof —was not a rich man.

Yefim was a sedate muzhik; he did not drink vodka, or smoke tobacco, or take snuff. All his life long he had never used a bad word, and he was a strict and upright man. He had served two terms as village elder and had come out without a deficit.

He had a large family,—two sons and a married grandson,—and all lived together. As for himself, he was hale, long-bearded, erect, and, though he was in his seventh decade, his beard was only beginning to grow gray.

Yeliseï was a little old man, neither rich nor poor; in former times he had gone about doing jobs in carpentry; but now, as he grew old, he began to stay at home, and took to raising bees. One of his sons had gone away to work, the other was at home. Yeliseï was a good-natured and jolly man. He used to drink vodka, and take snuff, and he liked to sing songs; but he was a peaceable man, and lived amicably with his family and his neighbors. As to his person, Yeliseï was a short, darkish little muzhik, with a curly beard; and like his name-saint, Elisha the prophet, he was entirely bald.

The old men had long ago promised and agreed to go together, but Tarasuitch had never found the leisure; his engagements had never come to an end. As soon as one was through with, another began: first the grandson got married; then they expected the younger son from the army; and then, again, he was occupied in building a new izba.

One festival day the old men met, and sat down together on the timber.

"Well," says Yeliseï, "when shall we set out, and fulfil our promise?"

Yefim knit his brow.

"We must wait awhile," says he. "This year it'll come hard for me. I am engaged in building this izba. I counted on spending about a hundred rubles; but I'm already on the third, and it isn't finished yet. You see, that'll take till summer. In the summer, if God grants, we will go without let or hindrance."

"According to my idea," says Yeliseï, "we ought not to put it off; we ought to go to-day. It's the very time—spring."

"It is a good time certainly; but this work is begun: how can I leave it?"

"Haven't you any one? Your son will attend to it."

"How attend to it? My eldest son is not to be trusted—he is given to drinking."

"We shall die, old friend; they'll have to live without us. Your son must learn."

"That's so; but I should like to see this job finished under my own eyes!"

"Ah! my dear man, you will never get all you want done. Only the other day, at my house, the women-folks were cleaning house, fixing up for Easter.

And both are necessary, but you'd never get done. And my oldest daughter-in-law, a sensible woman, says, 'Thank the Lord,' says she, 'Easter is coming; it doesn't wait for us, else,' says she, 'however much we did we should never get it all done.' "

Tarasuitch was lost in thought.

"I have put a good deal of money," says he, "into this building; and we can't go on this journey with empty hands. It won't take less than a hundred rubles."

Yeliseï laughed out:—

"Don't make a mistake, old friend," says he; "you have ten times as much property as I have. And you talk about money! Only say when shall we go? I haven't anything, but I'll manage it."

Tarasuitch also smiled.

"How rich you seem!" says he; "but where will you get it?"

"Well, I shall scrape some up at home—that'll be something; and for the rest,—I'll let my neighbor have ten of my hives. He has been after them for a long time."

"This is going to be a good swarming-year; you'll regret it."

"Regret it? No, old friend. I never regretted anything in my life except my sins. There is nothing more precious than the soul!"

"That's so. But it's not pleasant when things aren't right at home."

"But how will it be with us if our souls are not right? Then it will be worse. But we have made a vow—let us go! I beg of you, let us go!"

2

And Yeliseï persuaded his friend. Yefim thought about it, and thought about it; and in the morning he came to Yeliseï.

"Well, then, let us go," says he. "You are right. In death and in life, God rules. Since we are alive, and have strength, we must go."

At the end of a week the old men had made their preparations.

Tarasuitch had money in the house. He took one hundred rubles for his journey; two hundred he left for the old woman.

Yeliseï also was ready. He sold his neighbor the ten beehives. And the bees that would swarm from the ten hives, also, he sold to the neighbor. He received, all told, seventy rubles. The other thirty rubles he swept up as best he could. The old woman gave him all that she had saved up against her funeral; the daughter-in-law gave what she had.

Yefim Tarasuitch intrusted all his affairs to his oldest son,—he told him what meadows to rent, and where to put manure, and how to finish and roof in the izba. He thought about everything, he ordered how everything should be done.

But Yeliseï only directed his old woman to hive the young swarms of bees that he had sold, and give them to his neighbor without any trickery; but about household affairs, he did not have anything to say:—

"If anything comes up, light will be given what to do and how to do it. You people at home do as you think best."

The old men were now ready. The wives baked a lot of flat-cakes, sewed some bags, cut new leg-wrappers; they put on new boots, took some extra bast-shoes, and set forth. The folks kept them company to the common pasture, bade them good-by, and the old men set out on their journey.

Yeliseï set out in good spirits, and, as soon as he left the village, he forgot all about his cares. His only thoughts were how to please his companion on the way, how not to say a single churlish word to any one, and how to go in peace and love to the Places and return home. As he walked along the road, all the time he either whispered a prayer, or called to memory some saint's life which he knew. And if he met any one on the road, or came to any halting-place, he made himself as useful and as agreeable as possible to every one, and even said a word in God's service. He went on his way rejoicing. One thing Yeliseï could not do. He intended to give up snuff-taking, and he left his snuff-box; but it was melancholy. A man on the road gave him some. And now and again he would drop behind his companion, so as not to lead him into temptation, and take a pinch of snuff.

Yefim Tarasuitch also got along well—sturdily; he fell into no sin and he said nothing churlish, but he was not easy in his mind. He could not get his household affairs out of his mind. He kept thinking of what was doing at home. Had he forgotten to give his son some commands? and was his son doing as he was told? If he saw any one by the road planting potatoes, or spreading manure, he would think, "Is my son doing what I told him?" He was almost ready to turn back and show him how, and even do it himself.

3

Five weeks the old men had been journeying; their home-made lapti were worn out, and they had been obliged to buy new ones; and they came to the land of the Top-Knots.

From the time that they left home, they had paid for lodging and meals; but now that they had come among the Top-Knots, the people began to vie with each other in giving them invitations. They gave them shelter, and they fed them, and they would not take money from them, but even put bread, and sometimes flat-cakes, into their bags for the journey. Thus bravely the old men journeyed seven hundred versts. They passed through still another government, and came to a famine-stricken place.

They received them kindly and took them in, and would not take pay for lodgings; but they could no longer feed them. And they did not always let them have bread; and, again, it was not always to be obtained at all for love or money. The year before, so the people said, nothing had grown. Those who were rich had been ruined, and forced to sell out; those who lived in medium circumstances had come down to nothing; but the poor had either gone away altogether, or had come upon the Mir, or had almost perished in their homes. All winter they had been living on husks and pigweed.

One time the old men put up at a little place; they bought fifteen pounds of bread; and, having spent the night, they started off betimes, so as to get as far as possible before the heat of the day. They went ten versts, and reached a little river; they sat down, filled their cups with water, moistened the little loaves, ate their luncheon, and changed their shoes. They sat some time resting.

Yeliseï got out his little snuff-horn. Yefim Tarasuitch shook his head at him.

"Why," said he, "don't you throw away that nasty stuff?"

Yeliseï wrung his hands.

"The sin is too strong for me," said he; "what can I do?"

They got up, and went on their way. They went half a score of versts farther. They came to a great village; they went right through it. And already it had grown hot. Yeliseï was dead with fatigue; he wanted to rest, and have a drink, but Tarasuitch would not halt. Tarasuitch was the stronger in walking, and it was rather hard for Yeliseï to keep up with him.

"I'd like a drink," says he.

"All right. Get a drink. I don't want any."

Yeliseï stopped.

"Don't wait," says he; "I'm only going to run in for a minute here at this hut, and get a drink. I'll overtake you in a jiffy."

"All right."

And Yefim Tarasuitch proceeded on his way alone, and Yeliseï turned back to the hut.

Yeliseï went up to the hut. The hut was small, and plastered with mud; below it was black; above, white. The clay was peeling off; long, apparently, since it had been mended; and the roof in one place was broken through. The way to the hut led through a dvor or courtyard. Yeliseï went into the dvor and saw lying on the earth embankment a thin, beardless man, in shirt and drawers —in Little Russian fashion. The man evidently had laid himself down when it was cool, but now the sun was beating straight down upon him. And he lay there, and was not asleep. Yeliseï spoke to him and asked him for a drink. The man made no reply.

"Either he's sick or he's ugly," thought Yeliseï, and he went to the door. He heard a child crying in the hut. Yeliseï rapped with the ring:—

"Masters."

No reply. He rapped again on the door with his staff:—

"Christians!"

No one moved.

"Servants of God!"

No one answered. Yeliseï was about to proceed on his way, but he listened; some one seemed to be groaning behind the door.

"Can some misfortune have befallen these people? I must look and see." And Yeliseï went into the hut.

4

Yeliseï turned the ring—it was not fastened. He opened the door, and passed through the little vestibule. The door into the hut stood open; at the left was an oven; straight ahead was the front-room or "corner"; in the "corner" a shrine and a table; by the table a bench; on the bench, an old woman, in a single shirt, with disheveled hair, was sitting, resting her head on the table. At her elbow an emaciated little boy, pale as wax, with a distended belly, was tugging at the old woman's sleeve, and roaring at the top of his voice, asking for something.

Yeliseï went into the hut. In the hut the air was stifling; he looked around behind the oven: on the floor a woman was lying. She was lying on her back, and did not look up; only moaned, and sometimes stretched out her leg, sometimes drew it up again. And she threw herself from side to side, and the stench arising from her showed that she had soiled herself and no one had attended to her.

The old woman raised her head, and looked at the man.

"What do you want?" says she. "What do you want? We've nothing for you."

Yeliseï understood what she said; he went up to her. "I am a servant of God," says he; "I come to get a drink."

"Hain't got any, hain't got any. Hain't got anything to get it in. Go away!"

Yeliseï began to question her.

"Tell me, isn't there any one of you well enough to take care of the woman?"

"Hain't got any one—the man outside is dying, and here we are."

The boy had ceased crying when he saw the stranger; but when the old woman spoke, he began to tug again at her sleeve: "Bread, granny, bread!" and began screaming again.

Yeliseï was going to ask more questions of the old woman, when the muzhik came stumbling into the hut; he went along by the wall, and was going to sit on the bench, but failed of it, and fell into the room at the threshold. And he did not try to get up: he tried to speak. He would speak one word—then break off, his breath failed him—then he would speak another:—

"Sick," . . . said he, "and . . . starving. . . . Here . . . he . . . is . . . dying . . . starvation."

The muzhik indicated the boy with his head, and burst into tears.

Yeliseï shook off his sack from his shoulders, freed his arms, set the sack on the floor, then lifted it to the bench, and began to undo it. He undid it, took out bread, and a knife; then he cut off a slice, and offered it to the muzhik. The muzhik would not take it, but pointed to the boy and to the girl.

"Give it to them, please."

Yeliseï held it out to the boy. The boy smelt the bread, stretched himself up, seized the slice with both his little hands, and buried his nose in the slice. A little girl crept out from behind the oven, and stared at the bread. Yeliseï gave her some also. He cut off still another piece and gave it to the old woman. The old woman took it, and began to chew it.

"Would you bring some water?" she said; "their mouths are parched. I tried," says she, "yesterday, or to-day,—I don't remember which,—to get some. I fell, and couldn't get there; and the bucket is there yet, unless some one has stolen it."

Yeliseï asked where their well was. The old woman gave him the directions. Yeliseï went and found the bucket, brought water, gave the people some to drink.

The children were still eating the bread and drinking the water, and the old woman ate some too; but the muzhik refused to eat.

"It makes me sick at my stomach."

His wife, who did not notice anything at all, or come to herself, only tossed about on the boards.

Yeliseï went to the village, bought at the shop some millet, salt, flour, butter, and looked round for a hatchet. He split up some wood,—began to kindle a fire in the oven. The little girl began to help him. Yeliseï boiled some porridge and kasha, and fed the people.

5

The muzhik ate a little, and the old woman ate a little; but the little girl and the little boy licked the bowl clean, and lay down to sleep locked in each other's arms.

The muzhik and the old woman began to relate how all this had come upon them.

"We weren't rich, even before this," said they; "but when nothing grew, we had to give all we had for food last autumn. We parted with everything; then we had to go begging among our neighbors and kind people. At first they gave to us, but then they sent us away. Some would have gladly given to us, but they had nothing. Yes, and we were ashamed to beg; we got in debt to every one, both for money and flour and bread. I tried to get work," said the muzhik, "but there was no work. People everywhere were wandering about to work for something to eat. You'd work one day, and you'd go about for two hunting for work. The old woman and the little girl had to go a long way off begging. Not much was given them; no one had any bread to spare. And so we lived, hoping we should get along somehow till new crops came. But since spring they stopped giving at all, and then sickness came on. Things were just as bad as they could be. One day we had something to eat, but the next two nothing. We began to eat herbs. Yes, perhaps it was from eating herbs, or something of the sort, that my wife got sick. My wife became sick, and I have no strength," said the muzhik. "There was no way of curing us."

"I was the only one," said the old woman, "who kept up; but without eating, I lost my strength, and got puny. And the little girl got puny, and lost heart. We sent her to the neighbors, but she wouldn't go. She crept into the corner, and wouldn't come out. Day before yesterday a neighbor came round, yes, and she saw that we were starving, and were sick; but she turned round and went off. But her own husband had left her and she hadn't anything to feed her little children with. . . . And so here we lay,—waiting for death."

Yeliseï listened to their talk, and changed his mind about going to rejoin his companion that day, and he spent the night there.

In the morning Yeliseï got up, did the chores as if he were master of the house. He and the old woman kneaded the bread, and he lighted the fire in the oven. He went with the little girl to the neighbors', to get what they needed; for there was nothing to be found—nothing at all: everything had been disposed of; there was nothing for domestic purposes, and no clothing. And Yeliseï began to lay in a supply of what was needed. Some he himself made, and some he bought. Thus Yeliseï spent one day, spent a second, spent also a third.

The little boy got better, began to climb up on the bench, to caress Yeliseï. But the little girl became perfectly gay, and helped in everything. And she kept trotting after Yeliseï: "Grand-dad, dear little grand-daddy!"

And the old woman also got up, and went to her neighbor's house. And the muzhik began to walk, supporting himself by the wall. Only the peasant's wife lay unconscious; but even she, on the third day, came to herself, and began to ask for something to eat.

"Well," thinks Yeliseï, "I didn't expect to spend so much time; now I'll be going."

6

On the fourth day, meat-eating was allowed for the first time after the fast; and Yeliseï said to himself:—

"Come, now, I will feast with these people. I will buy them something for the Saints' day, and toward evening I will go."

Yeliseï went to the village again, bought milk, white flour, lard. He and the old woman boiled and baked; and in the morning Yeliseï went to mass, and when he came back, he ate meat with the people. On this day the wife also got up, and began to creep about. And the muzhik had shaved, put on a clean shirt,—the old woman had washed it out,—and gone to the village to ask mercy of a rich muzhik. Both meadow and corn-land had been mortgaged to the rich muzhik. So he went to ask if he would not give him back the meadow and corn-land till the new crops.

The husband returned toward evening, gloomy and in tears. The rich muzhik would not have pity on him. He said:—

"Bring your money."

Again Yeliseï falls into thought.

"How will he live now?" thinks he. "The men will be going out to mow; he has nothing. His hay-field is mortgaged. The rye is ripening; the men are beginning to harvest it (our good mother earth has done well for us this year), but these people won't have anything: their field had been mortgaged to the rich muzhik. If I go away, they'll be in trouble again."

And Yeliseï was much troubled by these thoughts, and did not take his departure that evening; he waited till morning. He went outdoors to sleep. He said his prayers and lay down, but he could not sleep.

"I must go—here I have been spending so much money and time—and I'm sorry for these people. You can't give to everybody, evidently. I meant to get them some water, and give them a slice of bread; but just see how it has taken me! Now—I must redeem their meadow and their field. And when I've redeemed their field, I must buy a cow for the children, and a horse to carry the muzhik's sheaves. There you are in a pretty pickle, brother Yeliseï Kuzmitch! You're anchored here, and you don't get off so easy!"

Yeliseï got up, took his kaftan from under his head, unfolded it, found his snuff-horn, took a pinch of snuff, tried to clear up his thoughts; but no, he thought and he thought, but could not think it out. He must go; but he pitied these people. And what to do, he knew not. He folded up his kaftan for a pillow, and lay down again. He lay and he lay, and the cocks were already singing when he finally fell into a doze.

Suddenly, something seemed to wake him up. He saw himself, as it were, all dressed, with his sack and his staff; and he had to go through a gate, but the gate was so nearly shut that only one person could get through at a time. And he went to the gate, and got caught on one side by his sack; he tried to detach it, and got caught on the other side by his leg-wrapper; and the leg-wrapper untied. He tried to detach it, but after all it was not the wattle which detained him, but the little girl holding him, and crying, "Grand-dad, dear little grand-daddy, bread!" He looked down at his leg, and the little boy was clinging to his leg-wrapper; the old woman and the muzhik were gazing from the window.

Yeliseï woke up, and said to himself aloud, "To-morrow," said he, "I will redeem the field and the meadow; and I will buy a horse, and flour enough to last till the new comes; and I will buy a cow for the children. For otherwise I should go across the sea to find Christ, and lose Him in my own soul. I must set these people right."

And Yeliseï slept till morning.

Yeliseï woke up early. He went to the rich muzhik; he redeemed the rye-field; he paid cash for it, and for the meadow-land. He bought a scythe,—the very one that had been disposed of, and brought it back. He sent the muzhik to mow, and he himself went round among the muzhiks; at last found a horse and telyega which an innkeeper was ready to sell. He struck a bargain and bought them. He bought, also, some flour, put the sack in the telyega, and went farther to buy a cow. Yeliseï was going along; he overtook two Top-Knots. They were women; and they were gossiping as they walked. And Yeliseï heard the women talking in their own speech, and he made out that they were talking about him.

"Heavens! at first they didn't know what to make of him; their idea was, he was a mere man. As he came by, it seems, he stopped to get a drink, and then he stayed. Whatever they needed, he bought. I myself saw him this very day buy of the tavern-keeper a nag and cart. Didn't know there were such folks in the world. Must go and see him!"

Yeliseï heard this, understood that they were praising him, and did not go to buy the cow. He returned to the tavern, and paid the money for the horse. He harnessed up, and drove with the wheat back to the hut. He drove up to the gate, reined in, and dismounted from the telyega. The household saw the horse; they wondered. And it occurred to them that he had bought the horse for them, but they dared not say so. The husband came out to open the gate.

"Where," says he, "did you get the nag, grandpa?"

"I bought it," says he. "I got it cheap. Mow a little grass, please, for the stall, for her to lie on over night. Yes, and fetch in the bag."

The husband unharnessed the horse, fetched the bag into the house; then he mowed a lot of grass and spread it in the stall. They went to bed. Yeliseï lay down out-of-doors, and there he had brought out his sack the evening before. All the folks were asleep. Yeliseï got up, shouldered his sack, fastened his leg-wrappers, put on his kaftan, and started on his way after Yefim.

7

Yeliseï had gone five versts and it began to grow light. He sat down under a tree, opened his sack, and began to reckon. He counted his money: there were left only seventeen rubles, twenty kopeks.

"Well," said he to himself, "with this I shan't get across the sea. And to beg in Christ's name—that might be a great sin. Friend Yefim will go alone; he'll set a candle for me. But the vow will remain on me till death. Thank the Lord, the Master is kind; He will have patience."

Yeliseï got up, lifted his sack up on his shoulders, and went back. Only, he went out of his way round the village, so that the people of it might not see him. And Yeliseï reached home quickly. When he started, it seemed hard to him, beyond his strength, to keep up with Yefim; but, going back, God gave him such strength that he walked along and did not know fatigue. He walked along gayly, swinging his staff, and made his seventy versts a day.

Yeliseï reached home. Already the fields had been harvested. The folks were delighted to see their old man; they began to ask questions,—how, and what, and why he had left his companion, why he did not go on, but came home. Yeliseï did not care to tell them about it.

"God did not permit me," says he. "I spent my money on the road, and fell behind my companion. And so I did not get there. Forgive me for Christ's sake."

And he handed the old woman what money he had left. Yeliseï inquired about the domestic affairs: it was all right; everything had been done properly; there was nothing left undone in the farm-work, and all were living in peace and harmony.

On this very same day, Yefim's people heard that Yeliseï had returned; they came round to ask after their old man. And Yeliseï told them the same thing.

"Your old man," says he, "went on sturdily; we parted," says he, "three days before Peter's Day; I intended to catch up with him, but then so many things happened: I spent my money, and, as I couldn't go on with what I had, I came back."

The people wondered how such a sensible man could have done so foolishly —start out, and not go on, and only waste his money. They wondered and forgot. And Yeliseï thought no more about it. He began to do the chores again; he helped his son chop wood against the winter; he threshed the corn with the women; he rethatched the shed, arranged about the bees, and gave his neighbor the ten hives with their increase. His old woman wanted to hide how many swarms had come from the hives that he had sold; but Yeliseï himself knew what hives had swarmed and what had not; and he gave his neighbor, instead of ten, seventeen swarms. Yeliseï arranged everything, sent his son off to work, and he himself settled down for the winter to make bast-shoes and chisel out beehives.

8

All that day when Yeliseï was staying in the sick folks' hut, Yefim waited for his companion. He went on a little way, and sat down. He waited and waited, and finally went to sleep; he woke up, and still sat there; no companion! He gazed with all his eyes. Already the sun had gone behind the trees—no Yeliseï.

"He can't have gone past me, or ridden by,—perhaps some one gave him a lift,—and not seen me while I was asleep, can he? He could not have helped seeing me. You see a long way on the steppes. If I should go back," he said to himself, "he would be getting ahead. We might miss each other; that would be still worse. I will go on; we shall meet at our lodging."

He went on to a village, asked the village policeman to send such and such an old man, if he come along, to yonder hut.

Yeliseï did not come to the lodging.

Yefim went farther; asked everybody if they had seen a bald, little old man. No one had seen him. Yefim wondered, and went on alone.

"We shall meet," he said to himself, "in Odessa somewhere, or on board ship."

And he ceased to think about it.

On the way he met a strannik.[1] The strannik wore a skullcap and cassock, and had long hair; had been to the Athos Monastery, and was going to Jerusalem for the second time. They met at the lodgings, got into conversation, and went on together.

They reached Odessa safely. They waited thrice twenty-four hours for a ship. Many pilgrims were waiting there. They were from different lands. Again Yefim made inquires about Yeliseï; no one had seen him.

Yefim asked for a passport; it cost five rubles. He paid forty silver rubles for a return ticket; bought bread and herring for the voyage. The vessel was loaded, the pilgrims embarked; Tarasuitch also took his place with the strannik. They hoisted anchor, set sail, flew across the sea. They sailed well all day; at evening a wind sprang up, rain fell; it began to get rough, and the waves dashed over the ship. The people were thrown about, women began to scream, and the weaker among the men began to run about the vessel, trying to find a place.

Fear fell upon Yefim also, but he did not show it. Exactly where he had sat down on coming on board, near some old men from Tambof, here also he kept sitting all night and all the next day; they only clung to their sacks, and said nothing. It cleared off on the third day. On the fifth day they reached Tsargrad.[2] Some of the stranniks were put ashore; they wanted to look at the temple of Sophia-Wisdom, where now the Turks hold sway. Tarasuitch did not land, but still sat on board. Only he bought some white loaves. They stayed twenty-four hours; again they flew over the sea. They made another stop at the city of Smyrna; at another city, Alexandria; and they happily reached the city of Jaffa. At Jaffa all the pilgrims disembarked. It was seventy versts on foot to Jerusalem. Also at landing, the people were panic-stricken; the ship was high, and the people had to jump down into boats; and the boat rocked, and there was danger that one might not strike it, but might fall in alongside; and two men were drenched, but all were landed happily.

They landed and started off on foot. On the third day after landing they reached Jerusalem. They established themselves in the city at the Russian hostelry; their passports were inscribed; they ate their dinner; then Yefim and the strannik went to the Holy Places. But to the Lord's sepulcher itself there was no longer any admittance.

They went to the Patriarchal Monastery; there all the worshipers collected; the women all sat down in one place, the men also sat down in another place. They were bidden to take off their shoes, and to sit in a circle. A monk came in with a towel, and began to wash all their feet: he washed them, wiped them, and kissed them; and thus he did to all. He washed Yefim's feet, and kissed them.

[1] A professional pilgrim, of the genus tramp.

[2] Constantinople, the *Tsar-city*.

They attended vespers and matins: they said their prayers, they placed candles, and presented prayers for their parents. And here also they were given something to eat, and wine was brought.

In the morning they went to the cell of Mary of Egypt, where she made her refuge. They set up candles, sang a Te Deum. Thence they went to the Monastery of Abraham. They saw the garden on Mount Moriah—the place where Abraham was going to sacrifice his son to God. Then they went to the place where Christ revealed himself to Mary Magdalene, and to the Church of James the brother of the Lord.

The strannik pointed out all these places, and always told where it was necessary to contribute money. They returned for dinner to the hostelry; and after dinner, just as they were getting ready to go to bed, the strannik began to groan, to shake his clothes, and to search. "I have been robbed," he says, "of my *portmonet*, with my money. Twenty-three rubles," said he, "there was in it—two ten-ruble notes, and three in change." The strannik mourned, mourned; nothing to be done: they lay down to sleep.

9

Yefim lay down to sleep, and temptation fell upon him.

"The strannik's money was not stolen," he said to himself; "he didn't have any. He never gave any. He told me where to give, but he himself did not give; yes, and he borrowed a ruble of me."

Thus Yefim argued, and then began to scold himself.

"Why," said he, "do I judge the man? I do wrong. I won't think about it."

As he grew sleepy, again he began to think how sharp the strannik was about money, and what an unlikely story he told about his *portmonet* having been stolen. "He hadn't any money," he said to himself. "It was a trick."

Next morning they got up, and went to early mass in the great Church of the Resurrection; to the tomb of the Lord. The strannik did not leave Yefim; he went with him everywhere.

They went to the church. A great crowd of people were collected together, of pilgrim-stranniks, Russians, and all peoples—of Greeks and Armenians, and Turks and Syrians. Yefim entered the sacred gates with the people. A monk led them. He led them past Turkish guards to the place where the Saviour was taken from the cross and anointed, and where the nine great candlesticks were burning. He pointed out everything, and told them everything. Here Yefim placed a candle. Then some monks led Yefim to the right hand up the little flight of steps to Golgotha, where the cross stood. Here Yefim said a prayer. Then they pointed out to Yefim the hole where the earth had opened down to hell; then they pointed out the place where they had fastened Christ's hands and feet to the cross; then they showed the tomb of Adam, over whose bones Christ's blood had flowed; then they came to the stone whereon Christ had sat when they put on him the crown of thorns; then to the pillar to which they bound Christ when they scourged him; then Yefim saw the stone with two hollows for Christ's feet. They were going to show them something more, but the crowd were in a hurry; they all rushed to the very grotto of the Lord's sepulcher. There the foreign mass had just ended, the orthodox mass was just beginning. Yefim went into the grotto with the throng.

He was anxious to get rid of the strannik, for continually in his thoughts he was sinning against the strannik: but the strannik would not be got rid of; in company with him he went to mass at the Lord's sepulcher. They tried to get nearer; they did not get there in time. The people were wedged so close that there was no going forward or back. Yefim stood, gazed forward, said his prayers; but it was of no use; he kept feeling whether his purse was still there. He was divided in his thoughts: one moment he imagined the strannik was deceiving him; the next he thought:—

"Or, if he is not deceiving me, and he was really robbed, why, then, it might be the same with me also."

10

Thus Yefim stood, and said his prayers, and looked forward toward the chapel where the sepulcher itself is; and on the sepulcher the thirty-six lamps were burning. Yefim stood, looked over the heads, when, what a marvel! Under the lamps themselves, where the blessed fire was burning before all, he saw a little old man standing, in a coarse kaftan, with a bald spot over his whole head, just as in the case of Yeliseï Bodrof.

"It's like Yeliseï," he thinks. "But it can't be him. He can't have got here before I did. No vessel had sailed for a week before us. He couldn't have got in ahead. And he wasn't on our vessel. I saw all the pilgrims."

While Yefim was thus reasoning, the little old man began to pray; and he bowed three times—once straight ahead, toward God, and then toward the orthodox throng on both sides. And as the little old man bent down his head to the right, then Yefim recognized him. It was Bodrof himself, with his blackish, curly beard, growing gray on the cheeks; and his eyebrows, and eyes, and nose, and all his peculiarities. It was Yeliseï Bodrof himself.

Yefim was filled with joy because his companion had come, and he wondered how Yeliseï had got there ahead of him.

"Well, well, Bodrof," he said to himself, "how did he get up there in front? He must have fallen in with somebody who put him there. Let me just meet him as we go out; I'll get rid of this strannik in his skullcap, and go with him, and perhaps he will get me a front place too."

And all the time Yefim kept his eyes on Yeliseï, so as not to miss him.

Now the mass was over; the crowd reeled, they tried to make their way, they struggled; Yefim was pushed to one side. Again the fear came on him that some one would steal his purse.

Yefim clutched his purse, and tried to break through the crowd, so as to get into an open space. He made his way into the open space; he walked and walked, he sought and sought for Yeliseï, and in the church also. And there, also, in the church he saw many people in cloisters; and some were eating, and drinking wine, and sleeping, and reading. And there was no Yeliseï anywhere. Yefim returned to the hostelry, but he did not find his companion. And that evening the strannik also did not come back. He disappeared, and did not return the ruble. Yefim was left alone.

On the next day Yefim again went to the Lord's sepulcher, with an old man from Tambof, who had come on the same ship with him. He wanted to get to the front but again he was crowded back; and he stood by a pillar, and prayed. He looked to the front: again under the lamps, at the very sepulcher of the Lord, in the foremost place, stood Yeliseï, spreading his arms like the priest at the altar; and the light shone all over his bald head.

"Well," thinks Yefim, "now I'll surely not miss him."

He tried to push through to the front. He pushed through. No Yeliseï! Apparently he had gone out.

And on the third day, again he gazed toward the Lord's sepulcher: in the same sacred spot stood Yeliseï, with the same aspect, his arms outspread, and looking up, almost as if his eyes were fixed upon him. And the bald spot on his whole head shone.

"Well," thinks Yefim, "now I'll not miss him; I'll go and stand at the door. There we shan't miss each other."

Yefim went and stood and stood. He stood there half the day; all the people went out—no Yeliseï.

Yefim spent six weeks in Jerusalem, and went everywhere; and in Bethlehem, and Bethany, and on the Jordan; and he had a seal stamped on a new shirt at the Lord's sepulcher, so that he might be buried in it; and he got some Jordan water in a vial, and some earth; and he bought some candles with the holy fire, and he had the prayer for the dead registered in the eight places; and having spent all his money, except enough to get him home, Yefim started on the home journey. He went to Jaffa, took passage in a ship, sailed to Odessa, and from there proceeded to walk home.

11

Yefim walked alone over the same road as before. As he began to near his home, again the worriment came upon him as to how his folks were getting along without him.

"In a year," thinks he, "much water leaks away. You spend a whole lifetime making a house, and it doesn't take long to go to waste."

How had his son conducted affairs in his absence? how had the spring opened up? how had the cattle weathered the winter? how had they finished the izba?

Yefim reached that place where, the year before, he had parted from Yeliseï. It was impossible to recognize the people. Where, the preceding year, there had been wretched poverty, now all were living in sufficient comfort. There had been good crops. The people had recovered and forgotten their former trouble.

One evening Yefim reached the very village where, the year before, Yeliseï had stopped. He had hardly entered the village, when a little girl in a white shirt sprang out from behind a hut:—

"Grandpa! Dear grandpa! Come into our house!"

Yefim was inclined to go on, but the little girl would not let him; she seized him by the skirts, pulled him along into the hut, and laughed.

There came out on the doorsteps a woman with a little boy; she also beckoned to him: "Come in, please, grandsire, d'yedushko,—and take supper with us, —you shall spend the night."

Yefim went in.

"All right," he said to himself; "I will ask about Yeliseï. I believe this is the very hut where he stopped to get a drink."

Yefim went in; the woman took his sack from him, gave him a chance to wash, and set him at the table. She put on milk, vareniki,[1] kasha-gruel,—she set them all on the table. Tarasuitch thanked and praised the people for being so hospitable to pilgrims. The woman shook her head:—

"We cannot help being hospitable to pilgrims. We owe our lives to a pilgrim. We lived, we had forgotten God, and God had forgotten us, so that all that we expected was death. Last summer it went so bad with us that we were all flat on our backs,—we had nothing to eat,—oh, how sick we were! And we should have died; but God sent us such a nice old man, just like you! He came in just at noon to get a drink; and when he saw us, he was sorry for us, yes, and he stayed on with us. And he gave us something to drink, and fed us, and put us on our legs; and he bought back our land, and he bought us a horse and cart and left them with us."

The old woman came into the hut; she took the woman's story out of her mouth.

"And we don't know at all," said she, "whether it was a man, or an angel of God. He loved us all so, and he was so sorry for us; and he went away without saying anything, and we don't know who we should pray God for. I can see it now just as it was; there I was lying expecting to die; I see a little old man come in . . . not a bit stuck up . . . rather bald . . . he asks for water. Sinner that I was, I thought, 'What is he prowling round here for?' And think what he did! As soon as he saw us, he took off his sack, and set it right down on that spot, and untied it."

And the little girl broke in.

"No," says she, "babushka; first he set his sack right in the middle of the hut, and then he put it on the bench."

And they began to discuss it, and to recall all his words and actions; both where he sat, and where he slept, and what he did, and what he said to any of them.

At nightfall came the muzhik on horseback; he, also, began to tell about Yeliseï, and how he had stayed with them.

"If he had not come to us," says he, "we should all have died in our sins. We were perishing in despair; we murmured against God and against men. But he set us on our feet; and through him we learned to know God, and we have come to believe that there are good people. Christ save him! Before, we lived like cattle; he made us human beings again."

The people fed Yefim, giving him all he wanted to drink; they settled him for the night, and they themselves lay down to sleep.

But Yefim was unable to sleep; and the thought would not leave his mind, how he had seen Yeliseï in Jerusalem three times in the foremost place.

"That's how he got there before me," he said to himself. "My labors may, or may not, be accepted; but the Lord has accepted his."

In the morning the people wished Yefim good speed; they loaded him with pirozhki for his journey, and they went to their work; and Yefim started on his way.

---

[1] A sort of triangular doughnuts, or dumplings, stuffed with cheese or curds.

12

Yefim had been gone exactly a year. In the spring he returned home.

He reached home in the evening. His son was not at home; he was at the tavern. His son came home tipsy. Yefim began to question him. In all respects he saw that the young man had got into bad ways during his absence. He had spent all the money badly, he had neglected things. The father began to reprimand him. The son began to be impudent.

"You yourself might have stirred about a little," says he, "but you went wandering. Yes, and you took all the money with you besides, and then you call me to account!"

The father grew angry, and beat his son.

In the morning Yefim Tarasuitch started for the starosta's to talk with him about his son; he passed by Yeliseï's dvor. Yeliseï's old woman was standing on the doorsteps; she greeted him.

"How's your health, neighbor?" said she; "did you have a good pilgrimage?"

Yefim Tarasuitch stopped.

"Glory to God," says he, "I have got back! I lost your old man, but I hear he is at home!"

And the old woman began to talk. She was very fond of prattling.

"He got back," says she, "good neighbor; he got back long ago. Very soon after the Assumption. And glad enough we were that God brought him. It was lonely for us without him. He isn't good for much work—his day is done; but he is the head, and we are happier. And how glad our lad was! 'Without father,' says he, 'it's like being without light in the eye.' It was lonely for us without him; we love him and we missed him so!"

"Well, is he at home now?"

"Yes, friend, he's with the bees: he's hiving the new swarms. Splendid swarms! such a power of bees God never gave, as far as my old man remembers. God doesn't grant according to our sins, he says. Come in, neighbor; how glad he'll be to see you!"

Yefim passed through the vestibule, through the yard, to the apiary, where Yeliseï was. He went into the apiary, he looked—there was Yeliseï standing under a little birch tree, without a net, without gloves, in his gray kaftan, spreading out his arms, and looking up; and the bald spot over his whole head gleamed just as when he stood in Jerusalem at the Lord's sepulcher; and over him, just as in Jerusalem the candles burned, the sunlight played through the birch tree; and around his head the golden bees were circling, flying in and out, and they did not sting him.

Yefim stood still.

Yeliseï's old woman called to her husband.

"Our neighbor's come," says she.

Yeliseï looked around, was delighted, and came to meet his companion, calmly detaching the bees from his beard.

"How are you, comrade, how are you, my dear friend!—did you have a good journey?"

"My feet went on the pilgrimage, and I have brought you some water from the river Jordan. Come . . . you shall have it . . . but whether the Lord accepted my labors . . ."

"Well, glory to God, Christ save us!"

Yefim was silent for a moment.

"My legs took me there, but whether it was my soul that was there or another's . . ."

"That is God's affair, comrade, God's affair."

"On my way back I stopped also . . . at the hut where you left me . . ."

Yeliseï became confused; he hastened to repeat:—

"It's God's affair, comrade, God's affair. What say you? shall we go into the izba?—I will bring you some honey."

And Yeliseï changed the conversation; he spoke about domestic affairs.

Yefim sighed, and did not again remind Yeliseï of the people in the hut, and the vision of him that he had seen in Jerusalem.

And he learned that in this world God bids every one do his duty till death —in love and good deeds.

1885

WHERE LOVE IS, THERE GOD IS ALSO

In the city lived the shoemaker, Martuin Avdyeitch. He lived in a basement, in a little room with one window. The window looked out on the street. Through the window he used to watch the people passing by; although only their feet could be seen, yet by the boots Martuin Avdyeitch recognized the people. Martuin Avdyeitch had lived long in one place, and had many acquaintances. Few pairs of boots in his district had not been in his hands once and again. Some he would half-sole, some he would patch, some he would stitch around, and occasionally he would also put on new uppers. And through the window he often recognized his work.

Avdyeitch had plenty to do, because he was a faithful workman, used good material, did not make exorbitant charges, and kept his word. If it was possible for him to finish an order by a certain time, he would accept it; otherwise, he would not deceive you,—he would tell you so beforehand. And all knew Avdyeitch, and he was never out of work.

Avdyeitch had always been a good man; but as he grew old, he began to think more about his soul, and get nearer to God. Martuin's wife had died when he was still living with his master. His wife left him a boy three years old. None of their other children had lived. All the eldest had died in childhood. Martuin at first intended to send his little son to his sister in the village, but afterward he felt sorry for him; he thought to himself:—

"It will be hard for my Kapitoshka to live in a strange family. I shall keep him with me."

And Avdyeitch left his master, and went into lodgings with his little son. But God gave Avdyeitch no luck with his children. As Kapitoshka grew older, he began to help his father, and would have been a delight to him, but a sickness fell on him, he went to bed, suffered a week, and died. Martuin buried his son, and fell into despair. So deep was this despair that he began to complain of God. Martuin fell into such a melancholy state, that more than once he prayed to God for death, and reproached God because He had not taken him who was an old man, instead of his beloved only son. Avdyeitch also ceased to go to church.

And once a little old man from the same district came from Troïtsa[1] to see Avdyeitch; for seven years he had been wandering about. Avdyeitch talked with him, and began to complain about his sorrows.

"I have no desire to live any longer," he said: "I only wish I was dead. That is all I pray God for. I am a man without anything to hope for now."

And the little old man said to him:—

"You don't talk right, Martuin: we must not judge God's doings. The world moves, not by our skill, but by God's will. God decreed for your son to die,— for you—to live. So it is for the best. And you are in despair, because you wish to live for your own happiness."

"But what shall one live for?" asked Martuin.

And the little old man said:—

"We must live for God, Martuin. He gives you life, and for His sake you must live. When you begin to live for Him, you will not grieve over anything, and all will seem easy to you."

Martuin kept silent for a moment, and then said, "But how can one live for God?"

And the little old man said:—

"Christ has taught us how to live for God. You know how to read? Buy a Testament, and read it; there you will learn how to live for God. Everything is explained there."

And these words kindled a fire in Avdyeitch's heart. And he went that very same day, bought a New Testament in large print, and began to read.

At first Avdyeitch intended to read only on holidays; but as he began to read, it so cheered his soul that he used to read every day. At times he would become so absorbed in reading, that all the kerosene in the lamp would burn out, and still he could not tear himself away. And so Avdyeitch used to read every evening.

And the more he read, the clearer he understood what God wanted of him, and how one should live for God; and his heart kept growing easier and easier. Formerly, when he lay down to sleep, he used to sigh and groan, and always thought of his Kapitoshka; and now his only exclamation was:—

"Glory to Thee! glory to Thee, Lord! Thy will be done."

And from that time Avdyeitch's whole life was changed. In other days he, too, used to drop into a public-house as a holiday amusement, to drink a cup of tea; and he was not averse to a little brandy either. He would take a drink with some acquaintance, and leave the saloon, not intoxicated exactly, yet in

---

[1] Trinity, a famous monastery, pilgrimage to which is reckoned a virtue.

a happy frame of mind, and inclined to talk nonsense, and shout, and use abusive language at a person. Now he left off that sort of thing. His life became quiet and joyful. In the morning he would sit down to work, finish his allotted task, then take the little lamp from the hook, put it on the table, get his book from the shelf, open it, and sit down to read. And the more he read, the more he understood, and the brighter and happier it grew in his heart.

Once it happened that Martuin read till late into the night. He was reading the Gospel of Luke. He was reading over the sixth chapter; and he was reading the verses:—

"*And unto him that smiteth thee on the one cheek offer also the other; and him that taketh away thy cloak forbid not to take thy coat also. Give to every man that asketh of thee; and of him that taketh away thy goods ask them not again. And as ye would that men should do to you, do ye also to them likewise.*"

He read farther also those verses, where God speaks:

"*And why call ye me, Lord, Lord, and do not the things which I say? Whosoever cometh to me, and heareth my sayings, and doeth them, I will shew you to whom he is like: he is like a man which built an house, and digged deep, and laid the foundation on a rock: and when the flood arose, the stream beat vehemently upon that house, and could not shake it; for it was founded upon a rock. But he that heareth, and doeth not, is like a man that without a foundation built an house upon the earth; against which the stream did beat vehemently, and immediately it fell; and the ruin of that house was great.*"

Avdyeitch read these words, and joy filled his soul. He took off his spectacles, put them down on the book, leaned his elbows on the table, and became lost in thought. And he began to measure his life by these words. And he thought to himself:—

"Is my house built on the rock, or on the sand? 'Tis well if on the rock. It is so easy when you are alone by yourself; it seems as if you had done everything as God commands; but when you forget yourself, you sin again. Yet I shall still struggle on. It is very good. Help me, Lord!"

Thus ran his thoughts; he wanted to go to bed, but he felt loath to tear himself away from the book. And he began to read farther in the seventh chapter. He read about the centurion, he read about the widow's son, he read about the answer given to John's disciples, and finally he came to that place where the rich Pharisee desired the Lord to sit at meat with him; and he read how the woman that was a sinner anointed His feet, and washed them with her tears, and how He forgave her. He reached the forty-fourth verse, and began to read:—

"*And he turned to the woman, and said unto Simon, Seest thou this woman? I entered into thine house, thou gavest me no water for my feet: but she hath washed my feet with tears, and wiped them with the hairs of her head. Thou gavest me no kiss: but this woman since the time I came in hath not ceased to kiss my feet. My head with oil thou didst not anoint: but this woman hath anointed my feet with ointment.*"

He finished reading these verses, and thought to himself:—

"*Thou gavest me no water for my feet, thou gavest me no kiss. My head with oil thou didst not anoint.*"

And again Avdyeitch took off his spectacles, put them down on the book, and again he became lost in thought.

"It seems that Pharisee must have been such a man as I am. I, too, apparently have thought only of myself,—how I might have my tea, be warm and comfortable, but never to think about my guest. He thought about himself, but there was not the least care taken of the guest. And who was his guest? The Lord Himself. If He had come to me, should I have done the same way?"

Avdyeitch rested his head upon both his arms, and did not notice that he fell asleep.

"Martuin!" suddenly seemed to sound in his ears.

Martuin started from his sleep:—

"Who is here?"

He turned around, glanced toward the door—no one.

Again he fell into a doze. Suddenly he plainly heard:—

"Martuin! Ah, Martuin! look to-morrow on the street. I am coming."

Martuin awoke, rose from the chair, began to rub his eyes. He himself could not tell whether he heard those words in his dream, or in reality. He turned down his lamp, and went to bed.

At daybreak next morning, Avdyeitch rose, made his prayer to God, lighted the stove, put on the cabbage-soup and the gruel, put the water in the samovar, put on his apron, and sat down by the window to work.

And while he was working, he kept thinking about all that had happened the day before. It seemed to him at one moment that it was a dream, and now he had really heard a voice.

"Well," he said to himself, "such things have been."

Martuin was sitting by the window, and looking out more than he was working. When any one passed by in boots which he did not know, he would bend down, look out of the window, in order to see, not only the feet, but also the face.

The House-porter passed by in new felt boots, the water-carrier passed by; then there came up to the window an old soldier of Nicholas's time, in an old pair of laced felt boots, with a shovel in his hands. Avdyeitch recognized him by his felt boots. The old man's name was Stepanuitch; and a neighboring merchant, out of charity, gave him a home with him. He was required to assist the dvornik. Stepanuitch began to shovel away the snow from in front of Avdyeitch's window. Avdyeitch glanced at him, and took up his work again.

"Pshaw! I must be getting crazy in my old age," said Avdyeitch, and laughed at himself. "Stepanuitch is clearing away the snow, and I imagine that Christ is coming to see me. I was entirely out of my mind, old dotard that I am!"

Avdyeitch sewed about a dozen stitches, and then felt impelled to look through the window again. He looked out again through the window, and saw that Stepanuitch had leaned his shovel against the wall, and was warming himself, and resting. He was an old broken-down man; evidently he had not strength enough even to shovel the snow. Avdyeitch said to himself:—

"I will give him some tea; by the way, the samovar has only just gone out." Avdyeitch laid down his awl, rose from his seat, put the samovar on the table, poured out the tea, and tapped with his finger at the glass. Stepanuitch turned around, and came to the window. Avdyeitch beckoned to him, and went to open the door.

"Come in, warm yourself a little," he said. "You must be cold."

"May Christ reward you for this! my bones ache," said Stepanuitch.

Stepanuitch came in, and shook off the snow, tried to wipe his feet, so as not to soil the floor, but staggered.

"Don't trouble to wipe your feet. I will clean it up myself; we are used to such things. Come in and sit down," said Avdyeitch. "Here, drink a cup of tea."

And Avdyeitch filled two glasses, and handed one to his guest; while he himself poured his tea into a saucer, and began to blow it.

Stepanuitch finished drinking his glass of tea, turned the glass upside down,[2] put the half-eaten lump of sugar on it, and began to express his thanks. But it was evident he wanted some more.

"Have some more," said Avdyeitch, filling both his own glass and his guest's. Avdyeitch drank his tea, but from time to time glanced out into the street.

"Are you expecting any one?" asked his guest.

"Am I expecting any one? I am ashamed even to tell whom I expect. I am, and I am not, expecting some one; but one word has kindled a fire in my heart. Whether it is a dream, or something else, I do not know. Don't you see, brother, I was reading yesterday the Gospel about Christ the Batyushka; how He suffered, how He walked on the earth. I suppose you have heard about it?"

"Indeed I have," replied Stepanuitch; "but we are people in darkness, we can't read."

"Well, now, I was reading about that very thing,—how He walked on the earth; I read, you know, how He came to the Pharisee, and the Pharisee did not treat Him hospitably. Well, and so, my brother, I was reading yesterday, about this very thing, and was thinking to myself how he did not receive Christ the Batyushka, with honor. Suppose, for example, He should come to me, or any one else, I said to myself, I should not even know how to receive Him. And he gave Him no reception at all. Well! while I was thus thinking, I fell asleep, brother, and I heard some one call me by name. I got up; the voice, just as if some one whispered, said, 'Be on the watch; I shall come to-morrow.' And this happened twice. Well! would you believe it, it got into my head? I scolded myself—and yet I am expecting Him, the Batyushka."

Stepanuitch shook his head, and said nothing; he finished drinking his glass of tea, and put it on the side; but Avdyeitch picked up the glass again, and filled it once more.

"Drink some more for your good health. You see, I have an idea that, when the Batyushka went about on this earth, He disdained no one, and had more to do with the simple people. He always went to see the simple people. He picked out His disciples more from among folk like such sinners as we are, from the working-class. Said He, whoever exalts himself, shall be humbled, and he who is humbled shall become exalted. Said He, you call me Lord, and, said He, I wash your feet. Whoever wishes, said He, to be the first, the same

---

[2] To signify he was satisfied, a custom among the Russians.

shall be a servant to all. Because, said He, blessed are the poor, the humble, the kind, the generous."

And Stepanuitch forgot about his tea; he was an old man, and easily moved to tears. He was listening, and the tears rolled down his face.

"Come, now, have some more tea," said Avdyeitch; but Stepanuitch made the sign of the cross, thanked him, turned down his glass, and arose.

"Thanks to you," he says, "Martuin Avdyeitch, for treating me kindly, and satisfying me, soul and body."

"You are welcome; come in again; always glad to see a friend," said Avdyeitch.

Stepanuitch departed; and Martuin poured out the rest of the tea, drank it up, put away the dishes, and sat down again by the window to work, to stitch on a patch. He kept stitching away, and at the same time looking through the window. He was expecting Christ, and was all the while thinking of Him and His deeds, and his head was filled with the different speeches of Christ.

Two soldiers passed by: one wore boots furnished by the crown, and the other one, boots that he had made; then the master of the next house passed by in shining galoshes; then a baker with a basket passed by. All passed by; and now there came also by the window a woman in woolen stockings and rustic bashmaks on her feet. She passed by the window, and stood still near the window-case.

Avdyeitch looked up at her from the window, and saw it was a stranger, a woman poorly clad, and with a child; she was standing by the wall with her back to the wind, trying to wrap up the child, and she had nothing to wrap it up in. The woman was dressed in shabby summer clothes; and from behind the frame, Avdyeitch could hear the child crying, and the woman trying to pacify it; but she was not able to pacify it.

Avdyeitch got up, went to the door, ascended the steps, and cried:—

"My good woman. Hey! my good woman!"

The woman heard him and turned around.

"Why are you standing in the cold with the child? Come into my room, where it is warm; you can manage it better. Here, this way!"

The woman was astonished. She saw an old, old man, in an apron, with spectacles on his nose, calling her to him. She followed him. They descended the steps and entered the room; the old man led the woman to his bed.

"There," says he, "Sit down, my good woman, nearer to the stove; you can get warm, and nurse the little one."

"I have no milk for him. I myself have not eaten anything since morning," said the woman; but, nevertheless, she took the baby to her breast.

Avdyeitch shook his head, went to the table, brought out the bread and a dish, opened the oven-door, poured into the dish some cabbage-soup, took out the pot with the gruel, but it was not cooked as yet; so he filled the dish with shchi only, and put it on the table. He got the bread, took the towel down from the hook, and spread it upon the table.

"Sit down," he says, "and eat, my good woman; and I will mind the little one. You see, I once had children of my own; I know how to handle them."

The woman crossed herself, sat down at the table, and began to eat; while Avdyeitch took a seat on the bed near the infant. Avdyeitch kept smacking and smacking to it with his lips; but it was a poor kind of smacking, for he had no teeth. The little one kept on crying. And it occurred to Avdyeitch to threaten the little one with his finger; he waved, waved his finger right before the child's mouth, and hastily withdrew it. He did not put it to its mouth, because his finger was black, and soiled with wax. And the little one looked at his finger, and became quiet; then it began to smile, and Avdyeitch also was glad. While the woman was eating, she told who she was, and whither she was going.

Said she:—

"I am a soldier's wife. It is now seven months since they sent my husband away off, and no tidings. I lived out as cook; the baby was born; no one cared to keep me with a child. This is the third month that I have been struggling along without a place. I ate up all I had. I wanted to engage as a wet-nurse— no one would take me—I am too thin, they say. I have just been to the merchant's wife, where lives a young woman I know, and so they promised to take us in. I thought that was the end of it. But she told me to come next week. And she lives a long way off. I got tired out; and it tired him too, my heart's darling. Fortunately our landlady takes pity on us for the sake of Christ, and gives us a room, else I don't know how I should manage to get along."

Avdyeitch sighed, and said:—

"Haven't you any warm clothes?"

"Now is the time, friend, to wear warm clothes; but yesterday I pawned my last shawl for a twenty-kopek piece."

The woman came to the bed, and took the child; and Avdyeitch rose, went to the partition, rummaged round, and succeeded in finding an old coat.

"Na!" says he; "it is a poor thing, yet you may turn it to some use."

The woman looked at the coat and looked at the old man; she took the coat, and burst into tears; and Avdyeitch turned away his head; crawling under the bed, he pushed out a little trunk, rummaged in it, and sat down again opposite the woman.

And the woman said:—

"May Christ bless you, little grandfather! He must have sent me to your window. My little baby would have frozen to death. When I started out it was warm, but now it has grown cold. And He, the Batyushka, led you to look through the window and take pity on me, an unfortunate."

Avdyeitch smiled, and said:—

"Indeed, He did that! I have been looking through the window, my good woman, for some wise reason."

And Martuin told the soldier's wife his dream, and how he heard the voice, —how the Lord promised to come and see him that day.

"All things are possible," said the woman. She rose, put on the coat, wrapped up her little child in it; and, as she started to take leave, she thanked Avdyeitch again.

"Take this, for Christ's sake," said Avdyeitch, giving her a twenty-kopek piece; "redeem your shawl."

She made the sign of the cross, and Avdyeitch made the sign of the cross and went with her to the door.

The woman went away. Avdyeitch ate some shchi, washed the dishes, and sat down again to work. While he was working he still remembered the window;

when the window grew darker he immediately looked out to see who was passing by. Acquaintances passed by and strangers passed by, and there was nothing out of the ordinary.

But here Avdyeitch saw that an old apple-woman had stopped in front of his window. She carried a basket with apples. Only a few were left, as she had evidently sold them nearly all out; and over her shoulder she had a bag full of chips. She must have gathered them up in some new building, and was on her way home. One could see that the bag was heavy on her shoulder; she tried to shift it to the other shoulder. So she lowered the bag on the sidewalk, stood the basket with the apples on a little post, and began to shake down the splinters in the bag. And while she was shaking her bag, a little boy in a torn cap came along, picked up an apple from the basket, and was about to make his escape; but the old woman noticed it, turned around, and caught the youngster by his sleeve. The little boy began to struggle, tried to tear himself away; but the old woman grasped him with both hands, knocked off his cap, and caught him by the hair.

The little boy was screaming, the old woman was scolding. Avdyeitch lost no time in putting away his awl; he threw it upon the floor, sprang to the door,—he even stumbled on the stairs, and dropped his spectacles,—and rushed out into the street.

The old woman was pulling the youngster by his hair, and was scolding, and threatening to take him to the policeman; the youngster was defending himself, and denying the charge.

"I did not take it," he said; "what are you licking me for? Let me go!"

Avdyeitch tried to separate them. He took the boy by his arm, and said:—

"Let him go, babushka; forgive him, for Christ's sake."

"I will forgive him so that he won't forget it till the new broom grows. I am going to take the little villain to the police."

Avdyeitch began to entreat the old woman:—

"Let him go, babushka," he said, "he will never do it again. Let him go, for Christ's sake."

The old woman let him loose; the boy started to run, but Avdyeitch kept him back.

"Ask the babushka's forgiveness," he said, "and don't you ever do it again; I saw you take the apple."

The boy burst into tears, and began to ask forgiveness.

"There now! that's right; and here's an apple for you."

And Avdyeitch took an apple from the basket, and gave it to the boy.

"I will pay you for it, babushka," he said to the old woman.

"You ruin them that way, the good-for-nothings," said the old woman. "He ought to be treated so that he would remember it for a whole week."

"Eh, babushka, babushka," said Avdyeitch, "that is right according to our judgment, but not according to God's. If he is to be whipped for an apple, then what ought to be done to us for our sins?"

The old woman was silent.

And Avdyeitch told her the parable of the master who forgave a debtor all that he owed him, and how the debtor went and began to choke one who owed him.

The old woman listened, and the boy stood listening.

"God has commanded us to forgive," said Avdyeitch, "else we, too, may not be forgiven. All should be forgiven, and the thoughtless especially."

The old woman shook her head, and sighed.

"That's so," said she; "but the trouble is that they are very much spoiled."

"Then, we who are older must teach them," said Avdyeitch.

"That's just what I say," remarked the old woman. "I myself have had seven of them,—only one daughter is left."

And the old woman began to relate where and how she lived with her daughter, and how many grandchildren she had. "Here," she says, "my strength is only so-so, and yet I have to work. I pity the youngsters—my grandchildren—but what nice children they are! No one gives me such a welcome as they do. Aksintka won't go to any one but me. 'Babushka, dear babushka, loveliest.' "

And the old woman grew quite sentimental.

"Of course, it is a childish trick. God be with him," said she, pointing to the boy.

The woman was just about to lift the bag up on her shoulder, when the boy ran up, and said:—

"Let me carry it, babushka; it is on my way."

The old woman nodded her head, and put the bag on the boy's back.

And side by side they passed along the street.

And the old woman even forgot to ask Avdyeitch to pay for the apple. Avdyeitch stood motionless, and kept gazing after them; and he heard them talking all the time as they walked away. After Avdyeitch saw them disappear, he returned to his room; he found his eye-glasses on the stairs,—they were not broken; he picked up his awl, and sat down to work again.

After working a little while it grew darker, so that he could not see to sew; he saw the lamplighter passing by to light the street-lamps.

"It must be time to make a light," he said to himself; so he got his little lamp ready, hung it up, and betook himself again to his work. He had one boot already finished; he turned it around, looked at it: "Well done." He put away his tools, swept off the cuttings, cleared off the bristles and ends, took the lamp, set it on the table, and took down the Gospels from the shelf. He intended to open the book at the very place where he had yesterday put a piece of leather as a mark, but it happened to open at another place; and the moment Avdyeitch opened the Testament, he recollected his last night's dream. And as soon as he remembered it, it seemed as if he heard some one stepping about behind him. Avdyeitch looked around, and saw—there, in the dark corner, it seemed as if people were standing; he was at a loss to know who they were. And a voice whispered in his ear:—

"Martuin—ah, Martuin! did you not recognize me?"

"Who?" exclaimed Avdyeitch.

"Me," repeated the voice. "It was I;" and Stepanuitch stepped forth from the dark corner; he smiled, and like a little cloud faded away, and soon vanished. . . .

"And it was I," said the voice.

From the dark corner stepped forth the woman with her child; the woman smiled, the child laughed, and they also vanished.

"And it was I," continued the voice; both the old woman and the boy with the apple stepped forward; both smiled and vanished.

Avdyeitch's soul rejoiced; he crossed himself, put on his spectacles, and began to read the Evangelists where it happened to open. On the upper part of the page he read:—

"*For I was an hungered, and ye gave me meat: I was thirsty, and ye gave me drink: I was a stranger, and ye took me in.*" . . .

And on the lower part of the page he read this:—

"*Inasmuch as ye have done it unto one of the least of these my brethren, ye have done it unto me*" (St. Matthew, chap. xxv.).

And Avdyeitch understood that his dream had not deceived him; that the Saviour really called on him that day, and that he really received Him.

1885

THE DEATH OF IVAN ILYITCH

1

In the great building of the law-courts, while the proceedings in the Mielvinsky suit were at a standstill, the members of the board and the prokuror met in Ivan Yegorovitch Shebek's private room, and the conversation turned on the famous Krasovsky suit. Feodor Vasilyevitch talked himself into a passion in pointing out the men's innocence; Ivan Yegorovitch maintained his side; but Piotr Ivanovitch, who had not entered into the discussion at first, took no part in it even now, and was glancing over the *Vyedomosti*, which had just been handed to him.

"Gentlemen!" said he, "Ivan Ilyitch is dead!"

"Is it possible?"

"Here! read for yourself," said he to Feodor Vasilyevitch, handing him the paper, which had still retained its odor of freshness.

Heavy black lines inclosed these printed words:—

"*Praskovia Feodorovna Golovina, with heartfelt sorrow, announces to relatives and friends the death of her beloved husabnd, Ivan Ilyitch Golovin, member of the Court of Appeal, who departed this life on the 16th February, 1882. The funeral will take place on Friday, at one o'clock in the afternoon.*"

Ivan Ilyitch had been the colleague of the gentlemen there assembled, and all liked him. He had been ill for several weeks, and it was said that his case was incurable. His place was kept vacant for him; but it had been decided that, in case of his death, Alekseyef might be assigned to his place, while either Vinnikof or Schtabel would take Alekseyef's place. And so, on hearing of Ivan Ilyitch's death, the first thought of each of the gentlemen gathered in that room was in regard to the changes and promotions which this death might bring about among the members of the council and their acquaintances.

"Now, surely, I shall get either Schtabel's or Vinnikof's place," was Feodor

Vasilyevitch's thought. "It has been promised me for a long time; and this promotion will mean an increase in my salary of eight hundred rubles, besides allowances."

"I must propose right away to have my brother-in-law transferred from Kaluga," thought Piotr Ivanovitch. "My wife will be very glad. Then it will be impossible for her to say that I have never done anything for her relations."

"I have been thinking that he wouldn't get up again," said Piotr Ivanovitch aloud. "It is too bad."

"But what was really the matter with him?"

"The doctors could not determine. That is to say, they determined it, but each in his own way. When I saw him the last time, it seemed to me that he was getting better."

"But I haven't been to see him since the Christmas holidays. I kept meaning to go."

"Did he have any property?"

"His wife had a very little, I think. But a mere pittance."

"Well, we must go to see her. They live a frightful distance off."

"That is, from you. Everything is far from you!"

"Now, see here! He can't forgive me because I live on the other side of the river," said Piotr Ivanovitch to Shebek, with a smile.

And then they talked about the long distances in cities, till the recess was over.

Over and above the considerations caused by the death of this man, in regard to the mutations and possible changes in the court that might result from it, the very fact of the death of an intimate friend aroused as usual in all who heard about it a feeling of pleasure that "it was he, and not I, who was dead."

Each one said to himself, or felt:—

"Well, he is dead, and I am not."

The intimate acquaintances, the so-called friends, of Ivan Ilyitch could not help having these thoughts, and also felt that now it was incumbent on them to fulfil the very melancholy obligation of propriety, in going to the funeral and paying a visit of condolence to the widow.

Feodor Vasilyevitch and Piotr Ivanovitch had been more intimate with him than the others.

Piotr Ivanovitch had been his fellow in the law-school, and had felt under obligations to Ivan Ilyitch.

Having, at dinner-time, informed his wife of Ivan Ilyitch's death, and his reflections as to the possibility of his brother-in-law's transfer into their circle, Piotr Ivanovitch, not stopping to rest, put on his dress-coat, and drove off to Ivan Ilyitch's.

At the door of Ivan Ilyitch's residence stood a carriage and two izvoshchiks. At the foot of the stairs, in the hallway by the hat-rack, pushed back against the wall, was the brocaded coffin-cover, with tassels and lace full of purified powdered camphor. Two ladies in black were taking off their shubkas. One whom he knew was Ivan Ilyitch's sister; the other lady he did not know. Piotr Ivanovitch's colleague, Schwartz, was just coming down-stairs; and, as he recognized the newcomer, he stopped on the upper step, and winked at him as much as to say:—

"Ivan Ilyitch was a bad manager; you and I understand a thing or two."

Schwartz's face, with its English side-whiskers, and his spare figure under his dress-coat, had, as always, an elegant solemnity; and this solemnity, which was forever contradicted by Schwartz's jovial nature, here had a peculiar piquancy, so Piotr Ivanovitch thought.

Piotr Ivanovitch gave precedence to the ladies, and slowly followed them up-stairs. Schwartz did not make any move to descend, but waited at the landing. Piotr Ivanovitch understood his motive; without doubt, he wanted to make an appointment for playing cards that evening. The ladies mounted the stairs to the widow's room; and Schwartz, with lips gravely compressed and firm, and with mischievous eyes, indicated to Piotr Ivanovitch, by the motion of his brows, the room at the right, where the dead man was.

Piotr Ivanovitch entered, having that feeling of uncertainty, ever present under such circumstances, as to what would be the proper thing to do. But he knew that in such circumstances the sign of the cross never came amiss. As to whether he ought to make a salutation or not, he was not quite sure; and he therefore took a middle course. As he went into the room, he began to cross himself, and, at the same time, he made an almost imperceptible inclination. As far as he was permitted by the motion of his hands and head, he took in the appearance of the room. Two young men, apparently nephews,—one, a scholar at the gymnasium,—were just leaving the room, making the sign of the cross. An old woman was standing motionless; and a lady, with strangely arched eyebrows, was saying something to her in a whisper. A hearty-looking, energetic sacristan in a frock was reading something in a loud voice, with an expression which forbade all objection. The muzhik, Gerasim, who acted as butler, was sprinkling something on the floor, passing slowly in front of Piotr Ivanovitch. As he saw this, Piotr Ivanovitch immediately became cognizant of a slight odor of decomposition.

Piotr Ivanovitch, at his last call on Ivan Ilyitch, had seen this muzhik in the library. He was performing the duties of nurse, and Ivan Ilyitch was extremely fond of him.

Piotr Ivanovitch kept crossing himself, and bowing impartially toward the corpse, the sacristan, and the ikons that stood on a table in the corner. Then, when it seemed to him that he had already continued too long making signs of the cross with his hand, he stopped short, and began to gaze at the dead man.

The dead man lay in the drapery of the coffin, as dead men always lie, a perfectly lifeless weight, absolutely unconscious, with stiffened limbs, with head forever at rest on the pillow; and showing, as all corpses show, a brow like yellow wax, with spots on the sunken temples, and a nose so prominent as almost to press down on the upper lip.

He had greatly changed, and was far more emaciated than when Piotr Ivanovitch had last seen him; but, as in the case of all the dead, his face was more beautiful, especially more dignified, than it had been when he was alive. On his face was an expression signifying that what was necessary to do, that had been done, and had been done in due form. Besides this, there was in his expression a reproach or warning to the living. This warning seemed ill-judged to Piotr Ivanovitch, or at least was not applicable to him. There was something displeasing in it; and therefore Piotr Ivanovitch again crossed himself hastily, and, it seemed to him, too hastily for proper decorum, turned around and went to the door.

Schwartz was waiting for him in the next room, standing with legs wide apart, and with both hands behind his back twirling his "cylinder" hat. Piotr Ivanovitch was cheered by the first glance at Schwartz's jovial, tidy, elegant figure. Piotr Ivanovitch comprehended that Schwartz was superior to these things, and did not give way to these harassing impressions. His appearance alone said:—

The incident of Ivan Ilyitch's funeral cannot serve as a sufficient reason for breaking into the order of exercises of the session; that is to say, nothing shall hinder us this very evening from opening and shuffling a pack of .cards while the servant is putting down four fresh candles; in general, there is no occasion to presuppose that this incident can prevent us from having a good time this evening, as well as any other.

He even said this in a whisper to Piotr Ivanovitch as he joined him, and proposed that they meet for a game at Feodor Vasilyevitch's. But evidently it was not Piotr Ivanovitch's fate to play cards that evening.

Praskovia Feodorovna, a short woman, and stout in spite of all her efforts to the contrary,—for her figure grew constantly wider and wider from her shoulders down,—dressed all in black, with lace on her head, and with the same extraordinarily arched eyebrows as the lady who had been standing by the coffin, came out from her rooms with other ladies; and as she preceded them through the door of the death-chamber, she said:—

"Mass will take place immediately. Please come in."

Schwartz, making a slight, indefinite bow, stood still, evidently undecided whether to accept or to decline this invitation. Praskovia Feodorovna, as soon as she recognized Piotr Ivanovitch, sighed, came quite close to him, took him by the hand, and said:—

"I know that you were a true friend of Ivan Ilyitch's." And she fixed her eyes on him, awaiting his action to respond to her words.

Piotr Ivanovitch knew that, just as in the other case it had been incumbent upon him to make the sign of the cross, so here he must press her hand, sigh, and say, "Why, certainly." And so he did. And having done so, he realized that the desired result was obtained,—that he was touched, and she was touched.

"Come," said the widow; "before it begins, I must have a talk with you. Give me your arm."

Piotr Ivanovitch offered her his arm; and they walked along to the inner rooms, passing by Schwartz, who winked compassionately at Piotr Ivanovitch. His jovial glance said:—

"It's all up with your game of *vint*; but don't be concerned, we'll find another partner. We'll cut in when you have finished."

Piotr Ivanovitch sighed still more deeply and grievously, and Praskovia Feodorovna pressed his arm gratefully.

When they entered her drawing-room, which had hangings of rose-colored cretonne, and was dimly lighted by a lamp, they sat down near a table,—

she on a divan, but Piotr Ivanovitch on a low ottoman, the springs of which were out of order, and yielded unevenly under his weight.

Praskovia Feodorovna wanted to suggest to him to take another chair; but to make such a suggestion seemed out of place in her situation, and she gave it up. As he sat down on the ottoman, Piotr Ivanovitch remembered how, when Ivan Ilyitch was decorating that drawing-room, he had asked his opinion about this very same rose-colored cretonne, with its green leaves.

As the widow passed by the table in going to the divan,—the whole room was crowded with ornaments and furniture,—she caught the black lace of her black mantilla on the woodwork. Piotr Ivanovitch got up, in order to detach it; and the ottoman, freed from his weight, began to shake and jostle him. The widow herself was busy disengaging her lace; and Piotr Ivanovitch sat down again, flattening out the ottoman which had rebelled under him. But still the widow could not get free, and Piotr Ivanovitch again arose; and again the ottoman rebelled, and even creaked.

When all this was arranged, she took out a clean cambric handkerchief, and began to weep. The episode with the lace and the struggle with the ottoman had thrown a chill over Piotr Ivanovitch, and he sat with a frown. This awkward situation was interrupted by Sokolof, Ivan Ilyitch's butler, with the announcement that the lot in the graveyard, which Praskovia Feodorovna had selected, would cost two hundred rubles. She ceased to weep, and, with the air of a martyr, looked at Piotr Ivanovitch, saying in French that it was very trying for her. Piotr Ivanovitch made a silent gesture, signifying his undoubted belief that this was inevitable.

"Smoke, I beg of you!" she said with a voice expressive of magnanimity as well as melancholy. And she discussed with Sokolof the price of the lot.

As Piotr Ivanovitch began to smoke, he overheard how she very circumstantially inquired into the various prices of land, and finally determined on the one which it suited her to purchase. When she had settled upon the lot, she also gave her orders in regard to the singers. Sokolof withdrew.

"I attend to everything myself," she said to Piotr Ivanovitch, moving to one side the albums that lay on the table; and then, noticing that the ashes were about to fall on the table, she hastened to hand Piotr Ivanovitch an ashtray, and continued:—

"It would be hypocritical for me to declare that grief prevents me from attending to practical affairs. On the contrary, though it cannot console me, yet it may divert my mind from my troubles."

Again she took out her handkerchief, as if preparing to weep; and suddenly, apparently making an effort over herself, she shook herself, and began to speak calmly:—

"At all events, I have some business with you."

Piotr Ivanovitch bowed, not giving the springs of the ottoman a chance to rise up against him, since only the moment before they had been misbehaving under him.

"During the last days, his sufferings were terrible."

"He suffered very much?" asked Piotr Ivanovitch.

"Oh! terribly! For hours before he died he did not cease to shriek. For three days and nights he shrieked all the time. It was unendurable. I cannot understand how I stood it. You could hear him through three doors! Akh! how I suffered!"

"And was he in his senses?" asked Piotr Ivanovitch.

"Yes," she said in a whisper, "to the last moment. He bade us farewell a quarter of an hour before he died, and even asked us to send Volodya out."

The thought of the sufferings of a man whom he had known so intimately, first as a jolly child and schoolboy, and then in adult life as his colleague, suddenly filled Piotr Ivanovitch with terror in spite of the unpleasant sense of this woman's hypocrisy and his own. Once more he saw that forehead, that nose nipping on the lip, and he felt frightened for himself.

"Three days and nights of horrible sufferings and death! Perhaps this may happen to me also, immediately, at any moment," he said to himself. And for an instant he felt panic-stricken. But immediately, though he himself knew not how, there came to his aid the common idea that this had happened to Ivan Ilyitch, and not to him, and therefore such a thing had no business to happen to him, and could not be possible; that, in thinking so, he had fallen into a melancholy frame of mind, which was a foolish thing to do, as was evident by Schwartz's face.

In the course of these reflections, Piotr Ivanovitch became calm, and began with interest to ask for the details of Ivan Ilyitch's decease, as if death were some accident peculiar to Ivan Ilyitch alone, and absolutely remote from himself.

After speaking at greater or less length of the details of the truly terrible physical sufferings endured by Ivan Ilyitch,—Piotr Ivanovitch listened to these details simply because Praskovia Feodorovna's nerves had been affected by her husband's sufferings,—the widow evidently felt that it was time to come to the point.

"Oh! Piotr Ivanovitch! how painful! how horribly painful! how horribly painful!" and again the tears began to flow.

Piotr Ivanovitch sighed, and waited till she had blown her nose. When she had blown her nose, he said:—

"Believe me . . ."

And again the springs of her speech were unloosed, and she explained what was apparently her chief object in seeing him: this matter concerned the problem of how she should make her husband's death secure her funds from the treasury.

She pretended to ask Piotr Ivanovitch's advice about a pension; but he clearly saw that she had already mastered the minutest points, even those that he himself knew not, in the process of extracting from the treasury the greatest possible amount in case of death. But what she wanted to find out, was whether it were not possible to become the recipient of still more money.

Piotr Ivanovitch endeavored to devise some means to this effect; but, having pondered a little, and out of politeness condemned our government for its niggardliness, he said that it seemed to him impossible to obtain more. Then she sighed, and evidently began to devise some means of getting rid of her visitor. He understood, put out his cigarette, arose, pressed her hand, and passed into the anteroom.

In the dining-room, where stood the clock that Ivan Ilyitch had taken such delight in, when he purchased it at a bric-à-brac shop, Piotr Ivanovitch met the priest and a few more acquaintances who had come to the funeral; and he recognized Ivan Ilyitch's daughter, a pretty young lady, whom he knew. She was all in black. Her very slender figure seemed more slender than usual. She looked melancholy, determined, almost irritated. She bowed to Piotr Ivanovitch as if he were in some way to blame. Behind the daughter, with the same melancholy look, stood a rich young man, a magistrate of Piotr Ivanovitch's acquaintance, who, as he heard, was her betrothed. He bowed to them disconsolately, and was about to pass into the death-chamber, when he saw coming up the stairs the slender form of Ivan Ilyitch's son,—a gymnasium student, and a striking image of Ivan Ilyitch. It was the same little Ivan Ilyitch whom Piotr Ivanovitch remembered at the law-school. His eyes were wet with tears, and had the faded appearance common to unhealthy boys of thirteen or fourteen. The boy, as soon as he saw Piotr Ivanovitch, scowled rudely and bashfully. Piotr Ivanovitch nodded at him, and entered the death-chamber.

The mass had begun; there were candles, groans, incense, tears, and sobs. Piotr Ivanovitch stood looking gloomily down at his feet. He did not once glance at the corpse, and to the end did not yield to the softening influences; and he was one of the first to leave. There was no one in the anteroom. Gerasim, the butler, rushed from the dead man's late room, tossed about all the fur garments with his strong hands, in order to find Piotr Ivanovitch's shuba, and handed it to him.

"Well, brother Gerasim," said Piotr Ivanovitch, so as to say something, "it's too bad, isn't it?"

"God's will. We shall all be there," said Gerasim, showing his close, white, peasant's teeth; and, like a man earnestly engaged in some great work, he opened the door with alacrity, called the coachman, helped Piotr Ivanovitch into the carriage, and then hastened back up the front steps, as if he were eager to find something else to do.

It was particularly agreeable to Piotr Ivanovitch to breathe the fresh air, after the odor of the incense, of the dead body, and carbolic acid.

"Where shall I drive to?" asked the coachman.

"It's not too late. I'll go to Feodor Vasilyevitch's, after all."

And Piotr Ivanovitch drove off. And, in fact, he found them just finishing the first rubber, so that it was convenient for him to cut in.

2

The past history of Ivan Ilyitch's life was most simple and uneventful, and yet most terrible.

Ivan Ilyitch died at the age of forty-five, a member of the Court of Justice. He was the son of a functionary who had followed, in various ministries and departments at Petersburg, a career such as brings men into a position from which, on account of their long service and their rank, they are never turned adrift, even though it is plainly manifest that their actual usefulness is at an end; and consequently they obtain imaginary, fictitious places, and from six to ten thousand that are not fictitious, on which they live till a good old age.

Such had been Ilya Yefimovitch Golovin, privy councilor, a useless member of various useless commissions.

He had three sons; Ivan Ilyitch was the second. The eldest had followed the same career as his father's, but in a different ministry, and was already nearing that period of his service in which inertia carries a man into emoluments. The third son had been a failure. He had completely gone to pieces in several positions, and he was now connected with railways; and his father and his brothers and especially their wives not only disliked to meet him, but, except when it was absolutely necessary, even forgot that he existed.

A sister was married to Baron Gref, who, like his father-in-law, was a Petersburg chinovnik. Ivan Ilyitch had been *le phénix de la famille*, as they used to say. He was neither so chilling and formal as the eldest brother, nor so unpromising as the youngest. He was the mean between them,—an intelligent, lively, agreeable, and polished man. He had studied at the law-school with his younger brother, who did not graduate but was expelled from the fifth class; Ivan Ilyitch, however, finished his course creditably. At the law-school he showed the same characteristics by which he was afterward distinguished all his life: he was capable, good-natured even to gayety, and sociable, but strictly fulfilling all that he considered to be his duty; duty, in his opinion, was all that is considered to be such by men in the highest station. He was not one to curry favor, either as a boy, or afterward in manhood; but from his earliest years he had been attracted by men in the highest station in society, just as a fly is by the light; he adopted their ways, their views of life, and entered into relations of friendship with them. All the passions of childhood and youth had passed away, not leaving serious traces. He had yielded to sensuality and vanity, and, toward the last of his life, to the higher forms of liberalism, but all within certain limits which his nature faithfully prescribed for him.

While at the law-school, he had done some things which hitherto had seemed to him very shameful, and which while he was engaged in them aroused in him deep scorn for himself. But afterward, finding that these things were also done by men of high position, and were not considered by them disgraceful, he came to regard them, not indeed as worthy, but as something to put entirely out of his mind, and he was not in the least troubled by the recollection of them.

When Ivan Ilyitch had graduated from the law-school with the tenth rank, and received from his father some money for his uniform, he ordered a suit of Scharmer, added to his trinkets the little medal with the legend *respice finem*, bade the prince and principal farewell, ate a dinner with his classmates at Donon's, and, furnished with new and stylish trunk, linen, uniform, razors, and toilet articles, and a plaid, ordered or bought at the very best shops, he departed for the province, as chinovnik and private secretary to the governor— a place which his father procured for him.

In the province, Ivan Ilyitch at once got himself into the same sort of easy and agreeable position as his position in the law-school had been. He attended to his duties, pressed forward in his career, and at the same time enjoyed life in a cheerful and circumspect manner. From time to time, delegated by his chief, he visited the districts, bore himself with dignity toward both his superiors and subordinates, and, without overweening conceit, fulfilled with punctuality and incorruptible integrity the duties imposed upon him, preëminently in the affair of the dissenters.[1]

Notwithstanding his youth, and his tendency to be gay and easy-going, he was, in matters of State, thoroughly discreet, and carried his official reserve even to sternness. But in society he was often merry and witty, and always good-natured, polite, and *bon enfant*, as he was called by his chief and his chief's wife, at whose house he was intimate.

While he was in the province, he had maintained relations with one of those ladies who are ready to fling themselves into the arms of an elegant young lawyer. There was also a dressmaker; and there were occasional sprees with visiting flügel-adjutants, and visits to some out-of-the-way street after supper; he had also the favor of his chief and even of his chief's wife, but everything of this sort was attended with such a high tone of good-breeding that it could not be qualified by hard names; it all squared with the rubric of the French expression, *Il faut que jeunesse se passe*.[2]

All was done with clean hands, with clean linen, with French words, and, above all, in company with the very highest society, and therefore with the approbation of those high in rank.

In this way Ivan Ilyitch served five years, and a change was instituted in the service. The new tribunals were established; new men were needed.

And Ivan Ilyitch was chosen as one of the new men.

He was offered the position of examining magistrate; and accepted it, notwithstanding the fact that this place was in another government, and that he would be obliged to give up the connections he had formed, and form new ones.

Ivan Ilyitch's friends saw him off. They were photographed in a group, they presented him a silver cigarette-case, and he departed for his new post.

As an examining magistrate, Ivan Ilyitch was just as *comme il faut*, just as circumspect, and careful to sunder the obligations of his office from his private life, and as successful in winning universal consideration, as when he was a chinovnik with special functions. The office of magistrate itself was vastly more interesting and attractive to Ivan Ilyitch than his former position had been.

To be sure, it used to be agreeable to him, in his former position, to pass with free and easy gait, in his Scharmer-made uniform, in front of trembling petitioners and petty officials, waiting for an interview, and envying him, as he went without hesitation into his chief's private room, and sat down with him to drink a cup of tea, and smoke a cigarette; but the men who had been directly dependent on his pleasure were few,—merely police captains and dissenters, if he were sent out with special instructions. And he liked to meet these men, dependent on him, not only politely, but even on terms of comradeship; he liked to make them feel that he, who had the power to crush them, treated them simply, and like friends. Such men at that time were few.

[1] The first body of *raskolniks*, or dissenters, called the "Old Believers," arose in the time of the Patriarch Nikon, who, in 1654, revised the Scriptures. A quarrel as to the number of fingers to be used in giving the blessing, and the manner of spelling Jesus, seems to have been the chief cause of the *raskol*, or schism. The Greek Church has now to contend with a host of different forms of dissent.

[2] "A man must sow his wild oats."

But now, as examining magistrate, Ivan Ilyitch felt that all, all without exception, even men of importance, of distinction, all were in his hands, and that all he had to do was to write such and such words on a piece of paper with a heading, and this important, distinguished man would be brought to him in the capacity of accused or witness, and, unless he wished to ask him to sit down, he would have to stand in his presence, and submit to his questions. Ivan Ilyitch never took undue advantage of this power; on the contrary, he tried to temper the expression of it. But the consciousness of this power, and the possibility of tempering it, furnished for him the chief interest and attractiveness of his new office.

In the office itself, especially in investigations, Ivan Ilyitch was very quick to master the process of eliminating all circumstances extraneous to the case, and of disentangling the most complicated details in such a manner that the case would be presented on paper only in its essentials, and absolutely shorn of his own personal opinion, and, last and not least, that every necessary formality would be fulfilled. This was a new mode of doing things. And he was one of the first to be engaged in putting into operation the code of 1864.

When he took up his residence in the new city, as examining magistrate, Ivan Ilyitch made new acquaintances and ties; he put himself on a new footing, and adopted a somewhat different tone. He held himself rather aloof from the provincial authorities, and took up with a better circle among the judges and wealthy nobles living in the city; and he adopted a tone of easy-going criticism of the government, together with a moderate form of liberalism and "civilized citizenship." At the same time, though Ivan Ilyitch in no wise diminished the elegance of his toilet, yet he ceased to shave his chin, and allowed his beard to grow as it would.

Ivan Ilyitch's life in the new city also passed very agreeably. The society which fronded against the government was good and friendly; his salary was larger than before; and, while he had no less zest in life, he had the additional pleasure of playing whist, a game in which, as he enjoyed playing cards, he quickly learned to excel, so that he was always on the winning side.

After two years of service in the new city Ivan Ilyitch met the lady who became his wife. Praskovia Feodorovna Mikhel was the most fascinating, witty, brilliant young girl in the circle where Ivan Ilyitch moved. In the multitude of other recreations, and as a solace from the labors of his office, Ivan Ilyitch established sportive easy-going relations with Praskovia Feodorovna.

At the time when Ivan Ilyitch was a chinovnik with special functions, he had been a passionate lover of dancing; but now that he was examining magistrate, he danced only as an occasional exception. He now danced with the idea that, "though I am an advocate of the new order of things, and belong to the fifth class, still, as far as the question of dancing goes, I can at least show that in this respect I am better than the rest."

Thus, it frequently happened that, toward the end of a party, he danced with Praskovia Feodorovna; and it was principally at the time of these dances, that he made the conquest of Praskovia Feodorovna. She fell in love with him. Ivan Ilyitch had no clearly decided intention of getting married; but when the girl fell in love with him, he asked himself this question: "In fact, why should I not get married?" said he to himself.

The young lady, Praskovia Feodorovna, came of a good family belonging to the nobility, far from ill-favored, had a small fortune. Ivan Ilyitch might have aspired to a more brilliant match, but this was an excellent one. Ivan Ilyitch had his salary; she, he hoped, would have as much more. She was of good family; she was sweet, pretty, and a thoroughly well-bred woman. To say that Ivan Ilyitch got married because he was in love with his betrothed, and found in her sympathy with his views of life, would be just as incorrect as to say that he got married because the men of his set approved of the match.

Ivan Ilyitch took a wife for two reasons: he gave himself a pleasure in taking such a wife; and, at the same time, the people of the highest rank considered such an act proper.

And so Ivan Ilyitch got married.

The wedding ceremony itself, and the first few days of their married life with its connubial caresses, their new furniture, their new plate, their new linen, everything, even the prospects of an increasing family, were all that could be desired. So that Ivan Ilyitch began to think that marriage not only was not going to disturb his easy-going, pleasant, gay, and always respectable life, so approved by society, and which Ivan Ilyitch considered a perfectly natural characteristic of life in general, but was also going to add to it. But from the first months of his wife's pregnancy, there appeared something new, unexpected, disagreeable, hard, and trying, which he could not have foreseen, and from which it was impossible to escape.

His wife, without any motive, as it seemed to Ivan Ilyitch, *de gaité de cœur*, as he said to himself, began to interfere with the pleasant and decent current of his life; without any cause she grew jealous of him, demanded attentions from him, found fault with everything, and caused him disagreeable and stormy scenes.

At first Ivan Ilyitch hoped to free himself from this unpleasant state of things by the same easy-going and respectable acceptation of life which had helped him in days gone by. He tried to ignore his wife's disposition, and continued to live as before in an easy and pleasant way. He invited his friends, he gave card-parties, he attempted to make his visits to the club or to friends; but his wife began one time to abuse him with rough and energetic language, and continued persistently to scold him each time that he failed to fulfil her demands, having evidently made up her mind not to cease berating him until he was completely subjected to her authority,—in other words, until he would stay at home, and be just as deeply in the dumps as she herself,—a thing which Ivan Ilyitch dreaded above all.

He learned that married life, at least as far as his wife was concerned, did not always add to the pleasantness and decency of existence, but, on the contrary, disturbed it, and that, therefore, it was necessary to protect himself from such interference. And Ivan Ilyitch tried to devise means to this end. His official duties were the only thing that had an imposing effect upon Praskovia Feodorovna; and Ivan Ilyitch, by means of his office, and the duties arising from it, began to struggle with his wife, for the defense of his independent life.

When the child was born, and in consequence of the various attempts and failures to have it properly nursed, and the illnesses, real and imaginary, of both mother and child, wherein Ivan Ilyitch's sympathy was demanded, but which were absolutely foreign to him, the necessity for him to secure a life outside of his family became still more imperative.

According as his wife grew more irritable and exacting, so Ivan Ilyitch transferred the center of his life's burdens more and more into his office. He began to love his office more and more, and became more ambitious than he had ever been.

Very soon, not longer than a year after his marriage, Ivan Ilyitch came to the conclusion that married life, while affording certain advantages, was in reality a very complicated and burdensome thing, in relation to which, if one would fulfil his duty, that is, live respectably and with the approbation of society, one must work out a certain system, just as in public office.

And such a system Ivan Ilyitch secured in his matrimonial life. He demanded of family life only such conveniences in the way of home dinners, a housekeeper, a bed, as it could furnish him, and, above all, that respectability in external forms which was in accordance with the opinions of society. As for the rest, he was anxious for pleasant amenities; and if he found them, he was very grateful. On the other hand, if he met with opposition and complaint, then he immediately took refuge in the far-off world of his official duties, which alone offered him delight.

Ivan Ilyitch was regarded as an excellent magistrate, and at the end of three years he was appointed deputy-prokuror. His new functions, their importance, the power vested in him of arresting and imprisoning anyone, the publicity of his speeches, his success obtained in this field,—all this still more attached him to the service.

Children came; his wife kept growing more irritable and ill-tempered; but the relations which Ivan Ilyitch maintained toward family life made him almost proof against her temper.

After seven years of service in one city, Ivan Ilyitch was promoted to the office of prokuror in another government. They moved; they had not much money, and the place where they went did not suit his wife. Although his salary was larger than before, yet living was more expensive; moreover, two of their children died; and thus family life became still more distasteful to Ivan Ilyitch.

Praskovia Feodorovna blamed her husband for all the misfortunes that came on them in their new place of abode. Most of the subjects of conversation between husband and wife, especially the education of their children, led to questions which were productive of quarrels, so that quarrels were always ready to break out. Only at rare intervals came those periods of affection which distinguish married life, but they were not of long duration. These were little islands in which they rested for a time; but then again they pushed out into the sea of secret animosity, which expressed itself by driving them farther and farther apart.

This alienation might have irritated Ivan Ilyitch, if he had not considered that it was inevitable; but he now began to look on this situation not merely as normal, but even as the goal of his activity in the family. This goal consisted in withdrawing as far as possible from these unpleasantnesses, or of giving them a character of innocence and respectability; and he attained this end by

380 THE DEATH OF IVAN ILYITCH

spending less and less time with his family; but when he was to do so, then he endeavored to guarantee his position by the presence of strangers.

But Ivan Ilyitch's chief resource was his office. In the world of his duties was concentrated all his interest in life. And this interest wholly absorbed him. The consciousness of his power of ruining any one whom he might wish to ruin; the importance of his position manifested outwardly when he came into court or met his subordinates; his success with superiors and subordinates; and, above all, his skill in the conduct of affairs,—and he was perfectly conscious of it,—all this delighted him, and, together with conversations with his colleagues, dinners and whist, filled all his life. Thus, for the most part, Ivan Ilyitch's life continued to flow in its even tenor as he considered that it ought to flow,—pleasantly and respectably.

Thus he lived seven years longer. His eldest daughter was already sixteen years old; still another little child had died; and there remained a lad, the one who was in school, the object of their wrangling. Ivan Ilyitch wanted to send him to the law-school; but Praskovia, out of spite toward him, selected the gymnasium. The daughter studied at home, and made good progress; the lad also was not at all backward in his studies.

3

Thus seventeen years of Ivan Ilyitch's life passed since the time of his marriage. He was already an old prokuror, having declined several transfers in the hope of a still more desirable place, when there occurred unexpectedly an unpleasant turn of affairs which was quite disturbing to his peaceful life.

Ivan Ilyitch had been hoping for the position of president in a university city; but Hoppe got in ahead of him, and obtained the place. Ivan Ilyitch became irritated, began to make recriminations, got into a quarrel with him and his next superior; signs of coolness were manifested toward him, and in the subsequent appointments he was passed over.

This was in 1880. This year was the most trying of Ivan Ilyitch's life. It happened, on the one hand, that his salary did not suffice for his expenses; on the other, that he was forgotten by all, and that what seemed to him a great, an atrocious, injustice toward himself was regarded by others as a perfectly natural thing. Even his father did not think it his duty to come to his aid. He felt that he was abandoned by all his friends, who considered that his position, worth thirty-five hundred rubles a year, was very normal and even fortunate. He alone knew that with the consciousness of the injustice which had been done him, and with his wife's everlasting rasping, and with the debts which began to accumulate, now that he lived beyond his means—he alone knew that his situation was far from normal.

The summer of that year, in order to lighten his expenses, he took leave of absence, and went with his wife to spend the summer at the country place belonging to Praskovia Feodorovna's brother.

In the country, relieved of his official duties, Ivan Ilyitch for the first time felt not only irksomeness, but insupportable anguish; and he made up his mind that it was impossible to live in such a way, and that he must take immediate and decisive steps, no matter what they were.

After a long, sleepless night, which he spent walking up and down the terrace,

Ivan Ilyitch decided to go to Petersburg, to bestir himself and to get transferred into another ministry so as to punish *them* who had not known how to appreciate him.

On the next day, notwithstanding all the protests of his wife and brother-in-law, he started for Petersburg.

He wanted only one thing,—to obtain a place worth five thousand a year. He would not stipulate for any special ministry, any special direction, any form of activity. All that he needed was a place,—a place with a salary of five thousand, in the administration, in the banks, on the railways, in the institutions of the Empress Maria, even in the customs service; but the sole condition was the five thousand salary, the sole condition to be relieved from the ministry where they did not know how to appreciate him.

And lo! this trip of Ivan Ilyitch's met with astonishing, unexpected success. At Kursk an acquaintance of his, F. S. Ilyin, came into the first-class carriage, and informed him of a telegram just received by the governor of Kursk to the effect that a change was about to be made in the ministry: in Piotr Ivanovitch's place would be appointed Ivan Semyonovitch.

This probable change, over and above its significance for Russia, had a special significance for Ivan Ilyitch, from the fact that by bringing up a new official, Piotr Petrovitch, and probably his friend Zakhar Ivanovitch, it was in the highest degree favorable for Ivan Ilyitch. Zakhar Ivanovitch was a colleague and friend of Ivan Ilyitch.

In Moscow the tidings were confirmed. And when he reached Petersburg, Ivan Ilyitch sought out Zakhar Ivanovitch, and obtained the promise of a sure position in his old ministry,—that of justice.

At the end of a week he telegraphed his wife:—

"Zakhar, in Miller's place; in the first report shall be appointed."

Ivan Ilyitch, thanks to this change of administration, suddenly obtained in his old ministry such an appointment as put him two grades above his colleagues,—five thousand salary, and thirty-five hundred for traveling expenses.

All his grievances against his former rivals and against the whole ministry were forgotten, and Ivan Ilyitch was entirely happy.

Ivan Ilyitch returned to the country, jocund, contented, as he had not been for a long time. Praskovia Feodorovna also brightened up, and peace was reestablished between them. Ivan Ilyitch related how he was honored by every one in Petersburg; how all those who had been his enemies were covered with shame and now fawned on him; how they envied him his position, and especially how dearly every one in Petersburg loved him.

Praskovia Feodorovna listened to this, and made believe that she believed it, and did not contradict him in anything, but only made plans for the arrangement of their new life in the city where they were going. And Ivan Ilyitch had the joy of seeing that these plans were his plans, that they coincided, and that his life, interrupted though it had been, was now about to regain its own character of festive pleasure and decency.

Ivan Ilyitch went back for a short visit only. On the 22d of September he was obliged to assume his duties; and, moreover, he needed time to get established in his new place, to transport all his possessions from the province, to buy new things, to give orders for still more,—in a word, to install himself as it seemed proper to his mind, and pretty nearly as it seemed proper to Praskovia Feodorovna's ideas.

And now, when all was ordered so happily, and when he and his wife were in accord, and, above all, lived together but a small portion of the time, they became better friends than they had been since the first years of their married life.

Ivan Ilyitch at first thought of taking his family with him immediately; but the insistence of his sister- and brother-in-law, who suddenly manifested an extraordinary friendliness and brotherly love for Ivan Ilyitch and his family, induced him to depart alone.

Ivan Ilyitch took his departure; and his jocund frame of mind, arising from his success and his reconciliation with his wife, the one consequent upon the other, did not for a moment leave him.

He found admirable apartments, exactly coinciding with the dreams of husband and wife,—spacious, lofty reception-rooms in the old style; a convenient, grandiose library; rooms for his wife and daughter; study-room for his son,—all as if expressly designed for them. Ivan Ilyitch himself took charge of the arrangements. He selected the wall-papers; he bought the furniture, mostly antique, to which he attributed a specially *comme-il-faut style*; hangings and all took form, and took form and approached that ideal which he had established in his conception.

When his arrangements were half completed, they surpassed his expectations. He perceived what a *comme-il-faut*, exquisite, and far from commonplace character all would have when completed. When he lay down to sleep, he imagined his "hall" as it would be. As he looked about his drawing-room, still unfinished, he already saw the fireplace, the screen, the little *étagère*, and those easy-chairs scattered here and there, those plates and saucers on the walls, and the bronzes, just as they would be when all was in place.

He was delighted with the thought of how he should astonish Pasha and Lizanka, who also had such good taste in these things. "They would never look for this. Especially that he would have the thought of going and buying, at such a low price, these old things that gave the whole an extraordinary character of gentility."

In his letters he purposely represented everything worse than it really was— so as to surprise them. All this so occupied him, that even his new duties, much as he enjoyed them, were not so absorbing as he expected. Even while court was in session, he had his moments of abstraction; he was cogitating as to what sort of cornices he should have for his curtains,—straight or matched. He was so interested in this, that often he himself took hold, rearranged the furniture, and even rehung the curtains himself.

One time, when he was climbing on a pair of steps, so as to explain to a dull-minded upholsterer how he wished a drapery to be arranged, he slipped and fell; but, being a strong, dexterous man, he saved himself. He only hit his side on the edge of the frame. He received a bruise, but it quickly passed away. Ivan Ilyitch all this time felt perfectly happy and well. He wrote, "I feel as if I were fifteen years younger."

He expected to finish in September, but circumstances delayed it till the middle of October. But it was all admirable; not only he himself said so, but all who saw it said the same.

In reality, it was exactly what is customary among those people who are not very rich, but who like to ape the rich, and therefore only resemble one another,—silken fabrics, mahogany, flowers, carpets, and bronzes, dark and shining, all that which all people of a certain class affect, so as to be comparable to all people of a certain class. And in his case, there was a greater resemblance, so that it was impossible to single out anything for attention; but still, this to him was something extraordinary.

When he met his family at the railway station, he took them to their apartments, freshly put in order for them; and the lackey, in a white necktie, opened the door into the vestibule, ornamented with flowers; and then they went into the parlor, the library, and ohed and ahed with delight; and he was very happy; he showed them everything, drank in their praises, and shone with satisfaction. On that very evening at tea, when Praskovia Feodorovna asked him, among other things, how he fell, he laughed, and illustrated in pantomime how he went head over heels, and scared the upholsterer.

"I'm not a gymnast for nothing. Another man would have been killed, but I just struck myself here a little; when you touch it, it hurts; but it's already wearing off—it's a mere bruise."

And they began to live in the new domicile, in which, as always, after one has become fairly established, it was discovered that there was just one room too few; and with their new means, which, as always, lacked a little of being sufficient; about five hundred rubles additional, and it would have been well.

All went extraordinarily well at first, while still their arrangements were not wholly regulated, and there was still much to do,—buying this thing, giving orders for that, rearranging, mending. Although there were occasional disagreements between husband and wife, yet both were so satisfied, and they had so many occupations, that no serious quarrel resulted. Still, when there was nothing left to arrange, they became a trifle bored, and felt that something was lacking; but now they began to form new acquaintances, new habits, and their lives became full.

Ivan Ilyitch spent the morning at court, but returned home to dinner; and at first he was in excellent humor, although sometimes he was a little vexed by something or other in the household management.

Any kind of spot on the table-cloth, on the draperies, any break in the curtain-cords, irritated him. He had taken so much pains in getting things in order, that any kind of harm befalling was painful to him.

But, on the whole, Ivan Ilyitch's life ran on, as in his opinion life ought to run, smoothly, pleasantly, and decently.

He rose at nine o'clock, drank his coffee, read the paper, then donned his uniform, and went down to court. There he instantly got himself into the harness to which he had been so long accustomed,—petitioners, inquiries at the chancery, the chancery itself, sessions public and administrative. In all this, it was necessary to devise means to exclude all those external concerns of life which forever tend to trespass on the accuracy of conducting official duties; it was necessary that he should tolerate no relations with people except on an official basis; and the cause for such relations must be official, and the relations themselves must be only official.

For example, a man comes, and wants to know something or other. Ivan Ilyitch, as a man apart from his office, cannot have any relations with this man; but if the relationship of this man to the magistrate is such that it can be expressed on letter-head paper, then, within the limits of these relations, Ivan Ilyitch would do all, absolutely all, in his power, and at the same time preserve the semblance of affable, philanthropical relations,—in other words, of politeness. The point where his official life and his private life joined was very strictly drawn. Ivan Ilyitch had a high degree of skill in separating the official side from the other without confounding them; and his long practice and talent gave him such *finesse*, that he sometimes, as a virtuoso, allowed himself, by way of a jest, to confound the humanitarian and his official relations.

This act in Ivan Ilyitch's case was played, not only smoothly, pleasantly, and decently, but also in a virtuoso manner. During the intervals, he smoked, drank tea, talked a little about politics, a little about affairs in general, a little about cards, and more than all about appointments; and when weary, but still conscious of his virtuosity, as of one who has well played his part, like one of the first violins of an orchestra, he went home.

At home the mother and daughter had been receiving or making calls; the son was at the gymnasium, preparing his lessons with tutors; and he learned accurately whatever was taught him in the gymnasium. All was excellent.

After dinner, unless he had guests, Ivan Ilyitch sometimes read some book which was much talked about; and during the evening he sat down to his work,—that is, read papers, consulted the laws, compared depositions and applied the law to them.

This was neither tedious nor inspiriting. It was tedious when he had the chance to play *vint*; but if there was no *vint*, then it was far better than to sit alone or with his wife.

Very delightful to Ivan Ilyitch were the little dinners to which he invited ladies and gentlemen holding high positions in society; and such entertainments were like the entertainments of people of the same class, just as his drawing-room was like all drawing-rooms.

One evening they even had a party; they danced, and Ivan Ilyitch felt gay, and all was good; only a great quarrel arose between husband and wife about the patties and sweetmeats. Praskovia Feodorovna had her ideas about them; but Ivan Ilyitch insisted on buying them all of an expensive confectioner, and he got a great quantity of patties; and the quarrel was because there was an extra quantity, and the confectioner's bill amounted to forty-five rubles.

The quarrel was sharp and disagreeable, inasmuch as Praskovia Feodorovna called him "Fool! Pig-head!"

And he, putting his hands to his head in his vexation, muttered something about divorce.

But the party itself was gay. The very best society were present; and Ivan Ilyitch danced with the Princess Trufonova, the sister of the well-known founder of the society called "*Unesi tui mayo gore.*"[1]

1 "Take away my sorrow."

Ivan Ilyitch's official pleasures were the pleasures of self-love; his pleasures in society were pleasures of vanity; but his real pleasures were the pleasures of playing *vint*. He confessed that, after all, after any disagreeable event befalling his life, the pleasure which, like a candle, glowed brighter than all others, was that of sitting down—four good players, and partners who did not shout—to a game of *vint*—and always four, for it is very bad form to have any one cut in, even though you say, "I like it very much"—and have a reasonable, serious game—when the cards run well,—and then to eat a little supper, and drink a glass of wine. And Ivan Ilyitch used to go to sleep, especially after a game of *vint*, when he had won a little something—a large sum is disagreeable—and feel particularly happy in his mind.

Thus they lived. The circle of their friends consisted of the very best society; men of high position visited them, and young men came.

As far as their views upon the circle of their acquaintance were concerned, husband, wife, and daughter were perfectly unanimous. And tacitly they each in the same way pushed aside, and rid themselves of, certain friends and relatives,—the undesirable kind, who came fawning around them in their drawing-room decorated with Japanese plates on the wall. Very soon these undesirable friends ceased to flutter around them, and the Golovins had only the very best society.

Young men were attracted to Lizanka; and the examining magistrate, Petrishchef, the son of Dmitri Ivanovitch Petrishchef, and the sole heir to his wealth, began to flutter around Liza so assiduously, that Ivan Ilyitch already asked Praskovia Feodorovna whether it would not be a good plan to take them on a troïka-ride together, or arrange some private theatricals.

Thus they lived. And thus all went along in its even course, and all was very good.

4

All were well. It was impossible to see any symptom of ill-health in the fact that Ivan Ilyitch sometimes spoke of a strange taste in his mouth and an uneasiness in the left side of his abdomen.

But it happened that this unpleasant feeling kept increasing; it did not as yet become a pain, but he was all the time conscious of a dull weight in his side, and of an irritable temper. This irritability, constantly increasing and increasing, began to disturb the pleasant, easy-going, decent life that had been characteristic of the Golovin family. The husband and wife began to quarrel more and more frequently; and before long their easy, pleasant relations were broken up, and even the decency was maintained under difficulties.

Scenes once more became very frequent. Once more, but quite infrequently, the little islands appeared, on which husband and wife could meet without an explosion. And Praskovia Feodorovna now said, with some justification, that her husband had a very trying disposition. With her peculiar tendency to exaggeration, she declared that he had always had such a horrible disposition, that nothing but her good nature had enabled her to endure it for twenty years.

It was indeed true that now he was the one that began the quarrels. His querulousness began always before dinner, and often, indeed, just as they sat down to eat the soup. Sometimes he noticed that a dish was chipped; sometimes the food did not suit him; now his son rested his elbows on the table; now it was the way his daughter dressed her hair. And he blamed Praskovia Feodorovna for everything. At first Praskovia Feodorovna answered him back, and said disagreeable things to him; but twice, during dinner-time, he broke out into such a fury that she perceived this to be an unhealthy state, which proceeded from the assimilation of his food; and she held her peace; she did not reply, and merely hastened to finish dinner.

Praskovia Feodorovna regarded her meekness as a great merit. As she had made up her mind that her husband had a horrible disposition, and was making her life wretched, she began to pity herself. And the more she pitied herself, the more she detested her husband. She began to wish that he would die; but she could not wish it, because then they would not have his salary any more. And this actually exasperated her still more against him. She regarded herself as terribly unhappy, from the very fact that his death could not relieve her; and she grew bitter, but concealed it; and this concealed bitterness strengthened her hatred of him.

After one scene in which Ivan Ilyitch was particularly unjust, and which he afterward explained on the ground of his irritability being the result of not being well, she told him that, if he was ill, then he ought to take some medicine; and she begged him to go to a famous physician.

He went. Everything was as he expected: everything was done according to the usual way,—the delay; and the pompous, *doctorial* air of importance, so familiar to him, the same as he himself assumed in court; and the tapping and the auscultation; and the leading questions requiring answers predetermined, and apparently not heard; and the look of superlative wisdom which seemed to say, "You, now, just trust yourself to us, and we will do everything; we understand without fail how to manage; everything is done in the same way for any man."

Everything was just exactly as in court. The airs he put on in court for the benefit of those brought before him, the same were assumed by the famous doctor for his benefit.

The doctor said, "Such and such a thing shows that you have such and such a thing in you; but if this is not confirmed according to the investigations of such and such a man, then you must suppose such and such a thing. Now, if we suppose such and such a thing, then"—and so on.

For Ivan Ilyitch, only one question was momentous: Was his case dangerous, or not? But the doctor ignored this inconvenient question. From a doctor's point of view, this question was idle, and deserved no consideration; the only thing to do was to weigh probabilities,—floating kidney, chronic catarrh, appendicitis.

It was not a question about Ivan Ilyitch's life, but there was doubt whether it was floating kidney, or appendicitis; and this doubt the doctor, in Ivan Ilyitch's presence, settled in the most brilliant manner in favor of the appendix, making a reserve in case an analysis of the urine should give new results, and then the case would have to be examined anew.

All this was exactly what Ivan Ilyitch himself had done a thousand times in the same brilliant manner for the benefit of the prisoner at the bar. Thus, even more brilliantly, the doctor made his *résumé*, and with an air of still more joyful triumph gazed down from over his spectacles on the prisoner at the bar. From the doctor's *résumé*, Ivan Ilyitch came to the conclusion that, as far as he was concerned, it was bad; but as far as the doctor, and perhaps the rest of the world, was concerned, it made no difference; but for him it was bad!

And this conclusion struck Ivan Ilyitch with a painful shock, causing in him a feeling of painful pity for himself, and of painful wrath against this physician who showed such indifference to such a vital question.

But he said nothing; then he got up, laid some money on the table, and, with a sigh, said:—

"Probably we sick men often ask you foolish questions," said he; "but, in general, is this trouble serious, or not?"

The doctor gave him a severe glance with one eye, through the spectacles, as if to say:—

"Prisoner at the bar, if you do not confine yourself to the limits of the questions already put to you, I shall be constrained to take measures for having you put out of the audience-chamber."

"I have already told you what I considered necessary and suitable," said the doctor; "a further examination will complete the diagnosis;" and the doctor bowed him out.

Ivan Ilyitch went out slowly, lugubriously took his seat in his sledge, and drove home. All the way he kept repeating what the doctor had said, endeavoring to translate all those involved scientific phrases into simple language, and find in them an answer to the question, "Is it a serious, very serious, case for me, or is it a mere nothing?"

And it seemed to him that the sense of all the doctor's words indicated a very serious case. The aspect of everything in the streets was gloomy. The izvoshchiks were gloomy; gloomy the houses, the pedestrians; the shops were gloomy. This pain, this obscure, dull pain, which did not leave him for a second, seemed to him, when taken in connection with the doctor's ambiguous remarks, to gather a new and more serious significance. Ivan Ilyitch, with a new sense of depression, now took heed of it.

He reached home, and began to tell his wife. His wife listened, but while he was in the midst of his account, his daughter came in with her hat on; she was ready to go out with her mother. She sat down with evident disrelish to listen to this wearisome tale, but she was not detained long; her mother did not hear him out.

"Well," said she, "I am very glad, for now you will be careful, and take your medicine properly. Give me the prescription, and I will send Gerasim to the apothecary's."

And she went to get dressed.

He could not get a long breath all the time that she was in the room, and he sighed heavily when she went out.

"Well," said he, "perhaps it's a mere nothing, after all." . . .

He began to take his medicine, and to follow the doctor's prescriptions, which were somewhat modified after the urine had been analyzed. But just here it so happened exactly that in this analysis, and in what ought to have followed it, there was come confusion. It was impossible to trace it back to the doctor, but the result was that what the doctor said to him did not take place. Either he had forgotten or neglected or concealed something from him.

But Ivan Ilyitch nevertheless began faithfully to follow the doctor's prescriptions, and in this way at first he found consolation.

Ivan Ilyitch's principal occupation, after he went to consult the doctor, consisted in carefully carrying out the doctor's prescription in regard to hygiene, and taking his medicine, and watching the symptoms of his malady, all the functions of his organism. Ivan Ilyitch became chiefly interested in human disease and human health. When people spoke in his presence of those who were sick, of those who had died, of those who were recuperating, especially from diseases like his own, he would listen, endeavoring to hide his agitation, would ask questions, and make comparisons with his own ailment.

The pain did not diminish, but Ivan Ilyitch compelled himself to feign that he was getting better. And he was able to deceive himself as long as there was nothing to irritate him. But the moment that he had any disagreeable scene with his wife, any failure at court, a bad hand at *vint*, then he instantly felt the full force of his malady; formerly he endured these reverses, hopefully saying to himself:—

"Now I shall straighten out this wretched business, shall conquer, shall attain success, win the next hand."

But now every little failure cut him down, and plunged him in despair. He said to himself:—

"Here I was just beginning to get a little better, and the medicine was already helping me, and here this cursed bad luck or this unpleasantness . . ."

And he would break out against his bad luck, or against the people that brought him unpleasantness, and were killing him; and he realized how this fit of anger was killing him, but he could not control it.

It would seem that it must be clear to him that these fits of anger against circumstances and people made his malady worse, and that, therefore, he ought not to notice disagreeable trifles; but he reasoned in precisely the opposite way: he said that he needed quiet; he was on the watch for everything which disturbed this quiet, and at every least disturbance his irritation broke out.

His condition was rendered worse by the fact that he read medical works, and consulted doctors. The progress of his disease was so gradual that he was able to deceive himself by comparing one evening with the next; there was little difference. But when he consulted the doctors, then it seemed to him that it was growing worse, and very rapidly also. And notwithstanding that he constantly consulted doctors.

During this month he went to another celebrity; the second celebrity said pretty much the same as the first had said, but he asked questions in a different way. And the consultation with this celebrity redoubled Ivan Ilyitch's doubt and fear.

A friend of a friend of his—a very good doctor—gave an absolutely different definition of his malady; and, notwithstanding the fact that he predicted recovery, his questions and hypotheses still further confused Ivan Ilyitch, and increased his doubts.

A homeopathist defined his disease in a still different manner, and gave him some pellets; and Ivan Ilyitch, without being suspected by any one, took them for a week. But at the end of the week, not perceiving that any relief came of them, and losing faith, not only in this, but in his former methods of treatment, he fell into still greater melancholy.

One time a lady of his acquaintance was telling him about cures effected by means of ikons. Ivan Ilyitch surprised himself by listening attentively, and believing in the reality of the fact. This circumstance frightened him.

"Is it possible that I have reached such a degree of mental weakness?" he asked himself. "Nonsense! All rubbish! One must not give way to mere fancies. Now I'm going to select one physician, and rigorously follow his advice. That's what I will do. That's the end of it. I will not bother my brain, and till summer I will strictly carry out his prescription; and then the result will be seen. Now for an end to these hesitations." . . .

It was easy to say this, but impossible to carry it out. The pain in his side kept troubling him, kept growing if anything worse, became incessant; the taste in his mouth became always more and more peculiar; it seemed to him that his breath was disagreeable, and that he was all the time losing his appetite and strength.

It was impossible to deceive himself; something terrible, novel, and significant, more significant than anything which had ever happened before to Ivan Ilyitch, was taking place in him. And he alone was conscious of it; those who surrounded him did not comprehend it, or did not wish to comprehend it, and thought that everything in the world was going on as before.

This more than aught else pained Ivan Ilyitch. His family,—especially his wife and daughter, who were in the very white-heat of social pleasures,—he saw, did not comprehend at all, were vexed with him because he was gloomy and exacting, as if he were to blame for it. Even though they tried to hide it, he saw that he was in their way, but that his wife had definitely made up her mind in regard to his trouble, and stuck to it, no matter what he might say or do.

This mental attitude was expressed in some such way as this:—

"You know," she would say to an acquaintance, "Ivan Ilyitch, like all easy-going men, can't carry out the doctor's prescriptions strictly. One day he will take his drops, and eat what is ordered for him, and go to bed in good season; then all of a sudden, if I don't look out, he will forget to take his medicine, will eat sturgeon,—though it is forbidden,—yes, and sit up at *vint* till one o'clock."

"Well, now, when?" asks Ivan Ilyitch, with asperity. "Just once at Piotr Ivanovitch's."

"And last evening with Shebek."

"All right,—I could not sleep from pain." . . .

"Yes, no matter what it comes from; only you will never get over it in this way, and will keep on tormenting us."

Praskovia Feodorovna's settled conviction in regard to his ailment,—and she impressed it on every one, and on Ivan Ilyitch himself,—was that he was to blame for it, and that his whole illness was a new affliction which he was causing his wife. Ivan Ilyitch felt that this was involuntary on her part, but it was not on that account any easier for him to bear it.

In court Ivan Ilyitch noticed, or thought he noticed, the same strange behavior toward him; now it seemed to him that he was regarded as a man who was soon to give up his place; again, his friends would suddenly begin to rally him about his low spirits, as if this horrible, strange, and unheard-of something that was breeding in him and ceaselessly sucking up his vitality, and irresistibly dragging him away, were a pleasant subject for raillery! Schwartz especially irritated him with his jocularity, his lively ways, and his *comme-il-faut-ness,* reminding Ivan Ilyitch of himself as he had been ten years before.

Friends came in to have a game of cards. They sat down, they dealt, new cards were shuffled, diamonds were thrown on diamonds,—seven of them. His partner said, "No trumps," and held up two diamonds. What more could be desired? It ought to have been a gay proud moment,—a clean sweep.

And suddenly Ivan Ilyitch was conscious of that living pain, of that taste in his mouth, and it seemed to him barbarous that he should be able thus to rejoice in' this hand. He looked at Mikhaïl Mikhaïlovitch, his partner, as he rapped the table with his big red hand, and courteously and condescendingly refrained from gathering up the tricks, but pushed them over to Ivan Ilyitch that he might have the pleasure of counting them, without inconveniencing himself, without putting his hand out.

"What! does he think that I am so weak that I can't put my hand out?" said Ivan Ilyitch to himself; then he forgot what were trumps; trumped his partner's trick, and lost the sweep by three points. And what was more terrible than all was that he saw how Mikhaïl Mikhaïlovitch suffers, and yet to him it was a matter of indifference. And it was terrible to think why it was a matter of indifference to him.

All could see that it was hard for him, and they said to him:—

"We can stop playing if you are tired. You rest awhile." . . .

Rest? No, he was not tired at all; they would finish the rubber. All were gloomy and taciturn. Ivan Ilyitch felt that he was the cause of their gloominess, and he could not enliven it. They had supper, and then went home; and Ivan Ilyitch was left alone, with the consciousness that his life is poisoned for him, and that he is poisoning the lives of others, and that this poison is not growing weaker, but is always working its way deeper and deeper into his being.

And with this consciousness, sometimes also with physical pain, sometimes with terror, he would have to go to bed, and frequently not sleep from anguish the greater part of the night. And in the morning he would have to get up again and dress and go to court and speak, write, and, unless he went out to ride, stay at home for those twenty-four hours, each one of which was a torture. And he had to live thus on the edge of destruction—alone, without any one to understand him and pity him.

5

Thus passed one month and two.

Before New Year's his brother-in-law came to their city, and stopped at their house. Praskovia Feodorovna had gone out shopping. Ivan Ilyitch was in court. When he came home, and went into his library, he found his brother-in-law there, a healthy, sanguine man, engaged in opening his trunk. He raised his head as he heard Ivan Ilyitch's steps, and looked at him a moment in silence. This look revealed all to Ivan Ilyitch. His brother-in-law opened his mouth to exclaim at him, and refrained. This motion confirmed everything.

"What? Have I changed?"

"Yes . . . there is a change."

And whenever afterward Ivan Ilyitch tried to bring the conversation round to the subject of his external appearance, his brother-in-law avoided it. Praskovia Feodorovna came in and his brother-in-law went to her room. Ivan Ilyitch locked the door, and began to look at himself in the glass, first front face, then his profile. He took his portrait painted with his wife, and compared it with what he saw in the mirror. The change was portentous. Then he bared his arm to the elbow, looked at it, pulled down his sleeve, sat down on the otomanka, and it became darker than night.

"It must not . . . it must not be!" said he to himself; jumped up, went to the table, unfolded a document, began to read it, but could not. He opened the door, went out into the "hall." The drawing-room door was shut. He tip-toed up to it, and began to listen.

"No, you exaggerate," Praskovia Feodorovna was saying.

"How do I exaggerate? Isn't it plain to you? He's a dead man. Look at his eyes, no light in them. . . . But what's the matter with him?"

"No one knows. Nikolayef"—that was another doctor— "says one thing, but I don't know about it. Leshchititsky"—that was the famous doctor— "says the opposite." . . .

Ivan Ilyitch turned away, went to his room, lay down, and began to think: "Kidney—a floating kidney!"

He recalled all that the doctors had told him,—how it was torn away, and how it was loose. And by an effort of his imagination he endeavored to catch this kidney, to stop it, to fasten it. "It is such a small thing to do," it seemed to him.

"No; I will make another visit to Piotr Ivanovitch."

This was the friend whose friend was a doctor.

He rang, ordered the horse to be harnessed, and got ready to go out.

"Where are you going, *Jean?*" asked his wife, with a peculiarly gloomy and unusually gentle expression.

This unusually gentle expression angered him. He looked at her grimly.

"I have got to go to Piotr Ivanovitch's."

He went to the friend whose friend was a doctor. They went together to this doctor's. He found him and had a long talk with him.

As he examined the anatomical and physiological details of what, according to the doctor, was taking place in him, he comprehended it perfectly.

There was one more trifle—the least bit of a trifle in the vermiform appendix. All that could be put to rights. Strengthen the force of one organ, weaken the activity of another—assimilation ensues, and all is set to rights.

He was a little late to dinner. He ate heartily, he talked gayly, but for a long time he was not able to make up his mind to go to work.

At last he went to his library, and immediately sat down to his labors. He read his documents, and labored over them; but he did not get rid of the consciousness that he had before him an important, private duty, which he must carry out to a conclusion.

When he had finished with his documents, he remembered that this private duty was the thought about the vermiform appendix. But he did not give in to it; he went to the drawing-room to tea. They had callers; there was conversation, there was playing on the pianoforte, and singing; the examining magistrate, the desirable match for their daughter, was there. Ivan Ilyitch spent the evening, as Praskovia Feodorovna observed, more cheerfully than usual; but he did not for a moment forget that he had before him those important thoughts about the vermiform appendix.

At eleven o'clock he bade his friends good-night, and retired to his own room. Since his illness began, he had slept alone in a little room off the library. He went to it, undressed, and took a romance of Zola's; but he did not read it; he thought. And in his imagination the longed-for cure of the vermiform appendix took place. Assimilation, secretion, were stimulated; regulated activity was established.

"Yes, it is just exactly so," said he to himself. "It is only necessary to help nature."

He remembered his medicine, got up, took it, lay on his back, waiting for the medicine to have its beneficent effect, and gradually ease his pain.

"Only take it regularly, and avoid unhealthy influences; even now I feel a little better, considerably better."

He began to punch his side; it was not painful to the touch.

"No, I don't feel it . . . already I feel considerably better."

He blew out the candle, and lay on his side. . . . "The vermiform appendix becomes regulated, is absorbed . . ."

And suddenly he began to feel the old, well-known, dull, lingering pain, stubborn, silent, serious; in his mouth the same well-known taste. His heart sank within him; his brain was in a whirl.

"My God! my God!" he cried, "again, again! and it will never cease!"

And suddenly the trouble presented itself to him absolutely in another guise.

"The vermiform appendix! the kidney!" he said to himself. "The trouble lies, not in the blind intestine, not in the kidney . . . but in life . . . and death! Yes, once there was life; but now it is passing away, passing away, and I cannot hold it back. Yes. Why deceive one's self? Is it not evident to every one, except myself, that I am going to die? and it is only a question of weeks, of days . . . maybe instantly. It was light, but now darkness. . . . Now I was here, but then I shall be there! Where?"

A chill ran over him, his breathing ceased. He heard only the thumping of his heart.

"I shall not be, but what will be? There will be nothing. Then, where shall I be when I am no more? Will that be death? No, I will not have it!"

He leaped up, wished to light the candle, fumbled about with trembling hands, knocked the candle and candlestick to the floor, and again fell back on the pillow.

"Wherefore? It is all the same," he said to himself, gazing into the darkness with wide-open eyes.

"Death! Yes, death! And *they* know nothing about it, and wish to know nothing about it; and they do not pity me. They are playing."—He heard through the door the distant sound of voices and *ritornelles*.—"To them it is all the same . . . and they also will die. Little fools! I first, and they after me. It will be their turn also. But they are enjoying themselves! Cattle!"

Anger choked him, and he felt an insupportably heavy burden of anguish.

"It cannot be that all men have been exposed to this horrible terror."

He lifted himself once more.

"No, it is not so at all. I must calm myself; I must think it all over from the beginning."

And here he began to reflect:—

"Yes, the beginning of the trouble. I hit my side, and I was just the same as before, one day and the next, only a little ache, then more severe, then the doctor, then low spirits, anxiety, the doctor again. And I am all the time coming nearer and nearer to the abyss. Less strength. Nearer, nearer! And how wasted I am! I have no light in my eyes. And death . . . and I thinking about the intestine! I am thinking only how to cure my intestine; but this is death!—Is it really death?"

Again fear fell on him. He panted, bent over, tried to find the matches, hit his elbow against the table. It hindered him, and hurt him; he lost his patience, pushed angrily against it with more violence, and tipped it over. And in despair, all out of breath, he fell back, expecting death instantly.

At this time the visitors were going. Praskovia Feodorovna was showing them out. She heard the table fall, and came in.

"What is the matter?"

"Nothing . . . I unintentionally knocked it over."

She went out, and brought in a candle. He was lying, breathing heavily, and quickly, like a man who has just run a verst; his eyes were staring at her.

"What is it, Jean?"

"No-o-thing. I . . . knock-ed . . . over. . . . Why say anything? she will not understand," he thought.

She did not in the least understand. She picked up the table, lighted the candle for him, and hurried out. She had to say good-night to her company.

When she came back, he was still lying on his back, looking up.

"What is the matter? Are you worse?"

"Yes."

She shook her head, and sat down.

"Do you know, Jean, I think we had better send for Leshchititsky? don't you?"

That meant, send for the celebrated doctor, and not mind the expense. He smiled bitterly, and said:—

"No."

She sat a moment, then came to him, and kissed him on the forehead. He abhorred her, with all the strength of his soul, at that moment when she kissed him; and he had to restrain himself from pushing her away.

"Good-night! God give you pleasant sleep!"

"Yes."

6

Ivan Ilyitch saw that he was going to die, and he was in perpetual despair. In the depths of his soul, he knew that he was going to die; but he not only failed to get used to the thought, but also simply did not comprehend it, could not comprehend it.

This form of syllogism, which he had studied in Kiziveter's "Logic,"—"Kaï is a man, men are mortal, therefore Kaï is mortal,"—had seemed to him all his life true only in its application to Kaï, but never to himself. It was Kaï as man, as man in general, and in this respect it was perfectly correct; but he was not Kaï, and not man in general, and he had always been an entity absolutely, absolutely distinct from all others; he had been Vanya with mamma and papa, with Mitya and Volodya, with his playthings, the coachman, with the nurse; then with Katenka, with all the joys, sorrows, enthusiasms of childhood, boyhood, youth.

Was it Kaï who smelt the odor of the little striped leather ball that Vanya had loved so dearly? Was it Kaï who had kissed his mother's hand? and was it for Kaï that the silken folds of his mother's dress had rustled so pleasantly? Was it he who made a conspiracy for the tarts at the law-school? Was it Kaï who had been so deeply in love? Was it Kaï who had such ability in conducting the sessions?

"And Kaï is certainly mortal, and it is proper that he should die; but for me, Vanya, Ivan Ilyitch, with all my feelings, my thoughts,—for me, that is another thing, and it cannot be that I must take my turn and die. That would be too horrible."

This was the way that he felt about it:—

"If I were going to die, like Kaï, then, surely, I should have known it; some internal voice would have told me; but nothing of the sort happened in me, and I myself, and my friends, all of us, have perceived that it was absolutely different in our case from what it was with Kaï. But now how is it?" he said to himself. "It cannot be, it cannot be, but it is! How is this? How understand it?"

And he could not understand it; and he endeavored to put away this thought as false, unjust, unwholesome, and to supplant it with other thoughts true and wholesome. But this thought, not merely as a thought, but, as it were, a reality, kept recurring and taking form before him.

And he summoned in place of this thought other thoughts, one after the other, in the hope of finding succor in them. He strove to return to his former course of reasoning, which hid from him of old the thought of death. But, strangely enough, all that which formerly hid, concealed, destroyed the image of death, was now incapable of producing that effect.

Ivan Ilyitch came to spend the larger part of his time in these attempts to restore the former current of feeling which put death out of sight. Sometimes he said to himself:—

"I will take up my duties again; they certainly kept me alive."

And he went to court, driving away every sort of doubt. He joined his colleagues in conversation, and sat down, according to his old habit, pensively looking with dreamy eyes on the throng, and resting his two emaciated hands on the arms of his oak chair, leaning over, just as usual, toward his colleague, running through the brief, whispering his comments; and then, suddenly lifting his eyes, and sitting straight, he pronounced the well-known words, and began business.

But suddenly, right in the midst of it, the pain in his side, entirely disregarding the time of public business, began its simultaneous business. Ivan Ilyitch perceived it, tried to turn his thoughts from it; but it took its course, and DEATH came up and stood directly before him, and gazed at him: and he was stupefied; the fire died out in his eyes, and he began once more to ask himself:—

"Is there nothing true save IT?"

And his colleagues and subordinates saw with surprise and concern that he, this brilliant, keen judge, was confused, was making mistakes.

He shook himself, tried to collect his thoughts, and in a way conducted the session till it adjourned, and then returned home with the melancholy consciousness that he no longer had the ability, as of old, to separate between his judicial acts and what he wished to put out of his thoughts; that even in the midst of his judicial acts, he could not deliver himself from IT. And what was worse than all, was the fact that IT distracted his attention, not to make him do anything, but only to make him look at IT, straight in the eye,—look at IT, and, though doing nothing, suffer beyond words.

And, while attempting to escape from this state of things, Ivan Ilyitch sought relief, sought other shelter; and other aids came along, and for a short time seemed to help him; but immediately they not so much failed, as grew transparent, as if IT became visible through all, and nothing could hide it.

It happened in this latter part of the time that he went into the drawing-room which he had decorated,—that very drawing-room where he had met with the fall, for which he—as he had to think with bitterness and scorn—for the decoration of which he had sacrificed his life; because he knew that his malady began with that bruise: he went in, and saw that on the varnished table was a scratch, cut by something. He sought for the cause of it, and found it in the bronze decoration of an album, which was turned up at the edge. He took the precious album, lovingly filled by him, and broke out in a passion against the carelessness of his daughter and her friends, who destroyed things so, who dog-eared photographs. He put this carefully to rights, and bent back the ornament.

Then the idea occurred to him to transfer this *établissement*, albums and all, to the other corner, where the flowers were. He summoned a servant. Either his wife or his daughter came to his help; they did not agree with him; they argued against the change: he argued, he lost his temper; but everything was good, because he did not think about IT, IT did not appear.

But here, as he himself was beginning to shift the things, his wife said:—

"Hold on! the men will attend to that; you will strain yourself again."

And suddenly IT gleamed through the shelter; he saw IT. IT gleamed; he was already hoping that IT had disappeared, but involuntarily he watched for the pain in his side—there it was, all the time, always making its advance; and he could not forget it, and IT clearly gazed at him from among the flowers. What was the purpose of it all?

"And it is true that here I have lost my life on that curtain as in a charge! Is it possible? How horrible and how ridiculous! It cannot be! It cannot be! but it is."

He went back to his library, went to bed, and found himself again alone with

IT. Face to face with IT. But to do anything with IT—impossible! Only to look at IT, and grow chill!

7

How it came about in the third month of Ivan Ilyitch's illness, it was impossible to say, because it came about step by step, imperceptibly; but it came about that his wife and daughter, and his son and the servants, and his acquaintances and the doctors, and chiefly he himself, knew that all the interest felt in him by others was concentrated in this one thing,—how soon he would vacate his place, would free the living from the constraint caused by his presence, and be himself freed from his sufferings.

He slept less and less; they gave him opium, and began to try hypodermic injections of morphine. But this did not relieve him. The dull distress which he experienced in his half-drowsy condition at first merely afforded the relief of change; but soon it came back as severe as ever, or even more intense than open pain.

They prepared for him special dishes, according to the direction of the physicians; but these dishes became ever more and more tasteless, more and more repugnant to him.

Special arrangements also had been made, so that he might perform the wants of nature; and each time it became more trying for him. The torture came from the uncleanliness, the indecency, of it, and the ill odor, from the knowledge that he required the assistance of another.

But from this very same disagreeable circumstance Ivan Ilyitch drew a consolation. His butler, the muzhik Gerasim, always came to set things to rights.

Gerasim was a clean, ruddy young muzhik, who had grown stout in waiting on the table in the city houses. He was always festive, always serene. From the very first, the sight of this man, always so neatly attired in his Russian costume, engaged in this repulsive task, made Ivan Ilyitch ashamed.

One time, after he had got up and was feeling too weak to lift his pantaloons, he threw himself into an easy-chair and was contemplating with horror his bare thighs with their strangely flabby muscles standing out.

Gerasim came in with light, buoyant steps, in thick boots, diffusing an agreeable odor of tar from his boots, and the freshness of the winter air. He wore a clean hempen apron and a clean cotton shirt, with the cuffs rolled up on his bare, strong young arms; and, not looking at Ivan Ilyitch, evidently curbing the joy in life which shone in his face, so as not to offend the sick man, he began to do his work.

"Gerasim," said Ivan Ilyitch, in a weak voice.

Gerasim started, evidently fearing that he had failed in some duty, and turned toward the sick man his fresh, good, simple young face, on which the beard was only just beginning to sprout.

"What can I do for you?"

"This, I am thinking, is disagreeable to you. Forgive me. I cannot help it."

"Do not mention it." And Gerasim's eyes shone, and he showed his white young teeth. "Why should I not do you this service? It is for a sick man."

And with expert, strong hands, he fulfilled his wonted task and went out with light steps. After five minutes he returned, still walking with light steps. He had made everything clean and sweet.

Ivan Ilyitch was still sitting in his arm-chair.

"Gerasim," he said, "be good enough to assist me. Come here."

Gerasim went to him.

"Lift me up. It is hard for me alone, and I sent Dmitri away."

Gerasim went to him. In just the same way as he walked, he lifted him with his strong arm, deftly, gently, and held him. With his other hand he adjusted his clothing, and then was about to let him sit down. But Ivan Ilyitch requested him to help him to the divan. Gerasim, without effort, and exercising no sensible pressure, supported him, almost carrying him, to the divan, and set him down.

"Thank you. How easily, how well, you do it all!"

Gerasim again smiled, and was about to go. But Ivan Ilyitch felt so good with him, that he wanted him to stay.

"Wait! Please bring me that chair . . . no; that one there. Put it under my feet. It is easier for me when my feet are raised."

Gerasim brought the chair, put it down noiselessly, arranged so that it sat even on the floor, and put Ivan Ilyitch's legs on the chair. It seemed to Ivan Ilyitch that he felt more comfortable while Gerasim was holding up his legs.

"It is better when my legs are up," said Ivan Ilyitch. "Bring me that cushion."

Gerasim did this. Again he lifted his legs, and arranged it all. Again Ivan Ilyitch felt better while Gerasim was holding his legs. When he put them down, he felt worse.

"Gerasim," said he, "are you busy just now?"

"Not at all," said Gerasim, having learned of city people how to speak with gentlefolk.

"What more have you to do?"

"What more have I to do? Everything has been done, except splitting wood against to-morrow."

"Then, hold my legs a little higher, can you?"

"Why not? Of course I can!"

Gerasim lifted his legs higher, and it seemed to Ivan Ilyitch that in this position he felt no pain at all.

"But how about the wood?"

"Don't be worried about that. We shall have time enough."

Ivan Ilyitch bade Gerasim to sit down and hold his legs, and he talked with him. And, strangely enough, it seemed to him that he felt better while Gerasim was holding his legs.

From that time forth Ivan Ilyitch would sometimes call Gerasim, and make him hold his legs on his shoulders, and he liked to talk with him. Gerasim did this easily, willingly, simply, and with a goodness of heart which touched Ivan Ilyitch. In all other people, good health, strength, and vigorous life affronted Ivan Ilyitch; but Gerasim's strength and vigorous life did not affront Ivan Ilyitch, but calmed him.

Ivan Ilyitch's chief torment was a lie,—the lie somehow accepted by every one, that he was only sick, but not dying, and that he needed only to be calm, and trust to the doctors, and then somehow he would come out all right. But *he* knew that, whatever was done, nothing would come of it, except still more excruciating anguish and death. And this lie tormented him; it tormented him that they were unwilling to acknowledge what all knew as well as he knew, but preferred to lie to him about his terrible situation, and made him also a party to this lie. This lie, this lie, it clung to him, even to the very evening of his death; this lie, tending to reduce the strange, solemn act of his death to the same level as visits, curtains, sturgeon for dinner—it was horribly painful for Ivan Ilyitch. And strange! many times, when they were playing this farce for his benefit, he was within a hair's-breadth of shouting at them:—

"Stop your foolish lies! you know as well as I know that I am dying, and so at least stop lying."

But he never had the spirit to do this. The strange, terrible act of his dissolution, he saw, was reduced by all who surrounded him to the grade of an accidental unpleasantness, often unseemly—when he was treated as a man who should come into the drawing-room and diffuse about him a bad odor—and contrary to those principles of "propriety" which he had served all his life. He saw that no one pitied him, because no one was willing even to appreciate his situation. Only Gerasim appreciated his situation, and pitied him. And, therefore, Ivan Ilyitch was contented only when Gerasim was with him.

He was contented when Gerasim for whole nights at a time held his legs, and did not care to go to sleep, saying:—

"Don't you trouble yourself, Ivan Ilyitch; I shall get sleep enough."

Or when suddenly, using *thou* instead of *you*, he would add:—

"If thou wert not sick . . . but since thou art, why not serve thee?"

Gerasim alone did not lie: in every way it was evident that he alone comprehended what the trouble was, and thought it unnecessary to hide it, and simply pitied his sick barin, who was wasting away. He even said directly when Ivan Ilyitch wanted to send him off to bed:—

"We shall all die. Then, why should I not serve you?" he said, meaning by this that he was not troubled by his extra work, for precisely the reason that he was doing it for a dying man, and he hoped that, when his time came, some one would undertake the same service for him.

Besides this lie, or in consequence of it, Ivan Ilyitch felt the greatest torment from the fact that no one pitied him as he longed for them to pity him. At some moments after long agonies he yearned more than all—although he would have been the last to confess it—he yearned for some one to pity him as a sick child is pitied. He longed to be caressed, to be kissed, to be wept for, as a child is caressed and comforted. He knew that he was a magistrate of importance, that his beard was turning gray, and that hence it was impossible; but nevertheless he longed for it. And in his relations with Gerasim there was something that approached this. And, therefore, his relations with Gerasim comforted him.

Ivan Ilyitch would have liked to weep, would have liked to be caressed, and have tears shed for him; and here came his colleague, the member Shebek, and, instead of weeping and being caressed, Ivan Ilyitch puts on a serious, stern, melancholy expression of countenance, and with all his energy speaks his opinions concerning the significance of a judgment of cassation, and obstinately stands up for it.

This lie surrounding him, and existing in him, more than all else poisoned Ivan Ilyitch's last days.

8

It was morning.

It was morning merely because Gerasim had gone, and Piotr, the lackey, had come. He put out the candles, opened one curtain, and began noiselessly to put things to rights. Whether it were morning, whether it were evening, Friday or Sunday, all was a matter of indifference to him, all was one and the same thing. The agonizing, shooting pain, never for an instant appeased; the consciousness of a life hopelessly wasting away, but not yet departed; the same terrible, cursed death coming nearer and nearer, the one reality, and always the same lie,—what matter, then, here, of days, weeks, and hours of the day?

"Will you not have me bring the tea?"

"He must follow form, and that requires masters to take tea in the morning," he thought; and he said merely:—

"No."

"Wouldn't you like to go over to the divan?"

"He has to put the room in order, and I hinder him; I am uncleanness, disorder!" he thought to himself, and said merely:—

"No: leave me!"

The lackey still bustled about a little. Ivan Ilyitch put out his hand. Piotr officiously hastened to him:—

"What do you wish?"

"My watch."

Piotr got the watch, which lay near by, and gave it to him.

"Half-past eight. They aren't up yet?"

"No one at all. Vasili Ivanovitch"—that was his son—"has gone to school, and Praskovia Feodorovna gave orders to wake her up if you asked for her. Do you wish it?"

"No, it is not necessary.—Shall I not try the tea?" he asked himself. "Yes . . . tea . . . bring me some."

Piotr started to go out. Ivan Ilyitch felt terror-stricken at being left alone. "How can I keep him? Yes, my medicine. Piotr, give me my medicine.—Why not? perhaps the medicine may help me yet."

He took the spoon, sipped it.

"No, there is no help. All this is nonsense and delusion," he said, as he immediately felt the familiar, mawkish, hopeless taste.

"No, I cannot have any faith in it. But this pain, . . . why this pain? Would that it might cease for a minute!"

And he began to groan. Piotr came back.

"Nothing . . . go! Bring the tea."

Piotr went out. Ivan Ilyitch, left alone, began to groan, not so much from the pain, although it was horrible, as from mental anguish.

"Always the same thing, and the same thing; all these endless days and nights. Would it might come very soon! What very soon? Death, blackness? No, no! Anything rather than death!"

When Piotr came back with the tea on a tray, Ivan Ilyitch stared long at him in bewilderment, not comprehending who he was, what he was. Piotr was abashed at this gaze; and when Piotr showed his confusion, Ivan Ilyitch came to himself.

"Oh, yes," said he, "the tea; very well, set it down. Only help me to wash, and to put on a clean shirt."

And Ivan Ilyitch began to perform his toilet. With resting spells he washed his hands and face, cleaned his teeth, began to comb his hair, and looked into the mirror. It seemed frightful, perfectly frightful, to him, to see how his hair lay flat upon his pale brow.

While he was changing his shirt, he knew that it would be still more frightful if he gazed at his body; and so he did not look at himself. But now it was done. He put on his khalat, wrapped himself in his plaid, and sat down in his easy-chair to take his tea. For a single moment he felt refreshed; but as soon as he began to drink the tea, again that same taste, that same pain. He compelled himself to drink it all, and lay down, stretching out his legs. He lay down, and let Piotr go.

Always the same thing. Now a drop of hope gleaming, then a sea of despair rising up, and always pain, always melancholy, and always the same monotony. It was terribly melancholy to the lonely man; he longed to call in some one, but he knew in advance that it is still worse when others are present.

"Even morphine again . . . to get a little sleep! . . . I will tell him, tell the doctor, to find something else. It is impossible, impossible so."

One hour, two hours, would pass in this way. But there! the bell in the corridor. Perhaps it is the doctor. Exactly: it is the doctor, fresh, hearty, portly, jovial, with an expression as if he said, "You may feel apprehension of something or other, but we will immediately straighten things out for you."

The doctor knows that this expression is not appropriate here; but he has already put it on once for all, and he cannot rid himself of it—like a man who has put on his dress-coat in the morning, and gone to make calls.

The doctor rubs his hands with an air of hearty assurance.

"I am cold. A healthy frost. Let me get warm a little," says he, with just the expression that signifies that all he needs is to wait until he gets warmed a little, and, when he is warmed, then he will straighten things out.

"Well, now, how goes it?"

Ivan Ilyitch feels that the doctor wants to say, "How go your little affairs?" but that he feels that it is impossible to say so; and he says, "What sort of a night did you have?"

Ivan Ilyitch would look at the doctor with an expression which seemed to ask the question, "Are you never ashamed of lying?"

But the doctor has no desire to understand his question.

And Ivan Ilyitch *says:*—

"It was just horrible! The pain does not cease, does not disappear. If you could only give me something for it!"

"That is always the way with you sick folks! Well, now, it seems to me I am warm enough; even the most particular Praskovia Feodorovna would not find anything to take exception to in my temperature. Well, now, how are you really?"

And the doctor shakes hands with him.

And, laying aside his former jocularity, the doctor begins with serious mien to examine the sick man, his pulse and temperature, and he renews the tappings and the auscultation.

Ivan Ilyitch knew for a certainty, and beyond peradventure, that all this was nonsense and foolish deception; but when the doctor, on his knees, leaned over toward him, applying his ear, now higher up, now lower down, and with most sapient mien performed various gymnastic evolutions on him, Ivan Ilyitch succumbed to him, as once he succumbed to the discourses of the lawyers, even when he knew perfectly well that they were deceiving him, and why they were deceiving him.

The doctor, still on his knees on the divan, was still performing the auscultation, when at the door were heard the rustle of Praskovia Feodorovna's silk dress, and her words of blame to Piotr because he had not informed her of the doctor's visit.

She came in, kissed her husband, and immediately began to explain that she had been up a long time; and only through a misunderstanding she had not been there when the doctor came.

Ivan Ilyitch looked at her, observed her from head to foot, and felt a secret indignation at her fairness and her plumpness, and the cleanliness of her hands, her neck, her glossy hair, and the brilliancy of her eyes, brimming with life. He hated her with all the strength of his soul, and her touch made him suffer an actual paroxysm of hatred of her.

Her attitude toward him and his malady was the same as before. Just as the doctor had formulated his treatment of his patient and could not change it, so she had formulated her treatment of him, making him feel that he was not doing what he ought to do, and was himself to blame; and she liked to reproach him for this, and she could not change her attitude toward him.

"Now, just see! he does not heed, he does not take his medicine regularly; and, above all, he lies in a position that is surely bad for him—his feet up."

She related how he made Gerasim hold his legs.

The doctor listened with a disdainfully good-natured smile, as much as to say:—

"What is to be done about it, pray? These sick folks are always conceiving some such foolishness. But you must let it go."

When the examination was over, the doctor looked at his watch; and then Praskovia Feodorovna declared to Ivan Ilyitch that, whether he was willing or not, she was going that very day to call in the celebrated doctor to come and have an examination and consultation with Mikhaïl Danilovitch—that was the name of their ordinary doctor.

"Now, don't oppose it, please. I am doing this for my own self," she said ironically, giving him to understand that she did it all for him, and only on this account did not allow him the right to oppose her.

He said nothing, and frowned. He felt that this lie surrounding him was so complicated that it was now hard to escape from it.

She did all this for him, only in her own interest; and she said that she was doing it for him, while she was in reality doing it for herself, as some incredible thing, so that he was forced to take it in its opposite sense.

The celebrated doctor, in fact, came about half-past eleven. Once more they had auscultations; and learned discussions took place before him, or in the next room, about his kidney, about the blind intestine, and questions and answers in such a learned form that again the place of the real question of life and death, which now alone faced him, was driven away by the question of the kidney and the blind intestine, which were not acting as became them, and on which Mikhaïl Danilovitch and the celebrity were to fall instantly and compel to attend to their duties.

The famous doctor took leave with a serious but not hopeless expression. And in reply to the timid question which Ivan Ilyitch's eyes, shining with fear and hope, asked of him, whether there was a possibility of his getting well, it replied that it could not vouch for it, but there was a possibility.

The look of hope with which Ivan Ilyitch followed the doctor was so pathetic that Praskovia Feodorovna, seeing it, even wept, as she went out of the library door in order to give the celebrated doctor his honorarium.

The raising of his spirits, caused by the doctor's hopefulness, was but temporary. Again the same room, the same pictures, curtains, wall-paper, vials, and his aching, pain-broken body. And Ivan Ilyitch began to groan. They gave him a subcutaneous injection, and he fell asleep.

When he woke up it was beginning to grow dusky. They brought him his dinner. He forced himself to eat a little *bouillon*. And again the same monotony, and again the advancing night.

About seven o'clock, after dinner, Praskovia Feodorovna came into his room, dressed as for a party, with her exuberant bosom swelling in her stays, and with traces of powder on her face. She had already that morning told him that they were going to the theater. Sarah Bernhardt had come to town, and they had a box which he had insisted on their taking.

Now he had forgotten about that, and her toilet offended him. But he concealed his vexation when he recollected that he himself had insisted on their taking a box, and going, on the ground that it would be an instructive, esthetic enjoyment for the children.

Praskovia Feodorovna, came in self-satisfied, but, as it were, feeling a little to blame. She sat down, asked after his health, as he saw, only for the sake of asking, and not so as to learn, knowing that there was nothing to learn, and began to say what was incumbent on her to say,—that she would not have gone for anything, but that they had taken the box; and that Elen and her daughter and Petrishchef—the examining magistrate, her daughter's betrothed —were going, and it was impossible to let them go alone, but that it would have been more agreeable to her to stay at home with him. Only he should be sure to follow the doctor's prescriptions in her absence.

"Yes—and Feodor Petrovitch"—the betrothed—"wanted to come in. May he? And Liza!"

"Let them come."

The daughter came in, in evening dress, with her fair young body,—her body that made his anguish more keen. But she paraded it before him, strong, healthy, evidently in love, and irritated against the disease, the suffering, and death which stood in the way of her happiness.

Feodor Petrovitch also entered, in his dress-coat, with curly hair *à la Capoul*, with long, sinewy neck tightly incased in a white standing collar, with a huge white bosom, and his long, muscular legs in tight black trousers, with a white glove on one hand, and with an opera hat.

Immediately behind him, almost unnoticed, came the gymnasium scholar, in his new uniform, poor little fellow, with gloves on, and with that terrible blue circle under the eyes, the meaning of which Ivan Ilyitch understood.

He always felt a pity for his son. And terrible was his timid and compassionate glance. With the exception of Gerasim, Vasya alone, it seemed to Ivan Ilyitch, understood and pitied him.

All sat down; again they asked after his health. Silence ensued. Liza asked her mother if she had the opera-glasses. A dispute arose between mother and daughter as to who had mislaid them. It was a disagreeable episode.

Feodor Petrovitch asked Ivan Ilyitch if he had seen Sarah Bernhardt. Ivan Ilyitch did not at first understand his question, but in a moment he said:—

"No . . . why, have you seen her yet?"

"Yes, in 'Adrienne Lecouvreur.' "

Praskovia Feodorovna said that she was especially good in that. The daughter disagreed with her. A conversation arose about the grace and realism of her acting,—the same conversation, which is always and forever one and the same thing.

In the midst of the conversation, Feodor Petrovitch glanced at Ivan Ilyitch, and grew silent. The others glanced at him, and grew silent. Ivan Ilyitch was looking straight ahead with gleaming eyes, evidently indignant at them. Some one had to extricate them from their embarrassment, but there seemed to be no way out of it. No one spoke; and a panic seized them all, lest suddenly this ceremonial lie should somehow be shattered, and the absolute truth become manifest to all.

Liza was the first to speak. She broke the silence. She wished to hide what all felt, but she betrayed it.

"One thing is certain,—*if we are going*, it is time," she said, glancing at her watch, her father's gift; and giving the young man a sign, scarcely perceptible, and yet understood by him, she smiled, and arose in her rustling dress.

All arose, said good-by, and went.

When they had gone, Ivan Ilyitch thought that he felt easier: the lying was at an end; it had gone with them; but the pain remained. Always this same pain, always this same terror, made it hard as hard could be. There was no easing of it. It grew ever worse, always worse.

Again minute after minute dragged by, hour after hour, forever the same monotony, and forever endless, and forever more terrible—the inevitable end.

"Yes, send me Gerasim," was his reply to Piotr's question.

9

Late at night his wife returned. She came in on her tiptoes, but he heard her; he opened his eyes, and quickly closed them again. She wanted to send Gerasim away, and sit with him herself. He opened his eyes, and said:—

"No, go away."

"You suffer very much."

"It makes no difference."

"Take some opium."

He consented, and drank it. She went.

Until three o'clock he was in a painful sleep. It seemed to him that they were forcing him cruelly into a narrow sack, black and deep; and they kept crowding him down, but could not force him in. And this performance, horrible for him, was accompanied with anguish. And he was afraid, and yet wished to get in, and struggled against it, and yet tried to help.

And here suddenly he broke through, and fell . . . and awoke.

There was Gerasim still sitting at his feet on the bed, dozing peacefully, patiently.

But he was lying there with his emaciated legs in stockings resting on his shoulders, the same candle with its shade, and the same never ending pain.

"Go away, Gerasim," he whispered.

"It's nothing; I will sit here a little while."

"No, go away."

He took down his legs, lay on his side on his arm, and began to pity himself. He waited only until Gerasim had gone into the next room, and then he no longer tried to control himself, but wept like a child. He wept over his helplessness, over his terrible loneliness, over the cruelty of men, over the cruelty of God, over the absence of God.

"Why hast Thou done this? Why didst Thou place me here? Why, why dost Thou torture me so horribly?"

He expected no reply; and he wept because there was none, and could be none. The pain seized him again; but he did not stir, did not call. He said to himself:—

"There, now, again, now strike! But why? What have I done to Thee? Why is it?"

Then he became silent; ceased not only to weep, ceased to breathe, and became all attention: as it were, he heard, not a voice speaking with sounds, but the voice of his soul, the tide of his thoughts, arising in him.

"What dost thou need?" was the first clear concept possible to be expressed in words which he heard.

" 'What dost thou need? What dost thou need?' " he said to himself. "What? Freedom from suffering. To live," he replied.

And again he gave his attention, with such effort that already he did not even notice his pain.

"To live? how live?" asked the voice of his soul.

"Yes, to live as I used to live—well, pleasantly."

"How didst thou live before when thou didst live well and pleasantly?" asked the voice.

And he began to call up in his imagination the best moments of his pleasant life. But, strangely enough, all these best moments of his pleasant life seemed to him absolutely different from what they had seemed then,—all, except the earliest remembrances of his childhood. There, in childhood, was something really pleasant, which would give new zest to life if it were to return. But the person who had enjoyed that pleasant existence was no more; it was as if it were the remembrance of some one else.

As soon as the period began which had produced the present *he*, Ivan

Ilyitch, all the pleasures which seemed such then, now in his eyes dwindled away, and changed into something of no account, and even disgusting.

And the farther he departed from infancy, and the nearer he came to the present, so much the more unimportant and dubious were the pleasures.

This began in the law-school. There was still something even then which was truly good; then there was gayety, there was friendship, there were hopes. But in the upper classes these good moments became rarer.

Then, in the time of his first service at the governor's, again appeared good moments; these were the recollections of love for a woman. Then all this became confused, and the happy time grew less. The nearer he came to the present, the worse it grew, and still worse and worse it grew.

"My marriage . . . so unexpected, and disillusionment and my wife's breath, and sensuality, hypocrisy! And this dead service, and these labors for money; and thus one year, and two, and ten, and twenty,—and always the same thing. And the longer it went, the more dead it became.

"It is as if all the time I were going down the mountain, while thinking that I was climbing it. So it was. According to public opinion, I was climbing the mountain; and all the time my life was gliding away from under my feet. . . . And here it is already . . . die!

"What is this? Why? It cannot be! It cannot be that life has been so irrational, so disgusting. But even if it is so disgusting and irrational, still, why die, and die in such agony? There is no reason.

"Can it be that I did not live as I ought?" suddenly came into his head. "But how can that be, when I have done all that it was my duty to do?" he asked himself. And immediately he put away this sole explanation of the enigma of life and death as something absolutely impossible.

"What dost thou wish now?—To live? To live how? To live as thou livest in court when the usher proclaims, 'The court is coming! the court is coming'?

"The court is coming—the court," he repeated to himself. "Here it is, the court. Yes; but I am not guilty," he cried with indignation. "What for?"

And he ceased to weep; and, turning his face to the wall, he began to think about that one thing, and that alone. "Why, wherefore, all this horror?"

But, in spite of all his thoughts, he received no answer. And when the thought occurred to him, as it had often occurred to him, that all this came from the fact that he had not lived as he should, he instantly remembered all the correctness of his life, and he drove away this strange thought.

10

Thus two weeks longer passed. Ivan Ilyitch no longer got up from the divan. He did not wish to lie in bed, and he lay on the divan. And, lying almost all the time with his face to the wall, he still suffered in solitude the same inexplicable sufferings, and still thought in solitude the same inexplicable thought.

"What is this? Is it true that this is death?"

And an inward voice responded:—

"Yes, it is true."

"Why these torments?"

And the voice responded:—

"But it is so. There is no why."

Farther and beyond this, there was nothing.

From the very beginning of his malady, from the time when Ivan Ilyitch for the first time went to the doctor, his life was divided into two conflicting tendencies, alternately succeeding each other. Now it was despair, and the expectation of an incomprehensible and frightful death; now it was hope, and the observation of the functional activity of his body, so full of interest for him. Now before his eyes was the kidney, or the intestine, which, for the time being, failed to fulfil its duty. Then it was that incomprehensible, horrible death, from which it was impossible for any one to escape.

These two mental states, from the very beginning of his illness, kept alternating with one another. But the farther the illness progressed, the more dubious and fantastical became his ideas about the kidney, and the more real his consciousness of approaching death.

He had but to call to mind what he had been three months before, and what he was now, to call to mind with what regularity he had been descending the mountain; and that was sufficient for all possibility of hope to be dispelled.

During the last period of this solitude through which he was passing, as he lay with his face turned to the back of the divan,—a solitude amid a populous city, and amid his numerous circle of friends and family,—a solitude deeper than which could not be found anywhere, either in the depths of the sea, or in the earth,—during the last period of this terrible solitude, Ivan Ilyitch lived only by imagination in the past.

One after another, the pictures of his past life arose before him. They always began with the time nearest to the present, and went back to the very remotest, —to his childhood, and there they rested.

If Ivan Ilyitch remembered the stewed prunes which they had given him to eat that very day, then he remembered the raw, puckery French prunes of his childhood, their peculiar taste, and the abundant flow of saliva caused by the stone. And in connection with these recollections of taste, started a whole series of recollections of that time,—his nurse, his brother, his toys.

"I must not think about these things; it is too painful," said Ivan Ilyitch to himself. And again he transported himself to the present,—the button on the back of the divan, and the wrinkles of the morocco. "Morocco is costly, not durable. There was a quarrel about it. But there was some other morocco, and some other quarrel, when we tore father's portfolio and got punished, and mamma brought us some tarts."

And again his thoughts reverted to childhood; and again it was painful to Ivan Ilyitch, and he tried to avoid it, and think of something else.

And again, together with this current of recollections, there passed through his mind another current of recollections about the progress and rise of his disease. Here, also, according as he went back, there was more and more of life. There was more, also, of excellence in life, and more of life itself. And the two were confounded.

"Just as this agony goes from worse to worse, so also all my life has gone from worse to worse," he thought. "One shining point, there back in the distance, at the beginning of life; and then all growing blacker and blacker, swifter and swifter, in inverse proportion to the square of the distance from death," thought Ivan Ilyitch.

And the comparison of a stone falling with accelerating rapidity occurred to his mind. Life, a series of increasing tortures, always speeding swifter and swifter to the end,—the most horrible torture.

"I am falling." . . .

He shuddered, he tossed, he wished to resist it. But he already knew that it was impossible to resist; and again, with eyes weary of looking, but still not able to resist looking at what was before him, he stared at the back of the divan, and waited, waited for this frightful fall, shock, and destruction.

"It is impossible to resist," he said to himself. "But can I not know the wherefore of it? Even that is impossible. It might be explained by saying that I had not lived as I ought. But it is impossible to acknowledge that," he said to himself, recollecting all the legality, the uprightness, the propriety of his life.

"It is impossible to admit that," he said to himself, with a smile on his lips, as if some one were to see that smile of his, and be deceived by it.

"No explanation! torture, death . . . why?"

11

Thus passed two weeks. In these weeks, there occurred an event desired by Ivan Ilyitch and his wife. Petrishchef made a formal proposal. This took place in the evening. On the next day, Praskovia Feodorovna went to her husband, meditating in what way to explain to him Feodor Petrovitch's proposition; but that very same night, a change for the worse had taken place in Ivan Ilyitch's condition. Praskovia Feodorovna found him on the same divan, but in a new position. He was lying on his back; he was groaning, and looking straight up with a fixed stare.

She began to speak about medicines. He turned his eyes on her. She did not finish saying what she had begun, so great was the hatred against her expressed in that look.

"For Christ's sake, let me die in peace!" said he.

She was about to go out; but just at this instant the daughter came in, and came near to wish him good-morning. He looked at his daughter as he had looked at his wife, and, in reply to her questions about his health, told her dryly that he would quickly relieve them all of his presence. Neither mother nor daughter said anything more; but they sat for a few moments longer, and then went out.

"What are we to blame for?" said Liza to her mother. "As if we had made him so! I am sorry for papa, but why should he torment us?"

At the usual time the doctor came. Ivan Ilyitch answered "yes," "no," not taking his angry eyes from him; and at last he said:—

"Now see here, you know that you don't help any, so leave me!"

"We can appease your sufferings," said the doctor.

"You cannot even do that; leave me!"

The doctor went into the drawing-room, and advised Praskovia Feodorovna that it was very serious, and that there was only one means—opium—of appeasing his sufferings, which must be terrible.

The doctor said that his physical sufferings were terrible, and this was true;

408 THE DEATH OF IVAN ILYITCH

but more terrible than his physical sufferings were his moral sufferings, and in this was his chief torment.

His moral sufferings consisted in the fact that that very night, as he looked at Gerasim's sleepy, good-natured face, with its high check-bones, it had suddenly come into his head:—

"But how is it if in reality my whole life, my conscious life, has been wrong?"

It came into his head that what had shortly before presented itself to him as an absolute impossibility—that he had not lived his life as he ought—might be true. It came into his head that the scarcely recognizable desires to struggle against what men highest in position considered good,—desires scarcely recognizable, which he had immediately banished,—might be true, and all the rest might be wrong. And his service, and his course of life, and his family, and these interests of society and office—all this might be wrong.

He endeavored to defend all this before himself. And suddenly he realized all the weakness of what he was defending. And there was nothing to defend.

"But if this is so," he said to himself, "and I am departing from life with the consciousness that I have wasted all that was given me, and that it is impossible to rectify it, what then?"

He lay flat on his back, and began entirely anew to examine his whole life.

When in the morning he saw the lackey, then his wife, then his daughter, then the doctor, each one of their motions, each one of their words, confirmed for him the terrible truth which had been disclosed to him that night. He saw in them himself, all that for which he had lived; and he saw clearly that all this was wrong, all this was a terrible, monstrous lie, concealing both life and death.

This consciousness increased his physical sufferings, added tenfold to them. He groaned and tossed, and threw off the clothes. It seemed to him that they choked him, and loaded him down.

And that was why he detested them.

They gave him a great dose of opium; he became unconscious, but at dinner-time the same thing began again. He drove them from him, and threw himself from place to place.

His wife came to him, and said:—

"Jean, darling, do this for me (*for me!*). It cannot do any harm, and sometimes it helps. Why, it is a mere nothing. And often well people try it."

He opened his eyes wide.

"What? Take the sacrament? Why? It's not necessary. But, however . . ."

She burst into tears.

"Will you, my dear? I will get our priest. He is so sweet!"

"Excellent! very good," he continued.

When the priest came, and confessed him, he became calmer, felt, as it were, an alleviation of his doubts, and consequently of his suffering; and there came a moment of hope. He again began to think about the blind intestine and the possibility of curing it. He took the sacrament with tears in his eyes.

When they put him to bed after the sacrament, he felt comfortable for the moment, and once more hope of life appeared. He began to think of the operation which they had proposed.

"I want to live, to live," he said to himself.

His wife came to congratulate him. She said the customary words, and added:— ·

"You feel better, don't you?"

Without looking at her, he said:—

"Yes."

Her hope, ·.er temperament, the expression of her face, the sound of her voice, all said to him one thing:—

"Wrong! all that for which thou hast lived, and thou livest, is falsehood, deception, hiding from thee life and death."

And as soon as he expressed this thought, his exasperation returned, and, together with his exasperation, the physical, tormenting agony; and, with the agony, the consciousness of inevitable death close at hand. Something new took place: a screw seemed to turn in him, twinging pain to show through him, and his breathing was constricted.

The expression of his face, when he said "yes," was terrible. After he had said that "yes," he looked straight into her face, and then, with extraordinary quickness for one so weak, he threw himself on his face and cried:—

"Go away! go away! leave me!"

12

From that moment began that shriek that did not cease for three days, and was so terrible that, when it was heard two rooms away, it was impossible to hear it without terror. At the moment that he answered his wife, he felt that he was lost, and there was no return, that the end had come, absolutely the end, and the question was not settled, but remained a question.

"U! uu! u!" he cried in varying intonations. He began to shriek, "N'ye khotchu—I won't;" and thus he kept up the cry on the letter u.

Three whole days, during which for him there was no time, he struggled in that black sack into which an invisible, invincible power was thrusting him. He fought as one condemned to death fights in the hands of the hangman, knowing that he cannot save himself, and at every moment he felt that, notwithstanding all the violence of his struggle, he was nearer and nearer to that which terrified him. He felt that his suffering consisted, both in the fact that he was being thrust into that black hole, and still more that he could not make his way through into it. What hindered him from making his way through was the confession that his life had been good. This justification of his life caught him, and did not let him advance, and more than all else tormented him.

Suddenly some force knocked him in the breast, in the side, still more forcibly compressed his breath; he was hurled through the hole, and there at the bottom of the hole some light seemed to shine on him. It happened to him as it sometimes does on a railway carriage when you think that you are going forward, but are really going backward, and suddenly recognize the true direction.

"Yes, all was wrong," he said to himself; "but that is nothing. I might, I might have done right. What is right?" he asked himself, and suddenly stopped.

This was at the end of the third day, two hours before his death. At this very same time the little student noiselessly stole into his father's room, and approached his bed. The moribund was continually shrieking desperately, and tossing his arms. His hand struck upon the little student's head. The little student seized it, pressed it to his lips, and burst into tears.

It was at this very same time that Ivan Ilyitch fell through, saw the light, and it was revealed to him that his life had not been as it ought, but that still it was possible to repair it. He was just asking himself, "What is right?" and stopped to listen.

Then he felt that some one was kissing his hand. He opened his eyes, and looked at his son. He felt sorry for him. His wife came to him. He looked at her. With open mouth, and with her nose and cheeks wet with tears, with an expression of despair, she was looking at him. He felt sorry for her.

"Yes, I am a torment to them," he thought. "I am sorry for them, but they will be better off when I am dead."

He wanted to express this, but he had not the strength to say it.

"However, why should I say it? I must do it."

He pointed out his son to his wife by a glance, and said:—

"Take him away . . . I am sorry . . . and for thee."

He wanted to say also, "*Prosti*—Forgive," but he said, "*Propusti*— Let it pass;" and, not having the strength to correct himself, he waved his hand, knowing that he would comprehend who had the right.

And suddenly it became clear to him that what oppressed him, and was hidden from him, suddenly was lighted up for him all at once, and on two sides, on ten sides, on all sides.

He felt sorry for them; he felt that he must do something to make it less painful for them. To free them, and free himself, from these torments, "How good and how simple!" he thought.

"But the pain," he asked himself, "where is it?—Here, now, where art thou, pain?"

He began to listen.

"Yes, here it is! Well, then, do your worst, pain!"

"And death? where is it?"

He tried to find his former customary fear of death, and could not.

"Where is death? What is it?"

There was no fear, because there was no death.

In place of death was light!

"Here is something like!" he suddenly said aloud. "What joy!"

For him all this passed in a single instant, and the significance of this instant did not change.

For those who stood by his side, his death-agony was prolonged two hours more. In his breast something bubbled up, his emaciated body shuddered. Then more and more rarely came the bubbling and the rattling.

"It is all over," said some one above him.

He heard these words, and repeated them in his soul.

"It is over! death!" he said to himself. "It does not exist more."

He drew in one more breath, stopped in the midst of it, stretched himself, and died.

1886

THE GODSON

*"Ye have heard that it hath been said, An eye for an eye, and a
tooth for a tooth: but I say unto you, That ye resist not evil: but
whosoever shall smite thee on thy right cheek, turn to him the other
also."*—MATT. v. 38, 39.
"Vengeance is mine; I will repay."—ROM. XII. 19.

A son was born to a poor muzhik. The muzhik was glad; went to invite a
neighbor to be his godfather. The neighbor declined. People are not eager to
stand as godparents to a poor muzhik. The poor muzhik went to another; this
one also declined.

He went through all the village: no one was willing to stand as godfather.
The muzhik went to the next village. And a passer-by happened to meet him
as he was going. The passer-by stopped.

"Good-morning," said he, "little muzhik, whither doth God lead you?"

"The Lord," says the muzhik, "has given me a little child, as a care during
infancy, as a consolation for old age, and to pray for my soul when I am dead.
But, because I am poor, no one in our village will stand as godfather. I am
trying to find a godfather."

And the passer-by said:—

"Take me for his godfather."

The muzhik was glad, thanked the passer-by, and said:—

"Whom now can I get for godmother?"

"Well, for godmother," said the passer-by, "invite the storekeeper's daughter.
Go into town; on the market-place is a stone house with shops; as you go
into the house, ask the merchant to let his daughter be godmother."

The muzhik had some misgivings.

"How, godfather elect," says he, "can I go to a merchant, a rich man? He
will scorn me; he won't let his daughter go."

"That's not for you to worry about. Go ask him. Be ready to-morrow
morning. I will come to the christening."

The poor muzhik returned home; went to the city, to the merchant's. He
reined up his horse in the dvor. The merchant himself came out.

"What is needed?" he asked.

"Look here, Mr. Merchant. The Lord has given me a little child, as a care
during infancy, as a consolation for old age, and to pray for my soul when I
am dead. Pray, let your daughter be his godmother."

"But when is the christening?"

"To-morrow morning."

"Well; very good. God be with you! she shall come to-morrow to the mass."

On the next day the godmother came; the godfather also came; they
christened the child. As soon as they had christened the child, the godfather

went off, and they knew not who he was. And they did not see him from that time forth.

2

The lad began to grow, to the delight of his parents; and he was strong and industrious, and intelligent and gentle. He reached the age of ten. His parents had him taught to read and write. What others took five years to learn, this lad learned in one year. And there was nothing left for him to learn.

Holy Week came. The lad went to his godmother, gave her the usual Easter salutation, returned home, and asked:—

"Batyushka and matushka,[1] where does my godfather live? I should like to go to him, to give him Easter greetings."

And the father said to him:—

"We know not, my dear little son, where thy godfather lives. We ourselves are sorry about it. We have not seen him since the day when he was at thy christening. And we have not heard of him, and we know not where he lives we know not whether he is alive."

The son bowed low to his father, to his mother:—

"Let me go, batyushka and matushka, and find my godfather. I wish to go to him and exchange Easter greetings."

The father and the mother let their son go. And the boy set forth to find his godfather.

3

The lad set forth from home, and walked along the highway. He walked half a day; a passer-by met him. The passer-by halted.

"Good-afternoon, lad," said he; "whither does God lead thee?"

And the boy replied, "I went," says he, "to my dear godmother, to give her Easter greetings. I went back home. I asked my parents where my godfather lived; I wished to exchange Easter greetings with him. My parents said, 'We know not, little son, where thy godfather lives. From the day when he was at thy christening, he has been gone from us; and we know nothing about him, and we know not whether he is alive.' And I had a desire to see my godfather, and so I am on my way to find him."

And the passer-by said:—

"I am thy godfather."

The lad was delighted and exchanged Easter greetings with his godfather.

"And where," said he, "dear godfather, art thou preparing to go now? If in our direction, then come to our house; but if to thy own house, then I will go with thee."

And the godfather said:—

"I have not time now to go to thy house; I have business in the villages. But I shall be at home to-morrow. Then come to me."

"But how, batyushka, shall I get to thee?"

"Well, then, go always toward the sunrise, always straight ahead. Thou wilt reach a forest; thou wilt see in the midst of the forest a clearing. Sit down

[1] Little father and mother.

in this clearing, rest, and notice what there may be there. Thou wilt come through the forest; thou wilt see a park, and in the park a palace with a golden roof. That is my house. Go up to the gates. I myself will meet thee there."

Thus said the godfather, and disappeared from his godson's eyes.

4

The lad went as his godfather had bidden him. He went and he went; he reached the forest. He walked into the clearing, and sees in the midst of the meadow a pine tree, and on the pine tree a rope fastened to a branch, and on the rope an oaken log weighing three puds.[1] And under the log was a trough with honey.

While the boy was pondering why the honey was put there, and why the log was hung, he heard a crackling in the forest, and he saw some bears coming, —a she-bear in advance, behind her a yearling, and then three young cubs. The she-bear stretched out her nose, and marched straight for the trough, and the young bears after her. The she-bear thrust her snout into the honey. She called her cubs: the cubs gamboled up to her, pressed up to the trough. The log swung off a little, came back, jostled the cubs. The she-bear saw it, and pushed the log with her paw. The log swung off a little farther, again came back, struck in the midst of the cubs, one on the back, one on the head.

The cubs began to whine, and jumped away. The she-bear growled, clutched the log with both paws above her head, pushed it away from her. The log flew high. The yearling bounded up to the trough, thrust his snout into the honey, and began to munch; and the others to come up again. They had not time to get there before the log returned, struck the yearling in the head, and killed him with the blow.

The she-bear growled more fiercely than before, clutched the log, and pushed it up with all her might. The log flew higher than the branch; even the rope slackened. The she-bear went to the trough, and all the cubs behind her. The log flew, flew up; stopped, fell back. The lower it falls, the swifter it falls. It goes very swiftly; it flew back toward the she-bear. It struck her a tremendous blow on the pate. The she-bear rolled over, stretched out her legs, and breathed her last. The cubs ran away.

5

The lad was amazed, and went farther. He came to a great park, and in the park was a lofty palace with a golden roof. And at the gate stood the godfather, smiling. The godfather greeted his godson, led him through the gate, and brought him into the park. Never even in dreams had the lad dreamed of such beauty and bliss as there were in that park.

The godfather led the lad into the palace. The palace was still better. The godfather led the lad through all the apartments. Each was better than the other, each more festive than the other; and he led him to a sealed door.

"Seest thou this door?" said he. "There is no key to it, only a seal. It can be opened, but I forbid thee. Live and roam wherever thou pleasest, and as thou pleasest. Enjoy all these pleasures; only one thing is forbidden thee. Enter not

[1] 108.33 pounds.

this door. But, if thou shouldst enter, then remember what thou sawest in the forest."

The godfather said this, and went. The godson was left alone, and began to live. And it was so festive and joyful, that it seemed to him that he had lived there only three hours, whereas he lived there thirty years.

And after thirty years had passed, the godson came to the sealed door, and began to ponder.

"Why did my godfather forbid me to go into this chamber? Let me go and see what is there."

He gave the door a push; the seals fell off; the door opened. The godson entered, and saw an apartment, larger than the rest, and finer than the rest; and in the midst of the apartment stood a golden throne.

The godson walked, walked through the apartment, and came to the throne, mounted the steps, and sat down. He sat down, and he saw a scepter lying by the throne.

The godson took the scepter into his hands. As soon as he took the scepter into his hands, instantly all the four walls of the apartment fell away. The godson gazed around him, and saw the whole world, and all that men were doing in the world.

He looked straight ahead: he saw the sea, and ships sailing on it. He looked toward the right: he saw foreign, non-Christian nations living. He looked toward the left side: there lived Christians, but not Russians. He looked toward the fourth side: there live our Russians.

"Now," said he, "I will look, and see what is doing at home—if the grain is growing well."

He looked toward his own field, and saw the sheaves standing. He began to count the sheaves [to see] whether there would be much grain; and he saw a telyega driving into the field, and a muzhik sitting in it.

The godson thought that it was his sire come by night to gather his sheaves. He looked; it was the thief, Vasili Kudriashof, coming. He went to the sheaves and began to lay hands upon them. The godson was provoked. He cried:—

"Batyushka, they are stealing sheaves in the field!"

His father woke in the night.

"I dreamed," said he, "that they were stealing sheaves. I am going to see." He mounted his horse and rode off.

He came to the field; he saw Vasili; he shouted to the muzhiks. Vasili was beaten. They took him and carried him off to jail.

The godson looked at the city where his godmother used to live. He saw that she was married to a merchant. And she was in bed, asleep; but her husband was up; he had gone to his mistress. The godson shouted to the merchant's wife:—

"Get up! thy husband is engaged in bad business."

The godmother jumped out of bed, dressed herself, found where her husband was, upbraided him, beat the mistress, and refused to have anything more to do with her husband.

Once more the godson looked toward his mother, and saw that she was lying down in the izba, and a robber was sneaking in, and beginning to break open the chests.

His mother awoke, and screamed. The robber noticed it, seized an ax, brandished it over the mother, and was about to kill her.

The godson could not restrain himself but let fly the scepter at the robber, struck him straight in the temple, and killed him on the spot.

6

The instant the godson killed the robber, the walls closed again, the apartment became what it was.

The door opened, the godfather entered. The godfather came to his son, took him by the hand, drew him from the throne, and said:—

"Thou hast not obeyed my command: one evil deed thou hast done,—thou openedst the sealed door; a second evil deed thou hast done,—thou hast mounted the throne, and taken my scepter into thy hand; a third evil deed thou hast done,—thou hast added much to the wickedness in the world. If thou hadst sat there an hour longer, thou wouldst have ruined half of the people."

And again the godfather led his son to the throne, and took the scepter in his hands. And again the walls were removed, and all things became visible.

And the godfather said:—

"Look now at what thou hast done to thy father. Vasili has now been in jail a year; he has learned all the evil that there is; he has become perfectly desperate. Look! now he has stolen two of thy father's horses, and thou seest how he has set fire to the dvor. This is what thou hast done to thy father."

As soon as the godson saw that his father's house was on fire, his godfather shut it from him, commanded him to look in the other direction.

"Here," says he, "it has been a year since thy godmother's husband deserted his wife; he gads about with others, all astray; and she, out of grief, has taken to drink; and his former mistress has gone wholly to the bad. This is what thou hast done to thy godmother."

The godfather also hid this, and pointed to his house. And he saw his mother: she was weeping over her sins; she repented, saying:—

"Better had it been for the robber to have killed me, for then I should not have fallen into such sins."

"This is what thou hast done to thy mother."

The godfather hid this also, and pointed down. And the godson saw the robber; two guards were holding the robber before the dungeon.

And the godfather said:—

"This man had taken nine lives. He ought himself to have atoned for his sins. But thou hast killed him: thou hast taken all his sins upon thyself. This is what thou hast done unto thyself. The she-bear pushed the log once, it disturbed her cubs; she pushed it a second time, it killed her yearling; but the third time that she pushed it, it killed herself. So has it been with thee. I give thee now thirty years' grace. Go out into the world, atone for the robber's sins. If thou dost not atone for them, thou must go in his place."

And the godson asked:—

"How shall I atone for his sins?"

And the godfather said:—

"When thou hast undone as much evil as thou hast done in the world, then thou wilt have atoned for thy sins, and the sins of the robber."

And the godson asked:—

"How undo the evil that is in the world?"

The godfather said:—

"Go straight toward the sunrise. Thou wilt reach a field, men in it. Notice what the men are doing, and teach them what thou knowest. Then go farther, notice what thou seest: thou wilt come on the fourth day to a forest; in the forest is a cell, in the cell lives a hermit; tell him all that has taken place. He will instruct thee. When thou hast done all that the hermit commands thee, then thou wilt have atoned for thy sins, and the sins of the robber."

Thus spoke the godfather, and let the godson out of the gate.

7

The godson went on his way. As he walked he said to himself:—

"How can I undo the evil that is in the world? Is evil destroyed in the world by banishing men into banishment, by putting them in prison, by executing them? How can I go to work to destroy evil, to say nothing of taking on one the sins of others?"

The godson thought and thought, but could not think it out. He went and went; he came to a field. In the field the grain had come up good and thick, and it was harvest-time. The godson saw that a little heifer had strayed into this grain, and the men had mounted their horses, and were hunting the little heifer through the grain, from one side to the other. Just as soon as the little heifer tried to escape from the grain, some one would ride up and frighten the little heifer back into the grain again. And again they would gallop after it through the grain. And on one side stood a peasant woman, weeping.

"They are running my little heifer," she said.

And the godson began to ask the muzhiks:—

"Why do you so? All of you ride out of the grain! Let the woman herself call out the heifer."

The men obeyed. The woman went to the edge, began to call, "Co', boss, co', boss."

The little heifer pricked up her ears, listened, listened; ran to her mistress, thrust her nose under her skirt, almost knocked her off her legs. And the muzhiks were glad, and the peasant woman was glad, and the little heifer was glad.

The godson went farther, and said to himself:—

"Now I see that evil is increased by evil. The more men chase evil, the more evil they make. It is impossible, of course, to destroy evil by evil. But how destroy it? I know not. It was good, the way the little heifer listened to its mistress. But suppose it hadn't listened, how would they have got it out?"

The godson pondered, could think of nothing, and so went on his way.

8

He went and went. He came to a village. He asked for a night's lodging at the last izba. The woman of the house consented. There was no one in the izba except the woman, who was washing up.

The godson went in, climbed on top of the oven, and began to watch what

the woman was doing; he saw that she was scrubbing the izba; she began to
rub the table, she scrubbed the table; she proceeded to wipe it with a dirty
towel. She was ready to wipe off one side—but the table was not cleaned.
Streaks of dirt were left on the table from the dirty towel. She was ready to
wipe it on the other side; while she rubbed out some streaks, she made others.
She began again to rub it from end to end. Again the same thing. She daubed
it with the dirty towel. She destroyed one spot, but she made another. The
godson watched and watched; and he said:—

"What are you doing, little mistress?"

"Why, dost not see?" she asked. "I am cleaning up for Easter. But here, I
can't clean my table; it's all dirty. I'm all spent."

"If you would rinse out your towel," said he, "then you could wipe it off."

The woman did so; she quickly cleaned off the table.

"Thank thee," says she, "for telling me how."

In the morning the godson bade good-by to the woman of the house and
started on his way. He went and he went and he came to a forest. He saw
muzhiks bending hoops. The godson came up, saw the muzhiks; but the hoop
would not stay bent.

The godson looked and noticed that the muzhiks' block was loose. There
was no support in it. The godson looked on, and said:—

"What are you doing, brothers?"

"We are bending hoops; and twice we have steamed them: we are all spent;
they will not bend."

"Well, now, brothers, just fasten your block; then you will make it stay
bent."

The muzhiks heeded what he said, fastened the block, and their work went
in tune.

The godson spent the night with them and then went on his way. All day and
all night he walked; just before dawn he met some drovers. He lay down
near them, and he noticed the drovers had halted their cattle, and were
struggling with a fire. They had taken dry twigs and lighted them, but they
did not allow them to get well started, but piled the fire with wet brushwood.
The brushwood began to hiss; the fire went out. The drovers took more dry
stuff, kindled it, again piled on the wet brushwood. Again it went out. They
struggled long, but could not kindle the fire.

And the godson said:—

"Don't be in such haste to put on the brushwood, but first start a nice little
fire. When it burns up briskly, then pile on."

Thus the drovers did. They started a powerful fire, and laid on the brushwood. The brushwood caught, the pile burned. The godson stayed a little while
with them, and went farther, and he pondered and pondered, but could not
tell for what purpose he had seen these three things.

9

The godson went and went. A day went by. He came to a forest; in the forest
was a cell. The godson went to the cell and knocked. A voice from the cell
asked:—

"Who is there?"

"A great sinner; I come to atone for the sins of another."

The hermit came forth, and asked:—

"What are these sins that thou bearest for another?"

The godson told him all,—about his godfather, and about the she-bear and her cubs, and about the throne in the sealed apartment, and about his godfather's prohibition; and how he had seen the muzhiks in the field, how they trampled down all the grain, and how the little heifer came of her own accord to her mistress.

"I understood," says he, "that it is impossible to destroy evil by evil; but I cannot understand how to destroy it. Teach me."

And the hermit said:—

"But tell me what more thou hast seen on thy way."

The godson told him about the peasant woman,—how she scrubbed; and about the muzhiks,—how they made hoops; and about the herdsmen,—how they lighted the fire.

The hermit listened, returned to his cell, brought out a dull hatchet.

"Come with me," says he.

The hermit went to a clearing away from the cell, and pointed to a tree.

"Cut it down," said he.

The godson cut it down; the tree fell.

"Now cut it into three lengths."

The godson cut it into three lengths. The hermit returned to the cell again and brought some fire.

"Now," said he, "burn these three logs."

The godson made a fire, burned the three logs. There remained three firebrands.

"Half bury them in the earth. This way."

The godson buried them.

"Thou seest the river at the foot of the mountain? Bring hither water in thy mouth, water them. Water this firebrand just as thou didst teach the baba; water this one as thou didst instruct the hoop-maker; and water this one as thou didst instruct the herdsmen. When all three shall have sprouted, and three apple trees sprung from the firebrands, then wilt thou know how evil is destroyed in men; then thou shalt atone for thy sins."

The hermit said this, and returned to his cell.

The godson pondered and pondered; but he could not comprehend the meaning of what the hermit had said. But he decided to do what he had commanded him.

10

The godson went to the river, "took prisoner" a mouthful of water, poured it on the firebrand. He went again and again. He also watered the other two. The godson grew weary and wanted something to eat. He went to the hermit's cell to ask for food. He opened the door, and the hermit was lying dead on a bench. The godson looked round and found some biscuits, and ate them. He found also a spade, and began to dig a grave for the hermit. At night he brought water, watered the brands, and by day he dug the grave. As soon as he had dug the grave, he was anxious to bury the hermit; people came from the village, bringing food for the hermit.

The people learned how the hermit had died, and had ordained the godson to take his place. The people helped bury the hermit, they left bread for the godson, they promised to bring more, and departed.

And the godson remained to live in the hermit's place, and the godson lived there, subsisting on what people brought him, and he fulfilled what was told him,—bringing water in his mouth from the river, and watering the brands.

Thus lived the godson for a year, and many people began to come to him. The fame of him went forth, that there was living in the forest a holy man, that he was working out his salvation by bringing water in his mouth from the river at the foot of the mountain, that he was watering the burned stumps. Many people began to come to him. And rich merchants began to come, bringing him gifts. The godson took nothing for himself, save what was necessary; but whatever was given him, he distributed among other poor people.

And thus the godson continued to live: half of the day he brought water in his mouth and watered the brands; and the other half he rested, and received the people.

And the godson began to think that this was the way he had been commanded to live, and that thus he would destroy sin, and atone for his sins.

Thus the godson lived a second year, and he never let a single day pass without putting on water; but as yet not a single brand had sprouted.

One time as he was sitting in his cell he heard a man riding past on horseback, and singing songs. The godson went out to see what kind of a man it was. He saw a strong young man. His clothes were good, and his horse and the saddle on which he sat were rich.

The godson stopped him, and asked who he was, and where he was going. The man halted.

"I am a robber," said he. "I ride along the highways, I kill men; the more men I kill, the gayer songs I sing."

The godson was horror-struck, and he asked himself:—

"How destroy the evil in this man? It is good for me to speak to those who come to me, for they are repentant. But this man boasts of his wickedness."

The godson said nothing, but, as he started to go off, he thought:—

"Now, how to act? If this cutthroat gets into the habit of riding by this way, he will frighten everybody; people will cease coming to me. And there will be no advantage to them,—yes, and then how shall I live?"

And the godson stopped. And he spoke to the highwayman.

"People come to me here," said he, "not to boast of their wickedness, but to repent, and put their sins away through prayer. Repent thou also, if thou fearest God; but if thou dost not desire to repent, then get thee hence, and never return, trouble me not, and frighten not the people from coming to me. And if thou dost not obey, God will punish thee."

The cutthroat jeered:—

"I am not afraid of God," said he, "nor will I obey you. You are not my master. You get your living by your piety," said he, "and I get my living by robbery. We must all get a living. Teach the peasant women that come to thee, but read me no lecture. And as for what you say about God, to-morrow I will kill two men more than usual. And I would kill you to-day, but I do not wish to soil my hands. But henceforth don't come into my way."

This threat the cutthroat uttered and rode off. But he came by no more, and the godson lived in his former style comfortably for eight years.

11

One time—it was at night—the godson went out to water his brands; he returned to his cell to rest, and he sat looking up and down the road, if any people should soon be coming. And on that day not a soul came. The godson sat alone by his door until evening; and it seemed lonely, and he began to think about his life. He remembered how the cutthroat had reproached him for getting his living by his piety, and the godson reviewed his life.

"I am not living," he said to himself, "as the hermit commanded me to live. The hermit imposed a penance on me, and I am getting from it bread and reputation among the people; and so led away have I been by it, that I am lonely when people do not come to me. And when the people come, then my only joy consists in the fact that they praise my holiness. It is not right to live so. I have been seduced by my popularity among the people. I have not atoned for my former sins, but I have incurred fresh ones. I will go into the forest, to another place, so that the people may not come to me. I will live alone, so as to atone for my former sins, and not incur new ones."

Thus reasoned the godson; and he took a little bag of biscuits and his spade, and went away from the cell into a ravine, so as to dig for himself a hut in a gloomy place, to hide from the people.

The godson was walking along with his little bag and his spade when the cutthroat overtook him. The godson was frightened, tried to run, but the cutthroat caught up with him.

"Where are you going?" said he.

The godson told him that he wanted to go away from people, to a place where no one would find him.

The cutthroat marveled.

"How will you live now, when people no longer will come to you?"

The godson had not thought of this before; but when the cutthroat asked him, he began to think about his sustenance.

"On what God will give," said he.

The highwayman said nothing, but rode on.

"Why was it," said the godson to himself, "that I said nothing to him about his life? Perhaps now he is repentant. To-day he seemed more subdued, and did not threaten to kill me."

And the godson shouted to the cutthroat:—

"But still it is needful for thee to repent. Thou wilt not escape from God."

The cutthroat wheeled his horse around, and, drawing a knife from his belt, shook it at the godson. The godson was frightened; he ran into the forest.

The cutthroat did not attempt to follow him, but only shouted:—

"Twice I have let you off; fall not in my hands a third time, else I will kill you!"

He said this, and rode off.

The godson went at eventide to water his brands; behold! one had put forth sprouts, an apple tree was growing from it.

12

The godson hid from the people, and began to live alone. His biscuits were used up.

"Well," he said to himself, "now I will seek for roots."

"But, as he began his search, he saw, hanging on a bough, a little bag of biscuits. The godson took it, and began to eat.

As soon as his biscuits were gone, again another little bag came, on the same branch. And thus the godson lived. He had only one grievance: he was afraid of the cutthroat. As soon as he heard the cutthroat, he would hide himself; he would think:—

"He will kill me, and I shall not have time to atone for my sins."

Thus he lived for ten years more. One apple tree grew, and thus there remained two firebrands as firebrands.

Once the godson arose betimes and proceeded to fulfil his task; he soaked the earth around the firebrands, but he became weary, and sat down to rest.

He sat down, and while he was resting he said to himself:—

"I have done wrong because I have been afraid of death. If it please God, I may thus atone even by death for my sins."

Even while these thoughts were passing through his mind, suddenly he heard the cutthroat coming; he was cursing.

The godson listened, and he said:—

"Without God, no evil and no good can come to me from any one."

And he went out to meet the cutthroat. He saw that the cutthroat was not riding alone, but had a man behind him on the saddle. And the man's hands and mouth were tied up. The man was silent, but the cutthroat was railing at him.

The godson went out to the cutthroat, and stood in front of the horse.

"Where," said he, "art thou taking this man?"

"I am taking him into the forest. This is a merchant's son. He will not tell where his father's money is hidden. I am going to thrash him until he will tell."

And the cutthroat started to ride on. But the godson would not allow it; he seized the horse by the bridle.

"Let this man go," said he.

The cutthoat was wroth with the godson and threatened him.

"Do you desire this?" he exclaimed. "I promise you I will kill you. Out of the way!"

The godson was not intimidated.

"I will not get out of thy way," said he. "I fear thee not. I fear God only. And God bids me not let thee go. Unloose the man."

The cutthroat scowled, drew out his knife, cut the cords, let the merchant's son go free.

"Off with you," says he, "both of you! and don't cross my path a second time."

The merchant's son jumped down and made off, and the cutthroat started to ride on, but the godson still detained him. He began to urge him to reform his evil life. The cutthroat stood still, heard every word; but he made no reply, and rode off.

The next morning the godson went to water his firebrands. Behold! the second one had sprouted—another apple tree was growing.

13

Ten years more passed.

One time the godson was sitting down, he had no desires and he had no fear, and his heart was glad within him. And he said to himself:

"What blessings men receive from God! but they torment themselves in vain. They ought to live and enjoy their lives."

And he remembered all the wickedness of men—how they torment themselves. And he felt sorry for them.

"Here I am," he said to himself, "living idly. I must go out and tell people what I know."

Even while he was pondering, he heard the cutthroat coming. He was about to let him pass; for he thought:—

"Whatever I say to him, he will not accept."

This was his first thought; but then he reconsidered it, and went out on the road. The cutthroat was riding by in moody silence; his eyes were on the ground.

The godson gazed at him, and he felt sorry for him; he drew near to him and seized him by the knee.

"Dear brother," said he, "have pity on thine own soul. Lo! the Spirit of God is in thee. Thou tormentest thyself, and others thou tormentest; and thou wilt be tormented still more grievously. But God loves thee so! With what bounty has He blessed thee! Ruin not thyself, brother! change thy life."

The cutthroat frowned, and he turned away.

"Out of my way!" he exclaimed.

The godson clutched the cutthroat's knee more firmly, and burst into tears.

The cutthroat raised his eyes to the godson. He looked and he looked, and then, dismounting from his horse, he fell on his knees before the godson.

"You have conquered me, old man," he cried. "Twenty years have I struggled with you. You have won me over. I have henceforth no power over you. Do with me as it seems to you good. When you spoke to me the first time," said he, "I only did the more evil. And your words made an impression on me only when you went away from men, and I learned that you gained no advantage from men."

And the godson remembered that the peasant woman succeeded in cleaning her table only after she had rinsed out her towel. When he ceased to think about himself, his heart was purified, and he began to purify the hearts of others.

And the cutthroat said:—

"But my heart was changed within me only when you ceased to fear death."

And the godson remembered that the hoopmakers only succeeded in bending their hoops after they had fastened their block: when he ceased to be afraid of death, he had fastened his life in God, and a disobedient heart became obedient.

And the cutthroat said:—

"But my heart melted entirely only when you pitied me and wept before me."

The godson was overjoyed; he led the cutthroat to the place where the firebrands had been.

They came to it, but out of the last firebrand also an apple tree had sprung!

And the godson remembered that the drovers' damp wood had kindled only when a great fire was built: when his own heart was well on fire, another's took fire from it.

And the godson was glad because now he had atoned for all his sins.

He told all this to the cutthroat, and died. The cutthroat buried him and began to live as the godson bade him, and thus became a teacher of men.

1886

HOW THE LITTLE DEVIL EARNED A CRUST OF BREAD

A poor muzhik was going out to plow, though he had eaten no breakfast; and he took with him, from the house, a crust of bread. The muzhik turned over his plow, unfastened the bar, put it under the bush; and then he left his crust of bread, and covered it with his kaftan. The horse was almost dead, and the muzhik was very hungry. The muzhik drove in the plow, unhitched the horse, gave her something to eat, and went to his kaftan to get a bite for himself. The muzhik picked up his kaftan; the crust was gone. He searched and searched; turned his kaftan inside out, shook it: there was no crust. The muzhik was amazed.

"This is a marvelous thing," he said to himself. "I haven't seen any one, and yet some one has carried off my crust."

But a little devil had stolen the crust while the muzhik was plowing, and had perched on a shrub to hear how the muzhik would swear, and call him, the devil, by name.

The muzhik was disappointed.

"Well, now, I am not going to die of starvation. Of course the one that took it must have needed it. Let him eat it, and be welcome."

And the muzhik went to the well, got a drink of water, sighed, caught his horse, harnessed her, and began to plow again.

The little devil was vexed because he had not led the muzhik into sin, and he went to tell about it to the biggest of the devils. He came to the big devil, and told him how he had stolen the crust from the muzhik, who, instead of getting angry, had said, "Be welcome."

The big devil was angry.

"Why," said he, "in this affair the muzhik has got the better of you: you yourself are to blame for it; you did not know how to do it. If," said he, "first muzhiks, and then peasant women, were to be caught by any such trick, it wouldn't be of any use for us to be in existence. It's no use doing the thing that way. Go back to the muzhik," said he, "earn that crust. If within three years' time you do not get the better of the muzhik, I'll give you a bath in holy water."

The little devil was alarmed; he ran back to earth and began to cogitate how he might atone for his fault. He thought and thought, and he thought out a scheme.

The little devil turned himself into a good man, and took service with the poor muzhik. And during a dry summer, he advised the muzhik to sow corn in a swamp. The muzhik took the laborer's advice and sowed in the swamp. The other muzhiks had everything burned up by the sun; but the poor muzhik had dense, high, full-eared corn. The muzhik had enough to live on till the next year; and even then, much corn remained.

That year, the laborer advised the muzhik to plant his grain on the high land. And the summer proved to be rainy. And the people had sowed their corn, but it sweat and the kernels did not fill out; but the muzhik had a quantity of corn ripen on the high land. And the muzhik had still much more corn than he needed, and he knew not what to do with it.

And the laborer taught the muzhik to grind the corn, and distil brandy. The muzhik distilled the brandy and began to drink himself, and gave others to drink.

The little devil came to the big one, and began to boast that he had earned the crust. The big one went to investigate.

He went to the muzhik's and saw how he invited the rich men, how he treated them all to brandy. The muzhik's wife offered the brandy to the guests. As she went round the table she hit against it and overturned a glass. The muzhik lost his temper, scolded his wife.

"Look you," says he, "you devilish fool! What makes you slop it so? you are wasting such good whisky, you bandy-legged [goose]!"

The little devil poked the big one with his elbow. "Just look!" said he, and thought how now he would not lack for crusts.

The man kept berating his wife; he himself began to pass round the brandy. A poor peasant came in from his work. He came in without being invited; he greeted those present; he sat down; he saw the people drinking brandy. He also would have liked to have a taste of the brandy. He sat and he sat and he kept swallowing his spittle, but the host did not offer any to him. He only muttered to himself:—

"Why must we furnish everybody with brandy?"

This pleased the big devil; but the little devil bragged.

"Just wait a little, and see what will come of it."

The rich muzhiks were drinking; the host also drank. They all began to fawn on one another, and flatter each other, and to tell rather buttery and scandalous stories. The big devil listened, and listened and he commended him for this.

"If," said he, "such flattery and such deception can come from this drunkenness, then they will all be in our hands."

"Just wait," said the little devil, "what more will come of it. There they are going to drink one little glass more. Now, like little foxes, they are wagging their tails at one another and trying to deceive one another; but just see how, in a short time, they will be acting like fierce wolves."

The muzhiks drained their glasses once more, and their talk became louder and rougher. In place of buttery speeches, they began to indulge in abuse; they began to get angry, and tweak one another's noses. The host also took part in the squabble. Even him they beat unmercifully.

The big devil looked on, and praised him for this also.

"This," said he, "is good."

But the little devil said:—

"Just wait! See what more will happen. Let them take a third drink. Now they are as mad as wolves; but give them time, let them drink once more; they will instantly begin to behave like hogs."

The muzhiks drank for the third time. They lost all control of themselves. They themselves had no idea what they stammered or shrieked, and they talked all at once. They started to go home, each in his own way, or in groups of two and three. They all fell into the gutter. The host went to see his guests out; he fell on his nose in a pool and got all smeared; he lay there like a boar, grunting.

This delighted the big devil still more.

"Well," says he, "this scheme of drunkenness was good. You have earned your crust. Now tell me," says he, "how did you make this liquor? You must have put into it some fox's blood, in the first place: that was what made the muzhik keen as a fox; and then some wolf's blood: that was what made him fierce as a wolf; and finally, of course, you added swine's blood: that made him act like a hog."

"No," said the little devil, "I did nothing of the sort. I only made it for him out of all the superfluous grain. This wild blood always exists in him, but has no way of getting out when the grain is properly used. At first he did not grudge even his last crust; but as soon as he began to have a superfluity of grain, he began to scheme how he might amuse himself. And I taught him the fun,— brandy-drinking. And as soon as he began to distil God's gift for his fun, the blood of the fox and the wolf and the hog began to show itself. Now all he needs, to be always a beast, is to keep on drinking brandy."

The chief of the devils praised the little devil, forgave him for the crust of bread, and made him one of his staff.

1886

HOW MUCH LAND DOES A MAN NEED?

1

A woman came from the city, to visit her younger sister in the country. The elder was a city merchant's wife; the younger, a country muzhik's. The two sisters drank tea together and talked. The older sister began to boast—to praise up her life in the city; how she lived roomily and elegantly, and went out, and how she dressed her children, and what rich things she had to eat and drink, and how she went to drive, and to walk, and to the theater.

The younger sister felt affronted, and began to depreciate the life of a merchant, and to set forth the advantages of her own,—that of the peasant.

"I wouldn't exchange my life for yours," says she. "Granted that we live coarsely, still we don't know what fear is. You live more elegantly; but you have to sell a great deal, else you find yourselves entirely sold. And the proverb runs, 'Loss is Gain's bigger brother.' It also happens, to-day you're rich, but to-morrow you're a beggar. But our muzhiks' affairs are more reliable; the muzhik's life is meager, but long; we may not be rich, but we have enough."

The elder sister began to say:—

"Enough,—I should think so! So do pigs and calves! No fine dresses, no good society. How your goodman works! how you live in the dunghill! and so you will die and it will be the same thing with your children."

"Indeed," said the younger, "our affairs are all right. We live well. We truckle to no one, we stand in fear of no one. But you in the city all live in the midst of temptations: to-day it's all right; but to-morrow up comes some improper person, I fear, to tempt you, and tempts your khozyaïn either to cards, or to wine, or to women. And everything goes to ruin. Isn't it so?"

Pakhom, the "goodman," was listening on the oven, as the women discussed.

"That's true," says he, "the veritable truth. As we peasants from childhood turn up mother earth, so folly stays in our head, and does not depart. Our one trouble is,—so little land. If I only had as much land as I wanted, I shouldn't be afraid of any one—even of the Devil."

The women drank up their tea, talked some more about dresses, put away the dishes, and went to bed.

But the Devil was sitting behind the oven; he heard everything. He was delighted because the peasant woman had induced her husband to boast with her; he had boasted that, if he had land enough, the Devil could not get him!

"All right," he thinks; "you and I'll have to fight it out. I will give you a lot of land. I'll get you through the land."

2

Next the muzhiks lived a lady. She had one hundred and twenty desyatins[1] of land. And she had always lived peaceably with the muzhiks, never taking any advantage of them. But a retired soldier engaged himself as her overseer, and he began to vex the muzhiks with fines. No matter how careful Pakhom was, either his horse would trample down the oats, or his cow would wander into the garden, or his calves would get into the meadows; there was a fine for everything.

Pakhom paid the fines, and scolded and beat the domestics. And during the summer Pakhom fell into many a sin on account of this overseer. And still he was glad that he had cattle in his dvor; though fodder was scarce, he was in no apprehension.

During the winter, the rumor spread that the lady was going to sell her

[1] Three hundred and twenty-four acres.

land, and that a dvornik from the highway had made arrangements to buy it.

The muzhiks heard it, and groaned.

"Now," think they, "the land will belong to the dvornik; he will make us pay worse fines than the lady did. It is impossible for us to live without this land. All of us around here live on it."

The peasants went to the lady in a body and began to beg her not to sell the land to the dvornik, but to let them have it. They promised to pay a higher price.

The lady agreed. The muzhiks tried to arrange, as a mir, to buy all the land. Once, twice, they collected in meeting, but there was a hitch in affairs. The evil one put them at variance; they were utterly unable to come to any agreement.

And the muzhiks determined to purchase the land individually, according to the ability of each. And the lady agreed to this also.

Pakhom heard that a neighbor had bought twenty desyatins[2] from the lady, and that she had given him a year in which to pay her half of the money. Pakhom was envious.

"They will buy all the land," he said to himself, "and I shall be behind them." He began to reason with his wife.

"The people are buying it up," said he. "We must buy ten desyatins too. Otherwise it will be impossible to live; the overseer was eating us up with fines."

They planned how to buy it. They had laid up a hundred rubles; then they sold a colt and half their bees; and they put their son out as a laborer, and they got some more from their brother-in-law; and thus they collected half of the money.

Pakhom gathered up the money, selected fifteen desyatins of the land with forest on it, and went to the lady to make the purchase. He negotiated for fifteen desyatins, struck a bargain, and paid down the earnest-money. They went to the city, ratified the purchase; he paid down half of the money; the remainder he bound himself to pay in two years.

And Pakhom now had his land. Pakhom took seed, and sowed the land that he had bought. In a single year he paid up the debt to the lady and to his brother-in-law. And Pakhom became a proprietor. He plowed all his land, and sowed it; he made hay on his own land; he cut stakes on his own land; and on his own land he pastured cattle. Pakhom would ride out over his wide fields to plow, or he would take note of his crops, or gaze at his meadows. And yet he was not happy. The grass seemed to him to be wasted, and the flowers flowering in it seemed entirely different. Formerly he used to ride over this land,—the land as land; but now the land began to be absolutely peculiar.

3

Thus Pakhom lived, and enjoyed himself. Everything would have been good, only the muzhiks began to trespass on his grain and meadows. He begged them to refrain, but they would not stop it. Now the cowboys let the cows into the meadow; now the horses escaped from the night-guard into his corn-field.

[2] Fifty-four acres.

And Pakhom drove them out, and forgave it, and never went to law; then he got tired of it, and complained to the volost-court.[1] And though he knew that the muzhiks did it from carelessness, and not from malice, he said to himself:—

"It is impossible to overlook it, otherwise they'll always be pasturing their cattle there. We must teach them a lesson."

He thus taught them in court once; he taught them twice: first one was fined, then another. The muzhiks, Pakhom's neighbors, began to harbor spite against him. Once more they began to trespass, and this time on purpose. Some one got into his woodland by night. They cut down a dozen of his lindens for basts. Pakhom went to his grove, saw what had been done, and turned pale. Some one had been there; the linden branches lay scattered about, the stumps stood out. The whole clump had been cut down to the very last; the rascal had cleaned it all out; only one was left standing.

Pakhom fell into a rage. "Akh!" said he to himself, "if I only knew who did that, I would give him a kneading."

He thought and he thought, "Who could it be?"

"No one more likely," said he to himself, "than Semka."

He went to search through Semka's dvor; he found nothing; they only exchanged some quarrelsome words. And Pakhom felt still more certain that Semyon had done it. He entered a complaint against him. They took it into court and had a long trial. The muzhik was acquitted, for there was no proof against him. Pakhom was still more affronted; he got incensed at the starshina and at the judges.

"You," said he, "are on the side of a pack of thieves. If you were decent men, you wouldn't acquit thieves."

Pakhom quarreled both with the judges and with his neighbors. They began even to threaten him with the "red rooster."[2] Pakhom had come to live on a broader scale on his farm, but with more constraint in the commune.

And about this time the rumor spread that the people were going to new places. And Pakhom said to himself:—

"There is no reason for *me* to go from my land; but if any of our neighbors should go, it would give us more room. I would take their land for myself; I would get it around here: life would be much better, for now it is too confined."

One time Pakhom was sitting at home; a wandering muzhik came along. They let the muzhik have a night's lodging; they gave him something to eat; they entered into conversation with him:—

"Whither, please, is God taking you?"

The muzhik said that he was on his way from down the Volga, where he had been at work. The muzhik related, a word at a time, how the people had gone colonizing there. He related how they had settled there, made a community, and given each *soul* ten desyatins of land. "But the land is such," said he, "that they sowed rye. Such stalks—the horses never saw the like—so thick! five handfuls made a sheaf. One muzhik," said he, "was perfectly

---

[1] The *volost* is a district including several villages.

[2] The picturesque Russian metaphor for a conflagration.

poor,—came with his hands alone,—and now he has six horses and two cows."

Pakhom's heart burned within him; he said to himself: "Why remain here in straitened circumstances, when it is possible to live well? I will sell my house and land here; then, with the money I get, I will start anew, and have a complete establishment. But here in these narrow quarters—it's a sin. Only I must find out all about it for myself."

He planned to be gone all summer, and started. From Samara he sailed down the Volga in a steamboat, then he went on foot four hundred versts. He reached the place. It was just so. The muzhiks were living on a generous scale, on farms of ten desyatins each, and they were glad to have accessions to their community. "And any one who has a little money can buy for three rubles as much of the very best land as he wishes, besides his allotment. You can buy just as much as you wish."

Pakhom made a thorough study of it; in the autumn he returned home, and proceeded to sell out everything. He sold his land to advantage, sold his dvor, sold all his cattle, withdrew his name from the community, waited till spring, and moved with his family to the new place.

4

Pakhom came with his family to the new place, and enrolled himself in a large village. He treated the elders to vodka, arranged all the papers. Pakhom was accepted; he was alloted, as for five persons, fifty desyatins[1] of the land, to be located in different fields, besides the pasturage. Pakhom settled down. He got cattle. He had three times as much land as he had had before, and the land was fertile. Life was tenfold better than what it had been in the old time; he had all the arable land and fodder that he needed. He could keep as many cattle as he liked.

At first, while he was getting settled, and putting his house in order, Pakhom was well pleased; but after he began to feel at home, even this farm seemed to him rather narrow quarters.

The first year Pakhom sowed wheat on his allotment; it came up well. He was anxious to sow wheat; but his allotment seemed to him altogether too small for his ambition.

Wheat is sowed there on grass or fallow land. They sow it one year, two years, and let it lie fallow till the feather-grass comes up again. There are many rival claimants for such land and there's not nearly enough to go round.

Quarrels also arose on account of this; one was richer than another: they all wanted to sow, but the poorer ones had to resort to merchants for loans.

Pakhom was desirous of sowing as much as possible. The next year he went to a merchant and hired land for a year. He sowed more; it came up well, but he had to go a long way from the village, not less than fifteen versts. He saw how muzhik-merchants in the vicinity lived in fine houses, and got rich.

"That's the thing," said Pakhom to himself. "If only I could buy the land, then I would have a fine house. It would all be in one piece."

And Pakhom began to cogitate how he might get a perpetual title.

Thus Pakhom lived three years. He hired land and sowed more wheat. The

[1] One hundred and thirty-five acres.

years were good, and the wheat grew well, and extra money was laid away.

As life passed, it became every year irksome to Pakhom to buy land with the men, to waste time over it; where the land is pretty good, the muzhiks instantly fly to it and divide it all up. He was always too late to buy cheap, and he had nothing to sow on.

But in the third year, he bought, on shares with a merchant, a pasturage of the muzhiks; and they had already plowed it. The muzhiks had been at law about it, and so the work was lost. "If I owned the land," he thinks, "I should not truckle to any one; and it would not be a sin."

And Pakhom began to inquire where he might buy land in perpetuity. And he struck upon a muzhik. The muzhik had five hundred desyatins[2] for sale; and, as he was anxious to get rid of it, he would sell at a bargain.

Pakhom began to dicker with him. He argued and argued, and finally the muzhik agreed to sell for fifteen hundred rubles, half the money on mortgage. They had already come to an agreement, when a peddler happened along, and asked Pakhom to let him have a little something to eat.

While they were drinking a cup of tea, they entered into conversation.

The peddler related how he was on his way from the distant Bashkirs.

"There," said he, "I bought of the Bashkirs fifteen hundred desyatins of land; and I had to pay only a thousand rubles."

Pakhom began to ask questions. The peddler told his story.

"All I did," said he, "was to satisfy the old men. I distributed some khalats and carpets, worth a hundred rubles, besides a chest of tea; and I gave a little wine to those who drank. And I got it for twenty kopeks a desyatin."
—He exhibited the title-deed.—"The land," says he, "is by a little river, and the steppe is all covered with grass."

Pakhom went on asking more questions,—How he managed it, and who?

"The land," said the merchant, "you wouldn't go round it in a year,—it's all Bashkirian. And the people are as stupid as rams. You could almost get it for nothing."

"Well," said Pakhom to himself, "why should I spend my thousand rubles for five hundred desyatins, and hang a burden of debt around my neck besides? But there, how much I could get for a thousand rubles!"

5

Pakhom asked how he went; and, as soon as he said good-by to the peddler, he determined to go. He left his house in his wife's care, took his man, and started. When they reached the city, he bought a chest of tea, gifts, wine, just as the merchant said. They traveled and traveled; they traveled five hundred versts.[1] On the seventh day they came to the range of the wandering Bashkirs. It was all just as the merchant had said. They all live in the steppe, along a little river, in felt-covered kibitkas. They themselves do not plow and they eat no bread. And their cattle graze along the steppe, and their horses are in droves. Behind the kibitkas the colts are tied, and twice a day they bring the mares to them. They milk the mares, and make kumys out of the milk. The women

2 Thirteen hundred and fifty acres.
1 Three hundred and thirty miles.

churn the mares' milk, and make cheese; and all the muzhiks can do is drink kumys and tea, to eat mutton, and play on their dudkas.[2] All are polite and jolly; they keep festival all summer. The people are very dark, and cannot speak Russian, but are affable.

As soon as the Bashkirs saw Pakhom, they came forth from their kibitkas; they surrounded their guest. The interpreter made his acquaintance. Pakhom told him that he had come to see about land. The Bashkirs were delighted, took him to a fine kibitka, spread rugs down, gave him a down-cushion to sit on, sat round him, and proceeded to treat him to tea and kymys. They slaughtered a ram, and gave him mutton.

Pakhom fetched from his tarantas his gifts, and began to distribute them among the Bashkirs.

Pakhom gave the Bashkirs his gifts, and divided the tea. The Bashkirs were overjoyed. They jabbered and jabbered together, and then commanded the interpreter to speak.

"Thy bid me tell you," says the interpreter, "that they have taken a fancy to you; and that we have a custom of doing everything possible to gratify a guest, and repay him for his gifts. You have given us gifts. Now tell what you wish from among our possessions, in order that we may give it to you."

"Above all else that you have," says Pakhom, "I would like some of your land. In my country," says he, "there is a scarcity of land. The land is cultivated to death. But you have much land, and good land. I never saw the like."

The interpreter translated for him. The Bashkirs talked and talked. Pakhom could not understand what they were saying; but he saw that they were good-natured, that they were talking at the top of their voices and laughing. Then they relapsed into silence, looked at Pakhom; and the interpreter said:—

"They bid me tell you that, in return for your kindness, they are happy to give you as much land as you wish. Only show us your hand—it shall be yours."

They were still talking, and began to dispute angrily. And Pakhom asked what they were quarreling about.

And the interpreter replied:—

"Some say that they ought to ask the head man about the land, and that without his consent it is impossible. And others say that it can be done without the head man."

6

The Bashkirs were quarreling; suddenly a man came in a foxskin shapka. They grew silent, and all stood up. And the interpreter said:—

"This is the head man himself."

Instantly Pakhom got out his best khalat, and gave it to the head man, together with five pounds of tea.

The head man accepted it, and sat down in the chief place. And immediately the Bashkirs began to tell him all about it.

The head man listened and listened; nodded his head, in sign of silence for all, and began to speak to Pakhom in Russian.

"Well," said he, "it can be done. Take it wherever you please. There is plenty of land."

[2] Reed-pipes.

"I shall get as much as I want," said Pakhom to himself. "I must secure it immediately, else they'll say it's mine, and then take it away."

"I thank you," says he, "for your kind words. I have seen that you have much land, and I need not very much. Only you must let me know what shall be mine. As soon as possible you must have it measured off and secured to me. God disposes of life and death. You good people make the grant, but the time may come when your children will take it away."

"You are right," says the head man; "it must be secured to you."

Pakhom began to speak:—

"I have heard that a merchant was here with you. You also gave him land, and struck a bargain. I should like to do the same."

The head man understood perfectly.

"This can all be done," says he. "We have a clerk; and we will go to the city, and will all put on our seals."

"And the price will be how much?" asked Pakhom.

"We have one price: one thousand rubles a day."

Pakhom did not understand. "What is this measure, the day? How many desyatins are there in it?"

"We can't reckon it," says he. "But we sell it by the day: all that you can go round in a day—that is yours; and the price of a day is one thousand rubles."

Pakhom was astonished.

"Look here," said he. "What I can go round in a day is a good deal of land!"

The head man laughed.

"It's all yours," said he. "Only one stipulation: if you don't come back within the day to the place from which you started, your money is lost."

"But how," says Pakhom, "can I mark where I am going?"

"Well, we'll stand on the place where it pleases you; we will be standing there; and you shall go and draw the circle, and take with you a hoe, and make a mark wherever you please; at the angle dig a little hole, put some turf in it; and we will go over it, from hole to hole, with the plow. Make your circle as large as you like, only at sunset you must be back at that place from which you set out. All that you encircle is yours."

Pakhom was delighted. They agreed to go out early. They talked it over, drank still more kumys, ate the mutton, and drank some more tea. It approached night-fall. They arranged for Pakhom to sleep in a down-bed, and the Bashkirs went off. They agreed to come together at early dawn the next day, and to go out at sunrise.

7

Pakhom lay in his down-bed; and there he could not sleep, all on account of thinking of his land.

"I will get hold of a great tract," said he to himself. "I can go over fifty versts in one day. A day now is worth a year. There'll be a good bit of land in a circle of fifty versts. I will sell off the worst parts, or let it to the muzhiks; and I will pick out what I like, and I will settle on it. I will have a two-ox plow, and I will take two men as laborers. I will cultivate fifty desyatins, and I will pasture my cattle on the rest."

Pakhom did not get a wink of sleep all night. Just before dawn he dropped into a doze. He just dropped into a doze and had a dream. He seemed to see himself lying in this very same kibitka, and listening to somebody cackling outside. And it seemed to him that he wanted to see who was laughing; and he got up and went out of the kibitka, and lo! that very same head man of the Bashkirs was sitting in front of the kibitka, and was holding his sides, and roaring and cackling about something.

He went up to him and asked:—

"What are you laughing at?"

And then it seemed to him that it was no longer the head man of the Bashkirs, but the peddler who had come to him and told him about the land.

And as soon as he saw that it was the peddler, he asked:—

"Have you been here long?"

And then it was no longer the peddler, but that muzhik who had come down the Volga so long ago.

And Pakhom saw that it was not the muzhik either, but the Devil himself, with horns and hoofs, sitting and laughing; and before him was lying a man barefooted, in shirt and drawers. And Pakhom looked more attentively to find out who the man was.

And he saw that the dead man was none other than—himself! Pakhom was frightened, and woke up.

He woke up.

"What was I dreaming about?" he asked himself. He looked around, he peered out of the closed door: it was already getting light, day was beginning to dawn.

"The people must be getting up," he thinks; "it's time to start."

Pakhom arose, aroused his man in the tarantas, told him to harness up, and then went to arouse the Bashkirs.

"Time," says he, "to go out on the steppe, to measure it off."

The Bashkirs got up, all collected; and the head man came forth. The Bashkirs again began by drinking kumys; they wished Pakhom to treat them to tea, but he was not inclined to delay.

"If we go . . . it is time to go now," said he.

8

The Bashkirs made ready; some got on horseback, some climbed into carts; they started. And Pakhom rode with his man in their tarantas, and took with him a hoe. They rode out into the steppe; the dawn was beginning. They reached a mound—*shikhan* in Bashkirian. They descended from their carts, dismounted from their horses, collected in a crowd. The chief man came to Pakhom, and pointed with his hand.

"Here," says he, "all is ours, as far as you can see. Take what you desire."

Pakhom's eyes burned. The whole region was grassy, flat as the palm of your hand, black as a pot; and where there was a hollow, it was filled with grass as high as one's breast.

The chief man took off his foxskin cap, and laid it on the ground.

"Here," says he, "is the spot. Start from here, come back here. All that you go round shall be yours."

Pakhom took out his money, laid it in the cap; took off his kaftan, stood in his blouse alone; girded himself around the belly with his sash, pulled it tighter; hung round his neck a little bag with bread, put a little flask with water into his belt, tightened his leg-wrappers, took the hoe from his man, and got ready to start.

He pondered and pondered on which side to take it; it was good everywhere. He said to himself:—

"It's all one; I will go toward the sunrise."

He faced toward the east and paced back and forth, waiting till the sun should show above the horizon.

He said to himself, "I will not lose any time. It's cool, and easier to walk."

As soon as the sunlight gushed out over the horizon, he threw his hoe over his shoulder, and started out on the steppe.

Pakhom proceeded neither slow nor fast. He went about a verst;[1] he halted and he dug a little pit and piled the turf in it, so that it might attract attention.

He went farther. As he went on, he quickened his pace. As he kept going on, he dug other little pits.

Pakhom looked around. The shikhan was still in sight in the sun, and the people were standing on it; the tires on the tarantas wheels glistened. Pakhom conjectured that he has been five versts. He began to get warm; he took off his blouse, threw it over his shoulder, and went on. It grew hot. He looked at the sun. It was already breakfast-time.

"One stage over," thinks Pakhom, "and four of them make a day; it's too early as yet to turn round. Only let me take off my boots."

He sat down and took off his boots, put them in his belt, and went on. It was easy walking. He said to himself, "Let me go five versts farther, then I will swing round to the left. This place is very good; it's a pity to give it up."

The farther he went, the better it became. He still went straight ahead. He looked round—the shikhan was now scarcely visible; and the people, like little ants, made a black spot on it; and something barely glistened.

"Well," said Pakhom, "I have enough in this direction; I must be turning round. I am sweaty enough. I should like a drink."

He halted, dug a pit, filled it with turf, unfastened his flask, took a drink, and turned sharply to the left. He went and went—the grass was deep, and it was hot.

Pakhom began to feel weary; he looked at the sun and saw that it was dinner-time.

"Well," said he, "I must have a rest."

Pakhom halted. He sat down and ate his bread and water, but did not try to lie down. He said to himself:—

"If I lie down, I may fall asleep."

He sat a little while; then he started on again; he found it easy walking; his strength was renewed by his meal, but now it was growing very hot—yes, and the sun began to decline; but still he kept going. He said:—

"Endure it for an hour, and you have an age to live."

He still went on a long distance in this direction. He kept intending to turn to the left, but lo! it was a low land and moist soil. It was a pity to throw it away! He said to himself:—

[1] Thirty-five hundred feet.

"This day has been a good one."

He still continued straight on. He took in the low land—dug his pit on the farther side of the low land, the hollow, and then turned the second corner.

Pakhom gazed back in the direction of the shikhan. The heat had caused a haziness, there was a quivering in the atmosphere, and through the haziness the people on the shikhan could scarcely be seen.

"Well," said Pakhom, "I have taken long sides—I must make this one shorter."

He started on the third side—he tried to hasten his pace. He looked at the sun—it was already far down the west, and on the third side he had only gone two versts; and back to the starting-point, there were fifteen versts.

"No," he said, "even though the tract should be uneven I must hurry back in a straight line. It wouldn't do to take too much; even as it is, I have already a good deal of land."

Pakhom dug his little pit in all haste, and headed straight for the shikhan.

9

Pakhom went straight toward the shikhan, and now it began to be heavy work for him. He was bathed in sweat; and his bare legs were cut and torn, and began to fail under him. He felt a desire to rest, but it was impossible; he could not stop till sunset. The sun did not delay, but was sinking lower and lower.

"Akh!" he says to himself, "can I have made a blunder? can I have taken too much? why don't you hurry along faster?"

He gazed at the shikhan—it gleamed in the sun; it was still a long distance to the place, and the sun was now not far from the horizon.

Still Pakhom hurried on; it was hard for him, but he kept quickening his pace, quickening his pace. He walked and walked—it was still always far away. He took to the double-quick. He threw away his blouse, his boots, his flask. He threw away his cap, but he clung to his hoe and helped himself along with it.

"Akh!" he said to himself, "I was too greedy; I have ruined the whole business; I shall not get there before sunset."

And his breath began to fail him all the worse because of his apprehension. Pakhom ran—his shirt and drawers clung to his body by reason of sweat—his mouth was parched. In his breast a pair of blacksmith's bellows, as it were, were working; and in his heart a mill was beating; and his legs were almost breaking down under him.

It became painful for Pakhom. He said to himself:—

"Suppose I should die from the strain?"

He was afraid of dropping dead, and yet he could not stop.

"If after running, I were to stop now, they would call me a fool."

He ran and ran. He was now getting near, and he could hear the Bashkirs shouting—screaming at him; and their screams made his heart pain him more than ever.

Pakhom ran on with the last of his strength, and the sun was still hovering on the horizon's edge; it went into the haze; there was a great glow, red as blood. Now—now it was setting! The sun had nearly set, but now Pakhom was not far from the place. He could see it; and the people on the shikhan gesticulating to him, urging him on. He saw the foxskin cap on the ground, he could even see the money in it. And he saw the head man sitting on the ground, holding his belly with his hands. And Pakhom remembered his dream.

"Much land," he said to himself, "but perhaps God has not willed me to live on it. Okh! I have ruined myself," he thinks. "I shall not get it."

Pakhom looked at the sun, but the sun had gone down under the earth; its body was already hidden, and its last segment had disappeared under the horizon.

Pakhom exerted his last energies, threw himself forward with his body; his legs just kept him from falling.

Just as Pakhom reached the shikhan, it suddenly grew dark. He saw that the sun had gone. Pakhom groaned.

"I have lost my labor," thinks he. He was just about to stop; but as he still heard the Bashkirs all screaming, he remembered that he was below them, and therefore the sun seemed to have set, although it had not set to those on top of the shikhan. Pakhom took a breath and ran up the shikhan. It was still light on the mound. Pakhom ran, and there was the cap. In front of the cap sat the head man, laughing and holding his sides.

Pakhom remembered his dream, groaned "Akh!" his legs gave way under him, and he fell forward, reaching out his arms toward the cap.

"Aï! brave lad!" shouted the head man. "You have got a good piece of land."

Pakhom's man ran to him, attempted to help him to his feet; but from his mouth poured a stream of blood, and he lay dead.

The Bashkirs clucked with their tongues, expressing their sorrow.

Pakhom's man took the hoe, dug a grave for him, made it just long enough, from head to foot,—three arshins,[1]—and buried him.

KHOLSTOMER

THE HISTORY OF A HORSE

1

Ever higher and higher rose the sky, wider spread the dawn, whiter grew the pallid silver of the dew, more lifeless the sickle of the moon, more vocal the forest. . . .

People were beginning to arise; and at the stables belonging to the barin were heard with increasing frequency the whinnying of the horses, the stamping of hoofs on the straw, and also the angry, shrill neighing of the animals collecting together, and even disputing with one another over something.

"We-e-lll you've got time enough; half-starved, ain't you?" said the old drover,

[1] About seven feet.

quickly opening the creaking gates. "Where you going?" he shouted, waving his hands at a mare which tried to run through the gate.

Nester, the drover, was dressed in a *kazakin*, or Cossack coat, with a decorated leather belt around his waist; his knout was slung over his shoulder, and a handkerchief, containing some bread, was tied into his belt. In his arms he carried a saddle and halter.

The horses were not in the least startled, nor did they show any resentment, at the drover's sarcastic tone; they made believe that it was all the same to them, and leisurely moved away from the gate,—all except one old dark bay mare, with a long flowing mane, who laid back her ears and quickly turned around. At this opportunity a young mare, who was standing behind, and had nothing at all to do with this, whinnied, and began to kick at the first horse she fell in with.

"No!" shouted the drover, still more loudly and fiercely, and turned to the corner of the yard.

Out of all the horses—there must have been nearly a hundred—that were moving off toward their breakfast, none manifested so little impatience as a piebald gelding, which stood alone in one corner under the shed, and gazed with half-shut eyes, and licked the oak stanchion of the shed.

It is hard to say what enjoyment the piebald gelding got from this, but his expression while doing so was solemn and thoughtful.

"Wake up!" again cried the drover, in the same tone, turning to him; and, going up to him, he laid the saddle and shiny saddle-cloth on a pile of manure near him.

The piebald gelding ceased licking the stanchion, and looked long at Nester without moving. He did not manifest any sign of mirth or anger or sullenness, but only drew in his whole belly and sighed heavily, heavily, and then turned away. The drover took him by the neck, and gave him his breakfast.

"What are you sighing for?" asked Nester.

The horse switched his tail as if to say, "Well, it's all right, Nester."

Nester put on the saddle-cloth and saddle, whereupon the horse pricked up his ears, expressing as plainly as could be his disgust; but he received nothing but execrations for this "rot," and then the saddle-girth was pulled tight.

At this the gelding tried to swell out; but his mouth was thrust open, and a knee was pressed into his side, so that he was forced to let out his breath. Notwithstanding this, when they got the bit between his teeth, he once more pricked back his ears, and even looked round. Though he knew that this was of no avail, yet he seemed to reckon it essential to express his displeasure, and that he always would show it. When he was saddled, he pawed with his swollen right leg, and began to champ the bit,—here also for some special reason, because it was time for him to know that there could be no taste in bits.

Nester mounted the gelding by the short stirrups, unwound his knout, freed his Cossack coat from under his knee, settled down in the saddle in the position peculiar to coachmen, hunters, and drovers, and twitched on the reins.

The gelding lifted his head, showing a disposition to go where he should be directed, but he stirred not from the spot. He knew that before he went there would be much shouting on the part of him who sat on his back, and many orders to be given to Vaska, the other drover, and to the horses. In fact, Nester began to shout:—

"Vaska! ha, Vaska! have you let out any of the mares,—hey? Where are you, you old devil? No-o! Are you asleep? Open the gate. Let the mares go first," and so on.

The gates creaked. Vaska, morose, and still full of sleep, holding a horse by the bridle, stood at the gate-post and let the horses out. The horses, one after the other, gingerly stepping over the straw and snuffing it, began to pass out,—the young fillies, the yearlings, the little colts; while the mares, heavy with young, stepped along heedfully, one at a time, lifting their bellies. The young fillies sometimes crowded in two at once, three at once, throwing their heads across one another's backs, and hitting their hoofs against the gates, each time receiving a volley of abuse from the drovers. The colts sometimes kicked the mares they did not know, and whinnied loudly in answer to the short neighing of their mothers.

A young filly, full of wantonness, as soon as she got outside the gate, tossed her head and shook it, began to back, and whinnied, but nevertheless did not venture to dash ahead of the old gray, grain-bestrewed Zhulduiba, who, with a gentle but solid step, swinging her belly from side to side, marched along, as always the dignified leader of the other horses.

After a few moments the yard but now so lively was left in melancholy loneliness; the posts stood out in sadness under the empty sheds, and only the sodden straw, soiled with dung, was to be seen.

Familiar as this picture of emptiness was to the piebald gelding, it seemed to have a melancholy effect on him. Slowly, as if making a bow, he lowered and lifted his head, sighed as deeply as the tightly drawn girth permitted, and, dragging his somewhat bent and decrepit legs, he started off after the herd, carrying the old Nester on his bony back.

"I know now. As soon as we get out on the road, he will go to work to make a light, and smoke his wooden pipe with its copper mounting and chain," thought the gelding. "I am glad of this, because it is early in the morning and the dew is on the grass, and this odor is agreeable to me, and brings up many pleasant recollections. I am sorry only that when the old man has his pipe in his mouth he always becomes excited, gets to imagining things, and sits on one side, infallibly on one side, and on that side it hurts. However, God be with him. It's no new thing for me to suffer for the sake of others. I have even come to find some equine satisfaction in this. Let him play that he's cock of the walk, poor fellow; but it's for his own pleasure that he looks so big, since no one sees him at all. Let him ride sidewise," said the horse to himself; and, stepping gingerly on his crooked legs, he walked along the middle of the road.

2

After driving the herd down to the river, near which the horses were to graze, Nester dismounted and took off the saddle. Meantime the herd began slowly to scatter over the as yet untrodden field, covered with dew and with vapor rising alike from the damp meadow and the river that encircled it.

Taking off the bridle from the piebald gelding, Nester scratched him under his neck; and the horse in reply expressed his happiness and satisfaction by shutting his eyes.

"The old dog likes it," said Nester.

The gelding really did not like this scratching very much, and only out of delicacy pretended that it was agreeable to him. He nodded his head as a sign of assent. But suddenly, unexpectedly, and without any reason, Nester, imagining perhaps that too great familiarity might give the gelding false ideas about what he meant,—Nester, without any warning, pushed away his head, and swinging the bridle, struck the horse very severely with the buckle on his lean leg, and, without saying anything, went up the hillock to a stump, near which he sat down as if nothing had happened.

Though this proceeding incensed the gelding, he showed no sign of it; and, leisurely switching his thin tail, and, sniffing at something, and merely for recreation cropping at the grass, he wandered down toward the river.

Not paying any heed to the antics played around him by the young fillies, the colts, and the yearlings, and knowing that the health of every one, and especially at his age, was subserved by getting a good drink of water on an empty stomach, and not eating till afterward, he turned his steps to where the bank was less steep and slippery; and, wetting his hoofs and gambrels, he thrust his snout into the river, and began to suck the water through his lips drawn back, to puff with his distending sides, and out of pure satisfaction to switch his thin, piebald tail with its leathery stump.

A chestnut filly, full of mischief, always nagging the old horse, and causing him manifold unpleasantnesses, came down to the water as if for her own necessities, but really merely for the sake of roiling the water in front of his nose.

But the piebald gelding had already drunk enough, and apparently giving no thought to the impudent mare, calmly put one miry leg before the other, shook his head, and, turning aside from the wanton youngster, began to eat. Dragging his legs in a peculiar manner, and not tramping down the abundant grass, the horse grazed for nearly three hours, scarcely stirring from the spot. Having eaten so much that his belly hung down like a bag from his thin, sharp ribs, he stood solidly on his four weak legs, so that as little strain as possible might come on any one of them,—at least on the right fore leg, which was weaker than all,—and went to sleep.

There is an honorable old age, there is an odious old age, there is a pitiable old age; there is also an old age that is both honorable and odious. The old age which the piebald gelding had reached was of this latter sort.

The old horse was of a great size,—more than nineteen hands high. His color was white, spotted with black; at least, it used to be so, but now the black spots had changed to a dirty brown. There were three of these spots: one on the head including an irregular-shaped star which ran down the side of the nose and half of the neck; the long mane, tangled with burrs, was partly white and partly brownish. The second spotted place ran along the right side, and covered half the belly; the third was on the flank, including the upper part of the tail and half of the loins; the rest of the tail was whitish, variegated.

The big bony head, with deep hollows under the eyes, and with pendent black lip, somewhat lacerated, hung heavily and low on the neck, which bent from its leanness, and seemed to be made of wood. From behind the pendent lip could be seen the dark-red tongue protruding on one side, and the yellow, worn tusks of his lower teeth. His ears, one of which was slit, fell over sidewise, and only occasionally he twitched them lazily to scare away the sticky flies. One long tuft still remaining of the forelock hung behind the ears; the broad forehead was hollowed and rough; the skin hung loose on the big cheek-bones. On the neck and head the veins stood out in knots, trembling and twitching whenever a fly touched them. The expression of his face was sternly patient, deeply thoughtful, and expressive of pain.

His fore legs were crooked at the knees. On both hoofs were swellings; and on the one which was half covered by the marking, there was near the knee at the back a sore boil. The hind legs were in better condition, but there had been severe bruises long before on the haunches, and the hair did not grow on those places. His legs seemed disproportionately long, because his body was so emaciated. His ribs, though also thick, were so exposed and drawn that the hide seemed dried in the hollows between them.

The back and withers were variated with old scars, and behind was still a freshly galled and purulent slough. The black stump of the tail, where the verte-bræ could be counted, stood out long and almost bare. On the brown flank near the tail, where it was overgrown with white hairs, was a scar as big as one's hand, that must have been from a bite. Another cicatrice was to be seen on the front shoulder. The houghs of the hind legs and the tail were foul from a recent bowel disorder. The hair all over the body, though short, stood out straight.

But in spite of the loathsome old age to which this horse had come, any one looking at him would have involuntarily thought, and an expert would have said immediately, that he must have been in his day a remarkably fine horse. The expert would have said also that there was only one breed in Russia that could give such broad bones, such huge joints, such hoofs, such slender leg-bones, such an arched neck, and, most of all, such a skull,—eyes large, black, and brilliant, and such a thoroughbred network of nerves over his head and neck, and such delicate skin and hair.

In reality there was something noble in the form of this horse, and in the terrible union in him of the repulsive signs of decrepitude, the increased var-iegatedness of his hide, and his actions, and the expression of self-dependence, and the calm consciousness of beauty and strength.

Like a living ruin he stood in the middle of the dewy field, alone; while not far away from him were heard the galloping, the neighing, the lively whinnying, the snorting, of the scattered herd.

3

The sun was now risen above the forest and shone brightly on the grass and the winding river. The dew dried away and fell off in drops. Like smoke the last of the morning mist rolled up. Little curly clouds made their appearance, but as yet there was no wind. On the other side of the gleaming river stood the verdant rye, bending on its stalks, and the air was fragrant with fresh verdure and flowers. The cuckoo cooed from the forest with echoing voice; and Nester, lying flat on his back, was reckoning up how many years of life lay before him. The larks arose from the rye and the meadow. The belated hare, overtaken by the horses, went leaping across the field, and when it reached the copse it sat up and cocked its ears to listen.

Vaska went to sleep, burying his head in the grass; the mares, making wide circuits around him, scattered over the field below. The older ones, neighing, traced a shining track across the dewy grass, and kept trying to find some place where they might be undisturbed. They no longer grazed, but only nibbled on the succulent grass-blades. The whole herd was imperceptibly moving in one direction.

And again the old Zhulduiba, stately stepping before the others, showed that it was possible to keep going farther. The young Mushka, who had cast her first foal, kept hinnying, and, lifting her tail, was scolding her violet-colored colt. The young Atlasnaya, with smooth and shining skin, dropping her head so that her black and silken forelock hid her forehead and eyes, was playing with the grass, nipping it and tossing it, and stamping her leg, with its furry fetlock. One of the older little colts,—he must have been imagining some kind of game,—lifting, for the twenty-sixth time, his rather short and tangled tail, like a plume, gamboled around his dam, who calmly picked at the herbage, having evidently already summed up her son's character, and only occasionally stopped to look askance at him out of her big black eye.

One of these same young colts—black as a coal, with a large head with a marvelous top-knot rising above his ears, and his tail still inclining to the side on which he had lain in his mother's belly—pricked up his ears, and opened his stupid eyes, as he stood motionless in his place, either out of jealousy or indignation, looking steadily at the colt jumping and dancing, and seemed not to understand at all why he did it.

Some suckled, butting with their noses; others, for some unknown reason, notwithstanding their mothers' invitation, would move along in a short, awkward trot, in a diametrically opposite direction, as if seeking something, and then, no one knows why, would stop short and hinny in a desperately penetrating voice. Some were lying on their sides in a row; some were taking lessons in grazing; some trying to scratch themselves with their hind legs behind the ear.

Two mares, still with young, went off by themselves, and, slowly moving their legs, continued to graze. Evidently their condition was respected by the others, and none of the young colts ventured to go near or disturb them. If any saucy young steed took it into his head to approach too near to them, then merely a motion of an ear or tail would be sufficient to show him all the impropriety of his behavior.

The yearlings and the young fillies pretend to be fullgrown and dignified, and rarely indulge in pranks, or join their gay companions. They ceremoniously nibble at the blades of grass, bending their swanlike, short-shorn necks, and, as if they also were blessed with tails, switch their little brushes. Just like the big horses, some of them lie down, roll over, and scratch one another's backs.

The jolliest band consists of the two-year-old and the three-year-old mares who have never foaled. They almost all wander off by themselves, and make a specially jolly virgin throng. Among them is heard a great tramping and stamping, hinnying and whinnying. They gather together, lay their heads over one another's shoulders, snuff the air, leap; and sometimes, lifting the tail like an oriflamme, proudly and coquettishly, in a half-trot, half-gallop, caracole in front of their companions.

Conspicuous for beauty and sprightly dashing ways, among all this young throng, was the wanton bay mare. Whatever she set on foot the others also did; wherever she went, there in her track followed also the whole throng of beauties.

The wanton was in a specially playful frame of mind this morning. The spirit of mischief was in her, just as it sometimes comes on men. Even at the riverside, playing her pranks on the old gelding, she had galloped along in the water, pretending that something had scared her, snorting, and then dashed off at full speed across the field; so that Vaska was constrained to gallop after her, and after the others who were at her heels. Then, after grazing a little while, she began to roll, then to tease the old mares, by dashing in front of them. Then she separated a suckling colt from its dam, and began to chase after it, pretending that she wanted to bite it. The mother was frightened, and ceased to graze; the little colt squealed in piteous tones. But the wanton young mare did not touch it, but only scared it, and made a spectacle for her comrades, who looked with sympathy on her antics.

Then she set out to turn the head of the roan horse which a muzhik, far away on the other side of the river, was driving with a *sokha*, or wooden plow, in the rye-field. She stood proudly, somewhat on one side, lifting her head high, shook herself, and neighed in a sweet, significant, and alluring voice. And frolic, gayety, and sentiment, and a touch of melancholy, were expressed in the sound of her neighing. In it were also desire and the promise of love and the melancholy that is born of love.

'Twas the time when the rail-bird, running from place to place among the thick reeds, passionately calls his mate; when also the cuckoo and the quail sing of love; and the flowers send to one another, on the breeze, their aromatic dust.

"And I am young and beautiful and strong," said the jolly wanton's neighing, "and till now it has not been given to me to experience the sweetness of this feeling, never yet has it been given me to feel it; and no lover, no not one, has yet come to woo me."

And the significant neighing rang with youthful melancholy over lowland and field, and it came to the ears of the roan horse far away. He pricked up his ears, and stopped. The muzhik kicked him with his wooden shoe; but the roan was bewitched by the silver sound of the distant neighing, and whinnied in reply. The muzhik grew angry, twitched him with the reins, and again kicked him in the belly with his bast shoe, so that he did not have a chance to complete all that he had to say in his neighing, but was forced to go on his way. And the roan horse felt a sweet sadness in his heart; and the sounds from the far-off rye-field, of that unfinished and passionate neigh, and the angry voice of the muzhik, long echoed in the ears of the herd.

If through one sound of her voice the roan horse could become so captivated as to forget his duty, what would have become of him if he had had full view of the beautiful wanton, as she stood pricking up her ears, inflating her nostrils, breathing in the air, and filled with longing, while her young and beauteous body trembled as she called to him?

But the wanton did not long ponder over her novel sensations. When the voice of the roan was still, she whinnied scornfully, and, sinking her head, began to paw the ground; and then she trotted off to wake up and tease the piebald gelding. The peibald gelding was a long-suffering butt for the amusement of this happy young wanton. She made him suffer more than men did. But in neither case did he give way to wrath. He was useful to men, but why should these young horses torment him?

4

He was old, they were young; he was lean, they were fat; he was sad, they were happy. So he was thoroughly strange, alien, an absolutely different creature; and it was impossible for them to have compassion on him. Horses have pity only on themselves, and only occasionally on those in whose skin they may easily imagine themselves. But, indeed, was not the piebald gelding himself to blame, in that he was old and gaunt and ugly? . . .

One would think that he was not to blame. But in equine ethics he was, and only those were right who were strong, young, and happy; those who had all life before them; those whose every muscle was tense with superfluous energy, and who curled their tails up into the air.

Maybe the piebald gelding himself understood this, and in tranquil moments was agreed that he was to blame because he had lived out all his life, that he must pay for his life; but he was after all only a horse, and he could not restrain himself often from feeling hurt, melancholy, and discontented, when he looked on all these young horses who tormented him for the very thing to which they would be subjected when they came to the end of their lives.

The reason for the heartlessness of these horses was a peculiarly aristocratic feeling. Every one of them was related, either on the side of father or mother, to the celebrated Smetanka; but it was not known from what stock the piebald gelding sprang. The gelding was a chance comer, bought at the market three years before for eighty paper rubles.

The young chestnut mare, as if accidentally wandering about, came up to the piebald gelding's very nose, and brushed against him. He knew beforehand what it meant, and did not open his eyes, but laid back his ears and showed his teeth. The mare wheeled around, and made believe that she was going to let fly at him with her heels. He opened his eyes, and wandered off to another part. He had no desire as yet to go to sleep, and began to eat.

Again the wanton young mare, accompanied by her confederates, went to the gelding. A two-year-old mare with a star on her forehead, very silly, always in mischief, and always ready to imitate the chestnut mare, trotted along with her, and, as imitators always do, began to play the same trick that the instigator had done.

The brown mare would march along at an ordinary gait, apparently bent on her own affairs, and would pass by the gelding's very nose, not looking at him, so that he really did not know whether to be angry or not; and this was really ridiculous.

This was what she did now; but the starred mare, following in her steps, and feeling very gay, hit the gelding on the chest. He showed his teeth once more, whinnied, and, with a quickness of motion unexpected on his part, sprang at the mare, and bit her on the flank. The young mare with the star flew out with her hind legs, and kicked the old horse heavily on his thin bare ribs. The old horse uttered a hoarse noise, and was about to make another lunge, but thought better of it, and, sighing deeply, turned away.

It must have been that all the young horses of the drove regarded as a personal insult the boldness which the piebald gelding permitted himself to show toward the starred mare; for all the rest of the day they gave him no chance to graze, and left him not a moment of peace, so that the drover several times rebuked them, and could not comprehend what they were doing.

The gelding was so abused that he himself walked up to Nester when it was time for the old man to drive back the drove, and he showed greater happiness and content than usual when Nester saddled him and mounted him.

God knows what the old gelding's thoughts were as he bore on his back the old man Nester. Did he think with bitterness of these importunate and merciless youngsters? or, with a scornful and silent pride peculiar to old age, did he pardon his persecutors? At all events, he did not make manifest any of his thoughts till he reached home.

That evening some cronies had come to see Nester; and, as the horses were driven by the cottages of the domestics, he noticed a horse and telyega standing at his doorstep. After he had driven in the horses, he was in such haste that he did not take the saddle off; he left the gelding in the yard, and shouted to Vaska to unsaddle the animal, then shut the gate, and hurried to his friends.

Perhaps, owing to the affront put on the starred mare, the descendant of Smetanka, by that "low trash" bought for a horse, and not knowing father or mother, and therefore offending the aristocratic sentiment of the whole community; or because the gelding with the high saddle without a rider presented a strangely fantastic spectacle for the horses,—at all events, that night something extraordinary took place in the paddock. All the horses, young and old, showing their teeth, tagged after the gelding, and drove him from one part of the yard to the other; the trampling of their hoofs echoed around him as he sighed and drew in his thin sides.

The gelding could not longer endure this, could not longer avoid their kicks. He halted in the middle of the paddock; his face expressed the repulsive, weak anger of helpless old age, and despair besides. He laid back his ears, and suddenly something happened that caused all the horses suddenly to become quiet. A very old mare, Viazopurikha, came up and sniffed the gelding, and sighed. The gelding also sighed. . . .

5

In the middle of the paddock, flooded with the moonlight, stood the tall, gaunt figure of the gelding, still wearing the high saddle with its prominent pommel. The horses, motionless and in deep silence, stood around him, as if they were learning something new and extraordinary from him. And, indeed, something new and extraordinary they learned from him.

This is what they learned from him. . . .

FIRST NIGHT

Yes, I was sired by Liubezni I. Baba was my dam. According to the genealogy my name is Muzhik I. Muzhik I., I am according to my pedigree; but generally I am known as Kholstomer, on account of a long and glorious gallop, the like of which never took place in Russia. In lineage no horse in the world stands higher than I, for good blood. I would never have told you this. Why should I? You would never have known me, for not even Viazopurikha knew me, though she and I used to be together at Khrenovo, and it is only just now that she recognized me. You would not have believed me had it not been for Viazopurikha's witness, and I should never have told you this. I do not need the pity of my kind. But you insisted upon it. Well, I am that Kholstomer whom the amateurs are seeking for and cannot find, that Kholstomer whom the count himself named, and whom he let go from his stud because I outran his favorite "Lebedi." . . .

When I was born I did not know what they meant when they called me a piebald: I thought that I was a horse. The first remark made about my hide, I remember, deeply surprised me and my dam.

I must have been foaled in the night. In the morning, licked clean by my dam's tongue, I stood on my legs. I remember I kept wanting something, and that everything seemed to me perfectly wonderful, and, at the same time, perfectly simple. Our stalls were in a long, warm corridor, with latticed gates, through which everything could be seen.

My dam tempted me to suckle; but I was so innocent as yet that I bunted her with my nose, now under her fore legs, now under her udder. Suddenly my dam gazed at the latticed gate, and, throwing her leg over me, stepped to one side. The groom on duty was looking in at us through the lattice.

"See, Baba has foaled!" he exclaimed, and began to draw the bolt. He came in over the staw bed, and took me up in his arms. "Come and look, Taras!" he cried; "see what a piebald colt, a perfect magpie!"

I tore myself away from him, and fell on my knees.

"See, a perfect little devil!" he said.

My dam became disquieted; but she did not take my part, and merely drew a long, long breath, and stepped to one side. The grooms came, and began to look at me. One ran to tell the equerry.

All laughed as they looked at my spotting, and gave me various odd names. I did not understand these names, nor did my dam either. Up to that time in all my family there had never been a single piebald known. We had no idea that there was anything disgraceful in it. And then all extolled my structure and strength.

"See what a lively one!" said the hostler. "You can't hold him."

In a little while came the equerry, and began to marvel at my coloring. He also seemed disgusted.

"What a nasty beast!" he cried. "The general will not keep him in the stud. Ekh! Baba, you have caused me much trouble," he said, addressing my dam. "You ought to have foaled a colt with a star, but this is completely piebald."

My dam made no reply, and, as always in such circumstances, merely sighed again.

"What kind of a devil was his sire? A regular muzhik!" he went on to say. "It is impossible to keep him in the stud; it's a shame! But we'll see, we'll see," said he; and all said the same as they looked at me.

After a few days the general himself came. He took a look at me, and again all seemed horror-struck, and scolded me and my mother also on account of my hide. "But we'll see, we'll see," said every one, as soon as they caught sight of me.

Until spring we young colts lived in separate stalls with our dams; only occasionally, when the snow on the roof of the sheds began to melt in the sun, they would let us out into the wide yard, spread with fresh straw. There for the first time I became acquainted with all my kin, near and remote. There I saw how from different doors issued all the famous mares of that time with their colts. There was the old Holland mare, Mushka, sired by Smetanka, Krasnukha, the saddle-horse Dobrokhotikha, all celebrities at that time. All, gathered together there with their colts, walked up and down in the sunshine, rolled over on the fresh straw, and sniffed of each other like ordinary horses.

I cannot even now forget the sight of that paddock, full of the beauties of that day. It may seem strange to you to think of me as ever having been young and frisky, but I used to be. This very same Viazopurikha was there then, a yearling, whose mane had just been cut,—a kind, jolly, frolicsome little horse. But let it not be taken as unkindly meant when I say that, though she is now considered a rarity among you on account of her pedigree, then she was only one of the meanest horses of that stud. She herself will corroborate this.

Though my piebald coat displeased the men, it was exceedingly attractive to all the horses. They all came round me, expressing their delight, and frisking with me. I even began to forget the words of the men about my hide, and felt happy. But I soon experienced the first sorrow of my life, and the cause of it was my dam. As soon as it began to thaw, and the swallows chirped under the eaves, and the spring made itself felt more and more in the air, my dam began to change in her behavior toward me.

Her whole nature was transformed. Suddenly, without any reason, she began to frisk, galloping around the yard, which certainly did not accord with her dignified growth; then she would pause and consider, and begin to whinny; then she would bite and kick her sister mares; then she began to smell of me, and neigh with dissatisfaction, then, trotting out into the sun she would lay her head across the shoulder of my two-year-old sister Kupchika, and long and earnestly scratch her back, and push me away from nursing her. One time the equerry came, commanded the halter to be put on her, and they led her out of the paddock. She whinnied; I replied to her, and darted after her, but she would not even look at me. The groom Taras seized me in both arms, just as they shut the door on my mother's retreating form.

I struggled, threw the groom on the straw; but the door was closed, and I only heard my mother's whinnying growing fainter and fainter. And in this whinnying I perceived that she called not for me, but I perceived a very different expression. In reply to her voice, there was heard in the distance a mighty voice, as I afterward learned, the voice of Dobrui I., who, with two grooms in attendance, was about to be united once more with my dam.

I don't remember how Taras got out of my stall; it was too grievous for me. I felt that I had forever lost my mother's love, and wholly because I was a piebald, I said to myself, remembering what the people said of my hide; and such passionate anger came over me, that I began to pound the sides of the stall with my head and feet, and I pounded them until the sweat poured from me, and I could not stand up from exhaustion.

After some time my dame returned to me. I heard her as she came along the corridor in a prancing trot, wholly unusual to her, and entered our stall. The door was opened for her. I did not recognize her, so much younger and handsomer had she grown. She snuffed at me, neighed, and began to snort. But in her whole expression I could see that she did not love me.

She told me about the beauty of Dobrui and her love for him. These meetings continued, and the relations between my dam and me kept growing cooler and cooler.

Soon they led us to pasture. I now began to experience new pleasures which consoled me for the loss of my mother's love. I had friends and companions. We learned together to eat grass, to neigh like the old horses, and to lift our tails and gallop in wide circles around our dams. This was a happy time. Everything was forgiven to me; all loved me and were loved by me, and looked indulgently on all that I did. This did not last long.

Very soon something terrible happened to me.

The gelding sighed deeply, deeply, and moved aside from the horses.

The dawn was already far advanced. The gates creaked. Nester came. The horses scattered. The drover straightened the saddle on the gelding's back, and drove away the horses.

6

SECOND NIGHT

As soon as the horses were driven in, they once more gathered around the piebald.

In the month of August, continued the piebald horse, I was separated from my mother, and I did not experience any unusual grief. I saw that she was already suckling a small brother—the famous Usan—and I was no longer what I had been before. I was not jealous, but I felt that I had become more than ever cool toward her. Besides, I knew that on leaving my mother I should be transferred to the general division of young horses, where we were stalled in twos and threes, and every day the whole herd went out to exercise.

I was in one stall with Milui. Milui was a saddle-horse, and afterward the emperor himself used to ride him, and he was represented in pictures and statuary. At that time he was a mere colt, with a shiny soft coat, a swanlike neck, and slender, straight legs. He was always lively, good-natured, and lovable; was always ready to frisk, and be caressed, and sport with either horse or man. He and I could not help being good friends, living together as we did; and our friendship lasted all the days of our youth. He was gay, and inclined to be giddy. Even then he began to feel the tender passion to disport with the fillies, and he used to make sport of my guilelessness. To my unhappiness, I myself, out of egotism, tried to follow his example, and very soon was in love. And this early inclination of mine was the cause, in great measure, of my fate. It happened that I was enamored. . . . Viazopurikha was older than I by a year; she and I were good friends, but toward the end of autumn I noticed that she began to avoid me. . . .

But I am not going to relate all the story of my unhappy first love; she herself remembers my senseless passion, which ended for me in the most important change in my life.

The hostlers came along, drove her away, and pounded me. In the evening they led me into a special stall. I whinnied the whole night long, as if with a presentiment of what was coming on the morrow.

In the morning the general, the equerry, the under grooms, and the hostlers came into the corridor where my stall was, and set up a terrible screaming. The general screamed to the head groom; the groom justified himself, saying that he had not given orders to send me away, but that the under groom had done it of their own free will. The general said that it had spoiled everything, but that it was impossible to keep young stallions. The head groom replied that he would have it attended to. They calmed down and went out. I did not understand it at all, but I perceived that something concerning me was under consideration. . . .

On the next day I had ceased forever to whinny; I became what I am now. All the light of my eyes was quenched. Nothing seemed sweet to me; I became self-absorbed, and began to be pensive. At first I felt indifferent to everything. I ceased even to eat, to drink, and to run; and all thought of sprightly sport was gone. Then it nevermore came into my mind to kick up my heels, to roll over, to whinny, without bringing up the terrible question, "Why? for what purpose?" And my vigor died away.

Once they led me out at eventide, at the time when they were driving the stud home from the field. From afar I saw already the cloud of dust in which could be barely distinguished the familiar lineaments of all of our dams. I heard the cheerful snorting, and the trampling of hoofs. I stopped short, though the halter-rope by which the groom held me cut my neck; and I gazed at the approaching drove as one gazes at a happiness which is lost forever and will never return again. They drew near, and my eyes fell upon forms so well known to me,—beautiful, grand, plump, full of life every one. Who among them all deigned to glance at me? I did not feel the pain which the groom in pulling the rope inflicted. I forgot myself, and involuntarily tried to whinny as of yore, and to gallop off; but my whinnying sounded melancholy, ridiculous, and unbecoming. Not one in the stud made sport of me, but I noticed that many of them from politeness turned away from me.

It was evident that in their eyes I was despicable and pitiable, and worst of all, ridiculous. My slender, weakly neck, my big head,—I had become thin, —my long, thick legs, and the awkward gait that I struck up, in my old fashion, around the groom, all must have seemed absurd to them. No one heeded my attempted whinnying, all turned away from me.

Suddenly I comprehended it all, comprehended how I was forever sundered from them, every one; and I know not how I stumbled home behind the groom.

I had already shown a tendency toward gravity and thoughtfulness; but now a decided change came over me. My spotted coat, which occasioned such a strange prejudice in men, my terrible and unexpected misfortune, and, moreover, my peculiarly isolated position in the stud—which I felt, but could never explain to myself—compelled me to turn my thoughts inward on myself. I pondered on the disgust that people showed when they berated me for being a piebald; I pondered on the inconstancy of maternal and of female affection in general, and its dependence on physical conditions; and, above all, I pondered on the characteristics of that strange race of mortals with whom we are so closely bound, and whom we call men,—those characteristics which were the source of the peculiarity of my position in the stud, felt by me but incomprehensible.

The significance of this peculiarity, and of the human characteristics on which it was based, was discovered to me by the following incident:—

It was winter, at Christmas-tide. All day long no fodder had been given to me, nor had I been led out to water. I afterward learned that this arose from our groom being drunk. On this day the equerry came to me, saw that I had no food, and began to use hard language about the missing groom, and went away.

On the next day, the groom with his mates came out to our stalls to give us some hay. I noticed that he was especially pale and depressed, and in the expression of his long back there was a something significant and demanding sympathy.

He angrily flung the hay behind the grating. I laid my head over his shoulder; but he struck me such a hard blow with his fist on the nose, that I started back. Then he kicked me in the belly with his boots.

"If it hadn't been for this scurvy beast," said he, "there wouldn't have been any trouble."

"Why?" asked another groom.

"Mind you, he doesn't come to inquire about the count's! But twice a day he comes out to look after his own."

"Have they given him the piebald?" inquired another.

"Whether they've given it to him or sold it to him, the dog only knows! The count's might all die o' starvation—it wouldn't make any difference; but see how it upset him when I didn't give *his* horse his fodder! 'Lie down!' says he, and then such a basting I got! No Christianity in it. More pity on the cattle than on a man. I don't believe he's ever been christened; he himself counted the blows, the barbarian! The general did not use the whip so. He made my back all welts. There's no soul of a Christian in him!"

Now, what they said about whips and Christianity, I understood well enough; but it was perfectly dark to me as to the meaning of the words, *my* horse, *his* horse, by which I perceived that men understood some sort of bond between me and the groom. Wherein consisted this bond, I could not then understand at all. Only long afterward, when I was separated from the other horses, I came to learn what it meant. At that time I could not understand at all that it meant that they considered *me* the property of a man. To say *my* horse in reference to me, a live horse, seemed to me as strange as to say, *my earth, my atmosphere, my water.*

But these words had a monstrous influence on me. I pondered on them ceaselessly; and only after long and varied relations with men did I come at last to comprehend the meaning that men find in these strange words.

The meaning is this: Men rule in life, not by deeds, but by words. They love not so much the possibility of doing or not doing anything, as the possibility of talking about different objects in words agreed on between them. Such words, considered very important among them, are the words, *my, mine, ours,* which they employ for various things, beings, and objects; even for the earth, people, and horses. In regard to any particular thing, they agree that only one person shall say, "It is *mine.*"

And he who in this play, which they engage in, can say *mine* in regard to the greatest number of things, is considered the most fortunate among them. Why this is so, I know not; but it is so. Long before, I had tried to explain this to my satisfaction, by some direct advantage; but it seemed that I was wrong.

Many of the men who, for instance, called me their horse, did not ride on me, but entirely different men rode on me. They themselves did not feed me, but entirely different people fed me. Again, it was not those who called me their horse who treated me kindly, but the coachman, the veterinary, and, as a general thing, outside men.

Afterward, as I widened the sphere of my experiences, I became convinced that the concept *my,* as applied not only to us horses, but to other things, has no other foundation than a low and animal, a human instinct, which they call the sentiment or right of property. Man says, *my house,* and never lives in it, but is only cumbered with the building and maintenance of it. The merchant says, *my shop,*—my clothing-shop, for example,—and he does not even wear clothes made of the best cloth in his shop.

There are people who call land theirs, and have never seen their land, and have never been on it. There are men who call other people theirs, but have never seen these people; and the whole relationship of these owners, to these people, consists in doing them harm.

There are men who call women theirs,—their wives or mistresses; but these women live with other men. And men struggle in life not to do what they consider good, but to call as many things as possible their own.

I am convinced now that herein lies the substantial difference between men and us. And, therefore, not speaking of other things where we are superior to men, we are able boldly to say that in this one respect at least we stand, in the scale of living beings, higher than men. The activity of men—at all events, of those with whom I have had to do—is guided by words; ours, by deeds.

And here the equerry obtained this right to say about me, *my horse;* and hence he lashed the hostler. This discovery deeply disturbed me; and these thoughts and opinions which my variegated coat aroused in men, and the thoughtfulness aroused in me by the change in my dam, together subserved to make me into that solemn and contemplative gelding that I am.

I was threefold unhappy: I was piebald; I was a gelding; and men imagined that I did not belong to God and myself, as is the prerogative of every living thing, but that I belonged to the equerry.

The consequences of their imagining this about me were many. The first was that they kept me apart from the others, fed me better, led me with a thong more frequently, and harnessed me up earlier. They harnessed me first when I was in my third year. I remember the first time; the equerry himself, who imagined that I was his, began, with a crowd of grooms, to harness me, expecting from me some ebullition of temper or contrariness. They put leather straps on me, and conducted me into the stalls. They laid on my back a wide leather cross, and attached it to the thills, so that I should not kick; but I was only waiting an opportunity to show my gait, and my love for work.

They marveled because I went like an old horse. They began to drive me, and I began to practise trotting. Every day I had greater and greater success, so that in three months the general himself, and many others, praised my gait. But this was a strange thing: for the very reason that they imagined that I was the equerry's, and not theirs, my gait had for them an entirely different significance.

The stallions, my brothers, were put through their paces; their time was reckoned; people came to see them; they were driven in gilded drozhskies. Costly saddles were put upon them. But I was driven in the equerry's simple drozhskies, when he had business at Chesmenko and other manor-houses. All this resulted from the fact that I was piebald, but more than all from the fact that I was, according to their idea, not the property of the count, but of the equerry.

To-morrow, if we are alive, I will tell you what a serious influence on me was exercised by this right of proprietorship which the equerry arrogated to himself.

All that day the horses treated Kholstomer with great consideration. But Nester's behavior toward him was as rough as ever. The muzhik's gray stallion, coming toward the drove, whinnied; and again the chestnut filly coquettishly replied to him.

7

THIRD NIGHT

The new moon was in the sky, and her narrow sickle poured a mild light on Kholstomer, standing in the middle of the yard; the horses had clustered around him.

The principal and most surprising consequence to me of the fact that I was not the count's property nor God's, but was the equerry's," continued the piebald, "was that what constitutes our chief activity—the mettlesome race—was made the cause of my banishment. They were driving Lebedi around the ring; and a jockey from Chesmenko was riding me, and entered the course. Lebedi dashed past us. He trotted well, but he seemed to want to show off. He had not that skill which I had cultivated in myself; that is, of compelling one leg instantly to follow on the motion of the other, and not to waste the least degree of energy, but use it all in pressing forward. Lebedi dashed by us. I dashed into the ring; the jockey did not hold me back.

"Say, will you time my piebald?' he cried; and, when Lebedi came abreast of us a second time, he let me out. Lebedi had the advantage of his momentum, and so I was left behind in the first heat; but in the second I began to gain on him; came up to him,—he was in a drozhsky,—caught up with him, passed beyond him, and won the race. They tried it a second time—the same thing. I was the swifter. And this filled them all with dismay. The general begged them to send me away as soon as possible, so that I might not be heard of again. "Otherwise the count will know about it, and there will be trouble,' said he. And they sent me to the horse-dealer. I did not remain there long. A hussar, who came along to get a remount, bought me. All this had been so unfair, so cruel, that I was glad when they took me from Khrenovaya, and forever separated me from all that had been near and dear to me. It was too hard for me among them. Before *them* stood love, honor, freedom; before me labor, humiliation,—humiliation, labor, to the end of my days. Why? Because I was piebald, and because I was compelled to be somebody's horse. . . ."

Kholstomer could not tell any more of his story that evening. In the paddock an event took place which filled all the horses with dismay. Kupchikha, a mare who had been overlong with foal and had at first been listening to Kholstomer's story, got up and went slowly over to the shelter of the shed, and there began to scream so piercingly that she attracted the attention of all the horses; then she lay down, then she got up again, then she lay down again. The old dams all understood what was her trouble, but the younger horses became greatly excited, and, leaving the gelding by himself, they went and stood around her.

By morning there was a new colt born, and it stood unsteadily on its legs. Nester shouted to the groom, and they took the dam and her little one to the stall, and separated them from the other horses.

8

FOURTH NIGHT

The next evening, when the gates were closed and all was still, the piebald continued thus:—

I had many experiences, both among men and among my own kind, while changing about from hand to hand. I stayed with two masters the longest: with a prince, an officer of hussars, and then with an old man who lived at Nikola Yavlennui Church.

I spent the happiest days of my life with the hussar.

Though he was the cause of my destruction, though he loved nothing and nobody, yet I loved him, and still love him, for this very reason.

He pleased me precisely because he was handsome, fortunate, rich, and therefore loved no one.

You understand this lofty equine sentiment of ours. His coldness, and my dependence on him, added greatly to the strength of my affection for him. "Beat me, drive me to death," I used to think in those happy days; "for that very reason I shall be all the happier."

He bought me of the horse-dealer to whom the equerry had sold me, for eight hundred rubles. He bought me because there was no demand for piebald horses. Those were my happiest days.

He had a mistress. I knew it because every day I took him to her; and I took her out driving, and sometimes took them together.

His mistress was a handsome woman, and he was handsome, and his coachman was handsome; and I loved them all because they were. And life was worth living then.

This is the way my life was spent: In the morning the groom came to rub me down,—not the coachman, but the groom. The groom was a young lad, taken from among the muzhiks. He would open the door, let the wind drive out the steam from the horses, shovel out the manure, take off the blanket, begin to flourish the brush over my body, and with the currycomb to brush out the rolls of sweaty hair on the floor of the stall, marked by the stamping of hoofs. I would make believe bite his sleeves, would push him with my leg.

Then we were led out, one after the other, to drink from a tub of cold water; and the youngster admired my sleek, spotted coat, which he had polished, my legs straight as an arrow, my broad hoofs, my glossy flank, and back wide enough to sleep on. Then he would throw the hay behind the broad rack, and pour the oats into the oaken cribs. Then Feofan and the old coachman would come.

The master and the coachman were alike. Neither the one nor the other feared any one or loved any one except themselves, and therefore everybody loved them. Feofan came in a red shirt, plush breeches, and coat. I used to like to hear him when, all pomaded for a holiday, he would come to the stable in his coat, and cry,—

"Well, you beast, are you asleep?" and poke me in the loin with the handle of his fork; but never so as to hurt, only in fun. I could instantly take a joke, and I would lay back my ears and show my teeth.

We had a chestnut stallion which belonged to a pair. Sometimes at night they would harness us together. This Polkan could not understand a joke, and was simply ugly as the devil. I used to stand in the next stall to him, and seriously quarrel. Feofan was not afraid of him. He used to go straight up to him, shout to him,—it seemed as if he were going to kick him,—but no, straight by, and put on the halter.

Once we ran away together, in a pair, down over the Kuznetskoye. Neither the master nor the coachman was frightened; they laughed, they shouted to the people, and they sawed on the reins and pulled up, and so I did not run over anybody.

In their service I wasted my best qualities, and half of my life. There they gave me too much water to drink, and spoilt my legs. . . .

But, in spite of everything, that was the best part of my life. At twelve o'clock they would come, harness me, oil my hoofs, moisten my forelock and mane, and put me between the thills.

The sledge was of cane, plaited, upholstered in velvet. The harness had little silver buckles, the reins were of silk, and once I wore a fly-net. The whole harness was such that, when all the straps and belts were put on and drawn, it was impossible to make out where the harness ended and the horse began. They would finish harnessing in the shed. Feofan would come out, his middle wider that his shoulders, with his red girdle up under his arms. He would inspect the harness, take his seat, straighten his kaftan, put his foot in the stirrup, get off some joke, always crack his whip, though he scarcely ever touched me with it,—merely for form's sake,—and cry, "Now off with you!" And, frisking at every step, I would prance out of the gate; and the cook, coming out to empty her dishwater, would pause in the road; and the muzhik, bringing in his firewood, would open his eyes. We would drive up and down, occasionally stopping. The lackeys come out, the coachmen drive up. And conversation would not flag. Always kept waiting. Sometimes for three hours we were kept at the door; occasionally we take a turn around, and talk awhile, and again we would halt.

At last there would be a tumult in the hallway; out would come the gray-haired Tikhon, with his paunch, in his dress-coat—"Drive on"; then there was none of that feeble way of saying, "Go ahead," as if I did not know that we were going forward and not backward. Feofan would cluck and drive up to the door, and the prince would come out quickly, unconcernedly, as if there was nothing wonderful either in this sledge or the horses, or Feofan himself, as he bends his back and holds out his hands in such a way that it would seem impossible to keep it up long.

The prince comes out in his shako and cloak, with a gray beaver collar concealing his ruddy face, with its black brows, a handsome face, which ought never to be covered. He would come out with clanking saber, jingling spurs, and copper-heeled boots; stepping over the carpet apparently in a hurry, and not paying any heed to me or to Feofan, whom everybody except himself looked at and admired.

Feofan clucks. I tug at the reins, and with a respectable rapid trot we are off and away. I glance round at the prince, and toss my aristocratic head and delicate topknot. . . .

The prince is in good spirits; he sometimes jests with Feofan. Feofan replies, half turning round to the prince his handsome face, and, not dropping his hands, makes an almost imperceptible motion with the reins which I understand: and on, on, on, with ever wider and wider strides, straining every muscle, and sending the muddy snow over the dasher, off I go! Then there was none of the absurd way that obtains to-day of crying "Oh!" as if the coachman were in pain, and couldn't speak. "G'long! Look out there! G'long! Look out there," shouts Feofan; and the people clear the way, and stand craning their necks to see the handsome gelding, the handsome coachman, and the handsome barin. . . .

I loved specially to outstrip some racer. When Feofan and I would see in the distance some team worthy of our mettle, flying like a whirlwind, we would gradually come nearer and nearer to him. And soon, tossing the mud over the dasher, I would be even with the passenger, and would snort over his head, then even with the saddle, with the bell-bow; then I would already see him and hear him behind me, gradually getting farther and farther away. But the prince and Feofan and I, we all kept silent, and made believe that we were merely out for a drive, and by our actions that we did not notice those with slow horses whom we overtook on our way. I loved to race, but I loved also to meet a good racer. One wink, sound, glance, and we would be off, and would fly along, each on his own side of the road. . . .

Here the gates creaked, and the voices of Nester and Vaska were heard.

9

FIFTH NIGHT

The weather began to change. The sky was overcast; and in the morning there was no dew, but it was warm, and the flies were sticky. As soon as the herd was driven in, the horses gathered around the piebald, and thus he finished his story:—

The happy days of my life were soon ended. I lived so only two years. At the end of the second winter, there happened an event which was most delightful to me, and immediately after came my deepest sorrow. It was at Shrovetide. I took the prince to the races. Atlasnui and Buichok also ran in the race.

I don't know what they were doing in the summer-house; but I know that he came, and ordered Feofan to enter the ring. I remember they drove me into the ring, stationed me, and stationed Atlasnui. Atlasnui was in racing gear, but I was harnessed in a city sleigh. At the turning stake I left him behind. A laugh and a cry of victory greeted my achievement.

When they began to lead me around, a crowd followed after, and a man offered the prince five thousand. He only laughed, showing his white teeth.

"No," said he, "this isn't a horse, it's a friend. I wouldn't sell him for a mountain of gold. Good day, gentlemen!"

He threw open the fur robes, and got in.

"To Ostozhenko."

That was where his mistress lived. And we flew. . . .

It was our last happy day. We reached her home. He called her *his*. But she loved some one else, and had gone off with him. The prince ascertained this at her room. It was five o'clock; and, not letting me be unharnessed, he started in pursuit of her. It had never happened before; they applied the knout to me, and made me gallop. For the first time, I began to flag, and, I am ashamed to say, I wanted to rest.

But suddenly I heard the prince himself shouting in an unnatural voice, "Hurry up!" and the knout whistled and cut me; and I dashed ahead again, my leg hitting against the iron of the dasher. We overtook her, after going twenty-five versts. I got him there; but I trembled all night, and could not eat anything. In the morning they gave me water. I drank it, and forever ceased to be the horse that I had been. I was sick. They tortured me and maimed me,—treated me as men are accustomed to do. My hoofs came off. I had abscesses, and my legs grew bent. I had no strength in my chest. Laziness and weakness were everywhere apparent. I was sent to the horse-dealer. He fed me on carrots and other things, and made me something quite unlike my old self, but yet capable of deceiving one who did not know. But there was no strength and no swiftness in me.

Moreover, the horse-dealer tormented me, by coming to my stall when customers were on hand, and beginning to stir me up, and torture me with a great knout so that it drove me to madness. Then he would wipe the bloody foam off the whip, and lead me out.

An old lady bought me of the dealer. She used to keep coming to Nikola Yavlennui, and she used to whip the coachman. The coachman would come and weep in my stall. And I knew that his tears had an agreeable salt taste. Then the old woman died. Her overseer took me into the country, and sold me to a peddler; then I was fed on wheat, and grew sicker still. I was sold to a muzhik. There I had to plow, had almost nothing to eat, and I cut my leg with a plowshare. I became sick again. A gipsy got possession of me. He tortured me horribly, and at last I was sold to the overseer here. And here I am. . . .

All were silent. The rain began to fall.

10

As the herd returned home the following evening, they met the master and a guest. Zhulduiba, leading the way, cast her eyes on two men's figures: one was the young master in a straw hat; the other a tall, stout, military man with wrinkled face. The old mare gazed at the man, and swerving went near to him; the rest, the younger ones, were thrown into some confusion, huddled together, especially when the master and his guest came directly into the midst of the horses, making gestures to each other, and talking.

"Here's this one. I bought it of Voyeïkof,—the dapple-gray horse," said the master.

"And that young black mare, with the white legs,—where did you get her? Fine one," said the guest.

They examined many of the horses as they walked around, or stood on the field. They remarked also the chestnut mare. "That's one of the saddle-horses, —the breed of Khrenovsky."

They quietly gazed at all the horses as they went by. The master shouted to Nester; and the old man, hastily digging his heels into the sides of the piebald, trotted out. The piebald horse hobbled along, limping on one leg; but his gait was such that it was evident that in other circumstances he would not have complained, even if he had been compelled to go in this way, as long as his strength held out, to the world's end. He was ready even to go at full gallop, and at first even broke into one.

"I have no hesitation in saying that there isn't a better horse in Russia than that one," said the master, pointing to one of the mares. The guest corroborated this praise. The master, full of satisfaction, walked up and down, made observations, and told the story and pedigree of each of the horses.

It was apparently somewhat of a bore to the guest to listen to the master; but he devised questions to make it seem as if he were interested in it.

"Yes, yes," said he, in some confusion.

"Look," said the host, not replying to the questions, "look at those legs, look. . . . She cost me dear, but I shall have a three-year-old from her that'll go!"

"Does she trot well?" asked the guest.

Thus they scrutinized almost all the horses, and there was nothing more to show. And they were silent.

"Well, shall we go?"

"Yes, let us go."

They went out through the gate. The guest was glad that the exhibition was over, and that he was going home, where he would eat, drink, smoke, and have a good time. As they went by Nester, who was sitting on the piebald and waiting for further orders, the guest struck his big fat hand on the horse's side.

"Here's good blood," said he. "He's like the piebald horse, if you remember, that I told you about."

The master perceived that it was not of his horses that the guest was speaking; and he did not listen, but, looking around, continued to gaze at his stud.

Suddenly, at his very ear, was heard a dull, weak, senile neigh. It was the piebald horse that began to neigh, but could not finish it. Becoming, as it were, confused, he broke short off.

Neither the guest nor the master paid any attention to this neigh, but went home. Kholstomer had recognized in the wrinkled old man his beloved former master, the once brilliant, handsome, and wealthy Sierpukhovskoï.

11

The rain continued to fall. In the paddock it was gloomy, but at the manor-house it was quite the reverse. The luxurious evening meal was spread in the luxurious dining-room. At the table sat master, mistress, and the guest who had just arrived.

The mistress of the house, in a delicate condition, as any one could see by her shape, and by the way she sat, by her plumpness, and especially by her eyes, which had a sweet introspection and serious look in them, was in her place behind the samovar.

The master held in his hand a box of specially fine decennial cigars, such as no one else had, according to his story, and proceeded to offer them to the guest. The master was a handsome young man of twenty-five, fresh, neatly dressed, smoothly brushed. He was dressed in a fresh, loosely fitting suit of clothes, made in London. On his watch-chain were big expensive charms. His cuff-buttons were of gold, large, even massive, set with turquoises. His beard was à la Napoléon III.; and his mustaches were waxed, and stood out in the way that is acquired nowhere else than in Paris.

The lady wore a silk-muslin dress, brocaded with large variegated flowers; on her head, large gold hairpins in her thick auburn hair, which was beautiful, though not entirely her own. Her hands were adorned with many bracelets and rings, all expensive.

The samovar was silver, the service exquisite. The lackey, magnificent in his dress-coat and white waistcoat and necktie, stood like a statue at the door, awaiting orders. The furniture was of bent wood, and bright; the wall-papers dark with large flowers. Around the table tinkled a cunning little dog, with a silver collar bearing an extremely hard English name, which neither of them could pronounce because they knew not English.

In the corner, among the flowers, stood the pianoforte, inlaid with mother-of-pearl. Everything breathed of newness, luxury, and rarity. Everything was extremely fine; but it all bore a peculiar impress of profusion, wealth, and an absence of intellectual interests.

The master was a great lover of racing, strong and hot-headed; one of those whom one meets everywhere, who drive out in sable furs, send costly bouquets to actresses, drink the most expensive wine, of the very latest brand, at the most expensive restaurant, offer prizes in their own names, and entertain the most expensive of . . .

The newcomer, Nikita Sierpukhovskoï, was a man of forty years, tall, stout, bald, with huge mustaches and side-whiskers. He ought to have been very handsome; but it was evident that he had wasted his forces—physical and moral and pecuniary.

He was so deeply in debt that he was obliged to go into the service so as to escape the sponging-house. He had now come to the government city as chief of the imperial stud. His influential relations had obtained this for him.

He was dressed in an army kittel and blue trousers. His kittel and trousers were such as only those who are rich can afford to wear; so with his linen also. His watch was English. His boots had peculiar soles, as thick as a finger.

Nikita Sierpukhovskoï had squandered a fortune of two millions, and was still in debt to the amount of one hundred and twenty thousand rubles. From such a course there always remains a certain momentum of life, giving credit, and the possibility of living almost luxuriously for another ten years.

The ten years had already passed, and the momentum was finished; and it had become hard for him to live. He had already begun to drink too much; that is, to get fuddled with wine, which had never been the case with him before. Properly speaking, he had never begun and never finished drinking.

More noticeable in him than all else was the restlessness of his eyes (they had begun to wander), and the uncertainty of his intonations and motions. This restlessness was surprising, from the fact that it was evidently a new thing in him, because it could be seen that he had been accustomed, all his life long, to fear nothing and nobody, and that now he endured severe sufferings from some dread which was thoroughly alien to his nature.

The host and hostess remarked this, exchanged glances, showing that they understood each other, postponed until they should get to bed the consideration of this subject, and, evidently, merely endured poor Sierpukhovskoï.

The sight of the young master's happiness humiliated Nikita, and compelled him to painful envy, as he remembered his own irrevocable past.

"You don't object to cigars, Marie?" he asked, addressing the lady in that peculiar tone, acquired only by practice, full of urbanity and friendliness, but not wholly satisfactory,—such as men who know the world use addressing women who are mistresses rather than wives. Not that he could have wished to insult her; on the contrary, he was much more anxious to gain her good-will and that of the host, though he would not for anything have acknowledged it to himself. But he had long been used to talking thus with such women. He knew that she would have been astonished, even affronted, if he had behaved to her as toward a lady. Moreover, it was necessary for him to preserve that peculiar shade of deference for the acknowledged wife of his friend. He treated such women always with consideration, not because he shared those so-called convictions that are promulgated in newspapers (he never read such trash), about esteem as the prerogative of every man, about the absurdity of marriage, etc., but because all well-bred men act thus, and he was a well-bred man, though inclined to drink.

He took a cigar. But his host awkwardly seized a handful of cigars, and placed them before the guest.

"No, just see how good these are! try them."

Nikita pushed away the cigars with his hand, and in his eyes flashed something like resentment and shame.

"Thanks,"—he took out his cigar-case,—"try mine."

The lady had tact. She perceived how it affected him. She began hastily to talk with him.

"I am very fond of cigars. I should smoke myself if everybody about me did not smoke."

And she gave him one of her bright, kindly smiles. He half smiled in reply. Two of his teeth were gone.

"No, take this," continued the host, who had not tact. "Those others are not so strong. *Fritz, bringen Sie noch eine Kasten,*" he said, "*dort zwei.*"

The German lackey brought another box.

"Do you like these larger ones? They are stronger. This is a very good kind. Take them all," he added, continuing to force them upon his guest.

He was evidently glad that there was some one on whom he could lavish his rarities, and he saw nothing out of the way in it. Sierpukhovskoï began to smoke, and hastened to take up the subject that had been dropped.

"How much did you have to go on Atlasnui?" he asked.

"He cost me dear,—not less than five thousand, but at all events I am secured. Plenty of colts, I tell you!"

"Do they trot?" inquired Sierpukhovskoï.

"First-rate. To-day Atlasnui's colt took three prizes: one at Tula, one at Moscow, and one at Petersburg. He raced with Voyeïkof's Voronui. The rascally jockey made four abatements, and almost put him out of the race."

"He was rather raw; too much Dutch stock in him, I should say," said Sierpukhovskoï.

"Well, but the mares are finer ones. I will show you to-morrow. I paid three thousand for Dobruina, two thousand for Laskovaya."

And again the host began to enumerate his wealth. The mistress saw that this was hard for Sierpukhovskoï, and that he only pretended to listen.

"Won't you have some more tea?" asked the hostess.

"I don't care for any more," said the host, and he went on with his story. She got up; the host detained her, took her in his arms, and kissed her.

Sierpukhovskoï smiled at first, as he looked at them, but his smile seemed to them unnatural; but when his host got up, and threw his arms around her, and went out with her as far as the *portière*, his face suddenly changed; he sighed deeply, and an expression of despair took possession of his wrinkled face. There was also wrath in it.

The host returned, and smiled as he sat down opposite Nikita. Neither of them spoke.

12

"Yes, you said that you bought him of Voyeïkof," said Sierpukhovskoï, with assumed indifference.

"Oh, yes! I was speaking of Atlasnui. I had a great mind to buy the mares of Dubovitsky. Nothing but rubbish was left."

"He was *burned* out," said Sierpukhovskoï, and suddenly stood up and looked around. He remembered that he owed this ruined man twenty thousand rubles, and that, if *burned* out were said of any one, it might by good rights be said about himself. He began to laugh.

Both preserved a long silence. The host was revolving in his mind how he might boast a little before his guest. Sierpukhovskoï was cogitating how he might show that he did not consider himself burned out. But the thoughts of both moved with difficulty, in spite of the fact that they tried to enliven themselves with cigars.

"Well, when shall we have something to drink, I wonder?" said Sierpukhovskoï to himself.

"At all events, we must have something to drink, else I shall die of the blues with him," said the host to himself.

"How is it? are you going to stay here long?" asked Sierpukhovskoï.

"About a month longer. Shall we have a little lunch? What say you? Fritz, is everything ready?"

They went back to the dining-room. There, under a hanging lamp, stood the table loaded with candles and very extraordinary things: siphons, and bottles with fancy stoppers, extraordinary wine in decanters, extraordinary liqueurs and vodka. They drank, sat down, drank again, sat down, and tried to talk. Sierpukhovskoï grew flushed, and began to speak unreservedly.

They talked about women: who kept such and such an one; the gipsy, the ballet-girl, the *soubrette*.[1]

"Why, you left Mathieu, didn't you?" asked the host.

This was the mistress who had caused Sierpukhovskoï's ruin.

"No, she left me. Oh, brother, how one remembers what one has squandered in life! Now I am glad, fact, when I get a thousand rubles; glad, fact, when I get out of everybody's way. I cannot in Moscow. Ah! what's to be said!"

The host was bored to listen to Sierpukhovskoï. He wanted to talk about himself,—to brag. But Sierpukhovskoï also wanted to talk about himself,—about his brilliant past. The host poured out some more wine, and waited till he had finished, so as to tell him about his affairs,—how he was going to arrange his stud as no one ever had before; and how Marie loved him, not for his money, but for himself.

"I was going to tell you that in my stud . . ." he began. But Sierpukhovskoï interrupted him.

"There was a time, I may say," he began, "when I loved, and knew how to live. You were talking just now about racing; please tell me what is your best racer."

The host was glad of the chance to tell some more about his stud, but Sierpukhovskoï again interrupted him.

[1] *Frantsuzhenka*, the little Frenchwoman.

"Yes, yes," said he. "But the trouble with you breeders is that you do it only for ostentation, and not for pleasure, for life. It wasn't so with me. I was telling you this very day that I used to have a piebald racer, with just such spots as I saw among your colts. Oh! what a horse he was! You can't imagine it; this was in '42. I had just come to Moscow. I went to a dealer, and saw a piebald gelding. All in best form. He pleased me. Price? Thousand rubles. He pleased me. I took him, and began to ride him. I never had, and you never had, and never will have, such a horse. I never knew a better horse, either for gait, or strength, or beauty. You were a lad then. You could not have known, but you may have heard, I suppose. All Moscow knew him."

"Yes, I heard about him," said the host, reluctantly. "But I was going to tell you about my . . ."

"So you heard about him. I bought him just as he was, without pedigree, without proof; but then I knew Voyeïkof, and I traced him. He was sired by Liubeznuï I. He was called Kholstomer.[2] He'd measure linen for you! On account of his spotting, he was given to the equerry at the Khrenovski stud; and he had him gelded and sold him to the dealer. There aren't horses like him any more, friend! Ah! what a time that was! Ah! vanished youth!" he said, quoting the words of a gipsy song. He began to get wild. "Eh! that was a golden time! I was twenty-five. I had eighty thousand a year income; then I hadn't a gray hair; all my teeth like pearls. . . . Whatever I undertook prospered. And yet all came to an end." . . .

"Well, you didn't have such lively races then," said the host, taking advantage of the interruption. "I tell you that my first horses began to run without . . ."

"Your horses! Horses were more mettlesome then . . ."

"How more mettlesome?"

"Yes, more mettlesome. I remember how one time I was at Moscow at the races. None of my horses were in it. I did not care for racing; but I had blooded horses, General Chaulet, Mahomet. I had my piebald with me. My coachman was a splendid young fellow. I liked him. But he was rather given to drink, so I drove. 'Sierpukhovskoï,' said they, 'when are you going to get some trotters?' —'I don't care for your low-bred beasts, the devil take 'em! I have a hack-driver's piebald that's worth all of yours.'—'Yes, but he doesn't race.'— 'I'll bet you a thousand rubles.' They took me up. He went round in five seconds, won the wager of a thousand rubles. But that was nothing. With my blooded horses I went in a troïka a hundred versts in three hours. All Moscow knew about it."

And Sierpukhovskoï began to brag so fluently and steadily that the host could not get in a word, and sat facing him with dejected countenance. Only, by way of diversion, he would fill up his glass and that of his companion.

It began already to grow light, but still they sat there. It became painfully tiresome to the host. He got up.

"Sleep,—let's go to sleep, then," said Sierpukhovskoï, as he got up, and went staggering and puffing to the room that had been assigned to him.

The master of the house rejoined his mistress.

[2] *Kholstomer* means a cloth-measurer; suggesting the greatest distance from finger to finger of the outstretched arms, and rapidity in accomplishing the motion.

"Oh, he's unendurable. He got drunk, and lied faster than he could talk."

"And he made love to me, too."

"I fear that he's going to beg some money of me."

Sierpukhovskoï threw himself on the bed without undressing, and drew a long breath.

"I must have talked a good deal of nonsense," he thought. "Well, it's all the same. Good wine, but he's a big hog. Something cheap about him. And I am a great hog myself," he remarked, and laughed aloud. "Well, I used to support others; now it's my turn. Perhaps the Winkler girl will help me. I'll borrow some money of her. He may come to it. I suppose I've got to undress. Can't get my boot off. Hey, hey!" he cried; but the man who had been ordered to wait on him had long before gone go bed.

He sat up, took off his kittel and his vest, and somehow managed to crawl out of his trousers; but it was long before his boots would stir; with his stout belly it was hard work to stoop over. He got one off; he struggled and struggled with the other, got out of breath, and gave it up. And so with one leg in the boot he threw himself down, and began to snore, filling the whole room with the odor of wine, tobacco, and vile old age.

13

If Kholstomer remembered anything that night, it was the frolic that Vaska gave him. He threw over him a blanket, and galloped off. He was left till morning at the door of a tavern, with a muzhik's horse. They licked each other. In the morning he went back to the herd, and itched all over.

"Something makes me itch fearfully," he thought.

Five days passed. They brought a veterinary. He said cheerfully:—

"The mange. You'll have to dispose of him to the gipsies."

"Better have his throat cut; only have it done to-day."

The morning was calm and clear. The herd had gone to pasture. Kholstomer remained behind. A strange man came along, thin, dark, dirty, in a kaftan spotted with something black. This was the knacker. He took Kholstomer by the halter, and without looking at him started off. The horse followed quietly, not looking round, and, as always, dragging his legs and kicking up the straw with his hind legs.

As he went out of the gate, he turned his head toward the well; but the knacker twitched the halter, and said:

"It's not worth while."

The knacker and Vaska, who followed, proceeded to a depression behind the brick barn, and stopped, as if there was something peculiar in this most ordinary place; and the knacker, handing the halter to Vaska, took off his kaftan, rolled up his sleeves, and produced a knife and whetstone from his boot-leg.

The piebald pulled at the halter, and out of sheer *ennui* tried to bite it, but it was too far off. He sighed, and closed his eyes. His lip hung down, showing his worn yellow teeth, and he began to drowse, lulled by the sound of the knife on the stone. Only his sick and swollen leg trembled a little.

Suddenly he felt that he was grasped by the lower jaw, and that his head was lifted up. He opened his eyes. Two dogs were in front of him. One was snuffing in the direction of the knacker, the other sat looking at the gelding as if he were expecting something especially from him. The gelding looked at them, and began to rub his jaw against the hand that held him.

"Of course they want to cure me," he said; "let it come!"

And the thought had hardly passed through his mind, before they did something to his throat. It hurt him; he started back, stamped his foot, but restrained himself, and waited for what was to follow. . . . What followed, was some liquid pouring in a stream down his neck and breast. He drew a deep breath, lifting his sides. And it seemed easier, much easier, to him.

The whole burden of his life was taken from him.

He closed his eyes, and began to droop his head,—no one held it. Then his legs quivered, his whole body swayed. He was not so much terrified as he was astonished. . . .

Everything was so new. He was astonished; he tried to run ahead, up the hill, . . . but, instead of this, his legs, moving where he stood, interfered. He began to roll over on his side, and, while expecting to make a step, he fell forward, and on his left side.

The knacker waited till the death-struggle was over, drove away the dogs which were creeping nearer, and then seized the horse by the legs, turned him over on the back, and, commanding Vaska to hold his leg, began to take off the hide.

"That was a horse indeed!" said Vaska.

"If he'd been fatter, it would have been a fine hide," said the knacker.

That evening the herd passed by the hill; and those who were on the left wing saw a red object below them, and around it some dogs busily romping, and crows and hawks flying over it. One dog, with his paws on the carcass, and shaking his head, was growling over what he was tearing with his teeth. The brown filly stopped, lifted her head and neck, and long sniffed the air. It took force to drive her away.

At sunset, in a ravine of the ancient forest, in the bottom of an overgrown glade, some large-headed wolf-whelps were beside themselves with joy. There were five of them,—four about of a size, and one little one with a head bigger than his body. A lean, hairless she-wolf, her belly with hanging dugs almost touching the ground, crept out of the bushes, and sat down in front of the wolves. The wolves sat in a semicircle in front of her. She went to the smallest, and, lowering her stumpy tail, and bending her snout to the ground, made a few convulsive motions, and opening her jaws filled with teeth, she struggled, and disgorged a great piece of horse-flesh.

The larger whelps made a movement to seize it; but she restrained them with a threatening growl, and let the little one have it all.

The little one, as if in anger, seized the morsel, hiding it under him, and began to devour it. Then the she-wolf disgorged for the second, and the third, and in the same way for all five, and finally lay down in front of them to rest.

At the end of a week there lay behind the brick barn only the great skull, and two shoulder-blades; all the rest had disappeared. In the summer a muzhik who gathered up the bones carried off also the skull and shoulder-blades, and put them to use.

The dead body of Sierpukhovskoï, who had been about in the world, and had eaten and drunken, was buried long after. Neither his skin nor his flesh nor his bones were of any use.

And just as his dead body, which had been about in the world, had been a great burden to others for twenty years, so the disposal of this body became only an additional charge on men. Long it had been useless to every one, long it had been only a burden. But still the dead who bury their dead found it expedient to dress this soon-to-be-decaying, swollen body in a fine uniform, in fine boots; to place it in a fine new coffin, with new tassels on the four corners; then to place this new coffin in another, made of lead, and carry it to Moscow; and there to dig up the bones of people long buried, and then to lay away this malodorous body devoured by worms, in its new uniform and polished boots, and to cover the whole with earth.

1886

THE REPENTANT SINNER

"And he said unto Jesus, Lord, remember me when thou comest into thy kingdom.
And Jesus said unto him, Verily I say unto thee, To-day shalt thou be with me in paradise."—LUKE XXIII. 42, 43.

Once there lived on earth a man seventy years old, and he had spent his whole life in sin. And this man fell ill, and did not make confession. And when death came, at the last hour he wept, and cried:—

"Lord, forgive me as thou didst the thief on the cross."

He had barely spoken these words, when his soul left his body. And the sinner's soul turned in love to God, and believed in His mercy, and came to the gates of paradise.

And the sinner began to knock, and ask admission to the kingdom of heaven.

And he heard a voice from within the gates:—

"What manner of man knocketh at the gates of paradise? and what have been the deeds done by this man in his life?"

And the voice of the accuser replied, and rehearsed all the sinful deeds of this man. And he did not mention one good deed.

And the voice from within the gates replied:—

"Sinners cannot enter into the kingdom of heaven. Get thee hence!"

And the man said:—

"Lord, I hear thy voice; but I see not thy face, and I know not thy name."

And the voice replied:—

"I am Peter the Apostle."

And the sinner said:—

"Have pity upon me, Peter Apostle! Remember human weakness and God's mercy. Wert thou not one of Christ's disciples? and didst thou not hear from His very lips His teaching? and hast thou not seen the example of His life? And remember, when He was in sorrow, and His soul was cast down, and thrice He asked thee to watch with Him and pray, and thou didst sleep, for thy eyes were heavy, and thrice He found thee sleeping. So it was with me.

"And remember also how thou didst promise Him not to deny Him till death, and how thrice thou didst deny Him when they took Him before Caiaphas. So it was with me.

"And remember, also, how the cock crew, and thou didst go out and weep bitterly. So it is with me. It is impossible for thee not to let me in."

And the voice from within the gates of paradise was silent.

And, after waiting awhile, the sinner began again to knock, and to demand entrance into the kingdom of heaven.

And a second voice was heard within the doors; and it said:—

"Who is this man, and how did he live in the world?"

And the voice of the accuser again rehearsed all the sinner's evil deeds, and mentioned no good deeds.

And the voice from within the gates replied:—

"Get thee gone! Sinners like thee cannot live with us in paradise."

And the sinner said:—

"Lord, I hear thy voice; but I see not thy face, and I know not thy name."

And the voice replied:—

"I am David, the tsar and prophet."

And the sinner did not despair, did not depart from the gates of paradise, but began to say:—

"Have mercy upon me, Tsar David, and remember human weakness and God's mercy. God loved thee, and magnified thee before the people. Thou hadst everything,—a kingdom and glory and wealth, and wives and children; and yet thou didst see from thy roof a poor man's wife; and sin came upon thee, and thou didst take Uriah's wife, and thou didst kill him by the sword of the Ammonites. Thou, a rich man, didst take the poor man's lamb, and kill the man himself. This was exactly what I did.

"And remember next how thou didst repent, and say, *I acknowledge my sin, and am grieved because of my transgressions.* So did I also. It is impossible for thee not to forgive me."

And the voice within the gates was silent.

And after waiting a little longer, yet again the sinner knocked, and demanded entrance into the kingdom of heaven.

And a third voice was heard from behind the gates; and it said:—

"Who is this man, and how did he live in the world?"

And the voice of the accuser replied, and for the third time rehearsed the man's evil deeds, and no good ones did it mention.

And the voice sounded from behind the gates:—

"Get thee gone! Sinners cannot enter into the kingdom of heaven."

And the sinner replied:—

"I hear thy voice; but thy face I see not, and thy name I know not."

And the voice replied:—

"I am John, the beloved disciple of Christ."

And the sinner rejoiced, and said:—

"Now it is impossible not to let me in! Peter and David would admit me because they know human weakness and God's mercy. But thou wilt admit me because thou hast much love. Hast thou not written, O John, in thy book, that God is love, and that whoever doth not love knoweth not God? And didst thou not in thine old age constantly say one single word to men,—'Brothers, love one another'? How, then, canst thou hate me and reject me? Either deny thy saying, or show love unto me, and let me into the kingdom of heaven."

And the gates of paradise opened; and John received the repentant sinner, and let him come into the kingdom of heaven.

1886

A SEED AS BIG AS A HEN'S EGG

Some children once found in a cave something as large as a hen's egg, with a groove about the middle, and like a seed. A passer-by saw the children playing with it, bought it for a trifle, took it to the city, and gave it to the tsar as a curiosity.

The tsar summoned his wise men, and commanded them to decide what kind of a thing it was,—an egg, or a seed. The wise men cogitated, cogitated; they could not give an answer. The thing was lying in the window; and a hen flew in, began to peck at it, and pecked a hole in it; and all knew that it was a seed.

The wise men went to the tsar, and said:—

"This is a kernel of rye."

The tsar marveled. He commanded the wise men to find out where and when this seed grew. The wise men cogitated, cogitated; they hunted in books, but they found no explanation. They came to the tsar, and said:—

"We cannot give an answer. In our books, there is nothing written about this; we must ask the muzhiks whether some one of their elders has not heard tell of when and where such a seed was sown."

The tsar sent, and commanded a very aged muzhik to be brought before him. They found such an old man, and brought him to the tsar. The green, toothless starik came in; he walked with difficulty on two crutches.

The tsar showed him the seed, but the old man was almost blind; he judged of it, as it were, partly by looking at it, partly by fumbling it in his hands.

The tsar began to ask him questions:—

"Do you not know where such a seed grows? Have you never sown any such kind of grain in your field? Or did you never in your life purchase any such seed?"

The old man was stupid; he could barely, barely hear, barely, barely understand. He began to make reply.

"No," said he, "I never sowed any such grain in my field, and I never harvested any such, and I never bought any such. When we bought grain, all such seed was small. But," said he, "you must ask my batyushka; maybe he's heard tell where such seed grew."

So the tsar sent for the old man's father, and bade him be brought before him. The ancient old man hobbled in on one crutch. The tsar began to show him the seed. The old man could still see with his eyes. He saw very well. The tsar began to question him:—

"Do you not know, my dear old man, where this seed can have grown? Have you never sown such grain in your field? or did you never in your life purchase such seed anywhere?"

Though the old man was rather hard of hearing, still he heard better than his son.

"No," says he, "I never sowed such seed in my field, nor such did I ever harvest; nor such did I ever buy, because in my day there was not money anywhere; we all lived on grain; and when it was necessary, we went shares with one another. I don't know where such seed is grown. Though our seed was much larger and more productive than that of nowadays, still I never saw such as this. But I have heard from my batyushka that, in his day, corn grew much higher than it does now, and was fuller, and had larger kernels. You must ask him."

The tsar sent for this old man's father. And they brought the grandfather also. They brought him to the tsar. The old man came before the tsar without crutches; he walked easily, his eyes were brilliant, he heard well, and spoke understandingly.

The tsar showed the seed to the old man. The old man looked at it. The old man turned it over and over.

"It is long," said he, "since I have seen such good old-fashioned grain."

The grandfather took a bite of the seed and chewed on the fragment.

"It's the very thing," said he.

"Tell me, little grandfather, where and when this kind of seed grows? Did you never sow such grain in your field? Or did you never in your life buy any such among people?"

And the old man said:—

"Such grain as this used to grow everywhere in my day. On such grain as this I have lived all my life," says he, "and fed my people. This kind of seed I have sown, and this kind I have reaped, and this kind I have sent to mill."

And the tsar asked, saying:—

"Tell me, little grandfather, did you buy such seed anywhere? or did you sow it in your field?"

The old man laughed.

"In my time," said he, "no one had ever conceived such a sin as to buy and sell grain. And they did not know about money. There was abundance of grain for all."

And the tsar asked, saying:—

"Tell me, little grandfather, when did you sow such grain, and where was your field?"

And the grandfather said:—

"My field was God's earth. Wherever there was tillage, there was my field.

The earth was free. There was no such thing as private ownership. All men claimed was their work."

"Tell me," said the tsar, "tell me two things more: one thing, Why did such seed use to spring up, and now does not? And the second thing, Why does your grandson walk on two crutches, and your son on one crutch, but here you go with perfect ease—and your eyes are bright, and your teeth strong, and your speech plain and clear? Tell me, little grandfather, why these things are so?"

And the old man said:—

"These two things both came about because men have ceased to live by their own work—and they have begun to hanker after other people's things. We did not live so in old times; in old times we lived for God. We had our own, and did not lust after others'."

1886

THE THREE HERMITS

"But when ye pray, use not vain repetitions, as the heathen do:
for they think that they shall be heard for their much speaking.
Be ye not therefore like unto them: for your Father knoweth what
things ye have need of, before ye ask him."—MATT. VI. 6, 7.

A bishop set sail in a ship from the city of Archangelsk to Solovki.[1] In the same ship sailed some pilgrims to the saints.

The wind was propitious, the weather was clear, the sea was not rough. The pilgrims, some of whom were lying down, some lunching, some sitting in little groups, conversed together.

The bishop also came on deck and began to walk up and down on the bridge. As he approached the bow, he saw a knot of people crowded together. A little muzhik was pointing his hand at something in the sea, and talking; and the people were listening.

The bishop stood still, and looked where the little muzhik was pointing; nothing was to be seen, except the sea glittering in the sun.

The bishop came closer and began to listen. When the little muzhik saw the bishop, he took off his cap, and stopped speaking. The people also, when they saw the bishop, took off their hats, and paid their respects.

"Don't mind me, brothers," said the bishop. "I have also come to listen to what you are saying, my good friend."

"This fisherman was telling us about some hermits," said a merchant, who was bolder than the rest.

"What about the hermits?" asked the bishop, as he came to the gunwale, and sat down on a box. "Tell me too; I should like to hear. What were you pointing at?"

"Well, then, yonder's the little island just heaving in sight," said the little

---

[1] The Slovetsky Monastery, at the mouth of the Dvina River.

peasant; and he pointed toward the port side. "On that very islet, three hermits live, working out their salvation."

"Where is the little island?" asked the bishop.

"Here, look along my arm, if you please. You see that little cloud? Well, just below it to the left it shows like a streak."

The bishop looked and looked; the water gleamed in the sun, but from lack of practice he could not see anything.

"I don't see it," says he. "What sort of hermits are they who live on the little island?"

"God's people," replied the peasant. "For a long time I had heard tell of them, but I never chanced to see them until last summer."

And the fisherman again began to relate how he had been out fishing, and how he was driven to that island, and knew not where he was. In the morning he started to look around, and stumbled upon a little earthen hut; and he found in the hut one hermit, and then two others came in. They fed him, and dried him, and helped him repair his boat.

"What sort of men were they?" asked the bishop.

"One was rather small, humpbacked, very, very old; he was dressed in well-worn stole; he must have been more than a hundred years old; the gray hairs in his beard were already turning green; but he always had a smile ready, and he was as serene as an angel of heaven. The second was taller, also old, in a torn kaftan; his long beard was growing a little yellowish, but he was a strong man; he turned my boat over as if it had been a tub,—and I didn't even have to help him: he was also a jolly man. But the third was tall, with a long beard reaching to his knee, and white as the moon; but he was gloomy; his eyes glared out from under beetling brows; and he was naked, all save a plaited belt."

"What did they say to you?" asked the bishop.

"They did everything mostly without speaking, and they talked very little among themselves; one had only to look, and the other understood. I began to ask the tall one if they had lived there long. He frowned, muttered something, grew almost angry: then the little old man instantly seized him by the hand, smiled, and the large man said nothing. But the old man said, 'Excuse us,' and smiled."

While the peasant was speaking, the ship had been sailing nearer and nearer to the islands.

"There, now you can see plainly," said the merchant. "Now please look, your reverence," said he, pointing.

The bishop tried to look, and he barely managed to make out a black speck— the little island.

The bishop gazed and gazed; and he went from the bow to the stern, and he approached the helmsman.

"What is that little island," says he, "that you see over yonder?"

"As far as I know, it has no name; there are a good many of them here."

"Is it true as they say, that some monks are winning their salvation there?"

"They say so, your reverence, but I don't rightly know. Fishermen, they say, have seen them. Still, folks talk a good deal of nonsense."

"I should like to land on the little island, and see the hermits," said the bishop. "How can I manage it?"

"It is impossible to go there in the ship," said the helmsman. "You might do it in a boat, but you will have to ask the captain."

They summoned the captain.

"I should like to have a sight of those hermits," said the bishop. "Is it out of the question to take me there?"

The captain tried to dissuade him.

"It is possible, quite possible, but we should waste much time; and I take the liberty of assuring your reverence, they are not worth looking at. I have heard from people that those old men are perfectly stupid; they don't understand anything, and can't say anything, just like some sort of sea-fish."

"I wish it," said the bishop. "I will pay for the trouble, if you will take me there."

There was nothing else to be done: the sailors arranged it; they shifted sail. The helmsman put the ship about and they sailed toward the island. A chair was set for the bishop on the bow. He sat down and looked. And all the people gathered on the bow, all looked at the little island. And those who had trustworthy eyes already began to see rocks on the island, and point out the hut. And one even saw the three hermits. The captain got out a spy-glass, gazed through it, handed it to the bishop.

"He is quite right," said the captain; "there on the shore at the right, standing on a great rock, are three men."

The bishop also looked through the glass; he pointed it in the right direction and plainly saw the three men standing there,—one tall, the second shorter, but the third very short. They were standing on the shore, hand in hand.

The captain came to the bishop:—

"Here, your reverence, the ship must come to anchor; if it suit you, you can be put ashore in a yawl, and we will anchor out here and wait for you."

Immediately they got the tackle ready, cast anchor, and furled the sails; the vessel brought up, began to roll. They lowered a boat, the rowers manned it, and the bishop started to climb down by the companionway. The bishop climbed down, took his seat on the thwart; the rowers lifted their oars; they sped away to the island. They sped away like a stone from a sling; they could see the three old men standing,— the tall one naked, with his plaited belt; the shorter one in his torn kaftan; and the little old humpbacked one, in his old stole,— all three were standing there, hand in hand.

The sailors reached shore and caught hold with the boat-hook. The bishop got out.

The hermits bowed before him; he blessed them; they bowed still lower. And the bishop began to speak to them:—

"I heard," says he, "that you hermits were here, working out your salvation, that you pray Christ our God for your fellow-men; and I am here by God's grace, an unworthy servant of Christ, called to be a shepherd to His flock; and so I desired also, if I might, to give instruction to you, who are the servants of God."

The hermits made no reply; they smiled, they exchanged glances.

"Tell me how you are working out your salvation, and how you serve God," said the bishop.

The middle hermit sighed, and looked at the aged one, at the venerable one;

the tall hermit frowned, and looked at the aged one, at the venerable one. And the venerable old hermit smiled, and said:—

"Servant of God, we have not the skill to serve God; we only serve ourselves, getting something to eat."

"How do you pray to God?" asked the bishop.

And the venerable hermit said:—

"We pray thus: 'You three, have mercy on us three.'"

And as soon as the venerable hermit said this, all three of the hermits raised their eyes to heaven, and all three said, "*Troe vas, troe nas, pomiluï nas!*"

The bishop smiled, and said:—

"You have heard this about the Holy Trinity, but you should not pray so. I have taken a fancy to you, men of God. I see that you desire to please God, but you know not how to serve Him. You should not pray so; but listen to me, I will teach you. I shall not teach you my own words, but shall teach you from God's scriptures how God commanded all people to pray to God."

And the bishop began to explain to the hermits how God revealed Himself to men. He taught them about God the Father, God the Son, and God the Holy Spirit, and said:—

"God the Son came upon earth to save men, and this is the way He taught all men to pray; listen, and repeat after me"—

And the bishop began to say:—

"*Our Father.*"

And one hermit repeated:—

"*Our Father.*"

And then the second repeated:—

"*Our Father.*"

And the third also repeated:—

"*Our Father.*"

"*Who art in heaven;*" and the hermits tried to repeat, "*Who art in heaven.*" But the middle hermit mixed the words up, he could not repeat them so; and the tall, naked hermit could not repeat them,—his mustache had grown so as to cover his mouth, he could not speak distinctly; and the venerable, toothless hermit could not stammer the words intelligibly.

The bishop said it a second time; the hermits repeated it again. And the bishop sat down on a little boulder, and the hermits stood about him; and they looked at his lips, and they repeated it after him until they knew it. And all that day till evening the bishop labored with them; and ten times, and twenty times, and a hundred times, he repeated each word, and the hermits learned it by rote. And when they got mixed up, he set them right, and made them begin all over again.

And the bishop did not leave the hermits until he had taught them the whole of the Lord's Prayer. They repeated it after him, and then by themselves.

First of all, the middle hermit learned it, and he repeated it from beginning to end; and the bishop bade him say it again and again, and still again to repeat it; and the others also learned the whole prayer.

It was already beginning to grow dark, and the moon was just coming up out of the sea, when the bishop arose to go back to the ship.

The bishop said farewell to the hermits; they all bowed very low before him. He raised them to their feet and kissed each of them, bade them pray as he had taught them; and he took his seat in the boat, and returned to the ship.

And while the bishop was rowed back to the ship, he heard all the time how the hermits were repeating the Lord's Prayer at the top of their voices.

They returned to the ship, and here the voices of the hermits could no longer be heard; but they could still see, in the light on the moon, the three old men standing in the very same place on the shore,—one shorter than the rest in the middle, with the tall one on the right, and the other on the left hand.

The bishop returned to the ship, climbed up on deck; the anchor was hoisted; the sails were spread, and bellied with wind; the ship began to move, and they sailed away.

The bishop came to the stern, and took a seat there, and kept looking at the little island. At first the hermits were to be seen; then they were hidden from sight, and only the island was visible; and then the island went out of sight, and only the sea was left playing in the moonlight.

The pilgrims lay down to sleep, and all was quiet on deck. But the bishop cared not to sleep; he sat by himself in the stern, looked out over the sea in the direction where the island had faded from sight, and thought about the good hermits.

He thought of how they had rejoiced in what they had learned in the prayer; and he thanked God because He had led him to the help of the hermits, in teaching them the word of God.

Thus the bishop was sitting and thinking, looking at the sea in the direction where the little island lay hidden. And his eyes were filled with the moonlight, as it danced here and there on the waves. Suddenly he saw something shining and gleaming white in the track of the moon. Was it a bird, a gull, or a boat-sail gleaming white? The bishop strained his sight.

"A sail-boat," he said to himself, "is chasing us. Yes, it is catching up with us very rapidly. It was far, far off, but now it is close to us. But, after all, it is not much like a sail-boat. Anyway, something is chasing us, and catching up with us."

And the bishop could not decide what it was,—a boat, or not a boat; a bird, or not a bird; a fish, or not a fish. It was like a man, but very great; but a man could not be in the midst of the sea.

The bishop got up and went to the helmsman.

"Look!" says he, "what is that? what is that, brother? what is it?" said the bishop.

But by this time he himself saw. It was the hermits running over sea. Their gray beards gleamed white, and shone; and they drew near the ship as if it were stationary.

The helmsman looked. He was scared, dropped the tiller, and cried with a loud voice:—

"Lord! the hermits are running over the sea as if it were dry land!"

The people heard and sprang up; all rushed aft. All beheld the hermits running, hand in hand. The end ones swung their arms; they signaled the ship to come to. All three ran over the water as if it were dry land, and did not move their feet.

It was not possible to bring the ship to before the hermits overtook it, came on board, raised their heads, and said with one voice:—

"We have forgotten, servant of God, we have forgotten what thou didst teach us. While we were learning it, we remembered it; but when we ceased for an hour to repeat it, one word slipped away; we have forgotten it: the whole was lost. We remembered none of it; teach it to us again."

The bishop crossed himself, bowed low to the hermits, and said:—

"Acceptable to God is your prayer, ye hermits. It is not for me to teach you. Pray for us sinners."

And the bishop bowed before the feet of the hermits. And the hermits paused, turned about, and went back over the sea. And until the morning, there was something seen shining in the direction where the hermits had gone.

1886

THE KREUTZER SONATA

1

"But I say unto you that every one that looketh on a woman to lust after her hath committed adultery with her already in his heart." — MATT. v. 28.

"The disciples say unto him, If the case of the man is so with his wife, it is not expedient to marry. But he said unto them, All men cannot receive this saying, but they to whom it is given."—MATT. XIX. 10, 11.

It was early spring. We had been traveling for more than twenty-four hours. Passengers with tickets for more or less distant places had been entering and leaving our carriage, but there were four of us who had been on the train from the very start:—a weary-faced lady, neither beautiful nor young, who wore a hat and a semi-masculine paletot, and smoked cigarettes; her companion, a talkative man of forty, with neat, new luggage; and thirdly a rather short and very reserved gentleman not by any means old, but with curly hair prematurely turning gray, with very nervous motions, and with extraordinarily brilliant eyes which kept roving from object to object. He wore an old paletot with a lamb's-wool collar, made by an expensive tailor, and a high lamb's-wool hat. Under his paletot, when it was thrown open, were visible a *poddyovka*, or sleeveless kaftan, and a Russian embroidered shirt. The peculiarity of this gentleman consisted in the fact that he from time to time produced strange noises like a cough or like a laugh begun and broken off. This gentleman, during the whole journey, had carefully avoided all acquaintance and intercourse with the other passengers. If any of his neighbors spoke to him, he replied briefly and stiffly, and for the most part he either read or smoked, gazing out of the window, or else, getting his provisions out of his old sack, drank tea or ate luncheon.

It seemed to me that he was oppressed by his loneliness, and several times I was tempted to speak with him; but whenever our eyes met, as often happened, since we sat diagonally opposite each other, he turned away and devoted him-self to his book or looked out of the window.

During one stop at a large station, just before the evening of our second day, this nervous gentleman left the carriage to get some hot water, and made him-self some tea. The gentleman with the neat new luggage, a lawyer, as I afterward learned, went out also with the cigarette-smoking lady in the semi-masculine paletot, to drink tea in the station. During the absence of the gentleman and lady several new persons entered our carriage, and among them a tall, closely shaven, wrinkled old man, evidently a merchant, in a shuba of American polecat fur and a cloth cap with a huge vizor. This merchant sat down opposite the lawyer, and immediately entered into conversation with a young man, apparently a merchant's *prikashchik*, or manager, who entered the carriage at the same station.

I was sitting diagonally opposite, and while the train was stationary and no one was passing between us, I could hear snatches of their conversation.

The merchant at first explained that he was on his way to an estate of his which was situated only one station distant. Then, as usual, they began to talk about prices, about trade, and how Moscow does business at the present time; and then they discussed the Fair at Nizhni-Novgorod.

The merchant's clerk began to tell about the merrymaking at the Fair, of some rich merchant whom both of them knew; but the old man did not let him finish: he began to tell about the merrymakings which had taken place in former times at Kunavino, and which he himself had enjoyed. He was evidently proud of the share which he had taken in them, and with manifest delight he related how he and this same common acquaintance had once got drunk at Kunavino, and played such tricks that he had to tell about it in a whisper, whereat the clerk burst out in a hearty fit of laughter which filled the whole carriage, and the old man also laughed, displaying two yellow teeth.

Not expecting to hear anything interesting, I got up to go out on the plat-form till the train should start. At the door I met the lawyer and his lady, talking in a very animated manner as they walked.

"You won't have time," said the sociable lawyer. "The second bell will ring in a moment."

And in fact I had not even time to walk to the end of the carriage before the bell rang. When I got back to my place the lively conversation was still going on. The old merchant sat silent in front of them, sternly looking straight ahead, and occasionally expressing his disapprobation by chewing on his teeth.

"Whereupon she explained to her husband up and down"—the lawyer was saying with a smile as I passed them—"that she could not and, moreover, she would not live with him since . . ."

And he proceeded to tell something more which I could not hear. Behind me came still other passengers, then came the conductor, followed by a guard on the run, and there was considerable noise for a time, so that I could not hear what they were talking about.

When it grew quieter the lawyer's voice was heard again; but the conversation had evidently gone over from a particular instance to general considerations. The lawyer was saying that the question of divorce was now occupying general attention in Europe, and that with us in Russia the phenomenon was appear-ing more and more frequently.

Noticing that his voice alone was heard, the lawyer cut his words short, and addressed himself to the old man.

"It didn't use to be so in old times; isn't that so?" he remarked, smiling pleasantly.

The old man was about to make some answer; but at this moment the train started, and, taking off his cap, he began to cross himself and to whisper a prayer. The lawyer, turning his eyes away, waited politely. Having finished his prayer and crossed himself thrice, the old man put on his cap and pulled it down, settling it in its place, and he began to speak.

"The same thing took place, sir, in old times, only less frequently," said he. "At the present time it can't help happening. People have grown cultured!"

The train, moving along more and more rapidly, thundered over the sleepers, and it was hard for me to hear; but it was interesting, and I took a seat nearer. My neighbor, the nervous, bright-eyed gentleman, was also evidently much interested, and listened, but without moving from his place.

"In what respect are we ill-educated?" asked the lady, with a scarcely perceptible smile. "Do you mean that it would be better for men and women to get married as they used to do in old times, when the bride and bridegroom never even saw each other?" she went on asking, replying after the fashion of many women, not to her neighbor's words, but to the words which she thought he would say.

"People did not know whether they would be able to love each other or not, but married whoever fell to their lot; yes, and often they were tortured their whole lives long! So you think that our old way was the best, do you?" she went on, addressing her discourse to me, and to the lawyer, and least of all to the old man with whom she was talking.

"We have already become very cultured," repeated the merchant, looking scornfully at the lady, and leaving her question unanswered.

"I should like to know how you explain the connection between culture and matrimonial quarrels," said the lawyer, with a scarcely perceptible smile.

The merchant was about to say something, but the lady interrupted him.

"No, that time has already passed," said she. But the lawyer checked her:—

"No, permit him to express his thought." . . .

"The absurdities of culture," said the old man, resolutely.

"People who do not love each other marry, and then they wonder that they get along inharmoniously," said the lady, hastily, glancing at the lawyer and then at me, and even at the clerk, who had got up in his seat and was standing with his elbow leaning on the back of the chair, and listening to the conversation with a smile. "You see animals only can be paired off in this way as the master may desire, but men and women have their own individual preferences and attachments," said the lady, evidently wishing to say something severe to the old merchant.

"When you speak thus, you speak to no purpose, madame," said the old man. "Animals are brutes, but man has a law."

"Well, how can one live with a man when there is no love?" insisted the lady, eager to express her opinion, which apparently seemed to her very novel.

"In former times they did not discuss this," said the old man, in a magisterial tone; "it is only a recent development. At any pretext the wife cries out:

'I will leave you.' Even among the peasantry this new method has come into fashion. 'Na,' says the muzhik's wife, 'here are your shirts and drawers, but I am going off with Vanka; his hair is curlier than yours.' Argument is no good. For a woman the first thing needed is fear."

The clerk looked at the lawyer and at the lady and at me, evidently repressing a smile, and ready either to laugh or to approve of the merchant's argument according as it was received by the company.

"Fear of what?" asked the lady.

"Why, of course, fear of her hu-us-band. . . . That kind of fear."

"But, batyushka, the day for that sort of thing has gone by," said the lady, with no little asperity.

"No, madame, the time for that can never go by. As Eve the woman was created out of the man's rib, so it will remain till the end of time," said the old man, and he nodded his head so sternly and triumphantly that the clerk instantly decided that the victory was on the merchant's side, and he burst out into a loud laugh.

"Yes, that is the way you men decide," said the lady, not yielding, and looking at us. "They give themselves full liberty, but you want to keep the woman in the terem.[1] To you, of course, all things are permitted."

"No one gives any such permission, but it is a fact man does not make his family increase, but woman is a fragile vessel," suggested the merchant. The dictatorialness of the merchant's tone evidently impressed his hearers, and even the lady felt crushed, but still she would not give in.

"Yes, but I think you will agree that a woman is a human being, and has feelings as well as a man. Well, then, what is she going to do if she does not love her husband?"

"Not love her husband?" exclaimed the merchant, repeating her words in a savage tone, making a grimace with his lips and his eyebrows. "Never fear, she should come to love him."

This unexpected argument especially pleased the clerk, and he gave vent to a grunt of approbation.

"But that is not so, she may not come to love him," insisted the lady; "and if there is no love, then they ought not to be compelled to this."

"But if a woman is false to her husband, what then?" asked the lawyer.

"That is not to be supposed," said the old man; "he must look out for that."

"But if it does happen, what then? It has occurred." . . .

"Yes, there are cases, but not among us," said the old man.

All were silent. The clerk changed his position, leaned forward a little more, and evidently wishing not to be left out of the conversation, began with a smile:—

"Well, there was a scandal arose in the house of a fine young fellow in our place. It was very hard to decide about it. It happened that the woman was very fond of amusements, and she began to play the devil; but her husband was a reasonable and progressive man. At first she flirted with a counting-house clerk. Her husband argued kindly with her; she would not stop. She did all sorts of

---

[1] The women's quarters in the ancient Russian ménage, which was thoroughly Oriental.

dirty tricks and even stole his money. And he flogged her. What good did that do? She only acted worse. Then she had an intrigue with an unchristened Jew, if I may say so. What could he do? He turned her off entirely, and so he lives like a bachelor, and she has become a gadabout."

"That was because he was a fool," said the old man. "If at the very beginning he had not given her her head, but had given her a good sound berating, she would have been all right, I tell you. She must not have her own way at first. Don't trust a horse in the field, or your wife in your house."

At this moment the conductor came along to take up the tickets for the next station. The old man surrendered his.

"Yes," said he, "we've got to restrain the female sex betimes, or else every thing will go to ruin."

"Yes, but you were just telling how you married men enjoyed yourselves at the fair at Kunavino," said I, unable to restrain myself.

"That was a personal matter," said the merchant, and he relapsed into silence.

When the whistle sounded the merchant got up, took his bag from under the seat, wrapped his shuba round him, and, lifting his cap, went out to the platform.

2

As soon as the old man had gone out, several voices spoke up at once.

"An old Testament patriarch," exclaimed the clerk.

"The 'Domostroï'[1] come to life," said the lady. "What savage notions of woman and marriage."

"Yes, indeed, we are still far from the European notions of marriage," said the lawyer.

"Well, the principal thing these men cannot understand," said the lady, "is that marriage without love is not marriage, that love alone consecrates marriage, and that the only true marriage is that which love consecrates."

The clerk listened and smiled, desiring to remember for future use as much as he could of the clever conversation.

In the midst of the lady's sentence, there was heard a sound just behind me like an interrupted laugh or a sob, and looking around we saw my neighbor, the bright-eyed, gray-haired, solitary gentleman, who during the conversation, which had evidently interested him, had unobtrusively drawn near us. He was standing with his hand resting on the back of the seat, and was evidently very much agitated; his face was red and the muscles of his cheek twitched.

"What is that love . . . that love . . . which consecrates marriage?" he asked, in a stammering voice.

The lady, seeing the agitated state of the speaker, tried to answer him as gently and circumstantially as possible.

"True love. It is that love between a man and a woman which makes marriage possible," said the lady.

---

[1] The "Domostroï" was the famous code of household manners and customs, compiled probably from earlier treatises by Monk Sylvester, who lived during the reign of Tsar Ivan IV. about the middle of the sixteenth century. It was rediscovered and published in 1849.

"Yes, but what do you mean by true love," said the bright-eyed gentleman, smiling awkwardly and timidly.

"Every one knows what true love is," said the lady, evidently wishing to cut short her speech with him.

"But I don't know," said the gentleman. "You must define what you mean by it."

"Why? . . . It is very simple," said the lady, but she hesitated. "Love . . . love is the, is the exclusive preference which a man or woman feels for one person out of all the rest in the world," said she.

"A preference for how long a time? For a month or two months or half an hour?" asked the gray-haired man, and laughed.

"No, but excuse me, you are evidently not talking about the same thing."

"Yes, I am talking about the same thing."

"She says," interrupted the lawyer, and indicating the lady, "that marriage ought to result in the first place from an attachment, from love, if you will, and that if such a love actually exists, then only marriage furnishes of itself, so to speak, some consecration. Therefore, every marriage where there is no genuine attachment as a foundation—love, if you say so—has no moral obligation. Do I express your idea correctly?" said he, addressing the lady.

The lady by an inclination of her head expressed her concurrence with his interpretation of her idea.

"Therefore . . ." the lawyer was about to continue, but the nervous gentleman, with his eyes all on fire, evidently restraining himself with difficulty, began, without allowing the lawyer to proceed:—

"No, I *am* speaking about the same thing, about the preference that one man or one woman has for one person above all others, and I simply ask, 'How long is this preference to last?' "

"How long? why, sometimes it lasts a whole lifetime," said the lady, shrugging her shoulders.

"Yes, but that is true only in novels, but never in real life. In real life this preference for one person rather than another may occasionally last for a year, more frequently it is measured by months, or even by weeks or days or hours," said he, evidently knowing that he was surprising every one by his opinion, and well satisfied with it.

"Oh, what are you saying?" . . . "No, excuse me!" . . . "Oh, no!" three of us exclaimed with one voice. Even the clerk uttered a disapproving grunt.

"Yes, I know," interrupted the gray-haired gentleman. "You are speaking of what is supposed to exist, but I am speaking of what does exist. Every man feels for every pretty woman what you call love."

"Oh, what you say is awful. Surely there exists among human beings that feeling which is called love, and which lasts not merely for months and years, but for whole lives!"

"No, I don't admit it. If it is granted even that a man may keep his preference for a given woman all his life, the woman in all probability will prefer some one else, and so it always has been in the world and always will be," said he; and, taking out a cigarette-case, he began to smoke.

"But it may be reciprocal," said the lawyer.

"No, it is impossible," he insisted, "just as impossible as that in a load of peas there should be two peas exactly alike, side by side. And over and above this improbability there is also the likelihood of satiety. That one or the other should love the same person a whole life long is as to say that a single candle would burn forever," said he, eagerly drawing in the smoke of his cigarette.

"But you are talking about carnal love; don't you admit that there is a love based on a unity of ideals, on a spiritual affinity?" asked the lady.

"Spiritual affinity! Unity of ideals!" repeated he, emitting his peculiar sound. "But in that case there is no reason why we should not sleep together,—excuse my brutality,—why, it is the very consequence of this unity of ideals that people go to bed together," said he, and he laughed nervously.

"But pardon me," said the lawyer, "what you say is contradicted by the facts. . . . We see that marriage exists, that all the human race, or the majority of it, lives a married life, and many live honorably all their days under the marriage relation."

The gray-haired gentleman again laughed.

"You were just saying that marriage is founded on love, but when I expressed my doubt of the existence of love except the sentimental kind, you try to prove the existence of love by the fact that marriages exist. But marriages in our day are all falsehood."

"Oh, no, excuse me," exclaimed the lawyer; "I only say that marriages have always existed and still exist."

"Exist? Yes, but why do they exist? They have existed and exist for people who see in marriage something sacred—a sacrament which is entered into before God—for such people it exists. Among us, people get married, seeing nothing in marriage except copulation, and the result is either deception or violence. When it is deception it is easy to endure. Husband and wife only deceive people into believing that they are living a monogamous marriage, but they are really practising polygamy and polyandry. It is filthy, but still it is the fashion; but when, as happens oftener than otherwise, men take on themselves an external obligation to live together all their lives long,—and even from the second month they hate each other, desire to separate, and yet they go on living, —then results that terrible hell from which they try to escape by intoxication, by fighting duels, by killing and poisoning themselves and others," said he, talking more and more rapidly, and growing more and more excited. It was embarrassing.

"Yes, without doubt there are critical episodes in married life," said the lawyer, wishing to cut short this unseemly and exciting conversation.

"I imagine you have guessed who I am," said the gray-haired gentleman, quietly and with a certain appearance of calmness.

"No, I have not that pleasure."

"The pleasure will not be great. My name is Pozdnuishef; I am the man in whose life happened that critical episode to which you just hinted—the episode of a man killing his wife," said he, swiftly glancing at each one of us.

No one found anything to say, and we all kept silence.

"Well, it is immaterial," said he, emitting his peculiar grunt. "However, excuse me, I will not trouble you any more."

"Don't mention it," said the lawyer, himself not knowing exactly what he was saying.

But Pozdnuishef, not heeding him, quickly turned round and went back to his place. The gentleman talked in whispers with the lady. I sat down with Pozdnuishef and said nothing, as I was unable to think of anything to say to him. It was too dark to read, and so I shut my eyes and pretended that I was going to sleep.

Thus we rode in silence till we reached the next station. At that station the gentleman and lady were transferred to another carriage, concerning which they had arranged beforehand with the conductor. The merchant's superintendent got into a comfortable position on his sofa and went to sleep. Pozdnuishef kept smoking, and drank his tea, which he got boiling hot at the station.

When I opened my eyes and looked at him, he suddenly turned to me with an expression of resolution and exasperation:—

"Maybe it is disagreeable for you to be sitting with me, now that you know who I am. If that is so, I will leave you."

"Oh, not at all, I beg of you."

"Well, then, wouldn't you like some? Only it is rather strong."

And he poured me out some tea.

"They say . . . but then they all lie . . ." said he.

"What are you speaking about?" I asked.

"Always about the same thing—about 'love'—and what people mean by it. Don't you want to sleep?"

"Not at all."

"Then, if you would like, I will relate to you how I was led by this very same kind of love to do what I did."

"I should indeed, unless it would be painful for you."

"No, it is hard for me to hold my tongue. You drink your tea—or is it too strong for you?"

The tea was really like beer, but I drank a glass of it. At this moment the conductor came along. Pozdnuishef silently followed him with angry eyes, and did not begin until he had left the car.

3

"Well, then, I will tell you. But are you sure you would like to have me?"

I assured him that I was very eager to hear him. He remained silent, rubbed his face with his hands, and began:—

"If I tell you, I must begin at the very beginning, I must tell you how and why I got married, and what I was before I married.

"Up to the time of my marriage I lived as all men live; that is, all the men in my circle. I am a landed proprietor and a university graduate, and I have been marshal of the nobility. Up to the time of my marriage I lived as all men live,—a dissipated life; and, like all the young men of our circle, though living a dissipated life, I was persuaded that I was living as I ought. Regarding myself, I thought that I was a charming person, that I was a perfectly moral man. I was no vulgar seducer, I had no unnatural tastes, I did not make this sort of thing my chief object in life, as did many of my intimates; I indulged in dissipation only moderately, decently, for my health's sake; I avoided such women as might, by the birth of a child, or by the force of attachment to me, entangle me. However, there may have been children and there may have been attachments; but I acted as if there was nothing of the sort, I not only considered this sort of thing moral, but I was proud of it."

He paused, emitted his peculiar sound, as he apparently always did when a new thought occurred to him.

"And precisely here is the chief viciousness of it all," he cried. "Depravity does not lie in anything physical; depravity does not imply any physical deformity; depravity, genuine depravity, consists in freeing oneself from the moral relations to women with whom you enter into physical relations. And this emancipation I arrogated to myself as a virture. I remember how one time I tormented myself because I had not paid a woman, who apparently loved me and had given herself to me, and I was only rendered happy again when I sent her the money, so as to show her thereby that I did not consider myself morally bound to her. Do not shake your head as if you agreed with me," he suddenly cried. "You see I know that kind of trick. All of you, in the best circumstances, unless you are a rare exception, have just such views as I had then. Well, no matter, please excuse me," he went on. "But this is the whole trouble and it is awful! awful! awful!"

"What is awful?" I asked.

"The abyss of error in which we live in relation to women, and our relations to them. It is true I cannot talk with any calmness in regard to this, and the reason I cannot is that episode which took place in my life. But ever since that episode occurred, my eyes have been opened, and I have seen everything in an entirely different light—exactly the opposite—exactly the opposite."

He smoked his cigarette, and, leaning his elbows on his knees, went on talking again. In the darkness I could not see his face, but above the rattle and rumble of the train I could hear his suggestive, pleasant voice.

4

"Yes, only by tormenting myself as I have, only by means of this have I learned where the root of the whole trouble is; have I learned what must be, and therefore have come to see the whole horror of what is.

"Now be kind enough to see, just here, how and when began that which led me to that episode of which I have spoken. It began when I was not quite sixteen years old. It happened when I was still in the gymnasium, and my oldest brother was a student in the first class. I had not known women at that time, but like all the unfortunate boys of our circle, I was by no means an innocent child. Two years before I had been corrupted by coarse boys; already woman, not any particular woman, but woman as a sweet something, woman, any woman —woman in her nakedness—had already begun to torment me. My solitudes were unchaste. I was tormented as ninety-nine per cent of our boys are tormented. I was horror-struck, I struggled, I prayed, and—I fell! My imagination was already corrupt. I, myself, was corrupt, but the final step had not yet been taken. I was ruined by myself, even before I had put my hands on another human being. But here a comrade of my brother, a gay young student, a so-called 'good fellow,'—in other words the greatest good-for-nothing possible,—who had already taught us to drink and to play cards, persuaded us after a drinking-bout to go there.

"We went. My brother also had been innocent, and he fell the same night;

and I, a boy of fifteen, polluted myself and accomplished the pollution of a woman, not at all understanding the enormity of what I was doing. You see I had never heard from any of my elders that what I was doing was wrong. And even now no one ever hears so. To be sure it is contained in the Ten Commandments, but the Ten Commandments seem to be used only in order to pass the priest's examination, and even then are not regarded as very important, not nearly so much so as the rule for the use of *ut* in conditional sentences.

"Thus I had never heard a single one of my elders, whom I respected, say that this was wrong. On the contrary, I heard men whom I respected declare that it was a good thing. I heard them say that my struggles and sufferings would be relieved after that. I heard it, and I read it, and heard my elders say that it was good for the health; from my comrades I heard that there was merit, that there was gallantry, in such conduct. So that, as a rule, there is nothing to be anticipated from it except beneficial effects. Danger of disease? But even that you see is taken care of. A solicitous government looks out for that. It looks after and regulates the activity of houses of 'indulgence,' and makes lewdness safe for gymnasium students. And doctors for a consideration do the same. Thus it comes about. They affirm that lewdness is good for the health, they make a regular institution of lewdness. I know of mothers who see to it that their sons' health is regulated in this way. And Science follows them into the houses of 'indulgence.' "

"Why Science?" I asked.

"What are doctors? The priests of Science. Who corrupt young men, declaring that this thing is necessary for the health? They do.

"But it is certain that if one per cent of the energy that is employed in the cure of syphilis were expended in the eradication of lewdness, syphilis would long ago have become only a memory. But instead the energy is expended, not in the eradication of lewdness, but in the guaranteeing the safety of lewdness. Well, that is not the trouble. The trouble consists in this, that with me, as with nine out of ten, if not even more, not only of our class, but of all, even of the peasantry, the horrible fact exists that I fell, not by reason of yielding to a single temptation of the charm of any special woman—no, no special woman led me astray; but I fell because those immediately around me saw, in what was really a fall, some a lawful act, a regulator advantageous for the health, others, a most natural and not only simple, but even innocent, diversion for a young man.

"I did not even realize that this was a fall; I simply began to give myself up to those pleasures, to those necessities, which, as it was suggested to me, were peculiar to a certain degree of lewdness,—gave myself up to this form of dissipation just as I had begun to drink and to smoke. And yet there was something peculiar and pathetic in this first fall. I well remember how immediately, even before I left that room, a feeling of sadness, of deep sadness, came over me, so that I felt like weeping, weeping the loss of my innocence, for a forever sullied relationship to womanhood. Yes, the natural, simple relationship that I had enjoyed with women was for evermore impossible. Purity of relationship with any woman was at an end, and could never be again. I had become what is called a libertine. And to be a libertine is to be in a physical condition like that of a morphiomaniac, a drunkard, or a smoker. As the morphiomaniac, the drunkard, the smoker, is no longer a normal man, so a man who uses women for his own pleasure is no longer normal, but is a man forever spoiled —is a libertine. As the drunkard and the morphiomaniac can be instantly recognized by his face, by his actions, so it is with the rake. The libertine may restrain himself, may struggle with his inclinations, but his simple, pure, frank, and fraternal relations with woman are no longer possible. By the very way in which he looks at a young woman, and stares at her, the libertine is to be recognized. And I became a libertine, and I remained one, and that was my ruin.

5

"Yes, so it was. So it went farther and farther, and every kind of depravity ensued. My God! When I remember all my abominable actions in this particular, I am overwhelmed with horror. I also remember how my comrades used to laugh at my so-called innocence. And when you hear about our gilded youth, our officers, our young Parisians . . .

"And all these gentlemen, and I, when we, libertines of thirty, having on our souls hundreds of the most varied and horrible crimes against woman, when we, rakes of thirty, come into the drawing-room or the ball-room, freshly washed, cleanly shaven, well-perfumed, in immaculate linen, in evening dress or uniform—what emblems of purity, how charming we are! . . .

"Just think what ought to be and what is! It ought to be that when such a gentleman comes into the society of my sister, or my daughter, I, knowing about his life, what it is, should go to him, draw him quietly to one side, and say in a confidential whisper:—

" 'Galubchik, you see I know exactly how you are living, how you are spending your nights and with whom. This is no place for you. Here are pure, innocent women and girls. Please go.'

"So it ought to be; but in reality, when such a gentleman makes his appearance, or when he dances with my sister or my daughter, clasping her in his arms, we rejoice if he is rich and well connected. Perhaps he honors my daughter after Rigolbozh. Even if traces of his disease still remain, it is of no consequence, the cure is easy nowadays. I know that some girls of the highest society have been given by their parents with enthusiasm to men affected with certain diseases. Oh, what rottenness! But the time is coming when this rottenness and falsehood will be cured."

Several times he emitted his strange noises and sipped his tea. His tea was terribly strong. There was no water at hand to weaken it. I was conscious that the two glasses which I had drunk had greatly excited my nerves. The tea also must have had a great effect on him, because he kept growing more and more excited. His voice kept growing louder and more energetic. He kept changing his position; at one moment he would pick up his hat, then he would put it on again; and his face kept strangely changing in the twilight in which we were sitting.

"Well, that was the way I lived until I was thirty years of age, never for a moment abandoning my intention of getting married and arranging for myself the most lofty and unsullied existence, and with this end in view I looked at every girl who came under observation," he continued. "I was soiled with the rottenness of lewdness, and at the same time I was looking round for a girl who by her purity might meet my demands. Many of them I instantly rejected on the ground that they were not sufficiently pure for me; at last I found one whom I thought worthy of me. She was one of the two daughters of a man in the government of Penza, who had formerly been very rich, but was at that time ruined. One evening, after we had been somewhere in a boat and were returning home by moonlight, and I was sitting next her and admiring her well-proportioned figure, clad in a jersey, and her curly locks, I suddenly made up my mind that she was the one. It seemed to me that evening that she understood everything I felt and thought, and I thought the most elevated thoughts. In reality it was simply the fact that her jersey was especially becoming to her and so were her curls, and that after I had spent a day in her immediate presence I wanted to be still closer to her.

"It is a marvelous thing how full of illusion is the notion that beauty is an advantage. A beautiful woman says all sorts of foolishness, you listen and you do not hear any foolishness, but what you hear seems to you wisdom itself. She says and does vulgar things, and to you it seems lovely. Even when she does not say stupid or vulgar things, but is simply beautiful, you are convinced that she is miraculously wise and moral.

"I returned home enthusiastic, and resolved that she was high above all moral perfection, and that she was therefore fit to be my wife; and the next day I made my proposal.

"See what an entanglement it was. Out of a thousand married men, not only in our rank, but unfortunately also in the people, there is scarcely one who, like Don Juan, would not have been married already not merely ten times, but even a hundred or a thousand times, before the marriage ceremony.

"It is true there are now, so I hear, and I believe it, some young men who live pure lives, feeling and knowing that this is no joke, but a serious matter.

"God help them! But in my time there was not one such out of ten thousand. And all know this and pretend that they do not know it. In all novels the feelings of the heroes, the ponds, the bushes around which they wander, are described in detail; but though their mighty love to some particular maiden is described, nothing is said about what the interesting hero was doing before, not a word about his frequenting 'houses of indulgence,' about his relations with chambermaids, cooks, and other women. . . . Improper novels of this kind —if there are any—are not put into the hands of those who most of all need to know about these things—that is, young women.

"At first they pretend before young women that this form of dissipation, which fills half of the life of our cities, and of our villages also, does not exist at all.

"Afterward they become so accustomed to this hypocrisy that at last they come actually to believe that all of us are moral men and live in a moral world! Girls, poor things, really believe in this with perfect seriousness.

"Thus did my unhappy wife believe. I remember how, after I became engaged to her, I showed her my diary, in which she might learn as much as she would like, even though it were very little, of my past, and especially regarding the last intrigue in which I had been engaged; for she might hear about this from others, and so I felt it necessary to tell her. I remember her horror, her despair, and disillusionment when she knew it all and realized what it meant. I saw that she was tempted to throw me over then. And why didn't she do it?" . . .

He emitted his peculiar sound, took another swallow of tea, and paused.

6

"No, on the whole it is much better, ever so much better so," he cried. "I deserved it. But that is not the point. I mean that in this business the only persons deceived are the poor unfortunate girls.

"Their mothers certainly know this, their mothers know it as well as any one, because they have been told by their husbands. And they pretend that they believe in the purity of men, though in reality they do not at all. They know by what bait to catch men for themselves and for their daughters. But you see we men don't know, and we don't know because we don't want to know; but women know perfectly well that the loftiest, and as we call it the most poetic, love depends, not on moral qualities, but on physical proximity and then on the way of doing up the hair, the complexion, the cut of the gown. Ask an experienced coquette who has set herself the task of entrapping a man, which she would prefer to risk: being detected in falsehood, cruelty, even immorality, in the presence of the one whom she is trying to entice, or to appear before him in a badly made or unbecoming gown,—and every time she would choose the first. She knows that man merely lies when he talks about lofty feelings—all he wants is the body—and so he pardons all vulgarities, but he would never pardon an ugly, unbecoming, unfashionable costume.

"The coquette knows this consciously; every innocent girl knows this unconsciously, just as animals know it.

"Hence these abominable jerseys, these tournures, these naked shoulders, arms, and almost bosoms. Women, especially those that have been through the school of marriage, know very well that talk on the highest topics is all talk; but what man wants is the body, and everything which displays it in a deceptive but captivating light, and they act accordingly. If we should once forget that we are accustomed to this indecency which has become second nature, and look at the life of our upper classes as it really is, in all its shamelessness, it would appear like one luxurious 'house of indulgence.'

"Don't you agree with me? Excuse me, I will prove it to you," he repeated, not allowing me a chance to speak.

"You say that the women in our society live for other aims than the women in the 'houses of indulgence,' but I say that it is not so, and I will prove it to you. If people differ by their aims, by the internal contents of their lives, then this difference will be shown, also, externally, and externally they will be different. But look at these unhappy, these despised women, and then on the ladies of our highest social circles; the same decorations, the same fashions, the same perfumes, the same bare shoulders, arms, and bosoms, the same extravagant exhibition of the tournure, the same passion for precious stones, for costly, brilliant things, the same gayeties, dances and music and singing. The methods of allurement used by the ones are used by the others.

7

"Yes, and I was captured by these jerseys and locks of hair and tournures.

"And it was very easy to capture me, because I had been brought up in those conditions in which young people, like cucumbers under glass, are turned out in love. You see our too abundant and exciting food, coupled with a perfectly idle existence, is nothing else than a systematic incitement to lust. You may be surprised or not, but it is so. I myself have seen nothing of this sort of thing until recently, but now I have seen it. This is the very thing that troubles me, that no one recognizes this, but every one says stupid things like the woman who just got out.

"Yes; not far from where I live some muzhiks were working this spring on the railway. The ordinary fare of the peasantry is meager,—bread, kvas, onions; the muzhik is lively, healthy, and sound. He goes to work on the railway, and his rations consist of kasha and one pound of meat. But in repayment of this he gives back sixteen hours' work, amounting to thirty puds, carried on a wheel-barrow. And it is always so with him.

"But we who eat daily two pounds of meat and game and fish and all kinds of stimulating foods and drinks—how does that go? In sensual excesses. If it goes that way, the safety-valve is open and all is satisfactory; but cut off the safety-valve,—as I kept it covered temporarily,—and immediately there will be an excitement which, coming through the prism of our artificial life, is expressed in a love of the first water, and is sometimes even platonic. And I fell in love as all young men do.

"And everything followed its course: transports and emotions and poetry. In reality, this love of mine was the result, on the one side, of the activity of the mamasha and the dressmakers; on the other, of the superfluity of stimulating food eaten by me in idleness. Had there not been, on the one hand, excursions in boats, had there not been dressmakers with close-fitting gowns, and the like, and had my wife been dressed in some unbecoming capote, and stayed at home, and had I, on the other hand, been a man in normal conditions, eating only as much food as I needed for my work, and had my safety-valve been open,—but then it chanced to be temporarily closed,—I should not have fallen in love, and there would not have been any trouble.

8

"Well, so it went on. My rank and fortune and good clothes and excursions in boats did the business. Twenty times it does not succeed, but this time it succeeded like a trap. I am not jesting. You see, nowadays marriages are always arranged like traps. Do you see how natural it is? The girl has arrived at maturity, and must be married. What could be more simple when the girl is not a monster, and there are men who wish to get married? This is the way it used to ·be done. The girl has reached the right age; her parents arrange a marriage. Thus it has been done, thus it is done throughout the world; among the Chinese, the Hindus, the Mahometans, and among the common Russian people; thus it is managed among at least ninety-nine per cent of the human race. It is only among a small one per cent, among us libertines and debauchees, that this custom had been found to be bad, and we have invented another. Now, what is this new way? It is this: the girls sit round, and the men come as at a bazaar and take their choice. And the girls wait and wonder, and have their own ideas, but they dare not say: 'Batyushka, take me,—no, me— not her, but me; look, what shoulders and all the rest.'

"And we, the men, walk by and stare at them and are satisfied. 'I know a thing or two, I am not caught.' They go by, they look, they are satisfied that this is all arranged for their special benefit. 'Look, don't get taken in—here's your chance!' "

"What is to be done, then?" I asked. "You would not have the young women make the offers, would you?"

"Well, I can't exactly say how; only if there is to be equality, then let it be equality. If it is discovered that the system of the go-between is humiliating, still this is a thousand times more so. Then the rights and chances were equal, but in our method the woman is either a slave in a bazaar, or the bait in the trap. You tell any mother or the girl herself the truth, that she is only occupied in husband-catching,—my God, what an insult! But the truth is they do this, and they have nothing else to do. And what is really dreadful is to see poor, and perfectly innocent, young girls engaged in doing this very thing. And again, it would not be so bad if it were only done openly, but it is all deception.

" 'Ah, the origin of species, how interesting it is! Ah, Lily is greatly interested in painting.'—And shall you be at the exhibition? How instructive! And the troïka rides and the theater and the symphony. Oh, how remarkable— 'My Lily is crazy over music!' 'And why don't you share these views?' And then the boat rides. And always one thought:— 'Take me, take my Lily. No, me!' 'Just try your luck!' Oh, vileness, oh, falsehood!" he concluded; and, swallowing the last of his tea, proceeded to gather together his cups and utensils.

9

"Do you know," he began, while he was packing up his tea and sugar in his bag, "the domination of women, which is the cause of the sufferings of the world, all proceeds from this?"

"How the domination of women?" I asked. "All rights, the majority of rights, belong to men."

"Yes, yes, that is the very thing," he exclaimed, interrupting me. "That is the very thing I wanted to say to you, and that is just what explains the extraordinary phenomenon that on the one side it is perfectly true that woman is reduced to the lowest degree of humiliation; on the other, she is the queen. Just exactly as the Jews, by their pecuniary power, avenge themselves for their humiliation, so it is with women. 'Ah, you want us to be merely merchants; very well, we as merchants will get you under our feet,' say the Jews. 'Ah, you wish us to be merely the objects of sensuality; very well, we as objects of sensual pleasure will make you our slaves,' say the women. A woman's lack of rights does not consist in the fact that she cannot vote or sit as judge,—for rights are not embraced in any such activities,—but in the fact that in sexual intercourse she is not the equal of the man: she must have the right to enjoy the man or to keep him at a distance according to her fancy, she must be able to choose her husband according to her own desire, instead of being the one chosen.

"You say that this would be unbecoming; very good, then let the man cease to have these rights. Now the woman lacks the right which the man possesses. And now, in order to get back this right, she acts on the passions of man; by means of his passions, she subdues him so that, while ostensibly he chooses, she is really the one. And having once got hold of this means, she abuses it, and acquires a terrible power over men."

"Yes, but where is this special power?" I asked.

"Where? Everywhere, in everything. Go in any large city among the shops. Millions there. You could estimate the amount of human labor expended in them, but in ninety per cent of these shops what will you find intended for men? All the luxury of life is demanded and maintained by women. Reckon up all the factories. The vast proportion of them are manufacturing unprofitable adornments, such as carriages, furniture, trinkets, for women. Millions of men, generations of slaves, perish in the galley-slave work in factories merely for the caprice of women. Women, like tsaritsas, hold as prisoners in slavery and hard labor about ninety per cent of the human race. And all this because they have been kept down, deprived of their equal rights with men. And so they avenge themselves by acting on our passions, by ensnaring us in their nets. Yes, everything comes from that.

"Women have made of themselves such a weapon for attacking the senses of men, that a man cannot with any calmness be in a woman's company. As soon as a man approaches a woman, he falls under the influence of her deviltry, and grows foolish. And there always used to be something awkward and painful, when I saw a lady dressed in a ball-gown; but now it is simply terrible. I regard it as something dangerous for men and contrary to law, and I feel the impulse to call for the police, to summon protection from the peril, to demand that the dangerous object be removed and put out of sight.

"Yes, you are laughing," he cried, "but this is no joke at all. I am convinced that the time is coming and perhaps very soon when men will recognize this and will be amazed that a society could exist in which actions so subversive to social quietude were permitted as those adornments of their body, permitted to women of our circle and meant to appeal to the passions. It is exactly the same as if all kinds of traps should be placed along our promenades and roads— it is worse than that. Why should games of chance be forbidden, and women not be forbidden to dress in a way to appeal to the passions? It is a thousand times more dangerous.

10

"Now, then, you understand me. I was what is called 'in love.' I not only imagined her as absolute perfection, I also imagined myself at the time of my marriage as absolute perfection. You see there is no scoundrel who is not able by searching to find a scoundrel in some respects worse than himself, and who therefore would not find an excuse for pride and self-satisfaction. So it was with me: I was not marrying for money, it was not a question of advantage with me as it was with the majority of my acquaintances, who married either for money or connections: I was rich, she was poor. That is one thing. Another thing which afforded me reason for pride was the fact that, while other men married with the intention of continuing to live in the same polygamy as they had enjoyed up to the time of their marriage, I had firmly resolved to live after my marriage as a monogamist, and my pride had no bounds in consequence of this resolution. Yes, I was a frightful hog, but I imagined that I was an angel!

"The time between my betrothal and my marriage was not very long. But I cannot remember that period of my engagement without shame. How vile it was! You see love is represented as spiritual and not sensual. Well, if it is love, it is spiritual; if it is a spiritual communion, then this spiritual intercourse ought to be expressed in words, in conversations, in colloquies. There was nothing of this. It used to be awfully hard to talk when we were alone together. What a labor of Sisyphus it used to be! No sooner had we thought of something to say and said it, than we would have to be silent and it would be necessary to think of something else. There was nothing to talk about. Everything that might be said of the life awaiting us, our arrangements, our plans, had been said, and what was there more? You see, if we had been animals then we should have known that it was not expected of us to talk; but here, on the contrary, it was necessary to talk, but there was nothing to say because what really interested us could not be expressed in words.

"And, moreover, there was that abominable custom of eating bonbons, that coarse gluttony, that gormandizing on sweets, and all those vile preparations for marriage; discussions about rooms, apartments, beds, night-gowns, khalats, linen, and toilets. Now you will admit that, if marriages were arranged in accordance with the 'Domostroï,' as that old man said, then the cushions, the dowry, the bed, and all that sort of thing would be merely particulars corresponding with the sacrament. But among us, when out of ten men who go to the altar probably scarcely nine believe, not merely in the sacrament, but do not even believe that what they are doing is anything binding; when out of a hundred men there is scarcely one who has not been practically married before, and out of fifty not more than one who is not ready to deceive his wife on any convenient pretext; when the majority regard the going to the church as merely a special condition for the possession of a certain woman,—think what a terrible significance, in view of all this, all these details must have! It comes to be something in the nature of a sale. They sell the libertine the innocent girl, and they surround the sale with certain formalities.

11

"That is the way all get married, and that is the way I got married, and the much-vaunted honeymoon began. What a vile name that is in itself!" he hissed spitefully. "I was making a tour of all the sights of Paris, and I went in to see the bearded woman and a water-dog. It seemed that the one was only a man décolleté, in a woman's gown, and the other was a dog fastened into a walrus-skin and swimming in a bath-tub full of water. The whole thing was very far from interesting; but when I left the place the showman conducted me out very obsequiously, and, addressing the public collected around the entrance, he pointed to me, and said:—

" 'Here, ask this gentleman if it is not worth looking at. Come in, come in, one franc apiece.'

"I was ashamed to say that it was not worth looking at, and the showman evidently counted on that. So is it, undoubtedly, with those that have experienced all the vileness of the honeymoon, and do not dispel the illusions of others. I also refrained from dispelling any one's illusions. But now I do not see why one should not tell the truth. It even seems to me that it is essential to tell the truth about this. It was awkward, shameful, vile, pitiable, and, above all, it was wearisome, unspeakably wearisome. It was something analogous to what I experienced when I was learning to smoke, when I was sick at my stomach and salivated, and I swallowed it down and pretended that it was very pleasant. Just as from that, the delights of marriage, if there are any, will be subsequent; the husband must educate his wife in this vice, in order to procure any pleasure from it."

"Vice? What do you mean?" I asked. "Why, you are talking about one of the most natural of human functions!"

"Natural?" he exclaimed. "Natural? No, I will tell you that I have come to the conviction that it is not natural. Nay, it is perfectly unnatural. Ask children, ask an innocent young girl.

"You said 'natural.'

"It is natural to eat. And it is agreeable, easy, and jolly, and not at all shameful, to eat; but this is vile and shameful and painful. No, it is not natural. And the pure maiden, I am convinced, will always hate it."

"But how," I asked, "how would the human race be perpetuated?"

"Well, why should not the human race perish?" he asked, with a touch of savage irony, as if he were expecting this unfair reply, as if he had heard it before. "Preach abstinence from procreation in the name of making it always possible for English lords to gormandize, and it will go! Preach abstinence from procreation in the name of giving a greater pleasure, it will go! But try to persuade people to refrain from procreation in the name of morality —ye fathers! what an outcry! The human race would not be extinguished, because an attempt was made to keep men from being swine. However, excuse me! this light is disagreeable to me; may I shade it?" he asked, pointing to the lamp.

I said that it was immaterial to me, and then—hastily, as in everything he did—he got up on the seat, and pulled down the woolen shade to the lamp.

"Nevertheless," said I, "if all men should adopt this for a law, the human race would be annihilated."

He did not immediately reply.

"You ask: 'How would the human race be perpetuated?'" said he, again taking his seat opposite me, and spreading his legs wide apart, and resting his elbows on his knees. "Why should it be continued—this human race of ours?" he exclaimed.

"Why do you ask such a question? Otherwise there would be no more of us."

"Well, why should there be?"

"What a question—why, to live, of course."

"But why should we live? If there is no other aim, if life was given only to perpetuate life, then there is no reason why we should live. And if this is so, then the Schopenhauers and Hartmanns, and all the Buddhists as well, are perfectly right. Now, if there is a purpose in life, then it is clear that life ought to come to an end when that purpose is attained. This is the logic of it," said he, with evident agitation, and seeming to set a high value on his thought. "This is the logic of it. Observe: if the aim of mankind is happiness, goodness, love if you prefer; if the aim of mankind is what is said in the prophecies that all men are to unite themselves in universal love, that the spears are to be beaten into pruning-hooks and the like, then what stands in the way of the attainment of this aim? Human passions do! Of all passions, the most powerful and vicious and obstinate is sexual, carnal love; and so if passions are annihilated and with them the last and most powerful, carnal love, then the prophecy will be fulfilled, men will be united together, the aim of mankind will have been attained, and there would be no longer any reason for existence. As long as humanity exists, this ideal will be before it, and of course this is not the ideal of rabbits or of pigs, which is to propagate as rapidly as possible, and it is not the ideal of monkeys or of Parisians, which is to enjoy all the refinements of sexual passion, but it is the ideal of goodness attained by self-restraint and chastity. Toward this men are now striving, and always have striven. And see what results.

"It results that sexual love is the safety-valve. If the human race does not as yet attain this aim, it is simply because there are passions, and the strongest of them the sexual. But since there is sexual passion, a new generation comes along, and of course there is always the possibility that the aim may be attained by some succeeding generation. But as long as it is not attained, then there will be other generations until the aim is attained, until the prophecies are fulfilled, until all men are joined in unity. And then what would be the result?

"If it be granted that God created men for the attainment of a certain end, then He must have created them mortal, without sexual passion, or immortal. If they were mortal, but without sexual passion, then what would be the result? —this: that they would live without attaining their aim, and then would die, so that, to attain the aim, God would have to create new men. But if they were immortal, then let us suppose—although it is harder for those men to correct mistakes and approach perfection than it is for the new generations— let us suppose, I say, that they reached their goal after many thousand years; but then, why should they? What good would the rest of their lives be to them? It is better as it is! . . .

"But perhaps you do not approve this form of expression, perhaps you are an evolutionist. Even then it comes to the same thing. The highest genus of animals, men, in order to get the advantage in the conflict with other creatures, must band together, like a hive of bees, and not propagate irregularly; must also, like the bees, nourish the sexless ones; in other words, must struggle toward continence, and never allow the kindling of the carnal lusts to which the whole arrangement of our life is directed."

He paused.

"Will the human race come to an end? Can any one who looks at the world as it is have the slightest doubt of it? Why, it is just as certain as death is certain. We find the end of the world inculcated in all the teachings of the Church, and in all the teachings of Science it is likewise shown to be inevitable.

12

"In our society it is just exactly reversed: if a man has felt it incumbent on him to be continent during his bachelorhood, then always after he is married he feels it no longer necessary to restrain himself. You see, the wedding journeys, this retirement to solitude which young people with the sanction of their parents practise, are nothing else than a sanction for lewdness. But the moral law when it is broken brings its own punishment.

"In spite of all my endeavors to make my honeymoon a success, it was a failure. The whole time was merely vile, shameful, and tiresome. But very soon it became also painfully oppressive. This state of things began almost at the first. I think it was on the third or fourth day, I found my wife depressed, and I began to inquire what was the matter, began to put my arms around her, which I supposed was all she could possibly desire; but she pushed away my arm and burst into tears.

"What was it? She could not tell me. But she was depressed and downhearted. Probably her highly wrought nerves whispered to her the truth as to the ignominy of our relations, but she could not tell me. I began to question her; she said something about being homesick for her mother. It seemed to me that this was not the truth. I tried to console her, but said nothing about her mother. I did not realize that she was simply bored, and that her mother was merely a pretext.

"But she immediately complained because I said nothing about her mother, as if I did not believe her. She told me that she could see I did not love her. I accused her of caprice, and immediately her face changed; in place of melancholy appeared exasperation, and she began in the bitterest terms to charge me with egotism and cruelty.

"I looked at her. Her whole face expressed the utmost coldness and hostility, almost hatred of me. I remember how alarmed I was on seeing this.

" 'How is this? What does it mean?' I asked myself; 'love is the union of souls, and instead of this what have we here? Why, it cannot be, this is not she.'

"I did my best to soothe her, but I came up against such an insuperable wall of cold, venomous hostility that, before I had time to think, something like exasperation took possession of me also, and we said to each other a quantity of disagreeable words. The impression of this first quarrel was horrible. I called it a quarrel, but it was not a quarrel; it was really only the discovery of the gulf which was in reality between us. Our passionate love had worn itself out in the satisfaction of the senses, and therefore we remained facing each other as we really were, in other words, two egotists alien to each other, desirous each of getting the greatest possible pleasure out of the other!

"I called what took place between us a quarrel, but it was not a quarrel; it was only the consequence of the cessation of our sensuality, disclosing our actual relation to each other. I did not realize that this cold and hostile relationship was our normal relation. I did not understand this because this hostility, in the first weeks of our marriage, was very quickly hidden again from us by the rising of a newly distilled sensuality, that is to say, passionate love.

"And so I thought that we had quarreled and become reconciled, and that this would be the end of it. But in the very first month, during our honeymoon, very quickly came another period of satiety, and again we ceased to be necessary to each other, and another quarrel ensued. The second quarrel surprised me even more than the first. I said to myself:—

" 'Of course the first could not have been the result of chance, but had to be the result of necessity, and so with this, and there will be others.'

"The second quarrel surprised me the more because it proceeded from the most trivial cause—something pecuniary; but I never grudged money, and certainly could never have grudged any to my wife. I only remember that she made some remark of mine seem to be the expression of my desire to control her through money to which I claimed an exclusive right—something impossible, stupid, cowardly, and natural neither to her nor to me.

"I grew angry, and began to reproach her for her lack of delicacy; she returned the charge, and so it went on as before. And I perceived in her words, and in the expression of her face and her eyes, the same harsh, cold hostility as had surprised me the first time. I remember having quarreled with my brother, my friend, even my father; but never did there arise between us such a peculiar venomous anger as was manifested now. But after a short time our mutual reciprocal hatred concealed itself again under our passionate love, that is, our sensuality, and I once more cherished the notion that these two quarrels had been mistakes which might be rectified.

"But when the third and the fourth quarrel ensued, I came to believe that it was not a mere chance, but that it had to be, and that it would still be so, and I was horror-struck at what was before me. In this connection I was tormented by the horrible idea that I was the only person who had this misfortune, and that no other couple had any such experiences as I was having with my wife. I had not then found out that this is a common lot—that all men think, just as I did, that it is a misfortune exclusively peculiar to them, and so conceal this exclusive and shameful misfortune, not only from others but also from themselves, and are unwilling to acknowledge it.

"It began with us at the very first and kept on all the time, and grew more severe and more bitter. In the depths of my soul I from the very first felt that I was lost, that marriage had not turned out at all as I had expected, that it was not only not a happiness, but was something very oppressive; but, like all other men, I was not willing to acknowledge this—and I should not acknowledge it even now, had it not been for the sequel—and I concealed it not only from others, but even from myself.

"Now I am amazed that I did not recognize my real position. It might have been seen in the fact that our quarrels sprang from causes so trivial that afterward, when they were ended, it was impossible to remember what brought them about. Reason was not quick enough to sophisticate sufficient pretexts for the hostility that constantly existed between us.

"But still more amazing was the insufficiency of the pretexts for reconciliation. Occasionally it was a word, or an explanation, even tears, but sometimes . . . oh, how shameful it is to remember it now! after the bitterest words exchanged, suddenly would come silence, glances, smiles, kisses, embraces! . . . Fu! abomination. Why was it that I failed to see all the vileness of this even then?" . . .

13

Two passengers entered and began to settle themselves at the end of the carriage. He ceased speaking while they were taking their places, but as soon as they became quiet he went on with his story, never for an instant losing the thread of his thoughts.

"What is chiefly vile about this," he went on to say, "is that it is taken for granted in theory that love is something ideal and elevated; whereas, in practice, love is something low and swinish, which it is shameful and disgusting to speak of or remember. You see, it was not without reason that nature made it shameful and disgusting. But if it is shameful and disgusting, then it ought to be so much the more to be made known. But with us, on the contrary, people pretend that what is low and shameful and disgusting is beautiful and elevated.

"What were the first symptoms of my love? Why, these—that I gave myself up to animal excesses, not only not feeling any shame at it, but feeling a certain pride at the possibility of these animal excesses, not thinking either of her spiritual life or even of her physical life. I wondered what was the cause of our animosity to each other, but the thing was perfectly clear: this animosity was nothing else than the protest of human nature against the animal which was crushing it. I was amazed at our hatred of each other. But you see it could not have been otherwise. This hatred was nothing else than identical with the hatred felt by the accomplices in a crime, both for the instigation and for the accomplishment of the deed. What else was it than a crime, when she, poor thing, became pregnant within the first month and our swinish relations continued.

"You think that I am wandering from my story? Not at all. I am all the time relating to you *how* I killed my wife. . . . At my trial I was asked why and how I killed her. . . . Fools! they think that I killed her with a dagger on the seventeenth of October. I did not kill her then, but long before. In exactly the same way they are all killing their wives now, all, all." . . .

"How so?" I asked.

"It is something amazing that no one wishes to know what is so clear and evident—what doctors ought to know and to proclaim, but they hold their tongues. You see, it is really awfully simple! Men and women are like animals, and they are so created that after sexual union pregnancy begins, then suckling— a condition of things during which sexual union is dangerous both for the woman and for the child. The number of women and of men is about even: what does that signify? Of course it is clear. It does not require great wisdom to draw from these things the conclusion which animals also draw—that continence is necessary. But no! Science has gone so far as to discover certain corpuscles which run about in the blood, and all sorts of useless stupidities, but it cannot comprehend this yet. At least it is not rumored about that Science is saying this.

"And now for women there are only two methods of escape: one is by making monsters of themselves, by destroying or annihilating in themselves, according to the requirements of the case, the faculty of being women, that is to say, mothers, so that men may have no interruption of their enjoyment. The second escape is not an escape at all, but a simple, brutal, direct violation of the laws of nature. Such is constantly taking place in all so-called virtuous families, and it is this: the woman, in direct opposition to her nature, is obliged while bearing and nursing a child to be at the same time her husband's mistress, is obliged to be what no other animal ever permits. And she can't have the strength for it.

"Hence in our social sphere hysteria and nerves, and among the people women possessed. You have observed among girls, pure girls I mean, there is no such thing as 'possession'; it is only among peasant women and among women who live with their husbands. So it is with us. And it is exactly the same in Europe. All the hospitals are full of hysterical women, who have broken the laws of nature. And these possessed women and the patients of Charcot are perfect cripples, and the world is full of half-crippled women. Only to think, what a mighty thing is taking place in a woman when she has conceived, or when she is nursing a baby. That which is growing is to continue ourselves, is to take our place. And this holy function is violated—for what? It is terrible to think about it. And yet they talk about the freedom, the rights, of women! It is just the same as if cannibals should feed up their prisoners for food, and at the same time talk, assert, that they were working for their freedom and rights."

All this was new, and surprised me.

"But what would you do?" I exclaimed. "If this came about, then a husband could have intercourse with his wife only once in two years; but a man . . ."

"Yes, yes, a man must have it," said he, taking the words out of my mouth. "Again, the priests of Science support you in your views. Suggest to a man that vodka, tobacco, opium, are indispensable to him, and all that sort of thing will become indispensable to him. It means that God did not understand what was needful, and that therefore, as He did not ask advice of the magi, he arranged things badly. Pray observe, the thing does not hang together. It is needful, it is indispensable, for a man to satisfy his carnal desires—so they decide; but here comes in the question of conception and nursing babies, which prevents the satisfaction of this necessity. How is the difficulty to be overcome? How manage it? Why! go to the magi; they will arrange it. They have thought it all out. Oh! when shall these magi be dethroned from their deceptions? It is time! You see how far things have already gone; men become mad and shoot themselves, and all from this one cause. And how could it be otherwise? Animals seem to know that their progeny perpetuate their kind, and they observe a certain law in this respect. Only man has not the wisdom to know this, and does not wish to know it. All He cares for is to have the greatest possible pleasure. And who is he? he is the tsar of nature, he is man!

"Pray observe, animals enjoy intercourse only when there is to be progeny, but the vile tsar of nature does it only for pleasure's sake, and at any time; and, moreover, he idealizes this monkey-like business, and calls it the pearl of creation, love! And in the name of this love, that is to say, this vileness, he destroys—what? one-half of the human race! In the name of his gratifications he makes of all women, who ought to be his coadjutors in the progress of humanity toward truth and happiness, enemies instead! Look around and tell me who everywhere acts as a hindrance to the progress of humanity—women. And what makes them so? Nothing but this!

"Yes, yes," he repeated several times, and he began to shift his position, to get out his cigarettes and to smoke, evidently desiring to calm himself a little.

14

"Thus I lived like a pig," he continued, in his former tone. "The worst of it was that, while I was living this vile life, I imagined that because I did not commit adultery with other women, therefore I was leading a perfectly virtuous family life, that I was a moral man, that I was in no manner to blame, but that if we had our quarrels she was to blame—her character!

"She was not to blame, of course. She was like all other women, like the majority. She had been educated in the way demanded by the position of women in our circle, and therefore as all women, without exception, belonging to the leisurely classes are educated and as they have to be educated.

"They talk nowadays about some new-fangled method of female education. All idle words: the training of women is exactly what it must be in view of the existent, sincere, and genuine notion of women universally held.

"And the education of women will always correspond to the notion of her held by men. Now we all know what that is, how men look on women: *Wein, Weib, und Gesang,* and so it goes in the verses of the poets. Take all poetry, all painting, all sculpture, beginning with erotic verse and naked Venuses and Phrynes, and you will see that woman is an instrument of pleasure; such she is at Truba and at Grachevka and at the finest ball. And mark the devil's subtlety: pleasure, satisfaction . . . then let it be understood that it is merely pleasure, that woman is a sweet morsel. In the early days, knights boasted that they made divinities of women—apotheosized them, and at the same time they looked on them as the instruments of their pleasure. But nowadays men declare that they respect women, some relinquish their places to them, or pick up their handkerchiefs, others admit their rights to occupy all responsibilities, to take part in government and the like. They do all this, but their view of them is always the same, she is still the instrument of enjoyment, her body is the means of enjoyment. And she knows all that. It is just the same as slavery.

"Slavery is nothing else than the enjoyment by the few of the compulsory labor of the many. And in order that slavery may come to an end, people must cease desiring to take advantage of the compulsory labor of others, must consider it sinful or shameful. But while they take away, while they abolish, the external form of slavery, while they so arrange it that it is no longer possible to buy and sell slaves in the market, and they believe and persuade themselves that slavery is abolished, they do not see and they do not wish to see that slavery still exists, for the reason that people, just the same as ever, like to profit by the labors of others, and consider it fair and honorable to do so. And as long as they consider this to be fair, there will always be men who will be stronger and keener than others, and will be able to do so.

"So it is with the emancipation of women. The slavery of woman consists in precisely this, that men desire to take advantage of her as an instrument of enjoyment, and consider it right to do so.

"Well, and now they emancipate woman, they give her all rights the same as to men, but they still continue to look on her as an instrument of enjoyment, and so they educate her with this end in view, both in childhood and by public opinion. But all the time she is just the same kind of a dissolute slave as before, and her husband is just the same kind of a dissolute slave-owner.

"They emancipate women in the colleges and in the law courts, but they look on her still as an object of enjoyment. Train her as she is trained among us, to regard herself in this light, and she will always remain a lower creature. Either she will, with the assistance of villainous doctors, prevent the birth of her offspring,—in other words, she will be a kind of prostitute, degrading herself, not to the level of a beast, but to the level of a thing; or she will be what she is, in the majority of cases, heart-sick, hysterical, unhappy, without the possibility of spiritual development.

"Gymnasia and universities cannot change this. It can be changed only by a change in the way men regard women, and the way women regard themselves. It can be changed only by woman coming to regard virginity as the highest condition, and not as it is now regarded, as a reproach and disgrace. Until this comes about, the ideal of every girl, whatever her education, will still remain that of attracting to herself as many men as possible, as many males as she can, in order that she may have a possibility of choice.

"The fact that one girl understands mathematics, and another can play on the harp, does not change this in the least. A woman is fortunate and attains all that she can desire when she obtains a husband, and therefore the chief task of woman is to learn how to bewitch him. So it has been, and so it will be. Just as this was characteristic of the maiden's life in our circle, so it continues to be even after she is married. In the maiden's life this was necessary for a choice; in the married woman's life it is needed for her ascendancy over her husband.

"The only thing which destroys this—curtails it for the time being—is the birth of children, and this is when she is not a monster; in other words, when she nurses her children. But here again the doctors interfere. In the case of my wife, although she wanted to suckle her first baby, and though she suckled the next five, the state of her health seemed precarious, and these doctors, who cynically undressed her and felt of her all over,—for which service I was obliged to be grateful to them and to pay money,—these gentle doctors found that she ought not to nurse her child; and so she, this first time, was deprived of the sole means of saving herself from coquetry. She hired a wet-nurse; in other words, we took advantage of the poverty, needs, ignorance of another woman, decoyed her away from her own child to ours, and, in payment for this, gave her a head-dress with laces. But that is not the point. The point is that during this period of emancipation from bearing and nursing babies, the female coquetry, which had hitherto lain dormant, manifested itself in her with greater strength, while correspondingly in me there appeared with especial violence the pangs of jealousy, which unceasingly tore me during all my married life, as they cannot fail to tear all husbands who live with their wives as I lived with mine—that is to say, unnaturally.

15

"During the whole course of my married life I never ceased to experience the pangs of jealousy, but there were periods when I suffered from them with especial acuteness; and one of these periods was after the birth of my first child, when the doctors forbade her to suckle it. I was especially jealous at this time; in the first place, because my wife suffered from that uneasiness characteristic of mothers, which is calculated to make an unreasonable interruption of the regular course of life; secondly, because when I saw how easily she renounced the moral responsibilities of a mother I naturally, even though unconsciously, concluded that it would be equally easy for her to renounce the duties of a wife; the more so because she was perfectly healthy, and, notwithstanding the prohibition of the dear doctors, she nursed the other children, and nursed them excellently."

"But you don't seem to like doctors?" said I, for I had noticed a particularly bitter tone in his voice every time he mentioned them.

"This is not a matter of love or of hate. They ruined my life, as they have ruined, and will still continue to ruin, the lives of thousands, hundreds of thousands, of people; and I cannot help connecting cause and effect. I understand that they, like lawyers and others, must earn money to live on, and I would willingly give them a half of my income; and, if it were only realized what they were doing, every one else would also, I am convinced, give a half of his property on condition that they would not meddle with our family lives, and would never come near us. I have never collected any statistics, still I know of a dozen cases—a multitude of them—in which they have killed the unborn child, declaring that the mother would not live if the child were born; and yet afterward the mother was admirably fortunate in childbearing; and again they have killed the mother under the pretext of some operation or other. You see, no one reckons up these murders, just as no one ever reckoned the murders of the Inquisition, because it has been supposed that this was done for the benefit of humanity. It is impossible to count the crimes committed by them. But all these crimes are nothing compared to the moral corruption of materialism which they introduced into the world, especially through women.

"I say nothing about the fact that, if we should follow their prescription, then, thanks to the infection everywhere, in everything, people would have to separate instead of drawing closer together; they would have, according to the teachings of the doctors, to sit apart, and never let the atomizer, with carbolic acid, out of their mouths. . . . Lately, however, they have discovered that even this is of no special use.

"But this is not to the point. The principal poison lies in the demoralization of the people, women especially.

"To-day, it is no longer enough to say, 'You are living a bad life; live better.' You can't say that to yourself or to another man. But if you are living a bad life, then the cause for it lies in the abnormal state of the nervous functions, and the like. And you have to consult the doctors, and they prescribe for thirty-five kopeks' worth of medicine at the apothecaries, and you take it.

"You will grow even worse, then have to take new drugs and consult other doctors. An excellent dodge!

"But that is not to the point. I only say that she suckled the children admirably, and that the only thing that saved me from the pangs of jealousy was her bearing and nursing her children.

"If it had not been for that, the inevitable end would have come about earlier.

"The children saved me and her. During eight years she gave birth to five children, and all except the first she nursed herself."

"Where are your children now?" I asked.

"My children?" he repeated, with a startled look.

"Forgive me! perhaps this question caused you painful memories."

"No, it's of no consequence. My sister-in-law and her brother took charge of my children. They would not give them to me. You see I am a kind of insane man. I am going away from them now. I have seen them, but they won't give them to me. For if they did, I should educate them so that they should not be like their parents. But it is necessary that they should be the same. Well, what is to be done? I can understand why they should not give them to me, or trust me. And besides, I don't know as I should have the strength to bring them up. I think not. I am a ruin, a cripple! One thing I have . . . I know. Yes, it is manifest that I know what it will be a long time before the rest of the world knows.

"Yes, my children are alive, and are growing up to be just such savages as all the rest around them are. I have seen them—three times I have seen them. I can't do anything for them—not a thing. I am going now to my own place in the south; I have a little house and a little garden there.

"Yes, it will not be soon that people will know what I know. It will soon be easy to find out how much iron and what other metals there are in the sun and the stars; but what shall cure our swinishness, that is hard, awfully hard!

"You have listened to me, and even for that I am grateful.

16

"You just mentioned the children. There, again, what terrible lying goes on concerning children. Children are a divine benediction. Children are a delight. Now this is all a lie. All this used to be so, but now there is nothing of the sort, nothing at all. Children are a torment, and that is all. The majority of mothers feel so, and some of them do not hesitate to say so, up and down. Ask the greater number of the mothers of our circle,—people of means,— and they will tell you that from terror lest their children should sicken and die they do not wish to have children; if they are born, they do not wish to suckle them, lest they should grow too much attached to them and cause them sorrow. The delight which the child affords them by its beauty, its tiny little arms, its little feet, its whole body,—the satisfaction afforded is less than the agony of apprehension which they experience, I do not say from illness or the loss of the child, but from the mere apprehension of the possibility of illnesses and death. Having weighed the advantages and disadvantages, it seems to be disadvantageous, and therefore that it is not desirable, to have children. They say this openly, boldly, imagining that these sentiments grow out of their love to their children, good, praiseworthy feelings in which they take pride. They do not notice this: that by this reasoning they directly renounce love and assert their egoism. For them there is less pleasure from the charm of a child than suffering from apprehension for it, and therefore they don't desire a child which they would come to love. They do not sacrifice themselves for the beloved creature, but they sacrifice for themselves the beloved creature that is to be.

"It is clear that this is not love, but egoism. But it is not for me to criticize these mothers of well-to-do families for their egoism, when you think of all they endure from the health of their children in our modern fashionable life, thanks again to these same doctors. How well I remember even now our life and the conditions of our life during the first period of our marriage, when we had three or four young children, and she was absorbed with them! It fills me even now with horror.

"It was no kind of a life. It was a perpetual peril, rescue from it followed by new peril; then new and desperate endeavors, and then a new rescue—all the time as if we were on board a sinking ship. It sometimes seemed to me that this was done on purpose; that she was pretending to be troubled about her children so as to get the upper hand of me, so alluringly, so simply all questions were decided for her advantage. It seemed to me sometimes that all that she said and did in these circumstances was done on purpose. But no, she herself suffered terribly and kept tormenting herself about the children, and about the care of their health and about their illnesses. It was a torture for her and for me also. And it was impossible for her not to torment herself.

"You see her attachment to her children,—the animal instinct to nurse them, to fondle them, to protect them was in her as it is in the majority of women; but she had not what animals have—a freedom from imagination and reason. The hen has no fear of what may befall her chick, she knows nothing about the diseases which may come upon it, knows nothing of all those remedies which men imagine they can employ to keep away sickness and death. And for the hen the young ones are no torment. She does for her chicks what is natural and pleasant for her to do, and her young are a delight to her. When the chicken shows signs of sickness her duties are distinctly determined: she warms and nourishes it. And in doing this she knows that she is doing her duty. If the chicken dies, she does not ask herself why it died, where it has gone to, she cackles for a while, then stops and goes on living as before.

"But for our unhappy women and for my wife there was nothing of the kind. Then, besides the question of diseases and how to cure them, of how to educate them, how to develop them, she had heard from all sides and had read endlessly varied and contradictory rules: you must feed it this way, no not this way, but so; how to dress it, what to give it to drink, when to bathe it, when to put it to sleep, when to take it out to walk, ventilation,—in regard to all this, we—and she especially—learned new rules every week. Just as if children began to be born only yesterday! Why! some child was not fed quite properly, or wasn't bathed at the right time, and it fell ill, and it showed that we were to blame—that we had not done what we should have done. Even when children are well, they are a torment. But when they fall ill, why then, of course, it is a perfect hell. It is presupposed that sickness may be cured and that there is such a science and there are such men—doctors, and that they know. Not that all know, but that the best of them do. And here is a sick child and it is requisite to get hold of this man, the very best of his profession, who can cure, and the child is saved; and if you don't get hold of this doctor, or if you don't live where this doctor lives, then the child is lost. And this belief was not exclusively confined to my wife, but it is the belief of all the women of her sphere, and on all sides she hears such talk as this:—

" 'Two of Yekaterina Semyonovna's children died because they did not call Ivan Zakharuitch in time, but Ivan Zakharuitch saved the life of Marya Ivanovna's oldest daughter; and here the Petrovitch children were sent in time to different hotels by this doctor's advice, and so their lives were saved; but those that had not been isolated, died. And such and such a woman had a feeble child, and by the doctor's advice they took it South, and it lived. . . .'

"How can one fail to torment oneself and grow excited all one's life long, when the life of her children, to whom she is devotedly attached, depends on her knowing in time what Ivan Zakharuitch will say about it? But no one knows what Ivan Zakharuitch will say—least of all himself, because he knows very well that he knows nothing at all and cannot give any help, and he only tergiversates at haphazard merely in order that people may not cease to believe in his knowledge.

"You see, if she had been simply an animal, she would not have tormented herself so; while if she had been a normal human being, then she would have had faith in God, she would have thought and spoken as true believers say:—

" 'God gave and God has taken and one can't escape from God.'

"So our whole life with our children was no joy but a torment for her, and, therefore, for me also. How could we help tormenting ourselves? And she constantly did torment herself. It used to be that just as we were calming down from any scene of jealousy or a simple quarrel, and were planning to begin a new life, to read something and to do something, and had only got fairly started, word would suddenly be brought that Vasya was vomiting, that Masha had the dysentery, or that Andryusha had a rash—and the end of it was that we had no kind of a life. Where should we send, what doctor should we get, in which room should we isolate the patient? And then began klysters, the taking of temperatures, the medicines, and the doctors. And this would scarcely be done with before something else would begin. There was no regular family life. But, as I have told you, there was a constant apprehension from real or fancied dangers. And that is the way it is in most families. In my family it was especially pronounced. My wife was affectionate and superstitious.

"Thus it was that the presence of children not only did not improve our life, but poisoned it. Moreover, the children gave us a new pretext for quarreling. From the time we began to have children, and the more in proportion as they grew up, the more frequently our children became the very means and object of our quarrels, not only the subject, but the very instrument of dissension; we, as it were, fought each other with our own children as weapons. Each of us had his own favorite child as a weapon of attack. I made more use of Vasya the eldest, and she of Liza. Later, when the children had begun to grow up, and their characters formed, it came about that they took sides with us according as we were able to attract them. They suffered terribly from this state of affairs, poor little things, but we in our incessant warfare had no time to think of them. The little girl was my special ally; the oldest boy, who resembled his mother and was her favorite, often seemed hateful to me.

17

"Well, thus we lived. Our relations grew more and more hostile, and at last it went so far that difference of views no longer produced enmity, but that enmity produced difference of views. Whatever she said I was ready in advance to disagree with her, and so it was with her.

"In the fourth year it was fairly admitted by both of us, though tacitly, that we could not understand each other—that we could not agree. We ceased to make any attempt to talk anything over to the end. In regard to the simplest things, especially the children, we each kept our own opinion unchangeably. As I now remember, the opinions which I advocated were not so precious in my sight that I could not give them up; but she had opposing notions, and to yield to them meant to yield to her. And this I could not do. Nor could she yield to me. She evidently counted herself always perfectly right toward me, and as for me, I was always a saint in my own eyes compared to her. When we were together we were almost reduced to silence, or to such conversation as I am convinced the beasts may carry on together:—'What time is it?'—'Is it bedtime?'—'What will you have for dinner to-day?'—'Where will you drive?'—'What is the news?'—'We must send for the doctor; Masha has a sore throat.'

"It required only to step a hair's width beyond this unendurably narrowing circle of conventional sentences in order to inspire a dissension,—skirmishes and expressions of hatred regarding the coffee, the table-cloth, the drive, the course of the game at whist,—in fact, over trifles which could not have had the slightest importance for either of us. In me, at least, hatred of her boiled terribly. I often looked at her when she was drinking tea, waving her foot, or conveying her spoon to her mouth, sipping from it and swallowing the liquid, and I hated her for this very trifle as if it were the worst of crimes. I did not notice that these periods broke out in me with perfect regularity and uniformity, corresponding to the periods of what we called 'love.' A period of 'love'—then a period of hatred; an energetic period of passion, then a long period of hatred; a feebler manifestation of passion, then a briefer outbreak of hatred.

"We did not then comprehend that this love and hatred were one and the same animal passion, only with opposite poles. It would have been horrible to live in this way if we had realized our situation; but we did not realize it and did not see it. In this lie the salvation as well as the punishment of a man is that when he is living irregularly he may blind himself so as not to see the wretchedness of his situation.

"Thus it was with us. She endeavored to forget herself in strenuous and ever absorbing occupations,—her housekeeping, the arrangement of the furniture, dressing herself and the family, and the education and health of the children. I had my own affairs to attend to,—drinking, hunting, playing cards, going to my office. We were both busy all the time. We both felt that the busier we were the more annoyed we might be with each other.

" 'It is very well for you to make up such grimaces,' I would think, mentally addressing her. 'How you tormented me all night with your scenes. But I have a meeting to attend.'

" 'It is all very well for you,' she would not only think, but even say aloud, 'but the baby kept me awake all night long.'

"These new theories of hypnotism, mental diseases, hysteria, are all an absurdity—not a simple absurdity, but a vile and pernicious one. In regard to my wife, Charcot would have infallibly said that she was a victim of hysteria, and he would have said of me that I was abnormal, and probably he would have tried to cure us. But there was no disease to cure.

"Thus we lived in a continual mist, not cognizant of the situation in which we found ourselves. And if the catastrophy which overtook us had not occurred, I should have continued to live on till old age in the same way, and on my death-bed I should have even thought that I had lived a good life,—not remarkably good, but not at all a bad life,—like that of all other men. I should never have understood that abyss of unhappiness and that abominable falsehood in which I was floundering.

"We were like two convicts, fastened to one chain and hating each other, each poisoning the life of the other and striving not to recognize the fact. I did not then realize that ninety-nine per cent of married people live in the same hell as mine, and that it must infallibly be so. I did not then realize that it was true of others or true of myself.

"It is amazing what coincidences may be found in a regular and even in an irregular life. Thus when parents are beginning to find that they are making each other's lives unendurable, it becomes imperative that they go to the city for the better education of their children. And so it was we found it necessary to move to the city."

He stopped speaking, and twice gave vent to those strange sounds which this time were quite like repressed sobs. We were approaching a station.

"What time is it?" he asked.

I looked at my watch. It was two o'clock.

"Aren't you tired?" he asked.

"No; but are you not tired?"

"I am suffocating. Permit me, I will go out and get a drink of water."

And he got up and went staggering through the carriage.

I sat alone, cogitating over what he had told me, and I fell into such a brown study that I did not notice him when he returned through the other door.

18

"Yes, I all the time wander from my story," he began; "I have pondered over it a good deal. I look on many things in a different way from what most do, and I want to talk it all out.

"Well, we began to live in the city. There a man may live a century and never dream that he has long ago died and rotted. One has no time to study himself—his time is wholly occupied: business, social relations, his health, art, the health of his children, and their education. Now he must receive calls from such and such people and must return them; now he must see this woman and hear some famous man or woman talk. You see, at any given moment there will be in the city surely one celebrity, and generally several, whom it is impossible for you to miss. Now you have to consult a doctor for yourself or for this one or that, then you have to see one of the tutors or the governess, and life is frittered away. Well, so it was we lived and suffered less from our life together. Moreover, we had at first the charming occupation of getting settled in a new city, in new quarters, and then again in traveling back and forth between the city and the country.

"Thus we lived one winter, and during the second winter the circumstance which I am going to relate took place, and though it seemed a trifling thing and attracted no attention, still it brought about all that succeeded.

"She became delicate in health, and the doctors forbade her to have any more children, and they taught her how to prevent it. This was repulsive to me. I had no patience with such an idea, but she with frivolous obstinacy insisted on having her own way, and I had to yield. The last justification of the swinish life—children—was taken away, and our life became viler than ever.

"To the muzhik, to the laboring man, children are a necessity; although it is hard for him to feed them, still he must have them and there the marital relations are justified. But to us, who already have children, more children are not a desideratum; they cause extra work, expense, further division of property —they are a burden.

"And therefore there is no justification for us of the swinish life. Either we artificially prevent the birth of children or we regard children as a misfortune, —as the consequence of carelessness, which is worse.

"There is no justification. But we have fallen morally so low that we do not see the need of any justification. The majority of men now belonging to the cultivated classes give themselves up to this form of debauchery without the slightest twinge of conscience.

"No one feels any conscientious scruples, because conscience is a non-existent quality except—if we may so say—the conscience of public opinion and of the criminal law. And in this respect neither the one nor the other is violated; no one has to bear the brunt of public scorn, for all do the same thing: both Marya Pavlovna and Ivan Zakharuitch. Why breed beggars or deprive oneself of the possibility of social life? . . . Or is there any reason to stand in awe of the criminal law or to fear it. Ugly peasant girls and soldiers' wives may throw their babies into ponds and wells, and they of course must go to prison, but all that sort of thing is done by us opportunely and neatly!

"Thus we lived two years. The means employed by the rascally doctors evidently began to take effect: physically she improved and she grew more beautiful, like the last beauty of the summer. She was conscious of this, and began to take care of herself. Her beauty became fascinating and disturbing to men. As she was in the prime of a woman of thirty and was no longer bearing children, she grew plump—stirring the passions. Even the sight of her made one uneasy. When she came among men she attracted all eyes. She was like a well-fed and bridled horse which had not been driven for some time and from which the bridle was taken off. There was no longer any restraint, as with ninety-nine per cent of our women. Even I felt this, and it was terrible to me."

19

He suddenly got up and sat down close by the window.

"Excuse me," he exclaimed, and looking out intently sat there for as much as three minutes. Then he sighed deeply and again sat down opposite me. His face had undergone a complete change, there came a piteous look into his eyes, and a strange sort of smile curved his lips.

"I had grown a little tired, but I will go on with my story. There is plenty of time left; it has not begun to grow light yet. Yes," he began again, after he had lighted a cigarette. "She grew plumper after she ceased to bear children, and her malady—the constant worriment over the children—began to disappear; it did not really disappear, but she, as it were, awoke from a drunken stupor; she began to remember, and she saw that there was a whole world, a divine world, with its joys about which she had entirely forgotten, but in which she did not know how to live—a divine world which she did not understand at all.

" 'How keep it from being wasted. Time is fleeting—it will not return.'

"Thus I imagined she thought or rather felt, and indeed it would have been impossible for it to be otherwise; she had been educated to believe that in this world there is only one thing worthy of any one's attention—love. She had become married, she had got some notion of what this love was, but it was very far from being what had been promised, from what she expected; she had undergone the loss of many illusions; she had borne many sufferings, and then that unexpected torment—so many children! This agony had worn her out. And now, thanks to the obliging doctors, she had found out that it was possible to avoid having children. She was glad of that, made the experiment, and began to live for the one thing which she knew about—for the sake of love. But the enjoyment of love with a husband who was consumed with the fiery passions of wrath and jealously was not the kind she wanted. She began to picture to herself another, a more genuine, a newer kind of connection—at least that is what I imagine was the case. And so she began to look around, as if she were expecting something.

"I noticed it, and was correspondingly troubled. It kept all the time happening that she, talking as her habit was with me through the medium of others, that is to say, talking with strangers, but making her remarks for my ears, expressed herself boldly, never at all dreaming that she, an hour before, had said diametrically the opposite, and expressed herself half seriously to the effect that that maternal solicitude was a delusion, that there was no sense in sacrificing her life for her children, that she was still young and could still enjoy life. She really occupied herself less with her children, certainly with less of desperate solicitude; but she gave more and more attention to herself, occupied herself with her external appearance, although she tried to keep it secret; also with her pleasures and with her accomplishments. She once more enthusiastically took up her piano practice which hitherto she had entirely neglected. That was the beginning of the end."

He once more turned to the window his weary-looking eyes, but straightway, evidently making an effort to control himself, he proceeded:—

"Yes, that man appeared."

He hesitated, and twice produced through his nose his peculiar sounds. I saw that it was trying for him to mention that man, to recall him, even to allude to him. But he made an effort, and as it were breaking through the barrier which hindered him, he resolutely went on:—

"A vile fellow he was in my eyes, in my estimation. And not because he played an important part in my life, but because he was really vile. However, the fact that he was bad serves merely as a proof of how irresponsible she was. If it had not been he, it would have surely been some one else."

He again ceased speaking.

"Yes, he was a musician, a fiddler—not a professional musician, but half professional, half society man. His father was a landed proprietor, a neighbor of my father's. His father went to ruin, and his children—three of them were boys —all managed to make their way; only this one, the youngest, was intrusted to his godmother and sent to Paris. There he was sent to the Conservatoire, because he had a talent for music, and he was graduated as a fiddler and played in concerts. He was the man." . . .

It was evident that he wished to say something harsh about him, but he restrained himself, and said, speaking rapidly:—

"Well, I don't know how he had lived up to that time, but that year he appeared in Russia and came to my house. . . . He had almond-shaped, humid eyes, handsome, smiling lips, little waxed mustaches, the latest and most fashionable method of dressing his hair, an insipidly handsome face, such as women call 'not bad,' a slender build, though not ill-shaped, and with a largely developed behind such as they say characterize Hottentot women. This it is said is musical! Slipping into familiarity, as far as was permitted him, but sensitive and always ready to stop short at the slightest resistance, with a regard to external appearances, and with that peculiar touch of Parisian elegance, caused by buttoned boots and bright-colored neckties and everything else which foreigners acquire in Paris, and which by their character of novelty always attract women. In his manners there was a factitious external gayety. A way, as you may know, of speaking about everything by means of hints and fragmentary allusions, as if the person with whom he was speaking knew all about it, and could fill out the missing links.

"Well, then, this man with his music was the cause of all the trouble. You see at the trial the whole affair was represented as having been caused by my jealousy. This was not so at all, that is to say, it was not exactly so; it was, and it was not. At the trial it was decided that I had been deceived and that I had committed the murder in defending my outraged honor,—so they called it in their language,—and on this ground I was acquitted. At the trial I did my best to explain my idea of it, but they understood that I had wished to rehabilitate my wife's honor.

"Her relations with that musician, whatever they were, did not have in my eyes that significance, nor in hers either. It simply had the significance I have already mentioned, that of my swinishness. All came from the fact that between us existed that terrible gulf, of which I have told you, that terrible tension of mutual hatred, whereby the first impulse was sufficient to precipitate the crisis. The quarrels between us, as time went on, became something awful and were remarkably striking, being mingled with intense animal passion.

"If he had not appeared, surely some one else would. If there had not been one pretext for jealousy, there would have been another. I insist upon it that all husbands living as I lived must either live wanton lives, or separate, or kill themselves or their wives as I did. If this does not occur in any given case, it is a rare exception. Why, before the end came, as I made it come, I was several times on the brink of suicide, and even she poisoned herself.

20

"Yes, this happened not long before the crisis.

"We had been living in a sort of armistice, and there was no reason for it to be broken. Suddenly a conversation began, in which I remarked that a certain dog had received a medal at an exhibition. She said:—

" 'Not a medal, but honorable mention.'

"A dispute began. We began to reproach each other, skipping from subject to subject.

" 'Well, I knew that long ago; it was always so.'

" 'You said so and so.'

" 'No, I said thus and so.'

" 'Do you mean to say I lie?'

"There is a feeling that you are on the edge of a frightful quarrel, and that you will be tempted to kill yourself or her. You know that it will begin in an instant and you dread it like fire and you want to control yourself, but anger seizes on your whole being. She is in the same or in an even worse condition, and she deliberately puts a wrong construction on every word you say, giving it a false signification, and every word she speaks is steeped in poison; wherever she knows I am most sensitive, there she strikes. The farther it goes, the more portentous it grows. I cry:—

" 'Silence,' or the like.

"She rushes from the room and takes refuge in the nursery. I try to detain her so that I may say out my say and prove my position, and I seize her by the arm. She pretends that I hurt her and screams:—

" 'Children, your father is striking me.'

"I cry:—

" 'Don't you lie!'

" 'And this is not the first time either,' she cries, or something to that effect.

"The children rush to her. She tries to calm them. I say,—

" 'Don't pretend.'

"She says:—

" 'For you everything is pretense. You strike a woman and then say that she is pretending. Now I understand you. This is the very thing you want.'

"I shout:—

" 'Oh, if you were only dead!'

"I remember how horror-struck I was at those terrible words. I would never have believed myself capable of uttering such coarse, terrible words, and I am amazed that they leap forth from my mouth. I shout out those terrible words and rush into my library, sit down and smoke. I hear her go into the vestibule, preparing to go out. I ask:—

" 'Where are you going?'

"She makes no reply.

" 'Well, the devil go with her!' I say to myself, as I return to the library and again sit down and smoke. A thousand different plans of how to avenge myself on her and how to get rid of her, how to set everything to rights again and how to act as if nothing had taken place, go rushing through my brain.

"And as I sit and think, I smoke, smoke, smoke! I conceive the plan of run- ning away from her, of hiding myself, of going to America. I actually go as far as to dream of getting rid of her, and I think how delightful it would be as soon as this is accomplished to make new ties with some beautiful woman, entirely new. I dream of getting rid of her by her dying or by securing a divorce, and I cogitate how this may be brought about. I see that my mind is wandering, that I am not thinking consecutively; but in order that I may not see that I am thinking the wrong kind of thoughts and am entirely at sea, I smoke.

"But life at home goes on. The governess comes and asks:—

" 'Where is madame? when will she be back?'

"The lackey asks:—

" 'Shall I serve tea?'

"I go into the dining-room. The children, especially the oldest one, Liza, who is already old enough to understand, look at me questioningly, disapprov- ingly. We silently drink our tea. Of her there is no sign. The whole evening passes; she does not come, and two thoughts mingle in my soul: wrath against her because she is tormenting me and all the children by her absence,—and yet, she will return in the end,—and fear that she will not come back, but will lay violent hands on herself.

"I should go out in search of her. But where to find her? At her sister's? But it would be stupid to go there with such an inquiry. Well, then, God go with her! if she wants to torment us, let her torment herself also. That is the very thing she would like. And next time she will be worse.

"But supposing she is not at her sister's, but has done something else—has even already laid hands on herself?

"Eleven o'clock, twelve o'clock. . . . I will not go into the sleeping-room —it would be stupid to lie down there and wait alone, but I will lie down where I am. I try to occupy myself with some work, to write letters, to read; but I can't do anything. I sit alone in my library, I torment myself with apprehensions, I am full of anger, I listen. Three o'clock, four—no sign of her. I fall asleep just before morning. When I wake up, there is no sign of her.

"Everything in the house goes on as usual; but all are in a state of dubiety, and look questioningly and reproachfully at me, supposing that it is all my fault. And within me is still the same struggle—anger because she torments me, and anxiety about her.

"About eleven o'clock in the morning her sister comes as her envoy; and she begins in the usual way:—

" 'She is in a terrible state of mind. Now what does it all mean? Some- thing must have happened.'

"I speak about the incompatibility of her temper, and I asseverate that I have done nothing.

" 'But you see that things cannot be allowed to go on in this way,' says she.

" 'It is all her affair, not mine,' I say. 'I shall not take the first step. If it be a separation, then let it be a separation.'

"My sister-in-law goes away without getting any satisfaction. I have spoken boldly that I would not take the first step; but as soon as she has gone, and I see the poor, frightened children, I am already prepared to take the first step. I should even be glad to do so, but I don't know how. Again I walk up and down and smoke, and after breakfast fortify myself with vodka and wine, and attain what I was unconsciously desirous of: I do not see the stupidity, the cowardice of my position.

"About three she returns. She meets me, but has nothing to say. I imagine that she has come to seek for a reconciliation, and I begin to tell her how I had been led on by her reproaches. She, with the same harsh, terribly harassed face, replies that she has not come to indulge in explanations, but to take the children away—that we cannot possibly live together.

"I begin to explain that I was not the one to blame, that it was she who had driven me out of my senses.

"She looks at me sternly, triumphantly, and then says:—

" 'Say no more, you will be sorry enough.'

"I reply that I cannot endure any comedy.

"Then she screams out something which I cannot comprehend and flees to her room. And she turns the key behind her; she has locked herself in. I knock; no answer, and full of wrath, I wait.

"At the end of half an hour Liza comes running in with tears in her eyes.

" 'What has happened?'

" 'I cannot hear mamma.'

"We go to her room. I press against the door with all my might. The bolt happens to be not wholly pushed in, and both halves of the door yield. I hasten to the bed. She is lying on it in an uncomfortable position in her petticoats and boots. On the table is an empty opium bottle. We bring her to consciousness. Tears and ultimate reconciliation. But it is no reconciliation; in the soul of each of us is the same old anger against each other, and an additional sense of exasperation for the pain which this quarrel has caused and which each blames the other for. But this trouble must be somehow ended, and life goes on in its old grooves. But in the same way such quarrels and even worse ones take place regularly all the time—now with a week's interval, now a month's interval, now every day, and it is always the same thing.

"One time I even applied for a foreign passport—the quarrel had lasted two days. But there ensued a semi-explanation, a semi-reconciliation, and I stayed.

21

"Such then were our relations when that man appeared. He came to Moscow —his name was Trukhachevsky—and he came to my house. It was in the morning. I received him. In former times we had been on familiar terms. He endeavored, sometimes using the more formal, sometimes the more familiar, form of address, to keep on his old footing of thee and thou, but I quickly settled the question by using the formal 'you' and he immediately took the hint. Even at the first glance he impressed me unfavorably. But strangely enough some peculiar fatal power impelled me not to keep him at a distance, to send him away, but rather to draw him nearer to me. Why, what could have been simpler than to have talked coolly with him a few minutes, and to have said 'good morning' without introducing him to my wife?

"But no, I talked with him deliberately about his playing, and remarked that we had been told that he had given up playing the fiddle. He replied that on the contrary he was playing now more than ever before. He recalled that the fact that I, too, had once played. I said that I had given up playing, but that my wife played very well. Wonderful thing! My relations to him that very first day, that very first hour of my meeting with him, were such as they could have been only after all that occurred subsequently. There was something strained in my relations with him; I noticed every word, every expression, said by him or myself, and attributed importance to them.

"I presented him to my wife. Immediately a conversation on music began between them, and he offered his services to practise with her. My wife, as was always the case with her at that later period of her life, was very elegant and fascinating, captivatingly beautiful. He evidently pleased her at first sight. Moreover, she was delighted with the prospect of having the gratification of playing with violin and piano, which she liked so much that she had once hired a fiddler from the theater, and her face expressed this pleasure. But as soon as she saw me, she instantly understood how I felt about it, and her expression changed, and our game of mutual deceit began. I smiled pleasantly, pretending it was very agreeable to me. He, looking at my wife as all immoral men look at pretty women, pretended that he was interested in nothing else but the topic of conversation, especially that part which did not interest him at all. She tried to seem indifferent, but my falsely smiling expression of jealousy, so well known to her, and his lecherous look evidently disturbed her. I saw that from his very first glance her eyes shone with peculiar brilliancy, and apparently as a consequence of my jealousy there passed between him and her something like an electrical shock, calling forth something like a uniformity in the expression of their eyes and their smiles. She blushed, he reddened. She smiled, he smiled. They talked about music, about Paris, about all sorts of trifles. He rose to take his leave, and stood smiling with his hat resting against his quivering thigh, and looked now at her, now at me, apparently waiting to see what we would do.

"I remember that moment especially because at that moment I might have refrained from inviting him to call again, and if I had, the trouble would not have happened. But I looked at him and her.

"'Do not think for an instant that I am jealous of you,' said I, mentally, to her, 'or that I am afraid of you,' said I, mentally, to him, and I invited him to come some evening and bring his fiddle and play with my wife. She looked at me in surprise, blushed, and as if startled, began to plead off, declaring that she did not play well enough. This refusal of hers irritated me still more, and I insisted on it with all the more vehemence. I remember the strange feeling I had as I looked at the back of his head and his white neck, strongly contrasting with his black hair which was combed back on both sides, as he left us with a springy gait like that of a bird. I cannot help acknowledging to myself that this man's presence was a torture to me.

"'It depends on me,' I said to myself, 'to act in such a way as never to see him again. But so to act would be equivalent to a confession that I fear him. No, I do not fear him; it would be too humiliating,' I said to myself. And there in the anteroom, knowing that my wife was listening to me, I insisted that he should come back that very evening and bring his fiddle with him. He promised that he would and took his departure.

"In the evening he came with his fiddle, and they played together. But for a long time the music did not go very well; we had not the pieces that he wanted, and those he had my wife could not play without preparation. I was very fond of music and sympathized with their playing, arranging the music-stand for him and turning over the leaves. They managed to play something—a few songs without words and a sonata by Mozart. He played excellently, and he had to the highest degree what is called 'temperament'—moreover, a delicate, noble art, entirely out of keeping with his character.

"He was, of course, far stronger than my wife, and he helped her and at the same time politely praised her playing. He behaved very well. My wife seemed interested only in the music, and was very simple and natural. Though I also pretended to be interested in the music, still, all the evening, I did not cease to be tortured by jealousy. From the first moment when his eyes fell on my wife I saw that the wild beast existing in them both, out of the reach of all the conditions of their position and the society in which they lived, was asking, 'Is it possible?' and answering its own question with a 'Yes, certainly it is.' I saw that he had never expected to find in my wife, in a society lady of Moscow, such a fascinating creature, and that he was delighted. Therefore there could be no doubt in his mind that she was harmonious with him. The whole question consisted in how the insufferable husband should not interfere with them. If I myself had been pure, I should not have understood this, but I, like the majority of men, had indulged in the same notions of women, until I was married, and therefore I could read his soul like a book.

"I was especially tormented by the fact that I could remark that her feelings and mine were in a state of constant irritation only occasionally interrupted by our habitual sensuality; while this man, both by his external elegance and by his novelty, by the fact that he was a stranger, but chiefly because of his indubitably great musical talent, by the proximity due to their playing together, by the influence produced by music, especially by a fiddle, on a very impressionable nature—all this, I say, made it inevitable that this man should please her, and more than that, that he should get a complete ascendancy over her, without the least hesitation, conquer, overwhelm, fascinate, enchain, and do with her whatever he willed. I could not help seeing that, and I suffered awfully. But in spite of this, or possibly in consequence of it, some force, against my will, compelled me to be especially polite and even affectionate to him. Whether I did this to show my wife, to show him, that I was not afraid of it, or whether I did it to deceive myself, I do not know; only I could not from the very first be natural with him. In order not to yield to my desire to kill him on the spot, I had to be friendly toward him. At dinner I treated him to expensive wines, I praised him for his playing and talked with him with a peculiarly affectionate smile, and invited him to dinner on the following Sunday, and to play again with my wife. I said I would ask some of my musical friends to hear him. And so it came to an end."

And Pozdnuishef, under the influence of powerful emotion, changed his position and emitted his peculiar sounds.

"It is strange what an effect the presence of that man had on me," he began once more, evidently making an effort to become calm.

"Two or three days after this I came home from an exhibition, and as I entered the vestibule I became conscious of a sudden feeling of oppression, exactly as if a stone had been rolled on my heart, and I could not explain it to myself. It was due to the fact that as I was passing through the vestibule I noticed something which reminded me of him. Only when I reached my library was I able to explain what it was, and I returned to the vestibule to verify it. Yes, I had not been mistaken, it was his cloak. A fashionable cloak, you know. Everything relating to him, although I could not explain the why and wherefore, I remarked with extraordinary attention. I asked if he was there, and the servant said 'yes.' I passed through the recitation-room, not the drawing-room, into the 'hall.' Liza, my daughter, was sitting with her book, and the nurse with the little girl was sitting at the table spinning a cover. The door into the 'hall' was closed, but I could hear the monotonous arpeggios and the sound of her voice and his. I listened, but could not decide what to do. Evidently the notes of the piano were played on purpose to drown out their words, perhaps their kisses. My God, what a storm arose in me! The mere thought of the wild beast which then awoke in me fills me with horror. My heart suddenly contracted, then stopped beating, and then it began to throb like a sledge-hammer.

"The chief feeling, as always in any outburst of anger, was pity for myself. 'Before the children, before the nurse,' I exclaimed inwardly. I must have been terrible to look at, because even Liza looked at me with frightened eyes.

" 'What is there for me to do?' I asked myself. 'Shall I go in? I cannot, for God knows what I should do. But neither can I go away. The nurse is looking at me as if she understood my position. But I cannot go in.' I said this to myself and hurriedly opened the door.

"He was sitting at the piano and was playing those arpeggios with his large white fingers bent back. She was standing at one corner of the grand bending over an open score. She was the first to see me or hear me and she looked at me. I know not whether she was startled or pretended not to be startled or really was not startled—at any rate, she did not show any agitation or even move, but merely blushed, but that was afterward.

" 'How glad I am that you have come. We can't decide what to play next Sunday,' said she, in a tone which she would never have employed in addressing me when we were alone. That and the fact that she said 'we,' connecting herself and him, exasperated me. I silently bowed to him. He pressed my hand, and instantly, with a smile which seemed to me derisive, began to explain that he had brought some music for Sunday, but that they could not agree what to play; whether something difficult and classical, such as a Beethoven violin sonata, or some easy trifles. All this was so natural and simple that it was impossible to find any fault with it, and yet I was convinced that it was all a falsehood, that they had been planning how to deceive me.

"One of the most torturing conditions for jealous men—and all of us are jealous in our fashionable society—are certain social conventions whereby the greatest and most dangerous proximity is permitted to a man and a woman. People would simply make themselves ridiculous if they tried to prevent this proximity at balls, between doctors and their female patients, between artists, and especially musicians. Two people occupy themselves with the noblest of arts—music; in order to accomplish this a certain proximity is required, and this proximity has nothing reprehensible in it, and only a stupid, jealous husband could find anything undesirable in it. But meantime all know that precisely by means of these very occupations, especially by music, the largest part of the adultery committed in the ranks of our society is committed.

"I especially confused them by the confusion which I myself showed; it was long before I could speak a word. I was like an upturned bottle from which the water will not flow because it is too full. I wanted to heap abuses on him, to drive him away; but I felt that it was my duty to be friendly and affectionate to him again, and so I was. I pretended that I approved of everything, and once more I felt that strange impulse which compelled me to treat him with a friendliness proportioned to the torment which his presence caused me.

"I told him that I had great confidence in his taste and I advised her to do the same. He stayed just as long as it was required to do away with the disagreeable impression made by my sudden appearance with such a scared face, and after a silence he took his departure, pretending that they had now determined what they would play the next day. I was perfectly convinced that in comparison with what was really occupying them, the question as to what they should play was perfectly immaterial.

"I accompanied him with more than ordinary courtesy to the vestibule—how could one fail to treat courteously a man who had come on purpose to disturb my peace of mind and destroy the happiness of a whole family?—and I pressed his soft white hand with especial affection.

22

"That whole day I did not speak to her—I could not. Her proximity produced in me such hatred of her that I feared for myself. At dinner she asked me in the presence of the children when I was going away. My duties called me the following week to a meeting in my district. I told her when. She asked me if I needed anything for my journey. I did not say anything, and I sat in silence at the table, and silently went to my library. Of late she had got out of the habit of coming to my library, especially at that time of day. I was lying down in my library, and was angry enough. Suddenly her well-known steps were heard coming, and the terrible, ugly thought leaped to my brain that she, like Uriah's wife, had already committed the sin and wanted to hide it, and that was why she was coming to me at such an unseasonable hour.

" 'Can it be that she is really coming to me?' I asked myself as I heard her approaching step.

" 'If she is coming to me, then it means I am right.'

"And in my soul arose an ineffable hatred of her. Nearer, nearer came her steps.

" 'Can it be that she is going by into the hall?'

"No, the door creaked and her tall, handsome figure appeared, and her face, her eyes, expressed timidity, and a desire to win my good-will, as I could easily see, and the significance of it I understood perfectly. I almost suffocated, so long I held my breath, and continuing to stare at her, I grasped my cigarette-case and began to smoke.

" 'Now how can you? Some one comes to sit with you and you go to smoking;'

and she sat down near me on the divan, and leaned up against me. I moved away, so as not to be in contact with her.

" 'I see that you are vexed because I am going to play on Sunday,' said she.

" 'Not in the least,' said I.

" 'But can't I see that you are?'

" 'Well, I congratulate you on your perspicacity. I see nothing except the fact that you behave like a coquette. To you all such kinds of vulgarity are pleasant, but to me they are horrible.'

" 'There, now, if you are going to abuse me like an izvoshchik, then I will go.'

" 'Go, then; but know that the honor of your family is not dear to you, neither are you dear to me—the devil take you—but the honor of the family is—'

" 'Now, what do you mean?'

" 'Get out of my sight! for God's sake, get out.'

"I know not whether she pretended that she did not comprehend, or really did not comprehend; but she only took offense, grew angry, and instead of leaving stood in the middle of the room.

" 'You have become positively unendurable,' she began. 'You have such a disposition that not even an angel could get along with you.' And, as always, trying to wound me as keenly as possible, she reminded me of the way I had treated my sister. It had happened that one time I forgot myself and spoke some very harsh words to my sister; she knew about it and that it tormented me, and so she wounded me in that place.

" 'After that, nothing that you could do would surprise me,' said she.

" 'Yes, insult me, humiliate me, disgrace me, and make me out to blame,' said I, to myself, and suddenly a terrible anger against her seized me, such as I had never before experienced. For the first time I felt the impulse to express this anger with physical force. I leaped up and moved toward her; but at the instant that I sprang to my feet, I became conscious of my anger and asked myself, 'Is it well to give way to this impulse?' and immediately the answer came that it was, that this would serve to frighten her; and on the spot, instead of withstanding my wrath, I began to fan it to a greater heat, and to rejoice because it grew more and more intense in me.

" 'Get out of here, or I will kill you,' I screamed, going closer to her and seizing her by the arm. In saying this I was conscious of raising my voice to a higher pitch, and I must have become terrible, because she became so frightened that she had not the strength to go, but merely stammered:—

" 'Vasya, what is it, what is the matter with you?'

" 'Go,' I cried, in a still louder tone. 'No one but you can drive me to madness. I won't be responsible for what I may do!'

"Having given free course to my madness I intoxicated myself with it, and I felt the impulse to do something extraordinary which should show the high-water mark of this madness of mine. I felt a terrible impulse to strike her, to kill her; but I knew that it was an impossibility, and therefore in order to give free course to my madness, I snatched up a paper-weight from the table, and shouting once more, 'Go!' I flung it down on the floor, near her. I aimed it carefully, so as to strike near her. Then she left the room, but remained standing in the doorway. And then while she was still looking—I did it so that she might see—I began to snatch up from the table various objects—the candlestick, the inkstand—and hurled them on the floor, still continuing to shout,—

" 'Go, get out of my sight! I won't be responsible for what I may do.'

"She went, and I immediately ceased.

"In the course of an hour the nurse came and told me that my wife was suffering from hysterics. I went to her; she was sobbing and laughing, and could not speak a word and was trembling all over. She was not pretending, but was really ill. Toward morning she grew calm, and we had a reconciliation under the influence of that passion which we call 'love.'

"In the morning, after our reconciliation I confessed to her that I was jealous of Trukhachevsky. She was not in the least confused, and laughed in the most natural manner. So strange even to her seemed, as she said, the possibility of being drawn to such a man.

" 'Is it possible that a respectable woman could feel anything for such a man beyond the pleasure which his music might afford? But if you wish, I am ready not to see him again. Even though all the guests are invited for Sunday, write him that I am ill, and that will be the end of it. Only one thing makes me indignant, and that is that any one could imagine, and especially he himself, that he is dangerous. I am too proud to permit myself to think of such a thing.'

"And evidently she was not prevaricating; she believed in what she was saying; she hoped by these words to evoke in herself scorn for him and to defend herself from him, but she did not succeed in this. Everything went against her, especially that cursed music.

"Thus the episode ended, and on Sunday the guests gathered and they played together again.

23

"I think it is superfluous to remark that I was very ostentatious; there would not be any living in our general society if it were not for ostentation. Thus on that Sunday I took the greatest pains to arrange for our dinner and for the evening musicale. I myself ordered the things for dinner and invited the guests.

"At six o'clock the guests had arrived, and he also, in evening dress with diamond shirt studs of bad taste. He was free and easy, made haste to answer all questions with a smile of sympathy and appreciation—you know what I mean, with that peculiar expression that signifies that everything you say or do is exactly what he expected. I remarked now with especial satisfaction everything about him calculated to give an unfavorable impression, because all this served to calm me, and prove that he stood in my wife's eyes on such a low level that, as she said, she could not possibly descend to it. I did not allow myself to be jealous. In the first place, I had already been through the pangs of that torment and needed rest; in the second place, I wanted to have faith in my wife's asseverations, and I did believe in them. But in spite of the fact that I was not jealous, still I was not at my ease with either of them, and during the dinner and the first half of the evening before the music began, I kept watching their motions and glances all the time.

"The dinner was like any dinner—dull and conventional. The music began rather early. Oh, how well I remember all the details of that evening. I remember how he brought his fiddle, opened the box, took off the covering which had been embroidered for him by some lady, took out the instrument and began to tune it. I remember how my wife sat with a pretendedly indifferent face under which I saw that she was hiding great diffidence,—the diffidence caused chiefly by distrust of her own ability,—how she took her seat at the grand piano with the same affected look and struck the usual *a*, which was followed by the pizzicato of the fiddle and the getting into tune. I remember how, then, they looked at each other, glanced at the audience, and then made some remark, and the music began. He struck the first chords. His face grew grave, stern, and sympathetic, and as he bent his head to listen to the sounds he produced, he placed his fingers cautiously on the strings. The piano replied. And it began." . . .

Pozdnuishef paused and several times emitted his peculiar sounds. He started to speak again but snuffed through his nose and again paused.

"They played Beethoven's Kreutzer Sonata," he finally went on to say. "Do you know the first *presto*—You know it?" he cried. "U! U! U! . . . That sonata is a terrible thing. And especially that movement. And music in general is a terrible thing. I cannot comprehend it. What is music? What does it do? And why does it have the effect it has? They say music has the effect of elevating the soul—rubbish! falsehood! It has its effect, it has a terrible effect,— I am speaking about its effect on me,—but not at all by elevating the soul. Its effect is neither to elevate nor to degrade, but to excite. How can I explain it to you? Music makes me forget myself, my actual position; it transports me into another state not my natural one; under the influence of music it seems to me that I feel what I do not really feel, that I understand what I do not really understand, that I can do what I can't do. I explain this by the fact that music acts like gaping or laughing; I am not sleepy but I gape, looking at any one else who is gaping; I have nothing to laugh at, but I laugh when I hear others laugh.

"Music instantaneously transports me into that mental condition in which he who composed it found himself. I blend my soul with his, and together with him am transported from one mood to another; but why this is so I cannot tell. For instance, he who composed the Kreutzer Sonata—Beethoven—he knew why he was in that mood. That mood impelled him to do certain things and therefore that mood meant something for him, but it means nothing for me. And that is why music excites and does not bring to any conclusion. Now they play a military march; the soldiers move forward under its strains, and the music accomplishes something; they play dance music and I dance, and the music accomplishes something; they perform a mass, I take the sacrament, again the music accomplishes its purpose. But in other cases there is only excitement, and it is impossible to tell what to do in this state of mind. And that is why music is so terrible, why it sometimes has such an awful effect. In China, music is regulated by government, and this is as it should be. Is it permissible that any one whatever shall hypnotize another person, or many persons, and then do with them what he pleases? And especially if this hypnotizer happens to be the first immoral man that comes along.

"And indeed it is a terrible means to place in any one's hands. For example, how could any one play this Kreutzer Sonata, the first *presto*, in a drawing-room before ladies dressed *décolletées?* To play that *presto* and then to applaud it, and then to eat ices and talk over the last bit of scandal? These things should be played only in certain grave, significant conditions, and only then when certain deeds corresponding to such music are to be accomplished: first play the music and perform that which this music was composed for. But to call forth an energy which is not consonant with the place or the time, and an impulse which does not manifest itself in anything, cannot fail to have a baneful effect. On me, at least, it had a horrible effect. It seemed to me that entirely new impulses, new possibilities, were revealed to me in myself, such as I had never dreamed of before.

" 'This is the way I should live and think—not at all as I have lived and thought hitherto,' seemed to be whispered into my soul. What this new thing was I now knew I could not explain even to myself, but the consciousness of this new state of mind was very delightful. All those faces—his and my wife's among them—presented themselves in a new light.

"After the *allegro* they played the beautiful but rather commonplace and far from original *andante*, with the cheap variations and the weak *finale*. Then at the request of the guests they played other things, first an elegy by Ernst and then various other trifles. All this was very good, but it did not produce on me a hundredth part of the impression which the first did. But all the music had the same background as the impression which the first produced.

"I felt gay and happy all the evening. I never saw my wife look as she did that evening: her gleaming eyes, her gravity and serenity of expression while she was playing, her perfectly melting mood, her tender, pathetic, and blissful smile, after they had finished playing; I saw it all, but attributed to it no other significance other than that she was experiencing the same thing as I was; that before her, as before me, new and hitherto unexampled feelings were revealed, dimly rising in her consciousness. The evening was pronounced a great success, and when it was over the guests took their departure.

"Knowing that I was to be going to the district meeting in two days, Trukha-chevsky, on bidding me farewell, said that he hoped that when he next came to Moscow he should have another pleasant evening like that. From this remark I was able to conclude that he did not deem it possible to visit my house during my absence, and that was agreeable to me. It seemed clear that as I should not return before his departure we should not meet again.

"For the first time I shook hands with him with genuine pleasure, and I thanked him for the gratification he had afforded us. He also bade my wife a final farewell, and their final farewell seemed to me most natural and proper. Everything was admirable. Both my wife and I were very well satisfied with the evening.

24

"Two days later I started for my district, taking leave of my wife in the happiest and calmest frame of mind.

"In the district there was always a pile of work and a special life, a special little world. For two days I worked ten hours a day in my office. On the third day a letter from my wife was brought to me in the office. I read it then and there.

"She wrote about the children, about her uncle, about the nurse-girl, about the things she had bought, and mentioned as something perfectly common-place the fact that Trukhachevsky had been to call, and had brought the music he had promised, and that he had offered to come and play again, but that she had declined.

"I did not remember that he had promised to bring any music. I had sup-posed that he had taken his final leave at that time, and so this gave me an unpleasant surprise. But I was so deeply engrossed in business that I could not stop to think it over, and it was not until evening, when I returned to my room, that I reread her letter.

"Besides the fact that Trukhachevsky had called again in my absence, the whole tone of the letter seemed to me unnatural. The frantic wild beast of jealousy roared in his cage and wanted to break forth; but I was afraid of this beast and I made haste to shut him up.

" 'What a vile feeling this jealousy is,' I said to myself. 'What can be more natural than what she has written?'

"And I lay on my bed and tried to think of the business which I should have to attend to the next day. I never go to sleep very quickly during these sessions in a new place, but this time I dropped asleep almost immediately. But as you know it often happens, I suddenly felt something like an electric shock, and started up wide awake. As I woke, I woke with a thought of her, of my carnal love for her, and of Trukhachevsky, and how all had been accomplished between him and her. Horror and rage crushed my heart. But I tried to reason myself out of it.

" 'What rubbish!' I exclaimed. 'There is not the slightest basis for any such suspicions. And how can I humiliate myself and her by harboring such horrible thoughts? Here is some one in the nature of a hired fiddler, with a reputation of being disreputable, and could a respectable woman, the mother of a family, *my wife*, suddenly fall a victim to such a man? What an absurdity.'

"That is what I argued on one side, but on the other, came these thoughts:—

" 'How could it fail to be so? Why is it not the simplest and most com-prehensible thing? Was it not for that I married her? Was it not for that I lived with her? Was it not that which makes me necessary to her? And would not therefore another man, this musician, be likewise necessary to her? He is an unmarried man, healthy,—I remember how lustily he crunched the gristle in the cutlet, and put the glass of wine to his red lips,—he is well-fed, sleek, and not only without principles, but evidently guided by the theory that it is best to take advantage of whatever pleasures present themselves. And between them is the tie of music; the subtle lust of the senses. What can restrain him? She? Yes, but who is she? She is as much of a riddle as she ever has been. I don't know her. I know her only as an animal; and nothing can restrain an animal, or is likely to.'

"Only at that instant I recalled their faces that evening after they had played the Kreutzer Sonata, and while they were performing some passionate piece, —I have forgotten what it was,—something sentimental to the degree of ob-scenity.

" 'How could I have come away?' I asked myself, as I recalled their faces. Was it not perfectly evident that the fatal step was taken by them that evening, and was it not evident that even from that evening on, not only was there no bar between them, but that both of them—she especially—felt some sense of shame after what happened to them? I recalled with what a soft, pathetic, and blissful smile she wiped away the perspiration from her heated face, as I approached the piano. Even then they avoided looking at each other, and only at dinner when he poured her out some water did they look at each other, and timidly smile. I remembered with horror that glance which I had intercepted, and that almost imperceptible smile.

" 'Yes, the fatal step has been taken,' said a voice within me; and instantly another voice seemed to say quite the contrary. 'You are crazy; this cannot be,' said this second voice.

"It was painful for me to lie there in the darkness. I lighted a match, and then it seemed to me terrible to be in that little room with its yellow wall-paper. I began to smoke a cigarette, and, as is always the case when one turns round in the same circle of irresolvable contradictions, I smoked; and I smoked one cigarette after another, for the purpose of befogging my mind and not seeing the contradictions.

"I did not sleep all night, and at five o'clock, having made up my mind that I could remain no longer in such a state of tension, but would instantly go back, I got up, wakened the bell-boy who waited on me, and sent him after horses. I sent a note to the Session stating that I had been called back to Moscow on extraordinary business, and therefore begged them to let another member take my place. At eight o'clock I took my seat in the tarantas and started."

25

The conductor came through the train, and noticing that our candle was almost burned out, extinguished it instead of putting in another. Out-of-doors it was beginning to grow light. Pozdnuishef ceased speaking and sighed heavily all the time the conductor was in the carriage. He proceeded with his story only when the conductor had taken his departure, and the only sound we could hear in the semi-darkness of the carriage was the rattle of the windows and regular snore of the merchant's clerk. In the twilight of the dawn I could not make out Pozdnuishef's face at all. I could only hear his passionate voice growing ever more and more excited:—

"I had to travel thirty-five versts by tarantas and eight hours by rail. It was splendid traveling with horses. It was frosty autumnal weather with a brilliant sun,—you know that kind of weather when the tires leave their print on the slippery road. The roads were smooth, the light was dazzling, and the atmosphere was exhilarating. Yes, it was jolly traveling by tarantas. As soon as it grew light, and I was fairly on my way, my heart felt lighter.

"As I looked at the horses, at the fields, at the persons I met, I forgot what my errand was. It sometimes seemed to me that I was simply out for a drive, and that there was nothing whatever to stir me so. And I felt particularly happy at thus forgetting myself. If by chance it occurred to me where I was bound, I said to myself:—

" 'Wait and see what will be; don't think about it now.'

"About half-way an event happened which delayed me, and still more tended to distract my attention; the tarantas broke down, and it was necessary to mend it. This break-down had a great significance because it caused me to reach Moscow at midnight instead of at five o'clock, as we had expected, and home at one o'clock, for I missed the express, and was obliged to take a way train. The search for a telyega, the mending of the tarantas, the settlement of the bill, tea at an inn, the conversation with the hostler,—all this served to divert me more and more. By twilight everything was ready, and I was on my way once more, and during the evening it was still pleasanter traveling than by day. There was a young moon, a slight touch of frost, the roads were still excellent, and so were the horses, the postilion was jolly, and so I traveled on and enjoyed myself, scarce thinking at all of what was awaiting me; or perhaps I enjoyed myself especially because I knew what was awaiting me, and I was having my last taste of the joys of life.

"But this calm state of mind, the power of controlling my feelings, came to an end as soon as I ceased traveling with the horses. As soon as I entered the railway carriage an entirely different state of things began. This eight-hour journey by rail was something horrible to me, and I shall never forget it as long as I live. Either because, as soon as I entered the carriage I vividly imagined myself as having already reached the end, or because railway travel has an exciting effect on people. As soon as I took my seat I had no longer any control over my imagination, which ceaselessly, with extraordinary vividness, began to bring up before me pictures kindling my jealousy; one after another they arose and always to the same effect: what had taken place during my absence, and how she had deceived me! I was on fire with indignation, wrath, and a peculiar sense of frenzy, caused by my humiliation, as I contemplated these pictures, and I could not tear myself away from them, could not help gazing at them, could not rub them out, could not help evoking them. And then the more I contemplated these imaginary pictures the more I was convinced of their reality. The vividness with which these pictures presented themselves before me seemed to serve as a proof of the actuality of what I imagined. A kind of a devil, perfectly against my will, suggested and stimulated the most horrible suggestions. A conversation I had once with Trukhachevsky's brother occurred to me, and with a sort of enthusiasm I lacerated my heart with this conversation, applying it to Trukhachevsky and my wife.

"It had taken place long before, but it came back clearly to me. I remember that once, Trukhachevsky's brother, in reply to a question whether he ever went to certain houses, stated that no decent man would ever go to such places, where there was danger of contracting disease, and that it was vile and disgusting; one could always find some society woman to serve his purpose. And now here was his brother and he had found my wife!

" 'To be sure she is no longer young; she has a tooth missing on one side of her mouth, her face is somewhat swollen,' I said, trying to look from his standpoint. 'But what difference does that make? One must take what one can get. Yes, he is conferring a favor on her to take her as his mistress,' said I, to myself. 'Then besides, there is no danger with her. . . . No, it is impossible!' I exclaimed in horror. 'There is no possibility of it, not the least, and there is not the slightest basis for any such conjectures. Has she not told me that to her it was a humiliating thought that I could be jealous of him. . . . Yes, but she is a liar, always a liar,' I would cry, and then begin the same thing over again.

"There were only two passengers in my carriage; an old woman with her husband, both of them very silent, and they got out at the first stop, and I was left alone. I was like a wild beast in a cage; now I would jump up and rush to the window, then staggering I would walk back and forth through the aisle trying to make the train go faster; but the carriage, with all its seats and its window-panes, shook just exactly as ours is doing now." . . .

And Pozdnuishef sprang to his feet and took a few steps and then sat down again.

"Oh, I dread, I dread these railway carriages—they fill me with horror—yes, I dread them awfully," he went on saying. "I said to myself, 'I must think of something else. All right, let me think of the landlord of the inn where I took tea. Well! Then before my eyes would arise the long-bearded dvornik and his grandson, a boy about as old as my Vasya.

" 'My Vasya! He will see a musician kissing his mother. What will happen to his poor soul at the sight? But what will she care? She is in love.'

"And again would arise the same visions.

" 'No, no! Well I will think about the inspection of the hospital. Yesterday that sick man complained of the doctor. A doctor with mustaches just like Trukhachevsky's. . . . And how brazenly he—they both deceived me, when he said that he was going away.' . . .

"And again it would begin. Everything I thought of had some connection with them. I suffered awfully. My chief suffering lay in my ignorance, in the uncertainty of it all, in my question whether I ought to love her or hate her. These sufferings were so intense that I remember the temptation came into my mind with great fascination to go out on the track and throw myself under the train on the rails, and so end it. Then, at least, there would be no further doubt. The one thing that prevented me from doing so was my self-pity which was the immediate source of my hatred of her. Toward him, also, I had a strange feeling of hatred, and a consciousness of my humiliation and of his victory, but toward her my hatred was awful.

" 'It is impossible to put an end to myself and to leave her behind. I must do something to make her suffer, so that she may appreciate that I have suffered,' I said to myself.

"I got out at all the stations in order to divert my mind. At one station I noticed that people were drinking in the buffet, and I immediately fortified myself with vodka. Next me stood a Jew and he also was drinking. He spoke to me and that I might not be alone in my carriage I went with him into his third-class compartment, though it was filthy and full of smoke and littered with the husks of seeds. There I sat down next him, and he went on chatting and relating anecdotes. I listened to him, but did not take in what he said because I kept thinking of my own affairs. He noticed this and tried to attract my attention; then I got up and went back to my own carriage.

" 'I must think it all over again,' I said to myself, 'whether what I think is true and whether there is any foundation for my anguish.' I sat down, desiring calmly to think it over, but instantly in place of calm deliberation, the same tumult of thought began; in place of argument, pictures and figments of the imagination.

" 'How often have I not tortured myself so,' I said to myself, for I remembered similar paroxysms of jealousy in times gone by, 'and then there was no ground for them. And so now, possibly, nay probably, I shall find her calmly sleeping; she will wake up and be glad to see me, and I shall be conscious both in her words and in her looks that nothing has taken place and that my suspicions were groundless. Oh! how delightful that would be!'

" 'But no, this has been so too frequently and now it will be so no longer' said some inner voice, and once more it would begin anew. Ah! what a punishment was here! I should not take a young man to a syphilitic hospital to cure him of his passion for women, but into my own soul, and give him a glimpse of the fiends that were rending it. You see it was horrible that I claimed an undoubted absolute right to her body just as if it had been my own body, and at the same time I was conscious that I could not control that body of hers, that it was not mine, and that she had the power to dispose of it as she chose, and that she did not choose to dispose of it as I wished. I could not even do anything to her or to him. He, like Vanka the cellarer before he was hanged, will sing a song of how he had kissed her on her sugary lips and the like. He would have the best of me. And with her I could do even less. If she had not yet done anything out of the way, but had it in mind to,—and I know that she did,—the case is still worse; it would be better to have it done with, so that I might know, so as to have this uncertainty settled.

"I could not tell what I desired. I desired her not to want what she could not help wanting. This was absolute madness.

26

"At the next to the last station, when the conductor came along to take the tickets, I picked up my belongings and went out on the platform, and the consciousness of what was about to take place still further increased my agitation. I became cold, and my jaws trembled so that my teeth chattered. Mechanically I followed the crowd out of the station, engaged an izvoshchik, took my seat in his cab and drove away. As I drove along, glancing at the occasional pedestrians, at the dvorniks and the shadows cast by the street lamps and my cab, now in front and now behind, my mind seemed to be a blank. By the time we had driven half a verst from the station my feet became cold, and I remembered that I had removed my woolen stockings in the train and put them into my gripsack.

" 'Where is my grip? Have I brought it with me?'

"Yes, I had. 'But where is my hamper?'

"Then I remembered that I had entirely forgotten about my baggage; but while I was thinking about it, I found my receipt and decided that it was not worth while to return for it, and so I drove home.

"In spite of my endeavors, I can never remember to this day what my state of mind was at that time,—what I thought, what I desired, I cannot tell. I only remember that I was conscious that something terrible and very vital in my life was in preparation. Whether this important event proceeded from the fact that I thought so or because I foreboded it, I do not know. Perhaps after what happened subsequently, all the preceding moments have taken on a gloomy shade in my recollection.

"I reached the doorstep. It was one o'clock. Several izvoshchiks were standing in front of the door waiting for fares in the light cast by the windows—the lighted windows were in our apartment, in the 'hall,' and the drawing-room. I made no attempt to explain to myself why our windows were still lighted so late at night, but still expectant of something dreadful about to happen, I mounted the steps and rang the bell. Yegor, the lackey, a good-natured, zealous, but extremely stupid fellow, answered it. The first thing that struck my eyes in the vestibule was a cloak hanging on a peg with other outside garments. I ought to have been surprised, but I was not, because it was what I expected.

" 'It is true,' I said to myself.

"When I asked Yegor who was there and he mentioned Trukhachevsky, I asked:—

" 'Is there any one else with them?' and he said:—

" 'No one.' I remember that in his reply, there was an intonation, as if he felt he was giving me a pleasure in dispelling my apprehension that any one else was there.

" 'It is true, it is true,' I seemed to say to myself.

" 'But the children?'

" 'Thank God, they are well. They have been asleep for a long time.'

"I could not breathe freely, nor could I prevent the trembling of my lower jaw.

" 'Yes, of course, it is not as I thought it might be; whereas formerly I imagined some misfortune and yet found everything all right, as usual, now it was not usual, now it was altogether what I had imagined and fancied that I only imagined, but it was now real. It was all . . .'

"I almost began to sob, but instantly a fiend suggested:—

" 'Shed tears, be sentimental; but they will calmly separate; there will be no proof, and you will be forever in doubt and torment.'

"Thereupon my self-pity vanished, and in its place came a strange feeling of gladness that my torture was now at an end, that I could punish her, could get rid of her, that I could give free course to my wrath. And I gave free course to my wrath—I became a wild beast, fierce and sly.

" 'No matter, no matter,' I said to Yegor, who was about to go to the drawing-room, 'attend to this instead: take an izvoshchik, and go as quickly as you can to the station for my luggage; here is the receipt. Off with you!'

"He went into the corridor to get his paletot. Fearing that he might disturb them, I accompanied him to his little room, and waited till he had got his things on. In the drawing-room, just through the wall, I could hear the sound of voices, and the clatter of knives and dishes. They were eating, and had not heard the bell.

" 'If only no one leaves the room now,' I said to myself.

"Yegor put on his paletot trimmed with astrakhan wool, and started. I let him out and shut the door behind him, and I felt a sense of dread at the idea of being left alone, of having to act instantly.

"How? I did not know as yet. All I knew was that all was ended, that there could be no longer any doubt as to her guilt, and that I should presently punish her, and put an end to my relations with her.

"Hitherto I had been troubled with vacillation, and I had said to myself: 'Maybe it is not so, maybe you are mistaken;' now this was at an end. Everything was now irrevocably decided. Clandestinely! alone with him! at night! This proved perfect forgetfulness of everything, or something even worse. Such audacity, such insolence, in crime was deliberately adopted in order that its very insolence might serve as a proof of innocence. All was clear, there could be no doubt! I was afraid of only one thing,—that they might escape, might invent some new deception, and deprive me of manifest proof, and the possibility of convincing myself. And so as to catch them as promptly as possible I went, not throught the drawing-room, but through the corridor and the nursery, on my tiptoes, into the 'hall' where they were sitting.

"In the first nursery-room the boys were sound asleep; in the second nursery-room the nurse stirred, and was on the point of waking up; and I imagined to myself what she would think if she knew it all; and then such a sense of self-pity came over me at this thought that I could not restrain my tears, and in order not to wake the children I ran out, on my tiptoes, into the corridor and into my own room, flung myself down on my divan, and sobbed.

" 'I, an upright man . . . I, the son of my own parents . . . I, who have dreamed all my life of the delights of domestic happiness . . . I, a husband who have never been unfaithful to my wife! . . . And here she, the mother of five children, and she is embracing a musician because he has red lips!

" 'No, she is not human. She is a bitch, a vile bitch! Next to the room where sleep her children, for whom, all her life, she has pretended to feel affection. And to write me what she wrote! And so insolently to throw herself into my arms! And how do I know? perhaps this same sort of thing has been taking place all the time! Who knows but the children whom I have always supposed to be mine may not have some lackey for their father!

" 'And if I had come home to-morrow she would have met me with her hair becomingly done up, and her graceful, indolent movements.' All the time I seemed to see her fascinating, abhorrent face . . . 'and this wild beast of jealousy would have taken his position forever in my heart, and torn it. What will the nurse think? . . . and Yegor? . . . and poor Lizotchka? She already has her suspicions. And this brazen impudence, and this falsehood! . . . And this animal sensuality which I know so well?' I said to myself.

"I tried to get up, but could not. My heart throbbed so that I could not stand on my legs.

" 'Yes, I shall die of a stroke. She will have killed me. That is just what she wants! What would it be to her to kill me? Indeed, it would be quite too advantageous, and I will not bestow that gratification on her. Yes, here I am sitting, and yonder they are eating and talking together, and . . .

" 'Yes, in spite of the fact that she is no longer in her first youth, he will not despise her . . . still, she is not bad-looking, and, what is the main thing, at least she is not dangerous for his precious health. Why, then, have I not strangled her already?' I asked myself, recalling that moment a week before when I drove her out of my library, and then smashed things. I had a vivid remembrance of the state of mind in which I was then; and not only had the remembrance, but I was conscious of the same necessity of striking, of destroying, as I had been conscious of before. I remember how I wanted to do something, and how all considerations except those that were necessary for action vanished from my mind. I came into the state of a wild animal, or rather, of a man under the influence of physical excitement in time of danger, when he acts definitely, deliberately, but without losing a single instant, and all the time with a single object in view.

"The first thing I did was to take off my boots, and then, in my stocking feet, I went to the wall, where various weapons and daggers were hung up over the divan, and I took down a curved Damascus dagger, which had never been used, and was very keen. I drew it out of its sheath. I remember the sheath slipped down behind the divan, and I remember I said to myself:—

" 'I must find it afterward or else it will get lost.' Then I took off my paletot which I had all the time been wearing and, gliding along in my stockings, I went *there*.

27

"And stepping up stealthily, I suddenly threw open the door. I remember the expression of both of their faces. I remember that expression because it afforded me a tormenting pleasure—it was an expression of horror. That was the very thing I needed! I shall never forget the expression of despairing horror which came into their faces the first second when they saw me. He was seated, it seems, at the table, but when he saw me or heard me, he leaped to his feet and stood with his back against the sideboard. His face bore the one unmistakable expression of horror. On her face also was an expression of horror, but there was something else blended with it. If it had not been for that something else, maybe what happened would not have happened; but in the expression of her face there was, or so there seemed to me at the first instant, a look of disappointment, of annoyance that her pleasure in his love and her enjoyment with him were interrupted. It was as if she desired nothing else than to be left undisturbed in her present happiness. This expression and the other lingered but an instant on their faces. The expression of horror on his face instantly grew into a look, which asked the question: 'Is it possible to lie out of it or not? If it is possible, now is the time to begin. If not, then something else must be done—but what?'

"He looked questioningly at her. On her face the expression of annoyance and disappointment changed as it seemed to me when she looked at him into one of solicitude for him.

"I stood for an instant on the threshold holding the dagger behind my back.

"During that second he smiled, and in a voice so indifferent that it was ludicrous, he began:—

" 'We have been having some music.'

" 'Why! I was not expecting you,' she began at the same instant, adopting his tone.

"But neither he nor she finished their sentences. The very same madness which I had experienced a week before took possession of me. Once more I felt the necessity of destroying something, of using violence; once more I felt the ecstasy of madness and I yielded to it. Neither finished what they were saying.

The something else which he was afraid of began, and it swept away instantaneously all that they had to say.

"I threw myself on her, still concealing the dagger in order that he might not prevent me from striking her in the side under the breast. I had chosen the spot at the very beginning. The instant I threw myself on her he saw my design, and with an action which I never expected from him, he seized me by the arm and cried:—

" 'Think what you . . . Help!'

"I wrenched away my arm, and without saying a word rushed at him. His eyes met mine; he suddenly turned as pale as a sheet, even to the lips, his eyes glittered with a peculiar light, and most unexpectedly to me he slipped under the piano and darted out of the door. I was just starting to rush after him when I was detained by a weight on my left arm. It was she! I tried to break away. She clung all the more heavily to my arm and would not let me go. This unexpected hindrance, the weight of her and her touch which was repulsive to me, still further inflamed my anger. I was conscious of being in a perfect frenzy and that I ought to be terrible, and I exulted in it. I drew back my left arm with all my might and struck her full in the face with my elbow. She screamed and let go my arm. I started to chase him, but remembered that it would be ridiculous for a man to chase his wife's lover in his stockings, and I did not want to be ridiculous, but I desired to be terrible.

"Notwithstanding the terrible frenzy in which I found myself, I never for an instant forgot the impression which I might produce on others, and this impression, even to a certain degree, governed me. I came back to her. She had fallen on a couch, and with her hand held up to her eyes, which I had bruised, was looking at me. In her face were such terror and hatred of me, her enemy, as a rat might show when the trap in which it had been caught was held up. At all events I could see nothing else in her face except terror and hatred of me. It was precisely the same terror and hatred which love to another would naturally evoke. But possibly I should have restrained myself and not done what I did if she had held her tongue. But she suddenly began to speak, and she seized my hand which held the dagger:—

" 'Come to your senses. What are you going to do? What is the matter with you? There has been nothing, no harm, I swear it.'

"I should have still delayed, but these last words, from which I drew exactly the opposite conclusion, that is, that my worst fears were realized, required an answer. And the answer had to correspond with the mood to which I had wrought myself up, which had gone on in a *crescendo* and was bound to reach its climax. Madness also has its laws.

" 'Do not lie, you wretch,' I cried, and with my left hand I seized her by the arm, but she tore herself away. Then, still clutching the dagger, I grasped her by the throat, pressed her over backward and began to strangle her. What a muscular throat she had! She grasped my hands with both hers, tearing them away from her throat, and I, as if I had been waiting for this opportunity, struck her with the dagger into the side under the ribs.

"When men say that in an attack of madness they don't remember what they did, it is all false, all nonsense. I remember every detail, and not for one second did I fail to remember. The more violently I kindled within me the flames of my madness, the more brightly burned the light of consciousness, so that I could not fail to see all that I did. I knew every second what I was doing. I cannot say that I knew in advance what I was going to do, but at the instant I did anything, and perhaps a little before I knew what I was up to, as if for the purpose of being able to repent, in order that I might say to myself: 'I might have stopped.' I knew that I struck below the ribs and that the dagger would penetrate. At the moment I was doing this, I knew that I was doing something, something awful, something which I had never done before and which would have awful consequences. But this consciousness flashed through my mind like lightning and was instantly followed by the deed. The deed made itself conscious with unexampled clearness. I felt and I remember the momentary resistance of her corset and of something else, and then the sinking of the blade into the soft parts of her body. She seized the dagger with her hands, wounding them, but she did not stop me.

"Afterward, in the prison, while a moral revolution was working itself out in me, I thought much about that moment—what I might have done, and I thought it all over. I remember that a second, only a second, before the deed was accomplished, I had the terrible consciousness that I was killing and had killed a woman—a defenseless woman—my wife. I recall the horror of this consciousness, and therefore I conclude—and indeed I dimly remember—that having plunged the dagger in, I immediately withdrew it, with the desire to remedy what I had done and to put a stop to it. I stood for a second motionless, waiting to see what would happen,—and whether I might undo what I had done.

"She sprang to her feet, and shrieked:—

" 'Nurse, he has killed me.'

"The nurse had heard the disturbance and was already on the threshold. I was still standing, expectant and irresolute. But at that instant the blood gushed from under her corset.

"Then only I realized that it was impossible to remedy it, and I instantly concluded that it was not necessary, that I myself did not wish to have it remedied, and that I had done the very thing I was in duty bound to do. I lingered until she fell and the nurse, with the exclamation 'Heavens,' rushed to her, and then I flung the dagger down and left the room.

" 'I must not get excited, I must know what I am doing,' said I to myself, looking neither at her nor at the nurse. The nurse screamed and called to the maid. I went along the corridor, and stopping to send the maid, I went to my room.

" 'What must I do now?' I asked myself, and instantly made up my mind. As soon as I reached my library I went directly to the wall and took down a revolver and contemplated it. It was loaded, and I laid it on the table. Then I picked up the sheath from behind the divan, and finally I sat down on the divan.

"I sat long in that attitude. My mind was without a thought, without a recollection. I heard some commotion *there*. I heard some one arrive, then some one else. Then I heard and saw Yegor bringing my luggage into my library. As if that would be useful to any one now.

" 'Have you heard what has happened?' I asked. 'Tell the dvornik to inform the police.'

"He said nothing, but went out. I got up, closed the door, got my cigarettes and matches, and began to smoke. I had not finished smoking my cigarette before drowsiness seized me and overcame me. I think I must have slept two hours. I remember I dreamed that she and I were friends, that we had quarreled, but had made it up, and that some trifle stood in our way; but still we were friends.

"A knock on the door awakened me.

" 'It is the police,' I thought as I woke; 'it seems I must have killed her. But maybe it is she herself and nothing has happened.'

"The knocking at the door was repeated. I did not answer, but kept trying to decide the question:—

" 'Had all that really taken place or not? . . . Yes it had.' I remembered the resistance of the corset and the sinking of the dagger, and a cold chill ran down my back.

" 'Yes, it is true. Yes, now I must have my turn,' said I to myself. But though I said this I knew I should not kill myself. Nevertheless, I got up and once more took the revolver into my hand. But strange as it may seem, I remember how many times before I had been near suicide, as, for instance, that very day on the railway train, and it had seemed to me very easy for the very reason that I thought that by that means I could fill her with consternation.

"Now I could not kill myself or think of such a thing. 'Why should I do it?' I asked myself; and there was no answer.

"The knocking still continued at the door.

" 'Yes, first I must find out who is knocking, I shall have time enough afterward . . .'

"I laid the revolver down and covered it with a newspaper. Then I went to the door and drew back the bolt. It was my wife's sister, a worthy but stupid widow.

" 'Vasya, what does this mean?' she asked, and her ever ready tears began to gush forth.

" 'What do you want?' I asked harshly. I saw that this was entirely unnecessary and that I had no reason to be gruff with her, but I could not adopt any other tone.

" 'Vasya, she is dying. Ivan Zakharuitch says so.'

"Ivan Zakharuitch was her doctor, her adviser.

" 'Why, is he here?' I asked, and all my rage against her flamed up once more. 'Well, suppose she is.'

" 'Vasya, go to her. Oh, how horrible this is!' she exclaimed.

" 'Must I go to her?' was the question that arose in my mind, and I instantly decided that I must go, that probably when a husband had killed his wife as I had, he must always go to her, that it was the proper thing to do.

" 'If it is always done, then I must surely go,' I said to myself. 'Yes, if it is necessary to, I shall; I can still kill myself,' I reasoned in regard to my intention of blowing my brains out; and I followed her.

" 'Now there will be phrases and grimaces, but I will not let them affect me,' said I to myself.

" 'Wait,' said I to my sister. 'It is stupid to go without my boots, let me at least put on my slippers.'

28

"Another remarkable thing:—Once more as I left my room and went through the familiar rooms, once more arose the hope that nothing had taken place, but the odor of the vile medical appliances, iodoform, the carbolic acid, struck my senses.

"Yes, all was a reality. As I went though the corridor past the nursery I caught sight of Lizanka. She looked at me with frightened eyes. It seemed to me then that all five of the children were there and that all of them were looking at me.

"I went to the door and the chambermaid opened it from the inside and passed out. The first thing that struck my eyes was her light gray gown lying on a chair and all discolored with blood. She was lying on our double bed, on my own side of it,—for it was easier of access on that side, and her knees were raised. She was placed in a very sloping position on pillows alone, with her kofta unbuttoned. Something had been placed over the wound. The room was full of the oppressive odor of iodoform. I was more than all struck by her swollen face, black and blue,—part of her nose and under her eyes. It was the effect of the blow that I had given her with my elbow, when she was trying to hold me back. Her beauty had all vanished, and her appearance was decidedly repulsive to me. I paused on the threshold.

" 'Go to her, go,' said her sister.

" 'Yes, she probably wants to confess to me,' I thought. 'Shall I forgive her? Yes, she is dying and it is permissible to forgive her,' I said mentally, striving to be magnanimous.

"I went close to her. She with difficulty raised her eyes to me—one of them was blackened, and she said with difficulty, with pauses between the words:—

" 'You have had your way . . . you have killed me.'

"And in her face, through her physical suffering and even the proximity of death, could be seen the old expression of cold animal hatred which I knew so well.

" 'The children . . . anyway . . . you shall not have . . . She' indicating her sister 'will take them.'

"As to what was the principal thing for me—her guilt, her unfaithfulness, she did not consider it worth while to say a word.

" 'Yes . . . delight yourself in what you have done.' said she, glancing at the door and sobbing. On the threshold stood her sister with the children. 'Oh, what have you done?'

"I looked at the children, at her bruised and discolored face, and for the first time forgot myself, my rights, my pride, for the first time recognized the human being in her. And so petty seemed all that had offended me, all my jealousy, and so significant the deed that I had done, that I had the impulse to bow down to her hand and to say, 'Forgive me,' but I had not the courage.

"She remained silent, closing her eyes, evidently too weak to speak further.

"Then her mutilated face was distorted with a frown. She feebly pushed me away.

" 'Why has all this taken place, why?'

" 'Forgive me,' I cried.

" 'Forgive? What nonsense! . . . If only I had not to die!' she cried, raising herself up, and her deliriously flashing eyes were fastened on me.

" 'Yes, you have wreaked your will. I hate you. Ai! Oh,' she screamed, evidently out of her head, evidently afraid of something. 'Shoot, I am not afraid. . . . Only kill us all. . . . He has gone. . . . He has gone.'

"The delirium continued to the very end. She did not recognize any one. On the same day at noon she died. Before that, at eight o'clock in the morning, I was arrested and taken to prison. And there, while I was confined for eleven months waiting for my trial, I had a chance to meditate on myself and my past life, and I came to understand it. On the third day I began to comprehend. On the third day they took me *there*."

He wanted to say something more, but not having the strength to hold back his sobs, he paused. Collecting his strength, he continued:—

"I began to comprehend only when I beheld her in her coffin." He sobbed, but immediately continued hastily:—

"Only when I beheld her dead face did I understand what I had done. I comprehended that I, I had killed her, that it was through me that she, who had been living, moving, warm, was now motionless, wax-like, and cold, and that there was no way of ever again making it right,—never, never again. He who has not lived through this cannot comprehend, U! U! U!" he cried several times, and said no more.

We sat a long time in silence. He sobbed and trembled before me. His face became pinched and long, and his mouth widened to its fullest extent.

"Yes," he said suddenly, "if I had known what I know now, then everything would have been entirely different. I would not have married her for . . . I would not have married at all."

Again we were long silent.

"Well, good-by—Prostite."

He turned from me and lay down on the seat, covering himself with his plaid.

At the station where I was to leave the train—it was eight o'clock in the morning—I went up to him to bid him farewell. Either he was asleep or was pretending to be sleeping; he did not move. I touched his hand. He uncovered himself, and it was plain that he had not been asleep.

"Proshchaïte—Farewell," said I, offering him my hand. He took it and almost smiled, but so piteously that I felt like weeping.

"Yes, good-by—Prostite," said he, repeating the very word with which he had closed his tale.

1889

THE STORY OF YEMILYAN
AND THE EMPTY DRUM

Yemilyan lived out as a day-laborer. Once upon a time he was on his way to the meadow where his work was, and lo and behold! a frog leaped out before him. He almost set his foot on it. But he stepped over it. Suddenly he heard some one calling to him from behind. He looked round and saw a beautiful girl standing there, and she said to him:—

"Yemilyan, why are you not married?"

"How could I be married, my pretty maid. Look at me; I have nothing at all. No one would take me."

"Well," said the girl, "take me for a wife."

The girl greatly pleased Yemilyan; said he:—

"I should like to; but where should we live?"

"That is something to think about," said the girl. "Hard work and little sleep is all that is required; but we can find clothes and food anywhere."

"Very good, I'm agreed; let us get married. Where shall we go?"

"Let us go to the city."

Yemilyan and the girl went to the city. The girl took him to a little cottage at the farther end of the city, and they were married and lived there.

One time the voyevode came to the city. He passed by Yemilyan's cottage, and Yemilyan's wife went out to look at him. When the voyevode saw her he was amazed.

"Where did such a beauty as that come from?"

He reined in his horse, and summoned Yemilyan's wife, and began to question her.

"Who are you?" he asked.

"The wife of the peasant Yemilyan," said she.

"How did it happen," said he, "that such a beautiful woman as you married a peasant? You ought to be a princess."

"Thank you," said she, "for your flattering remark, but I am satisfied with my husband."

The voyevode talked with her awhile, and then rode on his way. He reached his palace. But he could not help thinking of Yemilyan's wife. He lay awake all night long, planning how he might get her away from Yemilyan. He could not think of any way of doing it. He summoned his servants, and bade them devise some way. And the voyevode's servants said to him:—

"Take Yemilyan as your workman," said they. "We'll work him to death; his wife will be a widow, and then you can have her."

So the voyevode did; he sent for Yemilyan to come to him as a dvornik, and offered him a house for him and his wife.

The messengers came and told Yemilyan their story. But Yemilyan's wife said:—

"Very good," said she. "Go. Work there during the daytime, but at night return to me."

Yemilyan went. When he reached the palace, the voyevode's steward said to him:—

"Why have you come alone, without your wife?"

"Why should I bring her? Her place is at home."

In the voyevode's courtyard they gave him so much work to do that two men could not have accomplished it. Yemilyan took hold of the work, but it seemed hopeless for him to finish it. But lo and behold! when evening came it was all done. The steward saw that he had finished it, and gave him four times as much for the next day. Yemilyan went home and found the house all neatly swept and in order; the fire was burning in the stove, the baking and boiling were under way. His wife was sitting at the table sewing and waiting for her husband. When he entered she met him, got supper ready, and, after he had had all he wanted to eat and drink, she began to ask him about his work.

"Well," said he, "it went badly. They gave me more than I had strength to do. They are going to kill me with work."

"Now, then," said she, "don't you worry about your work, and don't look back and don't look forward to see if much has been done and much remains to be done. Only work. All will come out right."

Yemilyan went to bed. The next morning he went to his work again. He took hold of it, and not once did he look round. And lo and behold! it was all done by four o'clock, and while it was still light he went home for the night. And though they kept adding to his tasks, still Yemilyan always managed to finish it up and go home for the night.

Thus passed a week. The voyevode's servants perceived that they could not overcome the muzhik by "black work." They began to impose handiwork upon him, but this also proved vain. Carpentry work and mason work and the art of thatching—whatever they imposed upon him, that Yemilyan got done in ample time for him to go home and spend the night with his wife. Thus passed a second week. The voyevode summoned his servants, and said:—

"I should like to know if I feed you for doing nothing? Here two weeks have passed and I can't see that you have done anything at all. You were going to put Yemilyan out of the way for me, but from the window I see him going home every afternoon, singing songs. I should like to know if you are scheming to turn me into ridicule?"

The servants began to justify themselves:—

"We tried with all our might," said they, "to kill him off by 'black work,' but we could not do anything with him. Everything we gave him to work at he worked out, and we could not tire him. Then we gave him handiwork to do, thinking he would not have wit enough to do it, but in this too we failed to get him. It is like magic. As soon as he touches anything it is done. It must be that either he or his wife practises some witchcraft. We are tired to death of him. And now we are trying to think of something that he can't do. We have decided to make him build a new cathedral in one day. So will you summon Yemilyan and command him to build a new cathedral opposite your palace in one day? And if he does not have it done, then we will have his head cut off as a punishment."

The voyevode sent for Yemilyan.

"Well," said he, "this is my command. Build me a new cathedral on the square opposite my palace, so that it shall be all done to-morrow evening. If you get it built, I will reward you; if you fail, I shall punish you."

Yemilyan heard the command, he turned round and went home.

"Well," said he to himself, "that's the end of me."

He went to his wife and said:—

"Get yourself ready, wife; we must make our escape somewhere or other, else we shall be ruined."

"Why," said she, "are you such a coward that you must run away?"

"How can I help being?" said he. "The voyevode has ordered me to come to-morrow and build a new cathedral all in one day. And if I don't get it built, he threatens to cut off my head. The only thing left to do is to escape while there is time."

But his wife would not hear to this.

"The voyevode has many servants. They will catch us anywhere. You can't escape from him. But since you have the power, you must obey him."

"Yes, but how can one obey him, if one has not the power?"

"Listen, batyushka. Don't you worry. Eat your supper and go to bed. In the morning get up a little earlier than usual; you'll have it all done."

Yemilyan went to bed; his wife wakened him.

"Go," said she, "build your cathedral as quickly as possible. Here are nails and a hammer; there'll be work enough for you for the day."

Yemilyan went to the city; when he got there the new cathedral was already standing in the midst of the square, almost finished. Yemilyan went to work to finish it; by evening it was all complete.

The voyevode woke up, he looked out of his palace window, and saw that the cathedral was already built. Yemilyan was walking up and down, here and there driving in nails. And the voyevode was not pleased to see the cathedral; he was vexed because he had nothing to punish Yemilyan for, and could not take away his wife. So he called his servants again.

"Yemilyan has accomplished his task; there is nothing to punish him for. This task," said he, "was too small for him. Something craftier must be thought up. Put your wits to work, or else I will punish you instead of him."

And the voyevode's servants suggested that he should command Yemilyan to make a river which should flow round the palace, and that ships should be sailing on it. The voyevode summoned Yemilyan, and laid before him the new task.

"If you are able," said he, "in one night to build a cathedral, then you will be able to do this also. See to it that to-morrow everything be as I have commanded. And if it is not ready, then I will cut off your head."

Yemilyan was more than ever discouraged, and he returned to his wife in a very gloomy frame of mind.

"Why," said his wife, "are you so discouraged? Have you some new task imposed on you?"

Yemilyan told her.

"We must make our escape," said he.

But his wife said:—

"You can't run away; they will catch you everywhere; you must obey."

"Yes, but how can I obey?"

"Well, batyushka, there is nothing to be discouraged about. Eat your supper and go to bed. But get up earlier than usual; everything will be in order."

Yemilyan went to bed and slept. Early in the morning his wife waked him.

"Go," said she, "go to the city, all is ready. You will find one mound only at the harbor. Take your spade and level it off."

Yemilyan started. He reached the city; round the palace was a river, ships were sailing on it. Yemilyan reached the harbor, he saw the uneven place, and began to level it.

The voyevode woke up, he saw a river where no river had been; ships were sailing on it and Yemilyan was leveling a mound with his spade. The voyevode was horror-struck and was not rejoiced at the sight of the river and the ships; but he was vexed because he could not punish Yemilyan. He said to himself:—

"There is no task that he cannot accomplish it. What shall we try now?"

He summoned his servants and proceeded to consult with them.

"Think up some tasks," said he, "that will be above Yemilyan's powers. For whatever you have so far devised for him, he has done at once, and it is impossible to take his wife from him."

The servants cudgeled their brains, and at last had a bright idea. They came to the voyevode and said:—

"You must summon Yemilyan and say to him:—

" 'Go somewhere, you know not where, and bring back something, you know not what.' He won't be able to escape from this. Wherever he goes you will say that he went to the wrong place, and whatever he brings back you will say that he brought back the wrong thing. Then you will be able to punish him and take away his wife."

This pleased the voyevode.

"This time," said he, "you have had a bright idea."

He sent for Yemilyan and said to him:—

"Go somewhere, you know not where, and bring back something, you know not what, and if you don't bring it, I will cut your head off."

Yemilyan went to his wife, and told her what the voyevode had said. His wife put on her thinking-cap.

"Well," said she, "they've been teaching the voyevode something to his own ruin. We must work now wisely."

She sat down, pondered for a while, and then said to her husband:—

"You will have to take a long journey—to our babushka, our grandmother —to the ancient peasant mother—and you must ask for her good-will. And from her you will receive an object; then go straight-way to the voyevode, and I shall be there. For now I shall not get out of their hands. They will take me by force, but not for long. If you do all the old babushka commands, you will speedily rescue me."

The wife got her husband ready; she gave him a wallet and gave him a spindle.

"Here, take this," said she, "and give it to her. By this she will know that you are my husband."

She showed him the way. Yemilyan started; he went beyond the city, and he saw some bowmen drilling. Yemilyan stopped and watched them. After the bowmen had practised, they sat down to rest. Yemilyan approached them and asked:—

"Do you know, my brethren, where I must go, not knowing where, to get something, not knowing what?"

The bowmen listened to what he had to say, and they were filled with wonder.

"Who sent you to find out?" they inquired.

"The voyevode," said he.

"No," said they, "we cannot help you."

After Yemilyan had sat a little while, he proceeded on his way.

He went and he went, and at last he came to a forest. In the forest lived the old babushka.

The old woman was sitting in a cottage—the ancient peasant mother—she was spinning flax—and she was weeping. When the old woman saw Yemilyan, she cried out to him:—

"What have you come for?"

Yemilyan gave her the distaff, and told her his wife had sent it to her. And Yemilyan began to tell her all about his life, how he had married the girl, how he had gone to the city to live, how he had been taken as a dvornik, how he had served the voyevode, how he had built the cathedral and made the river with the ships, and how now the voyevode had commanded him to go somewhere, not knowing where, to get something, he knew not what.

The old woman listened to him and ceased to weep. She began to mutter to herself.

"That is very good," said she, "but sit down, little son, and eat."

Yemilyan ate his fill, and the old woman began to talk with him.

"Here is a little ball," said she; "roll it before you and follow it, wherever it may roll. You will have to go far, even to the sea. When you reach the sea, you will find there a great city. When you enter the city, ask for a night's lodgings at the last house. There you will find what you need."

"But how shall I know it, babushka?"

"Well, when you see what men obey sooner than father and mother, that is what you want; seize on it and take it with you. You will take it to the voyevode, but he will say to you that you have not brought the thing that was required, and then do you say to him: 'Well, if it is not what is wanted it must be broken;' then hit the thing a blow and take it down to the river, break it, and fling it into the water, and then you will recover your wife."

Yemilyan bade the old woman good-by, rolled the little ball ahead of him; it rolled and it rolled, and it took him to the sea, and by the sea was a great city. At the border of the city was a large house. Yemilyan there demanded hospitality for the night; it was granted, and he went to bed. He woke early in the morning and listened; the father was getting up, he called his son and sent him to split kindlings. But the son would not heed; "It is too early as yet," said he, "I shall have time enough." Yemilyan heard the mother get down from the oven and say:—

"Go, little son, your father's bones pain him; would you make him go?"

"There's plenty of time."

The son made a smacking noise with his lips, and dropped off to sleep again. As soon as he had fallen asleep there was a noise like thunder, and a loud crash in the street. The son leaped down, put on his clothes, and ran down into the street. Yemilyan also jumped down and followed him to see what the son obeyed better than his parents. Yemilyan ran down and saw a man going along the street, carrying a round object and beating on it with sticks, and it rumbled, and the son listened to it. Yemilyan ran closer and examined the object, and saw that it was round like a small tub, and both ends were covered with skin. And he insisted on knowing what it was called.

"A drum," they told him.

Yemilyan was amazed, and asked them to give it to him. They refused to give it to him. So Yemilyan ceased to ask for it, but he walked along following it. He walked all that day, and when the man that had it lay down to sleep, Yemilyan seized his drum and ran off with it.

He ran and he ran, and at last came back to his own city. He expected to see his wife at home, but she was not there.

On the next day they had brought her to the voyevode. Yemilyan went to the voyevode's, and bade them announce him in these words:—

"Here! the man who went he knew not where, has come back, bringing he knows not what."

The voyevode bade Yemilyan to return the next day.

Yemilyan then ordered them to say to the voyevode:—

"I," said he, "have come to-day. I have brought what he bade me bring; let the voyevode come to me or I will come to him."

The voyevode replied:—

"Where did you go?" he asked.

"I don't know," said he.

"And what did you bring with you?"

Yemilyan was about to show it to him, but the voyevode refused to look at it:—

"It's nothing," said he.

"Yes, it's nothing," said Yemilyan; "but then one must beat on it, and the devil is in it."

Yemilyan came with the drum and beat on it.

As soon as he began to beat on it, all the voyevode's army came and joined Yemilyan. They saluted him and waited till he should give the word of command.

The voyevode began to shout to his bowmen from the window of his palace, forbidding them to follow Yemilyan. They refused to obey him, and followed Yemilyan. The voyevode perceived this, and ordered them to restore his wife to Yemilyan, and then asked him to give him the drum.

"I cannot," said Yemilyan. "I must beat it," said he, "and throw the scrapings into the river."

Yemilyan went with the drum to the river, and the bowmen followed him. Yemilyan beat the drum by the river, broke it into pieces, and flung them into the river. And all the bowmen scattered in all directions. But Yemilyan took his wife and brought her home. And from that time forth the voyevode ceased to bother him, and he lived long and happily ever after.

1891

A DIALOGUE AMONG CLEVER
PEOPLE

Once some guests were gathered in a rich man's home, and it happened that a serious conversation about life arose.

They talked about persons absent and persons present, and they could not hit upon a single one contented with his life.

Not only did each one find something to complain of in his fortune, but there was not one who would consider that he was living as a Christian ought to live. All confessed that they were living worldly lives, concerned only about themselves and their families, thinking little about their neighbors, and still less about God.

Thus talked the guests, and all agreed in blaming themselves for their godless, unchristian lives.

"Then why do we live so?" cried one youth. "Why do we do what we ourselves do not approve? Have we not the power over our own lives? We ourselves are conscious that our luxury, our effeminacy, our wealth, and especially our pride—our separation from our brethren—are our ruin. In order to be important and rich we must deprive ourselves of everything that gives man joy in living; we crowd ourselves into cities, we make ourselves effeminate, we ruin our constitutions; and notwithstanding all our diversion, we die of ennui and of disgust because our lives are not what they ought to be.

"Why live so? Why destroy our lives so, and all the good which God has bestowed on us? I mean to give up living as I have. I will give up the studies I have begun; for, don't you see, they would lead me to no other than that tormenting life which all of us are now complaining of. I will renounce my property, and I will go and live with the poor in the country. I will work with them; I will learn to labor with my hands, and if my culture is necessary to the poor, I will share it with them, but not through institutions and books, but directly, living with them as if I were their brother. . . . Yes, I have made up my mind," he added, looking inquiringly at his father, who was also present.

"Your desire is a worthy one," said his father, "but foolish and ill-considered. Everything seems to you quite easy because you don't know life. How beautiful it seems to us! But the truth is, the accomplishment of this beautiful ideal is very difficult and complicated. It is hard enough to go well on a beaten track, but still more to trace out new paths. They can be traced out only by men who have arrived at full maturity and have assimilated all that is in the power of man to absorb. It seems to you easy to break out new paths in life, because, as yet, you have had no experience of life. This is all the heedlessness and pride of youth. We old people are needed to curb your impulses and to guide you by our experience, while you young people must obey us so as to profit by our experience. Your active life is still before you; now you are growing and developing. Get your education, and all the culture you can; stand on your own legs, have your own firm convictions, and then begin your new life, if you feel you have the strength for it. But now you must obey those that are guiding you for your own good, and you must not strike out into new paths in life!"

The youth made no reply, and the older persons present agreed with what his father said.

"You are right," said a middle-aged, married man, addressing the youth's father. "It is true that a youth having no experience of life may blunder in trying new paths of life, and his resolution may not be deeply settled; but, you see, we are all agreed on this point, that our lives are contrary to our consciences, and do not make us happy. And so we can't help regarding your desire to enter upon this new life as laudable.

"The young man may adopt his ideal through reason, but I am not a young man, and I am going to speak to you about myself. As I listened to our talk this evening the same thought entered my mind. The life which I am leading, it is plain to me, cannot give me a serene conscience and happiness. Both experience and reason prove this. Then what am I waiting for! You struggle from morning till night for your family, and the result is that both you and your family continue to live ungodly lives, and you are all the while worse and worse entangled in your sins. You work for your family, and it seems your family are not better off or happier because you work for them. And so I often think it would be better if I changed my whole life and did exactly what this young man proposed —ceased to bother about wife and children, and only thought about my soul. Not without reason does it say in St. Paul: 'He that is married takes thought about his wife, but he that is unmarried about God.'"

Before this married man had finished his remarks, all the women present, including his wife, fell upon him:

"You ought to have thought about all this earlier," said one of the elderly ladies. " 'Once harnessed, you must work.' According to your plan every man will be saying, 'I want to be saved,' when it seems to him hard to maintain and feed a family. It is all deception and baseness. No; a man ought to be able to live in a godly way even if he has a family. It is easy enough for him to save himself alone. And then the main thing—to act so is to act contrary to the teaching of Christ. God has commanded us to love others, but in this way you would offend others as if it were for God. No; a married man has his definite obligations, and he ought not to shirk them. It is another thing when your family has already been established. Then you may do as you please for yourself, but no one has any right to do violence to his family."

The married man did not agree with this. He said: "I have no wish to give up my family. All I say is that it is not necessary to maintain one's family and children in a worldly fashion, or to teach them to live for their own pleasures as we were just saying; but we ought to train them so that children in their early days 'may be accustomed to poverty, to labor, to help others; and, above all, to lead a fraternal life with all men. And to do this it is necessary to renounce all wealth and distinction."

"There is no sense in breaking in others while you yourself are not living a godly life," retorted his wife, with some heat. "Ever since your earliest youth you have lived for your own gratification. Why, then, should you wish to torment your children and family? Let them grow up in peace, and then they will do as they themselves are inclined; but don't you coerce them."

The married man held his peace, but an elderly man who was present took up the cudgels in his defense:—

"Let us admit," said he, "it is impossible for a married man who has accustomed his family to a certain degree of luxury, suddenly to deprive them of it all. It is true that if you have begun to educate your children, you had better carry out your plans than break them off. All the more, because the children, when they are grown up, will themselves choose the path which they think best. I admit that it is difficult, if not impossible, for a family man to change his life without working injury. But to us old men God has given this as a command. I will say of myself, I am living now without any responsibilities. I am living, to tell the truth, merely for my belly. I eat, I drink, I take my ease, and it is disgusting and repulsive to my nature.

"So then it is time for me to give up this life, to distribute my property, and to live the rest of my days as God has commanded a Christian to live."

The rest did not agree with the old man. His niece and goddaughter was present, all of whose children he had stood as sponsor for, always providing them with holiday gifts; and so was his son. All protested against his views.

"No," said his son, "you have worked hard in your day, you deserve to rest; and you have no right to torment yourself. You have lived sixty years in your own habits; it would be impossible for you to change them. You would only torment yourself for nothing."

"Yes, yes," exclaimed his niece, in confirmation of this, "you would be in want, you would be out of sorts, you would grumble, and you would commit worse sin. But God is merciful and pardons all sinners—much more such a good kind uncle as you are!"

"Yes, and why should we?" asked another old man, a contemporary of the old uncle. "You and I may not have two days longer to live. So what is the use of beginning?"

"What a marvelous thing!" exclaimed one of the guests—he had not spoken before—"What a marvelous thing! All of us confess that it is good to live a godly life, and that we live ill and suffer in soul and body; but as soon as it comes to the point, then it seems that it is impossible to break in the children, but they must be educated, not in the godlike way, but in the old-fashioned way. It is impossible for a young man to escape from his parents' will, but he must live, not in the godlike way, but in the old way. A married man cannot restrain his wife and children, but must live the ungodlike life, in the old way. The old men cannot begin, they are not accustomed to it; and besides this, they may not live two days longer. So the upshot is that it is impossible for any one to live well, but only to talk about it."

1893

WALK IN THE LIGHT WHILE
THERE IS LIGHT

A TALE OF THE TIME OF THE EARLY

CHRISTIANS

1

It was in the reign of the Roman Emperor Trajan, a century after the birth of Christ. It was at the time when the disciples of Christ's disciples were still living, and the Christians faithfully observed the laws of the Master as it is related in the Acts:—

And the multitude of them that believed were of one heart and of one soul; neither said any of them that aught of the things which he possessed was his own; but they had all things common. And with great power gave the Apostles witness of the resurrection of the Lord Jesus; and great grace was upon them all. Neither was there any among them that lacked; for as many as were possessors of lands or houses sold them and brought the prices of the things that were sold and laid them down at the Apostles' feet; and distribution was made unto every man according as he had need. (ACTS IV. 32–35.)

In these early times, a rich Syrian tradesman named Juvenal, a dealer in precious stones, was living in the province of Cilicia, in the city of Tarsus. He was of poor and simple origin; but, by dint of hard work and skill in his art, he had accumulated property and won the respect of his fellow-citizens. He had traveled widely in different lands; and though he was not a literate man, he had seen and learned much, and the city people regarded him highly for his intellect and his probity.

He held to the pagan faith of Rome, which was professed by all respectable people of the Roman Empire,—that faith burdened with ceremonies which the emperors since the days of Augustus had so strenuously inculcated, and which the reigning Emperor Trajan so strictly maintained.

The province of Cilicia was far from Rome, but it was administered by a Roman proconsul, and everything that took place in Rome found its echo in Cilicia, and the rulers were mimic emperors.

Juvenal remembered all that had been told him in his childhood about the actions of Nero in Rome. As time went on, he had seen how one emperor after another perished; and, like a clever man, he came to the conclusion that there was nothing sacred about the Roman religion, but that it was all the work of human hands. The senselessness of all the life which went on around him, especially that in Rome, where his business often took him, bewildered him. He had his doubts, he could not comprehend everything; and he attributed this to his lack of cultivation.

He was married, and four children had been born to him; but three had died young, and only one, a son named Julius, survived. Juvenal lavished on this son Julius all his affection and all his care. He especially wished so to educate his son that he might not be tortured by such doubts regarding life as had bewildered him. When Julius had passed the age of fifteen, his father intrusted his education to a philosopher who had settled in their city and devoted himself to the instruction of youth. Juvenal intrusted him to this philosopher, together with a comrade of his, Pamphilius, the son of a former slave whom Juvenal had freed.

The two boys were of the same age, both handsome, and good friends. They studied diligently, and both of them were of good morals. Julius distinguished himself more in the study of the poets and in mathematics; Pamphilius, in the study of philosophy.

About a year before the completion of their course of study, Pamphilius, coming to school one day, explained to the teacher that his widowed mother was going to the city of Daphne, and that he would be obliged to give up his studies.

The teacher was sorry to lose a pupil who had reflected credit on him; Juvenal also was sorry, but sorriest of all was Julius. But in spite of all their entreaties that he should stay and finish his studies, Pamphilius remained obdurate, and after thanking his friends for their love toward him and their solicitude for him, he took his departure.

Two years passed: Julius completed his studies; and during all that time he did not once see his friend.

One day, however, he met him in the street, invited him home, and began to ask him how and where he lived.

Pamphilius told him he still lived in the same place with his mother.

"We do not live alone," said he, "but many friends live with us, and we have all things in common."

"What do you mean 'in common'?" asked Julius.

"In such a way that none of us considers anything his private property."

"Why do you do that way?"

"We are Christians," said Pamphilius.

"Is it possible!" cried Julius. "Why, I have been told that Christians kill children and eat them. Can it be that you take part in doing such things?"

"Come and see," replied Pamphilius. "We do nothing of the sort; we live simply, trying to do nothing wrong."

"But how can you live, if you have no property of your own?"

"We support each other. If we give our brethren our labors, then they give us theirs."

"But if your brethren take your labors and don't reciprocate, then what?"

"We don't have such persons," said Pamphilius; "such persons prefer to live luxuriously, and they don't join us; life among us is simple, and without luxury."

"But are there not many lazy ones who would delight in being fed for nothing?"

"Yes, there are some such, and we willingly receive them. Not long ago a man of that character came to us—a runaway slave; at first, it is true, he was lazy, and led a bad life, but soon he changed his life, and has now become one of the good brethren."

"But supposing he had not ordered his life aright?"

"Well, there are some such. The old man Cyril says that we must treat such as if they were the very best of the brethren, and love them all the more."

"Can one love good-for-nothings?"

"It is impossible to help loving a human being."

"But how can you give all men whatever they ask of you?" asked Julius. "If my father gave all persons whatever they asked him for, very soon he wouldn't have anything left."

"I don't know," replied Pamphilius. "We always have enough left for our necessities. Even if it came about that we had nothing to eat or nothing to wear, then we ask the others and they give to us. Yes, it sometimes happens so. Only once did I ever have to go to bed without my supper, and that was because I was very tired and did not feel like going to ask any of the brethren."

"I don't know how you do," said Julius, "only what my father says: if he didn't have his own property, and if he gave to every one who asked him, he would die of starvation."

"We don't! Come and see. We live, and not only do not lack, but we have even more than we need."

"How can that be?"

"This is the way of it: We all profess one law, but our powers of fulfilling it vary in each individual; some have greater, some have less. One has already made great improvement in the good life, while another has only just begun in it. At the head of us all stands Christ, with His life, and we all try to imitate Him, and in this only we see our well-being. Certain of us, like the old man Cyril and his wife Pelagia, are our leaders; others stand next to them, and still others in a third rank, but all of us are traveling along the same path. Those in advance are already near to the law of Christ,—self-renunciation,—and they are willing to lose their life in order to save it. These need nothing; they have no regret for themselves, and to those that ask they give their last possession according to the law of Christ. There are others, feebler, who cannot give all they have, who have some pity on themselves, who grow weak if they don't have their usual dress and food, and cannot give everything away. Then there are others still weaker—such as have only just started on the path; these still live in the old way, keeping much for themselves and giving away only what is superfluous. Even these that linger in the rear give aid to those in the van. Moreover, all of us are entangled by our relationships with pagans. One man's father is a pagan and has a property, and gives to his son. The son gives to those that ask, but the father still continues to provide. The mother of another is a pagan, and has pity on her son, and helps him. A third has heathen children, while a mother is a Christian, and the children obey her, give to her, and beg her not to give her possessions away, while she, out of love to them, takes what they give her, and gives to others. Then, again, a fourth will have a pagan wife, and a fifth a pagan husband. Thus all are perplexed, and those in the van would be glad to give their all, but they cannot. In this way the feeble in faith are confirmed, and thus much of the superfluous is collected together."

In reply to this Julius said:—

"Well, if this is so, then it means you fail to observe the teaching of Christ, and only pretend to observe it. For if you don't give away your all, then there is no distinction between us and you. In my mind, if you are going to be a Christian, then you must fulfil the whole law; give everything away and remain a beggar."

"That is the best way of all," said Pamphilius. "Do so!"

"Yes, I will do so when I see that you do."

"We do not wish to set an example. And I don't advise you to join us and renounce your present life for a mere display; we act as we do, not for show, but as a part of our religion."

"What do you mean—your 'religion'?"

"Why, it means that salvation from the evils of the world, from death, is to be found only in life according to the teaching of Christ. And it makes no difference to us what men say about us. We are not doing this in the eyes of men, but because in this alone do we see life and welfare."

"It is impossible not to live for self," said Julius. "The gods instilled in us our instinct to love ourselves better than others and to seek happiness for ourselves. And you do the same thing. You confess that some of you have pity on yourselves; more and more they will look out for their own pleasures, and be ever more willing to give up your faith and do just what we are doing."

"No," replied Pamphilius; "our brethren will go in another path and will never weaken, but will become more and more confirmed in it: just as a fire will never go out when wood is added to it. In this is our faith."

"I don't find in what this faith consists."

"Our faith is this: that we understand life as Christ has interpreted it to us."

"How is that?"

"Christ uttered some such parable as this: Certain vine-dressers cultivated a vineyard, and they were obliged to pay tribute to the owner of the vineyard. We are the vine-dressers who live in the world and have to pay tribute to God and fulfil His will. But those that held to the worldly faith fancied that the vineyard was theirs, that they had nothing to pay for it, but only to enjoy the fruits of it. The Lord of the vineyard sent a messenger to these men to receive His tribute, but they drove him away. The Lord of the vineyard sent His Son after the tribute, but they killed Him, thinking that after that no one would interfere with them. This is the belief of the world, whereby all men live who do not acknowledge that life is given only for God's service. But Christ has taught us how false is the worldly belief that it would be better for man if he drove out of the vineyard the Master's messenger and His Son and avoided paying tribute, for He showed us that we must either pay tribute or be expelled from the vineyard. He taught us that all pleasures which we call pleasures— eating, drinking, amusements—cannot be pleasures if our life is devoted to them, that they are pleasures only when we seek another,—the fulfilment of the will of God; that only then these are pleasures, as a present reward following the fulfilment of the will of God. To wish to have pleasure without the labor of fulfilling the will of God, to separate pleasure from work, is the same as to tear off the stalks of flowers and plant them without seeds. We have this belief, and therefore we cannot seek for deception in place of truth. Our faith consists in this: that the welfare of life is not in its pleasures, but in the fulfilment of the will of God without a thought of its pleasures, or hoping for them. And thus we live, and the longer we live the more we see that pleasure and well-being, like a wheel behind the shafts, follow on the fulfilment of the will of God. Our Lord has said: *Come unto me all ye that labor and are heavy laden, and I will give you rest! Take my yoke upon you and learn of me, for I am meek and lowly in heart; and ye shall find rest unto your souls, for my yoke is easy and my burden is light.*"

Thus said Pamphilius.

Julius listened, and his heart was stirred within him; but what Pamphilius said was not clear to him: at one moment it seemed to him that Pamphilius was deceiving him, but when he looked into his friend's kindly eyes and remembered his goodness, it seemed to him that Pamphilius was deceiving himself.

Pamphilius invited Julius to visit him so as to examine into the life they led, and if it pleased him to remain and live with them.

And Julius promised, but he did not go to Pamphilius; and being drawn into his own life, he forgot about him.

2

Julius' father was rich, and as he loved his only son and was proud of him, he never stinted him for money. Julius lived the life of rich young men; in idleness, luxury, and dissipated amusements, which have always been, and are still, the same,—wine, gambling, and fast women.

But the pleasures to which Julius gave himself up kept demanding more and more money, and after a time he found he had not enough. Once he asked for more than his father generally gave him. His father gave it to him, but accompanied it with a rebuke. The son, conscious that he was to blame, and yet unwilling to acknowledge his fault, became angry, behaved rudely to his father, as those that are aware of their guilt, and are unwilling to confess it, are apt to do.

The money he obtained from his father was very quickly spent, and moreover, about the same time Julius and a companion happened to get into a drunken quarrel, and killed a man. The prefect of the city heard about it, and was desirous of subjecting Julius to punishment, but his father succeeded in bringing about his pardon. At this time, Julius, by his irregular life, required still more money. He borrowed it of a boon companion and agreed to repay it. Moreover his mistress asked him to give her a present; she desired a pearl necklace, and he knew that if he did not accede to her request, she would throw him over and take up with a rich man, who had already for some time been trying to entice her away from Julius.

Julius went to his mother and told her he had got to have some money; that if he did not succeed in raising as much as he needed, he should kill himself. For the fact that he had got into such a scrape he blamed his father, not himself. He said:—

"My father has accustomed me to a luxurious life, and then he began to blame me for wanting money. If at first he had given me what I needed without scolding, then with what he gave me afterward I should have regulated my life, and should not have needed much; but as he has always given me too little, I have had to apply to usurers, and they have extorted from me every-thing I had, and so nothing is left for me to live on, as a rich young man should, and I am put to shame before my companions; and yet my father can't seem to understand this at all. He has forgotten that he was young once himself. He got me into this position, and now, if he does not give me what I ask for, I shall kill myself."

The mother, who spoiled her son, went to his father. The father called the young man, and began to upbraid both him and his mother. The son answered the father rudely. The father struck him. The son seized his father's arm. The father called to his slaves and ordered them to take the young man and lock him up.

When he was left alone, Julius cursed his father and the day he was born. His own death or his father's presented itself before him as the only way of es-cape from the position in which he found himself.

Julius' mother suffered more than he did. She did not comprehend who was really to blame in all this. She felt nothing but pity for her beloved child. She went to her husband and begged him to forgive the youth, but he refused to listen to her, and began to reproach her for having spoiled her son; she blamed him, and the upshot of it was the husband beat his wife. But the wife made no account of the beating. She went to the son and persuaded him to go and beg his father's forgiveness and yield to his wishes. She promised him, if he would do so, she would give him the money he needed, and not let his father know.

The son consented, and then the mother went to her husband and urged him to pardon the young man. The father for a long time stormed at his wife and son, but at last decided to pardon him, but only on the condition that he should abandon his dissipated life and marry a rich tradesman's daughter, whose father wished her to enter into an engagement with him.

"He shall have money from me and his wife's dowry," said the young man's father, "and then let him enter upon a regular life. If he will agree to fulfil my wishes I will pardon him. But otherwise I will give him nothing, and at his first offense I will deliver him over into the hands of the prefect."

Julius agreed to everything, and was released. He promised to marry and to abandon his wicked ways, but he had no intention of doing so; and life at home now became a perfect hell for him: his father did not speak to him, and was quarreling about him with his mother, who wept.

On the next day his mother called him to her room and secretly gave him a precious stone which she had got from her husband.

"Go, sell it; not here, but in another city, and with the money do what you need, and I will manage to conceal the loss for a time, and if it is discovered I will blame it on one of the slaves."

Julius' heart was touched by his mother's words. He was horror-struck at what she had done; and he left home, but did not take the precious stone with him. He himself did not know where or wherefore he was going. He kept going on and on, away from the city, feeling the necessity of remaining alone, and thinking over all that had happened to him and was before him. As he kept going farther and farther away, he came entirely beyond the city limits and entered a grove sacred to the goddess Diana. Coming to a solitary spot, he began to think.

The first thought that occurred to him was to ask help of the goddess. But he no longer believed in his gods, and so he knew that no help was to be expected from them. But if no help came from them, then who would help him? As he thought over his position, it seemed to him too terrible. His soul was all confusion and gloom. But there was help for it. He had to appeal to his conscience, and he began to examine into his life and his acts. And both seemed to him wicked, and, more than all, stupid. Why was he tormenting himself so? He had few pleasures, and many trials and tribulations!

The principal thing was that he felt himself all alone. Hitherto he had had a beloved mother, a father; he certainly had friends; now he had no one. No one loved him. He was a burden to every one. He had succeeded in bringing trouble into all their lives: he had caused his mother to quarrel with his father; he had wasted his father's substance, gathered with so much labor all his life long; he had been a dangerous and disagreeable rival to his friends. There could be no doubt about it,—all would find it a relief if he were dead.

As he reviewed his life, he remembered Pamphilius, and his last meeting with him, and how Pamphilius had invited him to come there, to the Christians. And it occurred to him not to return home, but to go straight to the Christians, and remain with them.

"But was his position so desperate?" he asked himself, and again he proceeded to review what had happened, and again he was horror-struck because no one seemed to love him, and he loved no one. His mother, father, friends, did not love him, and must wish he were dead; but whom did he himself love? His friends? He was conscious that he did not love any one. All were rivals of his, all were pitiless toward him, now that he was in disgrace. "His father?" he asked himself, and horror seized him when at this question he looked into his heart. Not only did he not love him, but he hated him for his stinginess, for the affront he had put on him. He hated him, and, moreover, he saw plainly that for his own happiness his father's death was essential.

"Yes," Julius asked to himself, "and supposing I knew that no one would see it or ever find it out, what would I do if I could with one blow, once and for all, deprive him of life and set myself free?"

And Julius replied to this question:—

"Yes, I should kill him!"

He replied to this question, and was horror-struck at himself.

"My mother? Yes, I pity her, but I do not love her; it makes no difference to me what happens to her—all I need is her help. . . . Yes, I am a wild beast! and a wild beast beaten and tracked to its lair, and the only distinction is that I am able, if I chose, to quit this false, wicked life; I can do what the wild beast cannot—I can kill myself. I hate my father, there is no one I love . . . neither my mother, nor my friends—but how about Pamphilius?"

And again he remembered his one friend. He began to recall the last interview, and their conversation, and Pamphilius' words, how, according to their teaching, Christ had said: *Come unto me all ye that labor and are heavy laden, and I will give you rest.* Can that be true?

As he went on with his thoughts and recollections, he recalled Pamphilius' sweet, joyous, passionless face, and he felt inclined to believe in what Pamphilius said.

"What am I, in reality?" he asked himself. "Who am I? A man seeking well-being. I have sought for it in animal pleasures, and have not found it. And all living beings, like myself, also failed to find it. All are evil, and suffer. If any man is always happy, it is because he is seeking for nothing. He says that there are many such, and that all men will be such if they obey their Master's teachings. What if this is the truth? Whether it is the truth or not, it attracts me to it, and I am going."

Thus said Julius to himself, and he left the grove resolved never again to return home, and he bent his steps to the town where the Christians lived.

3

Julius went on boldly and cheerfully, and the farther he went and the more vividly he represented to himself the life of the Christians, remembering all to himself that Pamphilius had said, the more joyous he became in spirit.

The sun was already descending toward the west, and he felt the need of rest, when he fell in with a man who was resting and taking his nooning. This man was of middle age, and had an intellectual face. He was sitting and eating olives and cakes. When he saw Julius, he smiled and said:—

"How are you, young man? The way is still long. Sit down and rest."

Julius thanked him, and sat down.

"Where are you going?" asked the stranger.

"To the Christians," said Julius; and he gave a truthful account of his life and his decision.

The stranger listened attentively, and though he asked him about certain details, he did not express his opinion; but when Julius had finished, the stranger stowed away in his wallet the remains of his luncheon, arranged his attire, and said:—

"Young man, do not carry out your intention; you are making a mistake. I know life, and you do not. I know the Christians, and you do not know them. Listen, and I will explain your whole life and your ideas; and when you hear me you shall adopt the decision that seems to you the wiser. You are young, rich, handsome, strong; your passions are boiling in you. You wish to find a quiet refuge in which your passions would not disturb you, and you would not suffer from their consequences; and it seems to you that you might find such a refuge among the Christians.

"There is no such place, my dear young man, because what troubles you is not peculiar to Cilicia or to Rome, but to yourself. In the quiet of a village solitude the same passions will torment you—only a hundred times more violently. The fraud of the Christians, or their mistake—for I don't care to judge them—consists simply in this,—that they don't wish to understand the nature of man. The only person who can perfectly carry out their teachings is an old man who has outlived all his passions. A man in his prime, or a youth like you who has not yet learned life or himself, cannot submit to their law, because this law has for its basis, not the nature of man, but an idle philosophy. If you go to them, you will suffer what you suffer now, only in a far higher degree. Now, your passions entice you along false paths; but having once made a mistake in your direction, you can rectify it. Now, you still have the satisfaction of passion freed—in other words—of life.

"But, in their midst, controlling your passions by main force, you will make precisely the same mistakes, if not worse ones; and, besides that suffering, you will also have the incessant anguish of the unsatisfied human longings. Let the water out of a dam, and it will irrigate the soil and the meadows, and quench the thirst of animals; but if you keep it back it will tear away the earth and trickle away in mud. It is the same with the passions. The teachings of the Christians—beyond those doctrines from which they get consolation, and which I will not speak of—their teachings, I say, for life, consist in the following: They do not recognize violence, they do not recognize war or courts of justice, they do not recognize private property, they do not recognize the sciences, the arts, or anything which makes life cheerful and pleasant.

"All this would be good if all men were such as they describe their teacher to have been. But you see this is not so, and cannot be. Men are bad, and given over to their passions. It is this play of passions, and the collisions resulting from them, that keep men in those conditions of life in which they live. The barbarians know no restraint, and one savage, for the satisfaction of his own desires, would destroy the whole world, if all men submitted as these Christians submit. If the gods lodged in the human heart the sentiments of anger, of vengeance, even of evil against evil-doers, they must have done it because these sentiments are necessary for the life of men. The Christians teach that these feelings are wicked, and that men would be happy if they did not have them; there would be no murders, no punishments, no want. That is true; but one might as well take the position that men ought to refrain from eating for the sake of their happiness. In reality, it would put an end to greediness, hunger, and all the misfortunes that come from it. But this supposition could not change the nature of man. Even if two or three dozen people, believing in this, and actually refraining from food, should die of starvation, it would not change the nature of man. The same, exactly, with the other passions of men: indignation, wrath, vengeance, even love for women, for luxury, for splendor and pomp, are characteristic of the gods, and consequently they are the ineradicable characteristics of man.

"Annihilate man's nutrition, and you annihilate man. In exactly the same way annihilate the passions characteristic of man, and you annihilate humanity.

"The same is true also of private property, which the Christian would do away with. Look around you: every vineyard, every inclosure, every house, every ass,—everything has been produced by men under the conditions of private property. Abolish the right of private property, and not a vineyard would be planted, not a creature would be trained and pastured. The Christians assure you that they have no rights of private property; but they enjoy its fruits. They say they have all things in common, and everything they have is brought to one place; but what they bring together they receive from men who have private property. They merely deceive men, or in the very best light, deceive themselves. You say they themselves work in order to support life, but the work they do would not support them if they did not take advantage of what men possessing private property produced. Even if they could support themselves, it would be a mere existence, and there would be no place among them for the arts and sciences. [And indeed it is impossible for them to do otherwise. They do not even acknowledge the advantage of our arts and sciences.] All their doctrine tends to reduce them to a primitive condition, to barbarism, to the animal. They cannot serve humanity by arts and sciences, and as they do not know them, they renounce them; they cannot take advantage of the qualities which are the peculiar prerogative of man and ally him to the gods. They will not have temples, or statues, or theaters, or museums. They say these things are not necessary for them. The easiest way not to be ashamed of one's own baseness is to scorn nobility; and this they do. They are atheists. They do not recognize the gods, or their interference in the affairs of men. They acknowledge only the father of their teacher, whom they also call their father, and their teacher himself, who, according to their notions, has revealed to them all the mysteries of life. Their doctrine is a wretched deception.

"Notice one thing—our doctrine asserts that the world depends on the gods; the gods afford protection to men. In order that men may live well, they must reverence the gods, must search and think, and then our lives are regulated on the one hand by the will of the gods, on the other by the collective wisdom of all mankind. We live, think, search, and consequently approve the truth.

"But they have neither the gods nor their wills, nor the wisdom of humanity, but only one thing,—a blind faith in their crucified teacher, and in all he said to them.

"Now consider well: which is the more hopeful guide,—the will of the gods and the collective, free activity of human wisdom, or the compulsory blind belief in the words of one man?"

Julius was struck by what the stranger said to him, and especially by his last words. Not only was his purpose of going to the Christians shaken, but it now seemed to him strange enough that he, under the influence of his misfortunes, could ever have come to such a foolish decision. But the question still remained, What was he to do now, and how was he to escape from the difficult circumstances in which he was placed, and so, after he had related his situation, he asked the stranger's advice.

"That is the very thing that I wanted to speak about," continued the stranger. "What are you to do? Your way, as far as human wisdom is given me, is clear to me. All your misfortunes are the results of the passions peculiar to men. Passion has seduced you, has led you so far that you have suffered. Such are the ordinary lessons of life. These lessons must be turned to your advantage. You have learned much, and you know what is bitter and what is sweet; you cannot repeat the mistakes you have made. Profit by your experience. What has hurt you more than all is your quarrel with your father; this quarrel is the outcome of your position. Take another, and the quarrel will either cease, or at least it will not be so painfully apparent. All your tribulations have arisen from the irregularity of your position. You have yielded to the gaieties of youth; this was natural, and therefore it was certainly good. It was good while it was appropriate to your age. But that time has passed; you, with the powers of manhood, have yielded to the friskiness of youth, and it was bad. You have now reached the time when you must become a man, a citizen, and serve the state, and work for its welfare. Your father proposes to you to marry. His advice is wise. You have outlived one period of life—your youth—and have reached another. All your tribulations are the indications of a period of transition. Recognize that the period of youth is passed, and having boldly renounced all that belonged to it, and that is not appropriate to manhood, start on your new way. Marry, give up the amusements of youth, occupy yourself with trade, with social affairs, with arts and sciences, and you will find peace and joy as well as reconciliation with your father. The main thing that has disturbed you has been the unnaturalness of your position. Now you have reached manhood, and you must enter into matrimony, and be a man.

"And therefore my chief advice is: Fulfil your father's wishes, and marry. If you are attracted by that solitude which you expected to find among the Christians, if you are inclined toward philosophy and not to the activities of life, you can with profit devote yourself to this only after you have had experience of life in its actuality. But you will know this only as an independent citizen and head of a family. If then you feel drawn to a solitude, yield to it; then it will be a genuine inclination, and not a whim of discontent, as it is now. Then go."

These last words, more than anything else, persuaded Julius. He thanked the stranger, and returned home.

His mother received him joyfully. The father, also, on learning his intention to submit to his will and marry the girl whom he had chosen for him, was reconciled to him.

4

In three months Julius' wedding with the beautiful Eulampia was celebrated, and the young man, having changed his manner of life, began to live with his wife in their own house and to conduct a part of the business which his father intrusted to him.

Once upon a time he went on business to a not very distant city, and there, as he was sitting in a merchant's shop, he saw Pamphilius passing by with a girl whom he did not know. Both were walking, laden with heavy bunches of grapes, which they were selling. Julius, when he recognized his friend, went out to him and asked him to go into the shop and have a talk with him. The young girl, seeing Pamphilius' desire to go with his friend, and his reluctance to leave her alone, hastened to say that she did not need him, and that she would sit down with the grapes and wait for customers. Pamphilius thanked her, and went with Julius into the shop.

Julius asked his acquaintance, the merchant, permission to go with his friend into his private room, and, having received this permission, he went with Pamphilius into the apartment in the rear of the shop.

The friends inquired of each about the circumstances of their lives. Pamphilius' life had not changed since they had last seen each other: he had continued to live in the Christian community, he was not married, and he assured his friend that his life each year, day, and hour had been growing happier and happier.

Julius told his friend all that had happened to him, and how he had started to join the Christians, when his meeting with the stranger had opened his eyes to the mistakes of the Christians, and to his great obligation to marry, and how he had followed his advice and married.

"Well, tell me, are you happy now?" asked Pamphilius. "Have you found in marriage what the stranger promised you?"

"Happy?" repeated Julius. "What is being happy? If you mean by that word full satisfaction of my desires, then of course I am not happy. I am conducting my trade with success, men are beginning to respect me, and in both of these respects I find some satisfaction. Although I see many men who are richer and more regarded than I, yet I foresee the possibility of equaling them and even of excelling them. This side of my life is full; but my marriage, I will say frankly, does not satisfy me. I will say more: I am conscious that this same marriage, which ought to have given me joy, has not done so, and that the joy I experienced at first has kept growing less and less, and has at last vanished, and in its place, where joy had been, out of marriage arose sorrow. My wife is beautiful, intellectual, well educated, and good. At first I was perfectly happy. But now—this you can't know, having no wife—there have arisen causes of discord between us, at one time because she seeks my caresses when I am indifferent toward her, at another time the case is reversed. Moreover, for love, novelty is necessary. A woman less fascinating than my wife fascinates me more at first, but afterward becomes still less fascinating than my wife. I have already experienced this. No, I have not found satisfaction in matrimony. Yes, my friend," said Julius, in conclusion, "the philosophers are right; life does not give what the soul desires. This I have experienced in my marriage. But the fact that life does not give that happiness which the soul desires does not prove that your fraudulent practices can give it," he added with a smile.

"In what do you see we are fraudulent?" asked Pamphilius.

"Your fraud consists in this: that in order to free men from the evils connected with the facts of life, you repudiate all the facts of life—life itself. In order to free yourselves from disenchantment, you repudiate enchantment, you repudiate marriage itself."

"We do not repudiate marriage," said Pamphilius.

"If not marriage, then you repudiate love."

"On the contrary, we repudiate everything except love. For us it is the chief corner-stone of everything."

"I don't understand you," said Julius. "As far as I have heard from others and from yourself, and from the fact that you are not married yet, though you are as old as I am, I conclude that you don't have marriages among you. Those of you who are already married continue married, but the rest of you do not enter into new relations. You do not take pains to perpetuate the human race. And if there were no other people besides you, the human race would have long ago perished," said Julius, repeating what he had many times heard.

"That is unjust," said Pamphilius. "It is true we do not make it our aim to perpetuate the human race, and we take no anxious care about this, as I have many times heard from your wise men. We take for granted that our Heavenly Father has already provided for this: our aim is simply to live in accordance with His will. If the perpetuation of the race is consonant with His will, then it will be perpetuated; if not, then it will come to an end; this is not our business or our care; our care is to live in accordance with His will. His will is expressed both in our sermons and in our revelation, where it is said that the husband shall cleave unto the wife, and they twain shall be one flesh. Marriage amongst us is not only not forbidden, but is encouraged by our elders and teachers. The difference between marriage amongst us and marriage amongst you consists solely in this: that our law has revealed to us that every one who looks lustfully on a woman commits a sin; and therefore we and our women, instead of adorning ourselves and stimulating lust, try to avoid it as much as possible, so that the feeling of love, like that between brothers and sisters, may be stronger than that of lust, for one woman, which you call love."

"But still you cannot suppress the feeling for beauty," said Julius. "I am convinced, for example, that the beautiful young girl with whom you were carrying grapes, in spite of her garb, which concealed her charming figure, must awaken in you the feeling of love to a woman."

"I do not know as yet," said Pamphilius, reddening. "I have not thought about her beauty. You are the first person that has spoken of it. She is to me only as a sister. But I will continue what I was just going to say to you concerning the difference between our form of marriage and yours. The variance arises from the fact that, among you, lust, under the name of beauty and love and the service of the goddess Venus, is maintained and expressed in men. With us it is the contrary; carnal desire is not regarded as an evil,—for God has created no evil,—but a good, which becomes an evil when it is not in its place—a temptation, as we call it; and we try to avoid it by all the means in our power. And that is why I am not married as yet, though very possibly I might marry to-morrow."

"But what decides this?"

"The will of God."

"How do you find it out?"

"If one never seeks for its indications, one will never see them; but if one is all the time on the lookout for them, they become clear, as to you omens by sacrifices and birds are clear. And as you have your wise men who interpret for you the will of the gods by their wisdom, and by the vitals of the sacrificed victim, and by the flight of birds, so have we our wise men who explain to us the will of the Father by the revelation of Christ, by the promptings of their hearts, and the thoughts of other men, and chiefly by love to them."

"But all this is very indefinite," objected Julius. "What shows you, for example, when and whom you ought to marry? When I was about to marry, I had a choice between three girls. These girls were selected from the rest because they were beautiful and rich, and my father was satisfied whichever one of them I chose. Out of the three I chose my Eulampia because she was more beautiful and more attractive than the others. But what will govern you in your choice?"

"In order to answer you," said Pamphilius, "I must inform you, first of all, that as according to our doctrine all men are equal before our Father, so likewise they are equal before us both in their station and in their spiritual and physical qualities, and consequently our choice (if I may use this word so meaningless to us) cannot be in any way circumscribed. Any one of all the men and women of the world may be the wife of a Christian man or the husband of a Christian woman."

"That would make it still more impossible to decide," said Julius.

"I will tell you what our elder told me as to the difference between a Christian and a pagan marriage. The pagan—you, for example—chooses a wife who, according to his idea, will cause him, personally, more delight than any one else. In this choice his eyes wander about, and it is hard to decide; the more, because the enjoyment is before him. But the Christian has no such choice; or rather the choice for his personal enjoyment occupies not the first, but a subordinate place. For the Christian the question is whether by his marriage he is going contrary to God's will."

"But in what respect can there be in marriage anything contrary to God's will?"

"I might forget the 'Iliad,' which you and I read together, but you who live amid poets and sages cannot forget it. What is the whole 'Iliad'? It is a story of violations of the will of God in relation to marriage. Menelaus and Paris and Helen and Achilles and Agamemnon and Chreseis—it is all a description of the terrible tribulations that have ensued and are all the time coming from this violation."

"In what consists this violation?"

"It consists in this: that a man loves a woman for the personal enjoyment he gets from connection with her, and not because she is a human being like himself, and so he enters into matrimony for the sake of his pleasure. Christian marriage is possible only when a man has love for his fellow-men, and when the object of his carnal love has already been the object of fraternal love of man to man. As a house can be built satisfactorily and lastingly only when there is a foundation; as a picture can be painted only when there is something prepared to paint it on; so carnal love is lawful, reasonable, and lasting only when it is based on the respect and love of man to man. On this foundation only can a reasonable Christian family life be established."

"But still," said Julius, "I do not see why Christian love, as you call it, excludes such love for a woman as Paris experienced."

"I don't say that Christian marriage did not permit exclusive love for a woman; on the contrary, only then is it reasonable and holy; but exclusive love for a woman can take its rise only when the existent love to all men has not been previously violated. The exclusive love for a woman which the poets sing, calling it good, though it is not founded on love to men, has no right to be called love at all. It is animal passion, and very frequently passes over into hate. The best proof of this is how this so-called love, or *eros*, if it be not founded on brotherly love to all men, becomes brutal; this is shown in the cases where violence is offered to the very woman whom a man professes to love, and in so doing compels her to suffer, and ruins her. In violence it is manifest that there is no love to man—no, not if he torments the one he loves. But in un-Christian marriage violence is often concealed when the man that weds a girl who does not love him, or who loves some one else, compels her to suffer and does not pity her, provided only he satisfies his passion."

"Let us admit that this is so," said Julius, "but if a girl loves him, then there is no injustice, and I don't see any difference between Christian and pagan marriage."

"I do not know the details of your marriage," replied Pamphilius; "but I know that every marriage having for its basis personal advantage only cannot help being the cause of discord, just exactly as the mere act of feeding cannot take place among animals and men without quarrels and brawls. Every one wants the sweet morsel, and since there is an insufficiency of sweet morsels for all, the quarrel breaks out. Even if there is no outward quarrel, there is a secret one. The weak one desires the sweet morsel, but he knows that the strong one will not give it to him, and though he is aware of the impossibility of taking it directly away from the strong one, he looks at him with secret hatred and envy, and seizes the first opportunity of getting it away from him. The same is true of pagan marriages, only it is twice as bad, because the object of the hatred is a man, so that enmity is produced even between husband and wife."

"But how manage so that the married couple love no one but each other? Always the man or the girl is found loving this person or another. And then in your system the marriage is impossible. This is the very reason I see the justice of what is said about you, that you do not marry at all. It is for this reason you are not married, and apparently will not marry. How can it possibly be that a man should marry a single woman never having before kindled the feelings of love in some other woman, or that a girl should reach maturity without having awakened the feelings of some man? How must Helen have acted?"

"The elder Cyril thus speaks in regard to this: in the pagan world, men having no thought of love to their brethren, never having trained that feeling, think about one thing,—about the awakening of passionate love toward some woman, and they foster this passion in their hearts. And therefore in their world every Helen, and every woman like Helen, stimulates the love of many. Rivals fight with one another, and strive to supplant one another as animals do to possess the female. And to a greater or less degree their marriage is a constraint. In our community we not only do not think of the personal fascination of beauty, but we avoid all temptations which lead to that, and which in the heathen world are highly regarded as a merit and an object of adoration.

"We, on the contrary, think about those obligations of reverence and love to our neighbors which we have without distinction for all men, for the greatest beauty and the greatest ugliness. We use all our endeavors to educate this feeling, and so in us the feeling of love toward men gets the upper hand of the seduction of beauty, and conquers it, and annihilates the discords arising from sexual relations. The Christian marries only when he knows that his union with a woman causes no one any grief."

"But is this possible?" interrupted Julius. "Can men regulate their inclinations?"

"It is impossible if they have given them free course, but we can keep them from spreading and rising. Take, for example, the relations of a father to his daughter, of a mother to her sons, of brothers and sisters. The mother is to her son, the daughter to her father, the sister to her brother, not an object of personal enjoyment, but of pure love, and the passions are not awakened. They would be awakened only when the father should discover that she whom he had accounted his daughter was not his daughter, or the mother that her son was not her son, or that brother and sister were not brother and sister; but even then this passion would be very feeble and humble, and it would be in a man's power to repress it. The lustful feeling would be feeble, for it would be based on that of maternal, paternal, or fraternal love. Why then can't you believe that the feeling toward all women might be trained and controlled so that they would regard them in the same light as mothers, sisters, and daughters, and that the feeling of conjugal love might grow out of the basis of such an affection? As a brother permits the feeling of love toward the woman whom he has considered his sister to arise only when he has learned that she is not his sister, so when the Christian feels that his love does not injure any one, he permits this passion to arise in his soul."

"Well, but suppose two men love the same girl?"

"Then one sacrifices his happiness to the happiness of the other."

"But supposing she loves one of them?"

"Then the one whom she loves least sacrifices his feelings for the sake of her happiness."

"Well, supposing she loves both, and both sacrifice themselves, whom would she take?"

"In that case the elders would decide the matter, and advise in such a way that the greatest happiness would come to all, with the greatest amount of love."

"But it can't be done in such a way; and the reason is because it is contrary to human nature."

"Contrary to human nature! What is the nature of man? Man, besides being an animal, is a man, and it is true that such a relation to a woman is not consonant with man's animal nature, but is consonant with his rational nature. And when he employs his reason in the service of his animal nature, he does worse than a beast,—he descends to violence, to incest—a level to which no brute ever sinks. But when he employs his rational nature to the suppression of the animal, when the animal nature serves, then only he attains the well-being which satisfies him."

5

"But tell me about yourself personally," said Julius. "I see you with that pretty girl; you apparently live near her and serve her; can it be that you do not desire to be her husband?"

"I have not thought about it," said Pamphilius. "She is the daughter of a Christian widow. I serve them just as others do. You ask me if I love her in a way to unite my life with hers. This question is hard for me. But I will answer frankly. This idea has occurred to me; but there is a young man who loves her, and therefore I do not dare as yet to think about it. This young man is a Christian, and loves us both, and I cannot take a step which would hurt him. I live, not thinking about this. I try to do one thing: to fulfil the law of love to men—this is the only thing I demand; I shall marry when I see that it is proper."

"But it cannot be a matter of indifference to the mother whether she has a good industrious son-in-law or not. She would want you, and not any one else."

"No, it is a matter of indifference to her, because she knows that, besides me, all of us are ready to serve her as well as every one else, and I should serve her neither more nor less whether I were her son-in-law or not. If my marriage to her daughter results, I shall enter upon it with joy, and so I should rejoice even if she married some one else."

"That is impossible!" exclaimed Julius. "This is a horrible thing of you— that you deceive yourselves! And thus you deceive others. That stranger told me correctly about you. When I listen to you I cannot help yielding to the beauty of the life which you describe for me; but as I think it over, I see that it is all deception, leading to savagery, brutality, of life approaching that of brutes."

"Wherein do you see this savagery?"

"In this: that as you subject your own lives to labors, you have no leisure or chance to occupy yourselves with arts and sciences. Here you are in ragged dress, with hardened hands and feet; your fair friend, who might be a goddess of beauty, is like a slave. You have no hymns of Apollo, or temples, or poetry, or games,—none of those things which the gods have given for beautifying the life of man. To work, work like slaves or like oxen merely for a coarse existence—isn't this a voluntary and impious renunciation of the will and nature of man."

"The nature of man again!" said Pamphilius. "But in what does this nature consist? Is it in this, that you torment your slaves with unbearable labors, that you kill your brothers and reduce them to slavery, and make your women an object of enjoyment? All this is essential for that beauty of life which you consider a part of human nature. Or does it consist in this, that you must live in love and concord with all men, feeling yourself a member of one universal brotherhood?"

"You are also greatly mistaken if you think that we scorn the arts and sciences. We highly prize all the qualities with which human nature is endowed. But we look on all the qualities belonging to man as the means for the attainment of one single aim to which we devote our whole lives, and that is to fulfil the will of God. In art and science we do not see an amusement suitable only to while away the time of idle people; we demand from art and science what we demand from all human occupations,—that they hold the same activity of love to God and one's neighbor as permeates all the acts of a Christian. We call real science only those occupations which help us to live better, and art we regard only when it purifies our thoughts, elevates our souls, increases the force which we need for a loving, laborious life. Such science, as far as possible, we develop in ourselves and in our children, and such art we gladly cultivate in our free time. We read and study the writings bequeathed to us; we sing songs, we paint pictures, and our songs and paintings encourage our souls and cheer us up in moments of depression. And this is why we cannot approve of the application which you make of the arts and sciences. Your learned men employ their aptitudes and acquirements to the invention of new means of causing evil to men; they perfect the methods of war, in other words, of murder; they contrive new ways of money-making, that is to say, of enriching some at the expense of others. Your art serves for the erection and decoration of temples in honor of your gods, in whom the more cultivated of you have long ago ceased to believe, but belief in whom you inculcate in others, considering that, by such a deception, you keep them under your power. You erect statues in honor of the most powerful and cruel of your tyrants, whom no one respects, but all fear. In your theaters representations are permitted which hold criminal love up to admiration. Music serves for the delectation of your rich men who have eaten and drunken at their luxurious feasts. Pictorial art is employed in representing in houses of debauchery such scenes as no sober man unvitiated by animal passions could look at without blushing. No, not for this was man endowed with these lofty qualities which differentiate him from the beasts! It is impossible to use them for the mere gratification of your bodies. Consecrating our whole lives to the accomplishment of the will of God, we all the more employ our highest faculties in the same service."

"Yes," said Julius, "all this would be admirable if life in such conditions was possible; but it is not possible to live so. You deceive yourselves. You do not acknowledge our protection. But if it were not for the Roman legions, could you live in any comfort? You profit by our protection, though you do not acknowledge it. Some among you, as you yourself say, protect yourselves. You do not acknowledge private property, but take advantage of it; we have it and give it to you. You yourselves do not give away your grapes, but sell them and then make purchases. All this is a cheat. If you did what you say, then it would be so; but now you deceive others as yourselves."

Julius was indignant, and he spoke out what he had in his mind. Pamphilius was silent and waited his turn. When Julius had finished, Pamphilius said:—

"You are wrong in thinking that we do not acknowledge your protection, and yet take advantage of it. Our well-being consists in our not requiring protection, and this cannot be taken away from us. Even if material objects, which constitute property in your eyes, pass through our hands, we do not call them ours, and we give them to whoever needs them for subsistence. We sell goods to those that wish to buy them; yet it is not for the sake of increasing our private means, but solely that those that need may acquire what is required for supporting life. If any one desired to take these grapes away from us we should give them up without resistance. This is the precise reason why we have no fear, even of an invasion of the barbarians. If they proceeded to take from us the products of our toil, we should let them go; if they insisted on our working for them, we should joyfully comply with their demands, and not only would they have no reason to kill us or torture us, but it would be contrary to their interest to do so. The barbarians would speedily understand and like us, and we should have far less to endure at their hands than from the enlightened people that surround us now and persecute us.

"Your accusation against us consists in this,—that we do not wholly attain what we are striving for; that is, that we do not recognize violence and private property, and at the same time we take advantage of them. If we are deceivers, then it is no use to talk with us, and we are worthy neither of anger nor of being exposed, but only of scorn, and we should willingly accept your scorn, since one of our rules is the recognition of our insignificance. But if we are genuine in our striving toward what we profess, then your blaming us for deception would be unjust. If we strive, as I and my brethren strive, to fulfil our Teacher's law, then we strive for it, not for external ends,—for riches and honors, for you see all these things we do not recognize,—but for something else. You are seeking your best advantage, and so are we; the only difference is that we see our advantage in different things. You believe that your well-being consists in riches and honors; we believe in something else. Our belief shows us that our advantage is not in violence, but in submissiveness; not in wrath, but in giving everything away. And we, like plants in the light, cannot help striving in the direction where we see our advantage. It is true we do not accomplish all we wish for our own advantage; but how can it be otherwise? You strive to have the most beautiful woman for a wife, to have the largest property—but have you, or has any one else succeeded in doing this? If the arrow does not hit the bull's-eye, does the bowman any the less cease to aim at it, because he fails many times to hit it? It is the same with us. Our well-being, according to the teaching of Christ, is in love. We search for our advantage, but each one in his own way falls more or less short of attaining it."

"Yes, but why don't you believe in all human wisdom, and why do you turn your back on it, and put your faith in your one crucified Teacher? Your thraldom, your submissiveness before Him, is what repels me."

"Again you make a mistake, and any one makes a mistake who thinks that we, in fulfilling our doctrine, pin our faith to anything because the man we believe in commanded it. On the contrary, those that seek with all their soul for the instructions of Truth, for Communion with the Father, those that seek for true happiness, cannot help hitting upon that path which Christ traversed, and, therefore, cannot help following Him, seeing Him as their leader. All who love God meet on this path, and there you will be also! He is the Son of God and the mediator between God and men, and this is so, not because any one has told us this, and we blindly believe it, but because all those that seek God find His Son before them, and only through Him can they understand, see, and know God."

Julius made no reply to this, and sat for a long while silent.

"Are you happy?" he asked.

"I have nothing better to desire. But although, for the most part, I experience a sense of perplexity, a consciousness of some vague injustice, yet that is the very reason I am so tremendously happy," said Pamphilius, smiling.

"Yes," said Julius; "maybe I should have been happier if I had not met that stranger, and if I had joined you."

"Why! if you think so, what prevents your doing so even now?"

"How about my wife?"

"You say she has an inclination to Christianity, then she will come with you."

"Yes, but we have already begun a different kind of life; how can we break it off? We have begun; we must live it out," said Julius, picturing to himself the dissatisfaction which his father and mother and friends would feel, and, above all, the energy which it would require to make this change.

At this moment there appeared at the door of the shop this young girl, Pamphilius' friend, accompanied by a young man. Pamphilius joined them, and the young man said loud enough for Julius to hear that he had been sent by Cyril to buy leather. The grapes had been sold and wheat had been bought. Pamphilius proposed to the young man to go home with Magdalina while he himself should buy and bring home the leather. "It will be pleasanter for you," said he.

"No, it would be pleasanter for Magdalina to go with you," said the young man, and he took his departure. Julius introduced Pamphilius in the shop to a tradesman whom he knew. Pamphilius put the wheat into bags, and bestowing the smaller share on Magdalina, took up his own heavy load, said good-by to Julius, and left the city with the young girl. As he turned into a side street he looked round and nodded his head to Julius, and then still more joyously smiling said something to Magdalina, and thus they vanished from sight.

"Yes, I should have done better if I had gone to them," said Julius to himself, and in his imagination, commingling, arose two pictures: that of the lusty Pamphilius with the tall robust maiden carrying the baskets on their heads and their kindly radiant faces; then that of his own home which he had left that morning, and to which he should return, and then his pampered beautiful wife, of whom he had grown so tired, lying in her finery and bracelets on rugs and cushions.

But Julius had no time to think long; his acquaintances, the tradesmen, came, and they entered upon their usual proceedings, finishing up with a dinner with liquors and the night with women. . . .

6

Ten years passed. Julius saw nothing more of Pamphilius, and his interviews gradually faded from his remembrance, and his impressions of him and the Christian life grew dim.

Julius' life ran in the usual course. About that time his father died, and he was obliged to take the head of the whole business, which was complicated; there were old customers, there were salesmen in Africa, there were clerks, there were debts to be collected and to be paid. Julius, in spite of himself, was drawn into business and gave all his time to it. Moreover, new cares came upon him. He was selected for some civic function. And this new occupation, flattering to his pride, was attractive to him. Besides his commercial affairs, he was also interested in public matters, and having brains and the gift of eloquence, he proceeded to use his influence among his fellow-citizens, so as to acquire a high public position.

In the course of these ten years, a serious and, to him, unpleasant change had also taken place in his family life. Three children had been born to him, and this had estranged him from his wife. In the first place, his wife had lost a large part of her beauty and freshness; in the second place, she paid less attention to her husband. All her affection and tenderness were lavished on the children. Though the children were handed over to nurses and attendants, after the manner of the pagans, Julius often found them in their mother's rooms or found her in theirs. But the children for the most part were a burden to Julius, occasioning him more annoyance than pleasure.

Engrossed in his commercial and public affairs, Julius had abandoned his former dissipated life, but he took it for granted that he needed some refined recreation after his labors, and he did not find it with his wife. At this time she was more and more occupied with a Christian slave-woman, was more and more carried away by the new doctrine, and had renounced everything external and pagan which had constituted a charm for Julius. As he did not find this in his wife, he took up with a woman of frivolous character, and enjoyed with her those leisure moments which remained to him above his duties.

If Julius had been asked whether he was happy or unhappy in these years of his life, he could not have replied.

He was so busy! He hurried from affair to affair, from pleasure to pleasure,

but there was not one so satisfying to him that he would have it last. Everything he did was of such a kind that the quicker he got through with it the
better he liked it; and none of his pleasures was so sweet as not to be poisoned
by something, not to have mingled with it the weariness of satiety.

This kind of existence Julius was leading when an event happened which
very nearly revolutionized the whole nature of his life. At the Olympic games
he was taking part in the races, and as he was driving his chariot successfully near
the goal, he suddenly collided with another which he was just outstripping:
the wheel was broken, he was thrown out, and two of his ribs and an arm
were fractured. His injuries were serious, but not fatal; he was taken home,
and had to lie in bed for three months.

In the course of these three months, in the midst of severe physical sufferings, his thought began to ferment, and he had leisure to review his life as
if it were the life of a stranger, and his life presented itself before him in a
gloomy light, the more because during this time three unpleasant events,
deeply mortifying to him, occurred.

The first was that a slave in whom his father had reposed implicit trust,
having gone to Africa for him to purchase precious stones, had run away, causing great loss and confusion in Julius' business.

The second was that his concubine had deserted him, and accepted a new
protector.

The third and most unpleasant blow was that during his illness the election
for the position of administrator which he had been ambitious to fill, took
place, and his rival was chosen. All this, it seemed to Julius, resulted from
the fact that his chariot-wheel had swerved to the left the width of a finger.

As he lay alone on his couch, he began involuntarily to think how from
such insignificant circumstances his happiness depended, and these ideas led
him to still others, and to a recollection of his former misfortunes, of his attempt
to join the Christians, and of Pamphilius, whom he had not seen for ten years.

These recollections were still further strengthened by conversations with
his wife, who, during his illness, was frequently with him, and told him everything she could learn about Christianity from her slave-woman. This slave-
woman had lived for a time in the same community where Pamphilius lived,
and knew him. Julius wanted to see this slave-woman, and when she came to
his bedside she gave him a circumstantial account of everything, and particularly about Pamphilius.

"Pamphilius," the slave-woman said, "was one of the best of the brethren,
and was loved and regarded by them all. He was married to that same Magdalina
whom Julius had seen ten years previous. They already had several children.
Any man who did not believe that God had created men for their good should
go and observe the lives of these," said the slave-woman in conclusion.

Julius dismissed the slave-woman and remained alone, thinking over what he
had heard. It made him envious to compare Pamphilius' life with his own,
and he tried not to think about it.

In order to divert his mind, he took the Greek manuscript which his wife had
put into his hands, and began to read it. In the manuscript he reads as follows:—

There are two paths; one of life and one of death. The path of life consists in this; first, thou must love God, who created thee; secondly, thy neighbor as thyself; and do not unto another that which thou wouldst not have done unto thee. The doctrine included in these words is this:—

Bless those that curse you;

Pray for your enemies and for your persecutors; for what thanks have you if you love those that love you. Do not even the heathen the same?

Do you love them that hate you and you will not have enemies.

Abstain from sensual and worldly lusts.

If any one smite thee on the right cheek, turn to him the other also; and thou shalt be perfect. If any one compel thee to go one mile with him go with him twain;

If any one take what is thine, ask it not back, since this thou canst not do;

If any one take away thy outer garment, give also thy shirt;

Give to every one that asketh of thee and demand it not back, since the Father desires that His beneficent gifts be given unto all.

Blessed is he that giveth according to the Commandments.

My child! shun all evil and all appearance of evil. Be not given to wrath, since wrath leadeth to murder; nor to jealousy, nor to quarrelsomeness, since the outcome of all these is murder.

My child! be not lustful, since lust leadeth to fornication; be not obscene, for from obscenity proceedeth adultery.

My child! be not deceitful, because falsehood leadeth to theft; be not mercenary, be not ostentatious, since from all this proceedeth theft.

My child! be not a murmurer, since this leadeth to blasphemy; be not insolent or evil-minded, since from all this cometh blasphemy.

But be meek, for the meek shall inherit the earth.

Be long-suffering and gentle and mild and humble and good, and always beware of the words to which thou lendest thine ear.

Be not puffed up with pride and give not thy soul to insolence.

Yea, verily, let not thy soul cleave to the proud, but treat the just and the peaceful as thy friends.

All things that happen unto thee accept as for thy good, knowing that nothing can befall thee without God.

My child! be not the cause of discord, but act as a peacemaker when men are quarreling.

Widen not thy hands to receive, and make them not narrow when thou givest. Hesitate not about giving; and when thou hast given, do not repine, for thou knowest who is the beneficent giver of rewards.

Turn not from the needy but share all things with thy brother, and call nothing thine own property, for if you are all sharers in the imperishable, then how much more in that which perisheth.

Teach thy children from early youth the fear of God.

Correct not thy man-servant nor thy maid-servant in anger, lest they cease to fear God, who is above you both; for He cometh not to call men, judging by whom they are, but He calleth those whom the Spirit hath prepared.

But the path of Death is this: first of all it is evil and full of curses; here are murder, adultery, lust, fornication, robbery, idolatry, sorcery, poison, rape, false evidence, hypocrisy, duplicity, slyness, pride, wrath, arrogance, greediness, obscenity, hatred, insolence, presumption, vanity; here are the persecutors of the good, haters of the truth, lovers of falsehood, those that do not recognize rewards for justice, that do not cling to the good nor to just judgment, those that are vigilant, not for what is right but for what is wrong, from whom gentleness and patience hold aloof; here are those that love vanity and yearn for rewards, that have no sympathy with their neighbors, that work not for the overworked, that know not their Creator, slaughterers of children, breakers of God's images, who turn from the needy, persecutors of the oppressed, defenders of the rich, lawless judges of the poor, sinners in all things!

Children, beware of all such persons!

Long before he had read the manuscript to the end, Julius had the experience which men always have when they read books—that is to say, the thoughts of others—with a genuine desire for the Truth; he felt that he had entered with his whole soul into communion with the one that had inspired them. He read on and on, his mind foreseeing what was coming; and he not only agreed with the thoughts of the book, but he imagined that he himself had uttered them.

There happened to him that ordinary phenomenon, not noticed by many persons and yet most mysterious and significant, consisting in this, that the so-called living man becomes alive when he enters into communion—unites—with the so-called dead, and lives one life with them.

Julius' soul merged with the one who had written and composed these thoughts, and after this union had taken place he contemplated himself and his life. And he himself and his whole life seemed to him one horrible mistake. He had not lived, but by all his labors in regard to life, and by his temptations, he had only destroyed in himself the possibility of a true life.

"I do not wish to destroy life; I wish to live, to go on the path of life," he said to himself.

He remembered all that Pamphilius had said to him in their former interviews, and it seemed to him now so clear and indubitable that he was amazed that he could ever have believed in the stranger, and have renounced his intention of going to the Christians. He remembered also what the stranger had said to him:—

"Go when you have had experience of life."

"Well, I have had experience of life, and found nothing in it."

He also remembered how Pamphilius had said to him that whenever he should come to them they would be glad to receive him.

"No, I have erred and suffered enough," he said to himself. "I will renounce everything, and I will go to them and live as it says here."

He communicated his plan to his wife, and she was delighted with his intention. She was ready for everything. The only thing left was to decide how to carry it into execution. What should they do with the children? Should they take them along or leave them with their grandmother? How could they take them? How, after the tenderness of their nurture, subject them to all the trials of an austere life? The slave-woman proposed to accompany them. But the mother was troubled about her children, and declared that it would be better to leave them with their grandmother, and go alone. And they both decided to do this.

All was determined, and nothing but Julius' illness prevented its fulfilment.

7

In this condition of mind Julius fell asleep. The next morning he was told that a skilful physician traveling through the city desired to see him, and promised to give him speedy relief. Julius with joy received the physician. He proved to be none other than the stranger whom Julius had met when he started to join the Christians.

After he had examined his wounds, the physician prescribed certain simples for renewing his strength.

"Shall I be able to work with my arm?" asked Julius.

"Oh, yes, to drive a chariot, or to write; yes."

"But I mean hard work—to dig?"

"I was not thinking about that," said the physician, "because such work is not necessary to one in your position."

"On the contrary, it is very necessary to me," said Julius; and he told the physician that since the time he had last seen him he had followed his advice, had made trial of life, but life had not given him what it had promised him, but, on the contrary, had disillusioned him, and that he now was going to carry out the plan of which he had spoken to him at that time.

"Yes, evidently they have put into effect all their powers of deception and entangled you, if you, in your position, with your responsibilities, especially in regard to your children, cannot see their fallacies."

"Read this," was all that Julius said, producing the manuscript he had been reading. The physician took the manuscript and glanced at it.

"I know this," said he; "I know this fraud, and I am surprised that such a clever man as you are can fall into such a snare."

"I do not understand you. Where lies the snare?"

"The whole thing is in life; and here these sophists and rebels against men and the gods propose a happy path of life in which all men would be happy; there would be no wars, no executions, no poverty, no licentiousness, no quarrels, no evil. And they insist that such a condition of men would come about when men should fulfil the precepts of Christ; not to quarrel, not to commit fornication, not to blaspheme, not to use violence, not to bear ill-will against one another. But they make a mistake in taking the end for the means. Their aim is to keep from quarreling, from blasphemy, from fornication, and the like, and this aim is attained only by means of social life. And in speaking thus they say almost what a teacher of archery should say, if he said, 'You will hit the target when your arrow flies in a straight line directly to the target.'

"But the problem is, how to make it fly in a straight line. And this problem is solved in archery by the string being tightly stretched, the bow being elastic, the arrow straight. The same with the life of men;—the very best life for men —that in which they need not quarrel, or commit adultery, or do murder—is attained by the bowstring—the rulers; the elasticity of the bow—the force of the authorities; and the straight arrow—the equity of the law. But they, under the guise of living a better life, destroy whatever has improved or is improving it. They acknowledge no rulers, no authority, no laws."

"But they claim that even without rulers, authorities and laws human life will be vastly better if men would only fulfil the law of Christ."

"Yes, but what guarantee have we that men will fulfil that law? Absolutely none! They say: 'You have made trial of life with authorities and laws, and it has always been a failure. Try it now without authorities and laws, and you will soon see it becoming perfect. You cannot deny this, not having tested it by experience.' Here the sophistry of these impious men becomes evident. Are they more logical than the farmer who says: 'You sow the seed in the ground, and then cover it up with soil, and yet the crop falls far below your desires. My advice is: sow it in the sea, and the result will be far more satisfactory. And do not attempt to deny this theory. You cannot do so, never having tested it by experience.'"

"Yes, that's true," said Julius, who was beginning to waver.

"Not only this," continued the physician, "let us admit what is senseless, what is impossible—let us admit that the foundations of this Christian doctrine may be communicated to all men, like a dose of certain drops, and that suddenly all men should fulfil Christ's teachings, love God and their fellows, and fulfil the precepts. Let us admit this, and yet the way of life, according to their teaching, would not bear examination. There would be no life, and life would be cut short. Now the living live out their lives, but their children will not live their full time, or not one in ten will. According to their teaching all children must be the same to all mothers and fathers, theirs and others'. How will their children protect themselves when we see that all the passion, all the love, which the mother feels for these children scarcely protects them from destruction? What then will it be when this mother-passion is translated into a general commiseration, the same for all children? Who will take and protect the child? Who will spend sleepless nights watching with sick, ill-smelling children, unless it be the mother? Nature made a protective armor for the child in the mother's love; they take it away, giving nothing in its place. Who will educate the boy? Who will penetrate into his soul, if not his father? Who will ward off danger? All this is put aside! All life that is the perpetuation of the human race is put aside."

"That seems correct," said Julius, carried away by the physician's eloquence.

"No, my friend, have nothing to do with this nonsense, and live rationally; especially now, when such great, serious, and pressing responsibilities rest upon you. To fulfil them is a matter of honor. You have lived to reach your second period of doubt, but go onward, and your doubts will vanish. Your first and indubitable obligation is to educate your children, whom you have neglected; your obligation toward them is to make them worthy servants of their country. The existent form of government has given you all you have: you ought to serve it yourself and to give it capable servants in your children, and by so doing you confer a blessing on your children. The second obligation upon you is to serve the public. Your lack of success has mortified and discouraged you —this circumstance is temporary. Nothing is given to us without effort and struggle. And the joy of triumph is mighty only when the battle was hard. Begin a life with a recognition of your duty, and all your doubts will vanish. They were caused by your feeble state of health. Fulfil your obligations to the country by serving it, and by educating your children for this service. Put them on their feet so that they may take your place, and then calmly devote yourself to that life which attracts you; till then you have no right to do so, and if you did, you would find nothing but disappointment."

8

Either the learned physician's simples or his advice had their effect on Julius: he very speedily recovered his spirits, and his notions concerning the Christian life seemed to him idle vaporings.

The physician, after a visit of a few days, took his departure. Soon after, Julius got up, and, profiting by his advice, began a new life. He engaged tutors for his children, and he himself superintended their instruction. His time was wholly spent in public duties, and very soon he acquired great consideration in the city.

Thus Julius lived a year, and during this year not once did he remember the Christians. But during this time a tribunal was appointed to try the Christians in their city. An emissary of the Roman Empire had come to Cilicia to stamp out the Christian faith. Julius heard of the measures taken against the Christians, and though he supposed that it concerned the Christian community in which Pamphilius lived, he did not think of him. But one day as he was walking along the square in the place where his official duties called him, he was accosted by a poorly dressed, elderly man, whom he did not recognize at first. It was Pamphilius. He came up to Julius, leading a child by the hand.

"How are you, friend?" said Pamphilius. "I have a great favor to ask of you, but I don't know as you will be willing to recognize me as your friend, now that we Christians are being persecuted; you might be in danger of losing your place if you had any relations with me."

"I am not in the least afraid of it," replied Julius, "and as a proof of it I will ask you to come home with me. I will even postpone my business in the market so as to talk with you and be of service to you. Let us go home together. Whose child is this?"

"It is my son."

"Really, I need not have asked. I recognize your features in him. I recognize also those blue eyes, and I should not have to ask who your wife is: she is the beautiful woman whom I saw with you some years ago."

"You have surmised correctly," replied Pamphilius. "Shortly after we met, she became my wife."

The friends went to Julius' home. Julius summoned his wife and gave the boy to her, and brought Pamphilius to his luxurious private room.

"Here you can say anything; no one will hear us," said Julius.

"I am not afraid of being heard," replied Pamphilius; "since my request is not that the Christians, who have been arrested, may not be sentenced and executed, but only that they may be permitted publicly to confess their faith."

And Pamphilius told how the Christians arrested by the authorities had sent word to the community from the dungeons where they were confined. The elder Cyril, knowing of Pamphilius' relations with Julius, commissioned him to go and plead for the Christians. The Christians did not ask for mercy. They considered it their mission to bear witness to the truth of Christ's teaching. They could bear witness to this in the course of a long life of eighty years, and they could bear witness to the same by enduring tortures. Either way was immaterial to them; and physical death, unavoidable as it was, for them was alike free from terror and full of joy, whether it came immediately or at the end of half a century: but they wished their lives to be useful to men, and therefore they had sent Pamphilius to labor in their behalf, that their trial and punishment might be public.

Julius was dumfounded at Pamphilius' request, but he promised to do all in his power.

"I have promised you my intercession," said Julius, "but I have promised it to you on account of my friendship for you, and on account of the peculiarly pleasant feeling of tenderness which you have always awakened in me; but I must confess that I consider your doctrine most senseless and harmful. I can judge in regard to this, because not very long ago, in a moment of disappointment and illness, in a state of depression of spirits, I once more shared your views, and once more almost abandoned everything and went to you. I understand on what your error is based, for I have been through it; it is based on selfishness, on weakness of spirit, and the feebleness caused by ill health; it is a creed for women, but not for men."

"Why so?"

"Because although you acknowledge the fact that discord and violence are a part of human nature, you do not wish to take part in that violence or to teach others to do so. And without taking your share of the burden you nevertheless take advantage of the organization of society, which is based on violence. Do you call that fair? The world has always existed by means of its rulers: they assume the responsibility of governing, they protect us from enemies, domestic and foreign. We subjects, in return for this, pay the rulers deference and homage, obey their commands, and assist them by serving the State when we are needed. But you, out of pride, instead of taking part by your labors in the affairs of the empire, and in proportion to your services rising higher and higher in the estimation of men, you forthwith, by your pride, I say, regard all men as equal, so that you consider no one higher than yourselves, and consider yourselves equal to Cæsar.

"You yourself think so, and teach others to think so. And for the weak and the lazy this is a great temptation. Instead of laboring, every slave immediately counts himself equal to Cæsar. If men listened to you, society would be dissolved, and we should return to primitive savagery. You in the empire preach the dissolution of empire. But your very existence is dependent on the empire. If it was not for that, you would not be. You would all be slaves of the Scythians or the barbarians, the first who knew of your condition. You are like a tumor destroying the body, but able to make a show, and to feed on the body and nothing else. And the living body struggles with it and suppresses it! Thus do we act in regard to you, and we cannot do otherwise. And notwithstanding my promise to help you, and to comply with your request, I look on your doctrine as most harmful and low: low, because dishonorably and unjustly you devour the breast that nourishes you: take advantage of the blessings of the imperial order without sharing in its support, and yet trying to destroy it!"

"What you say would be just," said Pamphilius, "if we really lived as you think. But you do not know about our life, and you have formed a false conception of it. For you, with your habitual luxury, it is hard to imagine how little a man requires when he exists without superfluities. A man is so constituted that, when he is well, he can produce with his hands far more than he needs for the support of his life. Living in a community as we do, we are able by our labor to support without effort our children, and the aged and the sick and the feeble. You assert that we Christians arouse in the slave the desire to be the Cæsar; on the contrary, both by word and deed we fulfil one thing: patient submissiveness and work, the most humble work of all—the work of the working-man. We know nothing and we care nothing about affairs of state. We know one thing, but we know it beyond question,—that our well-being is only when the well-being of others is found, and we strive after this well-being; the well-being of all men is in their union. And union is attained not by violence, but by love. The violence of a brigand is as atrocious as is that of troops against their enemies, or of the judge against the culprit, and we can have no part in either. Nor can we profit by the work of others enforced by violence. Violence is reflected on us, but we do not inflict it, our share consists in submitting to it without protest."

"Yes," said Julius, "you preach love, but the result of your preaching is savagery, retrogression to primitive conditions of murder, robbery, and every kind of violence, which according to your doctrine must not be repressed in any way."

"No, that's not true," said Pamphilius, "and if you will examine the results of our teaching and the example of our lives you will see that they do not lead to murder, robbery and violence. On the contrary, those crimes can only be opposed by the means we practice. They existed long before Christianity and men found no way of coping with them. When violence meet violence, crimes are not checked but are provoked, because feelings of anger and bitterness are aroused.

"Look at the mighty Roman Empire, where legislation has been raised to a science, and the laws are thoroughly studied and administered, and the office of judge is highly regarded. Nevertheless debauchery and crime are everywhere prevalent. In the early days, when laws were not so numerous or so carefully administered, there was a higher standard of virtue; but simultaneously with the study and application of the laws there has been going on in the Roman Empire a steady deterioration of morals, accompanied by a vast increase in the number and variety of criminal offenses. Nor can it be otherwise. The only way to grapple with such crimes and with evil is the Christian way of love. The heathen weapons of vengeance, punishment and violence are inefficacious. All the preventive and remedial laws and punishments in the world will fail to eradicate people's propensities to do wrong. The root of evil must be got at, which is in the heart of man. That is what we aim at, while you try to repress the outward manifestations of evil. Not looking for its source and not knowing where it is, you can never hope to find it.

"Most crimes are perpetrated by men who desire to get more of this world's good than they can rightfully acquire. Some of these—as, for instance, monstrous commercial frauds—are perpetrated under the protection of the law, and those that are punishable are so cleverly managed that they often escape the penalty. Christianity removes all incentive to such crimes, because those that practise it refuse to take more than what is strictly needed for the support of life, and thereby give up to others their free labor. So that the sight of accumulated wealth is not a temptation, and those that are driven to desperation by hunger find what they need without having to use violent means of obtaining it. Some criminals avoid us altogether. Others join us and gradually become useful workers.

"As regards the crimes provoked by the play of passions: jealousy, carnal love, anger, and hatred. Laws never suppress such crimes. Obstacles only make them worse. But Christianity teaches men to curb their passions by a life of love and labor, so that the spiritual principle will overcome the fleshly. And as Christianity spreads, the number of crimes of this sort will diminish.

"There is still another class of crimes, which have their root in a sincere desire to help humanity. The wish to alleviate the sufferings of an entire people will impel certain men called revolutionists to kill a tyrant with the notion that they are benefiting a majority. The origin of such crimes is a mistaken conviction that evil may be done in order that good may follow. Crimes of this description are not lessened by laws against them, they are provoked by them. The men that commit crimes of this kind have a noble motive—a desire to do good to others. Most men of this kind, though mistaken in their hopes and beliefs, are impelled by the noble motive of desire to do good and they are ready to sacrifice their lives and all they have, and no danger or difficulty stands in their way. Punishment cannot restrain them. Danger only gives them new life and spirit. If they suffer, they are regarded as martyrs, and earn the sympathy of mankind, and they stimulate others to go and do likewise. We see this in the history of all nations. We Christians, though we clearly perceive the error of such conspirators, appreciate their sincerity and self-denial. But we believe that evil will only disappear when men understand the misery that results from it both for themselves and for others. Brotherhood can only be attained when we are all brothers.

"You may decide for yourself which of us—we Christians or you Romans —is more successful in the struggle with crime: we Christians, who preach and prove the joy and delight of a spiritual life, from which no evil can arise; or you Roman rulers and judges, who pass sentence according to the letter of a dead law and thus lash your victims into fury and drive them to the utmost hatred?"

"As long as I keep listening to you," said Julius, "I seem to get the impression that your point of view is correct. But tell me, Pamphilius, why are people against you? Why do they hunt you down and kill you? Why does your teaching of love lead to discord?"

"The reason for this is not in us but outside of us. Above and beyond the temporary laws established by the State and recognized by all men, there are eternal laws engraved in the hearts of men. We Christians obey these universal laws, discerning in the life of Christ their clearest and fullest expression, and condemning, as a crime, every form of violence which transgresses His commandments. We feel bound to observe the civil laws of the country in which we live, unless these laws are opposed to God's laws. 'Render unto Cæsar the things that are Cæsar's, and unto God the things that are God's.' We Christians strive to do away with all crimes, both those against the State and those that go counter to God's will, and, therefore, our fight with crime is more comprehensive than that carried on by the State. But this recognition of God's will as the highest law offends those that claim precedence for a private law, or that take some ingrained custom of their class as a law. Such men are animated by feelings of enmity for those that proclaim that man has a higher mission than to be merely subjects of a State or members of a Society. It was of such that Christ said: 'Woe unto you, Pharisees! for ye take away the key of knowledge: ye enter not in yourselves, and them that are entering in ye hinder.'

"We have no enmity towards any man, not even against those that persecute us, and our way of life injures no man. The only reason why men hate and persecute us is that our way of life is a constant rebuke to those whose conduct is based on violence. We have not the power of stopping this hostility, which does not have its source in us, because we cannot cease to realize that truth which we have accepted, because we cannot live contrary to our conscience and reason. In regard to this very hostility which our faith should arouse in others against us, our Teacher said, *Think not that I am come to send peace into the world; I came not to send peace, but a sword.*

"Christ experienced this hostility in His own life-time and more than once he warned us, His disciples, in regard to it. *Me,* He said, *the world hateth because its deeds are evil. If ye were of the world the world would love you, but since ye are not of this world therefore the world hateth you, and the time will come when he who killeth you will think he is serving God.* But we, like Christ, *fear not them which kill the body but are not able to kill the soul. And this is their condemnation, that light is come into the world, and men loved darkness rather than light because their deeds were evil.*

"In this there is nothing to worry over, because the truth will prevail. The sheep hear the shepherd's voice, and follow him because they know his voice. And Christ's flock will not perish but will increase, attracting to it new sheep from all the lands of the earth, for *The wind bloweth where it listeth and thou hearest the sound thereof, but canst not tell whence is cometh and whither it goeth . . .*"

"Yes," Julius said, interrupting him, "but are there many sincere ones among you? You are often blamed for only pretending to be martyrs and glad to lay down your lives for the truth, but the truth is not on your side. You are proud madmen, destroying the foundations of social life."

Pamphilius made no reply, and looked at Julius with melancholy.

9

Just as Julius was saying this, Pamphilius' little son came running into the room, and clung to his father. In spite of all the blandishments of Julius' wife, he would not stay with her, but ran to his father. Pamphilius sighed, caressed his son, and stood up; but Julius detained him, begging him to stay and talk some more, and have dinner with them.

"It surprises me that you are married and have children," exclaimed Julius. "I cannot comprehend how you Christians can bring up children when you have no private property. How can the mothers live in any peace of mind knowing the precariousness of their children's position?"

"Wherein are our children more precariously placed than yours?"

"Why, because you have no slaves, no property. My wife was greatly inclined to Christianity; she was at one time desirous of abandoning this life, and I had made up my mind to go with her. But what chiefly prevented was the fear she felt at the insecurity, the poverty, which threatened her children, and I could not help agreeing with her. This was at the time of my illness. All my life seemed repulsive to me, and I wanted to abandon everything. But then my wife's anxiety, and, on the other hand, the explanation of the physician who cured me, convinced me that the Christian life, as led by you, is impossible, and not good for families; but that there is no place in it for married people, for mothers with children; that in life as you understand it, life—that is the human race—would be annihilated. And this is perfectly correct. Consequently the sight of you with a child especially surprised me."

"Not one child only. At home I left one at the breast and a three-year-old girl."

"Explain to me how this happens. I don't understand. I was ready to abandon everything and join you. But I had children, and I came to the conclusion that, however pleasant it might be for me, I had no right to sacrifice my children, and for their sake I continued to live as before, in order to bring them up in the same conditions as I myself had grown up and lived."

"Strange," said Pamphilius; "we take diametrically opposite views. We say: 'If grown people live a wordly life it can be forgiven them, because they are already corrupted; but children! That is horrible! To live with them in the world and tempt them! *Woe unto the world because of offenses, for it must needs be that offenses come; but woe to that by whom the offense cometh.*'

"So spake our Teacher, and I do not say this to you as a refutation, but because it is actually so. The chiefest obligation that we have to live as we do arises from the fact that amongst us are children,—those beings of whom it is said, *Except ye become as little children ye shall not enter into the Kingdom of Heaven.*"

"But how can a Christian family do without definite means of subsistence?"

"According to our faith there is only one means of subsistence,—loving labor for men. For your means of livelihood you depend on violence. It can be destroyed as wealth is destroyed, and then all that is left is the labor and love of men. We consider that we must hold fast by that which is the basis of everything, and that we must increase it. And when this is done, then the family lives and prospers.

"No," continued Pamphilius; "if I were in doubt as to the truth of Christ's teaching, and if I were hesitating as to the fulfilling of it, then my doubts and hesitations would instantly come to an end if I thought about the fate of children brought up among the heathen in those conditions in which you grew up, and are educating your children. Whatever we, a few people, should do for the arrangement of our lives, with palaces, slaves, and the imported products of foreign lands, the life of the majority of men would still remain what it must be. The only security of that life will remain, love of mankind and labor. We wish to free ourselves and our children from these conditions, not by love, but by violence. We compel men to serve us, and—wonder of wonders!—the more we secure, as it were, our lives by this, the more we deprive ourselves of the only true, natural, and lasting security—love. The same with the other guarantee—labor. The more a man rids himself of labor and accustoms himself to luxury, the less he becomes fitted for work, the more he deprives himself of the true and lasting security. And these conditions in which men place their children they call *security!* Take your son and mine and send them now to find a path, to transmit an order, or to do any needful business, and see which of the two would do it most successfully; or try to give them to be educated, which of the two would be most willingly received? No, don't utter those horrible words that the Christian life is possible only for the childless. On the contrary, it might be said: to live the pagan life is excusable only in those who are childless. *But woe to him who offendeth one of these little ones.*"

Julius remained silent.

"Yes," said he, "maybe you are right, but the education of my children is begun, the best teachers are teaching them. Let them know all that we know. There can be no harm in that. But for me and for them there is still time. They may come to you when they reach their maturity, if they find it necessary. I also can do this, when I set them on their feet and am free."

"Know the Truth and you shall be free," said Pamphilius. "Christ gives full freedom instantly; earthly teaching never will give it. Good-by."

And Pamphilius went away with his son.

The trial was public, and Julius saw Pamphilius there as he and other Christians carried away the bodies of the martyrs. He saw him, but as he stood in fear of the authorities he did not go to him, and did not invite him home.

10

Twenty years more passed. Julius' wife died. His life flowed on in the labors of his public office, in efforts to secure power, which sometimes fell to his share, sometimes slipped out of his grasp. His wealth was large, and kept increasing.

His sons had grown up, and his second son, especially, began to lead a luxurious life. He made holes in the bottom of the bucket in which the wealth was held, and in proportion as the wealth increased, increased also the rapidity of its escape through these holes.

Julius began to have just such a struggle with his sons as he had had with his father,—wrath, hatred, jealousy.

About this time a new prefect deprived Julius of his favor.

Julius was forsaken by his former flatterers, and banishment threatened him. He went to Rome to offer explanations. He was not received, and was ordered to depart.

On reaching home he found his son carousing with boon companions. The report had spread through Cilicia that Julius was dead, and his son was celebrating his father's death! Julius lost control of himself, struck his son so that he fell, apparently lifeless, and he went to his wife's room. In his wife's room he found a copy of the gospel, and read:—

Come unto me all ye that labor and are heavy laden and I will give you rest. Take my yoke upon you and learn of me, for I am meek and lowly of heart, and ye shall find rest unto your souls. For my yoke is easy and my burden is light.

"Yes," said Julius, to himself, "He has been calling me long. I did not believe in Him, and I was disobedient and wicked; and my yoke was heavy and my burden was grievous."

Julius long sat with the gospel opened on his knee, thinking over his past life and recalling what Pamphilius had said to him at various times.

Then Julius arose and went to his son. He found his son on his feet, and was inexpressibly rejoiced to find he had suffered no injury from the blow he had given him. Without saying a word to his son, Julius went into the street and bent his steps in the direction of the Christian settlement. He went all day, and at eventide stopped at a countryman's for the night. In the room which he entered lay a man. At the noise of steps the man roused himself. It was the physician.

"No, this time you do not dissuade me!" cried Julius. "This is the third time I have started *thither*, and I know that there only shall I find peace of mind."

"Where?" asked the physician.

"Among the Christians."

"Yes, maybe you will find peace of mind, but you will not have fulfilled your obligations. You have no courage. Misfortunes have conquered you. True philosophers do not act thus. Misfortune is only the fire in which the gold is tried. You have passed through the furnace, and now you are needed, you are running away. Now test others and yourself. You have gained true wisdom, and you ought to employ if for the good of your country. What would become of the citizens if those that knew men, their passions and conditions of life, instead of devoting their knowledge and experience to the service of their country, should hide them away, in their search for peace of mind. Your experience of life has been gained in society, and so you ought to devote it to the same society."

"But I have no wisdom at all. I am wholly in error. My errors are ancient, but no wisdom has grown out of them. Like water, however old and stale it is, it never becomes wine."

Thus spake Julius; and seizing his cloak, he left the house and, without resting, walked on and on. At the end of the second day he reached the Christians.

They received him joyfully, though they did not know that he was a friend of Pamphilius, whom every one loved and respected. At the refectory Pamphilius recognized his friend, and with joy ran to him, and embraced him.

"Well, at last I have come," said Julius. "What is there for me to do? I will obey you."

"Don't worry about that," said Pamphilius. "You and I will go together."

And Pamphilius led Julius into the house where visitors were entertained, and showing him a bed, said:—

"In what way you can serve the people you yourself will see after you have had time to examine into the way we live; but in order that you may know where immediately to lend a hand, I will show you something tomorrow. In our vineyards the grape harvest is taking place. Go and help there. You yourself will see where there is a place for you."

The next morning Julius went to the vineyard. The first was a young vineyard hung with thick clusters. Young people were plucking and gathering them. All the places were occupied, and Julius, after going about for a long while, found no chance for himself.

He went farther. There he found an older plantation; there was less fruit, but here also Julius found nothing to do; all were working in pairs, and there was no place for him.

He went farther, and came to a superannuated vineyard. It was all empty. The vinestocks were gnarly and crooked, and, as it seemed to Julius, all empty. "Just like my life," he said to himself. "If I had come the first time it would have been like the fruit in the first vineyard. If I had come when the second time I started, it would have been like the fruit in the second vineyard; but now here is my life; like these useless superannuated vinestocks, it is good only for fire-wood."

And Julius was terrified at what he had done; he was terrified at the punishment awaiting him because he had ruined his life. And Julius became melancholy, and he said: "I am good for nothing; there is no work I can do now."

And he did not rise from where he sat, and he wept because he had wasted what could never more return to him. And suddenly he heard an old man's voice—a voice calling him. "Work, my brother," said the voice. Julius looked around and saw a white-haired old man, bent with years, and scarcely able to walk. He was standing by a vinestock and gathering from it the few sweet bunches remaining. Julius went to him.

"Work, dear brother; work is joyous;" and he showed him how to find the bunches here and there.

Julius went and searched; he found a few, and brought them and laid them in the old man's basket. And the old man said to him:—

"Look, in what respect are these bunches worse than those gathered in yonder vineyards? *Walk while ye have the light, lest darkness come upon you,* said our Teacher. *And this is the will of Him that sent me; that every one which seeth the Son and believeth on Him, may have everlasting life, and I will raise him at the last day.*

"*For God sent not His Son into the world to condemn the world; but that the world through Him might be saved.*

"*He that believeth on Him is not condemned: but he that believeth not is condemned already, because he hath not believed in the name of the only begotten Son of God.*

"*And this is the condemnation, that light is come into the world, and men loved darkness rather than light because their deeds were evil.*

"*For every one that doeth evil hateth the light, neither cometh to the light lest his deeds should be reproved.*

"*But he that doeth truth cometh to the light, that his deeds may be made manifest that they are wrought in God.*

"Be not unhappy, my son. We are all the children of God and His servants. We all go to make up His one army! Do you think that He has no servants besides you? And that if you, in all your strength, had given yourself to His service, would you have done all that He required all that men ought to do to establish His kingdom? You say you would have done twice, ten times, a hundred times more than you did. But suppose you had done ten thousand times ten thousand more than all men, what would that have been in the work of God? Nothing! To God's work, as to God Himself, there are no limits and no end. God's work is in you. Come to Him, and be not a laborer but a son, and you become a copartner with the infinite God and in His work. With God there is neither small nor great, but there is straight and crooked. Enter into the straight path of life and you will be with God, and your work will be neither small nor great, but it will be God's work. Remember that in heaven there is more joy over one sinner, than over a hundred just men. The world's work, all that you have neglected to do, has only shown you your sin, and you have repented. And as you have repented, you have found the straight path; go forward in it with God, and think not of the past, or of great and small. Before God, all living men are equal. There is one God and one life."

And Julius found peace of mind, and he began to live and to work for the brethren according to his strength. And he lived thus in joy twenty years longer, and he did not perceive how he died the physical death.

1893

OTHER COOPER SQUARE PRESS TITLES OF INTEREST

MARGARET SANGER
An Autobiography
New introduction by Kathryn Cullen-DuPont
516 pp., 1 b/w photo
0-8154-1015-8
$17.95

THE LANTERN-BEARERS AND OTHER ESSAYS
Robert Louis Stevenson
Edited by Jeremy Treglown
320 pp.
0-8154-1012-3
$16.95

THE SELECTED LETTERS OF MARK TWAIN
Edited by Charles Neider
352 pp., 1 b/w photo
0-8154-1011-5
$16.95

THE WAR OF 1812
Henry Adams
New introduction by Col. John R. Elting
392 pp., 27 maps
0-8154-1013-1
$16.95

Available at bookstores; or call 1-800-462-6420

 Cooper Square Press

150 Fifth Avenue
Suite 911
New York, NY 10011